Families & Change

Sixth Edition

This book is dedicated to Patrick C. McKenry (1949–2004) and Sharon J. Price,
our mentors and role models

Sara Miller McCune founded SAGE Publishing in 1965 to support the dissemination of usable knowledge and educate a global community. SAGE publishes more than 1000 journals and over 800 new books each year, spanning a wide range of subject areas. Our growing selection of library products includes archives, data, case studies and video. SAGE remains majority owned by our founder and after her lifetime will become owned by a charitable trust that secures the company's continued independence.

Los Angeles | London | New Delhi | Singapore | Washington DC | Melbourne

Families & Change

Coping With Stressful Events and Transitions

Sixth Edition

Kevin R. Bush
Miami University of Ohio

Christine A. Price
Montclair State University

Los Angeles | London | New Delhi
Singapore | Washington DC | Melbourne

FOR INFORMATION:

SAGE Publications, Inc.

2455 Teller Road

Thousand Oaks, California 91320

E-mail: order@sagepub.com

SAGE Publications Ltd.

1 Oliver's Yard

55 City Road

London, EC1Y 1SP

United Kingdom

SAGE Publications India Pvt. Ltd.

B 1/I 1 Mohan Cooperative Industrial Area

Mathura Road, New Delhi 110 044

India

SAGE Publications Asia-Pacific Pte. Ltd.

18 Cross Street #10-10/11/12

China Square Central

Singapore 048423

Acquisitions Editor: Joshua Perigo

Editorial Assistant: Sam Rosenberg

Production Editor: Vishwajeet Mehra and
    Zoheb Khan

Copy Editor: Diane DiMura

Typesetter: Hurix Digital

Indexer: Integra

Cover Designer: Candice Harman

Marketing Manager: Jennifer Jones

Printed in Canada

Library of Congress Cataloging-in-Publication Data

Names: Bush, Kevin R. (Kevin Ray), 1965- editor. | Price, Christine A, editor.

Title: Families & change : coping with stressful events and transitions / [edited by] Kevin R. Bush, Miami University of Ohio, Christine A. Price, Montclair State University.

Other titles: Families and change Description: Sixth Edition. | Thousand Oaks : SAGE Publications, Inc, 2020. | Revised edition of Families & change, [2017] | Includes bibliographical references

Identifiers: LCCN 2020021880 | ISBN 9781544371245 (paperback) | ISBN 9781544371252 (epub) | ISBN 9781544371191 (epub) | ISBN 9781544371269 (ebook)

Subjects: LCSH: Families–United States. | Social problems–United States. | Social change–United States.

Classification: LCC HQ536 .F332 2020 | DDC 306.85–dc23

LC record available at https://lccn.loc.gov/2020021880

This book is printed on acid-free paper.

20 21 22 23 24 10 9 8 7 6 5 4 3 2 1

Brief Contents

Detailed Contents

SECTION 5   CONTEXTUAL INFLUENCES ON FAMILY STRESS

Chapter 15 Stress and Coping With Intimate Partner Violence   357

Lyndal Khaw

List of Tables and Figures

Chapter 18: Family Socioeconomic Context and Mental Health in Parents and Children: A Heuristic Framework

Preface to the Sixth Edition

The sixth edition of *Families and Change: Coping With Stressful Events and Transitions* presents current literature detailing families' responses to varied transitions and stressful life events over the life span. Scholarly interest in family stress and the adjustment of families to change is not new. During the Progressive Era (1890–1920), the social and behavioral sciences took a specific interest in the social problems facing families as a result of industrialization and urbanization. The primary focus at that time was in social reform and the use of research to help in solving these problems. During the 1920s and 1930s, scholars began to explore the internal dynamics of families with particular emphasis on the well-being and personal adjustment of families and individuals. Researchers became interested in healthy lifestyles, mental health, and child development which led to the development of both family sociology and family therapy (Cole & Cole, 1993).

Two major societal disruptions—the Great Depression and World War II—prompted further attention on how families cope with unprecedented change. Angell (1936) and Cavan and Ranck (1938) identified various family characteristics that mediated the impact of the Depression—that is, family organization, integration, and adaptability. These findings remain largely unchallenged today (Boss, 1987). Hill (1949), in his study of wartime family separations, developed a framework for assessing family crisis—the ABC-X Model. This framework, with its emphasis on family resources and definitions that mediate the extent of the crisis response, serves today as the basis for most stress and coping theoretical models. The 1950s represented a focus on both the integrity of the American family as an institution and traditional family patterns. The social and political revolution of the 1960s, and the technological changes accompanying the greater industrialization, urbanization, and globalization of the 1970s, 1980s, 1990s, and 2000s resulted in a proliferation of research on how families cope and adapt to the multitude of changes and challenges they encounter.

In the 26 years between the publication of the first and sixth editions (1994–2020) of *Families and Change*, our society has witnessed significant familial, social, and global changes. Today, families live in a context filled with stressors associated with time demands, the economy, political strife, global insecurity, and the rapid pace of technological change. From a financial standpoint, families currently face the potential of another economic recession, threats to pensions, investments, savings, and benefits, and the reality of financing extended longevity (e.g., retirement and health-care costs). Technology has advanced so extensively that it has become both a benefit (e.g., convenience, social connections) and an invasive demand. Life has become more impersonal as human connections are replaced by virtual relationships and family time is usurped by screens. Industrialization and urbanization have expanded, leading to denser living environments and the associated stressors of expensive housing, traffic congestion, and increased cost of living. Extended longevity is offering the benefit of more time with family members yet there are associated sacrifices that accompany living longer (e.g., chronic and degenerative illness, caregiving demands, health-care costs).

Based on multiple indications, the stress and change that families are experiencing appear to be intensifying. Stressors inherent to daily life include the discrimination families often face based on race, religious beliefs, gender, and sexual orientation as well as the unpredictable yet stressful events of ongoing natural disasters including hurricanes, tornadoes, storms, floods, and earthquakes. With the blurring of gender roles and the increased diversity in family structure, the basic conceptualization of "family" has evolved. Although the family system may still be viewed as a "haven" from external stressors, families are also challenged to meet their increasingly complicated needs.

It is evident that many academic and social service professionals are involved in developing knowledge, as well as teaching classes and offering outreach programs in areas that focus on the stressors confronting families. As the nature of family stress and the stressors that families encounter expands and evolves, the emphasis on how families cope continues to grow. Before the development of the first edition of *Families and Change*, Pat McKenry and Sharon Price (the original editors) conducted an extensive review of more than 400 randomly selected undergraduate and graduate college and university catalogs concluding that more than 60% of these institutions offered courses that dealt with family problems, stress, or change. These courses were found in a variety of departments and disciplines. They also surveyed instructors of those courses and discovered that texts representing a compilation of recent research findings in this area were almost nonexistent. As a result, the first edition of *Families and Change* (1994) was published to address this void. According to recent data from the National Council of Family Relations[1] (NCFR; 2019), there are 267 universities and colleges in the United States that offer degrees in family science. It is likely that most of these family science programs offer one or more courses related to family stress. Similarly, many psychology and social work programs also offer courses related to family stress. Since the first edition of *Families and Change,* this text has been regularly updated to address the various problems, stressors, and societal changes that Western families face. Each of the six editions of *Families and Change* have reflected contemporary issues and transitions taking place in the larger society as well as in families. This has been achieved by incorporating current research findings, introducing new chapter subjects, and adding new topics to selected chapters. For example, in this edition, there is updated research in every chapter and most chapters contain new substantive content (e.g., skipped generation families in *Stress and Coping in Later Life*, the emerging gig economy in *Economic Stress and Families,* and separation-instigated violence in *Stress and Coping with Intimate Partner Violence*). Additionally, we have introduced chapters on family stressors associated with race and ethnicity, and the value of family stress and intervention.

---

[1] Since 1938, the National Council on Family Relations (NCFR) has been the premier professional association for understanding and strengthening families through interdisciplinary research, theory, and practice.

Finally, a chapter in the fifth edition, which combined the topics of physical and mental health, has been divided into two chapters addressing how families manage the stressors associated with physical illness and mental health, respectively.

In the sixth edition of *Families and Change,* as with previous editions, not all family stressors could be reviewed because of page constraints. The topics chosen represent contemporary issues that many families face today and that have received considerable social, professional, and research attention. Each chapter presents an overview of our current understanding of selected family transitions and stressors, real-life scenarios meant to illustrate content specific stressors families face, and most include possible mechanisms of intervention. However, each author was afforded the opportunity to present their area of expertise in the manner they viewed as appropriate. At the end of each chapter, authors have provided a minimum of three discussion questions to support student reflection and class discussion.

The topics in this book represent both predictable and unpredictable problems and stressors. Predictable family problems would include those stressors that are inherently stressful even though they are foreseen. We take the position that all abrupt or disjunctive changes, although moderated or buffered by the family's coping resources, are likely to be stress producing. Such predictable or normative changes include marriage, parenting, aging, death, and dying. Other problems are potentially more traumatic because they cannot be predicted—these would include community or intimate partner violence, physical illness, substance abuse, war, economic insecurity, and divorce. We take the position that many of these problems are interrelated and often combine to produce stress-related responses. For example, stress related to economic issues may lead to marital problems, including violence which may then initiate a cycle of divorce, personal and economic disorganization, and remarriage.

We also assume that family problems, change, and stress responses are not always "bad" for a family. The disequilibrium that develops requires a family to create new methods for handling problems. The encountering of stressful situations may result in new and creative solutions that are superior to those that were present when the problem occurred. This experience may enable a family to handle future crises in a more effective way, and therefore result in greater individual and group satisfaction with family life.

This text represents an integration of research, theory, and application, drawing on the interdisciplinary scholarship in each topic area. It is intended to serve as a basic or supplementary text for undergraduate and introductory graduate courses on family or social problems. This edition will also be useful to professionals who work in social work, education, counseling, and public health, who increasingly serve and support families confronting a multitude of problems.

Overview of Chapters

We begin this text (Chapter 1) with a discussion of the research on family stress and coping. The nature and origin of the problems and changes families face today are discussed, noting that while many of today's problems are not new, the degree of change in American society is unprecedented. The history of systematic inquiry into family problems and change is traced to individual physiological stress studies in the late 17th century; these studies have evolved into the current focus on whole-family interaction with an increased emphasis on resilience. An ecological or systems approach is presented as the integrating framework for studying families under stress. These perspectives facilitate an understanding of families as dynamic mechanisms, always in the process of growth and adaptation as they deal with change and stress over time.

In Chapter 2, Heather Helms, Kaicee Postler, and David Demo discuss everyday hassles and family stress. Specifically, they examine how daily stress and hassles are associated with family functioning, paying particular attention to the variability in family members' experiences and the invisible dimensions of family work. A stress-vulnerability-adaptation model is used to frame the research on daily hassles and family stress. The authors emphasize the diversity that exists across and within families as well as discuss the contextual factors that moderate how families manage stress. A feminist perspective is used when examining the gendered meanings applied to routine family activities. Finally, the authors discuss how existing policies and practices in the United States fail to mesh with the daily life of American families and propose policy interventions.

In Chapter 3, Suzanne Klatt and Anthony James discuss the role of mindfulness in how families respond to stress and stressors. They review theories related to family stress, conceptualize mindfulness, and then walk readers through two in-depth case studies that apply mindfulness to different contexts within each case study. The authors acknowledge mindfulness as being connected to a rich, deep cultural and religious history, and endeavor to shift toward a critically conscious approach to applying mindfulness to family stress by recognizing the systems of oppression that particular families face.

Gary Peterson, in Chapter 4, focuses on parenthood as a stressor. He emphasizes a "realistic" approach that integrates research on parental stress with family stress theory and recognizes that caring for and socializing children involves challenges and hassles as well as satisfactions and fulfillment. He addresses (a) why parental stress is so common, (b) why parental stress varies within the population of parents, (c) why parents vary in their capacities to cope with and adapt to stress, (d) what linkages exist between parental stress and the adjustment (or maladjustment) of parents and children, and (e) what strategies exist for controlling and reducing adverse parental stress. This approach helps one understand the wide range of circumstances varying from highly disruptive crises, to chronic stress, to normative challenges, and increases our understanding about how parental stress applies to both individuals and families.

In Chapter 5, Kami Gallus and Briana Nelson Goff present the varied challenges and processes facing families who have members with intellectual and developmental disabilities. Because of the complex terminology associated with this area of research, the authors first present an overview of terms used to describe individuals and families with special health-care needs. Gallus and Nelson Goff go on to present current research specific to this population and discuss relevant theoretical frameworks that can be used to better understand these families in their unique contexts. They also examine various family subsystems as well as several external resources available to families with special health-care needs.

Abbie Goldberg and Nora McCormick, in Chapter 6, discuss the challenges confronting lesbian, gay, bisexual, and queer (LGBQ) individuals as well as LGBQ-parent families. Using an ecological or systems approach, the authors review the situational and contextual forces that impact these populations as they move through the life course. These include issues surrounding "coming out," forming and maintaining intimate relationships, barriers faced in becoming parents, and the stressors related to relationships with their families of origin, schools, and the health-care system. Finally, Goldberg and McCormick present implications for professionals with regard to supporting LGBQ-parent families.

Áine Humble, in Chapter 7, focuses on individual and family challenges that result from aging. She frames the chapter around the concept of an "aging family" which pertains to the relationships, transitions, and social support networks of older family members. Using both ecological systems theory and the ABC-X model of family stress, Humble examines stressful events commonly associated with aging. Specifically, she focuses on two major transitional events that occur in later life: retirement and caregiving. The unfortunate experience of elder abuse is also discussed as is the stressors associated with skipped generation families. Finally, adaptive and coping strategies applied by individuals and their families in later life are also reviewed.

In Chapter 8, David Demo and Mark Fine provide a comprehensive overview of current research on divorce and its consequences for individuals and families. They use the divorce variation and fluidity model, an integrated process model, to illustrate the variability in which families experience divorce but also to explore how adjustment to divorce changes over time. Demo and Fine go on to describe historical trends and sociocultural patterns to provide a current context for divorce as well as present factors that may predict or cause divorce. Finally, interventions (i.e., parent education, divorce mediation) that may facilitate divorce adjustment are presented.

In Chapter 9, Chelsea Garneau and Braquel Egginton discuss the stressors associated with remarriage and stepfamily life. They provide a background on the terms and definitions of stepfamilies as well as present the prevalence and demographic characteristics of stepfamilies in general. Using a family systems perspective, they identify sources of stress within the larger family system and the various stepfamily subsystems (i.e., couples, parent, parent–child, stepparent–stepchild, and sibling subsystems) as well as the most common characteristics of resilient stepfamilies. Finally, Garneau and Egginton discuss psychoeducational and clinical approaches to easing stepfamily adjustment.

Bertranna Muruthi, Hyoun Kim, James Muruthi, and Jaehee Kim discuss, in Chapter 10, various aspects of resilience and adversity that immigrant families to the United States may experience. Using a family resilience framework, they highlight the importance of interactions among individuals within families, communities and the broader exosystemic contexts. The authors focus on how family processes (belief systems, organizational patterns and communications patterns) interact with broader sociostructural factors and influence immigrant families' adaption processes. They highlight the complexity of legal issues, such as various statuses and identities (e.g., undocumented, refugees, citizen children) among individuals and within families. The authors also highlight acculturation, adjustment of immigrant children, interparental conflict, parent–child conflict, and issues related to physical and mental health.

In Chapter 11, Suzanne Bartholomae and Jonathan Fox address the impact of economic stress on families using the family stress model (FSM) as a framework. The authors discuss ways that economic stress is measured and defined and review the current economic conditions of the American family. They discuss outcomes associated with economic stress, including a review of the research on economic well-being and its interaction with resources and problem solving. Finally, using a family economic life cycle, they examine family financial planning as a coping strategy to combat negative economic events.

In Chapter 12, Anthony James, Veronica Barrios, Roudi Roy, and Soyoung Lee discuss the stress-related experiences and responses that families encounter across the three largest ethnic minority groups (e.g., African American, Asian American, and Latinx American). The authors begin by reviewing both the ABC-X model and the SFS model to promote an understanding of family stress in the context of race or ethnicity. Case studies are then presented throughout the chapter that incorporate example stressors such as managing transnational families, cultural parenting expectations, and interactions with law enforcement. These scenarios illustrate how race and ethnicity can influence family stress processes across different cultural groups in the United States.

Kyung-Hee Lee and Shelly McDermid Wadsworth, in Chapter 13, use the life-course perspective to examine the impact of military life on individuals and families. By employing this framework, concepts such as *historical time*, *transitions*, *timing*, and *linked lives* are used to help facilitate an understanding of the stressors experienced by, and the resources available to veterans and their families. The authors first situate current wars and veterans in historical context followed by a discussion of the individual and family transitions that veterans, their spouses, and their children encounter. Finally, three interventions that target the challenges veterans and their families often encounter are introduced.

In Chapter 14, Margaret O'Dougherty Wright and Lucy Allbaugh discuss child maltreatment from an ecological and systems perspective placing considerable emphasis on adaptation and resilience of maltreated children. Data from longitudinal studies are used to examine both risk and protective factors that result in the diversity of outcomes found among maltreated children. Specifically, the chapter highlights what is known about factors that heighten risk for psychopathology and behavioral dysfunction following child maltreatment, as well as factors that promote positive adaptation and that protect against adverse, enduring effects. Promising interventions to foster resilience and recovery following child maltreatment are also reviewed.

Lyndal Khaw, in Chapter 15, provides a comprehensive overview of intimate partner violence (IPV). She describes several types of IPV recognizing the disparities that exist in the definitions, measures, and methods researchers employ to study this dimension of domestic violence. In an attempt to facilitate a better understanding of IPV, Khaw presents several theoretical explanations for why this violence takes place and effectively applies a simplified version of the contextual model of family stress to illustrate its complexity. Additional topics of importance to this area of research, such as same-sex relationships, male victimization, and the process of leaving an abusive partner are also addressed.

In Chapter 16, Amity Noltemeyer, Courtney McLaughlin, Mark McGowan, and Caitie Johnson discuss the impact on families of mass violence in schools and communities. They begin the chapter by presenting a hypothetical case study illustrating a family's experience with mass violence. The authors then review the trends of mass violence in the United States and provide a context for discussing both adaptive and maladaptive responses. Integrating an ecological and developmental perspective, the authors outline a theoretical framework to explain how this type of stressor can impact families and more specifically, how resilience takes place at both the individual and family level. Finally, they describe risk and protective factors that can influence family resilience, exploring implications for professionals working with families.

Jeremy Yorgason, Stephanie Richardson, and Kevin Stott, in Chapter 17, discuss physical illness in the context of the family. They integrate aspects of the Double ABC-X, family resilience, and the vulnerability-stress adaptation models to examine the complex interplay of illness characteristics and circumstances as well as the stressors families encounter and the resilience they display in the face of illness. By employing this approach, they recognize how health stressors are connected to individual and family outcomes through adaptive processes and enduring vulnerabilities. Research findings relating to three situations, including childhood illness, physical illness in marriage, and the declining health of aging parents, are discussed.

In Chapter 18, Kandaus Wickrama, Catherine Walker O'Neal, and Tae Kyoung Lee take an in-depth look at the association between family socioeconomic risk and family mental health. The authors center their attention on the severity of psychological symptoms with particular emphasis on depressive symptoms, and the onset of psychological disorders. They recognize the increased prevalence of mental health challenges for both parents and children during adolescence, young adulthood, and midlife. Finally, Wickrama and his coauthors present the family socioeconomic risk and family mental health (FSAMH) model to inform health policies as well as health intervention and prevention efforts.

In Chapter 19, Kevin Lyness and Judith Fischer discuss the challenges faced by families coping with alcohol and substance abuse. Specifically, their focus is on the experiences of children and adolescents (and their parents) as they struggle with this issue. They take a family developmental approach in their review of current literature as timing, perceptions, contextual factors, and resources depend on individual and family change over time. Lyness and Fisher employ a biopsychosocial model, which includes biological, psychological, and social influences and combine this with the family stress and coping model. They place particular emphasis on the mediating and moderating effects that intervene between two variables, that is, variables that mediate or modify the associations between parent and offspring substance abuse. Finally, they search for explanations of resilience in families coping with substance abuse and discuss issues relating to prevention and treatment.

In Chapter 20, Colleen Murray and Jordan Reuter discuss family experiences with death, dying, and grief. They emphasize that death is a normative and often predictable event, yet it is not viewed as normal and instead is frequently avoided by society. Murray and Reuter review several theories of grieving to illustrate the complex process of loss that individuals and families endure. Family adaptation to loss is described in terms of family vulnerability, belief systems, definitions and the appraisal of gender, culture, and religion. The developmental nature and the unique challenges of children's grief are examined with an emphasis on factors that influence this evolving process. Finally, the death of specific family members (i.e., children, spouse, sibling, parent) and the associated stressors relating to interpersonal and contextual factors are described.

REFERENCES

Angell, R. C. (1936). *The family encounters the depression*. New York, NY: Scribner.

Boss, P. G. (1987). Family stress. In M. B. Sussman & S. K. Steinmetz (Eds.), *Handbook of marriage and the family* (pp. 695–724). New York, NY: Plenum.

Cavan, R. S., & Ranck, K. H. (1938). *The family and the depression*. Chicago, IL: University of Chicago Press.

Cole, C. L., & Cole, A. L. (1993). Family therapy theory implications for marriage and family enrichment. In P. G. Boss, W. J. Doherty, R. LaRossa, W. R. Schumm, & S. K. Steinmetz (Eds.), *Sourcebook of family theories and methods: A contextual approach* (pp. 525–530). New York, NY: Plenum.

Hill, R. (1949). *Families under stress*. New York, NY: Harper & Row.

National Council on Family Relations (NCFR). (2020, February 11). *Degree programs in family science*. Retrieved from https://www.ncfr.org/degree-programs

Acknowledgments

As editors of the sixth edition of *Families and Change,* we would like to acknowledge the "passing of the torch" that has taken place over the past few editions. As many of you are aware, the first, second, and third editions of this book were the product of two well-respected and prolific scholars in the field of family science, Dr. Patrick McKenry and Dr. Sharon Price. At the time the third edition was being completed, Pat McKenry died. Pat and Sharon had been friends and coauthors for almost 30 years. They had a remarkable friendship; one that involved both hard work and unceasing humor. When SAGE requested a fourth edition of this book Sharon approached Christine Price (her niece) to join her in the editorial responsibilities. She felt the passing of this legacy was appropriate not only because of their family relationship but also because Pat had been a senior faculty friend and mentor to Christine during her years as an assistant professor at The Ohio State University. When discussions of a fifth edition took place, Sharon (who retired from The University of Georgia in 2000) decided that it was time to hand over the editorial responsibilities entirely to the next generation. Sharon and Christine were both thrilled when Kevin Bush, a former student of Pat McKenry's at The Ohio State University, a former faculty member at The University of Georgia, and a current professor and associate dean at Miami University accepted.

Because this book was the original creation of Sharon and Pat's combined efforts and their fingerprints are still present, we want to recognize and pay tribute to them both. We felt honored to take on the editorial responsibilities for the fifth and sixth editions of *Families and Change* and understood that we had big shoes to fill. Regarding this sixth edition, the suggestions and advice we received from those who used the fifth edition of this book were appreciated and important to the changes made in the content and format of the sixth edition. Also, the quality of the authors' contributions, their timely responses, and their enthusiasm were invaluable to this updated version. Some of the authors were colleagues of both Sharon and Pat for many years and have contributed to multiple editions. Following in the tradition that Sharon and Pat practiced in previous editions, we sought out both "senior" and "young" scholars to collaborate and contribute to this volume. We were very pleased that "senior" authors involved junior colleagues or students to be coauthors and some former second authors moved into the position of senior authors. In addition, several new authors were asked to contribute. We would like to extend a special thank you to all of the authors; your efforts and contributions are greatly appreciated.

Kevin R. Bush

Christine A. Price

Theoretical Foundations

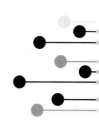

CHAPTER 1

Families Coping With Change

A Conceptual Overview

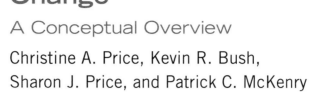

Christine A. Price, Kevin R. Bush,
Sharon J. Price, and Patrick C. McKenry

Families increasingly experience a wide variety of stressors associated with both positive and negative events. Industrialization, urbanization, increased population density (e.g., housing, traffic, demand on infrastructures), community violence, threats of terrorism, advances in technology (e.g., e-mails, texts, social media), financial challenges, and everyday hassles (e.g., errands, commuting, appointments) are frequently identified as making daily life more complicated and impersonal. Family roles are more fluid than the past, resulting in fewer social norms and a lack of support. Families have become more diverse as a result of changing family structures (e.g, divorce, single-parent families, lesbian, gay, bisexual, and queer-parent families, custodial grandfamilies, remarriage, cohabitation, intergenerational reciprocity), immigration, economics (e.g., increased cost of living and two earner families), geographic mobility, and other macro level factors. In addition to natural disasters (e.g., hurricanes, tornadoes, earthquakes) and societal stressors (e.g., discrimination based on race, religious beliefs, gender, and sexual orientation), U.S. families are facing the reality of wars involving American troops overseas, the threat of nuclear attack, and the reality of an ever-changing, and often divisive, political landscape. Additionally, contemporary families are still experiencing economic insecurity and stress due to the Great Recession and the associated economic downturn in the global economy (see Bartholomae & Fox, Chapter 11 in this volume). Sobering financial losses in pensions, investments, and savings accounts, employment instability, income volatility, and rising unsecured debt contribute to the financial struggle of individuals and families. Consider the accumulation of these events and it quickly becomes apparent that stress is a part of everyday life.

Families often face many unique problems, not because of one identifiable crisis, event, or situation, but because of continuous everyday societal change. Technology, for example, has enhanced everyday life in many ways but it has also brought about an increasingly overextended population that is bombarded with ongoing tweets, texts, and work-related demands. From an economic standpoint, members of the younger generation, in many families, are struggling with an increase in cost of living and overwhelming debt as they establish their independence. They are also faced with the reality that their life experiences may involve fewer opportunities and resources as compared to their parents and grandparents.

3

At the same time, due to medical advancements improving longevity and quality of life as we age, a demographic of adult children is faced with the undefined responsibilities of caregiving for their elders. Finally, the fluidity of family structures requires most families deal with cumulative, and sometime coinciding structural transitions during the life course (Teachman, Tedrow, & Kim, 2013; Walsh, 2013b).

All families experience stress as a result of change or pressure to change, whether or not change is "good" or "bad." The impact of change or the pressure to change depends on the family's perception of the situation as well as their coping abilities (Boss, 2013; Lavee, 2013; McCubbin & McCubbin, 2013). Boss (1988, 2002) defines *family stress* as pressure or tension on the status quo—a disturbance of the family's steady state. Life transitions and events often provide an essential condition for psychological development, and family stress is perceived as inevitable and normal or even desirable since people and, therefore, families, must develop, mature, and change over time. With change comes disturbance in the family system and pressure, what is termed *stress* (Boss, 2002; Boss, Bryant, & Mancini, 2017; Lavee, 2013). Changes affecting families also occur externally (e.g., unemployment, natural disasters, war, acts of terrorism), and these also create stress in family systems. This instability becomes problematic only when the degree of stress in a family system reaches a level at which family members becomes dissatisfied or show symptoms of decreased functioning (i.e., ability to carry out regular routines and interactions that maintain stability).

The Study of Family Stress and Change

Compared to the long history of research on stress and coping, theoretical and clinical interest in family-related stress is a rather recent phenomenon. Research on family stress and coping gradually evolved from various disciplines that have examined stress and coping from primarily an individualistic perspective.

According to the *Oxford English Dictionary*, the term *stress* can be traced back to the early 14th century when *stress* had several distinct meanings, including hardship, adversity, and affliction (Rutter, 1983). Even among stress researchers today, *stress* is variably defined as a stimulus, an inferred inner state, and an observable response to a stimulus or situation (e.g., Oken, Chamine, & Wakeland, 2015). There is also an ongoing debate concerning the extent to which stress is chemical, environmental, or psychological in nature (Folkman, 2013; Lazarus, 2006; Sarafino, 2006).

In the late 17th century, Hooke used *stress* in the context of physical science, although the usage was not made systematic until the early 19th century. Stress and strain were first conceived as a basis of ill health in the 19th century (Lazarus & Folkman, 1984). In the 20th century, Cannon (1932) laid the foundation for systematic research on the effects of stress in observations of bodily changes. He showed that stimuli associated with emotional arousal (e.g., pain, hunger, cold) caused changes in basic physiological functioning (Dohrenwend & Dohrenwend, 1974). Selye (1978) was the first researcher to define and measure stress adaptations in the human body. He defined *stress* as an orchestrated set of bodily defenses against any form of noxious stimuli and identified the term *General Adaptation Syndrome* (GAS) to describe the body's short- and long-term reaction to stress. In the 1950s, social scientists became interested in his conceptualization of stress, and Selye's work has remained influential in the stress and coping literature (e.g., Hatfield & Polomano, 2012; Lazarus & Folkman, 1984).

Meyer, in the 1930s, taught that life events may be an important component in the etiology of a disorder and the most normal and necessary life events may be potential contributors to pathology (Dohrenwend & Dohrenwend, 1974). In the 1960s, Holmes and Rahe (1967) investigated life events and their connection to the onset and progression of illness. Through their Social Readjustment Rating Scale (SRSS), which includes many family-related events, Holmes and Rahe associated the accumulation of life changes and those of greater magnitude to a higher chance of illness, disease, or death.

In the social sciences, both sociology and psychology have long histories of study related to stress and coping. Sociologists Marx, Weber, and Durkheim wrote extensively about "alienation." Alienation was conceptualized as synonymous with powerlessness, meaninglessness, and self-estrangement, clearly under the general rubric of stress (Lazarus & Folkman, 1984). In psychology, stress was implicit as an organizing framework for thinking about psychopathology, especially in the theorizing of Freud and later psychologically oriented writers. Freudian psychology highlighted the process of coping and established the basis for a developmental approach that considered the effect of life events on later development and the gradual acquisition of resources over the life cycle. Early psychologists used anxiety to denote stress, and it was seen as a central component in psychopathology through the 1950s. The reinforcement-learning theorists (e.g., Spence, 1956) viewed anxiety as a classically conditioned response that led to pathological habits of anxiety reduction. Existentialists (e.g., May, 1950) also focused on anxiety as a major barrier to self-actualization (Lazarus & Folkman, 1984). Developmentalists (e.g., Erickson, 1963) proposed various stage models that demand a particular crisis be negotiated before an individual can cope with subsequent developmental stages. Personal coping resources accrued during the adolescent–young adult years are thought to be integrated into the self-concept and shape the process of coping throughout adulthood (Moos, 1986). Crisis theorists (e.g., Caplan, 1964) conceptualized these life changes as crises, with the assumption that disequilibrium may provide stress in the short run but can promote the development of new skills in the long run.

The study of family stress began at the University of Michigan and the University of Chicago during the 1930s and the upheavals of the Depression (Boss, 2002). Reuben Hill, often referred to as the father of family stress research (Boss, 2006), was the first scholar to conceptualize family stress theory (Hill, 1949, 1958, 1971), when he developed the ABC-X model of family stress and his model of family crisis (Boss, 1988, 2002, 2006; Lavee, 2013). Subsequent generations of family stress researchers have made major contributions to this basic model (e.g., Boss, 1988, 2002, 2013; McCubbin, 1979; McCubbin & McCubbin, 1988; McCubbin & McCubbin, 2013). Developments in family stress theory include emphases on (a) family strengths or resilience (Walsh, 2006; Henry, Morris, & Harrist, 2015); (b) culture, race or ethnicity (Emmen et al., 2013; McCubbin, & McCubbin, 2013); (c) spirituality and faith (Boss, 2006; Walsh, 2013a); and ambiguous loss (Boss, 2002, 2013).

Family Stress Theory

Ecological/Systems Perspective

Family theorists typically have used an ecological or systems approach (e.g., Bronfenbrenner, 1979) in their conceptualization of families under stress. As a result, families are viewed as living organisms with both symbolic and real structures. They have boundaries to maintain and a variety of instrumental and expressive functions to perform to ensure growth and survival (Anderson, Sabatelli, & Kosutic, 2013; Boss, 1988, 2013). As any social system, families strive to maintain equilibrium. Families are the products of both subsystems (e.g., individual members, dyads) and suprasystems (e.g., community, culture, nation).

Although most general stress theories have focused only on the individual, the primary interest of family stress theory is the entire family unit. Systems theory states that the system is more than the sum of its parts (Anderson et al., 2013; Boss, 2006; Hall & Fagan, 1968). In terms of families, this means that a collection of family members is not only a specific number of people but also an aggregate of particular relationships and shared memories, successes, failures, and aspirations (Anderson et al., 2013; Boss, 1988, 2002). At the same time, systems theory also involves studying the individual to more completely understand a family's response to stress.

An ecological/systems approach allows the researcher to focus beyond the family and the individual to the wider social system (suprasystem). Families do not live in isolation; they are part of the larger social context. This external environment in which the family is embedded is referred to as the "ecosystem," according to ecological theory. This ecosystem consists of historical, cultural, economic, genetic, and developmental influences (Anderson et al., 2013; Boss, 1988, 2002). Thus, the family's response to a stressor event is influenced by living in a particular historical period, its cultural identification, the economic conditions of society, its genetic stamina and resistance, and its stage in the family life cycle.

ABC-X Model

The foundation for a systemic model of family stress lies in Hill's (1949) classic research on war-induced separation and reunion. Although his ABC-X formulation has been expanded (e.g., Boss, 1988, 2002, 2013; Burr, Klein, & Associates, 1994;

McCubbin, & McCubbin, 2013; McCubbin & Patterson, 1982; Walsh, 2013a), it has withstood careful assessment and is still the basis for analyzing family stress and coping (Boss, 2002, 2006; Darling, Senatore, & Strachan, 2012; Lavee, 2013). This family stress framework can be described as encompassing the following components: A (the provoking or stressor event of sufficient magnitude to result in change in a family)–interacting with B (the family's resources or strengths)–interacting with C (the definition or meaning attached to the event by the family)–produces X (stress or crisis). The main idea is that the X factor is influenced by several other moderating phenomena. Stress or crisis is not seen as inherent in the event itself, but conceptually as a function of the response of the disturbed family system to the stressor (Boss, 1988, 2002, 2006; Burr, 1973; Hill, 1949; Lavee, 2013; Walsh, 2013a; See Figure 1.1.).

Stressor Events

A stressor event is an occurrence that provokes a variable amount of change in the family system. Anything that alters some aspect of the system, such as the boundaries, structures, goals, processes, roles, or values, can produce stress (Boss, 2002; Burr, 1973; Lavee, 2013; Walsh, 2013a). This variable denotes something different than the routine changes within a system that are expected as part of its regular, ordinary operation. This variable is dichotomous, that is, an event either changes or does not change (Burr, 1982). The stressor event by definition has the potential to raise the family's level of stress. However, the degree of stress is dependent on the magnitude of the event as well as other moderating factors to be discussed. Also, both positive and

Figure 1.1 ABC-X Model of Family Crisis

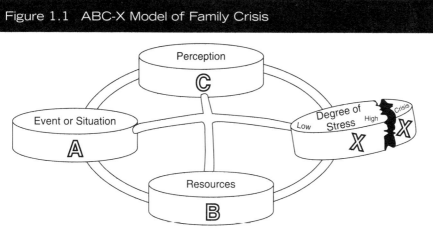

Source: Hill, R. (1958). Social stresses on the family: Generic features of families under stress. *Social Casework, 39,* 139–150. Reprinted with permission from *Families in Society* (www .familiesinsociety.org), published by the Alliance for Children and Families.

negative life events can be stressors. Research has clearly indicated that normal or positive life changes can increase an individual's risk for illness. Finally, stressor events do not always increase stress levels to the point of crisis. In some situations, the family's stress level can be successfully managed and the family can return to a new equilibrium.

Researchers have attempted to describe various types of stressor events (e.g., Boss, 1988, 2002; Hansen & Hill, 1964; McCubbin & McCubbin, 2013). Lipman-Blumen (1975) described family stressor events in terms of eight dimensions—these have been updated by adding two additional dimensions based on the research literature: (1) internal versus external, (2) pervasive versus bounded, (3) precipitate onset versus gradual onset, (4) intense versus mild, (5) transitory versus chronic, (6) random versus expectable, (7) natural generation versus artificial generation, (8) scarcity versus surplus, (9) perceived insolvable versus perceived solvable (e.g., ambiguous loss), and (10) substantive content (See Table 1.1 for definitions). The type of event may be highly correlated with the family's ability to manage stress. Other researchers (e.g., McCubbin, Patterson, & Wilson, 1981; Pearlin & Schooler, 1978) have classified stressor events in terms of their intensity or hardship on the family.

One dichotomous classification that is often used by family stress researchers and clinicians is normal or predictable events versus nonnormative or unpredictable events. Normal events are part of everyday life and represent transitions inherent in the family life cycle, such as birth or death of a family member, child's school entry, and retirement. These normative stressor events by definition are of short duration. Although predictable, such life-cycle events have the potential of changing a family's level of stress because they disturb the system equilibrium (Anderson et al., 2013; Henry et al., 2015). These events lead to crisis only if the family does not adapt to the changes brought about by these events (Carter & McGoldrick, 1989).

Nonnormative events are the product of unique situations that could not be predicted and are not likely to be repeated. Examples of nonnormative events would include natural disasters, loss of a job, or an automobile accident. Unexpected but welcome events that are not disastrous may also be stressful for families, such as a promotion or winning the lottery. Although these events are positive, they do change or disturb the family's routine and thus have the potential of raising the family's level of stress (Boss, 1988; Lavee, 2013).

There has been much interest in the study of isolated versus accumulated stressors. Specifically, life event scholars (e.g., Holmes & Rahe, 1967; McCubbin & McCubbin, 2013; McCubbin et al., 1981) suggest that it is the accumulation of several stressor events rather than the nature of one isolated event that determines a family's level of stress. The clustering of stressor events (normative and/or nonnormative) is termed *stress pileup*. An event rarely happens to a family in total isolation. Normal developmental changes are always taking place and nonnormative events tend to result in other stressors; for example, loss of job may result in a family having to move or marital disruption. By focusing only on certain

Table 1.1 Ten Dimensions of Family Stressor Events

1) *Internal versus External refers to whether the source of the crisis was internal or external to the social system affected.*
2) *Pervasive versus Bounded refers to the degree to which the crisis affects the entire system or only a limited part.*
3) *Precipitate onset versus Gradual onset marks the degree of suddenness with which the crisis occurred, i.e., without or with warning.*
4) *Intense versus Mild involves the degree of severity of the crisis.*
5) *Transitory versus Chronic refers to the degree to which the crisis represents a short- or long-term problem.*
6) *Random versus Expectable marks the degree to which the crisis could be expected or predicted.*
7) *Natural generation versus Artificial generation connotes the distinction between crises that arise from natural conditions and those that come about through technological or other human-made effects.*
8) *Scarcity versus Surplus refers to the degree to which the crisis represents a shortage or overabundance of vital commodities—human, material and nonmaterial.*
9) *Perceived insolvable versus Perceived solvable suggests the degree to which those individuals involved in the crisis believe the crisis is open to reversal or some level of resolution.*
10) *Substantive content (This dimension differs from the previous nine in that it subsumes a set of subject areas, each of which may be regarded as a separate continuum graded from low to high.) Using this dimension, one can determine whether the substantive nature of the crisis is primarily in the political, economic, moral, social, religious, health, or sexual domains or any combination thereof.*

Source: Adapted from Lipman-Blumen, J. (1975). A crisis framework applied to macrosociological family changes: Marriage, divorce, and occupational trends associated with World War II. *Journal of Marriage and the Family, 27,* 889–902.

events or stressors, researchers may fail to capture the complexity in the range and clustering of stressors (Pearlin, 1991; Yeh, Arora, & Wu, 2006).

Researchers have also offered alternative perspectives on stressor events. One such alternative is focusing on daily stressors and their relationship to stress outcomes (e.g., Darling et al., 2012; Harris, Marett, & Harris, 2011; Serido, Almeida, & Wethington, 2004; For review, see Helms, Postler, & Demo, Chapter 2 in this volume). Daily hassles not only parallel major life events in their potential to engender stress, but have an even stronger relationship than traditional life events measures in affecting relationship satisfaction, subjective well-being, and predicting physical health (Falconier et al., 2014; Graf et al., 2016).

Not all stressor events, however, are straightforward or easily understood. As a result, a state of ambiguity is created. Boss (1999, 2006, 2013; Boss, Bryant, & Mancini, 2017) addressed the issue of *ambiguous loss* that can result from incongruency between physical and psychological/emotional presence or absence. There are two major types of *ambiguous loss*: (1) a person being physically absent but psychologically or emotionally present (missing children, divorce, a family member in prison, soldiers missing in action, immigrants); and, (2) when a person is physically present but psychologically or emotionally absent (a person that has Alzheimer's disease or a chronic mental illness, chronic substance abuse; a spouse preoccupied with work; Boss, 1999, 2013). Ambiguous loss not only disrupts family functioning, it results in a lack of clarity regarding who is "in" and who is "outside" the family, as well as what are appropriate roles for family members. This type of ambiguity is the most stressful situation a person or family can experience. Boss attributed this high level of stress to (a) people feeling unable to problem solve because they do not know whether the problem is final or temporary, (b) the ambiguity preventing people from adjusting by reorganizing their relationship with the loved one, (c) families denying societal rituals associated with loss (e.g., funerals, death certificate) that in turn impede their ability to grieve, (d) friends or neighbors withdrawing rather than giving support, and (e) the extended continuation of ambiguous loss which leads to the physical and emotional exhaustion of affected family members (Boss, 1999, pp. 7–8).

Resources

The family's resources buffer or moderate the impact of the stressor event on the family's level of stress. Hansen (1965) uses the term *vulnerability* to denote the difference in families' physical and emotional responses to stressful stimuli (Gore & Colten, 1991). This moderator denotes variation in a family's ability to prevent a stressor event or change from creating disruptiveness in the system (Burr, 1973; Henry et al., 2015). When family members have sufficient and appropriate resources, they are less likely to view a stressful situation as problematic. McCubbin and Patterson (1985) defined *resources* as traits, characteristics, or abilities of (a) individual family members, (b) the family system, and (c) the community that can be used to meet the demands of a stressor event. Individual or personal resources include financial (economic well-being), educational (problem solving, information), health (physical and emotional well-being), and psychological resources which include self-esteem, optimism, sense of coherence, sense of mastery, and a positive family schema or ethnic identity (Everson, Darling, Herzog, Figley, & King, 2017; Garrard, Fennell, & Wilson, 2017; Lavee, 2013; McCubbin & McCubbin, 2013).

The term *family system resources* refers to internal attributes of the family unit that protect the family from the impact of stressors and facilitate family adaptation during family stress or crisis. Family cohesion (bonds of unity) and adaptability (ability to change) (Olson, Russell, & Sprenkle, 1979, 1983; Patterson, 2002) have received the most research attention (Lavee, 2013). These two dimensions are the major axes of the circumplex model (Olson et al., 1979). This model suggests that families who function moderately along the dimensions of cohesion and adaptability are likely to make a more successful adjustment to stress (Olson, Russell, & Sprenkle, 1980).

Community resources refer to those capabilities of people or institutions outside the family upon which the family can draw from to deal with stress (Boss, Bryant, & Mancini, 2017). Social support is one of the most important community resources, such as informal support from friends, neighbors and colleagues, as well as formal support from community institutions (Lavee, 2013). Social support may be viewed as informational in terms of facilitating problem solving and as tangible in the development of social contacts who provide help and assistance. In general, social support serves as a protector against the effects of stressors and promotes recovery from stress or crisis. Increasingly, the concept of community resources has been broadened to include the resources of cultural groups, for example, ethnic minority families (Emmen et al., 2013; Hill, 1999; McCubbin, Futrell, Thompson & Thompson, 1998; McCubbin, & McCubbin, 2013; Yeh et al., 2006) as well as those offered within established neighborhoods and communities (Distelberg & Taylor, 2015; Lum et al., 2016).

Definition of the Event/Perceptions

The impact of the stressor event on the family's level of stress is moderated by the definition or meaning the family gives to the event. This variable is also synonymous with family appraisal, perception, and assessment of the event. Thus, subjective definitions can vary from viewing circumstances as a challenge and an opportunity for growth, to the negative view that things are hopeless, too difficult, or unmanageable (Lavee, 2013; McCubbin & Patterson, 1985). Empirical findings suggest that an individual's cognitive appraisal of life events strongly influences the response (Lazarus & Launier, 1978), and may be the most important component in determining an individual's or family's response to a stressor event (Boss, 2002; Hennon et al., 2009).

This concept has a long tradition in social psychology in terms of the self-fulfilling prophecy that, if something is perceived as real, it is real in its consequences (Burr, 1982). Families who are able to redefine a stressor event more positively (i.e., reframe it) appear to be better able to cope and adapt. By redefining, families are able to (a) clarify the issues, hardships, and tasks to render them more manageable and responsive to problem-solving efforts; (b) decrease the intensity of the emotional burdens associated with stressors; and (c) encourage the family unit to carry on with its fundamental tasks of promoting individual member's social and emotional development (Lavee, 2013; McCubbin & McCubbin, 2013; McCubbin & Patterson, 1985).

Additional factors which could influence families' perceptions in a stressful situation include *spirituality, values and beliefs, culture,* and *stage of the family life cycle* (e.g., Emmen et al., 2013; McCubbin & McCubbin, 2013; Walsh, 2013a; Yeh et al., 2006). As noted earlier, there has been an increased emphasis on the role of spirituality, beliefs, and faith on family stress. Boss (2002, 2006) discussed several cases where a strong sense of spirituality results in a more positive attitude, hope, and optimism when families are confronted with a stressful situation. Faith can be a major coping mechanism promoting family resilience (Martin, Distelberg, & Elahad, 2015) and causing families to turn to their religious institutions and communities more than cognitive problem solving (Walsh, 2013a). Of course, spirituality can be experienced within or outside formal religious institutions. Regardless of the source, spiritual associations can bring a sense of meaning, wholeness, and connection with others. For example, religious communities provide guidelines for living and scripted ways to make major life transitions, as well as congregational support in times of need (Walsh, 2006, 2013a).

The belief system or value orientation of families may also influence their perceptions of stressful events. Families with a *mastery orientation* may believe they can solve any problem and control just about anything that could happen to them. For example, a recent study found that adolescent mastery orientation served to increase health promotion behaviors in teens despite family stress (Kwon & Wickrama, 2014). In contrast, families with a *fatalistic orientation* are more likely to believe that everything is determined by a higher power, therefore, all events are predetermined and not under their control. This orientation could be a barrier to coping because it encourages passivity, and active coping strategies have been found to be more effective than passive strategies (e.g., Boss, 2002; Yeh et al., 2006). The influence of belief and value orientations can also be mediated by culture (McCubbin & McCubbin, 2013; Yeh et al., 2006).

Culture influences the family stress process through (1) values or value orientations and (2) minority and immigrant status—both of which influence perceptions, coping strategies, and resources (Emmen et al., 2013; Folkman & Moskowitz, 2004; Yeh et al., 2006; Walsh, 2013a). Researchers of individual models of coping have made some strides in identifying how cultural values and social norms influence coping strategies. Scholars in this area have asserted that coping is not dualistic (e.g., Lazarus & Folkman, 1984) with only action oriented coping strategies resulting in positive outcomes, but rather cultural context also plays a part (Folkman & Moskowitz, 2004; Lam & Zane, 2004; Yeh et al., 2006). While taking direct action (e.g., confronting others, standing up for oneself) is a preferred and effective strategy in individualist cultural contexts; in collectivistic contexts, the emphasis on group harmony and interdependence leads individuals to enact coping strategies that focus on changing themselves to meet the needs of the group, instead of attempting to change the situation (Lam & Zane, 2004; Yeh et al., 2006). Scholars examining the cultural context of stress and family stress have focused on models that account for the depth and complexity of cultural and ethnic influences on family systems related to family stress and resilience. For example, McCubbin and McCubbin (2013) created the Relational and Resilience Theory of Ethnic Family Systems, which was designed to identify and validate competencies among ethnic/cultural families that facilitate successful adaption in the context of family stress. Similarly, McNeil Smith and Landor (2018) developed the sociocultural family stress model to help better understand the experience of family stress within racially and ethnically diverse families (see James, Barrios, Roy, & Lee, Chapter 12 in this volume).

The *stage of the family life cycle* can also influence a family's perceptions during a stressful event. Where the family currently exists in the family *life* cycle, points to the variation in structure, composition, interaction (between family members as well as between the family and the outside culture), and resources of that family (Henry et al., 2015; Price et al., 2000; Walsh, 2013b). Consequently, families at different stages of the life cycle vary in their response to stressful situations. This is particularly relevant as families move from one stage of development to another during normative transitions. It is during these periods of change (a child is born, children leave home, a family member dies) that families are likely to experience high levels of stress as they adjust rules, roles, and patterns of behavior (Aldous, 1996; Carter & McGoldrick, 2005). This stress is also affected by whether the transition is "on time" or "off time" as well as expected or unexpected (Rodgers & White, 1993). In general, off time (e.g., a child dies before a parent dies) and unexpected (a family member is diagnosed with a terminal illness) transitions create periods of greater stress. The significance of this stress could, at least partially, be attributed to the family members' perception of the stressful situation as being overwhelming or unfair.

Stress and Crisis

According to systems theory, stress represents a change in the family's steady state. Stress is the response of the family system to the demands experienced as a result of a stressor event. Stress itself is not inherently bad—it becomes problematic when the degree of stress in the family system reaches a level at which the family becomes disrupted or individual members become dissatisfied or display physical or emotional symptoms. The degree of stress ultimately depends on the family's definition of the stressor event as well as the adequacy of the family's resources to meet the demands of the change associated with the stressor event.

The terms *stress* and *crisis* have been used inconsistently in the literature. In fact, many researchers have failed to make a distinction between the two. Boss (1988, 2006) makes a useful distinction as she defines crisis as (a) a disturbance in the equilibrium that is overwhelming, (b) pressure that is so severe, or (c) change that is so acute that the family system is blocked and incapacitated. When a family is in a crisis state, at least for a time, it does not function adequately. Family boundaries are no longer maintained, customary roles and tasks are no longer performed, and family members are no longer functioning at optimal physical or psychological levels. The family has thus reached a state of acute disequilibrium and is immobilized.

Family stress, on the other hand, is merely a state of changed or disturbed equilibrium. Family stress therefore is a continuous variable (degree of stress), whereas family crisis is a dichotomous variable (either in crisis or not). A crisis does not have to permanently break up the family system. It may only temporarily immobilize the family system and then lead to a different level of functioning than that experienced before the stress level escalated to the point of crisis. Many family systems, in fact, become stronger after they have experienced and recovered from crisis (Boss, 1988, Walsh, 2013b).

Coping

Family stress researchers have increasingly shifted their attention from crisis and family dysfunction to the process of coping. Researchers have become more interested in explaining why some families are better able to manage and endure stressor events rather than documenting the frequency and severity of such events (e.g., Henry et al., 2015). In terms of intervention, this represents a change from crisis intervention to prevention (Boss, 1988; McCubbin et al., 1980; McCubbin & McCubbin, 2013).

The study of family coping has drawn heavily from cognitive psychology (e.g., Lazarus, 2006; Lazarus & Folkman, 1984) as well as sociology (e.g., Pearlin & Schooler, 1978; McCubbin, 2006). *Cognitive coping strategies* refer to the ways in which individual family members alter their subjective perceptions of stressful events. Sociological theories of coping emphasize a wide variety of actions directed at either changing the stressful situation or alleviating distress by manipulating the social environment (McCubbin et al., 1980; McCubbin & McCubbin, 2013). Thus family coping has been conceptualized in terms of three types of responses: (a) direct action (e.g., acquiring resources, learning new skills); (b) intrapsychic (e.g., reframing the problem); or (c) controlling the emotions generated by the stressor (e.g., social support, use of alcohol; Boss, 1988; Lazarus, 2006; Lazarus & Folkman, 1984; Pearlin & Schooler, 1978). These responses can be used individually, consecutively, or, more commonly, in various combinations. Specific coping strategies are not inherently adaptive or maladaptive; they are very much situation specific (e.g., Folkman & Moskowitz, 2004; Yeh et al., 2006). Flexible access to a range of responses appears to be more effective than the use of any one response (Moos, 1986; Yeh et al., 2006). Coping interacts with both family resources and perceptions as defined by the B and C factors of the ABC-X model. However, coping actions are different than resources and perceptions. Coping represents what people do—their concrete efforts to deal with a stressor (Folkman & Moskowitz, 2004; Pearlin & Schooler, 1978). Having a resource or a perception of an event does not imply whether or how a family will react (Boss, 1988; Lazarus & Folkman, 1984; Yeh et al., 2006).

Although coping is sometimes equated with adaptational success (i.e., a product), from a family systems perspective, coping is a process, not an outcome per se. *Coping* refers to all efforts expended to manage a stressor regardless of the effect (Lazarus, 2006; Lazarus & Folkman, 1984). Thus, the family strategy of coping is not instantly created but is progressively modified over time. Because the family is a system, coping behavior involves the management of various dimensions of family life simultaneously: (a) maintaining satisfactory internal conditions for communication and family organization, (b) promoting member independence and self-esteem, (c) maintenance of family bonds of coherence and unity, (d) maintenance and development of social supports in transactions with the community, and (e) maintenance of some efforts to control the impact of the stressor and the amount of change in the family unit (McCubbin et al., 1980). Coping is thus a process of achieving balance in the family system that facilitates organization and unity and promotes individual and family system growth and development (McCubbin & McCubbin, 2013). This is consistent with systems theory, which suggests that the families who most effectively cope with stress are strong as a unit as well as in individual members (Anderson et al., 2013; Buckley, 1967).

Boss (1988) cautions that coping should not be perceived as maintaining the status quo; rather, the active managing of stress should lead to progressively new levels of organization as systems are naturally inclined toward greater complexity. In fact, sometimes it is better for a family to "fail to cope" even if that precipitates a crisis. After the crisis, the family can reorganize into a better functioning system. For example, a marital separation may be very painful for a family, but it may be necessary to allow the family to grow in a different, more productive direction.

In addition to serving as a barrier to change and growth, maladaptive forms of coping serve as a source of stress. There are three ways that coping itself may be a source of additional hardship (Roskies & Lazarus, 1980). One way is by indirect damage to the family system. This occurs when a family member inadvertently behaves in such a way as to put the family in a disadvantaged position. For example, a father may become ill from overwork to ease his family's economic stress. The second way that coping can serve as a source of stress is through direct damage to the family system. In this instance, a family member may use an addictive behavior or violence to personally cope with stress, but this behavior will be disruptive, even harmful, to the family system. The third way that coping may increase family stress is by interfering with additional adaptive behaviors that could help preserve the family. For example, the denial of a problem may preclude getting necessary help and otherwise addressing the stressor event (Lavee, 2013; McCubbin et al., 1980).

Adaptation

Another major interest of family stress researchers has been the assessment of how families are able to *recover* from stress or crisis. Drawing from Hansen's (1965) work, Burr (1973) described this process in terms of a family's "regenerative power," denoting a family's ability to recover from stress or crisis. Accordingly, the purpose of adjustment following a crisis or stressful event is to reduce or eliminate the disruption in the family system and restore homeostasis (Lavee, 2013; McCubbin & McCubbin, 2013; McCubbin & Patterson, 1982). However, these authors also note that family stress has the potential of maintaining family relations and stimulating desirable change. Because system theorists (e.g., Anderson et al., 2013; Buckley, 1967) hold that all systems naturally evolve toward greater complexity, it may be inferred that family systems initiate and capitalize on externally produced change in order to grow. Therefore, reduction of stress or crisis alone is an incomplete index of a family's adjustment to crisis or stress.

McCubbin and Patterson (1982) use the term *adaptation* to describe a desirable outcome of a crisis or stressful state. *Family adaptation* is defined as the degree to which the family system alters its internal functions (behaviors, rules, roles, perceptions) or external reality to achieve a system (individual or family)-environment fit (Henry et al., 2015). Adaptation is achieved through reciprocal relationships in which (a) system demands (or needs) are met by resources from the environment and (b) environmental demands are satisfied through system resources (Hansen & Hill, 1964; McCubbin & McCubbin, 2013).

Demands on the family system include normative and nonnormative stressor events as well as the needs of individuals (e.g., intimacy), families (e.g., launching of children), and social institutions and communities (e.g., governmental authority; Lavee, 2013; McCubbin & Patterson, 1982). Resources include individual (e.g., education, psychological stability), family (e.g., cohesion, adaptability), and environmental (social support, medical services) attributes. Adaptation is different than adjustment. Adjustment is a short-term response or modification by a family that changes the situation temporarily. Adaptation implies a change in the family system that evolves over a longer period of time or is intended to have long-term consequences involving changes in family roles, rules, patterns of interaction, and perceptions (Henry et al., 2015; McCubbin, Cauble, & Patterson, 1982).

McCubbin and Patterson (1982) expanded Hill's (1949) ABC-X model by adding postcrisis/poststress factors to explain how families achieve a satisfactory adaptation to stress or crisis. Their model consists of the ABC-X model followed by their Double ABC-X configuration. (See Figure 1.2.)

McCubbin and Patterson's (1982) Double A factor refers to the stressor pileup in the family system, and this includes three types of stressors. The family must deal with unresolved aspects of the initial stressor event, the changes and events that occur regardless of the initial stressor (e.g., changes in family membership), and the consequences of the family's efforts to cope with the hardships of the situation (e.g., intrafamily role changes). The family's resources, the Double B factor, are of two types. The first are those resources already available to the family and that minimize the impact of the initial stressor. The second are those coping resources (personal, family, and social) that are strengthened or developed in response to the stress or crisis situation. The Double C factor refers to (a) the perception of the initial stressor event and (b) the perception of the stress or crisis. The perception of the stress or crisis situation includes the family's view of the stressor and related hardships and the pileup of events as well as the meaning families attach to the total family situation. The family's postcrisis or poststress perceptions involve values and beliefs, redefining (reframing) the situation, and endowing the situation with meaning.

The Double X factor includes the original family crisis/stress response and subsequent adaptation. The xX factor represents a continuum ranging from

Figure 1.2   Double ABC-X Model

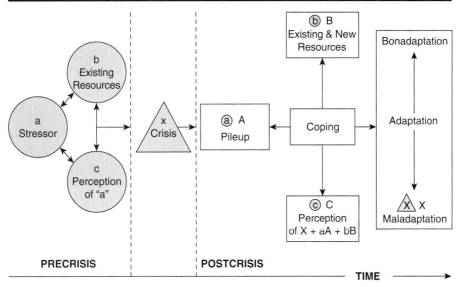

Source: From McCubbin, H. I., & Patterson, J. M. (1982). Family adaptation to crisis. In H. I. McCubbin, A. E. Cauble, & J. M. Patterson (Eds.), *Family stress, coping, and social support.* (pp. 26–47). Reprinted by permission of Charles C. Thomas, Publisher, Springfield, IL.

maladaptation (family crisis/stress) on one end to bonadaptation (family adjustment over time) on the other; and illustrates the extent of fit between individual family members, the family system, and the community in which they are imbedded (Lavee, 2013).

Boss (1988, 2002) has cautioned against the use of the term, *adaptation,* to describe the optimal outcome of a stressful or crisis state. She contends that the family literature appears to assume that calm, serenity, orderliness, and stability are the desired ends for family life. Like Hoffman (1981), Boss maintains that systems naturally experience discontinuous change through the life cycle in the process of growth. If adaptation is valued over conflict and change, then families are limited to a perspective that promotes adjustment to the stressor event at the expense of individual or family change. Boss contends that sometimes dramatic change must occur for individual and family well-being, including breaking family rules, changing boundaries, and revolution within the system. For example, an abused wife may need to leave or at least dramatically change her family system to achieve a sense of well-being for herself and perhaps for other family members. Therefore, in order to avoid circular reasoning, Boss prefers use of the term *managing* to refer to the coping process that results from the family's reaction to stress or crisis. Specifically, "unless crisis occurs, the family is managing its level of stress.

Managing high stress and being resilient are indeed the alternative outcome to falling into crisis" (Boss, 2002, p. 89).

Patterson (1988) revised the Double ABC-X model to include the community system as well as the individual and family system. This complex form of analysis requires that the (a) stressors; (b) resources; and (c) meanings/definitions of the individual, family, and community systems as well as their interactions be considered. Patterson's extension of the Double ABC-X model is consistent with biopsychosocial systems models that attempt to deal with the complex interplay and multiplicative interactions among biological, psychological, and social phenomena regarding health and illness (e.g., Masten & Monn, 2015; Repetti, Robles, & Reynolds, 2011). A few examples include research on parental coping in the context of child illness (Didericksen, Muse, & Aamar, 2019) and research linking marital conflict, children's stress reactivity (e.g., cortisol and alpha-amylase) and children's emotional and behavioral regulation strategies (Koss et al., 2014).

Resilience

Resilience has its roots in family stress and is both an individual and family phenomena. It has been defined as "the capacity to rebound from adversity strengthened and more resourceful . . . an active process of endurance, self-righting, and growth in response to crisis and challenges" (Walsh, 2006, p. 4). In addition, resiliency is referred to as the ability to stretch (like elastic) or flex (like a suspension bridge) in response to the pressures and strains of life (Boss, Bryant, & Mancini, 2017). In general, resilient families possess coping strengths that enable them to benefit from the challenges of adversity. The ability to successfully deal with a stressor event actually results in outcomes as good or better than those that would have been obtained in the absence of the adversity (Cicchetti & Garmezy, 1993; Hawley & DeHaan, 2003; Henry et al., 2015).

While early research and theorizing about the impact of stress on families focused mainly on the adverse effects of stressor events of families, more recent scholarship and theorizing have emphasized family resilience (Distelberg & Taylor, 2015; Henry et al., 2015; Lavee, 2013; Martin et al., 2015). Scholars have moved beyond viewing resiliency as a characteristic of an individual to providing a framework for viewing resiliency as a quality of families (Hawley & DeHaan, 2003; Henry et al., 2015). Following the family resilience model (FRM)—when family risk interacts with family protection and vulnerability in such ways that result in short-term and long-term family system adaptation, family resilience is present (Henry et al., 2015). Henry and colleagues (2015) describe the FRM as consisting of four key elements: (1) the presence of family risk, (2) family protection, (3) family vulnerability, and (4) short-term adjustment and long-term adaptation. Several key principles from individual resilience theories are applied, including variables that serve as protective or promotive functions in one circumstance, yet serve as risks or vulnerabilities in others (e.g., across cultural contexts).

Rather than a pathological view, or deficient model of families, the emphasis is on family wellness and strengths (Hawley & DeHaan, 2003; McCubbin & McCubbin, 1988, 2013; Walsh, 2006, 2013b). In contrast to Hill's (1949) original model which hypothesized that, following a crisis, families would return to functioning at a level below or above their previous level, resilient families are expected to return to a level at or above their previous level (Henry et al., 2015). A valuable conceptual contribution from the family resilience literature has been the recognition of a family ethos (i.e., a schema, world view, or sense of coherence) which describes a shared set of values and attitudes held by a family unit that serves as the core of the family's resilience (Hawley & DeHaan, 2003; McCubbin, 2006; McCubbin & McCubbin, 2013).

Conclusion

Families today are being challenged with a compelling number of changes and problems that have the capacity to produce stress and crisis. After many years of focusing on individual stress responses, researchers have begun systematic assessments of whole family responses, often by focusing on resiliency. Major theoretical paradigms that have been used to study family responses to stressor events include human ecology models (e.g., Bronfenbrenner, 1979) and family systems models (e.g., Anderson et al., 2013). Developing from Hill's (1949) work on the effect of wartime separation, various characteristics of stressor events as well as the mediating effects of perceptions and resources have been studied, suggesting that there is nothing inherent in the event per se that is stressful or crisis producing. More recently, family stress research has moved beyond the linear relationship of stressor, buffer or moderator, and response to look at coping and adaptation as a process that continues over time—that is, how families actually manage stress or crisis. Coping is conceptualized as an ongoing process that facilitates family organization but also promotes individual growth. Increasingly, the outcome of interest is adaptation, that is, the ability of a family to make needed changes and ultimately recover from stress and crisis. Adaptation, like coping, however, should not be perceived as a definitive end product because families are always growing and changing. Further, the serenity and stability synonymous with adaptation are not always functional for family members and for some families the response to a stressor event may result in a higher level of functioning. Finally, emphasis on the resilience of families has received increasing attention. By acknowledging the ability of families to successfully manage stressful events, scholars are broadening our understanding of how some families thrive in the face of adversity.

REFERENCES

Aldous, J. C. (1996). *Family careers: Rethinking the developmental perspective*. Thousand Oaks, CA: SAGE.

Anderson, S.A., & Gavazzi, S. M. (1990). A test of the Olson Circumplex Model: Examining its curvilinear assumption and the presence of extreme types. *Family Process, 29*, 309–324. https://doi.org/10.1111/j.1545-5300.1990.00309.x

Anderson, S.A., Sabatelli, R. M., & Kosutic, I. (2013). Systemic and ecological qualities of families. In G. W. Peterson & K. R. Bush (Eds.), *Handbook of marriage and the family* (3rd ed., pp. 121–138). New York, NY: Springer.

Boss, P. G. (1988). *Family stress management*. Newbury Park, CA: SAGE.

Boss, P. G. (1999). *Ambiguous loss,* Cambridge: Harvard University Press.

Boss, P. G. (2002). *Family stress management: A contextual approach* (2nd ed.). Thousand Oaks, CA: SAGE.

Boss, P. G. (2006). *Loss, trauma, and resilience: Therapeutic work with ambiguous loss*. New York, NY: Norton.

Boss, P. G. (2013). Resilience as tolerance for ambiguity. In D. S. Becvar (Ed.), *Handbook of family resilience* (pp. 285–297). New York, NY: Springer.

Boss, P. G., Bryant, C. M., & Mancini, J. A. (2017). *Family stress management: A contextual approach*. Thousand Oaks, CA: SAGE.

Brody, L. (1999). *Gender, emotion and the family*. Cambridge, MA: Harvard University Press.

Bronfenbrenner, U. (1979). *The ecology of human development*. Cambridge, MA: Harvard University Press.

Buckley, W. (1967). *Sociology and modern systems theory*. Englewood Cliffs, NJ: Prentice Hall.

Burr, W. R. (1973). *Theory construction and the sociology of the family.* New York, NY: Wiley.

Burr, W. R. (1982). Families under stress. In H. I. McCubbin, A. E. Cauble, & J. M. Patterson (Eds.), *Family stress, coping, and social support* (pp. 5–25). Springfield, IL: Charles C Thomas.

Burr, W. R., Klein, S. R., & Associates. (1994). *Reexamining family stress: New theory and research*. Thousand Oaks, CA: SAGE.

Cannon, W. B. (1932). *The wisdom of the body*. New York, NY: Norton.

Caplan, G. (1964). *Principles of preventive psychiatry.* New York, NY: Basic Books.

Carter, B., & McGoldrick, M. (1989). Overview: The changing family life cycle-A framework for family therapy. In B. Carter & M. McGoldrick (Eds.), *The changing family life cycle: A framework for family therapy* (pp. 3–28). Boston, MA: Allyn & Bacon.

Carter, B., & McGoldrick, M. (2005). *The expanded family life cycle: Individual, family, and social perspectives*. Boston, MA: Pearson.

Cicchetti, D., & Garmezy, N. (1993). Prospects and promises in the study of resilience. *Developmental and Psychopathology, 5*, 497–502. https://doi.org/10.1017/S0954579400006118

Darling, C. A., Senatore, N., & Strachan, J. (2012). Fathers of children with disabilities: Stress and life satisfaction. *Stress and Health: Journal of The International Society for the Investigation of Stress, 28*(4), 269–278. https://doi.org/10.1002/smi.1427

Didericksen, K.W., Muse, A., & Aamar, R. (2019). Rethinking parental coping with child health: A proposed theoretical model. *Marriage & Family Review, 55*(5), 423–446. https://doi.org/10.1080/01494929.2018.1501631

Distelberg, B., & Taylor, S. (2015). The roles of social support and family resilience in accessing healthcare and employment resources among families living in traditional public housing communities. *Child & Family Social Work, 20,* 494–506. https://doi.org/10.1111/cfs.12098

Dohrenwend, B. S., & Dohrenwend, B. P. (1974). *Stressful life events: Their nature and effects.* New York, NY: Wiley.

Emmen, R. G., Malda, M., Mesman, J., van Ijzendoorn, M. H., Prevoo, M. L., & Yeniad, N. (2013). Socioeconomic status and parenting in ethnic minority families: Testing a minority family stress model. *Journal of Family Psychology, 27*(6), 896–904. https://doi.org10.1037/a0034693

Erikson, E. H. (1963). *Childhood and society* (2nd ed.). New York, NY: Norton.

Everson, R. B., Darling, C. A., Herzog, J. R., Figley, C.R., & King, D. (2017). Quality of life among US Army spouses during the Iraq war. *Journal of Family Social Work, 20*(2), 124–143. https://doi.org/10.1080/10522158.2017.1279578

Falconier, M. K., Nussbeck, F., Bodenmann, G., Schneider, H., & Bradbury, T. (2014). Stress from daily hassles in couples: Its effects on intradyadic stress, relationship satisfaction, and physical and psychological well-being. *Journal of Marital and Family Therapy*, Advance online publication. https://doi.org/10.1111/jmft.12073

Folkman, S. (2013). Stress, coping, and hope. In B. I. Carr & J. Steel (Eds.), *Psychological aspects of cancer: A guide to emotional and psychological consequences of cancer, their causes, and their management* (pp. 119–127). New York, NY: Springer.

Folkman, S., & Moskowitz, J. T. (2004). Coping: Pitfalls and promise. *Annual Review of Psychology, 55,* 745–774. https://doi.org/10.1146/annurev.psych.55.090902.141456

Garrard, E. D., Fennell, K. M., & Wilson, C. (2017). "We're completely back to normal, but I'd say it's a new normal": A qualitative exploration of adaptive functioning in rural families following a parental cancer diagnosis. *Support Care Cancer, 25,* 3561–3568. https://doi.org/10.1007/s00520-017-3785-6

Gore, S., & Colten, M. E. (1991). Gender, stress and distress: Social-relational influences. In J. Eckenrode (Ed.), *The social context of coping.* New York, NY: Plenum.

Graf, A. S., Ramsey, M. A., Patrick, J. H., & Gentzler, A. L. (2016). Dark storm clouds and rays of sunshine: Profiles of negative and positive rumination about daily hassles and uplifts. *Journal of Happiness Studies, 17,* 2257–2276. https://doi.org10.1007/s10902-015-9693-x

Hall, A. D., & Fagan, R. E. (1968). Definition of system. In W. Buckley (Ed.), *Modern systems research for the behavioral scientist* (pp. 81–92). Chicago, IL: Aldine.

Hansen, D. A. (1965). Personal and positional influence in formal groups: Propositions and theory for research on family vulnerability to stress. *Social Forces, 44,* 202–210. https://doi.org/10.1093/sf/44.2.202

Hansen, D. A., & Hill, R. (1964). Families under stress. In H. Christensen (Ed.), *Handbook of marriage and the family* (pp. 215–295). Chicago, IL: Rand McNally.

Harris, J. K., Marett, K., & Harris, R. B. (2011). Technology-related pressure and work-family conflict: Main effects and an examination of moderating variables. *Journal of Applied Social Psychology, 41*(9), 2077–2103. https://doi.org/10.1111/j.1559-1816.2011.00805.x

Hatfield, L. A., & Polomano, R. C. (2012). Infant distress: Moving toward concept clarity. *Clinical Nursing Research: An International Journal, 21*(2), 164–182. https://doi.org/10.1177/1054773811410601

Hawley, D. R., & DeHaan, L. (2003). Toward a definition of family resilience: Integrating lifespan and family perspectives. In P. G. Boss (Ed.),

Family stress: Classic and contemporary readings (pp. 57–70). Thousand Oaks, CA: SAGE.

Hennon, C. B., Newsome, W. S., Peterson, G. W., Wilson, S. M., Radina, M. E., & Hildenbrand, B. (2009). Poverty, stress, resiliency: Using the MRM model for understanding poverty related family stress. In C. A. Broussard & A. L. Joseph (Eds.), *Family poverty in diverse contexts* (pp. 187–202). New York, NY: Routledge.

Henry, C. S., Morris, A. S., & Harrist, A. W. (2015). Family resilience: Moving into the third wave. *Family Relations: An Interdisciplinary Journal of Applied Family Studies, 64*(1), 22–43. https://doi.org/10.1111/fare.12106

Hill, R. (1949). *Families under stress.* Westport, CT: Greenwood.

Hill, R. (1958). Generic features of families under stress. *Social Casework, 39,* 139–150.

Hill, R. (1971). *Families under stress.* Westport, CT: Greenwood. (Original work published in 1949)

Hill, R. (1999). *The strengths of African American families: Twenty-five years later.* New York, NY: University Press of America.

Hillbrand, M., & Pallone, N. J. (1994). *The psychobiology of aggression: Engines, measurement, control.* New York, NY: Haworth.

Hoffman, L. (1981). *Foundation of family therapy: A conceptual framework for systemic change.* New York, NY: Basic Books.

Holmes, T. H., & Rahe, R. H. (1967). The social readjustment rating scale. *Journal of Psychosomatic Research, 11,* 213–218.

Koss, K. J., George, M. R. W., Cummings, E. M., Davies, P. T., El-Sheikh, M., & Cicchetti, D. (2014). Asymmetry in children's salivary cortisol and alpha-amylase in the context of martial conflict: Links to children's emotional security. *Developmental Psychobiology, 56,* 836–849. https://doi.org/10.1002/dev.21156

Kwon, J. A., & Wickrama, K. S. (2014). Linking family economic pressure and supportive parenting to adolescent health behaviors: Two developmental pathways leading to health promoting and health risk behaviors. *Journal of Youth and Adolescence, 43*(7), 1176–1190. https://doi.org/10.1007/s10964-013-0060-0

Lam, A. G., & Zane, N. W. S. (2004). Ethnic differences in coping with interpersonal stressors. *Journal of Cross-Cultural Psychology, 35,* 446–459. https://doi.org/10.1177/0022022104266108

Lavee, Y. (2013). Stress processes in families and couples. In G. W. Peterson & K. R. Bush (Eds), *Handbook of marriage and family* (3rd ed., pp. 159–176). New York, NY: Springer

Lazarus, R. S. (2006). Emotions and interpersonal relationships: Toward a person-centered conceptualization of emotions and coping. *Journal of Personality, 74*(1), 9–46. https://doi.org/10.1111/j.1467-6494.2005.00368.x

Lazarus, R. S., & Folkman, S. (1984). *Stress, appraisal, and coping.* New York, NY: Springer.

Lazarus, R. S., & Launier, R. (1978). Stress-related transactions between person and environment. In L. A. Pervin & M. Lewis (Eds.), *Perspectives in interactional psychology* (pp. 360–392). New York, NY: Plenum.

Lipman-Blumen, J. (1975). A crisis framework applied to macrosociological family changes: Marriage, divorce, and occupational trends associated with World War II. *Journal of Marriage and the Family, 27,* 889–902. https://www.jstor.org/stable/350840

Lum, T. Y. S., Lou, V. W. Q., Chen, Y., Wong, G., Hao, L., & Tong, T. (2016). Neighborhood support and aging-in-place preference among low-incomes elderly Chinese city-dwellers. *Journals of Gerontology Series B: Psychological Science & Social Sciences, 71*(1), 98–105. https://doi.org/10.1093/geronb/gbu154

Martin, A. S., Distelberg, B. J., & Elahad, J. A. (2015). The relationships between family resilience and aging successfully. *American Journal of Family Therapy, 43*, 163–179.

Masten, A. S., & Monn, A. R. (2015). Child and family resilience: Parallels and multilevel dynamics. *Family Relations, 64*, 5–21. https://doi.org/10.1080/01926187.2014.988593

May, R. (1950). *The meaning of anxiety*. New York, NY: Ronald.

McCubbin, H. I. (1979). Integrating coping behavior in family stress theory. *Journal of Marriage and the Family, 41*, 237–244. https://doi.org/10.1111/j.1741-3737.2002.00349.x

McCubbin, H. I., Cauble, A. E., & Patterson, J. M. (1982). *Family stress, coping, and social support*. Springfield, IL: Charles C. Thomas.

McCubbin, H. I., Joy, C. B., Cauble, A. E., Comeau, J. K., Patterson, J. M., & Needle, R. H. (1980). Family stress and coping: A decade review. *Journal of Marriage and the Family, 42,* 125–141. https://www.jstor.org/stable/351829

McCubbin, H., & McCubbin, M. (1988). Typology of resilient families: Emerging roles of social class and ethnicity. *Family Relations, 37,* 247–254. https://www.jstor.org/stable/584557

McCubbin, H. I., & Patterson, J. M. (1982). Family adaptation to crisis. In H. I. McCubbin, A. E. Cauble, & J. M. Patterson (Eds.), *Family stress, coping, and social support* (pp. 26–47). Springfield, IL: Charles C Thomas.

McCubbin, H. I., & Patterson, J. M. (1985). Adolescent stress, coping, and adaptation: A normative family perspective. In G. K. Leigh & G. W. Peterson (Eds.), *Adolescents in families* (pp. 256–276). Cincinnati, OH: Southwestern.

McCubbin, H. I., Patterson, J. M., & Wilson, L. (1981). *Family inventory of life events and changes (FILE): Research instrument*. St. Paul: University of Minnesota, Family Social Science. https://doi.org/10.1007/978-94-007-0753-5_101338

McCubbin, H. I., Futrell, J. A., Thompson, E. A., & Thompson, A. I. (1998). Resilient families in an ethnic and cultural context. In H. I. McCubbin, E. A. Thompson, A. I. Thompson, & J. A. Futrell (Eds.), *Resiliency in African-American families* (pp. 329–351). Thousand Oaks, CA: SAGE.

McCubbin, L. D. (2006). The role of indigenous family ethnic schema on well-being among Native Hawaiian families. *Contemporary Nurse, 23*(2), 170–180. https://doi.org/10.5172/conu.2006.23.2.170

McCubbin, L. D., & McCubbin, H. I. (2013). Resilience in ethnic family systems: A relational theory for research and practice. In D. S. Becvar (Ed.), *Handbook of family resilience* (pp. 175–195). New York, NY: Springer.

McNeil Smith, S., & Landor, A. M. (2018). Toward a better understanding of African American families: Development of the sociocultural family stress model. *Journal of Family Theory & Review, 10*(2), 434–450.

Moos, R. H. (1986). *Coping with life crises: An integrated approach*. New York, NY: Plenum.

Olson, D. H., Russell, C. S., & Sprenkle, D. H. (1979). Circumplex model of marital and family systems cohesion and adaptability dimensions, family types, and clinical applications. *Family Process, 18,* 3–28. https://doi.org/10.1111/j.1545-5300.1979.00003.x

Olson, D. H., Russell, C. S., & Sprenkle, D. H. (1980). Marital and family therapy: A decade review. *Journal of Marriage and the Family, 42,* 239–260. https://www.jstor.org/stable/351836

Olson, D. H., Russell, C. S., & Sprenkle, D. H. (1983). Circumplex Model of Marital and Family Systems: VI. Theoretical update. *Family Process, 22,* 69–81. https://doi.org/10.1111/j.1545-5300.1983.00069.x

Oken, B. S., Chamine, I., & Wakeland, W. (2015). A systems approach to stress, stressors and resilience in humans. *Behavioural Brain Research. 282,* 144–154. https://doi.org/10.1016/j.bbr.2014 .12.047

Patterson, J. M. (1988). Families experiencing stress. *Family Systems Medicine, 6,* 202–237. https://doi.org/10.1037/h0089739

Patterson, J. M. (2002). Integrating family resilience and family stress theory. *Journal of Marriage and the Family, 64,* 349–360.

Pearlin, L. (1991). The study of coping: An overview of problems and directions. In J. Eckenrode, *The social context of coping* (pp. 261–276). New York, NY: Plenum.

Pearlin, L., & Schooler, C. (1978). The structure of coping. *Journal of Health and Social Behavior, 19,* 2–21. https://www.jstor.org/stable/2136319

Price, S. J., McKenry, P. C., & Murphy, M. (2000). *Families across time: A life course perspective.* Los Angeles, CA: Roxbury.

Repetti, R. L., Robles, T. F., & Reynolds, B. (2011). Allostatic processes in the family. *Development and Psychopathology, 23,* 921–938.

Rodgers, R. H., & White J. M. (l993). Family developmental theory. In P. G. Boss, W. J. Doherty, R. LaRossa, W. R. Schumm, & S. K. Steinmetz (Eds.), *Sourcebook of family theories and methods: A contextual approach* (pp. 225–254). New York, NY: Plenum.

Roskies, E., & Lazarus, R. (1980). Coping theory and the teaching of coping skills. In D. Davidson & S. Davidson (Eds.), *Behavioral medicine: Changing health lifestyles* (pp. 38–69). New York, NY: Brunner/Mazel.

Rutter, M. (1983). Stress, coping, and development: Some issues and questions. In N. Garmezy & M. Rutter (Eds.), *Stress, coping, and development* (pp. 1–41). New York, NY: McGraw-Hill.

Sarafino, E. P. (2006). *Health psychology: Biopsychosocial interactions* (5th ed). Hoboken, NJ: Wiley.

Schulz, M. S., Cowan, P. A., Cowan, C. P., & Brennan, R. T. (2004). Coming home upset: Gender, marital satisfaction, and the daily spillover of workday experience into couple interactions. *Journal of Family Psychology, 18*(1), 250–263. https://doi.org/10.1037/0893-3200.18.1.250

Selye, H. (1978). *The stress of life.* New York, NY: McGraw-Hill.

Serido, J., Almeida, D. M., & Wethington, E. (2004). Chronic stressors and daily hassles: Unique and interactive relationships with psychological distress. *Journal of Health and Social Behavior, 45,* 17–33. https://doi.org/10.1177 /002214650404500102

Spence, K. W. (1956). *Behavior therapy and conditioning.* New Haven, CT: Yale University Press.

Teachman, J., Tedrow, L., & Kim, G. (2013). The demography and families. In G. W. Peterson, & K. R. Bush (Eds.), *Handbook of marriage and the family* (3rd ed., pp. 39–62). New York, NY: Springer.

Walsh, F. (2006). *Strengthening family resilience.* New York, NY: Guilford Press.

Walsh, F. (2013a). Religion and spirituality: A family systems perspective in clinical practice. In K. I. Pargament, A. Mahoney, & E. P. Shafranske (Eds.), *APA handbook of psychology religion, and spirituality (Vol 2): An applied psychology of religion and spirituality* (pp. 189–205). Washington, DC: American Psychological Association.

Walsh, F. (2013b). Community-based practices of a family resilience framework. In D. S. Becvar. (Ed.), *Handbook of family resilience* (pp. 65–82). New York, NY: Springer.

Yeh, C. J., Arora, A. K., & Wu, K. A. (2006). A new theoretical model of collectivistic coping. In P. P. Wong, & L. J. Wong (Eds.), *Handbook of multicultural perspectives on stress and coping* (pp. 55–72). New York, NY: Springer.

Family Stress and Adjustment

CHAPTER

2

Everyday Hassles and Family Relationships

Heather M. Helms, Kaicee B. Postler, and David H. Demo

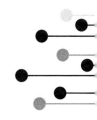

For many American families, daily life involves negotiating a maze of activities that includes cooking; cleaning; running errands; paying bills; dropping off and picking up children; commuting to and from work; tending to pets; scheduling appointments; attending events (community, religious, and school related); returning phone calls, e-mails, and texts; caring for aging family members; and remembering birthdays—often while parents fulfill the duties of full- or part-time jobs. These routinized experiences define the rhythm of family life, and family members can experience them at times as rewarding and at other times as hassles. Whether family members perceive a particular event to be a hassle, a pleasure, or both can depend on any number of factors. For example, women and men define and react to hassles differently; socioeconomic resources, cultural context, and work schedules make it easier for some families and harder for others to deal with daily hassles; and differences in personality characteristics and coping resources influence how individual family members experience and respond to everyday hassles.

In this chapter, we discuss the everyday hassles that researchers have examined in studies of daily stress and family life. We first define the kinds of events that constitute such hassles and then describe the methods researchers use to study them, including the means by which researchers explore invisible dimensions of family life. We then examine how everyday hassles are associated with family functioning, paying particular attention to the variability in family members' experiences. We present Karney and Bradbury's (1995) vulnerability-stress-adaptation (VSA) model as a helpful way to frame the research on daily hassles and family relationships, focusing on the diversity that exists both across and within families in each of the three domains proposed in the model. Because elements of context such as socioeconomic factors, workplace policies, and macrosocietal patterns (e.g., institutionalized discrimination based on race, gender, and sexual orientation) potentially introduce differential opportunities and constraints for family members that are likely to affect the links between each element of the model, we adapt Karney and Bradbury's model by nesting it within the ecological niches that families inhabit. In so doing, we underscore how contextual factors moderate the associations between vulnerability, stress, and adaptation. Furthermore, given the gendered meanings attached to many routinized family activities and the often divergent experiences of women and men in families, our approach is necessarily feminist. We conclude the chapter with a discussion of how existing social policies in the United States fail to mesh with the daily reality of most American families and thus contribute to family members' experiences of everyday hassles. We close with implications and suggestions for family policy interventions.

What are Everyday Hassles?

Everyday hassles are the proximal stressors, strains, and transactions of day-to-day life that can be viewed as common annoyances. These events are relatively minor and arise out of routinized daily activities, such as the tasks involved in maintaining a home, caring for family members, working at a paid job, and participating in community activities (e.g., Serido, Almeida, & Wethington, 2004). Both anticipated and unanticipated events constitute daily hassles (Wheaton, Young, Montazer, & Stuart-Lahman, 2012). For example, commuting to work in morning traffic, chauffeuring children to and from school and activities, and working longer hours at particular times of the year (e.g., holiday season for retailers, tax season for accountants) are all daily hassles that families routinize and anticipate. Unanticipated daily hassles, in contrast, are distinct in their episodic nature. Examples of such hassles include an argument with a spouse, a midday phone call concerning a sick child who needs to be picked up from a childcare center, a flat tire on the way to work, or an unexpected text from a boss demanding attention during nonwork hours. Although many unexpected daily hassles are relatively minor, they often disrupt the flow of everyday life and thus add to family stress.

Whether anticipated or unanticipated, everyday hassles are distinct from other daily stressors that are severe in nature (e.g., microaggressions, discrimination, racism) and the major life events or transitions discussed in other chapters of this book (e.g., death of a loved one, divorce, job loss, immigration). First, everyday hassles represent a more frequent and continuous form of stress than the relatively rare events that constitute major life changes. Because of their frequency, everyday hassles may be more important determinants of family stress than major, but less frequent, life events (Repetti & Wood, 1997b; Serido et al., 2004). Accordingly, the aggregate effects of everyday hassles have the potential to compromise family and individual well-being and even increase vulnerability to major life events. Second, hassles are characterized by relatively minor ongoing stressors that occupy daily living. Although they may contribute to a major life stressor or co-occur with other more toxic forms of daily stress, everyday hassles are viewed as conceptually distinct from other forms of daily stress (Serido et al., 2004). These conceptually distinct forms of stress may interact; families experiencing major life changes also confront daily hassles and continuous toxic stressors. For example, a family member who is adjusting to a major life event, such as immigration to the United States, may feel heightened stress if they miss an appointment or has to pick up a sick child from school. The stress from a relatively minor everyday hassle is likely to be heightened for a recent immigrant who may also be exposed to more severe chronic stressors related to English competency, legal status, or discriminatory practices at work.

Methods for Studying Everyday Hassles and Family Relationships

Researchers who study the links between everyday hassles and family relationships have utilized a variety of methods to assess family members' experiences of daily stress. In early studies, researchers defined *hassles* as "those irritating, frustrating, distressing demands and troubled relationships that grind on us day in and day out" (Miller & Wilcox, 1986, p. 39). Participants in these studies were presented with lists of various kinds of hassles and were asked to rate the frequency and severity with which they had experienced each hassle in the past month (Kanner, Coyne, Schaefer, & Lazarus, 1981). One criticism of this method is that it does not take into account the complexity of individuals' experiences of daily hassles. For example, Lazarus (1999) argued that the likelihood that an individual perceives or experiences a particular event as a hassle depends on the person's appraisal of the event as well as their coping resources. To account more fully for individual differences in appraisals of daily hassles, DeLongis, Folkman, and Lazarus (1988) revised Kanner et al.'s (1981) measure of daily hassles to enable respondents to rate how much of a hassle or an uplift they found each category (e.g., work, health, family, friends) to be on a particular day. DeLongis et al.'s revised checklist demonstrates an important shift in scholars' thinking about daily hassles, from viewing hassles as inherently stressful events to viewing them as experiences that individuals might appraise as hassles, uplifts, or both.

Feminist scholars who have used qualitative methods to study everyday, routinized experiences within families have also emphasized the multidimensional nature of daily hassles. Focusing on the routine, gendered experiences of everyday family life, feminist researchers have conducted in-depth, face-to-face interviews to uncover valuable insights regarding daily hassles. These studies provide rich sources of information about the nuances of daily family life that include participants' own, often quite complex, appraisals of their experiences. Through the use of these methods, feminist scholars have learned that although women may label many of the routinized tasks of daily life as essential and often unpleasant hassles, they also view these tasks as expressions of care for the people they love. For example, caring for an elderly partner or parent may include providing transportation to activities and doctor's appointments, grocery and clothes shopping, cleaning, and help with personal care. Women are more often responsible for carrying out these types of tasks than are men and, on average, experience them as more stressful than do men; yet regardless of the stress that accompanies the added responsibilities of caregiving, many women derive meaning and satisfaction from attending to the needs of their loved ones (Walker, Pratt, & Eddy, 1995).

In addition to underscoring the complex and sometimes contradictory nature of family members' experiences of daily hassles, a rich history of qualitative research has uncovered routinized aspects of daily family life previously overlooked by researchers. This body of work directs our attention beyond the activities typically identified in survey studies to include (a) emotion work (Dressel & Clark, 1990), (b) kin work (DiLeonardo, 1987), (c) marriage work (Oliker, 1989), (d) the scheduling of family time (Roy, Tubbs, & Burton, 2004), (e) the feeding of the family (DeVault, 1991), (f) the enactment of family rituals (Oswald, 2000), (g) household labor (Coltrane, 2000), (g) childcare and care for aging or sick family members (Abel & Nelson, 1990), (h) volunteer or service work (Hunter, Pearson, Ialongo, & Kellam, 1998), and, most recently, (i) the impact of information and communication technology (ICT) on work and family (Golden, 2013).

At the start of the 21st century, researchers began to examine whether and how fluctuations in daily hassles affected daily interactions in families. The methods used in these labor-intensive studies generally featured precise temporal sequencing of daily stressors and subsequent interactions with family members. The development of innovative research tools, such as time diaries and experience sampling, permitted researchers to obtain detailed accounts of daily hassles and resolve problems associated with retrospective recall that limited earlier research. Perhaps the greatest benefit of this body of research is that the methods allow for a within-person examination of the day-to-day or even hourly fluctuations in everyday hassles and their links with family relationships and functioning (Almeida, Stawski, & Cichy, 2010).

Influenced by family systems and stress transmission literatures as well as ecological and psychobiological perspectives, contemporary scholars have conducted daily experience studies focusing on how one family member's daily stress is linked to another family member's affect or behavior, as well as the reactivity of men versus women to daily stressors, and—most recently—family members' physiological arousal. Reed Larson's seminal work in the area of emotional transmission across family relationships is noteworthy in its utilization of the experience sampling method (ESM; Larson & Almeida, 1999)—an approach in which family members carried preprogrammed alarm watches throughout the day for 7 consecutive days and were signaled at random moments. When signaled, family members completed brief questionnaires about their activities, companions, and emotional states at those moments. In addition, researchers have coupled multiple methods (i.e., observations of marital and parent–child interactions, daily diary self-report data of mood and workload) with self-collected saliva samples gathered by each family member at multiple time points on each day of the study (Saxbe, Repetti, & Nishina, 2008; Seltzer et al., 2009; Stawski, Cichy, Piazza, & Almeida, 2013). In combination, these time-intensive and comprehensive methods have allowed researchers to examine the complex associations between family members' everyday hassles, their physiological arousal, and subsequent marital and family functioning in multiple contexts throughout the day.

Early work in this area was criticized for its reliance on relatively small, nonrepresentative samples (Perry-Jenkins, Newkirk, & Ghunney, 2013), the use of self-administered checklists to assess daily hassles and stressors, and the time-intensive demands placed on respondents, which often lead to attrition or missing data (Almeida, Wethington, & Kessler, 2002). To address these concerns, researchers have begun to examine the links between everyday hassles and family functioning in understudied populations, including same-sex couples, older adults, cohabiters, families with children, military families, and families of color (Cinchy, Stawski, & Almeida, 2012; Doyle & Molix, 2014; Lara-Cinisomo et al., 2012; Totenhagen, Butler, & Ridley, 2012; Totenhagen & Curran, 2011; Villeneuve et al., 2014). Informing this body of work is the Daily Inventory of Stressful Events (DISE), a semistructured telephone interview designed for use with a nationally representative sample of 1,483 adults (i.e., the National Study of Daily Experiences; Almeida, Stawski, & Cichy, 2010). The DISE methodology involves eight consecutive daily telephone interviews in which participants respond to a series of semistructured, open-ended questions about the occurrence of daily stressors across several domains, including arguments or disagreements, work or school, home life, discrimination, and issues involving close friends or relatives. Participants are asked to provide narrative descriptions of all the daily stressors they mention as well as the perceived severity of the stressors. All interviews are recorded, transcribed, and coded. Almeida's methodology is unique in that rather than relying on participants' self-reported appraisals of stressors, it uses investigator ratings of objective threat and severity to determine the type of threat each stressor poses (i.e., loss, danger, disappointment, frustration, and opportunity) as well as its severity. Participants' highly specific, brief narratives provide detailed explanations about the types of events that men and women typically experience as daily hassles, and the investigator ratings reduce some of the bias associated with self-reported appraisals of stressors. Almeida's methodology reflects scholars' calls for studying the intensity, duration, and source of stress in understanding daily hassles (Randall & Bodenmann, 2009). In addition, interviewing participants over eight consecutive days enables researchers to examine within-person fluctuations in daily hassles and well-being over time as well as the cumulative effects of hassles rather than relying on single reports about particular days or subjective estimates of hassles over several days.

Understanding the Links between Everyday Hassles and Family Well-Being

In this section, we examine how family members manage daily hassles and discuss the links between everyday hassles and individual and family functioning. We begin with a discussion of Karney and Bradbury's (1995) VSA model, and then use this model to frame a review of the literature on the effects of everyday hassles for families and their members.

The Vulnerability-Stress-Adaptation Model

The application of theory to the study of everyday hassles and family relationships is as varied as the methodologies used. Studies range from the atheoretical to research grounded in life course theory (e.g., Almeida & Horn, 2004; Moen, 2003), the ecological perspective (e.g., Repetti & Wood, 1997a/1997b), feminist perspectives (e.g., Daly, 2001; DeVault, 1991), emotional transmission paradigms (e.g., Larson & Almeida, 1999), more recently, biopsychosocial approaches (e.g., Saxbe et al., 2008; Slatcher, 2014), boundary theory (e.g., Boswell & Olson-Buchanan, 2007), spillover theory (e.g., Harris, Marett, & Harris, 2011), and conservation of resources theory (e.g., Harris, Harris, Carlson, & Carlson, 2015). Originally designed to provide an integrative framework for understanding the empirical research on marital quality and stability, Karney and Bradbury's (1995) VSA model is helpful in that it parsimoniously integrates and expands principles from various social and behavioral theoretical perspectives to explain the ways in which family members' experiences of potentially stressful events may be linked to relational outcomes. In our application of Karney and Bradbury's model, we treat everyday hassles as stressful events and explore how they interact with enduring vulnerabilities and adaptive processes to predict family well-being. In addition, the opportunities and constraints afforded by the ecological niches that family members inhabit are viewed as central to each element of the model, and we illustrate the adapted model in Figure 2.1.

Figure 2.1   Adapted Vulnerability-Stress-Adaptation Model

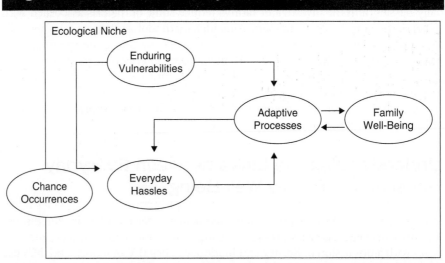

Source: Karney, B. R., & Bradbury, T. N. (1995). The longitudinal course of marital quality and stability: A review of theory, method, and research. *Psychological Bulletin, 118,* 3–34.

At the most basic level of their model, Karney and Bradbury (1995) identified three elements that contribute to our understanding of the links between everyday hassles and family relationships. Adaptive processes, which play a central role in the model, are the ways in which individuals and families cope with everyday hassles. They are critical to our application of the model because they moderate the associations between daily hassles and family well-being. Family well-being and functioning changes as a function of the way family members behave in response to everyday hassles, and, in turn, family well-being can affect how family members appraise daily hassles. For example, some studies suggest that employed spouses and parents withdraw from family interaction following workdays characterized by interpersonal difficulties and high work demands (Repetti & Wood, 1997a; Schulz, Cowan, Cowan, & Brennan, 2004). This type of social withdrawal has short-term benefits, in that solitary time can rejuvenate spouses and parents and buffer children and partners from the transmission of negative emotions. Rejuvenated parents and protected children are then better able to deal with additional hassles as they unfold. However, the short-term benefits of emotional withdrawal for the individual and the family may be offset over time as repeated instances of withdrawal may erode feelings of closeness in the family, leading to negative interactions, resentment, and more hassles which ultimately decrease family functioning and overall well-being (Story & Repetti, 2006).

The model also proposes a reciprocal relationship between adaptive processes and daily hassles. The level of stress is partially determined by the number, severity, and centrality of daily hassles that the family and its members encounter (Almeida, Wethington et al., 2002; Randall & Bodenmann, 2009). Interpersonal tensions or arguments have been linked with both physical symptoms and psychological distress, whereas everyday hassles that disrupt daily routines, threaten physical health, or generate feelings of self-doubt are rated as highly psychologically distressing by adults (Almeida, 2004; Stawski et al., 2013). Furthermore, the manner in which family members deal with hassles can exacerbate or alleviate family stress. To put it simply, certain days, weeks, and months are better than others; some hassles are easier to manage than others; and some people cope with everyday hassles better than others (Almeida, 2004).

In a study of divorced single mothers, Hodgson, Dienhart, and Daly (2001) found that careful planning, scheduling, and multitasking were important coping strategies for mothers of young children. To the extent that the mothers in their study were able to navigate daily hassles, they maintained a sense of control over their family routines. For example,

> I have a certain amount of minutes allotted to get in and out of the day-care center . . . then I have half an hour to get to work so I have it timed to about, I have like six minutes to get them in and out . . . . I can't always, things don't always go that way, smoothly, you know those six minutes to get him dropped off in the morning, I can't guarantee that that happens five days a week, 52 weeks of the year. . . . if I didn't leave the daycare

right at the right minute then there's a school bus that I follow all the way down [Highway] 21 . . . there was construction last fall on 21, you know, and there have been situations where I've forgotten things or (child) hasn't settled into daycare. . . . He needed a few extra minutes of comforting. . . . I drop him off the minute it opens and the minute it closes is the minute I'm there to pick him up. (Hodgson et al., pp. 14–15)

This mother's words illustrate that, as the model suggests, even with the most careful planning around rigid work and childcare schedules, chance events (e.g., bad weather, road construction, forgetfulness, an upset child) can lead to unanticipated hassles, disrupted plans, and the need for additional adaptation. For single mothers with young children, backup plans and the anticipation of the unexpected are essential coping strategies for dealing with daily hassles.

A family's ability to adapt to daily hassles is also influenced by the enduring vulnerabilities that the family and its members possess. Karney and Bradbury (1995) defined *enduring vulnerabilities* as family members' relatively stable intrapersonal characteristics (e.g., personality, child temperament) and family background variables (e.g., structural and behavioral patterns in family of origin). In her seminal research using daily diary methods, Repetti and colleagues (e.g., Repetti & Wood, 1997a) documented that the extent to which parents are able to refrain from engaging in negative interaction with their children following high-stress depends, in part, on the parents' own general level of psychological functioning. Using mood data collected at the end of study participants' workdays as well as self-report and observational data collected in the first few minutes of mother–child interaction at a work-site childcare center, Repetti and Wood found that mothers with higher levels of type A behaviors, depression, and anxiety were more likely than other mothers to engage in aversive interactions with their preschoolers on days during which they had experienced either overloads or negative interpersonal interactions at work. Such enduring vulnerabilities can both contribute to family members' appraisals of daily hassles and affect how they adapt to those hassles.

In the VSA model, adaptive processes are hypothesized to be positively associated with family well-being; that is, families and their members function better to the extent that they deal with daily hassles in constructive ways. In addition, the model proposes an inverse association between family well-being and enduring vulnerabilities and family well-being and daily hassles. High levels of enduring vulnerabilities and daily hassles are linked with low levels of family well-being. However, adaptive processes are expected to moderate this link in such a way that families with average levels of enduring vulnerabilities and daily hassles have lower levels of family well-being when adaptive processes are poor and higher levels of family well-being when adaptive processes are average or good.

A strength of the VSA model is that it provides an integrative framework that scholars can apply to gain a better understanding of everyday hassles and family stress. The components of the applied model—daily hassles, enduring vulnerabilities, and adaptive processes—and the general paths in the model can help us understand the complex and reciprocal processes operating among the model's components. The model is limited by its inattention to the ecological niches and sociocultural characteristics that families and their members inhabit, which leads it to ignore the potential variability that may exist in model paths based on between- and within-family differences. For example, contemporary American families are likely to work evenings, nights, rotating hours, or weekends, and some have access to workplace policies, such as telecommuting and flextime that may enhance their ability to manage everyday hassles (Berg, Kossek, Misra, & Belman, 2014). However, low-income families are disproportionately more likely to work nonstandard shifts with little access to family-supportive workplace policies than their high-income counterparts who are disproportionately more likely to utilize and have access to these policies and also the associated gains to well-being (Mills & Täht, 2010). Though some parents may organize nonstandard shift work to reduce daily hassles (e.g., working opposite shifts to allow one parent to be home with the children), constraints created by a work schedule that is "out of sync" with family life and compounded by limited financial resources pose significant challenges for managing everyday hassles:

> We interviewed Betty Jones, a low-income solo African American mother who worked the late afternoon and evening shift as a custodian in an Oakland hospital. Her car had broken down months before and she couldn't afford repairs, so her 11-year-old son Tyrone (all names have been changed) took responsibility for bringing himself and his 6-year-old sister to school on a city bus. After school, Tyrone picked up his younger sister and they walked to a bus stop to begin an hour-long daily ride, including a transfer, from Oakland to San Leandro where their grandmother lived. The grandmother took them with her to her evening job as a custodian in an office building. After she got off work at 10 or 11pm, she drove the kids back to their apartment in a low-income area of Oakland. This scheduling exhausted all of them, and Betty, the children's mother, was concerned about her own mother's willingness to continue watching after grandchildren while cleaning offices at night. Like others we interviewed with very tight budgets, Betty wanted to send her kids to the after-school program located at the public school but she found the fees exorbitant; her income was more than used up by basics like food, rent, and utilities. Betty's swing shift job as a hospital custodian precluded the presence of her children. (Thorne, 2004, pp. 168–169)

In other words, just as the "out-of-sync" nonstandard work schedule has the potential to undermine family well-being, providing families some degree of flexibility and autonomy in their work is related to higher well-being. It is beyond the scope of this chapter to develop a comprehensive model that can better account for variability in the ecological niches that families inhabit, but we suggest that the current model should be expanded to consider contextual factors to better reflect the growing body of research on everyday hassles and family relationships.

Everyday Hassles

A growing number of researchers using widely varying methodologies have explored the everyday hassles that family members typically experience as well as the different meanings that men and women ascribe to these hassles. With a sample of 1,031 adults, each of whom completed an average of seven daily phone interviews, Almeida and Horn (2004) found that women reported experiencing everyday hassles more frequently than did men. However, they found no differences in the numbers of days that men and women reported experiencing multiple hassles. In addition, a negative relationship between age and reports of everyday hassles was found, with a decrease in reports of hassles occurring in old age (i.e., ages 60–74). Compared with older adults, young and midlife adults reported experiencing a hassle or multiple hassles on more days, and they perceived their hassles to be more severe.

The content of the everyday hassles that individuals reported included arguments or tensions, overloads (i.e., having too little time or resources), and hassles regarding respondents' social networks, health care, home management, and work or school. Arguments or tensions accounted for half of all daily stressors reported by men and women, and most of these tensions involved spouses or partners. Overload and network hassles were much less common, occurring on 6% and 8% of the study days, respectively. Women were more likely than men to report hassles involving their social networks (i.e., relatives or close friends), whereas men reported more overloads related to work or school than did women (Almeida, 2004). Compared with older adults, the younger and midlife adults in Almeida and Horn's study experienced a greater proportion of overloads and reported that hassles caused greater disruption in their daily routines.

Feminist scholars have focused on gender differences in family members' experiences and the subjective meanings that family members ascribe to routinized hassles. For example, feminist researchers have demonstrated that women perform the bulk of family labor (e.g., cooking, housecleaning, laundry), parenting, and caregiving, and this work has multiple and sometimes contradictory meanings for the individuals who perform it. Studies involving national surveys and time diaries confirm a gender gap in household labor but suggest that it may be narrowing somewhat in the 21st century (Sayer, 2005). These results show that men are spending more time on routine household chores and childcare than in the past. Women, however, continue to perform about twice the amount of housework as their husbands, and mothers spend substantially more solo time caring for children than do fathers (Bianchi, Sayer, Milkie, & Robinson, 2012; Sullivan, 2018). Furthermore, even though men's and women's time allocation has become more similar, the types of activities performed remain strongly gendered. Women spend a greater percentage of total time in unpaid labor on routine, time-consuming, and less optional housework (e.g., laundry, cooking), whereas men spend a greater percentage of time on occasional household tasks that require less time and regularity (e.g., mowing the lawn, car maintenance). Relative to fathers, mothers experience childcare as more stressful and tiring, which may reflect the fact that mothers do more multitasking and physical care, provide care on a more rigid timetable, spend more time alone with children, and have more overall responsibility for managing care (Connelly & Kimmel, 2014; Craig, 2006; Offer & Schneider, 2011). In addition, gender disparities in free time have increased, with women reporting almost 4 hours less free time each week than men (Sayer, 2005). When paid and unpaid work hours are combined, married mothers work more total hours per week than married fathers (Bianchi & Raley, 2005; Sayer, 2005). Finally, the increased use of 24/7 information and communication technology (ICT) by 21st century families may lead to gendered patterns of spillover between hassles at work and home. For example, Chelsey (2005) found that increased ICT leads to more family demands spilling over into the workplace for women (e.g., caring for family needs while at work), and more work demands spilling over to the home for men (e.g., handling work demands while at home). The gendered nature of family work is not without costs, as evidenced in findings demonstrating that women report more stress from both external daily hassles and internal (relationship) daily hassles, and, relative to men's, women's internal and external hassles place both partners' relationship satisfaction at risk (Falconier, Nussbeck, Bodenmann, Schneider, & Bradbury, 2014).

Even in situations where couples define their division of family work as equal, inequalities abound when examining the management of everyday hassles. Regarding the everyday hassles associated with organizing family members' schedules, Jeannie [a mother of two children ages 9 and 12] observed: "I mean the thing is it generally falls on the woman. It's really kind of hard to expect [this to happen] and maybe it's just because of . . . nature. When I first got married and had kids I thought [we should share childcare] fifty-fifty because everything else was fifty-fifty" (Kaplan, 2010, pp. 598–599). Inequalities may also manifest in the degree of worry mothers and fathers express about their children. For example, Eleanor, a mother of a 12- and 14-year-old, commented, "[My husband] doesn't worry as much as I about my daughter . . . Sometimes I say to him, 'Don't you know when she's coming home?' And he's sort of, 'Oh, she'll be home.' So we have a different standard of worry" (Kaplan, 2010, pp. 603–604). These mothers' experiences of tending to the everyday needs of their children underscore feminist characterizations of the often "invisible" nature of the work required to care for children and maintain a home and suggest that if this type of family work were measured directly in large-scale survey studies, gender differences may be even more pronounced.

To understand the links between everyday hassles and family relationships, one must recognize that family labor is multidimensional and time intensive, involves both routine and occasional tasks, and is highly variable across and within households. Furthermore, because much of the "worry-shift" is mundane, tedious, boring, and generally performed without pay, most women and men report that they do not like doing it (DeVault, 1991; Kaplan, 2010; Robinson & Milkie, 1998). The sheer volume of family labor and caregiving, as well as the ongoing and relentless nature of many of these responsibilities, requires planning, preparation, scheduling, and multitasking—tasks that often fall disproportionately on the shoulders of women. Thus, although caring for family members includes enjoyable aspects, the work itself often creates hassles that impact family relationships (Connelly & Kimmel, 2014). Peg, a school psychologist working 45 hours per week and a married mother of three young children, explains the division of family labor in her home and her frustrations with the arrangement:

> He's not a morning person. He has coffee and sits. That's one of the biggest gripes. When I've had a tough morning, I'll say, "Am I the only one who hears people say, 'more orange juice?'" . . . Things build to a head and then I have what you call a meltdown. "I can't do this anymore. This isn't fair. This isn't right. I'm not the only adult in the house!" Then for a few days he'll try to make lunch. It's generally when I'm feeling pressured . . . and the stress level just gets to me and then I let it all out. It changes for a short period of time but then reverts right back to the same. (Deutsch, 1999, pp. 50, 53)

Ethan, Peg's husband who works 60 hours per week in the biotechnology business, recognizes the inequality but explains it differently: "[Peg] just naturally jumps in where I kind of wait for her to take the initiative. . . . Maybe I'm not helping as much as I could because I feel like that" (Deutsch, 1999, p. 51). Ethan's response implies that "helping" with the children in the morning is an option for him—something he can opt out of if he does not feel like participating.

One explanation for the differences between women and men in the ways they experience everyday hassles focuses on the extent to which individuals interpret their involvement in family labor to be freely chosen or voluntary. In an exploration of the contextual conditions surrounding family members' experience of emotions, Larson, Richards, and Perry-Jenkins (1994) were the first to discover how married spouses' perceptions of choice played a key role predicting fluctuations in their moods throughout the day. Their rich data on the contrasting moods of husbands and wives at work and at home highlighted how differently men and women experience these contexts and the everyday hassles they encounter. For example, employed wives recorded their most positive moods while at work and an emotional decline at home during the evening hours, which were filled with housework and childcare. In contrast, husbands recorded their most negative emotions in the workplace; at home their moods lightened, in part, because non-work time included leisure activities. However, even when men performed housework or childcare, their moods while doing these tasks were more positive than were those of their wives when they performed the same activities. Further analyses revealed that performing housework and childcare tasks elicited more positive reactions from husbands than from wives because the husbands perceived that they had more choice regarding their involvement in these domains than did the wives.

The reverse is true for paid work. Husbands in Larson et al.'s (1994) study reported low levels of choice while at work, potentially related to constraints associated with gendered expectations for men to be providers. Employed wives reported more positive moods at work than did employed husbands. For many (but not all) women, an unhurried work pace and a friendly work environment contributed to their positive moods while on the job, demonstrating the importance of social support in the workplace for women's mental health. Collectively, these findings suggest that the transfer of women's and men's routinized experiences in the workplace or at home to emotional distress is a gendered process. The translation of work and family experiences into emotional health or distress may depend, in part, on the degree to which the individual perceives the activity to be freely chosen and whether it provides opportunities for positive social interaction, rather than the characteristics of the activity per se.

In sum, the studies reviewed above suggest that scholars may achieve a better understanding of everyday hassles by considering the ecological contexts in which the hassles occur. A family's construction of gendered expectations is one such context (Allen & Walker, 2000) and contributes to differences in women's and men's perceptions of and reactions to daily hassles. In addition, research has shown that a family's socioeconomic status (Grzywacz, Almeida, Neupert, & Ettner, 2004; Maisel & Karney, 2012), exposure to chronic stressors at work or at home (Serido et al., 2004), nonstandard work schedules (Almeida, 2004), increased use of ICT, and minority stress linked to individuals' race, ethnicity, sexual orientation, or immigration status (Lincoln & Chae, 2010; Riggle, Rostosky, & Horne, 2010; Trail, Goff, Bradbury, & Karney, 2012) may exacerbate (or buffer) the impact of everyday hassles on family well-being. For example, aspects of the larger sociopolitical climate including anti-immigration policies and deportation enforcement initiatives enacted by the United States Department of Justice under the direction of the Trump administration have increased fear and stress, including risk for and fear of deportation and separation, among immigrant families in the United States. Increases in Immigration and Customs Enforcement (ICE) raids, efforts to build a border wall between the United States and Mexico, the weakening of the Deferred Action for Childhood Arrivals (DACA), and the practice of the detention and separation of families at the U.S. border impact everyday hassles for Latinx immigrant families regardless of their legal status (e.g., Dreby, 2015). As spoken by a Mexican immigrant wife and mother who experienced immense anxiety about deportation, "Sometimes I dream that I go get [my daughter] at the school and there I find all the other mothers who tell me, 'Don't go back to the apartments.' . . . Or sometimes I dream that my husband gets arrested by the police at work; they call me and tell me that he is in jail" (Dreby, 2015, p. 38). As this example illustrates, everyday hassles are embedded in a larger context that amplifies the impact that seemingly minor irritations (e.g., picking up a sick child from school, a traffic stop for a broken taillight) have on family and personal well-being. Laws and policies that institutionalize discrimination are an important dimension of context that scholars have begun to study and address via publicly disseminated policy statements documenting their harmful effect on families (e.g., American Psychological Association [APA], 2019; Bouza et al., 2018; Vesely, Bravo, & Guzzardo, 2019).

Adaptive Processes

According to the VSA, the processes that family members use to cope with everyday hassles have important implications for how those hassles affect family interactions. In general, two different patterns of responses have been identified following workdays characterized by heavy workloads or negative interactions with coworkers: (1) increases in marital or parent–child conflict and (2) social withdrawal. These patterns, however, vary across studies, within couples, and by reporter.

In one of the first daily diary studies of married couples with children, Bolger, DeLongis, Kessler, and Wethington (1989) found that on days when husbands experienced an argument at work with a coworker or supervisor, they were more likely to return home from work and argue with their wives, but not with their children. For wives, however, the researchers found no significant associations between arguments at work and subsequent arguments with spouses or children. In contrast, another diary study conducted by Story and Repetti (2006) found that wives, but not husbands, reported more marital anger toward their spouse and were more withdrawn from family interaction following workdays characterized by heavy workloads and unpleasant social interactions. In an interesting twist, husbands' reports of their wives' behavior suggested that husbands did not notice their wives' displays of anger or withdrawal on these same days. This may be partially explained by the finding that everyday hassles at work were found to contribute to wives' negative moods, which in turn colored wives' perceptions of their interactions at home. Although husbands did not perceive their wives to be more angry or withdrawn following difficult days at work, wives perceived that they were more irritable and less emotionally available, in part, due to their negative moods. For some families, daily stressors experienced at work may also spill over into interactions with children. For example, Repetti's (1994) early work demonstrated that fathers engaged in more expressions of anger toward children and more harsh discipline following days characterized by negative social interactions at work. In addition, both mothers and fathers have been shown to be less behaviorally and emotionally engaged with their children following busy workdays (Repetti, 1994; Repetti & Wood, 1997a).

Daily relationship stress—or hassles related to the sharing of housework, different goals, and partners' annoying habits—may also be important in understanding the link between everyday hassles (e.g., at work) and couple functioning (Falconier et al., 2014; Ledermann, Bodenmann, Rudaz, & Bradbury, 2010). For example, a study of 345 married and unmarried Swiss couples found that the everyday hassles that partners experienced impacted their overall relationship quality and communication effectiveness via elevations in daily relationship stressors

(Ledermann et al., 2010). In a second Swiss study of 110 couples, Falconier et al. (2014) found that women's daily hassles predicted their own physical well-being and anxiety and both partners' relationship stress. Women's relationship stress, in turn, was related to women's depression and both partners' relationship satisfaction. Men's daily hassles were related to their own relationship stress, depression, anxiety, and physical well-being. Men's relationship stress predicted their own depression and relationship satisfaction. Taken together, these findings suggest that although daily hassles are inherently beyond couples' control, couples who adopt effective strategies to reduce relationship stress may be able to protect their relationship quality and satisfaction from the negative effects of everyday hassles.

How might family members buffer others from the effects of the everyday hassles they encounter? Repetti and Wood's (e.g., 1997b) early research suggested that parents' behavioral and emotional withdrawal may actually protect children from the transmission of their parents' negative work experiences. Another early study (Bolger et al., 1989) found that when husbands experienced greater-than-usual demands at the workplace, they performed less household labor and childcare when they returned home, and their wives compensated for their withdrawal by performing more of the work at home. The parallel pattern did not occur when wives experienced overloads at work. When wives experienced overloads at work, they too performed less work at home (i.e., behavioral withdrawal), but their husbands did not reciprocate by performing more. Bolger et al. (1989) label this an "asymmetry in the buffering effect" (p. 182) and suggest that, in the short term, wives' stepping in for husbands may alleviate husbands' stress and avoid the transmission of stress from husbands' daily hassles to children. However, this short-term adaptive process may prove harmful over time for families—most particularly for wives. Coping in this manner in repeated instances over time may be one factor in explaining the consistent finding that marriage benefits the emotional health of men more than that of women (Amato, Johnson, Booth, & Rogers, 2003). To the extent that women's emotional health plays a key role in child well-being (Demo & Acock, 1996), a pattern of asymmetrical buffering may be detrimental for children in families as well.

Additionally, several researchers have inquired as to how patterns of emotional transmission from daily hassles in the workplace to home vary based on the quality of the marital relationship (Schulz et al., 2004; Story & Repetti, 2006). Story and Repetti (2006) found that both husbands and wives in higher-conflict marriages were more likely than their peers in less conflicted marriages to express anger toward their spouse and withdraw from family interaction on evenings following stressful days at work. Similarly, Schulz et al. (2004) found that husbands in more satisfying marriages were less likely than maritally dissatisfied husbands to express anger or criticism toward their wives following emotionally upsetting days at work. Taken together, this research suggests that husbands and wives in higher conflict families are more likely to express negative feelings toward their spouses following high-stress days. Spouses in these families also frequently withdraw from family interaction following difficult workdays, perhaps in an attempt to disengage from further negative interactions.

One unexpected finding indicated that some wives in more satisfying marriages actually withdraw more and express more anger following demanding days at work than do wives in less satisfying marriages (Schulz et al., 2004). The authors suggest that a more satisfying marital relationship may create a context in which husbands encourage wives to express their frustrations as a way of coping. It may be that more maritally satisfied husbands facilitate wives' temporary withdrawal from family interactions by increasing their own involvement with childcare and housework so that their wives can recuperate (e.g., "Mommy needs some time to relax and unwind because she had a hard day at work."). In turn, wives in more satisfying marital relationships may feel freer than their maritally dissatisfied counterparts to express anger and withdraw from family interaction after difficult workdays because their husbands are willing to hear their complaints and increase their supportive behavior. This research suggests that the nature of the marital relationship may affect the extent to which everyday hassles at work spill over into family interactions and that these patterns may vary by gender. Similarly, the results of other studies suggest that additional family vulnerabilities or strengths (e.g., child conduct problems, overly controlling parenting) may influence the extent to which daily hassles transfer to family stress (Larson & Gillman, 1999; Margolin, Christensen, & John, 1996).

Research from a 10-year, multisite qualitative study suggests that buffering children from the effects of parents' everyday hassles may be a luxury afforded to only middle-class and more affluent families (Dodson & Dickert, 2004). In their study of low-income families, Dodson and Dickert (2004) found that parents engaged children, most typically eldest daughters, in childcare and housework tasks as a strategy to compensate for the inflexible work hours, low wages, and nonstandard shifts of working-poor parents. Whereas studies of both working- and middle-class families have found that girls, more than boys, assume household labor responsibilities when mothers' work demands are high (e.g., Crouter, Head, Bumpus, & McHale, 2001), low-income families differ in that girls' contributions to family labor are essential for family survival because the demands of parents' work render mothers and fathers unavailable to attend to even the most basic everyday hassles of family life. In this way, parents' workplace demands have direct impacts on eldest daughters' daily experiences in that these girls must contend with the everyday hassles and responsibilities customarily assigned to parents. As a teacher of the low-income adolescent girls participating in Dodson and Dickert's (2004) study observed, "They have to take their little brother to the bus stop in the morning and sometimes that means getting to school late or they are babysitting . . . they are like little mothers" (p. 326). One 15-year-old daughter's own words illustrate that the girls themselves are keenly aware of their responsibilities as childcare providers and assistant housekeepers: "I have to take care of the house and take care of the kids and I don't go outside. I have to stay home. They have to go to work so I take over" (p. 324).

The results of Dodson and Dickert's (2004) study suggest that although this adaptive strategy has both short-term benefits (e.g., children are cared for and housework is completed) and long-term benefits (e.g., family cohesion or loyalty, higher levels of social responsibility for adolescents), families use it at considerable cost to eldest daughters. When eldest daughters assume responsibility for the everyday hassles associated with family care, their own education and goals are secondary to the needs of the family. In Dodson and Dickert's study, teachers, parents, and the girls themselves described lost opportunities for education and extracurricular involvement and, perhaps most disconcerting, lost hope for the eldest daughters' futures.

A relatively new line of research has examined the influence of information and communication technology (ICT) on everyday hassles, including how it may help buffer families from daily hassles or how it may create additional everyday hassles by blurring the lines between work and home. In some ways, the use of ICT can be viewed as an adaptive process that provides support for handling everyday hassles. A recent qualitative study demonstrated that for some couples the use of ICT makes it easier to manage daily schedules, communicate work and family needs, and organize their own and their family's time. For example, in Golden's (2013) qualitative study, an employee from a high tech organization in the Northeast reflected on managing daily routines with ICT:

> If it's something like a doctor's appointment, or even an after-hours event I have. I'll put it on there [virtual calendar system] just so when I look at my calendar, it's there as a reminder that, hey, you've gotta go do this tonight or Saturday morning don't forget to take the car in . . . My wife and I also use a function of [e-mail] which, there's a shared calendar function.

Similarly, Golden (2013) found that individuals use ICT to increase their work flexibility (e.g., by completing some work tasks from home), manage doing work from home (e.g., answering e-mails in nonwork hours), and remain available to family demands during work hours (e.g., accepting instant messages, e-mails, or calls from spouse and children). Although workplace flexibility may benefit family well-being, technology-enabled flexibility (e.g., via cell phones, tablets, home-accessible e-mail) may also increase the potential of work to impede on family life for those "fortunate" enough to have it (e.g., Golden, 2013; Heijstra & Rafnsdottir, 2010). Therefore, although ICT may at times buffer the impact of everyday hassles, it may also contribute to family stress.

ICT blurs the boundaries between work and home by providing 24/7 access and availability to interact with individuals or tasks previously segregated into work and home spaces. This increased technology may make it difficult for workers to disconnect from work at home (Chelsey & Johnson, 2015; Golden, 2013; Madden & Jones, 2008), especially for employees with high levels of ambition and involvement in their work or those whose identity is tied to their career (Boswell & Olson-Buchanan, 2007). Even individuals who do not actively complete work tasks from home may become distracted by work during family time via technological communication (Boswell & Olson-Buchanan, 2007). Additionally, a recent study from the Pew Internet and American Life Project found that increased access to technology is related to higher expectations from employers that workers remain engaged in work and available at all times (Chelsey & Johnson, 2015). These new demands represent additional everyday hassles that families must learn to manage. One adaptive process involves setting intentional boundaries and limits regarding work-related technology use at home (e.g., turning off notifications) which reduces ICT interruptions and subsequent work-to-family conflict (Fenner & Renn, 2010). Setting boundaries in this way may be difficult, however, as many individuals report feeling pressure to stay connected to work. A recent study reported that 50% of workers complete work tasks during nonwork hours (e.g., at home, on vacation; Madden & Jones, 2008).

Enduring Vulnerabilities

Individual differences or enduring vulnerabilities in personality and emotional functioning can both contribute to everyday hassles and affect how family members adapt to them. For example, enduring vulnerabilities play an important role in determining how family members process, interpret, and react to the everyday hassles they encounter. In addition, the extent to which individuals possess relatively stable traits can render them resilient or vulnerable to the transfer of stress from everyday hassles. For example, studies have found exaggerated stress responses to hassles among individuals with higher levels of negative affectivity, neuroticism, type A personality traits, depression, and introversion (e.g., Almeida, McGonagle, Cate, Kessler, & Wethington, 2002; Falconier et al., 2014) and lower levels of mastery and self-esteem (Almeida, McGonagle et al., 2002; Pearlin, 1999).

Gender differences may influence the extent to which enduring vulnerabilities moderate the links between daily hassles and family stress may differ for men and women. Almeida, McGonagle et al. (2002) asked 166 married couples to complete daily diaries for 42 consecutive days. In each diary entry, participants responded to a short questionnaire about a variety of daily stressors, including arguments with their spouse, as well as a questionnaire designed to assess psychological distress. The analyses addressed the moderating effects of psychological characteristics (i.e., neuroticism, mastery, self-esteem, and extraversion) on the link between marital arguments and psychological distress. They found that the extent to which wives felt distressed following marital arguments was exacerbated by high levels of neuroticism and attenuated by high levels of mastery, self-esteem, and extraversion. In contrast, self-esteem alone moderated the link between marital arguments and psychological distress for husbands. Almeida, McGonagle et al. (2002) suggested that because personality has been shown to be particularly salient for coping with stressors that are highly threatening or uncontrollable, the different patterns that emerged for husbands and wives in their sample imply that wives may perceive marital arguments as more threatening than do husbands.

Intervention: Toward a New Family-Responsive Policy Agenda

Feminists argue for gender equity in daily tasks as a solution to the disproportionate burdens that mothers, wives, and daughters carry in families (Allen, Walker, & McCann, 2013), but they also warn that even with gender equity, many contemporary families would still have too many hassles to manage on their own (Coontz, 2015). In contrast, those ascribing to structural-functionalist views suggest that families function best when women focus on children and home management and men focus on breadwinning (Popenoe, 2009). Rare among scholars but quite prevalent in popular culture are self-help perspectives that frame the link between everyday hassles and family well-being as a private matter that individuals can solve by using time more efficiently. Still others emphasize government- or employer-subsidized child- and eldercare services as mechanisms for outsourcing many of the everyday hassles associated with caregiving while also acknowledging that government and workplace policies may actually amplify sources of hassles if ineffectively administered (Bogenschneider, 2000, 2014).

We argue that contemporary American families need better opportunities both at home and in the workplace to meet family members' diverse needs without inadvertently creating additional stressors for individuals already living in chronically stressful situations (Perry-Jenkins et al., 2013; Roy et al, 2004). We support Moen's (2003) conclusion that we must "re-imagine and reconfigure work hours, workweeks, and occupational career paths in ways that address the widening gaps between the time needs and goals of workers and their families at all stages of the life course on the one hand and the time available to them on the other" (p. 7). For example, some families may want to devote more time to paid work outside the home and therefore need ways to simplify aspects of their daily home lives and outsource everyday tasks to readily available, high-quality substitutes. As Valcour and Batt (2003) note, for parents who want to focus more of their time on family obligations, flexibility in the workplace is of paramount importance. They quoted a mother of three children (including 4-year-old twins) who has been married to a business administrator for 15 years:

> I was lucky to work out a job sharing arrangement because there was another woman in my department who did the same thing as me and was also struggling after she had her second baby. So we went to the human resource person and she was supportive but said the company doesn't have this in place. So we did the research and went to the president of the division and we went through a couple of struggles, but eventually they accepted it. I'm so glad it worked out, because it has been great for me and my family. (p. 320)

As this woman's experience illustrates, workplace policies that enable family members to care for the needs of their members without jeopardizing their financial security or jobs are likely to be particularly beneficial for families caring for young children or sick or aging family members.

Although the needs and desires of family members in diverse family forms are likely to change over the life course, they exist in a sociohistorical context that has seen little development in family-responsive workplace policies (Perry-Jenkins et al., 2013). For example, the everyday hassles that today's families encounter are situated in a society that is still predicated on a breadwinner-husband–homemaker-wife script in which the breadwinner is assured an adequate wage for family provision and a full-time, linear rise up the occupational ladder, and the home-maker manages the everyday non-work aspects of her husband's life as well as the daily hassles of managing a home and family (Coontz, 2000; Moen, 2003). This outdated script contrasts starkly with the contemporary reality that the majority of American families (e.g., single-parent and dual-earner families) experience as they work in an economy where family-wage jobs are reserved for the highly edu-cated, secure manufacturing jobs are few, job growth is limited to low-wage 24/7 service-sector positions with little security or hope for advancement, and income gains are disproportionately situated among more advantaged individuals (Autor & Dorn, 2013). Further, relative to high-wage workers, low-wage workers are less likely to be employed at firms large enough to entitle them to health insurance and family leave, and also less likely to be able to afford the insurance premiums and 12 weeks of unpaid leave (Perry-Jenkins et al., 2013). In addition, existing gov-ernment and workplace policies have been slow to recognize that working family members have legitimate family demands on their time that may require greater flexibility in the workplace. As long as the culture of the workplace equates work commitment with overwork and fails to recognize the legitimacy of family care-giving as an employee right, those seeking a reasonable balance between work and family life are likely to be penalized (Jacobs & Gerson, 2005). This point is docu-mented by a father of two children (ages 8 and 14) who is employed as a manufac-turing production supervisor and married to a part-time educational coordinator:

> I wish there were more flexibility, especially in our production environ-ment. I've worked all my life around a rotating-work schedule, but this year alone I lost three excellent employees. They had each become single parents for one reason or another, and there's no way you can get child care in off hours and weekends. It just breaks my heart. Traditionally produc-tion has been a male-oriented thing, where one partner stays home with the children and the other one works crazy schedules. . . . the world is changing and the schedule is not. (quoted in Valcour & Batt, 2003, p. 310)

The mismatch between the work environments that family members inhabit and the needs of contemporary families creates a context in which everyday has-sles emerge and multiply (Perry-Jenkins et al., 2013). The policies most effective at improving family well-being take a holistic approach by integrating service delivery, prevention programs, universal high-quality services, and programs that are flexible to families' needs (Hengstebeck, Helms, & Crosby, 2016).

Valcour and Batt (2003) suggest that employers first adopt and promote a family-responsive attitude toward employees and then demonstrate support for this attitude through company policy. A primary objective of this approach is to reduce the often unspoken costs to employees who choose nonstandard work arrangements or take advantage of family-friendly policies (Jacobs & Gerson, 2005). Such an attitude recognizes that all employees, regardless of whether they have spouses, partners, children, or other kin at home, are members of families and experience everyday hassles and demands from personal involvements outside the workplace (Perry-Jenkins et al., 2013). Valcour and Batt (2003) note that family-responsive employers must offer employees the following: (a) a broad range of work-life programs that provide employees with control over their working time and support in meeting their family and personal needs; (b) adequate pay, benefits, and employment security; (c) work designed to provide employees with discretion and control in meeting work and life demands; and (d) a workplace culture, transmitted formally by organizational policies and informally by supervisors and coworkers, that values and supports the work-life integration of all employees (Thompson & Prottas, 2005; Valcour & Batt, 2003, pp. 312–313). Jacobs and Gerson (2005) further emphasize that family responsive reforms must uphold both two essential principles: (1) gender equality in opportunity structures and (2) support for employees regardless of socioeconomic location.

Moen (2003) argues that it is not enough for corporations to list such policies on the books. Employers must make continuous efforts to enforce these policies to cultivate a corporate climate that is truly responsive to the needs of families. Moen also suggests that employers and government officials need to keep better records of the variations (and the reasons for them) in employees' work-hour and career-path arrangements in order to track the implications of these variations for employees and corporations. The information gained through such tracking may help to convince employers and policymakers of the heterogeneity in employees' experiences both at work and at home and thus persuade them to change outdated workplace policies based on the breadwinner-homemaker template. Finally, and perhaps most important for families' experiences of everyday hassles and stress, employers and policymakers must view employees' vulnerabilities and family circumstances as key human resource, workforce, and labor issues. For family members struggling in uncertain economic times and working in low-wage jobs with inflexible work schedules, everyday hassles such as minor car accidents, sick children, and parent–teacher conferences scheduled during work hours can add strains that they may find hard to manage. Policies that focus on the risks, vulnerabilities, and family lives of workers are likely to attenuate the transfer of stress from everyday hassles to family relationships.

DISCUSSION QUESTIONS

1. What are everyday hassles? How do they differ from more severe daily stressors? Provide some examples of anticipated and unanticipated everyday hassles, including how they may impact families who are (or are not) dealing with additional chronic stressors.

2. What, if any, differences exist in the experiences of everyday hassles for men and women? What implications does this have for couples' relationships and overall family functioning?

3. What recommendations do you have for families to manage the stress of everyday hassles?

4. How might increases in technology help and/or hinder how families experience and manage everyday hassles?

5. What policy recommendations were suggested to help families manage everyday hassles? How might these changes support families?

REFERENCES

Abel, E. K., & Nelson, M. K. (Eds.). (1990). *Circles of care: Work and identity in women's lives.* Albany: State University of New York Press.

Allen, K. R., & Walker, A. J. (2000). Constructing gender in families. In R. M. Milardo & S. Duck (Eds.), *Families as relationships* (pp. 1–17). Chichester, England: Wiley.

Allen, K. R., Walker, A. J., & McCann, B. R. (2013). Feminism and families. In G. W. Peterson & K. R. Bush (Eds.), *Handbook of marriage and the family* (pp. 139–158). New York, NY: Springer.

Almeida, D. M. (2004). Using daily diaries to assess temporal friction between work and family. In A. C. Crouter & A. Booth (Eds.), *Work-family challenges for low-income parents and their children* (pp. 127–136). Mahwah, NJ: Erlbaum.

Almeida, D. M., & Horn, M. C. (2004). Is daily life more stressful during middle adulthood? In C. D. Ryff & R. C. Kessler (Eds.), *A portrait of midlife in the United States* (pp. 425–451). Chicago: University of Chicago Press.

Almeida, D. M., McGonagle, K. A., Cate, R. C., Kessler, R. C., & Wethington, E. (2002). Psychological moderators of emotional reactivity to marital arguments: Results from a daily diary study. *Marriage and Family Review, 34,* 89–113.

Almeida, D. M., Stawski, R. S., & Cichy, K. E. (2010). Combining checklist and interview approaches for assessing daily stressors: The Daily Inventory of Stressful Events. In R. J. Contrada & A. Baum (Eds.), *The handbook of stress science: Biology, psychology, and health* (pp. 583–596). New York, NY: Springer.

Almeida, D. M., Wethington, E., & Kessler, R. C. (2002). The daily inventory of stressful events: An interview-based approach for measuring daily stressors. *Assessment, 9,* 41–55.

Amato, P. R., Johnson, D. R., Booth, A., & Rogers, S. J. (2003). Continuity and change in marital quality between 1980 and 2000. *Journal of Marriage and Family, 65,* 1–22.

American Psychological Association. (2019). Immigration policy: A psychological perspective. https://www.apa.org/advocacy/immigration/fact-sheet.pdf

Autor, D. H., & Dorn, D. (2013). The growth of low-skill service jobs and the polarization of the US labor market. *The American Economic Review, 103*(5), 1553–1597.

Berg, P., Kossek, E. E., Misra, K., & Belman, D. (2014). Work-life flexibility policies: Do unions affect employee access and use? *Industrial & Labor Relations Review, 67*(1), 111–137.

Bianchi, S. M., & Raley, S. B. (2005). Time allocation in families. In S. M. Bianchi, L. M. Casper, & R. B. King (Eds.), *Work, family, health, and well-being* (pp. 21–42). Mahwah, NJ: Erlbaum.

Bianchi, S. M., Sayer, L. C., Milkie, M. A., & Robinson, J. P. (2012). Housework: Who did, does or will do it, and how much does it matter? *Social Forces, 91*(1), 55–63.

Bogenschneider, K. (2000). Has family policy come of age? A decade review of the state of U.S. family policy in the 1990s. *Journal of Marriage and the Family, 62,* 1136–1159.

Bogenschneider, K. (2014). *Family policy matters: How policymaking affects families and what professionals can do.* New York, NY: Routledge.

Bolger, N., DeLongis, A., Kessler, R. C., & Wethington, E. (1989). The contagion of stress across multiple roles. *Journal of Marriage and the Family, 51,* 175–183.

Boswell, W. R., & Olson-Buchanan, J. B. (2007). The use of communication technologies after hours: The role of work attitudes and work-life conflict. *Journal of Management, 33*(4), 592–610.

Bouza, J. R., Camacho-Thompson, D. E., Carlo, G., Franco, X., Garcia Coll, C., Halgunseth, L. C., Marks, A., Livas Stein, G., Suárez-Orozco, C., & White, R. M. B. (2018). The science is clear: Separating families has long-term damaging psychological and health consequences for children, families, and communities. *Society for Research in Child Development: Statement of the Evidence.* http://www.srcd.org/sites/default/files/resources/FINAL_The%20Science%20is%20Clear_0.pdf

Chelsey, N., & Johnson, B. E. (2015). Technology use and the new economy: Work extension, network connectivity, and employee distress and productivity. In S. K. Ammons & E. L. Kelly (Eds.), *Work and family in the new economy* (pp. 61–99). Bingley, UK: Emerald Group Publishing.

Cichy, K., Stawski, R. S., & Almeida, D. M. (2012). Racial differences in exposure and reactivity to daily family stressors. *Journal of Marriage and Family, 74*(3), 572–586.

Coltrane, S. (2000). Research on household labor: Modeling and measuring the social embeddedness of routine family work. *Journal of Marriage and the Family, 62,* 1208–1233.

Connelly, R., & Kimmel, J. (2014). If you're happy and you know it: How do mothers and fathers in the US really feel about caring for their children? *Feminist Economics.*

Coontz, S. (2015). Revolution in intimate life and relationships. *Family Theory & Review, 7,* 5–12.

Craig, L. (2006). Does father care mean fathers share?: a comparison of how mothers and fathers in intact families spend time with children. *Gender & Society 20*(2), 259–281.

Crouter, A. C., Head, M. R., Bumpus, M. F., & McHale, S. M. (2001). Household chores: Under what conditions do mothers lean on daughters? In A. J. Fuligini (Ed.), *Family obligation and assistance during adolescence* (pp. 23–41). New York, NY: Wiley.

Daly, K. J. (2001). Deconstructing family time: From ideology to lived experience. *Journal of Marriage and Family, 63,* 283–294.

DeLongis, A., Folkman, S., & Lazarus, R. S. (1988). The impact of daily stress and health on mood: Psychological and social resources as mediators. *Journal of Personality and Social Psychology, 54,* 486–495.

Demo, D. H., & Acock, A. C. (1996). Family structure, family process, and adolescent well-being. *Journal of Research on Adolescence, 6*, 457–488.

Deutsch, F. M. (1999). *Halving it all: How equally shared parenting works*. Cambridge, MA: Harvard University Press.

DeVault, M. L. (1991). *Feeding the family: The social organization of caring as gendered work*. Chicago: University of Chicago Press.

DiLeonardo, M. (1987). The female world of cards and holidays: Women, families, and the work of kinship. *Signs, 12*, 440–453.

Dodson, L., & Dickert, J. (2004). Girls' family labor in low-income households: A decade of qualitative research. *Journal of Marriage and Family, 66*, 318–332.

Doyle, M., & Molix, L. (2014). Love on the margins: The effects of social stigma and relationship length on romantic relationship quality. *Social Psychological and Personality Science, 5*(1), 102–110.

Dreby, J. (2015). *Everyday illegal: When policies undermine immigrant families*. Oakland: University of California Press.

Dressel, P., & Clark, A. (1990). A critical look at family care. *Journal of Marriage and the Family, 52*, 769–782.

Falconier, M. K., Nussbeck, F., Bodenmann, G., Schneider, H., & Bradbury, T. (2014). Stress from daily hassles in couples: Its effects on intradyadic stress, relationship satisfaction, and physical and psychological well-being. *Journal of Marital and Family Therapy*, Advance online publication. doi: 10.1111/jmft.12073

Fenner, G. H. & Renn, R. W. (2010). Technology-assisted supplemental work and work-to-family conflict: The role of instrumentality beliefs, organization expectations and time management. *Human Relations, 63*, 63–82. doi: 10.1177/0018726709351064

Golden, A. G. (2013). The structuration of information and communication technologies and work-life interrelationships: Shared organizational and family rules and resources and implications for work in a high-technology organization. *Communication Monographs, 80*(1), 101–123. doi: 10.1080/03637751.2012.739702

Grzywacz, J. G., Almeida, D. M., Neupert, S. D., & Ettner, S. L. (2004). Socioeconomic status and health: A micro-level analysis of exposure and vulnerability to daily stressors. *Journal of Health and Social Behavior, 45*, 1–16.

Harris, K. J., Harris, R. B., Carlson, J. R., & Carlson, D. S. (2015). Resource loss from technology overload and its impact on work-family conflict: Can leaders help? *Computers in Human Behavior, 50*, 411–417.

Harris, J. K., Marett, K., & Harris, R. B. (2011). Technology-related pressure and work-family conflict: Main effects and an examination of moderating variables. *Journal of Applied Social Psychology, 41*(9), 2077–2103.

Hengstebeck, N. D., Helms, H. M., & Crosby, D. A. (2016). Family policies. In C. Shehan (Ed.), *Encyclopedia of family studies* (pp. 748–753). Hoboken, NJ: Wiley-Blackwell.

Heijstra, T. M., & Rafnsdottir, G. L. (2010). The internet and academics' workload and work-family balance. *The Internet and Higher Education, 13*(3), 158–163. doi:10.1016/j.iheduc.2010.03.004

Hodgson, J., Dienhart, A., & Daly, K. J. (2001). Time juggling: Single mothers' experience of time-press following divorce. *Journal of Divorce and Remarriage, 35*, 1–28.

Hunter, A. G., Pearson, J. L., Ialongo, N. S., & Kellam, S. G. (1998). Parenting alone to multiple caregivers: Child care and parenting arrangements in black and white urban families. *Family Relations, 47*, 343–353.

Jacobs, J. A., & Gerson, K. (2005). *The time divide*. Cambridge, MA: Harvard University Press.

Kanner, A. D., Coyne, J. C., Schaefer, C., & Lazarus, R. S. (1981). Comparisons of two modes of stress measurement: Daily hassles and uplifts versus major life events. *Journal of Behavioral Medicine, 4*, 1–39.

Kaplan, E. B. (2010). Doing care on the run: Family strategies for the contested terrain of gender and institutional intransigence. *Journal of Contemporary Ethnography, 39*, 587–618.

Karney, B. R., & Bradbury, T. N. (1995). The longitudinal course of marital quality and stability: A review of theory, method, and research. *Psychological Bulletin, 118*, 3–34.

Lara-Cinisomo, S., Chandra, A., Burns, R. M., Jaycox, L. H., Tanielian, T., Ruder, T., & Bing, H. (2012). A mixed-method approach to understanding the experiences of non-deployed military caregivers. *Maternal and Child Health Journal, 16*, 374–384.

Larson, R. W., & Almeida, D. M. (1999). Emotional transmission in the daily lives of families: A new paradigm for studying family process. *Journal of Marriage and the Family, 61*, 5–20.

Larson, R. W., & Gillman, S. (1999). Transmission of emotions in the daily interactions of single-mother families. *Journal of Marriage and the Family, 61*, 21–37.

Larson, R. W., Richards, M. H., & Perry-Jenkins, M. (1994). Divergent worlds: The daily emotional experiences of mothers and fathers in the domestic and public spheres. *Journal of Personality and Social Psychology, 67*, 1034–1046.

Lazarus, R. S. (1999). *Stress and emotion: A new synthesis*. New York, NY: Springer.

Ledermann, T., Bodenmann, G., Rudaz, M., & Bradbury, T. N. (2010). Stress, communication, and marital quality in couples. *Family Relations, 59*(2), 195–206.

Lincoln, K. D., & Chae, D. H. (2010). Stress, marital satisfaction, and psychological distress among African Americans. *Journal of Family Issues, 31*, 1081–1105.

Madden, M., & Jones, S. (2008). *Networked workers*. Pew Research Center. https://www.pewinternet.org/2008/09/24/networked-workers/

Maisel, N. C., & Karney, B. R. (2012). Socioeconomic status moderates associations among stressful events, mental health, and relationship satisfaction. *Journal of Family Psychology, 26*(4), 654–660.

Margolin, G., Christensen, A., & John, R. S. (1996). The continuance and spillover of everyday tensions in distressed and nondistressed families. *Journal of Family Psychology, 10*, 304–321.

Miller, M. J., & Wilcox, C. T. (1986). Measuring perceived hassles and uplifts among the elderly. *Journal of Human Behavior and Learning, 3*, 38–45.

Mills, M., & Täht, K. (2010). Nonstandard work schedules and partnership quality: Quantitative and qualitative findings. *Journal of Marriage and Family, 72*, 860–875.

Moen, P. (Ed.). (2003). *It's about time: Couples and careers*. Ithaca, NY: Cornell University Press.

Offer, S., & Schneider, B. (2011). Revisiting the gender gap in time-use patterns: Multitasking and well-being among mothers and fathers in dual-earner families. *American Sociological Review, 76*(6), 809–833.

Oliker, S. J. (1989). *Best friends and marriage*. Berkeley: University of California Press.

Oswald, R. F. (2000). A member of the wedding? Heterosexism and family ritual. *Journal of Social and Personal Relationships, 17*(3), 349–368.

Pearlin, L. I. (1999). Stress and mental health: A conceptual overview. In A. V. Horwitz & T. L. Scheid (Eds.), *A handbook for the study of mental health: Social contexts, theories, and systems* (pp. 161–175). New York, NY: Cambridge University Press.

Perry-Jenkins, M., Newkirk, K., & Ghunney, A. K. (2013). Family work through time and space: An ecological perspective. *Journal of Family Theory & Review, 5*, 105–123.

Popenoe, D. (2009). *Families without fathers: Fathers, marriage and children in American society.* New Brunswick, NJ: Transaction.

Randall, A. K., & Bodenmann, G. (2009). The role of stress on close relationships and marital satisfaction. *Clinical Psychology Review, 29*(2), 105–115.

Repetti, R. L. (1994). Short-term and long-term processes linking job stressors to father–child interaction. *Social Development, 3,* 1–5.

Repetti, R. L., & Wood, J. (1997a). The effects of daily stress at work on mothers' interactions with preschoolers. *Journal of Family Psychology, 11,* 90–108.

Repetti, R. L., & Wood, J. (1997b). Families accommodating to chronic stress. In B. H. Gottlieb (Ed.), *Coping with chronic stress* (pp. 191–220). New York, NY: Plenum.

Riggle, E. D., Rostosky, S. S., & Horne, S. G. (2010). Psychological distress, well-being, and legal recognition in same-sex couple relationships. *Journal of Family Psychology, 24*(1), 82–86.

Robinson, J. P., & Milkie, M. A. (1998). Back to the basics: Trends in and role determinants of women's attitudes toward housework. *Journal of Marriage and the Family, 60,* 205–218.

Roy, K. M., Tubbs, C. Y., & Burton, L. M. (2004). Don't have no time: Daily rhythms and the organization of time for low-income families. *Family Relations, 53*(2), 168–178.

Saxbe, D. E., Repetti, R. L., & Nishina, A. (2008). Marital satisfaction, recovery from work, and diurnal cortisol among men and women. *Health Psychology, 27,* 15–25.

Sayer, L. C. (2005). Gender, time and inequality: Trends in women's and men's paid work, unpaid work and free time. *Social Forces, 84,* 285–303.

Schulz, M. S., Cowan, P. A., Cowan, C. P., & Brennan, R. T. (2004). Coming home upset: Gender, marital satisfaction, and the daily spillover of workday experience into couple interactions. *Journal of Family Psychology, 18,* 250–263.

Seltzer, M. M., Almeida, D. M., Greenberg, J. S., Savla, J., Stawski, R. S., Hong, J., & Taylor, J. L. (2009). Psychosocial and biological markers of daily lives of midlife parents of children with disabilities. *Journal of Health and Social Behavior, 50*(1), 1–15.

Serido, J., Almeida, D. M., & Wethington, E. (2004). Chronic stressors and daily hassles: Unique and interactive relationships with psychological distress. *Journal of Health and Social Behavior, 45,* 17–33.

Slatcher, R. B. (2014). Family relationships and cortisol in everyday life. In C. Agnew & S. South (Eds.), *Interpersonal relationships and health: Social and clinical psychological mechanisms* (pp. 71–88). New York, NY: Oxford University Press.

Story, L. B., & Repetti, R. L. (2006). Daily occupational stressors and marital behavior. *Journal of Family Psychology, 20,* 690–700.

Stawski, R. S., Cichy, K. E., Piazza, J. R., & Almeida, D. M. (2013). Associations among daily stressors and salivary cortisol: Findings from the National Study of Daily Experiences. *Psychoneuroendocrinology, 38*(11), 2654–2665.

Sullivan, O. (2018). The gendered division of household labor. In B. J. Risman, C. Froyum, & W. J. Scarborough (Eds.), *Handbook of the sociology of gender* (pp. 377–392). Cham, Switzerland: Springer. doi:10.1007/978-3-319-76333-0_27

Thompson, C. A., & Prottas, D. J. (2005). Relationships among organizational family support, job autonomy, perceived control, and employee well-being. *Journal of Occupational Health Psychology, 11*(1), 100–118.

Thorne, B. (2004). The crisis of care. In A. C. Crouter & A. Booth (Eds.), *Work-family challenges for low-income parents and their children* (pp. 165–178). Mahwah, NJ: Erlbaum.

Totenhagen, C. J., Butler, E. A., & Ridley, C. A. (2012). Daily stress, closeness, and satisfaction in gay and lesbian couples. *Personal Relationships, 19*(2), 219–233.

Totenhagen, C. J., & Curran, M. A. (2011). Daily hassles, sacrifices, and relationship quality for pregnant cohabitors. *Family Science, 2*(1), 68–72.

Trail, T. E., Goff, P. A., Bradbury, T. N., & Karney, B. R. (2012). The costs of racism for marriage: How racial discrimination hurts, and ethnic identity protects, newlywed marriages among Latinos. *Personality & Social Psychology Bulletin, 38*(4), 454–65.

Valcour, P. M., & Batt, R. (2003). Work-life integration: Challenges and organizational responses. In P. Moen (Ed.), *It's about time: Couples and careers* (pp. 310–331). Ithaca, NY: Cornell University Press.

Vesely, C. K., Bravo, D. Y., & Guzzardo, M. T. (2019). Immigrant families across the life course: Policy impacts on physical and mental health. *National Council on Family Relations: Policy Brief, 4*(1), 1–8. https://www.ncfr.org/sites/default/files/2019-07/Immigrant_Families_Policy_Brief_July_23_2019.pdf

Villeneuve, L., Dargis, L., Trudel, G., Boyer, R., Préville, M., & Bégin, J. (2014). Daily hassles, marital functioning and psychological distress among community-dwelling older couples. *European Review of Applied Psychology, 64*(5), 251–258.

Walker, A. J., Pratt, C. C., & Eddy, L. (1995). Informal caregiving to aging family members: A critical review. *Family Relations, 44,* 402–411.

Wheaton, B., Young, M., Montazer, S., & Stuart-Lahman, K. (2012). Social stress in the twenty-first century. In C. S. Aneshensel, J. C. Phelan, & A. Bierman (Eds.), *Handbook of the sociology of mental health* (2nd ed., pp. 299–323). Springer.

CHAPTER 3

Mindfulness and Family Stress

Suzanne Klatt and Anthony G. James

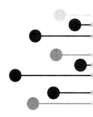

Families and Mindfulness

The area of family stress includes many components, but central in the study, understanding, and explanation of the scholarship on family stress is how families respond to stress and stressors. This chapter focuses on the role of mindfulness, one of several contemplative practices, in how families and their members respond (or react) to stress and stressors. We approach this chapter with a discussion of the current family science literature on stress and coping (or change) followed by an introduction to mindfulness. We then bring this discussion to life by providing two case studies highlighting how mindfulness practices can be an effective tool to help families cope with stress and stressors.

Key to this discussion is the effectiveness of the tool, mindfulness in this case. All families face stress, and thus, have to respond to that stress (or stressors) in some way or another. What matters is the effectiveness of the tool being tried. We hope to make a case for the value of mindfulness as a tool to help families best adapt to changing environments. First, we review some models for understanding family stress.

Family Stress Literature

Family stress is neither inherently positive nor negative; but rather an event (stress) initiating the need to change or respond (See Price, Bush, Price & McKenry, Chapter 1 in this Volume). The influence that a particular stressor (or pressure to change) has on a family system depends on a wide range of factors. These include, most importantly, the family's perception of the stressor, the coping ability of individual members and the family system as a whole, access to resources both within the family system and external to the family, and characteristics of the stressor itself (Lavee, 2013; McCubbin & McCubbin, 2013).

As previously mentioned the family stress literature consists primarily of two broad components: (1) stressful events or experiences that families may have, and (2) how families respond to or cope with said experiences. This chapter will focus more on how families adapt or respond to stressful experiences, whether chronic or acute. The prevailing thought is that the more tools or resources that families have to adapt to stress the better off they are going to be. Mindfulness is one such tool at the disposal of families, and we will discuss here the research and theory that place mindfulness in the context of family stress literature. Moreover, our approach will show how mindfulness can fit into prominent family stress theories (ABC-X and AaBbCc-Xx; Hill, 1958; McCubbin & Patterson, 1983).

ABC-X Models

For both models, resources to adapt to stress are prominent features. Because both are covered in more depth earlier in the current volume, we only briefly describe them here. The A in the ABC-X model represents the stressful event, the B represents the resources that families have to respond to said event, the C represents the perspective of the event that the family has, and "X" represents the resultant crises that the family experiences having undergone the stressful event. An extension of this model was put forth by McCubbin and Patterson (1983) and essentially has the same components except it adds to it the fact that families can experience multiple stressors overtime. One of the assumptions of the ABC-X model is that families experience a stressful event, they address it or adapt and move on. However, many would agree that families can have chronic stressors or that one stress can lead to another stress and this causes what is known as stress pileup. Thus, a new model was needed to account for the multiple stressors that families can experience, the demand on existing resources from previous or other stressors family experience, how the new plus existing stressors changes the perspective of the current stressful event, and the accumulation of family adjustments to the combined stressors (McCubbin & Patterson, 1983).

Minority Stress Models

A prominent framework for understanding how minority families (in the United States) experience stress is the mundane extreme environmental stress theory (MEES; Peters & Massey, 1983). This theory used *mundane* in the sense that bigotry and discrimination was so common and ubiquitous, that it become mundane in the daily lives of minority groups, but also created an extreme environment for families embedded in such a context (Carroll, 1998). To be sure, the previously cited studies focused specifically on African American families, and how existing in such a mundane extreme environment deteriorates the health and well-being of these families. McNeil Smith and Landor (2018) expanded on this framework, via the sociocultural family stress model. This model included an intersectional approach, which allows broader application to many structures of families and the many processes within them.

Adjacent Explanatory Theory and Concepts

Several other theories or concepts, beyond specific stress models, will be important to content presented in this chapter. We want to provide readers with some background information on this content prior to the application of it later in the chapter.

Bioecological Theory

Though bioecological theory is a theory of human development, and not specifically a family stress theory, it can be used to understand how stress potentially influences stress that people experience or how they respond to said stress. Within this theory is the PPCT (proximal processes, person characteristics, context, time) model, which specifies the variety of human development (Bronfenbrenner & Morris, 2006). Proximal processes refers to the daily interactions people have that shape their development. Person characteristics refers to the idiosyncratic qualities people bring to human interactions that regulate their developmental and lived experiences. For instance, being a woman walking alone at night has different potential relative to a man repeating that action under similar conditions. In this case, the person characteristic gender presents different potentials under the same action. Context, in the model, refers to the multiple layers of context people are embedded (e.g., micro, meso, exo, macro). Finally, context can refer to the opportunities and constraints presented to individuals in a given historical time or in a given developmental period.

Stress Duration

Again, many people experience stress but how they experience stress varies. Two concepts important to this literature concern how long individuals or families experience stress. Stress can be chronic (e.g., a person living with asthma is a chronic stressor) or acute (e.g., a person fractures their arm, which is treated and then healed). Whether stress is chronic or acute has implications for the extent to which it influences family dynamics.

Conceptualizing Mindfulness

Mindfulness is a difficult concept to define (Van Dam et al., 2018) and there is not a full consensus on its definition (Anālayo, 2016). Contemporary messages about mindfulness lead us to believe it is a panacea for all of our woes. The term frequently appears in media and pop culture as a noun, verb, adverb, and adjective. *Time* magazine covers (2014, 2016) featuring young thin white women seemingly meditating in ethereal poses, and media messages reproducing consumerism via individual wellness panaceas is not the message we hope to reproduce here. We recognize mindfulness as connected to a rich, deep cultural and religious history, and endeavor to shift toward a critically conscious (Freire, 1970) approach to mindfulness and family stress by recognizing the systems of oppression particular families face. In this chapter, we acknowledge cultural representations of mindfulness and do our best to conceptualize some of the ways mindfulness is situated within a Western secular format as a program, informal or formal practice, state (Lau, Bishop, Segal, Buis, Anderson, Carlson, Devins, 2006), trait or disposition (Brown et al., 2007; Kabat-Zinn, 1990), and skill. Additionally, we note its commodification and concurrently utilize a critical family ecological framework to consider how mindfulness occurs within families (Walsh, 2016; Wilson, 2016).

The origin of the term *mindfulness* derives from the Pali word *Sati* meaning "to remember." When referenced in Buddhism, "as a mental factor it signifies presence of mind, attentiveness to the present" (Bodhi, 2000, p. 86). While it derives from Eastern religion, philosophy, and practices, it is also a component of Western Buddhism(s), Buddhist psychology, integrative health, education, business (and more) practices and programs. We refer to its Eastern roots as an ethical decision to honor the Central, East, and Southeast Asian peoples and cultures where mindfulness arose. Reviewing all types of meditation and the various instructions associated with particular types of meditation is beyond the scope of this chapter. This chapter is about mindfulness meditation although meditation generally is practiced among religious folks, atheists, and agnostics. The 2014 religious landscape research study (Pew Research Center, 2014) found the highest percentage of persons who meditate daily in the United States are Jehovah Witnesses (77%) and Buddhists (66%). Many other groups (historically Black Protestant, Evangelical Protestant, Catholic, mainline Protestant, Muslim, Hindu, Jewish, agnostic, atheist, and those identifying "nothing in particular") report meditating as well.

While mindfulness as a construct is based on Buddhism (Kabat-Zinn, 2003) many people in Western contexts learn about mindfulness as a component of a health-related program, experiential learning in P–16 education, or community education programs. Mindfulness as a robust academic theme and emerging discipline surfaced in the late 1970s with a few publications in the 1980s, incremental increases starting around 2010 and exponentially expanding through today (American Mindfulness Research Association, 2019). Mindfulness-based stress reduction (MBSR) is the prominent model emerging early in this trajectory. As the first and most researched of these evidence based programs, the creator of MBSR, Jon Kabat-Zinn, describes mindfulness as "paying attention in a particular way: on purpose, in the present moment, and non-judgmentally" (1994). Bishop and colleagues are attentive to the quality of one's experience describing mindfulness as "a process of regulating attention in order to bring a quality of non-elaborative awareness to current experience and a quality of relating to one's experience within an orientation of curiosity, experiential openness, and acceptance" (Bishop et al., 2004, p. 234).

Criticism of the empirical evidence for mindfulness includes poor methodology, lack of attention to potential adverse effects, and lack of information about teacher training (Van Dam et al., 2018). Facilitators with extensive mindfulness practice are more equipped to support quality program delivery (Segal et al., 2002). In this chapter, the mindfulness practices referenced in case examples were facilitated by a highly trained facilitator with extensive and ongoing practice history over 20 years. We utilize peer and systematically reviewed research citations when possible to support our claims that promote using mindfulness as a tool for managing stress in families.

Family Pathways to Mindfulness

Families learn about and experience mindfulness in many ways including intensive practice-based programs such as MBSR and intensive skill-based programs such as dialectical behavior therapy (DBT). Families also become aware of mindfulness through family-focused interventions often based on MBSR and DBT models, family therapy, as well as various exercises, practices, and programs adjusted to meet the developmental, topical, or contextual needs of a particular individual, family, group, or community. In this section, we tune into MBSR and DBT as core Western approaches, with Mindful Schools (mindfulschools.org; www.mindfulschools.org) as a developmentally appropriate program, and referencing Langer's (1989) cognitive approach. There is purposeful attention to the (in)accessibility of mindfulness and family-based mindfulness programs to families currently and historically marginalized or oppressed. We provide two corresponding family cases connecting individual family member experiences to real and potential family impacts via the ABC-X and AaBbCc-Xx models in spaces where vulnerable and oppressed families converge.

Mindfulness-Based Stress Reduction (MBSR)

The contemporary secular mindfulness movement harkens back to the late 1970s. MBSR (Kabat-Zinn, 2011) emerged at that time and is the most empirically supported mindfulness program to date and serves as a model for multiple other mindfulness-based interventions (MBIs) and programs including mindfulness-based cognitive therapy (Segal, 2002). Jon Kabat-Zinn utilized various mindfulness practices recruiting hospital patients considered to be non-responding or who would "fall through the cracks" of a health-care or "disease care" setting (Kabat-Zinn, 2011). During the MBSR 8-week program folks are guided in formal practices (e.g., sitting meditation, walking, body scan, gentle mindful movement) weekly with experiential exercises about the impact of stress on the body and mind, and opportunities to express practice experiences. Participants are given materials to practice formally on their own between weeks (home practice) and practice informally as they interact in the world.

The MBSR program is helpful with nonclinical and clinical health challenges (Grossman, Niemann, Schmidt & Wallach, 2004). It improves mental health (Fjorback, Arendt, Ørnbøl, Fink, & Walach, 2011), showing moderate effectiveness with depression, anxiety, distress, and stress (Khoury, Sharma, Rush, & Fournier, 2015), and when adapted, MBSR improves psychological functioning among youth vulnerable to community trauma (Sibinga, Webb, Ghazarian, & Ellen, 2016), with particular improvements in interpersonal relationships, physical health, school achievement, and hostility (Sibinga, Kerrigan, Steward, Johnson, Magyari, & Ellen, 2011). Health-care professionals participating in MBSR see increased quality of life and reduced stress (Shapiro, Astin, Bishop, & Cordova, 2005). Increasing the amount of mindfulness practice time in MBSR leads to significantly more positive intervention outcomes (Parsons, Crane, Parsons, Fjorback, & Kuyken, 2017). Lloyd, White, Eames, and Crane (2018) make a call for more research attention to "home practice" as this is a large component of MBSR with limited research connecting it to outcomes. We also wonder how home practice impacts families, particularly as it relates to well-being and stress management.

MBSR and DBT were designed to address physical pain and emotional suffering. Dialectical cognitive therapy (DBT) is a skill-based program originally designed for people experiencing suicidal ideation, parasuicidal behavior, relationship difficulties, and symptoms often related to borderline personality disorder (BPD; Linehan, 1993, 2020). Clients categorized as BPD are often doubly stigmatized both socially due to mental health stigma and medically by helpers or clinicians who, while often well meaning, are frustrated with or do not want to work with BPD clients.

Dialectical Behavior Therapy (DBT)

Research in DBT is relatively new and even more sparse as it relates to adolescents (James, Taylor, Winmill, & Alfoadari, 2008). Quite promising though is the research on adult clients diagnosed with BPD showing effectiveness in controlling and stabilizing self-destructive behavior and violence and decreasing the frequency of use of psychiatric crisis services (DeCou et al., 2019). DBT is adjusted to meet the needs of couples and to address intimate partner violence (Rathus, Cavuoto, & Passarelli, 2006). Dialectical behavior therapy for adolescents (DBT-A; Miller, Rathus & Linehan, 2007) was developed with adolescents in mind and utilizes a biosocial model (Linehan, 2015) recognizing challenges with emotional dysregulation due to the interaction of an environment that is invalidating and some sort of biological predisposition. There is a small to medium effect size for depression, self-injury, anxiety, and suicide risk for DBT-A therapy participants (Hunnicutt Hollenbaugh & Lenz, 2018).

DBT utilizes mindfulness, interpersonal effectiveness, emotional regulation, and distress tolerance as skills. There are now multiple workbooks outlining particular DBT skill-development exercises for multiple purposes and populations. The program typically lasts 6 to 12 months, includes multihour groups where participants learn a skill, practice it, and then utilize it in the milieu. Other unique components of DBT include a systematic implementation and dialectic framework. For example, clients utilizing multiple systems (e.g., outpatient mental health, inpatient, case management, therapy) will encounter DBT-trained persons who utilize similar language during crisis. The dialectic is a broad framework supporting acceptance and change as central opposites occurring simultaneously. Practically, this means accepting ourselves just as we are while concurrently moving toward change in particular (Linehan, 1993, 2020). One similarity to Kabat Zinn's MBSR is including both formal practice time and informal learning experiential practices as part of the group meetings and extending into daily life.

MBSR and other mindfulness programs should be adapted to meet the needs of marginalized populations (Vallejo & Amaro, 2009). Professionals, researchers, educators, and program specialists modify both DBT and MBSR curriculum to meet developmental needs and contexts as well. Mindfulness with youth emerged much later and programs such as Mindful Schools have an intensive manualized training path (see McKeering & Hwang, 2018 for review of adolescent programs). A few programs designed specifically for families, although sometimes inaccessible to highly stressed families, include mindfulness-based relationship enhancement (Carson et al., 2004), a family program similarly structured to MBSR although targeting nondistressed couples in order to cultivate their relationships. Participants show improved relationship stress, overall stress, happiness, and coping efficacy with greater improvements among those who practice more (Carson et al., 2004). The Mindfulness-Enhanced Strengthening Families Program (MSFP), combines mindfulness activities with an already evidence based family program (Coatsworth, Duncan, Berrena, Bamberger, Loeschinger, Greenberg, Nix, 2014).

Perspective Taking

Perspectives change as a result of mindfulness in various ways. Participating in mindfulness meditation exercises may impact one's experience of time (Droit-Volet, Chaulet, & Dambrun, 2018). At its inception, MBSR targeted adults experiencing chronic pain (Kabat-Zinn, 1982) and as a result of MBSR mindfulness instruction, the intensity of physical pain is not reduced, rather the unpleasantness of it is reduced (Perlman, Salomons, Davidson, & Lutz, 2010). Mindfulness shifts the emotional appraisal of that pain (Brown & Jones, 2010). Our family relationships are influenced by how we perceive each other (Adair & Frederickson, 2015). There is a direct link between mindfulness and an individual family member's perception of the quality of their relationships (Parent et al., 2014).

What about when we consider mindfulness without connecting it to practice? Langer (1989), inquired about mindfulness as a cognitive phenomenon where mindlessness is contrasted with mindfulness. She explores what it means to be mindful. When mindful, one allows new cognitive categories to be created, is aware of more than one perspective, and open to new information and flexible perspective taking. In a sense this is also about how individuals see and experience each moment when more or less mindful. Later researchers wonder about mindfulness as a disposition (DM) or trait. DM is (a) inversely related to psychopathological symptoms (depression), (b) associated with better emotional regulation and processing, and (c) positively linked to "adaptive cognitive processes" (decreased pain catastrophizing and rumination) (Tomlinson, Yousaf, Vitterso, & Jones, 2018).

Structural Support for Mindfulness Practice

There are many universities and organizations exploring mindfulness from a variety of perspectives: the Mindfulness Center at Brown University; UMass

Medical School Center for Mindfulness in Medicine, Health Care, and Society; and UCSD Center for Mindfulness, to name a few. The mission varies widely across centers and institutions, but all generally include the provision of services engaging in and teaching mindful practices within the university and local community, as well as promoting research in this area. For example, the Miami University Mindfulness & Contemplative Inquiry Center placed within the College of Education, Health, and Society and part of the Institute for Community Justice and Well-Being is a university-wide center serving students, faculty, researchers, and the wider community through the creation, co-creation, and development of related interdisciplinary scholarship and research, curricular initiatives, and public events. This collaboration fosters a culture of contemplation and holistic engagement and actively pursues a just, compassionate, and sustainable society. Part of the Center's mission is to work with individuals, groups, organizations, and communities requesting evidence-based mindfulness program facilitation, targeted support or programming based on identified wants and needs, or create community around mindfulness and other contemplative practices. This chapter derives from some of that work.

Integrating Mindfulness into Family Stress Literature

The following case examples highlight mindfulness entry points and specific ways mindfulness can provide families with a resource for coping with stress (B in the ABC-X model) or shift perceptions of stress (C in the ABC-X model). These cases and this chapter situate mindfulness in the context of families and their intersection with alternative education and after-school programs, spaces often part of the lives of minoritized or systematically oppressed families.

Case 1: Managing Chronic Stress Through Mindfulness

This case begins with a White female teacher, Jean,[1] with a long history living in a midwestern rural town and family she describes as "Appalachian with a family holler." Growing up was difficult for Jean although she did make it to college later in life and became a teacher. She grew up in a chaotic and emotionally and sometimes physically abusive family and is no longer connected with her family of origin. She has three children of her own and a life partner, Kelly, who was recently diagnosed with a chronic health issue. Kelly can no longer work and Jean continues to work at Mendon Alternative High School and has increased home responsibilities. Mendon students are referred from multiple public rural and urban districts due to behaviors their home schools have deemed unmanageable, disruptive, and

---

[1] These cases derive from actual cases and are adjusted slightly to protect participants.

unable to be supported at their home school. Facilitators trained in MBSR, DBT, Mindful Schools, and other evidence-based programs work in partnership with a cluster of similar schools and begin by asking students and employees about their strengths, needs, and wants. Jean participates in a focus group. Jean is not interested in mindfulness for herself although she thinks that students would benefit after she learns about initial school-based research related to mindfulness and schools. A mindfulness facilitator visits her classroom once or twice a week and Jean listens to the information about mindfulness and participates in practices along with youth twice a week. She comments to the facilitator, "I could have used this when I was young." After positive feedback from the teachers, staff, and many students, the programming continues and is extended to meet the particular needs and wants of teachers and other staff. Jean participates in these abbreviated and teacher–staff-targeted MBSR components. The facilitator emphasizes "acceptance and change" (DBT) as part of this program delivery. School-based data indicate improvements in overall staff and teacher morale. When asked about the program during its mid and end point, Jean's reflections are focused more on her interactions with her partner than at school. In particular, she has more patience and care toward her partner and "doesn't get as worked up." Jean reports sleeping through the night for the first time in months toward the end of the 6-week mindfulness program.

In this case, the family was dealing with a chronic stressor that created additional hardships and crises for the family (A). Though the family no doubt had resources to help them get along, those tools did not appear to drastically change family dynamics for the better. However, through a university partnership, the family member (Jean) was introduced to a tool, mindfulness (B), which she utilized at work and brought home to her family in order to help cope with the stressor. Subsequently, through gaining this tool, Jean's perception of family members and improved workplace morale shifted her ability to manage the stress (C), which subsequently altered the resulting stress the event has on the family (X).

Case 2: Managing the Mundane Experience of Stress

This case begins with an 8-year-old female, Tonya, attending after-school programming in her neighborhood. Tonya lives with her dad and three older siblings. Her dad works multiple jobs, is not around much, and her siblings or a neighbor watch her at home when he is not there. She typically gets along well with other youth at the after-school program although she had been having some problems in the 3 weeks prior to the mindfulness facilitator's arrival. The after-school program serves mostly African American youth between the ages of 5 and 12 who participate in after-school programming at a local club. Over 90% of youth participating in this after-school setting are on free and reduced lunch, live in high-poverty neighborhoods, and go to poor-performing schools. Tonya and 20 other students participated in the Mindful Schools curriculum once or twice a week in addition to their regular after-school activities. Each visit takes about 15 minutes and includes a theme, brief developmentally appropriate formal practice, educational component, brief experiential activity and suggestions for between meeting "practice" or attention to the theme. Youth in this setting showed significant decreases in anxiety pre- and post-mindful schools program start and completion. The program leader checks in with participants occasionally to ask if they "used their mindfulness" and if so, how. Tonya reported a specific story about how she used her mindfulness when her sibling was yelling at her. She typically would hit him leading to an afternoon of yelling, crying, and not being able to get her homework done. After being in the program for a few weeks, Tonya detailed a new option she had not tried yet at home. She decided to do mindful breathing on the bus to the after-school program and when she got home from the after-school program. She shared a specific detailed story about how she used mindfulness at home; when her brother started yelling, she left, went to her room, took some breaths, and then just colored. She noticed that her tummy did not hurt later that day, too. By the end of the program, Tonya's teacher reported that she was doing something similar at the after-school program and had asked the after-school program director to take mindful breaths with her when she arrived off the bus.

In this case, Tonya's life is saturated with chronic stress (e.g., poverty, lack of parent engagement), but there are also moments of acute stress due to normative interactions between siblings (X). However, these chronic and acute stressors can combine to produce somatic responses that manifest as the source of her stomach aches. Thus, the mindful program provided her with a breathing exercise (B) that she can implement when she experiences stress. This also changes her perception of stress (C) because she gains agency over coping strategies that produce outcomes that do not end with the aforementioned somatic response (X).

Discussion

Meditations on Systematic Oppression

We use family stress theory as a lens to postulate about mindfulness as both a resource or mechanism for perceptual change, as it relates to individuals and families' response to stress. The Pali word for mindfulness meaning, *to remember,* calls us to remember minoritized and systematically oppressed families and individuals not prominently reflected in the mindfulness literature and health-care literature generally. What may be hidden in this discussion of family stress and mindfulness interventions for Jean and Tonya are the many ongoing stressors created by heterosexist and racist U.S. policies and practices. In the United States, one glaring instance of this can be the long battle of GLBTQ persons and families who only recently gained the right to even be considered as actual families. At the time of Jean's case, she could legally be fired for being gay. This fact kept her from talking about her home life at work, leaving her with little relational support in a workplace that is quite stressful. Such an example highlights the many systems (e.g., family policy, health, workplace, cultural values) that create stress for minority families. There is disproportionate exposure to stress among ethnic and racial minority groups and in particular Black and U.S. Hispanics (Sternthal, Slopen, & Williams, 2011; see James, Barrios, Roy, & Lee, Chapter 4 in this volume for more on this). Among Black families, this stress cannot be separated from overtly discriminatory housing policies (redlining, National Housing Act of 1934; realtor discrimination, GI Bill of 1944) and the continued discrimination and segregation without legal recourse occurring until the 1968 Fair Housing Act. Even while policies change, there is a continuous and nuanced process of racial and ethnic socialization occurring among African American families (James, Coard, Fine, & Rudy, 2018). There may be additional stressors for Tonya and her family, too, as she attends a school where 90% or more students receive free and reduced lunch (e.g., Ohio Department of Education, 2015). These policies co-created the multigenerational segregated poverty experienced by Tonya and her family.

Interestingly, in the early days of MBSR, Kabat-Zinn (2011) recognized oppressive systems as an impetus for recruiting folks whose needs and pain are not eased through a "disease care" system and may benefit from a mindfulness-based program. Linehan (1993, 2020) too utilizes mindfulness as a tool to address people, mostly women, diagnosed with BPD, a doubly stigmatized diagnosis within a mental health system not designed to meet their needs and concurrently pushing them away. This chapter is about family stress and how mindfulness may be one of many ways to address it. We use the ABC-X model to highlight two cases and bring some attention to additional chronic ongoing stressors minoritized and systemically oppressed individuals and families face at potentially exacerbating their reaction or response due to the additional ongoing stressors.

Acceptance and Change

Linehan's DBT model (1993, 2020) emphasizes a dialectic, or joining of opposites and in particular: acceptance and change. This stance is important for facilitators working with families similar to Jean and Tonya. The systemic oppressive practices are not their fault, yet they impact the real lived experiences of such families and many minoritized individuals and families. When utilizing tools such as mindfulness to create change, whether that change is designed to impact a mental health symptom, health issue, family, teaching quality, or agency morale, taking a stance of *acceptance of the person just as they are* is key especially when minoritized and systematically oppressed individuals and families have not caused the additional conditions (e.g., discriminatory policies, culturally condoned heterosexist, racist, and other related practices across multiple systems including healthcare, education, and "justice" to name a few) heightening their stress response. In other words, mindfulness facilitators, individuals, and families can endeavor for changes while accepting people for who they are.

For future research we might ask the following questions: "What strengths do the minoritized and systematically oppressed develop to manage through their lives?" "How can 'home practice' or 'informal practice' be cultivated through various forms of inquiry in order to understand and expand the availability of mindfulness among families who may not have access to traditional programming?" "Could there be a family 'dispositional mindfulness'?" "How can we as practitioners, researchers, and facilitators be open to new categories and new possibilities (Langer, 1983, 2020) designed to empower and support mindfulness for families using a more participatory and culturally proficient lens (Lindsey, Nuri-Robins, Terrell, & Lindsey, 2010)?"

DISCUSSION QUESTIONS ●

1. Refer back to the four DBT skills referenced in this chapter. How might each one of these skills impact families? How could these skills potentially benefit your own family?

2. Choose one of the cases listed above. Based on the information provided, brainstorm and then list (a) at least three additional potential stressors associated with the family over the life course and (b) how an intensive mindfulness program such as MBSR or DBT might impact family member perspectives about these stressors?

3. Consider multiple reasons why individuals or families are minoritized due to social identity

(national origin, first language, socioeconomic status, religious or spiritual affiliation, ethnicity, race, gender, physical/emotional/developmental (dis)ability, sexuality, gender, etc.). Weave at least one additional minoritized social identity within one of the cases listed in this chapter. What are additional family stressors that may arise? Brainstorm additional strengths this family will develop to respond to these stressors. How might mindfulness practices or programs impact the family?

REFERENCES

Adair, K. C., Frederickson, B. L. (2015). Be open: Mindfulness predicts reduced motivated perception. *Personality & Individual Difference, 83,* 198–201.

American Mindfulness Research Association. (2019). *Mindfulness journal publications by year 1980–2018.* Retrieved from https://goamra.org /resources/

Anālayo, B. (2016). Early Buddhist mindfulness and memory, the body, and pain. *Mindfulness, 7*(6), 1271–1280.

Bishop, S. R., Lau, M., Shapiro, S., Carlson, L., Anderson, N. D., & Carmody, J., (2004). Mindfulness: A proposed operational definition. *Clinical Psychology: Science and Practice, 11*(3), 230–241. doi/10.1093/clipsy.bph077

Bodhi, B. (2000). *A comprehensive manual of Abhidhamma*. Seattle, WA: Buddhist Publication Society Pariyatti Editions.

Bronfenbrenner, U., & Morris, P. A. (2006). The bioecological model of human development. In R. M. Lerner & W. Damon (Eds.), *Handbook of child psychology: Theoretical models of human development., Vol. 1* (6th ed., pp. 793–828). Hoboken, NJ: Wiley.

Brown, C. A., Jones, A. K. (2010). Meditation experience predicts less negative appraisal of pain: Electrophysiological evidence for the involvement of anticipatory neural responses. *Pain, 150,* 428–438.

Brown, K. W., Ryan, R. M., & Creswell, J. D. (2007). Mindfulness: Theoretical foundations and evidence for its salutary effects. *Psychological Inquiry, 18*(4), 211–237.

Carroll, G. (1998). Mundane extreme environmental stress and African American families: A case for recognizing different realities. *Journal of Comparative Family Studies, 29*(2), 271–284.

Carson, J. W., Carson, K. M., Gil, K. M., & Baucom, D. H. (2004). Mindfulness-based relationship enhancement. *Behavior Therapy, 35*(3), 471–494.

Coatsworth, J. D., Duncan, L. G., Berrena, E., Bamberger, K. T., Loeschinger, D., Greenberg, M. T., & Nix, R. L. (2014). The Mindfulness-Enhanced Strengthening Families Program: Integrating brief mindfulness activities and parent training within an evidence-based prevention program. *New Directions for Human Development, 142,* 45–58.

DeCou, C. R., Comtois, K. A., & Landes, S. J. (2019). Dialectical behavior therapy is effective for the treatment of suicidal behavior: A meta-analysis. *Behavior Therapy, 50*(1), 60–72.

Droit-Volet, S., Chaulet, M., & Dambrun, M. (2018). Time and meditation: When does the perception of time change with mindfulness practice? *Mindfulness, 9,* 1557–1570.

Fjorback, L. O., Arendt, M., Ørnbøl, E., Fink, P., & Walach, H. (2011). Mindfulness-based stress reduction and mindfulness-based cognitive therapy: A systematic review of randomized controlled trials. *Acta Psychiatrica Scandinavica, 124*(2), 102–119.

Freire, P. (1970), *Pedagogy of the oppressed*. New York, NY: Continuum.

Grossman, P., Niemann, L., Schmidt, S., & Walach, H. (2004). Mindfulness-based stress reduction and health benefits: A meta-analysis. *Journal of Psychosomatic Research, 57*(1), 35–43.

Hill, R. (1958). Generic features of families under stress, *Social Casework 49,* 139–150.

Hunnicutt Hollenbaugh, K. M., & Lenz, A. S. (2018). Preliminary evidence for the effectiveness of dialectical behavior therapy for adolescents. *Journal of Counseling & Development, 96*(2), 119–131.

James, A. G., Taylor, A., Winmill, L., & Alfoadari, K. (2008). A preliminary community study of dialectical behaviour therapy (DBT) with adolescent females demonstrating persistent, deliberate self-harm (DSH). *Child and Adolescent Mental Health, 13*(3),148–152.

James, A. G., Coard, S. I., Fine, M. A., & Rudy, D. (2018). The central roles of race and racism in reframing family systems theory: A consideration of choice and time. *Journal of Family Theory & Review, 10*(2), 419–433.

Kabat-Zinn, J. (1982). An outpatient program in behavioral medicine for chronic pain patients based on the practice of mindfulness meditation: Theoretical considerations and preliminary results. *General Hospital Psychiatry, 4,* 33–47.

Kabat-Zinn, J. (1990). *Full-catastrophe living: Using the wisdom of your body and mind to face stress, pain* and illness: The program of the Stress Reduction Clinic at the University of Massachusetts Medical Center. New York, NY: Dell.

Kabat-Zinn, J. (1994). *Wherever you go, there you are: Mindfulness meditation in everyday life*. New York, NY: Hyperion.

Kabat-Zinn, J. (2003). Mindfulness-based interventions in context: Past, present, and future. *Clinical Psychology: Science and Practice, 10*(2), 144–156.

Kabat-Zinn, J. (2011). Some reflections on the origins of MBSR, skillful means, and the trouble with maps. *Contemporary Buddhism, 12*(1), 281–306.

Khoury, B., Sharma, M., Rush, S. E., & Fournier, C. (2015). Mindfulness-based stress reduction in healthy individuals: A meta-analysis. *Journal of Psychosomatic Research, 78*(6), 519–528.

Langer, E. J. (1989). *Mindfulness*. Cambridge, MA: Da Capo Press.

Lau, M., Bishop, S., Segal, Z., Buis, T., Anderson, N., Carlson, L., & Devins, G. (2006). The Toronto Mindfulness Scale: Development and validation. *Journal of Clinical Psychology, 62*(12), 1445–1467.

Lavee, Y. (2013). Stress processes in families and couples. In G. W. Peterson & K. R. Bush (Eds), *Handbook of marriage and family* (3rd ed., pp. 159–176). New York, NY: Springer.

Lindsey, R. B., Nuri-Robins, K., Terrell, R. D., & Lindsey, D. B. (2019). *Cultural proficiency: Manual for school leaders* (4th ed.). Thousand Oaks, CA: Corwin.

Linehan, M. M. (1993). *Cognitive-behavioral treatment of borderline personality disorder*. New York, NY: Guilford Press.

Linehan, M. M. (2015). *DBT skills training manual* (2nd ed.). New York, NY: Guilford Press.

Linehan, M. M. (2020). *Building a life worth living: A memoir*. New York, NY: Random House.

Lloyd, A., White, R., Eames, C., & Crane, R. (2018). The utility of home-practice in mindfulness-based group interventions: A systematic review. *Mindfulness, 9*, 673–692.

McCubbin, H. I., & Patterson, J. M. (1983). The family stress process: The Double ABC-X model of adjustment and adaptation. *Marriage & Family Review, 6*(1/2), 7–37.

McCubbin, L. D., & McCubbin, H. I. (2013). Resilience in ethnic family systems: A relational theory for research and practice. In D. S. Becvar (Ed.), *Handbook of family resilience* (pp. 175–195). New York, NY: Springer.

McKeering, P., & Hwang, Y. S. (2019). A systematic review of mindfulness-based school interventions with early adolescents. *Mindfulness, 10*(4), 593–610.

McNeil Smith, S., & Landor, A. M. (2018). Toward a better understanding of African American families: Development of the sociocultural family stress model. *Journal of Family Theory & Review, 10*(2), 434–450.

Miller, A. L., Rathus, J. H., & Linehan, M. M. (2007). *Dialectical behavior therapy with suicidal adolescents*. New York, NY: Guilford Press.

Ohio Department of Education. (2015). *[Graph illustration of Free and Reduced Price Meal Eligibility]. Data For Free and Reduced Lunch*. Retrieved from http://education.ohio.gov/Topics/Student-Su pports/Food-and-Nutrition/Resources-and-Tools -for-Food-and-Nutrition/MR81-Data-for-Free -and-Reduced-Price-Meal-Eligibil

Parent, J., Clifton, J., Forehand, R., Golub, A., Reid, M., & Pichler, E. R. (2014). Parental mindfulness and dyadic relationship quality in low-income cohabiting black stepfamilies: Associations with parenting experienced by adolescents. *Couple and Family Psychology: Research and Practice, 3*(2), 67–82.

Parsons, C. E., Crane, C., Parsons, L. J., Fjorback, L. O., & Kuyken, W. (2017). Home practice in mindfulness-based cognitive therapy and mindfulness-based stress reduction: A systematic review and meta-analysis of participants' mindfulness practice and its association with outcomes. *Behaviour Research and Therapy, 95*, 29–41.

Perlman, D. M., Salomons, T. V., Davidson, R. J., & Lutz, A. (2010). Differential effects on pain intensity and unpleasantness of two meditation practices. *Emotion 10*, 65–71.

Peters, M. F., & Massey, G. (1983). Mundane extreme environmental stress in family stress theories: The case of Black families in White America. *Marriage & Family Review, 6*(1/2), 193–218.

Pew Research Center. (2014). [Graph Illustration Religious Landscape Study, conducted June 4-Sept. 30, 2014] *Frequency of meditation among U.S. religious groups*. Retrieved from https://www.pewresearch.org/fact-tank/2018/01/02/meditation-is-common-across-many-religious-groups-in-the-u-s/

Rathus, J. H., Cavuoto, N., & Passarelli, V. (2006). Dialectical behavioral therapy (DBT): A mindfulness-based treatment for intimate partner violence. In R. Baer (Ed.), *Mindfulness-based treatment approaches: Clinician's guide to evidence base and applications* (pp. 333–358). Boston, MA: Academic Press.

Segal, Z. V., Williams, J. M. G., & Teasdale, J. D. (2002). *Mindfulness-based cognitive therapy for depression: A new approach to preventing relapse.* Guilford Press.

Shapiro, S. L., Astin, J. A., Bishop, S. R., & Cordova, M. (2005). Mindfulness-based stress reduction for health care professionals: Results from a randomized trial. *International Journal of Stress Management, 12*(2), 164–176.

Sibinga, M. S., Kerrigan, D., Steward, M., Johnson, K., Magyari, T., & Ellen, J. M. (2011). Mindfulness-based stress reduction for urban youth. *Journal of Alternative and Complementary Medicine, 17*(3), 213–218.

Sibinga, M. S., Webb, L., Ghazarian, S. R., & Ellen, J. M. (2016). School-based mindfulness instruction: An RCT. *Pediatrics, 137*(1), 1–8.

Sternthal, M. J., Slopen, N., & Williams, D. R. (2011). Racial disparities in health: How much does stress really matter? *Du Bois Review, 8*(1), 95–113.

Tomlinson, E. R., Yousaf, O., Vietterso, A. D., & Jones, L. (2018). Dispositional mindfulness and psychological health: A systematic review. *Mind fulness* (9), 23–43.

Van Dam, N. T., Van Vugt, M. K., Vago, D. R., Schmalz, L., Saron, C. D., Oldendzki, A., Meissner, T., Lazar, S. W., Kerr, C. E., Gorchov, J., Fox, K. C. R., Field, B. A., Britton, W. B., Brefczynski-Lewis, J. A., & Meyer, D. E. (2018). Mind the hype: A critical evaluation and prescriptive agenda for research on mindfulness and meditation. *Perspectives Psychological Science, 13*(1), 36–61.

Vallejo, Z., & Amaro, H. (2009). Adaptation of mindfulness-based stress reduction program for addiction relapse and prevention. *The Humanistic Psychologist, 37*(2), 192–206. https://doi.org/10.1080/08873260902892287

Walsh, Z. (2016). A meta-critique of mindfulness critiques: From McMindfulness to critical mindfulness. In R. Purser, D. Forbes, & A. Burke (Eds.), *Handbook of mindfulness* (pp. 153–166). New York, NY: Springer.

Wilson, J. (2016). Selling mindfulness: Commodity lineages and the marketing of mindful products. In R. Purser, D. Forbes, & A. Burke (Eds.), *Handbook of mindfulness: Mindfulness in behavioral health* (pp. 109–119). New York, NY: Springer.

Developmental Family Stress

CHAPTER 4

Parental Stress Viewed Through the Lens of Family Stress Theory

Gary W. Peterson

During the socialization process in many cultures most of us are strongly encouraged through multiple influences to value children and become parents as a fundamental experience in a person's life. Females, in particular, are traditionally socialized to view motherhood as a primary source of life satisfaction and, more recently, men have been encouraged to identify with fatherhood more than in the past (Bigner, 2010; Holden, 2015; Marsiglio & Roy, 2013). Positive cultural images of parenthood, partly based in pronatalist and religious influences, are key sources of the pervasive idea that raising children is almost always a life-fulfilling experience.

Pronatalism is a complex set of beliefs and actions that promote childbearing and parenthood as highly desirable outcomes. These beliefs and actions are powerfully encouraged by social justifications, beliefs about personal welfare, religious views, biological reasons, and to ensure the existence of the human species (Green, 2017). Pronatalism can be promoted through public policies aimed at creating financial, legal, and social incentives such as tax incentives or government programs that reward having and caring for children. Those who support pronatalist social policies often seek ways to limit the use of birth control through abortion and contraception (Green, 2017).

An example of a conservative religious group that is also pronatalist is the Quiverfull fundamentalist sect located in the United States and to some extent internationally. The Quiverfulls are an evangelical group of Christians who promote procreation and parenthood by believing strongly that children are blessings given by God and reject all forms of contraception, including natural family planning, sterilization, and abortion (Blumberg, 2015). This sect defines any form of birth control by married couples to be wrongful disobedience to the word of God, which is captured in the Biblical phrase "Be fruitful and multiply" (Kaufmann, 2011). Happiness and reduced stress are supposed to result from parenthood, especially for Quiverfull women, when they reject any form of birth control and accept their biblically mandated roles of motherhood. Husbands are ordained by God to be leaders of patriarchal family systems and are strongly encouraged to be involved parents as strong authority figures. Quiverfulls further argue that parental stress is divinely controlled and lessened because God is all-knowing and will not give each parent or adult more children than that which they can reasonably cope (Blumberg, 2015).

Other positive and even romanticized views of parenting have their basis in secular beliefs that children almost always make parents' lives complete and more meaningful. Raising children is seen as a source of fun, novelty, stimulation and a means of solidifying ties among parents, grandparents, kin, and parental surrogates (Cloud, 2011; Eibach & Mock, 2011). Parenthood provides a socially defined marker of mature status, a sense of permanence, and feelings of personal efficacy (Bigner, 2010; Holden, 2015). Recent evolutionary views also reinforce pronatalist perspectives by proposing that, due to natural selection processes, our genetic heritage provides a significant biological propensity for adults to assume parental roles. Although these natural tendencies to become parents can be changed, considerable effort is needed to consciously alter such predispositions (Buss, 2005). This means that pronatalist and unrealistically positive views of parenting often are dominant, while more objective assessments of the challenges and stresses involved are neglected. The purpose of this chapter is to apply concepts from family stress theory to provide a more realistic and balanced conception of parenting, which includes the pervasive and variable presence of both normative and nonnormative forms of parental stress.

The Reality of Parenthood and Parental Stress

More realistic views of parenthood often explicitly or implicitly reject the idea that motherhood and fatherhood are exclusively negative or positive experiences. Instead, newer more reality-based conceptions recognize that caring for, disciplining, and socializing children often involves a blend of positive, negative, and rather mundane experiences for parents (Basile, 2014; Cloud, 2011, Eibach & Mock, 2011). An array of common parental experiences include powerful bonds and attachments, personal fulfillment, great satisfactions from children's achievements, and great sadness when they fail. Children and youth often contribute to parents' daily hassles, tensions, anxiety, distress, depression, and severe trauma. Parenthood can be characterized as a deeply meaningful challenge in life but also one of the most arduous responsibilities that adults will ever face. Romanticized conceptions are increasingly seen as illusory, simplistic and distorted images of a much more complex circumstance (Cloud, 2011; Eibach & Mock, 2011).

A more realistic view of parenthood is that of a complex circumstance of life where stress is a normative experience that changes from moment to moment and over the long term. A growing segment of the U.S. population appears to be more realistic about parenthood and is choosing such alternatives as voluntary childlessness more frequently and feeling more comfortable with this child-free option. Recent evidence indicates that a child-free lifestyle often can have few psychological costs for those who make this life choice (Bures, Koropeckyj-Cox, & Loree, 2009; Kelly, 2009; Koropeckyj-Cox et al., 2007; Umberson et al., 2010).

Feminist thought also questions the "normative imperative" for women to bear children as a primary means for defining meaningful identities for themselves.

Although most feminists acknowledge that motherhood can be a rewarding experience, they also argue that we should reject the idealized "cult of motherhood" and recognize that being a mother is not always the most important thing that women can do nor the only way women can be fulfilled. In the end, motherhood is more frequently viewed as a personal choice, just like many other pathways in life that are increasingly available to women (Basile, 2014; Hu, 2015).

Realistic views also are reflected in the work of economists who seek to establish the economic value of children as either assets or liabilities rather than simply viewing parenthood through idealized conceptions of inevitable happiness (Folbre, 2008). Economic metaphors are used to show how parents' investments and balance sheet decisions are used to define the great variability that exists in the positive and negative stress experienced by parents from raising the young (Eibach & Mock, 2011).

A key source of parents' stresses is their social cognitions or mental models of themselves as parents, which can lead them to evaluate the challenges and benefits of parenting in realistic ways (Eibach & Mock, 2011; Finegood, Raver, DeJoseph & Blair 2017; Vernhet et al., 2019). These mental models of parenthood are shaped by their own self-perceptions, how they perceive others (e.g., their children and youth) as well as attitudes, attributions, and expectations they have developed within particular cultural contexts. How parents appraise themselves in terms of such social meanings is important for defining the onset, continuity, intensity, and management of parental stress (Deater-Deckard, Smith, Ivy, & Petrill, 2005; Eibach & Mock, 2011). Stressful experiences occur and require management throughout the life course, often on a daily basis. Such everyday experiences of parental stress can occur when parents are fatigued by an infant's inconsistent sleep–awake patterns, a toddler who bites a classmate in childcare, a teenage daughter who demands later curfew hours for dating, the difficult behavior of an autistic child, or when a teenage son is arrested for possession of marijuana (Rich, 2017).

Parents become stressed by difficult job circumstances that compel them to spend less positive time, be less supportive, and to use less effective discipline with their children (Kremer-Sadlik & Paugh, 2007). Stress for parents also becomes problematic when work demands are high and when parents lack feelings of self-control in their work environments (Ohu et al., 2018). In fact, parental stress can result from variability in several external circumstances including socioeconomic resources, family structural characteristics, work- and career-related factors, as well as childcare arrangements. Recent findings make clear that the multiple roles of parents often influence the degree of stress they experience within the parent–child relationship (Deater-Deckard, 2004; Rich, 2017; Umberson et al., 2010).

The point of these diverse examples is that some degree of parental stress is likely to be a universal experience for parents and their surrogates, including grandparents, aunts, uncles, stepparents, foster parents, and others who perform parental roles. The ubiquitous nature of these experiences underscores the importance of understanding how stress contributes to the effective or ineffective functioning of parents and other caregivers (Crnic et al., 2005; Crnic & Low, 2002; Hennon et al., 2008; Letiecq et al., 2008). In contrast, despite its universality, the precise manner and degree that parental stress is experienced may vary greatly across parents and depends upon many factors (Deater-Deckard, 2004). Individuals, in certain social circumstances, such as some single parents and lower SES families are more likely to experience parental stress due to limited resources of a financial, social and psychological nature (e.g., limited energy, time, and money). These deficiencies leave parents more vulnerable to typical stressors that are pervasive, vary widely in intensity, and subject to diverse circumstances (Crouter & Booth, 2004).

The primary purpose of this chapter is to interpret the research on parental stress using concepts central to family stress theory, which can provide greater understanding to this aspect of the parent–child relationship (Hennon et al., 2009; Hennon & Peterson, 2007; Hill, 1949; Lavee, 2013; McCubbin & Patterson, 1983; Patterson, 2002). Key concepts from family stress theory used to accomplish this goal are stress and crisis, stressor event (or stressor), resources, definition of the stressor (or perception), coping, and adaptation. A case study will be presented and used periodically to illustrate points in this chapter.

Addressing these issues and concepts will provide greater understanding about (a) why the experience of parental stress is so common, (b) why the degree of stress varies widely within the population of parents, (c) why parents vary in their capacities to cope with and adapt to stress, (d) what linkages exist between parental stress and the adjustment (or maladjustment) of parents and children, and (e) what strategies exist for controlling and reducing adverse parental stress.

Rethinking the research literature on parental stress in terms of family stress theory also provides a more systemic or family systems view of this area of knowledge. Previous research and the conceptualization of parental stress has been largely an application of psychological theory (Crnic & Low, 2002; Deater-Deckard, 2004) by emphasizing stress as experienced through the internal dynamics of individuals (e.g., parents) who experience psychological "distress" (or similar forms of affect such as anxiety, depression, trauma, strain, uneasiness), while limited attention has been devoted to "relationship" or "systemic" conceptions. In contrast, this chapter reinterprets parental stress more extensively as changes in systemic family relationships that encompass parent–child relationships without ignoring the individual psychological experience of stress (Lavee, 2013).

Case Study: Tiffany

Tiffany is a 40-year-old divorced mother of three, Matt (17), Joey (10), and Pamela (3), of whom she has full legal and physical custody. The children see their father only on holidays and sometimes during the summers because he lives and works inconsistently in another state. Tiffany works as a custodian 40-hours per week on the third shift (11 p.m. to 7 a.m.). She prefers the third shift because it allows her to send off the older two children to school in the mornings and be at home in the afternoons when they return. She also has a second, part-time job on weekends, just to afford necessities. Tiffany's family is currently living in a mobile home that she is purchasing because their previous mobile home was destroyed by a flood during an extended rain storm. At the time of the flood, Tiffany and her family had to flee their home and lost most of their belongings. Tiffany often feels exhausted and overwhelmed by the accumulation of her many responsibilities, including being a single parent who has primary responsibility to provide financially for her family. Fortunately, she is able to rely on her oldest son, Matt, to care for the two younger children on the weekends when she works. Also, her great aunt is a retired special education teacher who loves to spend time with Tiffany's children and usually comes over during the day to watch Pamela (who was diagnosed with autism recently), while Tiffany sleeps in preparation for her night shift. Tiffany has a very busy and stressful life in which she must have a lot of stamina, patience, and be very resourceful to cope with it all.

The "Systemic" Factor X: Parental Stress and Family Stress Theory

The foundation of family stress theory is provided in Reuben Hill's (1949) classic work on the ABC-X model. Hill proposed that family crisis or stress (the X factor) results from a complex three-way combination of (1) the stressor event (the A factor), (2) the resources that families have available (the B factor), and (3) the definitions or meanings that families assign to the stressor (the C factor). Stressful or crisis situations do not result directly from the event by itself but are a product of the event, the interpretations of family members and how much family systems have abilities to cope and recover (Boss, 2002; Lavee, 2013; Patterson, 2002). In the most general sense, *family stress* is defined as a change or disturbance in the steady state of the family system which can have consequences that range along a continuum from very positive to very negative (Allen, 2017; Boss, 2014).

Originally, family stress theory examined only the circumstances of a "crisis" in which sudden, dramatic events had occurred (e.g., the flood that destroyed Tiffany's previous mobile home or a when a child is suddenly diagnosed with life threatening cancer) that may seriously incapacitate the family. In contrast, more recent conceptualizations of the X factor have dealt with more normative, milder, cumulative, and long-term changes. Another increased focus for understanding family and parental stress is the systemic nature of these changes within parent-child relationships and the larger family system (Boss, 2014; Crnic et al., 2005; Crnic & Low, 2002; Hill, 1949; Lavee, 2013).

Family stress scholars view change in family systems as the stress and tension within families and parent–child relationships that varies widely (Boss, 2002,

2014; Hennon et al., 2008; Patterson, 2002). Various life transitions provide the essential ingredients for normal psychosocial development of individuals, but do so in conjunction with pressures for change in the roles and expectations that shape the larger family system. Because family members and family systems are subject to persistent developmental change, stress in the form of systemic change becomes inevitable during everyday life, both within families and parent–child relationships (Lavee, 2013). An important contribution of family stress theory is to move the construct of "stress" from being used solely at the psychological level to both the parent-child relationship and family systems levels of analysis (Allen, 2017; Boss, 2002; Hennon et al., 2009; Lavee, 2013).

At the psychological level, parental stress (sometimes called "distress") is commonly viewed as an aversive emotional reaction by an individual parent to the demands of childcare and child socialization (Crnic et al., 2005; Crnic & Low, 2002; Deater-Deckard, 2004). In contrast, stresses at relationship or family systems levels are defined as pressure or tension for development within a relationship system that is synonymous with change (Allen, 2017; Boss, 2002; Lavee, 2013). Depending on how parents and other family members view such pressures for change, this may contribute either to psychological distress or positive psychological feelings of individuals as they cope with challenging circumstances. Consequently, family level and parental or individual stress involve awareness of changes within a family's structure, role relationships, and corresponding expectations that affect either the stability of family systems or family members' personal assessments of these changes. Changes that may evoke such stressful reactions include dramatic crisis events, changes in family members' behavior, alteration in the family's authority structure, mundane daily hassles, and the pileup of several of these challenging circumstances at the same time (i.e., strain) (Allen, 2017: Lavee, 2013; McCubbin, & Patterson, 1983).

From a systems perspective, parental stress also must be viewed in terms of *reciprocal* or even *multidirectional* processes (Kuczynski & De Mol, 2015). Stress experienced by parents is a product of connections with others (e.g., relationships with coworkers or with a person's spouse or partner). Parental stress also is an *activator* of parental behavior and other responses that have developmental consequences for other family members, most importantly children and youth (Deater-Deckard, 2004; Deater-Deckard et al., 2005). Children themselves are another primary source of parental stress that shape the responses of parents to the young in a bidirectional or transactional manner (Bush & Peterson, 2013; Neece et al., 2012). For example, Matt's high level of maturity, respect, and love that he displays within the family allows Tiffany to trust him to provide social support in the form of watching his siblings. Moreover, this trust lead's to Tiffany's willingness to grant him more autonomy, responsibility and privileges, including such things as use of the family car. Parental stress or positive feelings are a product of mothers' and fathers' circumstances based on their bidirectional or transactional connections with children and with other individuals, both inside and beyond family boundaries. Such systems-based conditions include sudden job loss, severe spousal conflict, parental divorce or remarriage, disengagement from families or excessive intrusions by extended family members to name just a few circumstances (Gerard, Krishnakumar, & Buehler, 2008; Peterson & Bush, 2015, Rich, 2017).

Parental stress also operates as a "systemic activator" within parent–child relationships by fostering changes in parents' socializing behavior, which leads sometimes to dysfunctional parenting (Crnic & Low, 2002; Deater-Deckard et al., 2005; Deater-Deckard, 2004). Stressful responses by parents may then have consequences for the social, emotional, and cognitive development of children (Buehler & Gerard, 2002; Bush & Peterson, 2008; Cappa, Begle, Conger, Dumas, & Conger, 2011; Gerard et al., 2008; Jones et al., 2009). For example, highly stressed compared to less stressed parents are more inclined to be anxious, emotionally reactive, preoccupied with adult-centered goals, less able to maintain effective childrearing, and less likely to supervise their young effectively. Thus, parental stress tends to *spill over* systemically into parent–child relationships by contributing to parental behaviors that are less responsive, less likely to demonstrate rational control, and to be less warm, while being more neglectful, punitive, or even abusive toward children (Buehler & Gerard, 2002; Bush & Peterson, 2008; Carapito, Ribeiro, Pereira, & Roberto, 2018; Gerard et al., 2008). For example, Tiffany reports feeling very stressed about her finances toward the end of the month. During these times, she is more focused on providing food for her family and ensuring that the rent is paid instead of consciously demonstrating high-quality parenting behaviors. Declines in parenting quality may lead, in turn, to negative outcomes in children such as noncompliance, less effective social skills, problems with peer adjustment, feelings of rejection, lowered self-esteem, aggressive behavior, social withdrawal, and distressed psychological experiences (Bush & Peterson, 2013; Carapito et al., 2018, Crnic et al., 2005; Crnic & Low, 2002; Deater-Deckard, 2004; Deater-Deckard et al., 2005; Gerard et al., 2008). In contrast, parents who have lower stress and perceive positive change within the family system tend to be more responsive, warm, rational, and to use moderate control (i.e., firm control, reasoning, consistent rule enforcement, and better monitoring rather than punitive or neglectful behavior) with children (Bush & Peterson, 2013; Crnic et al., 2005; Deater-Deckard, 2004; Deater-Deckard et al., 2005; Gerard et al., 2008). Child outcomes associated with positive parental behaviors include high self-esteem, effective school achievement, competent social skills, effective peer adjustment, as well as a balance between conforming to parents and making progress toward autonomy. These child and adolescent qualities are key aspects of social competence, or what a variety of cultures often view as adaptive attributes by the young (Bush & Peterson, 2013; Peterson & Bush, 2015).

The systemic *connections* between parental stress and child characteristics are not limited to circumstances where social influence is viewed as flowing only from parent to child. Instead, children and their perceived attributes have considerable influence on the stress experienced by parents (Bush & Peterson, 2013; Cappa et al., 2011; Deater-Deckard, 2004; Gerard et al., 2008). The existing literature generally supports the family systems hypothesis that relationships, such as those between parents and children, are extensively interdependent, reciprocal, or transactional (Kuczynski & De Mol, 2015; Neece et al., 2012). Moreover, parents who report greater intimacy and communication in their marriages tend to be less stressed and are more responsive, affectionate, and moderately controlling with children (Bush & Peterson, 2013; Gerard et al., 2008). Clearly, the parent–child relationship is systemic in nature by having reciprocal or multidirectional connections, with parental stress being both a "product" and an "activator" of changes within the family system (Deater-Deckard, 2004; Kuczynski, & De Mol, 2015; Neece et al., 2012).

Stressors or Stressor Events for Parents: Factor A

Stressors or stressor events (the A factor) consist of occurrences that may be of sufficient magnitude to bring about changes within the larger family system, the parent–child subsystem and feelings of tension by parents (Boss, 2014). However, because many stressful circumstances do not occur for parents as discrete events, the general term *stressor* is now preferred. This distinction is important because parents may be dealing with circumstances that develop gradually over an extended time period and multiple stressors can accumulate to gradually determine the overall level of parental stress (McCubbin & Patterson, 1983; Rich, 2017).

Although a stressor has the *potential* to evoke systemic change and psychological responses, the occurrences that challenge parent–child relationships do not inevitably lead to the onset of stress. Stressors may threaten the status quo of families and parent–child relationships, but they are *not solely responsible* for fostering stress by imposing demands on individuals (e.g., parents) and relationships. By themselves, stressors (a) do not have all the necessary ingredients (i.e., the B factor, *resources,* and the C factor, *definitions*) for parental stress, (b) have no inherent positive or negative qualities, and (c) may never immobilize the parent–child relationship and bring about individual stress by parents. Instead, stressors are undefined phenomena that are capable of only applying pressures that range from developing dramatically to unfolding gradually. Rather than always being major disruptions, many stressors are of mild to moderate strength that can accumulate and "pile up" over time (Buehler, & Gerard, 2013; McCubbin & Patterson, 1983; Patterson, 2002).

Despite the fact that stressors have no inherent meaning, scholars have developed classification systems to identify common ways that parents and families tend to define and respond to them (Allen, 2017). A number of stressors often receive fairly common individual definitions that fit approximately into the categories of a classification system. Most classification systems include three common categories: normative stressors, nonnormative stressors, and chronic stressors. An important caution to keep in mind, however, is that specific stressors do not always fit exclusively within a single category, which means that any classification system inherently has imperfections.

Normative Stressors

An initial kind of change, *normative stressors*, are part of everyday life (e.g., daily hassles) or are longer term developmental transitions that occur normally during the family life course (see Price, Bush, Price, & McKenry, Chapter 1 in this volume).

Daily Hassles

Parents' daily hassles include constant caregiving demands and pressures from everyday tasks involved in caring for and socializing children (Finegood et al., 2017; Helms, Postler, & Demo, Chapter 2 in this volume). Many everyday child-rearing experiences are sources of self-defined competence and satisfactions by parents as they engage in playful activities with children, solve parent–child challenges, and enjoy the developmental progress of their young (Bush & Peterson, 2008, 2013; Peterson & Bush, 2015). In contrast, other parenting experiences are less positive, such as when Tiffany reports dealing with her children's whining, their annoying conduct due to underdeveloped self-control, endless cleaning-up activities, loss of sleep, toilet training, constant interruptions, lack of personal time, and seemingly endless errands. Some hassles are infrequent and situational, whereas others occur repeatedly as part of everyday life (Crnic et al., 2005; Crnic & Low, 2002, Kalil et al., 2014; Yoon et al., 2015). By itself, each hassle may have limited consequences, but the cumulative impact of daily hassles may lead to substantial amounts of parental stress (Finegood et al., 2017; Helms, Postler, & Demo, Chapter 2 in this volume; Hennon et al., 2009).

Single-parent families may be subject to problems stemming from the rapid accumulation of daily hassles and other stressors. One reason for this "accumulation" problem is that adult partners are now absent or are no longer sharing the everyday challenges of child-rearing. For example, although Tiffany's ex-husband pays some child support (he is only inconsistently employed), he is not involved with the children regularly to share everyday tasks. The daily hassles of single parents may be complicated by stress resulting from economic disadvantage, employment conflicts, and limited social support. Single parents often must face an accumulation of challenges that leads to feelings of isolation, exhaustion, depression, distress, and diminished feelings of parental efficacy (Kremer-Sadlik & Paugh, 2007; Ontai et al., 2008). Although many single parents provide positive environments for children, this accumulation of daily hassles may push parent–child relationships gradually in problematic directions over time (Ontai et al., 2008). When daily hassles occur regularly, parents who once were satisfied and competent, may gradually become fatigued, dysfunctional, and subjected to growing stress (Dunning & Giallo, 2012). These evolving circular processes may give rise to unresponsive, and less satisfied parents, along with children who demonstrate acting out and problematic behaviors (Crnic et al., 2005; Crnic & Low, 2002; Neece et al., 2012).

Developmental Transitions

Other sources of normative stress are the developmental transitions of the young, the social meanings associated with these changes, and the resulting need for modifications within parent–child relationships. Developmental transitions have the potential for stressors to accumulate and can result in disruptive change, psychological distress, or, in contrast, a growing sense of parental competence. One of these pivotal times of change and possible stress occurs during the transition to parenthood. Newborns require almost constant care through feeding, cleaning, changing, and dealing with an infant's sleep patterns. Relentless parental responsibilities during this period include monitoring their infant's health, applying preventative measures, and arranging treatment for problematic health issues (Medina et al., 2009). Parents who cope effectively are those who sooth newborns when they cry and provide other forms of sensitive responsiveness that foster the establishment of secure parent–child attachment. Sensitive responsiveness involves managing stress so that parenting is attentive, empathic, and reads the infant's cues accurately. Sensitive parents also avoid high intrusiveness and are emotionally responsive to infants (Solomon & George, 2008).

The birth of an infant often abruptly disrupts the routine patterns of parents in ways requiring concentrated attention to the needs of the newborn (Epifanio et al., 2015). Parents experience sleep disturbances because newborns often wake up every few hours for feeding. Because new mothers often leave the workplace, families with newborns can experience decreases in income, which may increase the stress of fathers as they take second jobs or work more hours to supplement family finances (Medina et al., 2009). The decreased time and energy experienced by marital partners often results in decreased marital satisfaction, less mutual expressions of love, and greater conflict between spouses (Lawrence et al., 2008). How parents manage these potential sources of stress may depend on how well they maintain marital relationships and successful co-parenting (or establish a parental alliance). High-quality marital relationships are predictive of effective co-parenting where parents work together to support each other's parenting with competence (Bouchard, 2014). Competent parenting involves providing support, resolving child-rearing disagreements, dividing family duties fairly, and managing interaction patterns. Co-parenting involves providing mutual social support and helps reduce stress while increasing parents' abilities to respond to infants with sensitivity (Schoppe-Sullivan & Mangelsdorf, 2013). Co-parenting also involves being responsive to infants, maintaining couple satisfaction, and diminishing parental stress (McHale & Lindahl, 2011).

Another example of a developmental transition occurs during the adolescent years, when greater stress may be experienced by parents when their role is expected to change toward granting autonomy to the young (Collins & Steinberg, 2006; Kagitcibasi, 2013; Liga et al., 2015). Consistent with normative expectations, parents in the United States often grant autonomy through a gradual process of relationship renegotiation that allows adolescents greater self-determination (Bush & Peterson 2008; Collins & Steinberg, 2006; Kagitcibasi, 2013; Peterson & Bush, 2015). This process of "letting go" in western cultures is not a sudden transfer of authority to the young. Instead, competent parents and developing teenagers engage in renegotiation processes that are necessary, mutual, and accelerate during adolescence (Collins & Steinberg, 2006; Kagitcibasi, 2013; Peterson & Bush, 2013). This letting-go process presents potential stressors, especially when parents resist granting autonomy to the young and resist the need to redefine gradually their roles as authority figures. This effort to delay youthful autonomy may erupt into heightened conflict and stress between adolescents and parents (Bush & Peterson, 2008; Collins & Steinberg, 2006; Peterson & Bush, 2015). Consequently, this desire of adolescents for greater autonomy may result in feelings of distress and separation anxiety by parents who resist this loss of control (Collins & Steinberg, 2006; Liga et al, 2015). Moderate levels of parent–adolescent conflict and distress may be normative energizers for growing autonomy. In contrast, parent–adolescent conflict that escalates to very high levels may lead to greater emotional distance, severe conflict, and greater stress for parents when the autonomy-granting process malfunctions (Collins & Steinberg, 2006; Peterson & Bush, 2015). Many families also experience multiple developmental transitions simultaneously, such as when Tiffany gave birth to Pamela, she was also going through the complexities of Matt's transition into adolescence.

Nonnormative Stressors

Parents also face stressor events that are nonnormative through unpredictable occurrences that substantially disrupt the everyday pattern of parent–child relationships (Allen, 2017; Hill, 1949; see Chapter 1). Nonnormative stressor events are often sudden, dramatic occurrences that have high potential of disrupting the lives of parents and family members. Most often, these stressors are products of unique situations that are unlikely to be repeated very often. Examples include a natural disaster (e.g., Tiffany's flood, hurricanes, tornados); the sudden death of a child; a sudden, disabling injury to a family member; or winning the state lottery. All are unexpected and have the potential to disrupt family relationships and require structural changes that can lead to greater stress for parents (Allen, 2017; Hill, 1949; see Chapter 1). These events, however, are not inherently stressful in exactly the same way for all parents. Instead, nonnormative stressors vary in their disruptive qualities depending upon the parents' subjective interpretations and the resources (or vulnerabilities) they have available.

Off-Time Developments

People generally anticipate that certain life circumstances, such as retirement, the death of an elderly family member, and the advent of grandparenthood, will occur as part of normal family transitions at expected times of the life course (Boss, 2002; Hennon et al., 2009; Hennon & Peterson, 2007). However, when normal events occur at unanticipated times, they can become sources of disruptive distress for parents. For example, during children's school-age years, the death of a parent or the death of a child is an off-time event and often is very traumatic for surviving parents and other family members (Murray et al., 2010). In similar fashion, parents often experience considerable upheaval and stress when learning about their teenage daughter's pregnancy, the stigma she may face, how becoming a parent prematurely will disrupt her life, and the assumption of grandparenthood earlier than a parent expected. The premature transition of a young daughter into parenting roles also places her at risk for problems due to inexperience, maternal depression, and considerable parental stress. High levels of maternal depression, anxiety and stress can reduce the responsiveness of young mothers to infants and may have negative consequences for the development of young children (Devereux et al., 2009; Huang et al., 2014).

Initial Awareness or Diagnosis

Another type of nonnormative stressor for parents may result from acute situations involving the initial awareness or diagnosis of unexpected circumstances and deviant or abnormal child characteristics. Examples include initial awareness of delinquency, conduct disorders, attention deficit behavior, autism, physical illness, poor mental health, and birth defects (Ambert, 1997; Ben-Sasson, Soto, Martínez-Pedraza, & Carter 2013, Hennon & Peterson, 2007; Lambek et al., 2014; Ryan et al., 2007; Vernhet et al., 2019). The initial diagnosis that Pamela has autism, for example, was defined by Tiffany as an acute stressor that disrupted her life and the lives of her family members. Likewise, parents have greater tendencies to experience acute stress or crisis when their son phones home from jail stating that he has been arrested for shoplifting. When parents are initially confronted with their child's delinquency or externalizing behavior, they often experience distress, worry, and feelings of great concern (Ambert, 1997, 1999; Caldwell, Horne, Davidson, & Quinn, 2007; Gavazzi, 2011; Mackler et al., 2015).

Chronic Stressors

Over time, as parents continue to be challenged by nonnormative stressors, these sudden, disruptive events may become converted into more moderate, chronic stressors as parents become more accustomed (or adapted) to these challenges. Chronic stressors are atypical circumstances that may be initiated by either the characteristics of children and youth or by other circumstances in the social environment. Stressors that are chronic continue over extended periods of time are difficult to amend and can accumulate.

Chronic Stressors From the Social Environment

Some of these persistent stressors result from the social context of families such as socioeconomic circumstances that compete with parenting roles. Chronic stressors such as work roles, poverty, immigration to a new culture, and marital conflict may have stressful effects, both for parents and their young. Included among such stressors are parents' daily employment demands that compete with parenting due to long work hours, shift work, and unusually dangerous or stressful jobs (e.g., police work or combat military personnel) that contribute to parental stress and spillover into parent–child relationships (Collins, 2019; Escalante, 2019; Haines, Marchand, & Harvey, 2006; Bianchi & Milkie, 2010). Another source of chronic parental stress within ethnic-minority, immigrant families, *generational dissonance,* results from differential rates of immigrant acculturation as the younger generation accepts the new culture more rapidly than parents (Berry, Phinney, David, Sam, & Vedder, 2005; Birman & Poff, 2011; Gonzales, Fabrett, & Knight, 2009). Difficulties often arise when new cultural changes practiced by the younger generation cause parents to view their youth as betraying their culture of origin. The resulting increases in acculturative stress and parent–adolescent conflict may lead to greater distance between the generations (Berry et al., 2005, Birman, & Poff, 2011). Moreover, both persistent family poverty and prolonged marital conflict also can function as chronic stressors that can increase parental stress, spill over into the parent–child relationship and have detrimental consequences for the psychosocial outcomes of children and youth (Buehler, Benson, & Gerard, 2006; Finegood et al., 2017; Gerard et al., 2008; Lin et al., 2017; Santiago et al., 2012; Scarmella et al., 2008).

Chronic Stressors: Child Effects

Another source of chronic stress, specific child characteristics, often contribute to parental stress when the shock of the initial recognition of a child's characteristic subsides and realities set in about the long-term challenges. Often referred to as the *child effects* perspective, this source of parental stress results from the impact of children's health, physical handicaps, and well-being on the socioemotional lives of parents (Ambert, 1997; Bush & Peterson, 2013; Neece et al., 2012; Rich, 2017). Having children who have congenital birth defects, physical discrepancies, long-term illnesses, problematic behavior patterns (e.g., aggressiveness and disruptive behavior), socioemotional problems, attention-deficit/hyperactivity disorder (ADHD), autism, and schizophrenia, can create stressful circumstances for parents over the long term (Ambert, 1997; Beernink, Swinkels, Van der Gaag, & Buitelaar, 2012; Deater-Deckard, 2004; Hastings, 2002; Silva & Schalock, 2012, Vernhet et al., 2019). These accumulating conditions can result from treatment costs, social stigma, demanding supervision requirements, and constant demands for care even during the parents' later years of life. These difficult circumstances create considerable potential for parents to experience stress, anger, embarrassment, guilt, despair, and a diminished sense of parental efficacy (Ambert, 1997, 1999; Caldwell et al., 2007).

Parents' Recovery Factors: Resources, Coping, and Adaptation: Factor B

The level of disruptive change within parent–child relationships, the psychological experience of parents, and the length of stress or crisis may partially be determined by Factor B's recovery factors referred to as parental resources, coping, and adaptation. Resources are the *potential* strengths of parents that may be drawn upon as the possible basis for progress toward renewal. In contrast, coping involves actually *taking direct actions* (e.g., acquiring resources, learning new skills, and asking for assistance), *altering one's interpretations* (e.g., reframing circumstances), and *managing one's emotions* (e.g., positively through social support or negatively through substance abuse). Finally, *adaptation* or *resilience* refers to the ability of parents and other family members to recover from stress and crisis and establish a new level of functioning (Henry et al., 2015; Hill, 1949).

Parental Resources

The first aspect of the B factor, parental resources, identifies *potential* factors that may contribute to pressures for change and foster distress as well as potential sources of recovery (Allen, 2017; Boss, 2002; Hennon et al., 2009; Hennon et al., 2007; Patterson, 2002). *Positive resources* are the traits, qualities, characteristics, and abilities of parents, parent–child relationships, family systems, and the larger social context that can possibly be brought to bear on the demands of stressors. These characteristics of individuals or the social context have potential or *latent* capacity to buffer stress by decreasing the negative effects of stressors. Resources also includes *negative resources,* or the potential or latent vulnerabilities of parents and parent–child relationships to stressors and crisis events. Negative resources at individual and relationship levels have the possibility of accentuating stress by increasing the adverse effects of stressors (McCubbin & Patterson, 1983; Patterson, 2002).

A distinguishing characteristic of resources (both positive and negative) is their *potential* rather than *actual* nature (Hennon et al., 2007; McCubbin & Patterson, 1983; Patterson, 2002). This means that parents, with seemingly equivalent resources, often vary in the extent to which they can put these reserves into action within the parent–child relationship. Variability in accessing resources underscores the idea that resources are only capacities that may or may not be put into action by parents (Henry et al., 2015). Resources are often classified based on their origins as within the person, within the familial environment, or other social contexts.

Personal Resources of Parents

The individual or personal resources of parents include economic well-being, knowledge (e.g., of child development), interpersonal skills, physical health, mental health and psychopathology (e.g., depression). Illustrative of individual resources are psychological and emotional qualities that are components of parents' competence or incompetence as socializers and caregivers for children. Parental competence, a complex array of individual resources (among other resources), is composed of such qualities as psychological maturity, empathy, warmth, secure self-image, good mental health, parental self-efficacy, parental satisfaction, capacity to express affection, and ability to use firm, rational control with the young (Bush & Peterson, 2008, 2013; Katsikitis et al., 2013; Glatz & Trifan, 2019; Liu et al., 2012; Peterson & Bush, 2013, 2015). Such personal competencies function as potential resources that may empower parents to marshal their resources and manage stress.

The contrasting personal qualities, or negative and positive personal resources, shape the psychological experiences of parents. Adults who have psychological or emotional problems, such as extensive depression, anger, and anxiety, often are at risk for having these personal issues becoming evident within the parent–child relationship and increasing the vulnerability of parents for higher levels of parenting stress. Parents who are self-preoccupied, depressed, highly anxious, distant, hostile, or abusers of substances are less likely to dealing effectively with stressors or crisis events (Biondic, Wiener, Martinussen, 2019; Delvecchio, Di Riso, Chessa, Salcuni, Mazzeschi, & Laghezza, 2014; Gavazzi, 2011; Hanington, Heron, Stein, & Ramchandani, 2012; Johansson et al., 2017; Holden, 2015). Highly stressed parents also are less likely to demonstrate the patience, sensitivity, and responsiveness that is needed to raise children effectively (Bush & Peterson, 2008; Crnic et al., 2005; Deater-Deckard, 2004; Lee et al., 2018).

Familial and Social Resources

Parents also draw on resources and experience vulnerabilities that are situated both within the family system and the surrounding socioecological context (Hennon et al., 2009; Hennon & Peterson, 2007). For example, parental efficacy (or a sense of feeling competent as a parent) may be influenced by the quality of the neighborhoods that families live in or through expertise provided to them online or through social media (DeHoff et al., 2016). These contingent social environments can provide either the capacities for social support or dangerous circumstances (e.g., gang influences) that can diminish parental competence and increase parental stress (Henry et al., 2008; Ontai et al., 2008). The potential to acquire assistance or social support from social networks has been associated with a variety of positive mental health outcomes for parents, including lower psychological distress (McHale et al., 2002) and better capacities to deal with stressful events (DeHoff et al., 2016; Henry et al., 2008). Supportive partners, extended kin, friends, church members and neighbors can potentially assist parents to deal with stressors and crises by providing advice, emotional support, material assistance, and encouragement. Potential for this kind of assistance causes parents to believe they have someone to turn to when stressors arise, which, in turn, fosters feelings of security and being valued (Hennon et al., 2007).

Scholars differ in the types of social support they identify, but most distinguish between capacities to communicate caring or *emotional support* and concrete assistance that helps parents' to deal with tasks and responsibilities or *instrumental support* (Hennon et al., 2009; Hennon et al., 2008). Although conceptualized as separate phenomena to clarify their meaning, emotional and instrumental support are not always mutually exclusive. The two types of support often do overlap, as demonstrated when Tiffany's aunt quickly cancels her cherished plans to play golf with her friends to assist Tiffany and her children. Her niece needs her help to babysit Pamela and Joey due to emergency circumstances at her workplace that require her presence. The child care that Tiffany's aunt provides is instrumental support, while her selfless actions to postpone her golf plans on short notice also provides emotional support to her niece.

The parents' marital relationship also is a critical, immediate aspect of social networks from which potential sources of support can increase or decrease the vulnerability of parents (Boss, 2002; Crnic et al., 2005; Crnic & Low, 2002; Gerard et al., 2008; Lin et al., 2017; Ontai et al., 2008). Scholars have frequently concluded that the role of potential social support beyond family boundaries is of secondary importance to the role of marital relationships. Research indicates that maternal stress is reduced when a spouse uses humor and listening skills to smooth over difficult moments that frustrate their partner (Lamb, 2013). In fact, the overall importance of husbands supporting their wives cannot be overstated because mothers continue to have more responsibility, more involvement, and experience greater parental stress from parenting (Crnic et al., 2005; Hennon et al., 2007; Lamb, 2013). Marriages characterized by a lack of shared housework and caregiving, low support from fathers, marital dissatisfaction, marital hostility, and high marital conflict function as negative resources that add to parental stress (Deater-Deckard et al., 2005; Gerard et al., 2008; Grych, Oxtoby, & Lynn, 2013; Lin et al., 2017).

Social support from outside the family also has the potential to ameliorate parental depression and increase coping abilities during times of stress (Hennon et al., 2008; Lamb, 2013). Support from outside family boundaries becomes especially important when parents do not have adult partners, the involvement of partners in caregiving is inadequate, or alternative significant others (e.g., older siblings) are not available (Ontai et al., 2008). Moreover, social support has the potential to affect the quality of parenting indirectly by enhancing, maintaining, or impairing the emotional well-being of mothers and fathers (Lamb, 2013). Support that reduces parental distress assists parents to be more nurturant and rational and to use more moderate forms of control, while avoiding harsh or rejecting forms of discipline (Crnic et al., 2005 Deater-Deckard, 2004).

Consistent with conceptions of resources and vulnerabilities, an important idea is that social networks are not always supportive but may function to increase parental stress. For example, Tiffany's mother is good at providing instrumental support in emergencies (e.g., picking up the children, helping out with bills between paydays). In contrast, her mother was not in favor of Tiffany's divorce and tended to agree with Tiffany's ex-husband about issues within their co-parenting relationship. Tiffany can't rely on her mother for emotional support on these issues and feels that her mother wants her to return to an unsupportive, ex-husband. Consequently, the relationship between Tiffany and her mother has become strained similar to the stress, conflict, frustration, and disappointment that families of unmarried teenage mothers experience sometimes with their own mothers (Devereux et al., 2009; Huang et al., 2014). The social support provided by parents and extended kin members may include judgmental and restrictive qualities that increase the stress of the new parent significantly. For teenage mothers, effective social support should involve providing assistance, while also continuing to foster autonomy that acknowledges the young parent's viewpoints, accepts the teen's feelings, and resists being too intrusive into the young person's life (Devereux et al., 2009; Huang et al., 2014). Such an approach has the potential to reduce stress, provide assistance for the demands of parenting, and promotes the long-term psychosocial maturity of young parents.

Parental Coping

From a family stress and crisis perspective, coping goes beyond being a potential resource by describing how parents can actually manage, endure, and recover from stressors (Patterson, 2002). Instead of being a potential ability, the process of coping involves actively seeking to maintain the status quo or to achieve new levels of family organization. Coping by parents involves *making actual responses to or redefining* the circumstances at hand (Dewar, 2016; Jones et al., 2009). Specific coping strategies are not inherently adaptive or maladaptive, but are useful to a degree that depends on the precise nature of the circumstances that are faced (Dewar, 2016; Hennon et al., 2009; Patterson, 2002).

The process of coping that involves using available resources and the parents' perceptions are conceptually distinct phenomena but often are interrelated in reality for many circumstances. The types of coping responses that parents use can vary with the specific stressor or crisis that is faced (Hennon et al., 2007; Hennon et al., 2008). For example, parents who face serious financial stress that can add to parenting distress, are better prepared to deal with this circumstance when they maintain positive self-evaluations, beliefs in their own mastery, and abilities to take charge of and resolve their financial difficulties. Coping strategies for chronic economic problems include financial problem solving, receiving social support (e.g., from a relative or financial counselor), acceptance of the situation, positive thinking, finding supplemental employment, and seeking positive distractions at select times to manage the accumulation of parental stress (Dewar, 2016; Morse et al., 2014).

Several additional strategies for coping with parental stress, such as cognitive coping, can be found in the literature on parent–child relationships. Cognitive strategies include passive approaches like denial or avoidance, as well as active approaches involving positive reappraisal and problem-focused response strategies (Crnic et al., 2005; Crnic & Low, 2002; Dewar, 2016). Parents who face economic problems or children with mental health issues can cope (i.e., reduce their stress) through positive reframing, problem solving, clear communication, affective responsiveness, and behavioral control (Dewar, 2016; Morse et al., 2014). These "active" coping strategies are more successful for reducing stress and restoring constructive parental behaviors than are "passive" cognitions involving a fatalistic acceptance of one's circumstances. Other coping strategies involve drawing on or orchestrating resources from the social environment, perhaps in the form of parent education, to learn more about high-quality parenting, child development, and how stress can be managed (Dewar, 2016; Hennon et al., 2007; Hennon et al., 2013).

Parents are more likely to become less stressed when they can become more capable of practicing better parenting through the actual use of social support that is available (DeHoff et al., 2016). Moreover, exposure to parent education that provides knowledge of child development, realistic expectations for the young, and the development of quality parenting skills can be effective means of coping. Subsequently, these parents are likely to be more capable of accessing resources, managing their responses, and developing the necessary social support networks to buffer stress levels and maintain high quality parenting (Hennon et al., 2007). Critical attributes for parental coping are the willingness and ability to take advantage of potential parenting resources and available social support (Hennon et al., 2013). For example, a single mother who is struggling to supervise a delinquent teenage son might gain assistance from her social network of parents, siblings, neighborhood friends, local social service agencies, online sources, and family life educators (DeHoff et al., 2016). Similarly, Tiffany is fortunate to have her aunt who not only provides emotional support and direct instrumental assistance through childcare, but also helps Tiffany to connect with community resources (e.g., parental groups, agencies, and online resources that specialize in autism). However, failure to actually use potential resources may occur if parent's feelings of pride, embarrassment, personal responsibility or exhaustion become obstacles to making use of these supports.

Parental Adaptation

Family stress theory also identifies *adaptation* as another important recovery factor, which refers to the ability of parents and other family members to recover from stress and crisis. Recovery in the family system and parent–child relationships may occur either by eliminating relationship disruptions and returning to preexisting patterns or by moving to new levels of relationship organization and stability (Hill, 1949; McCubbin & Patterson, 1983). Recently, the concept of adaptation has been expanded to view the recovery process as family resilience, which involves thinking about the multiple ways that parents and families face hardships, express strengths, and use protective factors to keep growing and changing (Henry et al., 2015).

A prominent example of parental adaptation research is the work on the experiences of parents following marital separation or divorce (Braver & Lamb, 2013; Demo & Buehler, 2013; Hetherington & Stanley-Hagan, 2002; Pedro-Carroll, 2011). Stress is a common experience for custodial mothers when role transitions are forced on them as ex-marital partners withdraw and become less involved in parental roles. Subsequently, many custodial mothers must shoulder new responsibilities as providers, build new support networks, and incorporate aspects of the father's role into their parenting repertoires. Such changes often occur under difficult economic circumstances that contribute to psychological problems such as distress, anxiety, and depression. Subsequently, these negative mental health conditions place mothers at risk for declines in the quality of their performance as parents. During early phases of separation and divorce, custodial mothers who experience increased irritability and stress often become (a) less capable of monitoring children, (b) more permissive in their parenting, (c) more punitive in their parenting, and (d) more inclined to engage in coercive exchanges with children (Hetherington & Stanley-Hagan, 2002). Fortunately, the stressful circumstances for many of these mothers subside over time as they cope more effectively (Hetherington & Stanley-Hagan, 2002; Pedro-Carroll, 2011). A frequent outcome of a stressor or crisis initiated by divorce or separation is that parents eventually begin to define their situation as more manageable, actively cope more effectively to manage stress, and restore the quality of their child-rearing behavior approximately 1 to 2 years after the divorce stressor began (Braver & Lamb, 2013; Demo & Buehler, 2013; Hetherington & Stanley-Hagan, 2002; Pedro-Carroll, 2011).

Parental Definitions: Factor C

Family stress theory also proposes that events or phenomena by themselves do not create the actual experience of stress or crisis. Instead, parents and other family members impose subjective "definitions" or personal cognitive appraisals on their circumstances. These definitions are shaped, in part, by varied expectations for parenting that are prevalent within different cultural, ethnic and socioeconomic groups (Finegood et al. 2017; Jones et al., 2009; Marsiglio & Roy, 2013; Peterson & Bush, 2013). Consequently, the meanings that individuals and families assign to phenomena (the C factor) help to determine whether they experience stressor or crisis events in the form of positive, negative, or neutral definitions (Boss, 2002; McCubbin & Patterson, 1983; see Chapter 1).

Although the appraisals of each person or family are at least somewhat unique, a typology of appraisals has been developed based on general patterns that have been identified (Hennon et al., 2009). *Benign* appraisals, for example, signify that a stressor situation is not hazardous, whereas, *challenges* are demanding appraisals that may pose some difficulty but are likely to be handled appropriately. Appraisals classified as *threatening,* in turn, are circumstances having the potential to cause considerable harm or loss to the family, though such negative outcomes have not yet happened (e.g., growing financial difficulties that may lead to bankruptcy or a child's first signs of disruptive behavior in school). If managed appropriately, threatening forms of appraisal can be avoided. If the threatening definition cannot be dealt with effectively, however, eventual harm can result for a family or parent–child relationship. Finally, a fourth category, *harm/loss,* represents situations appraised as having already damaged the family system. Such conditions may arise when the progression of a child's cancer is found to be progressing more rapidly than expected or when a teenage son's chronic delinquent behavior results in repeated periods of problematic behavior and incarceration.

The overall significance of appraisal categories is that virtually identical events may evoke varied responses from different parents and other family members. Subjective appraisals of similar circumstances either increase to decrease parental stress associated with changes and challenging events through such diverse feelings as mastery, hopelessness, denial of reality, or acceptance in the face of unpredictable circumstances (Boss, 2002; Finegood et al. 2017; Jones et al., 2009; Marsiglio & Roy, 2013; McCubbin & Patterson, 1983). Variability in appraisals that leads to different stress levels is rooted in many sources, including such things as previous life experience, diversity in ethnic and cultural background, differences in family traditions, and a particular person's beliefs and available resources (Boss, 2002).

These ideas from family stress theory are reinforced by research findings concerning the subjective experiences of parents. Of special importance are findings indicating that parental beliefs, values, attitudes, expectations, and "developmental scenarios" provide meaning for parents' relationships with their children and help to determine how they will respond to the young. Specifically, parents make attributions about their children's moods, motives, intentions, responsibilities, and competencies that shape the parents' emotional responses (e.g., positive stress or distress) as well as their subsequent child-rearing approaches (Bush & Peterson, 2013; Marsiglio & Roy, 2013; Peterson & Bush, 2013). Parents tend to hold their children accountable for negative behavior when they believe that the young are intentionally misbehaving and could instead choose to exercise self-control. Parents who make such attributions are more likely to be distressed and to use punitive behavior with their children, partly because they perceive children as "knowing better." In contrast, parents who view younger children (e.g., infants and toddlers) as being immature, not yet fully competent, or as lacking in intention for their actions often have more positive feelings and are less inclined to experience stress. Parents who experience greater negative stress, in turn, tend to become more punitive and rejecting toward children. Diminished parental stress tends to result in greater expressions of nurturance and moderate forms of reasoning, monitoring, and consistent rule enforcement. Consequently, awareness of parental beliefs and subjective definitions are critical for understanding how parents' positive or negative stress can influence how parents respond to their children (Deater-Deckard, 2004, Deater-Deckard et al., 2005; Peterson & Bush, 2013).

A closely related means of conceptualizing how subjective appraisals can lead to parenting stress and behavior is the degree to which parents view their children's characteristics as deviating from social standards of normality within a specific culture or ethnic group (Goodnow, 2005; Jones et al., 2009; Richman & Mandara, 2013). Parents can define their children as deviating from their expectations in either positive or negative directions, with greater deviations from accepted norms possibly leading to greater distress or satisfaction by parents (Goodnow, 2005; Jones et al., 2009; Richman & Mandara, 2013). The most frequent parental responses to perceived negative deviations (e.g., aggressive or conduct disorder behavior) are (a) adverse appraisals (e.g., psychological distress) and (b) the communication of parent's negative feelings toward children through punitive, withdrawn, or rejecting behaviors. In contrast, some parents may experience satisfaction or positive feelings (positive stress) regarding specific developmental changes (e.g., successful school achievement), which is viewed as affirming both their own sense of parental competence and their beliefs about what is viewed as youthful competence (Peterson & Bush, 2013, 2015). Common responses to positive interpretations include parental supportive behavior and moderate control strategies, such as the use of reasoning and rule-based supervision. The specific responses of parents to children are often shaped, not only by children's actual characteristics, but also how parents define these qualities, which may or may not reflect objective standards (Goodnow, 2005).

Conclusion

This chapter has demonstrated that scholarship on parental stress can be conceptualized with constructs from family stress theory in ways that add to our understanding of individual and relationship levels of family systems. When faced with demanding situations, parental stress or crisis are complex products of several factors: (a) the nature of the stressor or crisis event; (b) the potential recovery factors in the form of resources, coping styles, and adaptive abilities available to parents; and (c) the subjective definitions or appraisals that parents assign to the stressor events. These seemingly separate ideas are only truly meaningful when they are virtually indistinguishable and function together in real time.

Applying family stress concepts to parental stress helps us to gain greater understanding about the possible range of circumstances that can exist from highly disruptive (nonnormative) crises to chronic stress and more normative challenges. A major contribution of family stress theory is the insight it provides about how parental stress applies to both the individual and relationship or systemic levels of family life. Applying family stress theory concepts to the scholarship on parental stress helps to show more clearly (a) that parental stress is normal, (b) why the intensity of parental stress varies widely across individual parents and parent–child relationships, (c) why parents and families cope with and adapt to stress differently, and (d) how individual parenting stress and systemic stress influence the socialization performance of parents' and the psychosocial well-being of the young. Parental stress can function to disrupt, inhibit, or energize mothers and fathers, depending on numerous individual and socioenvironmental factors. As my mother used to tell me, "the really meaningful things in life are often complicated and don't come easily!"

DISCUSSION QUESTIONS ●

1. Has parenting been romanticized in reference to how stressful it is? If romanticism is evident, give examples that support your answer.

2. Does viewing parenting from the perspective of concepts from family stress theory provide a more realistic view of what is experienced by parents? Give examples of why this is true.

3. Is parental stress something that we can and should strive to completely eliminate in parent–child relationships? Provide an argument that supports your answer.

4. How can parental stress be viewed as a systemic concept within parent–child and family relationships?

5. Please critique this statement: All stressor events or stressors are essentially the same by having inherent meanings and similar consequences for parents.

6. What are the factors of the ABC-X model that may function to modify how stressor events or stressors have different meanings and consequences for parents? Be able to give examples and describe why seemingly similar stressors can have varied meanings and consequences for different parents.

7. Describe the role of recovery factors for parental stress. Distinguish between the concepts of resources, coping, and adaptation as recovery factors for parents who experience stress.

8. Do parents often view stressful events differently? What is the role of parental definitions of stressful circumstances and what causes these differences in meaning to exist?

9. Is all parental stress bad for parents? Why or why not? Can you identify an example of parental stress that has positive developmental consequences for parents and children?

REFERENCES

Allen, K. R. (2017). Family stress and resilience theory. In K. R. Allen & A. C. Henderson, *Family theories: Foundations and applications* (pp. 209–229). Chichester, England: Wiley Blackwell.

Ambert, A. (1997). *Parents, children, and adolescents: Interactive relationships and development in context.* Binghamton, NY: Haworth.

Ambert, A. (1999). The effect of male delinquency on mothers and fathers: A heuristic study. *Sociological Inquiry, 69,* 368–384.

Basile, L. M. (2014, July 6). Why we need to stop romanticizing the mother–daughter relationship. *Huffpost.* https://www.huffpost.com/entry/why-we-need-to-stop-romanticizing-the-mother-daughter-relationship_b_5234432

Beernink, A. E., Swinkels, S. H. N., Van der Gaag, R. J., & Buitelaar, J. K. (2012). Effects of attentional/hyperactive and oppositional/aggressive problem behaviour at 14 months and 21 months on parenting stress. *Child and Adolescent Mental Health, 17,* 113–120.

Ben-Sasson, A., Soto, T. W,. Martínez-Pedraza, F., & Carter, A. S. (2013). Early sensory over-responsivity in toddlers autism spectrum disorders as a predictor of family impairment and parenting stress, *Journal of Child Psychology and Psychiatry, 54,* 846–853.

Berry, J. W., Phinney, J. S., Sam, D. L., & Vedder, P. (2005). Immigrant youth: Acculturation, identity, and adaptation. *Applied Psychology: An International Review, 55,* 303–332.

Bianchi, S. M., & Milkie, M. A. (2010). Work and family research in the first decade of the 21st century. *Journal of Marriage and the Family, 72,* 705–725.

Bigner, J. (2010). *Parent–child relations: An introduction to parenting.* Upper Saddle River, NJ: Merrill-Pearson Education.

Biondic, D., Wiener, J., & Martinussen, R. (2019). Parental psychopathology and parenting stress in parents of adolescents with attention-deficit hyperactivity disorder. *Journal of Child and Family Studies, 28,* 2107–2119.

Birman, D., & Poff, M. (2011). Student intergenerational differences in acculturation. *Encyclopedia of Early Child Development.* http://www.child-encyclopedia.com/sites/default/files/textes-experts/en/664/intergenerational-differences-in-acculturation.pdf

Blumberg, A. (2015, May 26). What you need to know about the 'Quiverfull' movement. *Huffpost.* https://www.huffpost.com/entry/quiverfull-movement-facts_n_7444604

Boss, P. G. (2002). *Family stress management* (2nd ed.). Mountain View, CA: SAGE.

Boss, P. G. (2014) Family Stress. In A. C. Michalos (Ed.), *Encyclopedia of quality of life and well-being research* (p. 445). New York, NY: Springer.

Bouchard, G. (2014). The quality of the parenting alliance during the transition to parenthood. *Canadian Journal of Behavioral Science, 46,* 20–28.

Buehler, C., Benson, M. J., & Gerard, J. M. (2006). Interparental hostility and early adolescent problem behavior: The mediating role of specific aspects of parenting. *Journal of Research on Adolescence, 16,* 265–292.

Buehler, C., & Gerard, J. M. (2002). Marital conflict, ineffective parenting, and children's and adolescent's maladjustment. *Journal of Marriage and the Family, 64,* 78–92.

Buehler, C., & Gerard, J. M. (2013). Cumulative family risk predicts increases in adjustment difficulties across early adolescence. *Journal of Youth Adolescence, 42,* 905–920.

Braver, S., & Lamb, M. E. (2013). Marital dissolution. In G. W. Peterson & K. R. Bush (Eds.),

Handbook of marriage and the family (3rd ed., pp. 487–516). New York, NY: Springer.

Bures, R. M., Koropeckyj-Cox, T., & Loree, M. (2009). Childlessness, parenthood, and depressive symptoms among middle-aged and older adults. *Journal of Family Issues, 30,* 670–687.

Bush, K. R., & Peterson, G. W. (2008). Family influences on childhood development. In T. P. Gullotta (Ed.), *Handbook of childhood behavioral issues* (pp. 43–67). New York, NY: Taylor & Francis.

Bush, K. R., & Peterson, G. W. (2013). Parent–child relationships in diverse contexts. In G. W. Peterson & K. R. Bush (Eds.), *Handbook of marriage and the family* (3rd ed., pp. 275–302). New York, NY: Springer.

Buss, D. M. (2005). *The handbook of evolutionary psychology.* New York, NY: Wiley.

Caldwell, C. L., Horne, A. M., Davidson, B., & Quinn, W. H. (2007). Effectiveness of multiple family group intervention for juvenile first offenders in reducing parenting stress. *Journal of Child and Family Studies, 16,* 443–459.

Cappa, K. A, Begle, A. Conger, J. C., Dumas, J. E., & Conger, A. J. (2011). Bidirectional relationships between parenting stress and child coping competence: Findings from the pace study. *Journal of Child and Family Studies, 20,* 334–342.

Carapito, E., Ribeiro, M. T., Pereira, A.S., & Roberto, M. S. (2018). Parenting stress and preschoolers' socio-emotional adjustment: The mediating role of parenting styles in parent–child dyads. *Journal of Family Studies,* https://www.tandfonline.com/doi/abs/10.1080/13229400.2018.1442737

Cloud, J. A. (2011, March 4). Kid crazy: Why we exaggerate the joys of parenthood. *Time.* http://healthland.time.com/2011/03/04/why-having-kids-is-foolish/

Collins, C. (2019). *Making motherhood work: How women manage careers and caregiving.* Princeton, NJ: Princeton University Press.

Collins, W. A., & Steinberg, L. A. (2006). Adolescent development in interpersonal context. In W. Damon & R. M. Lerner (Eds.), *Handbook of child psychology, Volume 3: Social, emotional, and personality development* (6th ed., pp. 1003–1068). New York, NY: Wiley.

Crouter, A. C., & Booth, A. (2004). *Work-family challenges for low-income parents and their children.* Mahwah, NJ: Erlbaum.

Crnic, K., Gaze, C., & Hoffman, C. (2005). Cumulative parenting stress across the preschool period: Relations to maternal parenting and child behavior at age 5. *Infant & Child Development, 14,* 117–132.

Crnic, K., & Low, C. (2002). Everyday stresses and parenting. In M. H. Bornstein (Ed.), *Handbook of parenting: Vol. 5. Practical issues in parenting* (2nd ed., pp. 243–267). Mahwah, NJ: Erlbaum.

Deater-Deckard, K. D. (2004). *Parenting stress.* New Haven, CT: Yale University Press.

Deater-Deckard, K. D., Smith, J., Ivy, L., & Petrill, S. A. (2005). Differential perceptions of and feelings about sibling children: Implications for research on parenting stress. *Infant and Child Development, 14,* 211–225.

DeHoff, B. A., Staten, L. K., Rodgers, R. C., & Denne, S. C. (2016). The role of online social support in supporting and educating parents of young children with special health care needs in the United States: A scoping review. *Journal of Medical Internet Research, 18,* https://www.ncbi.nlm.nih.gov/pmc/articles/PMC5216258/

Delvecchio, E., Di Riso, D., Chessa, D., Salcuni, S., Mazzeschi, C., & Laghezza, L. (2014). Expressed emotion, parental stress, and family dysfunction. among parents of nonclinical Italian children. *Journal of Child & Family Studies, 23,* 989–999.

Demo, D. H. & Buehler, C. (2013). Theoretical approaches to studying divorce. In M. A. Fine & F. D. Fincham (Eds.), *Handbook of family theories: A content-based approach* (pp. 263–279). New York, NY: Routledge.

Devereux, P. G., Weigel, D. J., Ballard-Reisch, D., Leigh G. K., & Cahoon, K. L. (2009). Immediate and longer-term connections between support and stress in pregnant/parenting and non-pregnant/non-parenting adolescents. *Child and Adolescent Social Work Journal, 26*, 431–446.

Dewar, G. (2016). Parenting stress: 10 evidence-based tips for making life better. *Parental Science.* https://www.parentingscience.com/parenting-stress-evidence-based-tips.html

Dunning, M. J., & Giallo, R. (2012). Fatigue, parenting stress, self-efficacy and satisfaction in mothers of infants and young children. *Journal of Reproductive and Infant Psychology, 30*, 145–159.

Eibach, R. P., & Mock, S. E. (2011). Idealizing parenthood to rationalize parental investments. *Psychological Science, 22*, 203–208.

Epifanio, M. S., Genna, V., De Luca, C., Roccella, M., & La Grutta, S. (2015, June, 24). Paternal and maternal transition to parenthood: The risk of postpartum depression and parenting stress. *Pediatric Reports, 7.* https://www.ncbi.nlm.nih.gov/pubmed/26266033

Escalante, A. (2019, March 6). Why millions of mothers are overwhelmed by stress. *Psychology Today.* https://www.psychologytoday.com/us/blog/shouldstorm/201903/why-millions-mothers-are-overwhelmed-stress.

Finegood, E. D., Raver, C. C., DeJoseph, M. L., & Blair, C. (2017). Parenting in poverty: Attention bias and anxiety interact to predict parents' perceptions of daily parenting hassles. *Journal of Family Psychology, 31*, 51–60.

Folbre, N. (2008). *Valuing children: Rethinking the economics of the family*. Cambridge, MA: Harvard University Press.

Gavazzi, S. M. (2011). *Families with adolescents: Bridging the gaps between theory, research, and practice.* New York, NY: Springer.

Gerard, J. M., Krishnakumar, A., & Buehler, C. (2008). Marital conflict, parent–child relations, and youth adjustment: A longitudinal investigation of spillover effects. *Journal of Family Issues, 27*, 951–975.

Glatz, T., & Trifan, T. A. (2019). Examination of parental self-efficacy and their beliefs about the outcomes of their parenting practices. *Journal of Family Issues, 40*, 1321–1345.

Gonzales, N. A., Fabrett, F. C., & Knight, G. P. (2009). Psychological impact of Latino youth acculturation and enculturation. In F. A. Villaruel, G. Carlo, M. Azmitia, J. Grau, N. Cabrera, & J. Chahin (Eds.), *Handbook of U.S. Latino psychology* (pp. 115–134). Thousand Oaks, CA: SAGE.

Goodnow, J. J. (2005). Family socialization: New moves and next steps. *New Directions for Child and Adolescent Development, 109,* 83–90.

Green, E. (2017, December 6). The rebirth of America's pro-natalist movement. *The Atlantic.* https://www.theatlantic.com/politics/archive/2017/12/pro-natalism/547493/

Grych, J. H., Oxtoby, C., & Lynn, M. (2013). The effects of interparental conflict on children. In M. A. Fine & F. D. Fincham (Eds.), *Handbook of family theories: Content-based approach* (pp. 228–245). New York, NY: Routledge.

Haines, V. Y., Marchand, A., & Harvey, S. (2006). Crossover of workplace aggression experiences in dual-earner couples. *Journal of Occupational Health Psychology, 11*, 305–314.

Hanington, L., Heron, J., Stein, A., & Ramchandani, P. (2012). Parental depression and child outcomes–is marital conflict the missing link? *Child Care, Health & Development, 38*, 520–529.

Hastings, R. P. (2002). Parental stress and behaviour problems of children with developmental disability. *Journal of Intellectual and Developmental Disability, 27,* 149–160.

Hennon, C. B., Newsome, W. S., Peterson, G. W., Wilson, S. M., Radina, M. E., & Hildenbrand, B. (2009). Poverty, stress, resiliency: Using the MRM Model for understanding and abating poverty-related family stress. In C. A. Broussard & A. L. Joseph (Eds.), *Family poverty in diverse contexts* (pp. 187–202). New York, NY: Routledge.

Hennon, C. B., & Peterson, G. W. (2007). Estrés parental: Modelos teóricos y revisión de la literatura [Parenting stress: Theoretical models and a literature review]. In R. Esteinou (Ed.), *Fortalezas y desafíos de las familias en dos contextos: Estados Unidos de América y México* [Strengths and challenges of families in two contexts: The United States of America and Mexico] (pp. 167–221). México, D. F.: Centro de Investigaciones y Estudios Superiores en Antropología Social (CIESAS) y Sistema Nacional para el Desarrollo Integral de la Familia (DIF). [Research Center and Superior Studies in Social Anthropology and National System for the Integral Development of the Family].

Hennon, C. B., Peterson, G. W., Hildenbrand, B., & Wilson, S. M. (2008). Parental stress amongst migrant and immigrant populations: The MRM and CRSRP models for interventions [Stress Parental em Populações Migrantes e Imigrantes: Os Modelos de Intervenção MRM e CRSRP]. *Pesquisas e Práticas Psicossociais, 2,* 242–257.

Hennon, C. B., Peterson, G. W., Polzin, L., & Radina, M. E. (2007). Familias de ascendencia mexicana residentes en Estados Unidos: recursos para el manejo del estrés parental [Resident families of Mexican ancestry in United States: Resources for the handling of parental stress]. In R. Esteinou (Ed.), *Fortalezas y desafíos de las familias en dos contextos: Estados Unidos de América y México* [Strengths and challenges of families in two contexts: The United States of America and Mexico] (pp. 225–282). México, D. F.: Centro de Investigaciones y Estudios Superiores en Antropología Social (CIESAS) y Sistema Nacional para el Desarrollo Integral de la Familia (DIF).

Hennon, C. B., Radina, M. E., & Wilson, S. M. (2013). Family life education: Issues and challenges in professional practice. In G. W. Peterson & K. R. Bush (Eds.), *Handbook of marriage and the family* (3rd ed., pp. 815–843). New York, NY: Springer.

Henry, C. S., Merten, M. J., Plunkett, S. W., & Sands, T. (2008). Neighborhood, parenting, and adolescent factors and academic achievement in Latino adolescents from immigrant families. *Family Relations, 57,* 579–590.

Henry, C. S., Morris, A. H., & Harrist, A. W. (2015). Family resilience: Moving into the third wave. *Family Relations, 64,* 22–43.

Hetherington, E. M., & Stanley-Hagan, M. (2002). Parenting in divorced and remarried families. In M. H. Bornstein (Ed.), *Handbook of parenting: Vol. 3. Being and becoming a parent* (2nd ed., pp. 287–316). Mahwah, NJ: Erlbaum.

Hill, R. (1949). *Families under stress.* New York, NY: Harper.

Holden, G. W. (2015). *Parenting: A dynamic perspective* (2nd ed). Thousand Oaks, CA: SAGE.

Hu, N. (2015, October 22). The cult of motherhood: Motherhood is a personal choice. *The Harvard Crimson.* https://www.thecrimson.com /column/femme-fatale/article/2015/10/22/femme -fatale-cult-motherhood/

Huang, C. Y., Costeines, J., Kaufman, J. S., & Ayala, C. (2014). Parenting stress, social support, and depression for ethnic minority adolescent mothers: Impact on child development. *Journal of Child and Family Studies, 23,* 255–262.

Johansson, M., Svensson, I., Stenström, U., & Massoudi, P. (2017). Depressive symptoms and parental stress in mothers and fathers 25 months after birth. *Journal of Child Health Care, 21,* 65–73.

Jones, L., Rowe, J., & Becker, T. (2009). Appraisal, coping, and social support as predictors of psychological distress and parenting efficacy in parents of premature infants. *Children's Health Care, 38,* 245–262.

Kagitcibasi, C. (2013). Adolescent autonomy-relatedness and the family in cultural context: What is optimal? *Journal of Research on Adolescence, 23,* 223–235.

Kalil, A., Dunifon, R., Crosby, D., & Su, J. H. (2014). Work hours, schedules, and insufficient sleep among mothers and their young children. *Journal of Marriage and Family, 76,* 891–904.

Katsikitis, M., Bignell, K., Rooskov, N., Elms, L., & Davidson, G. (2013). The family strengthening program: Influences on parental mood, parental sense of competence and family functioning. *Advances in Mental Health, 11*(2), 143–151.

Kaufmann, E. (2011). *Shall the religious inherit the earth: Demography and politics in the twenty-first century.* London, England: Profile Books.

Kelly, M. (2009). Women's voluntary childlessness: A radical rejection of motherhood? *Women's Studies, Gender, and Sexuality. 37,* 157–172.

Koropeckyj-Cox, T., Pienta, A. M., & Brown, T. H. (2007). Women of the 1950s and the "normative" life course: The implications of childlessness, fertility timing, and marital status for psychological well-being in late midlife. *International Journal of Aging and Human Development, 64,* 299–330.

Kuczynski, L., & De Mol, J. (2015). *Theory and method.* In W. F. Overton & P. C. Molenaar (Eds.), *Handbook of child psychology and developmental science* (7th ed., Vol. 1, pp. 323–368). Hoboken, NJ: Wiley.

Kremer-Sadlik, T., & Paugh, A. L. (2007). Everyday moments—Finding "quality time" in American working families. *Time & Society, 16,* 287–308.

Lamb, M. E. (2013). The changing faces of fatherhood and father–child relationships: From fatherhood as status to dad. In M. A. Fine & F. D. Fincham (Eds.), *Handbook of family theories: Content-based approach* (pp. 87–102). New York, NY: Routledge, Taylor Francis Group.

Lambek, R., Sonuga-Barke, E., Psychogiou, L., Thompson, M., Tannock, R., Damm, D. & Thomsen, P. (2014). The parental emotional response to children index: A questionnaire measure of parents' reactions to ADHD, *Journal of Attention Disorders, 3,* 1–14.

Lavee, L. (2013). Stress processes in families and couples. In G. W. Peterson & K. R. Bush (Eds.), *Handbook of marriage and the family* (3rd ed., pp. 159–176). New York, NY: Springer.

Lawrence, E., Rothman, A. D., Cobb, R. J., Rothman, J. T., & Bradbury, T. N. (2008). Marital satisfaction across the transition to parenthood. *Journal of Family Psychology, 22,* 41–50.

Lee, S. J., Pace, G. T., Lee, J. Y., & Knauer, H. (2018). The association of fathers' parental warmth and parenting stress to child behavior problems. *Children and Youth Services Review, 91,* 1–10.

Letiecq, B. L., Bailey, S. J., & Porterfield, F. (2008). "We have no rights, we get no help": The legal and policy dilemmas facing grandparent caregivers. *Journal of Family Issues, 29*(8), 995–1012.

Liga, F., Ingoglia, S., Lo Cricchio, M. G., & Lo Coco, A. (2015). Mothers' parenting stress and adolescents' emotional separation: The role of youngsters' self-orientation. *International Journal of Developmental Science, 9,* 147–156.

Lin, X., Zhang, Y., Chi, P., Ding, W., Heath, M. A., Fang, X., & Xu, S. (2017). The mutual effect of marital quality and parenting stress on child and parent depressive symptoms in families of children with oppositional defiant disorder. *Frontiers in Psychology, 8,*1810. https://www.ncbi.nlm.nih.gov/pmc/articles/PMC5654759/

Liu, C., Chen, Y., Yeh, Y., & Hsieh, Y. (2012). Effects of maternal confidence and competence on maternal parenting stress in newborn care. *Journal of Advanced Nursing, 68,* 908–918.

Mackler, J. S., Kelleher, R. T, Shanahan, L., Calkins, S. D., Keane, S. P., & O'Brien, M. (2015). Parenting stress, parental reactions, and externalizing behavior from ages 4 to 10. *Journal of Marriage and Family 77,* 388–406.

Marsiglio, W., & Roy, K. (2013). Fathers' nurturance of children over the life course. In G. W. Peterson & K. R. Bush (Eds.), *Handbook of marriage and the family* (3rd ed., pp. 353–376). New York, NY: Springer.

McCubbin, H. I., & Patterson, J. M. (1983). Family stress and adaptation to crises: A Double ABC-X Model of family behavior. In D. H. Olson & R. C. Miller (Eds.), *Family studies review yearbook: vol. 1* (pp. 87–106). Beverly Hills, CA: SAGE.

McHale, J., Kazan, I., Erera, P., Rotman, T., DeCourcey, W., & McConnell, M. (2002). Co-parenting in diverse family systems. In M. H. Bornstein (Ed.), *Handbook of parenting, Vol.3: Being and becoming a parent* (2nd ed., pp. 75–108). Mahwah, NJ: Erlbaum.

McHale, J., & Lindahl, K. (2011). *Co-parenting: Theory, research, and clinical applications.* Washington, DC: American Psychological Association.

Medina, A. M., Lederhos, C. L., & Lillis, T. S. (2009). Sleep disruption and decline of marital satisfaction across the transition to parenthood. *Families, Systems, & Health, 27,* 153–160.

Morse, R., Rojahn, J., & Smith, A. (2014). Effects of behavior problems, family functioning, and family coping on parent stress in families with a child with Smith-Magenis Syndrome. *Journal of Developmental & Physical Disabilities. 26,* 391–401.

Murray, C. I., Toth, K., Larsen, B.L., & Moulton, S. (2010). Death, dying and grief in families. In C. Price, S. Price, & P. C. McKenry (Eds.), *Families and change: Coping with stressful events and transitions* (4th ed., pp. 73–95). Thousand Oaks, CA: SAGE.

Neece, C. L., Green, S. A., & Baker, B. L. (2012). Parenting stress and child behavior problems: A transactional relationship across time. *American Journal of Intellectual and Developmental Disabilities. 117,* 48–66.

Ohu, E. A., Spitzmueller, C., Zhang, J., Thomas, C. L., Osezua, A., & Yu, J. (2018, December 27). When work–family conflict hits home: Parental work–family conflict and child health. *Journal of Occupational Health Psychology.* Advance online publication. http://dx.doi.org/10.1037/ocp000014

Ontai, L., Sano, Y., Hatton, H., & Conger, K. J. (2008). Low-income rural mothers' perceptions of parental confidence: The role of family health problems and partner status. *Family Relations, 57,* 324–334.

Patterson, J. M. (2002). Integrating family resilience and family stress theory. *Journal of Marriage and Family, 64,* 349–360.

Pedro-Carroll, J. (2011). How parents can help children cope with separation/divorce. In R. E. Tremblay, M. Boivin, & R. Peters (Eds.), *Encyclopedia on early childhood development.* http://www.child-encyclopedia.com/divorce-and-separation/according-experts/how-parents-can-help-children-cope-separationdivorce

Peterson, G. W., & Bush, K. R. (2013). Conceptualizing cultural influences on socialization: Comparing parent–adolescent relationships in the U.S. and Mexico. In G. W. Peterson & K. R. Bush (Eds.), *Handbook of marriage and the family* (3rd ed., pp. 177–208). New York, NY: Springer.

Peterson, G. W., & Bush, K. R. (2015). Families and adolescent development. In T. P. Gullotta & G. R. Adams (Eds.), *Handbook of adolescent behavioral problems: Evidence-based approaches to prevention and treatment* (2nd ed., pp. 44–69). New York, NY: Springer.

Rich, J. D. (2017, October, 31). Stressed out parents: Children can pick up on your stress and act out (which leads to more stress!). *Psychology Today.* https://www.psychologytoday.com/us/blog/parenting-purpose/201710/stressed-out-parents

Richman, S. B., & Mandara, J. (2013). Do socialization goals explain differences in parental control between black and white parents? *Family Relations 62,* 625–636.

Ryan, L. G., Miller-Loessi, K., & Nieri, T. (2007). Relationships with adults as predictors of substance use, gang involvement, and threats to safety among disadvantaged urban high-school adolescents. *Journal of Community Psychology,* 35, 1053–1071.

Santiago, C. D., Etter, E. M., Wadsworth, M. E. & Raviv, T. (2012). Predictors of responses to stress among families coping with poverty-related stress. *Anxiety, Stress, & Coping,* 25, 239–258.

Scarmella, L. V., Neppl, T. K., Ontai, L. I., & Conger, R. D. (2008). Consequences of socioeconomic disadvantage across three generations: Parenting behavior and child externalizing problems, *Journal of Family Psychology,* 18, 725–753.

Schoppe-Sullivan, S. J., & Mangelsdorf, S. C. (2013). Parent characteristics and early coparenting behavior at the transition to parenthood. *Social Development,* 22, 363–383.

Silva, L. M. T., & Schalock, M. (2012). Autism parenting stress index: Initial psychometric evidence, *Journal Autism Development Disorder,* 42, 566–574.

Solomon, J., & George, C. (2008). The measurement of attachment security and related constructs in infancy and early childhood. In J. Cassidy & P. R. Shaver (Eds.), *Handbook of attachment* (2nd ed., pp. 383–416). New York, NY: Guilford Press.

Umberson, D., Pudrovska, T., & Reczek, C. (2010). Parenthood, childlessness, and well-being: A life course perspective. *Journal of Marriage & Family,* 72, 612–629.

Vernhet, C., Dellapiazza, F., Blanc, N., Cousson-Gélie, F., Miot, S., Roeyers, H., & Baghdadli, A. (2019). Coping strategies of parents of children with autism spectrum disorder: A systematic review. *European Child & Adolescent Psychiatry,* 28, 747–758.

Yoon, Y., Newkirk, K. & Perry-Jenkins, M. (2015). Parenting stress, dinnertime rituals, and child well-being in working-class families. *Family Relations,* 64, 93–107.

Intellectual and Developmental Disabilities

Understanding Stress and Resilience in Family Systems

Kami L. Gallus and
Briana S. Nelson Goff

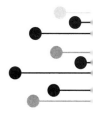

Vignette

Jared and Ashley had been married for 8 years when they learned they were expecting their first child. They had always wanted a big family, but the last several years had brought much heartache due to years of negative pregnancy tests, failed fertility treatments, and miscarriages. Overjoyed at the news of their pregnancy, Jared and Ashley immediately called their families to relay the news. Over the next several months, they prepared for the birth of their first-born child. After finding out they were expecting a baby girl, Ashley began preparing the nursery and shopping for dresses and bows. With their daughter's birth approaching, Jared and Ashley found themselves talking about the activities they would enjoy and memories they would create with their daughter. At the start of labor contractions, Jared and Ashley rushed to the hospital. After eight exhausting hours, Ashley gave birth to a beautiful baby girl. The joy of seeing their daughter for the first time was stifled as a sudden hush fell over the delivery room. After some consultation, a doctor returned to give Jared and Ashley the news that their daughter had indicators of Down syndrome. Suddenly, Jared and Ashley found themselves in unfamiliar territory. As new parents of a child with a developmental disability, Jared and Ashley joined an increasing number of U.S. families with a child with a special health-care need.

Families and Special Health-Care Needs

According to the U.S. Department of Health and Human Services (2013), more than 1 in 5 households with children ages birth to 17 years have at least one child with a special health-care need. The Maternal and Child Health Bureau defines *children with special health-care needs* as having "an increased risk for a chronic physical, developmental, behavioral, or emotional condition and who also require health and related services of a type or amount beyond that required by children generally" (McPherson et al., 1998, p. 138). Special health-care needs is a broad and inclusive term that emphasizes characteristics shared by individuals with a wide range of chronic health issues and disabilities (McPherson et al., 1998). Conditions that qualify for this designation include developmental delays and disabilities (e.g., autism spectrum disorder, Down syndrome); physical disabilities (e.g., spina bifida, muscular dystrophy); mental health diagnoses (e.g., depression, anxiety); learning disabilities, intellectual disabilities, and other long-standing medical conditions (e.g., asthma, epilepsy, diabetes; Child and Adolescent Health Measurement Initiative, 2012).

Rather than focusing on a specific diagnosis or type of disability, the term special health-care needs places emphasis on the functioning and service need consequences of a condition or disability. Common functional limitations that may affect the day-to-day life of individuals with special health-care needs can include difficulties with general comprehension, self-care, and interpersonal communication. These ongoing limitations affect an individual's ability to participate in daily educational, employment, and social activities. Specialized services and support systems may be needed to assist families in caring for their family member at home and in the community, including in-home nursing care, mental health counseling, special education programming, or therapies (e.g., physical, speech, occupational; McPherson et al., 1998).

With an estimated 23% of U.S. households having at least one child under the age of 18 years meeting the criteria for a special health-care need, the prevalence of these families is increasing (U.S. Department of Health and Human Services, 2013). There are multiple challenges related to the care of their children that families may encounter including developmental, medical, educational, social, and financial burdens (Lindley & Mark, 2010) as well as caregiver stress and fatigue, marital distress, and difficulty maintaining employment (Pilapil, Coletti, Rabey, & DeLaet, 2017). Coping with the initial uncertainty of a diagnosis, understanding potential physical or developmental limitations, identifying and accessing specialized services and supports, dealing with chronic and sometimes severe health problems, accessing and navigating community resources, and planning for the future are common strains described by families (Flaherty & Masters Glidden, 2000; Glidden, Billings, & Jobe, 2006). Although having a child with special health-care needs may result in greater demands on family resources, the presence of family coping strategies, social support, and community resources can effectively reduce the stress associated with having a loved one with a disability (Asberg, Vogel, & Bowers, 2007).

Based on the broad spectrum of conditions and disabilities encompassed by the term, the considerable variation in medical complexity, functional limitations, and resource requirements (Davis & Brosco, 2007), and the diversity among families of children with special health-care needs, it is often a challenge for professionals to understand the unique health-care requirements of an individual and the needs of their family. In recognition of this complexity, the current chapter focuses on the special health-care needs and family processes associated with intellectual and developmental disabilities. We present an overview of terms used to describe individuals and families in this population, highlight research specific to intellectual and developmental disabilities as well as relevant theoretical frameworks used to understand families in their unique contexts. We also provide a discussion of the various subsystems in families, as well as several external resources available to families with special health-care needs.

Intellectual and Developmental Disabilities

Children develop a wide range of skills during the early years of life including the development of fine and gross motor skills, language and speech, cognitive functioning, and activities of daily living. While every child develops at his or her own pace, developmental milestones give a general idea of the common skills children can expect to develop as they grow and age. When a child does not meet age-specific milestones across two or more developmental domains, this lag in development is referred to as a *developmental delay* (Moeschler & Shevell, 2014). Developmental delays can be significant or minor, temporary or persistent, and most commonly originate in gestation due to genetic causes or complications of pregnancy or birth (e.g., infection, prematurity).

In comparison, severe, persistent mental or physical developmental impairments are referred to as *developmental disabilities* (U.S. Department of Health and Human Services, 2000). This term refers to an expansive group of conditions that impact a person's daily functioning, due to considerable deficits in physical or cognitive functioning (National Institutes of Health [NIH], 2010). Developmental disabilities manifest before the age of 22 and usually last throughout life with significant deficits appearing in at least three of the following areas: self-care, receptive and expressive language, learning, mobility, self-direction, independent living, and money management. Some developmental disabilities may be solely physical (e.g., epilepsy or blindness) or solely cognitive (e.g., dyslexia). Others involve both physical and cognitive disabilities stemming from genetic or other causes, such as Down syndrome and fetal alcohol syndrome.

The American Association on Intellectual and Developmental Disabilities defines *intellectual disability* as originating before the age of 18 and being characterized by significant limitations both in intellectual functioning (reasoning, learning, problem solving) and in adaptive behavior, which covers a range of everyday social and practical skills (managing money, schedules, routines, and social interactions; Schalock et al., 2010). Previously termed *mental retardation*, intellectual disability is the most common developmental disability, with an estimated prevalence rate of approximately 1% of the population (American Psychiatric Association [APA], 2013). The term does not refer to a singular condition; rather, it involves a diagnosis with thousands of genetic (e.g., Down syndrome, Fragile X syndrome) or environmental (e.g., fetal alcohol syndrome, malnutrition) causes. For 30% to 50% of individuals with intellectual disability and their families, there is no known etiology to account for cognitive impairment (see Percy, 2007). Since intellectual and developmental disabilities frequently co-occur, professionals often work with individuals who have both types, resulting in combining the terms to *intellectual and developmental disabilities* (Schalock et al., 2010).

Disability as a Social Construct

Historically, disability focused on illness, personal deficit, and categorization (Schalock, 2011). The social construct of intellectual and developmental disabilities, which lies within the general construct of disability (Schalock & Luckasson, 2013), has changed over time; thus, influencing the terminology, explanations, and definitions as well as the policies and services implemented. Most recently, the social construct of intellectual and developmental disabilities evolved from a person-oriented approach to a more inclusive approach, shifting from a description of a personal limitation or deficit to a characteristic that originates from organic or social factors (DePoy & Gilson, 2004). As such, disability is not considered an invariant trait of the person, but instead focuses on the interaction between an individual and their environment, which can be strengthened by the services and supports available (Schalock, Luckasson, & Shogren, 2007). The current social construct of intellectual and developmental disabilities focuses on enhancing human potential through individualized supports that emphasize social inclusion and personal development (Schalock, 2011).

Just as there are varied abilities and needs among all individuals with intellectual and developmental disabilities, there are differences in the experiences and challenges families encounter as a child with disabilities grows and develops across the life span. The functionality of the person as well as available social supports are key predictors for the overall health, stability, and well-being of the individual and the family. As with many of life's challenges, having a child with intellectual and developmental disabilities is often stressful, but the experiences of families vary based on individual and contextual factors (Grant, Ramcharan, & Flynn, 2007; McConnell & Savage, 2015). Overall, families of children with intellectual and developmental disabilities exhibit patterns of resilience and effective coping strategies with their parenting responsibilities (Hastings & Taunt, 2002; McConnell & Savage, 2015).

By providing a clear definition of intellectual and developmental disabilities and identifying associated contextual and social factors, theoretical approaches can help professionals conceptualize the impact special health-care needs may have on individuals and families. Specifically, families of individuals with intellectual and developmental disabilities experience unique contexts associated with characteristics and impairments of their family members' disabilities. Although other stressful events and transitions may occur for extended periods (e.g., family violence, physical and mental illness) or may involve variations in impairment (e.g., mental illness, addictions), having a child with intellectual and developmental disabilities is a stressor that often co-occurs with other stressful events and transitions and requires lifelong responsibilities and resources. Parents may take on permanent roles as "caregivers" and experience divergent patterns and experiences across the life course (Hayes & Watson, 2013; Nelson Goff et al., 2016). Unlike chronic disabilities, other types of family stressors offer hope for remission (i.e., as with health issues or recovery from addiction) or "respite," even if recurrence or relapse ensues. As we apply theoretical frameworks to families of individuals with intellectual and developmental disabilities, it is critical to note these unique and complex factors.

Theoretical Frameworks: Intellectual and Developmental Disabilities and Families as Complex Systems

Literature suggests that families of individuals with intellectual and developmental disabilities may experience unique stressors due to the nonnormative and chronic challenges they face. While all families experience stress with change, families with intellectual and developmental disabilities may be at greater risk due to the emotional and psychological distress of an initial diagnosis as well as the extended caregiving roles and resource demands (DePape & Lindsay, 2015). Theoretical frameworks can assist researchers and practitioners in better understanding the stressors experienced by families with intellectual and developmental disabilities, as well as the coping strategies and resources employed in response to a disability diagnosis.

Family Stress Theories

Stress theories such as the transactional stress model (Lazarus & Folkman, 1984), the ABC-X/Double ABC-X model (Hill, 1949, 1958; McCubbin & Patterson, 1983), and ambiguous loss (Boss, 1999, 2007) have been applied to families of a child with intellectual and developmental disabilities to describe how stressors associated with the child's diagnosis may affect parental stress and adjustment to the diagnosis. Much of the early research in the field of intellectual and developmental disabilities focused on the limitations and negative experiences of parents (Hodapp, 2007). Recent models allow for both positive and negative outcomes for parents of children with intellectual and developmental disabilities. The transactional stress model (Lazarus & Folkman, 1984) holds that appraisals of stressors are important mechanisms through which stress is translated and therefore experienced by parents. Likewise, the ABC-X/Double ABC-X model (Hill, 1949, 1958; McCubbin & Patterson, 1983) conceptualizes perceptions, resources, and coping as important factors in understanding the impact of the stressor on the family system. Hastings and Taunt (2002) and McStay, Trembath, and Dissanayake (2014) applied these theories to parents of children with a developmental disability and called for a greater understanding of how appraisal or perceptual mechanisms and other factors influence the adjustment process of parents.

Because families of individuals with intellectual and developmental disabilities often encounter specific and unique challenges that other families may not experience, the diagnosis of a family member with a disability may be a potential stressor or crisis for the family system. The chronic nature of the condition may contribute not only to the initial stress but also exacerbate daily or chronic stress including behavioral problems and special health-care needs of the individual, increased financial expenses, life cycle transitions, and caregiver stress, and compassion fatigue due to the ongoing demands (DePape & Lindsay, 2015; Marquis, Hayes, & McGrail, 2019; O'Brien, 2007). However, it is also important to recognize the variety of factors related to the stressor event, that influence a stressor's initial impact on the family, as well as the resources available to mitigate the family's experience of the stressor. Thus, current theoretical approaches address both the initial appraisal of the developmental disability diagnosis as a stressor event, as well as the numerous contextual factors that influence the family's process of adjustment to the diagnosis (Nelson Goff et al., 2013).

Two specific theories frequently applied to the experiences of families facing intellectual and developmental disabilities include ambiguous loss (Boss, 1999, 2007) and the contextual model of family stress (Boss, 2002). Because much research literature focuses on the individual disabilities, without addressing the experiences or contexts of the family, it is important to recognize the systemic theories as they apply to individuals with intellectual and developmental disabilities within the family system and broader sociocultural contexts. These are just two theories that provide frameworks that can be applied to intellectual and developmental disabilities and similar special health-care needs in families.

Ambiguous Loss

Boss (1999) defined *ambiguous loss* as an incongruence between the psychological and physical family. In families of individuals with intellectual and developmental disabilities, a potential ambiguous loss may result from the family's experience of having a family member who is both physically present, yet psychologically absent (i.e., the child is different from what was expected or planned, as the parents must deal with the "absence" of a typically developing child and face the "presence" of a child with a disability). A significant component of Boss's ambiguous loss is the concept of *boundary ambiguity*, which refers to the experience of not knowing who is in or out of the family or relationship (Boss, 2006). The ambiguity that stems from the diagnosis of intellectual and developmental disabilities primarily exists on two levels—the uncertainty of the level of impairment, which leaves future abilities and functioning unknown, and the family's grief over the loss of the envisioned typically developing child. The uncertainty and grief that accompany the ambiguity can be paralyzing for some families, as it complicates both the loss and the processes of mourning (Boss, 1999). Like an ambiguous loss, a disability diagnosis represents a long-term, often permanent change in life's trajectory. It includes a number of unknown elements and requires that the family adapt to the incongruence between the psychological (expected) and physical (present) family (see Bentley, Zvonkovic, McCarty, & Springer, 2015;

O'Brien, 2007, for additional application of ambiguous loss in families facing an initial diagnosis).

In the opening chapter vignette, it is clear that the parents-to-be, Jared and Ashley, spent time preparing for their new baby, yet, were confronted with the unexpected reality of their child's Down syndrome diagnosis. This experience is an illustration of ambiguous loss, as Jared and Ashley had planned to welcome a typically developing child, only to learn that their family was going to be different. Although their physical family still consists of two parents and a newborn daughter, their psychological family changed from what was expected. Jared and Ashley's initial appraisal of the stressor (i.e., the disability diagnosis) can further be described through the lens of the contextual model of family stress (Boss, 2002), which builds on the original ABC-X/Double ABC-X model (Hill, 1949, 1958; McCubbin & Patterson, 1983).

Contextual Model of Family Stress

Boss's (2002) contextual model of family stress provides another conceptualization tool for considering families facing an intellectual and developmental disability diagnosis. Based on the original ABC-X model (Hill, 1949, 1958), in this model, the stressor, A, can be seen as the point of the disability diagnosis. Resources, the B component, are defined as helpful coping mechanisms available to the family across the individual, family, and community levels. For Jared and Ashley, identifying resources to assist them and accessing services to support their daughter will help to facilitate their adjustment process and manage the unexpected challenges the family may face. As described previously, the contextual model extends perceptions, C, to include the concepts of boundary ambiguity and socially constructed perceptions and meanings. McCubbin and Patterson (1983) expanded Hill's original model to include the pileup of stressors (aA), additional resources (bB), perceptions (cC), and level of adaptation (xX) of the family over time in their experience of the stressor event. Families with a disability diagnosis may experience ambiguity in different settings and at various times across the life span, as their family member with a disability continues to change and develop. Elements of the external context (i.e., culture, historical, economic, developmental, and heredity) and internal context (i.e., structural, psychological, and philosophical factors that are part of the family) are additional factors that accumulate to determine the degree of stress the family may experience (Boss, 2002). Further, the internal and external contextual components may create challenges and conflicts that contribute to the family stress. This theoretical model brings the various sociocultural, contextual factors into consideration to better understand a family's experiences when encountering intellectual and developmental disabilities diagnoses. The internal subsystems and external contextual factors associated with this model of family stress are described in the next sections as they relate to families encountering a loved ones' diagnosis with intellectual and developmental disabilities.

Internal Context: Understanding the Impact of Developmental Disabilities and Subsystems of Families

Some studies have shown that families of individuals with intellectual and developmental disabilities experience specific stressors that may negatively affect the marital relationship and be associated with poorer couple and family adjustment (Hayes & Watson, 2013; McGlone, Santos, Kazama, Fong, & Mueller, 2002; Stoneman & Gavidia-Payne, 2006). Conversely, high marital quality and successful family functioning can be protective factors against stress in families of children with intellectual and developmental disabilities (Kersh, Hedvat, Hauser-Cram, & Warfield, 2006; Mitchell, Szczerepa, & Hauser-Cram, 2016). The following sections provide a description of the impact of disabilities on the various internal family subsystems.

Parents of Children with Intellectual and Developmental Disabilities

When a child has intellectual and developmental disabilities, parental responsibilities increase in complexity and often are combined with a need to manage feelings of grief and loss. Caregiver stress may be related not only to the everyday stressors of caring for a child with a developmental disability, but also to immediate demands, like medical problems or financial issues, as well as future concerns (DePape & Lindsay, 2015). Parents often experience a heightened sense of responsibility and stress in their roles as caregivers (Hayes & Watson, 2013; see Marquis et al., 2019, for a review of the factors related to mental and physical health outcomes of parents).

Parental reactions to the initial intellectual and developmental disability diagnosis and the evolution of parental response over time are varied. Nelson Goff and colleagues (2013) found parental reactions to an initial developmental disability diagnosis of a child involved a variety and range of emotions, described by one participant as "a complete rollercoaster of emotions" (p. 451). Parents often report a process of adjustment, beginning with their original feelings of grief and loss, followed by more general acceptance and understanding of the diagnosis (DePape & Lindsay, 2015; Nelson Goff et al., 2013). Parents of children with intellectual and developmental disabilities frequently report positive personal effects, including personal growth, strengthening of their interpersonal relationships, and a sense of empowerment and purpose (Cless & Stephenson, 2018; DePape & Lindsay, 2015; Farkas et al., 2019).

To date, research involving parents of children with intellectual and developmental disabilities predominantly includes mothers as the primary participants (See Cless & Stephenson, 2018, for a review of literature). When comparing mothers of children with disabilities with mothers of typically developing children, researchers found that mothers of the former group spent more time engaged as the primary caregiver for their child(ren), less time socializing with other parents, and less time engaged in activities outside the home (Crowe, 1993; Smith et al.,

2010). Research suggests that mothers of children with intellectual and developmental disabilities also may experience greater stress than fathers, both in the level of daily stressors and in cumulative stress experienced over time (Brown, 2012; Dabrowska & Pisula, 2010). Research on fathers has increased recently, but remains limited (see Bentley et al., 2015; Kersh et al., 2006; Ricci & Hodapp, 2003).

The impact of having a child with intellectual and developmental disabilities on the marital/couple relationship has been addressed in some empirical research. While some literature indicates that the presence of a child with a disability has a slightly negative impact on the parents' marriage (Namkung, Song, Greenberg, Mailick, & Floyd, 2015; Risdal & Singer, 2004), others have not found a negative effect on the couple relationship (Freedman, Kalb, Zablotsky, & Stuart, 2012).

In general, data from studies of parents of children with intellectual and developmental disabilities are mixed, but suggest that negative outcomes are not as severe as often reported or presumed. Marquis et al. (2019) indicated mixed results in their review of the current research on parents of children with disabilities. They also suggested, however, that there may be other factors impacting the quality and stability of the couple relationship, such as type and severity of the child's disability and level of caregiver burden and well-being. It is also critical to recognize the role the couple and co-parenting relationship may have in reducing stress, providing social support, and increasing connection between the parents.

Siblings of Individuals with Intellectual and Developmental Disabilities

The sibling relationship may by the longest, most dynamic, and influential relationship an individual can experience due to the vast amount of time spent together in childhood and the significant overlap in lifespan (Cicirelli, 1995). However, this relationship may vary for siblings of individuals with intellectual and developmental disabilities (see Chapter 17 in this volume for a discussion of sibling of children affected by childhood illnesses). Research exploring the impact of living with a sibling with a disability suggests that siblings without a disability experience a wide variety of effects (Schuntermann, 2007; Shivers, 2018; Stoneman, 2005). While some research indicates greater risk of impairment in siblings (e.g., depression and anxiety; see Hodapp & Urbano, 2007; O'Neill & Murray, 2016; Petalas, Hastings, Nash, Lloyd, & Dowey, 2009; Shivers, Deisenroth, & Taylor, 2013; Williams et al., 2010), other research indicates positive benefits associated with having a sibling with intellectual and developmental disabilities (Floyd, Costigan, & Richardson, 2016; Floyd, Purcell, Richardson, & Kupersmidt, 2009; Skotko, Levine, & Goldstein, 2011; Smith, Elder, Storch, & Rowe, 2015). Researchers comparing siblings of individuals with and without developmental disabilities find either no differences between sibling groups (Hastings & Petalas, 2014; Neely-Barnes & Graff, 2011; Quintero & McIntyre, 2010; Rodgers et al., 2016) or mixed results, indicating both positive and negative outcomes (Graff et al., 2012; Petalas, Hastings, Nash, Reilly, & Dowey, 2012).

Specific negative outcomes for siblings primarily relate to gender of the sibling (i.e., more impairment in male siblings or when the sibling with a developmental disability is male), family-system impairments (i.e., parental conflict or financial problems), or more severe behavior problems in the individual with intellectual and developmental disabilities (Hastings, 2007; Shivers, 2018; Shivers et al., 2013; Tomeny, Baker, Barry, Eldred, & Rankin, 2016). More research is necessary to understand the unique factors and processes that affect the individual functioning and relationship when one sibling has a disability; however, we can conclude that having a sibling with intellectual and developmental disabilities does not automatically increase negative outcomes in siblings (Shivers, 2018).

Grandparents of Children with Intellectual and Developmental Disabilities

Little research has explored the experiences of extended family members of individuals with intellectual and developmental disabilities. To date, research primarily focuses on the experiences of grandparents. Research suggests that grandparents may experience similar emotional reactions as parents to the news of a grandchild's diagnosis with intellectual and developmental disabilities (Lee & Gardner, 2010), describing the experience as an emotional rollercoaster that elicits a range of initial reactions (Woodbridge, Buys, & Miller, 2009). Yet, the effect that grandparents can have on parents' abilities to cope and a family's adjustment following the birth of a child with a disability is significant (Trute, 2003; Woodbridge & Buys, 2018). Extended family members, particularly grandparents, can provide significant support, assistance, and information, among other substantial and meaningful resources (e.g., childcare, money; Kahana et al., 2015; Lee & Gardner, 2010; Seligman & Darling, 2007). Schilmoeller and Baranowski (1998) found that grandparents provide support to their children and grandchildren in one of three primary ways—providing money when needed, taking time to do things with their grandchild with a disability, and engaging in activities with their adult child. While some researchers have found varied effects on grandparents (see Findler, 2014; Miller, Buys, & Woodbridge, 2012; Woodbridge et al., 2009, 2011; Woodbridge & Clapton, 2012), it is necessary to recognize the meaningful and important roles and contributions made by grandparents and other extended family members (Lee & Gardner, 2010; Woodbridge & Buys, 2018).

External Context: Resources and Support Systems in Coping, Adaptation, and Building Resilience

In addition to the internal contextual elements of the family system, there are a number of external components important to recognize. As Boss (2002) described, external contextual factors may include culture and history, as well as external systems in which the family is embedded. While external systems are components of all children's developmental experiences, they play a unique role in the lives of children with intellectual and developmental disabilities and their families who must navigate multiple, complex systems (e.g., social services, schools, health care) less frequently encountered by families of children without disabilities. Successfully mastering these systems is a complex task with many components, including interventions, policies, legal issues, and structural barriers. Although impossible to describe all of the components and aspects of each external system, we briefly emphasize the key external contexts for families of individuals with intellectual and developmental disabilities.

Social Support Systems

Social withdrawal may occur for families of children with intellectual and development disabilities often due to the competing demands of multiple commitments. Eventually, families may reintegrate into social networks as they access services and engage with support groups (Divan, Vajaratkar, Desai, Strik-Lievers, & Patel, 2012). How society reacts to individuals with disabilities contributes to a sense of isolation; for example, families may encounter stigma and negative experiences, including discrimination and marginalization. This isolation and social stigma may increase stress and caregiver burden experienced by parents (Marquis et al., 2019).

Acquiring social support is a coping strategy frequently reported by parents of children with intellectual and developmental disabilities (Luther, Canham, & Cureton, 2005; Nelson Goff et al., 2013; Twoy, Connolly, & Novak, 2007). Connections with both formal programs and services, as well as informal support networks, is a critical factor in caregiver health and well-being (Marquis et al., 2019). Families often seek support from friends, extended family members, faith-based groups, other families, school personnel, health-care professionals, and formal support groups. Parents may enter into new social support networks as they connect with other families of children with intellectual and developmental disabilities and the multitude of professionals involved in providing services (Divan et al., 2012). It is recommended that families seek out resources to assist with individual and family adjustment and to promote resilience (Grant et al., 2007; McConnell & Savage, 2015).

Health-Care Systems

Families of individuals with intellectual and developmental disabilities often spend a significant amount of time in medical facilities, interacting with a plethora of health-care and allied health professionals. The attitudes and practices of medical professionals can have a significant effect on parents' perspectives about their child's condition and their caregiving abilities. Nelson Goff et al. (2013) reported that a primary theme among parents of children with Down syndrome included negative experiences with medical personnel related to their child's diagnosis, including pressure to have prenatal testing or to terminate the pregnancy, negative and misinformation about Down syndrome, and a general lack of compassion. Findings suggest the need for compassion, understanding, and honesty, as well as training for health-care professionals on working with individuals with intellectual and developmental disabilities, from prenatal diagnosis to ongoing health-care needs.

Skotko and colleagues (Skotko, Capone et al., 2009; Skotko, Kishnani et al., 2009) identified a variety of recommendations for health-care professionals delivering diagnoses, including providing current and accurate information and materials on local support groups as well as disclosing the news in a private setting. To improve family adjustment and to support the well-being of all family members, continual, specific, and coordinated services need to be provided (Lefebvre & Levert, 2012). Interventions that promote more positive developmental outcomes for families, particularly during life-cycle transitions, can help build family resilience through the creation of therapeutic collaboration (Shapiro, 2002). Specifically, collaborative efforts that help parents increase resources to meet the diverse demands of caring for a child with intellectual and developmental disabilities are warranted. Naar-King, Siegel, Smyth, and Simpson (2003) identified the importance of providing integrated care (i.e., medical and behavioral health services) for families of children with intellectual and developmental disabilities. Caregivers often indicate a need for better information about their health-care concerns or problems related to disabilities, including prognosis, rehabilitation, care, and services (Lefebvre & Levert, 2012). Empowering families and individuals with intellectual and developmental disabilities to develop health literacy and actively engage in collaborative and integrated health care is critical to meeting long-term needs (Ruiz, Giuriceo, Caldwell, Snyder, & Putnam, 2019; Summar, 2018).

Educational Systems

Navigating the educational system can be an especially difficult task for families of children with intellectual and developmental disabilities, as schools are primarily designed to provide educational services to children without disabilities. Programs and services available for children with intellectual and developmental disabilities can be limited or inadequate to meet the range of needs that may be present. Children with intellectual and developmental disabilities benefit from school systems that allow flexibility to meet each child's unique needs (Francis et al., 2016). This often requires extra administrative, social, and educational support during the child's transition to and immersion in school (Janus, Kopechanski, Cameron, & Hughes, 2008).

Parents should be familiar with the statutes and provisions through the *Individuals With Disabilities Education Improvement Act* (*IDEA*, 2004), as well as their roles as collaborative team members in the educational decisions made as part of the Individualized Education Program (IEP) process for students with disabilities (see Francis & Nagro, 2018, for a summary of *IDEA* and special education law). Parents and school personnel can collaboratively find the best methods to educate a child with intellectual and developmental disabilities. It is important for parents and school personnel to establish clear expectations and work collaboratively to ensure mutually beneficial outcomes (Francis & Nagro, 2018; Ryndak, Jackson, & White, 2013). Developing these family–professional partnerships is critical to ensure effective educational programs as well as long-term success for individuals with intellectual and developmental disabilities and their families.

Employment and Education for Adults with Intellectual and Developmental Disabilities

Today, there are over 270 programs that support the participation of students with intellectual disabilities in higher education in the United States (Think College, 2019). Most of these programs are certificate or nondegree programs, where students actively participate in campus activities and courses and typically earn a credential rather than a degree (Grigal et al., 2015). Research suggests significant positive employment outcomes for individuals with intellectual disability who participate in postsecondary education programs (Moore & Schelling, 2015).

Despite gains in educational access, the phenomenon of students with intellectual and developmental disabilities taking college courses is still rare; thus, resulting in this population being significantly underrepresented in the labor force (Butterworth et al., 2011). Using a nationally representative random sample, Siperstein, Parker, and Drascher (2013) found that only 34% of Americans with intellectual and developmental disabilities ages 21 to 64 years were employed, compared to 76% of working-age adults without disabilities. Moreover, among the small percentage of individuals with intellectual and developmental disabilities who are employed, most are paid below the national minimum wage and work part-time, thus making them ineligible to receive employee benefits, such as paid time off or health insurance (Siperstein et al., 2013).

Individuals whose primary educational experience included segregated special education classrooms are often ill-prepared for the social demands of an integrated work setting in their communities (The Arc, 2016). Likewise, employers are often misinformed or unaware that individuals with disabilities are potentially valuable employees (Luecking, 2011). A near century-old federal policy, *The Fair Labor Standards Act of 1938* (U.S. Department of Labor, n.d.) that states individuals with disabilities can be paid below the national minimum wage, continues to be cited allowing employers to legally pay these employees significantly below minimum wage. Leading researchers with expertise in employment conclude that while numerous effective interventions exist to help people with intellectual and developmental disabilities obtain and maintain employment, programs tend to be inconsistently implemented (Nord, Luecking, Mank, Kiernan, & Wray, 2013). Low employment rates and subminimum wages received by individuals with intellectual and developmental disabilities suggest personal, systemic, social, and policy barriers, which create significant employment challenges (Nord et al., 2013; Siperstein et al., 2013).

While some external systems described may have both positive and negative effects on the family, the importance of these external components cannot be ignored. External systems provide necessary treatments, interventions, services, information, and supports critical to family systems' positive adjustment and outcomes. Providing families with accurate information regarding diagnosis, connecting them with effective resources and supports, and encouraging the development of positive perspectives and advocacy skills are important in developing resilience and promoting success for families.

Developing Resilience and Ensuring Success for Individuals With Intellectual and Developmental Disabilities and Their Families

Historically, research has focused on the challenges of having a family member with a disability (Hodapp, 2007), and only more recently have shifts revealed the positive experiences and outcomes (Hastings & Taunt, 2002; Skotko et al., 2016). Families still face social stigma and negative perceptions of individuals with intellectual and developmental disabilities. While many parents experience a heightened sense of responsibility and increased demands on time and resources (McConnell & Savage, 2015) resulting in increased caregiver stress (Hayes & Watson, 2013; Marquis et al., 2019), the overall experience for most parents of children with intellectual and developmental disabilities is one of resilience and positive growth.

Families of children with intellectual and developmental disabilities often require a variety of resources to manage common stressors. Grant et al. (2007) described the key elements that enhance the resilience of families—establishing a sense of meaning, gaining a sense of control over the situation, maintaining personal identities for each family member (separate from the disability), and boundary maintenance within the family system (e.g., having a clear structure and defined roles and rules within the family). Parents also may develop new roles and skills, such as those needed to successfully advocate for their child to ensure they receive necessary resources and services (Krueger et al., 2019).

Implications for Research and Professional Practice

There are a number of research topics that require further exploration in the area of individuals and families with special health-care needs. Acknowledging the diverse experiences of parenting children with intellectual and developmental disabilities is important, as are longitudinal studies that address family functioning at all developmental levels (Keogh, Bernheimer, & Guthrie, 2004). Further refinement and testing of theoretical models as they apply to individuals with intellectual and developmental disabilities and their families is needed. While the current models of family stress and crisis described here are relevant, research applying theoretical frameworks to this population is limited.

Further research is needed to explore the experiences of families from more varied populations (Cuskelly, Hauser-Cram, & Van Riper, 2009; Hodapp, 2007), as a distinct lack of diversity in the research remains a critical limitation. In order to provide enhanced services, additional research should address the unique individual, family, and contextual factors that families experience, including those who may not have the resources or voices to advocate for themselves. More emphasis needs to be placed on the experiences of lower socioeconomic families, single-parent families, and varying levels of impairment (e.g., severe behavioral disorders, comorbidity, later-life behavior regression; Marquis et al., 2019).

Additional research is needed to understand differences in the adjustment process of families across different disabilities, as well as longitudinal research across the life span. Finally, most research on families in this area continues to focus primarily on mothers with limited emphasis on the experiences of fathers or the broader impact on the couple and family system, including both internal and external contextual factors (Boss, 2002). A greater understanding of how family systems interact internally and with external services may assist not only professionals in developing and providing direct services but also those shaping policies relevant to the rights of individuals and families.

An important next step is to further awareness of the long-term needs of families of individuals with intellectual and developmental disabilities (Marquis et al., 2019; Nelson Goff et al., 2016). As individuals with intellectual and developmental disabilities are living longer, achieving better education and training, and attaining greater rights and opportunities (e.g., employment, marriage), families are facing new experiences. These advancements require ongoing efforts by researchers, professionals, and family members to understand the impact of these changes on the family and social systems of care that provide services to individuals with intellectual and developmental disabilities.

Conclusion

This chapter focused on understanding the unique experiences of individuals with intellectual and developmental disabilities and how their families access and navigate external systems and contexts. It is critical for professionals to recognize the unique experiences and stressors experienced by these families, while also acknowledging the many ways they are like all other families. Despite the potential stressors, family members of individuals with intellectual and developmental disabilities often report that they are content and see their lives as including both challenging and satisfying experiences (Asberg et al., 2007; Farkas et al.,

2019; Grant et al., 2007; Nelson Goff et al., 2013). Research is clear that families of individuals with intellectual and developmental disabiliites are not inherently impaired or permanently disrupted. In fact, for many families, the positive aspects may even outnumber the difficulties and challenges. The "negative narrative" (Hastings, 2016) is not the reality for most families; instead, a balanced and empowered depiction is a more accurate representation. Professionals working with families of individuals with intellectual and developmental disabilities must understand and address the unique stressors as well as the positive experiences, coping strategies, and resilience families encounter (Grant et al., 2007; McConnell & Savage, 2015). Ultimately, we must begin to celebrate the positive impact individuals with intellectual and developmental disabilities bring to the family system as well as the broader community.

DISCUSSION QUESTIONS

1. Describe three reasons why families of individuals with intellectual and developmental disabilities may experience greater levels of stress and crisis.

2. Using the contextual model of family stress, identify how specific internal and external contextual factors in families of individuals with intellectual and developmental disabilities may serve to (1) improve or benefit the family and (2) reduce family functioning or add stress to the family.

3. Discuss areas where research on families of individuals with intellectual and developmental disabilities are currently limited, and identify how those limitations could be addressed in future research.

REFERENCES

American Psychiatric Association. (2013). *Diagnostic and statistical manual of mental disorders (DSM-5)*. Washington, DC: Author.

Asberg, K. K., Vogel, J. J., & Bowers, C. A. (2007). Exploring correlates and predictors of stress in parents of children who are deaf: Implications of perceived social support and mode of communication. *Journal of Child and Family Studies, 17*(4), 486–499. Retrieved from https://doi.org/10.1007/s10826-007-9169-7

Bentley, G. E., Zvonkovic, A. M., McCarty, M., & Springer, N. (2015). Down syndrome and fathering: An exploration of ambiguous loss. *Fathering, 13*(1), 1–17.

Boss, P. G. (1999). *Ambiguous loss: Learning to live with unresolved grief*. Cambridge, MA: Harvard University Press.

Boss, P. G. (2002). *Family stress management: A contextual approach*. Thousand Oaks, CA: SAGE.

Boss, P. G. (2006). *Loss, trauma, and resilience: Therapeutic work with ambiguous loss*. New York, NY: Norton.

Boss, P. G. (2007). Ambiguous loss theory: Challenges for scholars and practitioners. *Family Relations, 56*, 105–111. Retrieved from https://doi.org /10.1111/j.1741-3729.2007.00444.x

Brown, M. (2012). *Dyadic coping, relationship satisfaction, and parenting stress among parents of children with an autism spectrum disorder: The role of couple relationship*. (Unpublished doctoral dissertation). Texas Tech University, Lubbock, TX.

Butterworth, J., Hall, A. C., Smith, F. A., Migliore, A., Winsor, J., Ciulla Timmons, J., & Domin, D. (2011). *StateData. The national report on employment services and outcomes*. Boston, MA: Institute for Community Inclusion, University of Massachusetts Boston.

Child and Adolescent Health Measurement Initiative. (2012). *Who are children with special health care needs (CSHCN)*. Data Resource Center, supported by Cooperative Agreement 1–U59–MC06980–01 from the U.S. Department of Health and Human Services, Health Resources and Services Administration (HRSA), Maternal and Child Health Bureau (MCHB). Retrieved from https://www.cahmi.org/wp-content/uploads/2014 /06/CSHCNS-whoarecshcn_revised_07b-pdf.pdf

Cicirelli, V. G. (1995). *Sibling relationships across the life span*. New York, NY: Plenum.

Cless, J. D., & Stephenson, C. (2018). Perspectives from mothers: Recognizing their strengths and contributions beyond caregiving. In B. S. Nelson Goff & N. Piland Springer (Eds.), *Intellectual and developmental disabilities: A roadmap for families and professionals* (pp. 76–89). New York, NY: Routledge/Taylor & Francis.

Crowe, T. K. (1993). Time use of mothers with young children: The impact of a child's disability. *Developmental Medicine and Child Neurology, 35*(7),

621–630. Retrieved from https://doi.org/10.1111 /j.1469-8749.1993.tb11700.x

Cuskelly, M., Hauser-Cram, P., & Van Riper, M. (2009). Families of children with Down syndrome: What we know and what we need to know. *Down Syndrome: Research & Practice, 12*(3), 202–210. doi:10.3104/reviews/2079

Dabrowska, A., & Pisula, E. (2010). Parenting stress and coping styles in mothers and fathers of pre-school children with autism and Down syndrome. *Journal of Intellectual Disability Research, 54*(3), 266–280. Retrieved from https://doi.org/10 .1111/j.1365-2788.2010.01258.x

Davis, M. M., & Brosco, J. P. (2007). Being specific about being special: defining children's conditions and special health care needs. *Archives of Pediatrics & Adolescent Medicine, 161*(10), 1003–1005. doi:10.1001/archpedi.161.10.1003

DePape, A. M., & Lindsay, S. (2015). Parents' experiences of caring for a child with autism spectrum disorder. *Qualitative Health Research, 25*(4), 569–583. doi:10.1177/1049732314552455

DePoy, E., & Gilson, S. F. (2004). *Rethinking disability: Principles for professional and social change*. Belmont, CA: Thompson Brooks/Cole.

Divan, G., Vajaratkar, V., Desai, M. U., Strik–Lievers, L., & Patel, V. (2012). Challenges, coping strategies, and unmet needs of families with a child with autism spectrum disorder in Goa, India. *Autism Research, 5*(3), 190–200. doi:10. 1002/aur.1225

Farkas, L., Cless, J., Cless, A., Nelson Goff, B. S., Bodine, E., & Schmelzle, A. (2019). The ups and downs of Down syndrome: A qualitative study of positive and negative parenting experiences. *Journal of Family Issues, 40*, 518–539. doi:10.1177/0192513X18812192

Findler, L. (2014). The experience of stress and personal growth among grandparents of children with and without intellectual disability. *Intellectual and Developmental Disabilities, 52*(1), 32–48. doi:10.1352/1934-9556-52.1.32

Flaherty, E., & Masters Glidden, L. (2000). Positive adjustment in parents rearing children with Down syndrome. *Early Education and Development, 11*(4), 407–422. doi:10.1207/s15566935eed1104_3

Floyd, F. J., Costigan, C. L., & Richardson, S. S. (2016). Sibling relationships in adolescence and early adulthood with people who have intellectual disability. *American Journal on Intellectual and Developmental Disabilities, 121*(5), 383–397. doi:10.1352/1944-7558-121.5.383

Floyd, F. J., Purcell, S. E., Richardson, S. S., & Kupersmidt, J. B. (2009). Sibling relationship quality and social functioning of children and adolescents with intellectual disability. *American Journal on Intellectual and Developmental Disabilities, 114*(2), 110–127. doi:10.1352/2009.114.110-127

Francis, G. L., Blue-Banning, M., Turnbull, A. P., Hill, C., Haines, S. J., & Gross, J. M. S. (2016). Culture in inclusive schools: Parental perspectives on trusting family-school partnerships. *Education and Training in Autism and Developmental Disabilities, 51*(3), 281–293. Retrieved from http://daddcec.org/

Francis, G., & Nagro, S. (2018). The education system: Building partnerships and inclusive communities. In B. S. Nelson Goff & N. Piland Springer (Eds.), *Intellectual and developmental disabilities: A roadmap for families and professionals* (pp. 158–170). New York, NY: Routledge/Taylor & Francis.

Freedman, B. H., Kalb, L. G., Zablotsky, B., & Stuart, E. A. (2012). Relationship status among parents of children with autism spectrum disorders: A population-based study. *Journal of Autism and Developmental Disorders, 42*(4), 539–548. doi:10.1007/s10803-011-1269-y

Glidden, L. M., Billings, F. J., & Jobe, B. M. (2006). Personality, coping style and well-being of parents rearing children with developmental disabilities. *Journal of Intellectual Disability Research, 50*(12), 949–962. doi:10.1111/j.1365-2788.2006.00929.x

Graff, C., Mandleco, B., Dyches, T. T., Coverston, C. R., Roper, S. O., & Freeborn, D. (2012). Perspectives of adolescent siblings of children with Down syndrome who have multiple health problems. *Journal of Family Nursing, 18*(2), 175–199. doi:10.1177/1074840712439797

Grant, G., Ramcharan, P., & Flynn, M. (2007). Resilience in families with children and adult members with intellectual disabilities: Tracing elements of a psycho-social model. *Journal of Applied Research in Intellectual Disabilities, 20*(6), 563–575. doi:10.1111/j.1468-3148.2007.00407.x

Grigal, M., Hart, D., Smith, F. A., Domin, D., & Weir, C. (2015). *Think College National Coordinating Center: Annual report on the transition and postsecondary programs for students with intellectual disabilities (2014–2015).* Boston, MA: University of Massachusetts Boston, Institute for Community Inclusion

Hastings, R. P. (2007). Longitudinal relationships between sibling behavioral adjustment and behavior problems of children with developmental disabilities. *Journal of Autism and Developmental Disorders, 37*(8), 1485–1492. doi:10.1007/s10803-006-0230-y

Hastings, R. P. (2016). Do children with intellectual and developmental disabilities have a negative impact on other family members? The case for rejecting a negative narrative. *International Review of Research in Developmental Disabilities, 50*, 165–194. doi:10.1016/bs.irrdd.2016.05.002

Hastings, R. P., & Petalas, M. A. (2014). Self-reported behaviour problems and sibling relationship quality by siblings of children with autism spectrum disorder. *Journal of Applied Research in Intellectual Disabilities, 27*(4), 363–363. doi:10.1111/cch.12131

Hastings, R. P., & Taunt, H. M. (2002). Positive perceptions in families of children with developmental disabilities. *American Journal on Mental Retardation, 107*(2), 116–127. doi10 .1352/0895-8017(2002)107<0116:PPIFOC>2 .0.CO;2

Hayes, S. A., & Watson, S. L. (2013). The impact of parenting stress: A meta-analysis of studies comparing the experience of parenting stress in parents of children with and without autism spectrum disorder. *Journal of Autism and Developmental Disorders, 43*(3), 629–642. doi:10.1007/ s10803-012-1604-y

Hill, R. (1949). *Families under stress.* New York, NY: Harper.

Hill, R. (1958). Generic features of families under stress. *Social Casework, 49,* 139–150. doi:10.1177/1044389458039002-318

Hodapp, R. M. (2007). Families of persons with Down syndrome: New perspectives, findings, and research and service needs. *Mental Retardation and Developmental Disabilities Research Reviews, 13*(3), 279–287. doi:10.1002/mrdd.20160

Hodapp, R. M., & Urbano, R. C. (2007). Adult siblings of individuals with Down syndrome versus with autism: Findings from a large-scale US survey. *Journal of Intellectual Disability Research, 51,* 1018–1029. doi:10.1111/j.1365-2788.2007.00994.x

Individuals with Disabilities Education Act, 20 U.S.C. § 1400 *et seq.* (2004).

Janus, M., Kopechanski, L., Cameron, R., & Hughes, D. (2008). In transition: Experiences of parents of children with special needs at school entry. *Early Childhood Education Journal, 35*(5), 479–485. doi:10.1007/s10643-007-0217-0

Kahana, E., Lee, J. E., Kahana, J., Goler, T., Kahana, B., Burk, E., & Barnes, K. (2015). Childhood autism and proactive family coping: Intergenerational perspectives. *Journal of Intergenerational Relationships, 13*(2), 150–166. doi :10.1080/15350770.2015.1026759

Keogh, B. K., Bernheimer, L. P., & Guthrie, D. (2004). Children with developmental delays twenty years later: Where are they? How are they? *American Journal on Mental Retardation, 109*(3), 219–230. doi:10.1352/0895-8017(2004)109< 219:CWDDTY>2.0.CO;2

Kersh, J., Hedvat, T. T., Hauser-Cram, P., & Warfield, M. E. (2006). The contribution of marital quality to the well-being of parents of children with developmental disabilities. *Journal of Intellectual Disability Research, 50*(12), 883–893. doi:10.1111/j.1365-2788.20

Krueger, K., Cless, J., Dyster, M., Reves, M., Steele, R., & Nelson Goff, B. S. (2019). Understanding the systems, contexts, behaviors, and strategies of parents advocating for their children with Down syndrome. *Intellectual and Developmental Disabilities, 57,* 146-157. doi:10.1352/1934-9556-57.2.146

Lazarus, R. S., & Folkman, S. (1984). *Stress, appraisal, and coping.* New York, NY: Springer.

Lee, M., & Gardner, J. E. (2010). Grandparents' involvement and support of families with disabilities. *Educational Gerontology, 36,* 467–499. doi:10.1080/03601270903212419

Lefebvre, H., & Levert, M. (2012). The close relatives of people who have had a traumatic brain injury and their special needs. *Brain Injury, 26*(9), 1084–1097. doi:10.3109/02699052.2012.666364

Lindley, L. C. & Mark, B. A. (2010). Children with special health care needs: Impact of health care expenditures on family financial burden. *Journal of Child and Family Studies, 19,* 79–89. doi.org/10 .1007/s10826-009-9286-6

Luecking, R. G. (2011). Connecting employers with people who have intellectual disability. *Intellectual and Developmental Disabilities, 49,* 261–273. doi:10.1352/1934-9556-49.4.261

Luther, E. H., Canham, D. L., & Cureton, V. Y. (2005). Coping and social support for parents of children with autism. *The Journal of School Nursing, 21*(1), 40–47. doi:10.1177/10598405050210010901

Marquis, S., Hayes, M. V., & McGrail, K. (2019). Factors affecting the health of caregivers of children who have an intellectual/developmental disability. *Journal of Policy and Practice in Intellectual Disabilities.* Advance online publication. doi:10.1111/jppi.12283

McConnell, D., & Savage, A. (2015). Stress and resilience among families caring for children with intellectual disability: Expanding the research agenda. *Current Developmental Disorders Reports, 2*(2), 100–109. doi:10.1007/s40474-015-0040-z

McCubbin, H. I., & Patterson, J. M. (1983). The family stress process: The Double ABC-X model of adjustment and adaptation. *Marriage & Family Review, 6*(1/2), 7–37. doi:10.1300/J002v06n01_02

McGlone, K., Santos, L., Kazama, L., Fong, R., & Mueller, C. (2002). Psychological stress in adoptive parents of special-needs children. *Child Welfare, 81*(2), 151–171.

McPherson, M., Arango, P., Fox, H., Lauver, C., McManus, M., Newacheck, P. W., Perrin, J. M., Shonkoff, J. P., & Strickland, B. (1998). A new definition of children with special health care needs. *Pediatrics, 102*(1), 137–139. doi:10.1542/peds.102.1.137

McStay, R. L., Trembath, D., & Dissanayake, C. (2014). Stress and family quality of life in parents of children with autism spectrum disorder: Parent gender and the Double ABC-X model. *Journal of Autism and Developmental Disorders, 44*(12), 3101–3118. doi:10.1007/s10803-014-2178-7

Miller, E., Buys, L., & Woodbridge, S. (2012). Impact of disability on family: Grandparents' perspectives. *Journal of Intellectual Disability Research, 56*(1), 102–110. doi:10.1111/j.1365-2788.2011.01403.x

Mitchell, D. B., Szczerepa, A., & Hauser-Cram, P. (2016). Spilling over: Partner parenting stress as a predictor of family cohesion in parents of adolescents with developmental disabilities. *Research in Developmental Disabilities, 49–50,* 258–267. doi:10.1016/j.ridd.2015.12.007

Moeschler, J. B., & Shevell, M. (2014). Comprehensive evaluation of the child with intellectual disability or global developmental delays. *Pediatrics, 134*(3), e903-e918. doi:10.1542/peds.2014-1839

Moore, E. J., & Schelling, A. (2015). Postsecondary inclusion for individuals with an intellectual disability and its effects on employment. *Journal of Intellectual Disabilities, 19*(2), 130–148. doi:10.1177/1744629514564448

Naar-King, S., Siegel, P. T., Smyth, M., & Simpson, P. (2003). An evaluation of an integrated health care program for children with special needs. *Children's Health Care, 32*(3), 233–243. doi:10.1207/S15326888CHC3203_4

Namkung, E. H., Song, J., Greenberg, J. S., Mailick, M. R., & Floyd, F. J. (2015). The relative risk of divorce in parents of children with developmental disabilities: Impacts of lifelong parenting. *American Journal on Intellectual and Developmental Disabilities, 120*(6), 514–526. doi:10.1352/1944-7558-120.6.514

National Institutes of Health. (2010). *Fact sheet—Intellectual and developmental disabilities.* Retrieved from http://report.nih.gov/nihfactsheets/ViewFactSheet.aspx?csid=100

Neely-Barnes, S. L., & Graff, J. C. (2011). Are there adverse consequences to being a sibling of a person with a disability? A propensity score analysis. *Family Relations, 60*(3), 331–341. doi:10.1111/j.1741-3729.2011.00652.x

Nelson Goff, B. S., Monk, J. K., Staats, N., Malone, J., Tanner, A., & Springer, N. (2016). Comparing parents of children with Down syndrome at different life span stages. *Journal of Marriage* and *Family, 78,* 1131–1148. doi:10.1111/jomf.12312

Nelson Goff, B. S., Springer, N., Foote, L. C., Frantz, C., Peak, M., Tracy, C., ...& Cross, K. A. (2013). Receiving the initial Down syndrome diagnosis: A comparison of prenatal and postnatal parent group experiences. *Intellectual and Developmental Disabilities, 51*(6), 446–457. doi:10.1352/1934-9556-51.6.446

Nord, D., Luecking, R., Mank, D., Kiernan, W., & Wray, C. (2013). The state of the science of employment and economic self-sufficiency for people with intellectual and developmental disabilities. *Intellectual and Developmental Disabilities, 51,* 376–384. doi:10.1352/1934-9566-51.5.376

O'Brien, M. (2007). Ambiguous loss in families of children with autism spectrum disorders. *Family Relations, 56*(2), 135–146. doi:10.1111/j.1741-3729.2007.00447.x

O'Neill, L. P., & Murray, L. E. (2016). Anxiety and depression symptomatology in adult siblings of individuals with different developmental disability diagnoses. *Research in Developmental Disabilities, 51,* 116–125. doi:

Percy, M. (2007). Factors that cause or contribute to intellectual and developmental disabilities. In I. Brown and M. Percy (Eds.), *A comprehensive guide to intellectual and developmental disabilities* (pp. 125–148). Baltimore, MD: Brookes.

Petalas, M. A., Hastings, R. P., Nash, S., Lloyd, T., & Dowey, A. (2009). Emotional and behavioural adjustment in siblings of children with intellectual disability with and without autism. *Autism, 13*(5), 471–483. doi:10.1177/1362361309335721

Petalas, M. A., Hastings, R. P., Nash, S., Reilly, D., & Dowey, A. (2012). The perceptions and experiences of adolescent siblings who have a brother with autism spectrum disorder. *Journal of Intellectual and Developmental Disability, 37*(4), 303–314. doi:10.3109/13668250.2012.734603

Pilapil, M., Coletti, D. J., Rabey, C., & DeLaet, D. (2017). Caring for the caregiver: Supporting families of youth with special health care needs. *Current Problems in Pediatric and Adolescent Health Care, 47*(8), 190–199. doi:10.1016/j.cppeds.2017.07.003

Quintero, N., & McIntyre, L. L. (2010). Sibling adjustment and maternal well-being: An examination of families with and without a child with an autism spectrum disorder. *Focus on Autism and Other Developmental Disabilities, 25*(1), 37–46. doi:10.1177/1088357609350367

Ricci, L. A., & Hodapp, R. M. (2003). Fathers of children with Down's [sic] syndrome versus other types of intellectual disability: Perceptions, stress and involvement. *Journal of Intellectual Disability Research, 47*(4/5), 273–284. doi:10.1046/j.1365-2788.2003.00489.x

Risdal, D., & Singer, G. (2004). Marital adjustment in parents of children with disabilities: A historical review and meta-analysis. *Research & Practice for Persons with Severe Disabilities, 29*(2), 95–103. doi:10.2511/rpsd.29.2.95

Rodgers, J. D., Warhol, A., Fox, J. D., McDonald, C. A., Thomeer, M. L., Lopata, C., ... & Sheffield, T. (2016). Minimal risk of internalizing problems in typically-developing siblings of children with high-functioning autism spectrum disorder. *Journal of Child and Family Studies, 25*(8), 2554–2561. doi:10.1007/s10826-016-0407-8

Ruiz, S., Giuriceo, K., Caldwell, J., Snyder, L. P., & Putnam, M. (2019). Care coordination models improve quality of care for adults aging with intellectual and developmental disabilities. *Journal of Disability Policy Studies.* Advance online publication. doi:10.1177%2F1044207319835195

Ryndak, D. L., Jackson, L. B., & White, J. M. (2013). Involvement and progress in the general curriculum for students with extensive support needs: K–12 inclusive-education research and implications for the future. *Inclusion, 1,* 28–49. doi:10.1352/2326-6988-1.1.028

Schalock, R. L. (2011). The evolving understanding of the construct of intellectual disability. *Journal of Intellectual and Developmental Disability, 36*(4), 227–237. doi:10.3109/13668250.2011.624087

Schalock, R. L., Borthwick-Duffy, S. A., Bradley, V. J., Buntinx, W. H. E., Coulter, D. L., Craig, E. M., . . . & Yeager, M. H. (2010). *Intellectual disability: Definition, classification, and systems of support* (11 ed.). Washington, DC: American Association on Intellectual and Developmental Disabilities.

Schalock, R. L., & Luckasson, R. A. (2013). What's at stake in the lives of people with intellectual disability? Part I: The power of naming, defining, diagnosing, classifying, and planning supports. *Intellectual and Developmental Disabilities, 51*(2), 86–93. doi:10.1352/1934-9556-51.2.086

Schalock, R. L., Luckasson, R. A., & Shogren, K. A. (2007). The renaming of mental retardation: Understanding the change to the term intellectual disability. *Intellectual and Developmental Disabilities, 45*(2), 116–124. doi:10.1352/1934-9556(2007)45[116:TROMRU]2.0.CO;2

Schilmoeller, G. L., & Baranowski, M. D. (1998). Intergenerational support in families with disabilities: Grandparents' perspectives. *Families in Society, 79*(5), 465–476. doi:10.1606/1044-3894.714

Schuntermann, P. (2007). The sibling experience: Growing up with a child who has pervasive developmental disorder or mental retardation. *Harvard Review of Psychiatry, 15*(3), 93–108. doi:10.1080/10673220701432188

Seligman, M., & Darling, R. B. (2007). *Ordinary families, special children: A systems approach to childhood disability* (3rd ed.). New York, NY: Guilford Press.

Shapiro, E. R. (2002). Chronic illness as a family process: A social-developmental approach to promoting resilience. *Journal of Clinical Psychology, 58*(11), 1375–1384. doi:10.1002/jclp.10085

Shivers, C. (2018). The sibling experience: More than my brother's keeper. In B. S. Nelson Goff & N. Piland Springer (Eds.), *Intellectual and developmental disabilities: A roadmap for families and professionals* (pp. 104–116). New York, NY: Routledge/Taylor & Francis.

Shivers, C. M., Deisenroth, L. K., & Taylor, J. L. (2013). Patterns and predictors of anxiety among siblings of children with autism spectrum disorders. *Journal of Autism and Developmental Disorders, 43*(6), 1136–1346. doi:10.1007/s10803-012-1685-7

Siperstein, G. N., Parker, R. C., & Drascher, M. (2013). National snapshot of adults with intellectual disabilities in the labor force. *Journal of Vocational Rehabilitation, 39*(3), 157–165. doi:10:3233/JVR-130-658

Skotko, B. G., Capone, G. T., Kishnani, P. S., & Down Syndrome Diagnosis Study Group. (2009). Postnatal diagnosis of Down syndrome: Synthesis of the evidence on how best to deliver the news. *Pediatrics, 124*(4), e751–e758. doi:10.1542/peds.2009-0480

Skotko, B. G., Kishnani, P. S., Capone, G. T., & Down Syndrome Diagnosis Study Group. (2009). Prenatal diagnosis of Down syndrome: How best to deliver the news. *American Journal of Medical Genetics, 149A,* 2361–2367. doi:10.1002/ajmg

Skotko, B. G., Levine, S. P., & Goldstein, R. (2011). Having a brother or sister with Down syndrome: Perspectives from siblings. *American Journal of Medical Genetics Part A, 155*(10), 2348-2359. doi:10.1002/ajmg.a.34228

Skotko, B. G., Levine, S. P., Macklin, E. A., & Goldstein, R. D. (2016). Family perspectives about Down syndrome. *American Journal of Medical Genetics Part A, 170,* 930–941. doi:10.1002/ajmg.a.37520a.33082

Smith, L. E., Hong, J., Seltzer, M. M., Greenberg, J. S., Almeida, D. M., & Bishop, S. L. (2010).

Daily experiences among mothers of adolescents and adults with autism spectrum disorder. *Journal of Autism and Developmental Disorders, 40*(2), 167–178. doi:10.1007/s10803-009-0844-y

Smith, L. O., Elder, J. H., Storch, E. A., & Rowe, M. A. (2015). Predictors of sense of coherence in typically developing adolescent siblings of individuals with autism spectrum disorder. *Journal of Intellectual Disability Research, 59*, 26–38. doi:10.1111/jir.12124

Stoneman, Z. (2005). Siblings of children with disabilities: Research themes. *Mental Retardation, 43*(5), 339–350. doi:10.1352/0047-6765(2005)43[339:SOCWDR]2.0.CO;2

Stoneman, Z., & Gavidia-Payne, S. (2006). Marital adjustment in families of young children with disabilities: Associations with daily hassles and problem-focused coping. *American Journal on Mental Retardation, 111*(1), 1–14. doi:10.1352/0895-8017

Summar, K. (2018). The medical perspective: Developing health literacy in families. In B. S. Nelson Goff & N. Piland Springer (Eds.), *Intellectual and developmental disabilities: A roadmap for families and professionals* (pp. 133–147). New York, NY: Routledge/Taylor & Francis.

The Arc. (2016). *Public policy and legal advocacy: Education issues for people with disabilities.* Retrieved from http://www.thearc.org/what-we-do/public-policy/policy-issues/education

Think College. (2019). *College search.* Retrieved from https://thinkcollege.net/college-search

Tomeny, T. S., Baker, L. K., Barry, T. D., Eldred, S. W., & Rankin, J. A. (2016). Emotional and behavioral functioning of typically-developing sisters of children with autism spectrum disorder: The roles of ASD severity, parental stress, and marital status. *Research in Autism Spectrum Disorders, 32*, 130–142. doi:10.1016/j.rasd.2016.09.008

Trute, B. (2003). Grandparents of children with developmental disabilities: Intergenerational support and family well-being. *Families in Society, 84*(1), 119–126. doi:10.1606/1044-3894.87

Twoy, R., Connolly, P. M., & Novak, J. M. (2007). Coping strategies used by parents of children with autism. *Journal of the American Academy of Nurse Practitioners, 19*(5), 251–260. doi:10.1111/j.1745-7599.2007.00222.x

U.S. Department of Health and Human Services. (2000). *Developmental disabilities assistance and Bill of Rights Act amendments of 2000*, PL 106-402, 45 CFR 1385.3-Definitions.

U.S. Department of Health and Human Services, Health Resources and Services Administration, Maternal and Child Health Bureau. (2013). *The national survey of children with special health care needs chartbook 2009–2010.* Rockville, MD: U.S. Department of Health and Human Services. Retrieved from https://mchb.hrsa.gov/cshcn0910/more/pdf/nscshcn0910.pdf

U.S. Department of Labor. (n.d.). *Compliance assistance: Wages and the Fair Labor Standards Act (FLSA).* Retrieved from https://www.dol.gov/whd/flsa/

Williams, P. D., Piamjariyakul, U., Graff, J. C., Stanton, A., Guthrie, A. C., Hafeman, C., & Williams, A. R. (2010). Developmental disabilities: Effects on well siblings. *Issues in Comprehensive Pediatric Nursing, 33*(1), 39–55. doi:10.3109/01460860903486515

Woodbridge, S., & Buys, L. (2018). Grandparents: Meaningful contributors to a changing family landscape. In B. S. Nelson Goff & N. Piland Springer (Eds.), *Intellectual and developmental disabilities: A roadmap for families and professionals* (pp. 117–130). New York, NY: Routledge/Taylor & Francis.

Woodbridge, S., Buys, L., & Miller, E. (2009). Grandparenting a child with a disability: An emotional rollercoaster. *Australasian Journal on Ageing, 28*(1), 37–40. doi:10.1111/j.1741-6612.2008.00344

Woodbridge, S., Buys, L., & Miller, E. (2011). My grandchild has a disability: Impact on grandparent identity, roles and responsibilities. *Journal of Aging Studies, 25*, 355–363. doi:10.1016/j.jaging.2011.01.002

Woodbridge, S., & Clapton, J. (2012). What should I do now? Exploring family roles and relationships when a child has a disability—The grandparent's perspective. *Journal of Intellectual Disability Research, 56*, 736. doi:10.1111/j.1365-2788.2012.01583_8.x

CHAPTER

6

LGBQ-Parent Families

Development and Functioning
in Context

Abbie E. Goldberg and Nora M. McCormick

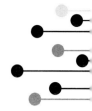

Vignette

Anya and Vivian are a female same-sex couple who have been together for 10 years. Anya is a 33-year-old White social worker and Vivian is a 35-year-old African American music teacher. They reside in the rural Midwest, where they met attending graduate school. Six years ago, the couple adopted Keisha, a two-year-old biracial (White and African American) girl through the foster care system. Both women felt strongly about adopting a child and Vivian expressed a sincere desire to adopt a child of color from the foster care system. Because of the number of children available for adoption via foster care, she felt irresponsible not choosing that route. Initially, Anya's parents were resistant to the adoption because they felt the couple already faced enough trouble in the world as an interracial female couple. Also, Anya's family had never completely accepted Vivian, which the couple suspected was due more to her race than their same-sex relationship. Upon adopting Keisha, however, Anya's parents went from being distant and fairly uninvolved in their lives to asking to babysit all the time.

Currently, Anya and Vivian's biggest stressor is Keisha's school. They are the only same-sex parent family in the school, which was not a problem from kindergarten through second grade because of Keisha's "cool teachers." However, in third grade, Keisha is now facing some teasing at school and has an unresponsive, unsympathetic teacher. Feeling helpless and desperate, Anya and Vivian have become more cautious about coming out to Keisha's teachers and school officials; and have considered switching Keisha to the local charter school. The couple has even entertained the idea of Vivian returning to her former career as a lawyer, a job she hated but which paid better than her job as a teacher. This change would enable the couple to relocate to a more urban, progressive, and diverse community that might more readily accept their family—and ideally provide greater access to schools, religious institutions, and health-care providers that are validating of their family structure.

Introduction

An ecological or systems approach to human development recognizes that individuals exist within, are influenced by, and interact with multiple intersecting contexts, including their families, friends, neighborhoods, communities, and workplaces, as well as broader societal institutions, ideologies, and discourses (Bronfenbrenner, 1977; Whitchurch & Constantine, 1993). Such interactions shift throughout the life cycle, as individuals develop, establish relationships, and create families and communities. This approach is particularly useful in the study of lesbian, gay, bisexual, and queer (LGBQ) individuals, whose lives, relationships, and families are increasingly visible in society, and yet who continue to encounter stigma and discrimination in a range of contexts (Goldberg, 2010). Indeed, continual and pervasive exposure to stigma and lack of access to equal rights may lead LGBQ persons and their families to experience psychosocial stress (also termed *minority stress*; Meyer, 2003). Such stress arises from the stigmatization that minorities tend to experience, as well as the power imbalance that exists between minorities and the broader systems with which they interact (e.g., families, schools, health care, the legal sphere), and places minorities at risk for adverse mental health outcomes, such as depression and anxiety (Goldberg & Smith, 2011; Meyer, 2003).

This chapter discusses research on various aspects of LGBQ individuals' experiences. Special attention is paid to the situational and contextual forces that impact LGBQ people's experiences as they move through the life course, particularly those that may pose challenges for sexual minorities and their families. Topically, this chapter begins with a discussion of LGBQ people's *coming out experiences,* as well as their experiences *forming and maintaining intimate relationships*, with attention to the barriers they face in doing so (e.g., lack of recognition and stigma). Next, the multiple barriers that LGBQ people face in *becoming parents* are discussed (e.g., challenges in accessing fertility treatments; discrimination in the adoption process) with attention to the resourcefulness that they display in the face of such barriers. The research on *LGBQ parents and their children* is also highlighted, with a focus on the stressors that LGBQ-parent families experience in relation to three major overlapping contexts: their families of origin, schools, and the health-care system. A discussion of the *implications of this research*, along with suggestions for teachers, therapists, social workers, health-care providers, and other professionals with regard to supporting LGBQ-parent families, conclude the chapter. Of note is that we do not discuss transgender (trans) parenting, as this is beyond the scope of this chapter.

Coming Out and Being Out

The process of coming out is one that is unique to the life experience and life cycle of sexual minorities. According to Cass's (1979) stage model, which is perhaps the most widely known framework for understanding the coming out process, individuals move from a state of questioning and confusion ("Could I be gay?") to acceptance of one's nonheterosexual identity ("I am gay, and I will be okay.") to pride and synthesis of their LGBQ identity ("This is a part of who I am and I need to let people know who I am."). Thus, the coming out process is conceptualized as one that is relatively linear and proceeds according to a series of predefined and continuous stages. Contemporary scholars, however, have asserted that coming out is an ongoing process for sexual minorities that is not necessarily linear, but is dynamic and iterative, marked by contradiction and complexity (Orne, 2011; Yon Leau & Munoz-Laboy, 2010). Further, scholars have increasingly argued for a conceptual distinction between individual sexual identity and group membership identity (McCarn & Fassinger, 1996), noting that, for example, a woman may come to terms with her same-sex erotic feelings and intimacy (and may ultimately identify as a lesbian) without identifying with or becoming active within the lesbian community. Thus, failure to disclose one's sexual orientation in diverse contexts should not necessarily be interpreted as implying an incomplete or inauthentic sexual identity (Orne, 2011).

Scholars have also increasingly emphasized the importance of considering the varied situational and contextual forces that impact individual decisions to come out (Orne, 2011). In deciding whether to disclose their sexual orientation, LGBQ people must consider their immediate social contexts and potential threats associated with disclosure (e.g., verbal or physical harassment, social humiliation and rejection, loss of housing or employment), how well they know the individual at hand, and the ease of concealment (Cohen & Savin-Williams, 2012). Broader contextual factors, including aspects of one's family, friendship network, workplace, neighborhood, and community, will also influence the coming out processes; indeed, as we saw in the opening vignette, LGBQ individuals who find themselves in settings that are not LGBQ-affirming may in turn be more hesitant to disclose their sexuality. Individuals from highly religious or politically conservative families, for example, may be particularly fearful of rejection and social alienation (Cohen & Savin-Williams, 2012; Jadwin-Cakmak, Pingel, Harper, & Bauermeister, 2015) and may resist or delay coming out to family members. Social class and occupation may also shape how, and the degree to which, sexual minorities are out in various aspects of their lives (Moore, 2011; Willis, 2011). For example, working-class sexual minorities, who are often employed in male-dominated, blue-collar workplaces, may experience less freedom to be "out" at work than their middle-class counterparts (McDermott, 2006). As illustrated in the opening vignette, geographic location may also shape sexual minorities' negotiations around outness, insomuch as there may be fewer visible (i.e., out) LGBQ persons in rural and nonmetropolitan areas than urban areas (Kinkler & Goldberg, 2011; Mendez, Holman, Oswald, & Izenstark, 2016). In the absence of a visible LGBQ community or role models, sexual minorities may experience greater hesitation or anxiety surrounding disclosure (Goldberg, 2010).

Race and ethnicity may also shape coming out and outness. LGBQ racial/ethnic minorities may face multiple forms of marginalization and oppression, in that they are vulnerable to racism in the LGBQ community, and may also be vulnerable to heterosexism and homophobia in their racial/ethnic communities and within their own families (Ghabriel, 2017; Nadal & Corpus, 2013). Awareness of hostile attitudes regarding homosexuality within their immediate and extended families may lead LGBQ racial/ethnic minorities to conceal their sexual orientation because they do not wish to lose the emotional and material support those family members provide (Malebranche, Fields, Bryant, & Harper, 2009), particularly if they depend on them for financial resources (Moore, 2011). They may also hesitate to come out because of strong cultural restrictions on sexuality and gender roles (Bridges, Selvidge, & Matthews, 2003) or because they do not wish to show disrespect for their cultural upbringing (Nadal & Corpus, 2013). Merighi and Grimes (2000), for example, found that African American, Mexican American, and Vietnamese American gay men struggled with wanting to establish their own gay identity while also respecting certain cultural norms and ideals. They were aware their families would respond to their coming out as the "end to the family lineage" and as a source of shame and embarrassment, and thus they were cautious about making their sexual identity widely known.

Social class and geographic location may also intersect with individuals' racial and sexual identities in key ways that have implications for outness. Moore (2011) studied a sample of Black lesbians in New York and found that the middle-class and upper middle-class lesbians in her sample tended to reside in economically stable and safer communities, which facilitated their outness. In contrast, working-class women tended to reside in urban areas where "strangers . . . may be more menacing, and safety in these communities is a sobering concern—not just around sexuality but around any visible identity that targets one as an easy mark," which had the effect of limiting their ability to live open lives (Moore, 2011, p. 202).

Outness may benefit individuals' mental health and relationship functioning. For example, being out to others may facilitate a sense of pride in one's identity, enhance opportunities to meet potential partners, and enable access to LGBQ-specific supports and resources, thus reducing isolation and intrapersonal distress (Vaughan & Waehler, 2010). At the same time, closeting oneself is a protective and adaptive strategy in certain contexts, and individuals who are "strategically out" (i.e., not out to every person or in every context in their lives) are not necessarily less psychologically healthy than those who are (Orne, 2011; Twist, Bergdall, Belous, & Maier, 2017). Further, sexual minorities who closet themselves in certain situations do not necessarily experience ambivalence or inner conflict, but recognize that such closeting is often necessary to survival (Moore, 2011; Willis, 2011). It is important to recognize that the function, meaning, and implications of outness will vary depending on situational context, such that, individuals who are very out in unsupportive or homophobic contexts may suffer mental health consequences (Goldberg & Smith, 2013a; Legate, Ryan, & Weinstein, 2012). Significantly, sexual minorities are increasingly using the Internet to come out, either as a precursor or supplement to face-to-face disclosures (Chester et al., 2016).

Same-Sex Relationships

Coming out may precede or occur alongside the formation of same-sex relationships. Same-sex unions share many characteristics with heterosexual unions but are uniquely impacted by sexual stigma, which manifests itself institutionally, interpersonally, and intrapersonally (Goldberg, 2010). Despite the stigmatized nature of same-sex relationships, studies that compare same- and different-sex relationships in terms of perceived quality and satisfaction have found few differences between the two groups (Goldberg, Smith, & Kashy; 2010; Rostosky & Riggle, 2019). Some studies have found that female same-sex couples report higher relationship quality than heterosexual couples (Kurdek, 2001; Meuwly, Feinstein, Davila, Nunez, & Bodenmann, 2013), a finding that may in part reflect the absence of structural barriers and relationship constraints (e.g., legal recognition, children) that have historically governed heterosexual relationships, wherein relationships that are not highly rewarding may be more easily terminated (Goldberg & Kuvalanka, 2012). Federal marriage equality, in turn, provides hard-won legal recognition of same-sex relationships that may serve as a "barrier to leaving," particularly when coupled with children (Goldberg & Romero, 2019).

Existing work on same-sex *parents* suggests that female couples may be somewhat more likely to separate than their heterosexual counterparts, yet the same does not appear to be true for male couples (Farr & Goldberg, 2019; Goldberg & Garcia, 2015). Factors that may help to explain these differences include (a) a higher income among gay men, which protects against stress and relationship dissolution; and (b) a greater likelihood of adopting children with special needs among lesbian women, the demands of which contribute to intrapersonal and interpersonal stress (Farr & Goldberg, 2019).

Characteristics of Healthy Relationships: Same-Sex Couples

Of interest are the characteristics of healthy or stable relationships among same-sex couples. That is, what factors appear to promote relationship quality? And, by extension, what variables appear to contribute to instability in same-sex relationships?

Equality

Some scholars suggest that perceptions of egalitarianism in the relationship— that is, the extent to which partners perceive themselves as sharing decision-making power, household management, for example—may be particularly important in same-sex couples, in that both partners may be particularly sensitive to power imbalances due to their stigmatized status in society (Goldberg, 2013). Female same-sex partners in particular may be especially likely to value equality in their intimate relationships, given their common socialization as women, and, therefore, their exposure to inequity in a variety of interpersonal and institutional contexts (Goldberg, 2013). Both female and male same-sex couples also tend to share housework more equitably than heterosexual couples (Goldberg, 2013; Solomon, Rothblum, & Balsam, 2005). Such sharing appears to be facilitated by financial, educational, occupational, and social resources (Goldberg, Smith, &

Perry-Jenkins, 2012), such that the sharing of domestic labor is enhanced among financially comfortable couples who rely on paid help, or have flexible work schedules (Goldberg, 2013).

Perceptions of equality have in turn been linked to relationship outcomes in same-sex couples. For example, Kurdek (2007) found that lesbian and gay partners' satisfaction with the division of labor affected relationship satisfaction and stability over time, via the mediating influence of perceived equality in the relationship. Discrepancies between ideal and actual levels of equality are also related to lower relationship quality for both lesbian and gay couples (Tornello, Kruczkowski, & Patterson, 2015).

Conflict and Difference

Few couples can avoid any conflict or disagreement in their relationships. Lesbian, gay, and heterosexual couples tend to report a similar frequency of arguments in their relationships (Peplau & Fingerhut, 2007) and to disagree about similar topics, such as finances, sex, and household tasks (Kurdek, 2006). Likewise, research suggests that higher levels of conflict are associated with lower levels of relationship quality in both heterosexual and same-sex relationships (Balsam et al., 2008; Goldberg & Sayer, 2006). Yet some sources of conflict may be specific to same-sex couples. Given the unique relational context of same-sex relationships (e.g., partners' shared gender socialization and status as stigmatized minorities), same-sex couples may encounter certain unique intra- and interpersonal processes that impact conflict management and relationship quality. For example, internalized homophobia has been linked to higher levels of relationship conflict (Totenhagen, Randall, & Lloyd, 2018).

Partners within same-sex couples may also differ from one another in important ways that may cause conflict. For example, racial/ethnic differences between partners may create the potential for stress and misunderstanding. Racial/ethnic minority LGBQ individuals with White partners may experience alienation within their relationships if they feel that their partners cannot empathize with the intersecting forces of sexism, heterosexism, and racism that they face on a daily basis (Balsam, Molina, Beadnell, Simoni, & Walters, 2011). White partners may feel guilty about internalized or institutional racism and attempt to compensate for their privilege, a strategy that may leave both partners feeling frustrated. Furthermore, interracial same-sex couples—such as Vivian and Anya, in the opening vignette—may be more identifiable than two women or men of the same ethnic group, thereby eliciting homophobic and racist reactions from outsiders (Rostosky, Riggle, Savage, & Gilbert, 2008; Steinbugler, 2005), possibly placing them at risk for victimization. This perceived risk may lead couples to avoid racially homogeneous settings and to prefer diverse racial atmospheres (Rostosky et al., 2008; Steinbugler, 2005). Interracial same-sex couples may also face negativity from family and friends, which in turn is linked to lower relationship quality and trust and higher likelihood of intimate partner aggression (Rosenthal & Starks, 2015).

Despite the challenges that interracial same-sex couples face, they often maintain healthy committed relationships.

Partners within same-sex couples may also differ in sexual identity. In couples where one partner identifies as bisexual or queer (i.e., nonmonosexual) and one partner identifies as lesbian or gay (i.e., monosexual), rates of conflict may be higher than if both partners were monosexual (Goldberg, Garcia, & Manley, 2017). It may be that nonmonosexual women and their partners are aware of stereotypes related to nonmonosexuality (e.g., the idea that bisexual people are confused about their sexuality or less committed to monogamy; Ross, Dobinson, & Eady, 2010). This awareness could prompt arguments (e.g., due to worries about infidelity on the nonmonosexual partner's part) or regular check-ins about the relationship, which may result in more conflicts being raised generally. In addition, bisexual-identified individuals partnered with monosexual-identified individuals have been found to experience unique, bisexual-specific minority stressors that they need support to address (Vencill, Carlson, Iantaffi, & Miner, 2017).

Social Support and Recognition

The intimate relationships of LGBQ individuals are necessarily impacted by their social networks. The support (or lack of support) they receive from their families of origin, friends, communities, workplaces, and state and national governments has profound implications for their individual and relational health (Goldberg & Smith, 2011). Individuals in same-sex couples have been found to perceive less social support from family members compared to individuals in heterosexual couples (Goldberg & Smith, 2008; Kurdek, 2001), which may impact their relationship quality (Goldberg et al., 2010), mental health (Goldberg & Smith, 2008, 2011; Graham & Barnow, 2013), and parenting processes (Green, Rubio, Rothblum, Bergman, & Katuzny, 2019). Certain sexual minorities are especially at risk for diminished familial support, including LGBQ racial/ethnic minorities and sexual minorities in interracial relationships (Rosenthal & Starks, 2015; Rostosky et al., 2008).

Sexual minorities have also historically faced legal nonsupport and lack of recognition, whereby both their intimate relationships and parent–child relationships have not been granted the same legal protections and securities afforded to heterosexual couples (Goldberg & Kuvalanka, 2012; Shapiro, 2013). Until 2015, when federal marriage equality in the United States became a reality, same-sex couples in committed relationships lacked all of the benefits that marriage affords, including automatic financial decision-making authority on behalf of a spouse, the ability to make medical decisions for an incapacitated partner, and the ability to file joint income tax returns, among numerous other benefits (Shapiro, 2013). Although the institution of marriage is viewed as problematic by some same-sex couples—including those who have chosen to marry, and those who have not—most would agree that same-sex couples should at least have the choice to marry (Goldberg & Romero, 2019). For those couples who choose to marry, marriage offers numerous legal and symbolic benefits, which may strengthen relationships and, in turn, individual well-being. Indeed, a number of studies have documented the positive effects of getting married on same-sex partners' sense of security, recognition as a couple, mental health, and physical health (Goldberg, Smith, McCormick, & Overstreet, 2019; Lannutti, 2011; Shulman, Gotta, & Green, 2012; Solomon et al., 2005). These findings may also reflect the positive impact that pro-gay (e.g., marriage equality) legislation can have on community attitudes, resulting in less stigma directed at same-sex couples (and, in turn, greater personal and relational well-being; Kail, Acosta, & Wright, 2015; Ogolsky, Monk, Rice, & Oswald, 2019). Notably, however, some qualitative research suggests that some sexual minorities demonstrate ambivalence about the idea of marriage (e.g., they hold concerns about "assimilating" to a heterosexual way of life; Lannutti, 2011).

Becoming Parents, Forming Families

Many sexual minorities may become parents in the context of heterosexual relationships: That is, they become parents before coming out as LGBQ, and then, in some cases, enter same-sex relationships, wherein their children may ultimately be raised in LGBQ-parent stepfamilies (Tasker, 2013). Other LGBQ people become parents in the context of same-sex committed relationships,[1] a phenomenon that has become increasingly common due in part to advancements in reproductive technology and increasingly tolerant attitudes regarding same-sex parenting and adoption (Goldberg, 2010).

Gates (2015) estimates that between 2 million and 3.7 million children under 18 years of age in the United States have at least one sexual minority parent. Further, as of 2013, more than three-quarters of same-sex couples raising children under age 18 were female (77%; Gates, 2015). Among married same-sex couples with children, the proportion of female couples is slightly lower, at 71% (Gates, 2015). Significantly, LGBQ parents currently represent a sizeable minority of *adoptive* and *foster* parents, specifically. Among couples with children, same-sex couples are at least three times more likely than heterosexual couples to be raising an adopted or foster child, with nearly 27,000 same-sex couples raising an estimated 58,000 adopted and foster children in the United States (Gates, 2015). If the same-sex couple is married, they are five times more likely than heterosexual married couples to be raising an adopted or foster child (Gates, 2015).

Donor Insemination

Same-sex couples who wish to become parents may consider several potential routes to parenthood: donor insemination (among lesbian couples),

---

[1] These families are often referred to as "planned" or "intentional" LGBQ-parent families.

adoption, surrogacy, or more complex parenting arrangements (e.g., a female couple and a male couple may choose to coparent). The most common routes to parenthood among intentional LGBQ-parent families are donor insemination and adoption.[2] Each of these presents unique challenges. Lesbian couples who pursue insemination must decide who is going to be the biological parent (i.e., experience pregnancy and childbirth, and be genetically related to the child), which may be an easy decision in some cases (e.g., if one partner wants to be pregnant, and one does not) but a difficult and sensitive decision in others (Goldberg, 2006). Female couples also must decide whether to inseminate using sperm from a known or unknown donor. Women who choose unknown donors often do so out of a desire to avoid unclear or fuzzy boundaries, or potential custody challenges (Goldberg, 2006). Women who pursue insemination via known donors may also experience legal worries, but feel strongly that their child deserves access to their biological heritage (Goldberg & Allen, 2013; Chapman, Wardrop, Zappia, Watkins, & Shields, 2012 Hayman, Wilkes, Halcomb, & Jackson, 2015; Titlestad & Robinson, 2019). They may also choose known donors because they wish to avoid interfacing with official, potentially heterosexist institutions such as sperm banks and fertility clinics (Priddle, 2015).

Social change, combined with the increasing visibility of female same-sex couples with children, has gradually facilitated greater awareness and more sensitive treatment of sexual minority women who seek out donor insemination; yet reports of insensitive and inappropriate treatment by health-care providers continue to appear in the literature (Goldberg, 2006; Spidsberg, 2007). For example, sexual minority women routinely encounter clinic forms that are inappropriate for LGBQ patients (e.g., they assume a heterosexual two-parent family), as well as health-care providers who fail to acknowledge the nonbirthing partner at office visits and prenatal classes (Goldberg, 2006). Women who are more masculine-presenting are especially vulnerable to discrimination in the perinatal care environment (Scout, Lombardi, & White, 2010).

Adoption

Some same-sex couples pursue adoption as a means of becoming a parent. They are more often "preferential adopters" than heterosexual couples, meaning that they choose adoption first, before pursuing biological routes to parenthood (Goldberg, 2012; Jennings, Mellish, Tasker, Lamb, & Golombok, 2014). Types of adoption include international adoption (i.e., from abroad), public domestic adoption (through the child welfare system), and private domestic adoption (e.g., through a lawyer or agency). Sending countries (i.e., countries willing to work with the United States to coordinate international adoptions) have historically been resistant to same-sex couples, so same-sex couples have adopted internationally by having one parent present as a single parent during the adoption process.

---

[2] For a review of the limited research on surrogacy by LGBQ people, see Berkowitz (2013).

A decline in the number of sending countries open to single parents, much less same-sex couples, has meant that this option is no longer viable for most sexual minorities. In turn, most same-sex couples currently pursue public domestic adoption or private domestic adoption. Notably, private domestic adoptions in the United States are increasingly "open," as opposed to "closed," with openness (which occurs on a continuum) involving an exchange of information or communication between birth parents and adoptive parents before and after placement of the child. Closed adoptions, where birth parents and adoptive parents do not exchange identifying information and there is no contact between the two parties, are increasingly rare.

Same-sex couples may choose private domestic open adoption because they are attracted to the possibility of maintaining contact with birth parents or being able to provide their child with (possibly ongoing) information about their birth parents (Goldberg, Downing, & Sauck, 2007; Goldberg, Kinkler, Richardson, & Downing, 2011). They may also be drawn to open adoption because of the greater likelihood of adopting an infant compared to international or public adoption (Downing, Richardson, Kinkler, & Goldberg, 2009). Prospective adoptive parents have historically selected international adoption in part to avoid the long wait associated with domestic private adoptions of healthy infants (Hollingsworth & Ruffin, 2002), a reason that may be especially prominent among sexual minorities. That is, same-sex couples may worry that birth mothers (who often choose the adoptive parents in open adoptions) are unlikely to choose them because of their sexual orientation, resulting in a long or endless waiting period for a child placement (Goldberg et al., 2007; Goldberg, 2012).

Same-sex couples who seek to adopt through the child welfare system are typically in part motivated by finances or altruistic reasons (e.g., the wish to give a child a permanent family; Goldberg, 2012). As described in the opening vignette, it was important to Vivian to "adopt a child of color . . . and there are so many in the foster care system that it seemed irresponsible not to choose that route." Additionally, sexual minorities may also choose to adopt through foster care because they believe that they have the best chance of adopting through this route, in that the number of children in foster care far exceeds the number of heterosexual prospective adoptive parents. Although sexual minorities may be welcomed by some child welfare workers and social service agencies, reports of insensitive practices by child welfare workers continue to appear in the literature (Goldberg, 2012; Goldberg et al., 2007; Riggs, 2011).

Upon settling on an adoption route, prospective adoptive parents choose an agency or lawyer, a process that can be particularly challenging and time consuming for same-sex couples. Given their vulnerability in the adoption process, it is not surprising that many same-sex couples expend significant time and effort researching potential adoption agencies for evidence that they are open to working with sexual minorities (Goldberg et al., 2007; Kimberly & Moore, 2015). Even when same-sex couples select agencies that they believe to be accepting and affirming, they may still encounter heterosexist treatment, via forms, materials, and support groups that seem to focus on heterosexual couples only (e.g., they presume a history of infertility; Farr & Goldberg, 2018; Goldberg et al., 2007). They may also confront adoption professionals who hold discriminatory stereotypes and attitudes toward LGBQ people, and who therefore sabotage potential adoptive placements (Farr & Goldberg, 2018). Sexual minorities with less traditional gender expressions may be vulnerable to particularly high levels of scrutiny and discrimination (Farr & Goldberg, 2018). Because of their vulnerability in the adoption process, LGBQ prospective parents may be cautious about not "making waves" (e.g., confronting discrimination) out of fear of further jeopardizing their chances of adopting (Goldberg, 2012; Wood, 2016). Sexual minorities with few resources (e.g., social, financial, geographic) may be particularly careful about making waves; indeed, same-sex couples who have few financial resources, or who live in rural areas, for example, may have few choices in terms of what agency or lawyer to work with (Kinkler & Goldberg, 2011; Riggs, 2011).

Other Challenges

Sexual minorities, regardless of what route to parenthood they choose, are typically vulnerable to additional challenges as they make their way toward parenthood. For example, LGBQ people do not benefit from the societal support that heterosexual couples receive when they become parents: They may face nonsupport from other (heterosexual) parents, as well as resistance from their families of origin (Goldberg, 2010). Female same-sex couples who become parents via insemination also encounter the unique challenge of negotiating various asymmetries in their relationship (i.e., during pregnancy, with regard to breastfeeding, and in the partners' genetic relatedness to the child; Goldberg & Perry-Jenkins, 2007). Such asymmetries may create feelings of jealousy on the part of the nonbiological mother or conflicts over who the child "belongs" to (Goldberg, Downing, & Sauck, 2008)—asymmetries which are in part facilitated by broader social norms that value biological over social parenthood. Same-sex couples can now, in the era of federal marriage equality, petition to jointly adopt a child—whereas in the past, some states did not allow same-sex couples to co-adopt; one partner had to adopt as a single parent, and then, in some cases, the other partner could complete a second-parent adoption and become the child's other legal parent. Couples may be required to be in a legally recognized relationship (e.g., married) to jointly adopt. However, same-sex married couples who wish to adopt do continue to face legal challenges and hurdles in their quest to do so, depending on where they live. For example, a number of states are in the process of considering or trying to pass legislation to create broad religious exemptions, that would enable, for example, religiously affiliated placement agencies to turn away same-sex couples seeking to adopt or foster (Moreau, 2019).

There is evidence that many LGBQ people adopt transracially or transculturally, as was the case of Anya in the opening vignette (Gates, Badgett, Macomber, & Chambers, 2007; Goldberg, 2009). National survey data show that 17% of White same-sex couples are raising children of color, as compared to 3% of different-sex couples (Gates, 2014). In turn, same-sex transracial adoptive households may face additional challenges related to their multiple stigmatized and highly visible family structure, in that these families are vulnerable to the stresses associated with both heterosexism *and* racism (Goldberg, 2009, 2012). For example, because of their visibility, parents and children may be faced with intrusive questions about the why's and how's of their family's creation (Gianino, Goldberg, & Lewis, 2009). LGBQ parents of children of color employ a variety of strategies in an effort to facilitate their children's positive identity development, including (a) initiating parent–child conversations aimed at instilling pride, (b) seeking communities that reflect their child's identities, and (c) educating about racism and heterosexism (Goldberg, Sweeney, Black, & Moyer, 2016).

LGBQ-Parent Families: Experiences and Challenges

Next, the experiences of LGBQ parents and their children are explored, with attention to parent, family, and child functioning and well-being. Then, the challenges that LGBQ-parent families encounter in the family, school, and health-care spheres are examined.

Parent and Child Functioning

Despite concerns that the sexual orientation of LGBQ parents will negatively affect children in both indirect and direct ways, research is consistent in indicating that sexuality is not relevant to men and women's parenting capacities and parent–child relationships. Studies that have compared lesbian, gay, and heterosexual parents in terms of mental health, parenting stress, parenting skills, and parental warmth and involvement have found few differences according to family structure (Bos, Knox, van Gelderen, & Gartrell, 2016; Goldberg & Smith, 2011, 2014; Golombok et al., 2003, 2014; Green et al., 2019). Similarly, studies suggest that children who grow up with LGBQ parents do not appear to differ remarkably from children of heterosexual parents in terms of their emotional and behavioral adjustment. Studies have found few differences between children in lesbian, gay, and heterosexual parent families in terms of self-esteem, depression, behavioral problems, or social functioning (Goldberg & Smith, 2013b; Golombok et al., 2003; van Gelderen, Bos, Gartrell, Hermanns, & Perrin, 2012). Interestingly, a few recent studies have found that children of gay fathers actually show higher levels of psychological adjustment compared to heterosexual and lesbian parent families (e.g., Carone, Lingiardi, Chirumbolo, & Baiocco, 2018; Golombok et al., 2014; Green et al., 2019). Other work has shown higher levels of social competence and lower levels of aggressive behavior and conduct problems among teens raised by lesbian mothers, when compared to an age- and gender-matched group of adolescents with heterosexual parents (Bos, van Gelderen, & Gartrell, 2015; Gartrell & Bos, 2010). Qualitative work has found that young adults cite various strengths associated with growing up with LGBQ parents, including resilience, valuing of diversity, and empathy and compassion toward marginalized groups (Cody, Farr, McRoy, Ayers-Lopez, & Ledesma, 2017).

When looking beyond family structure at the family processes associated with more positive adjustment outcomes in children with LGBQ parents, several factors emerge as important. Research indicates that among same-sex couples with children, positive coparenting (Green et al., 2019), positive parent–child relationships (Bos et al., 2015), satisfaction with the division of labor (Feuge, Cossette, Cyr, & Julien, 2019), and support from friends (Green et al., 2019) have all been linked to more positive psychological outcomes in children. Additionally, within adoptive samples, children who were adopted at an early age show better psychological outcomes than children adopted later (Goldberg & Smith, 2013b).

That LGBQ parents and their children demonstrate such positive outcomes suggests remarkable resilience, given that they develop in a heterosexist society and are exposed to stigma and nonsupport in multiple intersecting, overlapping contexts (Goldberg, 2010). Specifically, LGBQ parents and their children are vulnerable to nonsupport and alienation from their *families of origin*. They are also vulnerable to misunderstanding and mistreatment in the *school context*. Finally, they also confront lack of recognition and support in the *health-care system*. LGBQ-parent families' experiences navigating challenges in these domains will be discussed next.

The Family of Origin Context

LGBQ parents may perceive less support from members of their family of origin than heterosexual parents (Goldberg & Smith, 2008; but see Sumontha, Farr, & Patterson, 2016), but may also report greater support from family members than LGBQ nonparents (DeMino, Appleby, & Fisk, 2007). It seems that family members may become more supportive once a child enters the picture. Goldberg (2006) found that lesbian women's perceptions of support from their own and their partners' families increased across the transition to parenthood. Thus, some family members may push their feelings about nonheterosexuality aside and seek to repair problematic or damaged relationships in the interest of developing a relationship with a new grandchild (or niece, or nephew; Goldberg, 2012). In fact, in some cases, family ties may be strengthened by the arrival of a child, such that LGBQ parents enjoy closer ties to their parents after becoming parents themselves (Goldberg, 2012). Indeed, as Anya and Vivian experienced, Anya's family went from having a "distant" relationship with the couple to asking if they could babysit Keisha. Of course, not all family members become more supportive or involved across the transition to parenthood. Some LGBQ parents confront reduced support from their families upon announcing their intention to parent. For example, their families may express opposition to their decision to parent on moral or religious grounds, or because they believe that life as an LGBQ-parent family will simply be too difficult (Goldberg, 2012).

The level of support that LGBQ-parent families receive may depend on whether the child is biologically related to the family of origin. That is, biological mothers' families may be more involved in children's lives than nonbiological mothers' families (Patterson, Hurt, & Mason, 1998), although some work has found that establishment of *legal* ties by nonbiological mothers may encourage greater investment and involvement by extended family members (Hayman, Wilkes, Halcomb, & Jackson, 2013; Hequembourg, 2004), presumably signaling their commitment to the child and validating the parent–child relationship. Family support may also vary depending on the racial/ethnic match between parent and child, such that LGBQ parents who adopt across racial lines may encounter particular resistance and nonsupport from family members—as we saw in the case of Anya, in the opening vignette (Goldberg, 2009; Johnson & O'Connor, 2002). Family members may be uncomfortable acknowledging their new grandchild (or niece, or nephew) based upon their own racist beliefs or find it difficult to embrace a child that looks different from them (Goldberg, 2012). Family members may also voice concerns about the challenges and vulnerabilities children might be exposed to because of their multiple marginalized statuses (Goldberg, 2009; Johnson & O'Connor, 2002).

Lack of family of origin support may have negative implications for LGBQ-parent families. Some work has shown that parents who perceive their families as less supportive report less positive parenting and coparenting (Green et al., 2019; Sumontha et al., 2016). Similar to heterosexual couples, same-sex couples tend to shift their focus from their friends to their family of origin when they become parents, and may struggle more with parenting responsibilities if the level of support they anticipate receiving from family does not materialize (Carter & McGoldrick, 1996; DeMino et al., 2007). Significantly, the legalization of same-sex adoption may allow families of origin some comfort in knowing that contact with their nonbiological grandchildren, nieces, and nephews is legally protected should the same-sex couple's relationship end, which in turn may increase their level of support and involvement (DeMino et al., 2007).

The School Context

As illustrated in the opening vignette, both LGBQ parents and their children are also vulnerable to alienation and stigma within the school setting (Goldberg & Smith, 2014). A survey conducted by the Gay, Lesbian and Straight Education Network (GLSEN) found that more than half (53%) of over 500 LGBT parents described various forms of exclusion from their children's school communities (i.e., being excluded or prevented from fully participating in school activities and events, being excluded by school policies and procedures, and being ignored; Kosciw & Diaz, 2008). Further, 26% of LGBT parents reported being mistreated by other parents (e.g., being stared at or ignored). Parents whose children's schools had school policies that protected both students and their parents from harassment or exclusion based on actual or perceived sexual orientation or gender identity reported lower levels of mistreatment than parents whose children's schools did not have such policies. The survey also found that 40% of the 154 students surveyed reported being verbally harassed in school because of their family (e.g., being called names such as "fag" and "lesbo"). Such teasing may be more prominent at certain developmental periods and relatively minimal at others, as illustrated in Keisha's case in the opening vignette. Indeed, Gartrell et al. (2000) found that 18% of lesbian mothers reported that their 5-year-old children had experienced some type of homophobia from peers or teachers. However, by the age of 10, almost half of children had reportedly experienced some form of homophobia (e.g., in the form of teasing; Gartrell, Deck, Rodas, Peyser, & Banks, 2005). As social norms change, instances of teasing may be less common—a more recent study of same-sex parents with adopted 8-year-old children found that only 8% of parents reported that their children had been teased or bullied for having LGBQ parents (Farr, Oakley, & Ollen, 2016). Significantly, though, children who had been bullied were also reported to have more behavioral issues by parents and teachers, highlighting the negative impact of homophobic bullying (Farr et al., 2016).

Where LGBQ parents live, and the type of school their children attend, may impact children's social experiences, as well as their exposure to teasing and bullying specifically. In turn, middle- and upper middle-class LGBQ parents may be better able to protect their children from bullying, in that social and financial resources allow them some choice in where they live, and they may favor areas and schools that are known to be more inclusive and progressive (Goldberg & Smith, 2014; Goldberg, Allen, Black, Frost, & Manley, 2018). Indeed, in the case of Anya and Vivian, both were considering career changes that would allow them to move to a more progressive area where their family and child would be better received.

It is notable that despite their potential vulnerability to teasing and stigma, the academic progress and performance of children of LGBQ parents appears to be on par with that of children of heterosexual parents (Potter, 2012; Rosenfeld, 2010). Growing up with LGBQ parents is not related to delayed progression through elementary school (Allen, Pakaluk, & Price, 2013; Lavner, Waterman, & Peplau, 2012; Rosenfeld, 2010), nor is it related to lower academic achievement (Gartrell & Bos, 2010; Potter, 2012; Wainright et al., 2004). These positive outcomes may in part reflect LGBQ parents' high levels of involvement in their children's schooling. Aware of the possibility for exclusion, same-sex couples with children may go "above and beyond" to ensure that their children's classrooms and assignments are inclusive of same-sex parent families, and may engage in other forms of implicit and explicit advocacy, such as joining the school diversity committee (Goldberg, Black, Sweeney, & Moyer, 2017; Goldberg, Black, Manley, & Frost, 2017). They may come out to schools and teachers purposefully, even when fearful of potential stigma, in part to model pride and self-advocacy for their children (Cloughessy, Waniganayake, & Blatterer, 2018; Goldberg, Black, Sweeney, & Moyer, 2017).

The Health-Care Context

Another major context that LGBQ-parent families interface with, and that may be biased against them, is health care. Implicit preferences for heterosexual people versus lesbian and gay people as well as bias against LGBQ parents are pervasive among heterosexual health-care providers (Nicol, Chapman, Watkins, Young, & Shields, 2013; Sabin, Riskind, & Nosek, 2015), such that LGBQ-parent families have mixed experiences in the health-care system. Starting with family creation, LGBQ couples face potential stigma from health-care providers who do not support their intention to parent children. In a recent systematic review of the literature on lesbians becoming mothers, Gregg (2018) found that across all studies reviewed, lesbian women seeking maternity care experienced some amount of heteronormativity or homophobia in their health-care encounters. Types of homophobia included exclusion, heterosexual assumptions, inappropriate questioning, and refusal of services (see Hayman et al., 2013). For example, nonbiological mothers often felt as though they had to fight to be acknowledged as parents (see Malmquist & Nelson, 2014; Wojnar & Katzenmeyer, 2014). Further, after giving birth, women in same-sex couples have reported reluctance to approach providers about depressive symptoms for fear of judgement that may be compounded by their sexual orientation (Alang & Fomotar, 2015). Notably, there is little research on health-care provider attitudes toward gay men becoming fathers, although existing work suggests that providers may possess similarly negative attitudes (Carroll, 2018; Perrin, Pinderhughes, Mattern, Hurley, & Newman, 2016; Perrin, Hurley, Mattern, Flavin, & Pinderhughes, 2019). Existing studies show that many gay men are discouraged from even trying to pursue fatherhood for fear of the stigma they will face (Baiocco et al., 2014; Bauermeister, 2014). Although little work has focused on bisexual parents' interactions with health-care providers, one recent study of male-partnered bisexual women showed that most had positive experiences with perinatal providers, although some expressed concerns about biphobia and others had preferences for LGBQ-affirming providers (Goldberg, Ross, Manley, & Mohr, 2017).

In seeking care for their children, same-sex couples may anticipate or endure stigma from providers. Studies show that same-sex couples fear anxiety about prejudicial treatment by child health professionals (e.g., Chapman, Watkins, Zappia, Combs, & Shields, 2012; Hayman et al., 2013) and face implicit and explicit discrimination and prejudice (Andersen, Moberg, Tops, & Garmy, 2017; Dahl, Fylkesnes, Sorlie, & Malterud, 2016; Wells & Lang, 2016). Some research suggests that providers show comparatively less stigma directed toward the children of LGBQ couples (Andersen et al., 2017; Perrin et al., 2016, 2019). Online survey research on gay fathers across the United States found that fathers faced stigma from medical professionals directed toward themselves, but reported relatively little to none toward their children (Perrin et al., 2016, 2019).

Beyond health-care providers, it is important to understand how health-care policy also impacts LGBQ-parent families. Past negative interactions with health-care providers inhibit people from accessing health care, as does a lack of health insurance (Hutchinson, Thompson, & Cederbaum, 2006; United States Department of Health & Human Services, 2000). Children of same-sex parents are less likely to have private health insurance than their peers with married different-sex parents (Gonzales & Blewett, 2013). This difference will inevitably diminish amid the recent legalization of same-sex marriage throughout the United States (Webster & Telingator, 2016), but LGBQ parents still face administrative hurdles to obtain health insurance based on state-sponsored discrimination policies (Potter & Allen, 2016). Indeed, as of June 2019, 36 states did not expressly ban health insurance discrimination based on sexual orientation or gender identity (Movement Advancement Project, 2019) and in May 2019, the Department of Health and Human Services issued a rule to expand federal laws that allow health-care providers and entities to cite their religious or moral beliefs in denying services to patients, such as LGBQ parents (Office for Civil Rights, 2019). The potentially difficult task for LGBQ people to acquire adequate health care and insurance can be further compounded by additional minority statuses based on race, ethnicity, and class (Cahill, 2009; Gonzales & Henning-Smith, 2017; Potter & Allen, 2016). Despite the legalization of same-sex marriage, it is clear that federal and state health policies are still negatively impacting the wellness of LGBQ-parent families.

Conclusions and Suggestions for Practitioners

LGBQ parents and their children are vulnerable to social and legal challenges at multiple stages of the life course and in multiple settings. For example, Anya, Vivian, and Keisha encountered nonsupport from their family, school, and community at various points during their lives. Such challenges undermine the integrity of sexual minorities' family relationships and threaten their emotional and physical well-being. And yet, LGBQ parents and their children demonstrate remarkable resilience in the face of such challenges. This resilience is likely facilitated by the formation of strong and stable relationships that are characterized by equality, mutuality, and compassion (Rostosky & Riggle, 2019), access to and engagement with an active or visible LGBQ community (Russell & Richards, 2003; Titlestad & Robinson, 2019), and perceptions of support and affirmation from one's family or friendship network (Goldberg, 2012; Russell & Richards, 2003). Of course, the fact that LGBQ-parent families demonstrate remarkable resilience by no means legitimates the heterosexism that they face in their everyday lives. Scholars, practitioners, educators, and policymakers are urged to work on behalf of LGBQ persons and families to identify and ameliorate the conditions that underlie and perpetuate the social stress and oppression that they must endure. By destabilizing systems of oppression and inequality, we can begin to improve the social conditions in which LGBQ-parent families live.

Therapists and practitioners who work with same-sex couples should be attentive to the unique dimensions of their relationships as compared to heterosexual relationships, but at the same time should remain cognizant of the ways in which same-sex couples' relational difficulties may reflect "universal" relationship conflicts. Furthermore, therapists should be sensitive to the many variables and contexts that impact the formation, nature, and stability of same-sex relationships, such as similarities and differences between partners in terms of outness, race, and so on. Finally, and perhaps most importantly, therapists should maintain a heightened awareness of the ways in which both subtle and overt forms of societal stigma and exclusion may contribute to existing individual and relational problems. For example, in treating a socially isolated lesbian couple, a therapist should recognize the potential systemic causes of their isolation, and should resist blaming the couple for their lack of social connectedness.

Practitioners (e.g., gynecologists, social workers, pediatricians) and institutions (e.g., fertility clinics, adoption agencies, and hospitals) that work with LGBQ individuals and couples during the transitional stage of becoming parents should strive to communicate a philosophy of inclusion and acceptance (Webster & Telingator, 2016). For health-care providers and institutions, standardized forms for coparents as opposed to "mothers" and "fathers" reflect attentiveness to LGBQ couples while trainings can help sensitize staff to the needs of LGBQ families. For example, LGBQ parents report feeling more supported by health-care providers when both parents are equally respected and given a say in their child's health (Wells & Lang, 2016). Facilitators of prenatal education classes and adoption support groups can strive to utilize inclusive language (e.g., terms such as *partner*; Goldberg, 2006, 2012). Pink triangles, rainbow decals, and other symbols of LGBQ affirmation can be easily posted inconspicuously in health and adoption-related offices and client rooms.

School educators and personnel are encouraged to take steps to reduce stigmatization of LGBQ-parent families by actively creating a climate of acceptance and inclusion of these families within schools and classrooms (Goldberg & Smith, 2014). School educators and administrators, for example, may choose to seek ongoing training and education about diverse families (e.g., via organizations such as GLSEN; www.glsen.org). Such training will support them in advocating for diverse families and actively fighting discrimination and prejudice against children resulting from their parents' sexual orientations.

Finally, at the policy and legal level, greater protections are clearly needed for LGBQ-parent families. Federal and state laws that discriminate against LGBQ people and families (e.g., by allowing adoption agencies to turn away prospective parents or insurance companies to turn away parents based on their sexual orientation) render them vulnerable to stigma, poorer health, and serve to legitimate treatment of children and families as second-class citizens. Likewise, the absence of federal employment policies that protect LGBQ workers from employment discrimination hurts these individuals and their families. Maintaining and spreading legal protection of LGBQ-parent families will help to (a) foster acceptance; (b) ensure the protection of these families via the provision of standard rights and benefits; and (c) promote the stability and security of LGBQ-parent families and their children, thereby contributing to their health and well-being.

DISCUSSION QUESTIONS

1. Considering the research presented in this chapter, what advice would you give to an interracial same-sex couple considering parenthood? Specifically, what are some key considerations they might make with regard to where they live, choosing a parenthood route, and preparing their extended kin for their family's expansion?

2. If you were a therapist and treating a same-sex couple in couples therapy, what institutional, interpersonal, and intrapersonal factors or processes would you be especially attuned to?

3. What policies and laws need to be passed to better protect and support LGBQ-parent families?

REFERENCES

Alang, S. M., & Fomotar, M. (2015). Postpartum depression in an online community of lesbian mothers: Implications for clinical practice. *Journal of Gay and Lesbian Mental Health, 19*(1), 21–39.

Allen, D. W., Pakaluk, C., & Price, J. (2013). Nontraditional families and childhood progress through school: A comment on Rosenfeld. *Demography, 50*(3), 955–961.

Andersen, A. E., Moberg, C., Bengtsson Tops, A., & Garmy, P. (2017). Lesbian, gay and bisexual parents' experiences of nurses' attitudes in child health care: A qualitative study. *Journal of Clinical Nursing, 26*(23/24), 5065–5071.

Baiocco, R., Argalia, M., & Laghi, F. (2014). The desire to marry and attitudes toward same-sex

family legalization in a sample of Italian lesbians and gay men. *Journal of Family Issues, 35*(2), 181–200.

Balsam, K. F., Beauchaine, T. P., Rothblum, E. D., & Solomon, S. E. (2008). Three-year follow-up of same-sex couples who had civil unions in Vermont, same-sex couples not in civil unions, and heterosexual married couples. *Developmental Psychology 44*(1), 102–116.

Balsam, K. F., Molina, Y., Beadnell, B., Simoni, J. M., & Walters, K. (2011). Measuring multiple minority stress: The LGBT People of Color Microaggressions Scale. *Cultural Diversity and Ethnic Minority Psychology, 17,* 163–174.

Bauermeister, J. A. (2014). How statewide LGB policies go from "under our skin" to "into our hearts": Fatherhood aspirations and psychological well-being among emerging adult sexual minority men. *Journal of Youth and Adolescence*, *43*(8), 1295–1305.

Berkowitz, D. (2013). Gay men and surrogacy. In A. E. Goldberg & K. R. Allen (Eds.), *LGBT- parent families: Innovations in research and implications for practice* (pp. 71–85). Springer.

Bos, H. M. W., Knox, J. R., van Rijn-van Gelderen, L., & Gartrell, N. K. (2016). Same-sex and different-sex parent households and child health outcomes: Findings from the National Survey of Children's Health. *Journal of Developmental and Behavioral Pediatrics*, *37*(3), 179–187.

Bos, H. M. W., van Gelderen, L., & Gartrell, N. (2015). Lesbian and heterosexual two-parent families: Adolescent–parent relationship quality and adolescent well-being. *Journal of Child and Family Studies*, *24*(4), 1031–1046.

Bridges, S. K., Selvidge, M. M. D., & Matthews, C. R. (2003). Lesbian women of color: Therapeutic issues and challenges. *Journal of Multicultural Counseling and Development*, *31*, 113–130.

Bronfenbrenner, U. (1977). Toward an experimental ecology of human development. *American Psychologist*, *32*, 513–531.

Cahill, S. (2009). The disproportionate impact of antigay family policies on Black and Latino same-sex couple households. *Journal of African American Studies*, *13*(3), 219–250.

Carone, N., Lingiardi, V., Chirumbolo, A., & Baiocco, R. (2018). Italian gay father families formed by surrogacy: Parenting, stigmatization, and children's psychological adjustment. *Developmental Psychology*, *54*(10), 1904–1916.

Carroll, M. (2018). Managing without moms: Gay fathers, incidental activism, and the politics of parental gender. *Journal of Family Issues*, *39*(13), 1–26.

Carter, E., & McGoldrick, M. (1988). *The changing family life cycle: A framework for family therapy* (2nd ed.). Gardner Press.

Cass, V. C. (1979). Homosexual identity formation: Testing a theoretical model. *Journal of Homosexuality*, *4*, 219–235.

Chapman, R., Wardrop, J., Zappia, T., Watkins, R., & Shields, L. (2012). The experiences of Australian lesbian couples becoming parents: Deciding, searching and birthing. *Journal of Clinical Nursing*, *21*(13/14), 1878–1885.

Chapman, R., Watkins, R., Zappia, T., Combs, S., & Shields, L. (2012). Second-level hospital health professionals' attitudes to lesbian, gay, bisexual and transgender parents seeking health for their children. *Journal of Clinical Nursing*, *21*(5/6), 880–887.

Chester, M. R., Sinnard, M. T., Rochlen, A. B., Nadeau, M. M., Balsan, M. J., & Provence, M. M. (2016). Gay men's experiences coming out online: A qualitative study. *Journal of Gay and Lesbian Social Services*, *28*(4), 317–335.

Cloughessy, K., Waniganayake, M., & Blatterer, H. (2018). "This is our family. We do not hide who we are": Stigma and disclosure decisions of lesbian parents in Australian early childhood settings. *Journal of GLBT Family Studies*, *14*(4), 381–399.

Cody, P. A., Farr, R. H., McRoy, R. G., Ayers-Lopez, S. J., & Ledesma, K. J. (2017). Youth perspectives on being adopted from foster care by lesbian and gay parents: Implications for families and adoption professionals. *Adoption Quarterly*, *20*(1), 98–118.

Cohen, K., & Savin-Williams, R. (2012). Coming out to self and others: Developmental milestones. In P. Levounis, J. Drescher, & M. Barber (Eds), *The LGBT casebook* (pp. 17–33). American Psychiatric Publishing.

Dahl, B., Margrethe Fylkesnes, A., Sørlie, V., & Malterud, K. (2013). Lesbian women's experiences with healthcare providers in the birthing context: A meta-ethnography. *Midwifery, 29*(6), 674–681.

DeMino, K. A., Appleby, G., & Fisk, D. (2007). Lesbian mothers with planned families: A comparative study of internalized homophobia and social support. *American Journal of Orthopsychiatry, 77,* 165–173.

Downing, J. B., Richardson, H. B., Kinkler, L. A., & Goldberg, A. E. (2009). Making the decision: Factors influencing gay men's choice of an adoption path. *Adoption Quarterly, 12,* 247–271.

Farr, R. H., & Goldberg, A. E. (2018). Sexual orientation, gender identity, and adoption law. *Family Court Review, 56*(3), 374–383.

Farr, R. H., & Goldberg, A. E. (2019). Same-sex relationship dissolution and divorce: How will children be affected? In A. E. Goldberg & A. P. Romero (Eds.), *LGBTQ divorce and relationship dissolution: Psychological and legal perspectives and implications for practice* (pp. 151–172). Oxford University Press.

Farr, R. H., Oakley, M. K., & Ollen, E. W. (2016). School experiences of young children and their lesbian and gay adoptive parents. *Psychology of Sexual Orientation and Gender Diversity, 3*(4), 442–447.

Feugé, É. A., Cossette, L., Cyr, C., & Julien, D. (2019). Parental involvement among adoptive gay fathers: Associations with resources, time constraints, gender role, and child adjustment. *Psychology of Sexual Orientation and Gender Diversity, 6*(1), 1–10.

Gartrell, N., Banks, A., Reed, N., Hamilton, J., Rodas, C., & Deck, A. (2000). The National Lesbian Family Study: 3. Interviews with mothers of five-year-olds. *American Journal of Orthopsychiatry, 70,* 542-548.

Gartrell, N., & Bos, H. M. W. (2010). US National Longitudinal Lesbian Family Study: Psychological adjustment of 17-year-old adolescents. *Pediatrics, 126,* 28–36.

Gartrell, N., Deck, A., Rodas, C., Peyser, H., & Banks, A. (2005). The National Lesbian Family Study: 4. Interviews with the 10-year-old children. *American Journal of Orthopsychiatry, 75,* 518–524.

Gates, G. J. (2014). *Percent raising non-white children among couples with children under age 18.* Retrieved from https://www.drgaryjgates.com/couples-families-kids?lightbox=dataItem-ip8sjqae3

Gates, G. J. (2015). *Demographics of married and unmarried same-sex couples: Analyses of the 2013 American Community Survey.* Los Angeles. Retrieved from http://williamsinstitute.law.ucla.edu/wp-content/uploads/Demographics-Same-Sex-Couples-ACS2013-March-2015.pdf

Gates, G. J., Badgett, M. V. L., Macomber, J. E., & Chambers, K. (2007). *Adoption and foster care by gay and lesbian parents in the United States.* Washington, DC: The Urban Institute.

Ghabrial, M. A. (2017). "Trying to figure out where we belong": Narratives of racialized sexual minorities on community, identity, discrimination, and health. *Sexuality Research and Social Policy, 14*(1), 42–55.

Gianino, M., Goldberg, A. E., & Lewis, T. (2009). Family outings: Disclosure practices among adopted youth with gay and lesbian parents. *Adoption Quarterly, 12,* 205–228.

Goldberg, A. E. (2006). The transition to parenthood for lesbian couples. *Journal of GLBT Family Studies, 2,* 13–42.

Goldberg, A. E. (2009). Lesbian and heterosexual preadoptive couples' openness to transracial adoption. *American Journal of Orthopsychiatry, 79,* 103–117.

Goldberg, A. E. (2010). *Lesbian and gay parents and their children: Research on the family life cycle.* Washington, DC: American Psychological Association.

Goldberg, A. E. (2012). *Gay dads: Transitions to adoptive fatherhood*. New York, NY: New York University Press.

Goldberg, A. E. (2013). "Doing" and "undoing" gender: The meaning and division of housework in same-sex couples. *Journal of Family Theory and Review, 5*, 85–104.

Goldberg, A. E., & Allen, K. R. (2013). Same-sex relationship dissolution and LGB stepfamily formation: Perspectives of young adults with LGB parents. *Family Relations. 62*, 529–544.

Goldberg, A. E., Allen, K. R., Black, K. A., Frost, R. L., & Manley, M. H. (2018). "There is no perfect school": The complexity of school decision-making among lesbian and gay adoptive parents. *Journal of Marriage and Family, 80*(3), 684–703.

Goldberg, A. E., Black, K. A., Manley, M. H., & Frost, R. L. (2017). "We told them that we are both really involved parents": Sexual minority and heterosexual adoptive parents' engagement in school communities. *Gender & Education, 5*, 614–631.

Goldberg, A. E., Black, K. A., Sweeney, K., & Moyer, A. (2017). Lesbian, gay, and heterosexual adoptive parents' perceptions of inclusivity and receptiveness in early childhood education settings. *Journal of Research in Childhood Education, 31*, 141–159.

Goldberg, A. E., Downing, J. B., & Sauck, C. C. (2007). Choices, challenges, and tensions: Perspectives of lesbian prospective adoptive parents. *Adoption Quarterly, 10*, 33–64.

Goldberg, A. E., Downing, J. B., & Sauck, C. C. (2008). Perceptions of children's parental preferences in lesbian two-mother households. *Journal of Marriage and Family, 70*, 419–434.

Goldberg, A. E., & Garcia, R. (2015). Predictors of relationship dissolution in lesbian, gay, and heterosexual adoptive parents. *Journal of Family Psychology, 29*, 394–404

Goldberg, A. E., Garcia, R., & Manley, M. H. (2017). Monosexual and nonmonosexual women in same-sex couples' relationship quality during the first five years of parenthood. *Sexual and Relationship Therapy, 33*(1/2), 190–212.

Goldberg, A. E., Kinkler, L. A., Richardson, H. B., & Downing, J. B. (2011). Open adoption among lesbian, gay, and heterosexual couples: A qualitative study. *Journal of Marriage and Family, 73*, 502–518.

Goldberg, A. E., & Kuvalanka, K. A. (2012). Marriage (in)equality: The perspectives of adolescents and emerging adults with lesbian, gay, and bisexual parents. *Journal of Marriage and Family, 74*, 34–52.

Goldberg, A. E., & Perry-Jenkins, M. (2007). The division of labor and perceptions of parental roles: Lesbian couples across the transition to parenthood. *Journal of Social & Personal Relationships, 24*, 297–318.

Goldberg, A. E., & Romero, A. P. (Eds.). (2019). *LGBTQ divorce and relationship dissolution: Psychological and legal perspectives and implications for practice*. New York, NY: Oxford University Press.

Goldberg, A. E., Ross, L. E., Manley, M. H., & Mohr, J. J. (2017). Male-partnered sexual minority women: Sexual identity disclosure to health care providers during the perinatal period. *Psychology of Sexual Orientation and Gender Diversity, 4*(1), 105–114.

Goldberg, A. E., & Sayer, A. G. (2006). Lesbian couples' relationship quality across the transition to parenthood. *Journal of Marriage and Family, 68*, 87–100.

Goldberg, A. E., & Smith, J. Z. (2008). Social support and well-being in lesbian and heterosexual preadoptive parents. *Family Relations, 57*, 281–294.

Goldberg, A. E., & Smith, J. Z. (2011). Stigma, social context, and mental health: Lesbian and gay couples across the transition to adoptive parenthood. *Journal of Counseling Psychology, 58,* 139–150.

Goldberg, A. E., & Smith, J. Z. (2013a). Work conditions and mental health in lesbian and gay dual-earner parents. *Family Relations, 62,* 727–740.

Goldberg, A. E., & Smith, J. Z. (2013b). Predictors of psychological adjustment among early-placed adopted children with lesbian, gay, and heterosexual parents. *Journal of Family Psychology, 27,* 431–442.

Goldberg, A. E., & Smith, J. Z. (2014). Preschool selection considerations and experiences of school mistreatment among lesbian, gay, and heterosexual adoptive parents. *Early Childhood Research Quarterly, 29*(1), 64–75.

Goldberg, A. E., Smith, J. Z., & Kashy, D. A. (2010). Pre-adoptive factors predicting lesbian, gay, and heterosexual couples' relationship quality across the transition to adoptive parenthood. *Journal of Family Psychology, 24,* 221–232.

Goldberg, A. E., Smith, J. Z., McCormick, N. M., & Overstreet, N. M. (2019). Health behaviors and outcomes of parents in same-sex couples: An exploratory study. *Psychology of Sexual Orientation and Gender Diversity, 6*(3), 318–335.

Goldberg, A. E., Smith, J. Z., & Perry-Jenkins, M. (2012). The division of labor in lesbian, gay, and heterosexual new adoptive parents. *Journal of Marriage and Family, 74,* 812–828.

Goldberg, A. E., Sweeney, K., Black, K. A., & Moyer, A. (2016). Lesbian, gay, and heterosexual adoptive parents' socialization approaches to children's minority statuses. *Counseling Psychologist, 44*(2), 267–299.

Golombok, S., Mellish, L., Jennings, S., Casey, P., Tasker, F., & Lamb, M. E. (2014). Adoptive gay father families: Parent–child relationships and children's psychological adjustment. *Child Development, 85*(2), 456–468.

Golombok, S., Perry, B., Burston, A., Murray, C., Mooney-Somers, J., Stevens, M. & Golding, J. (2003). Children with lesbian parents: A community study. *Developmental Psychology, 39,* 20–33.

Gonzales, G., & Blewett, L. A. (2013). Disparities in health insurance among children with same-sex parents. *Pediatrics, 132*(4), 703–711.

Gonzales, G., & Henning-Smith, C. (2017). The Affordable Care Act and health insurance coverage for lesbian, gay, and bisexual adults: Analysis of the behavioral risk factor surveillance system. *LGBT Health, 4*(1), 62–67.

Graham, J. M., & Barnow, Z. B. (2013). Stress and social support in gay, lesbian, and heterosexual couples: Direct effects and buffering models. *Journal of Family Psychology, 27*(4), 569–578.

Green, R-.J., Rubio, R. J., Rothblum, E. D., Bergman, K., & Katuzny, K. E. (2019). Gay fathers by surrogacy: Prejudice, parenting, and well-being of female and male children. *Psychology of Sexual Orientation and Gender Diversity, 6*(3), 269–283.

Gregg, I. (2018). The health care experiences of lesbian women becoming mothers. *Nursing for Women's Health, 22*(1), 41–50.

Hayman, B., Wilkes, L., Halcomb, E. J., & Jackson, D. (2013). Marginalised mothers: Lesbian women negotiating heteronormative health care services. *Contemporary Nurse, 44*(1), 120–127.

Hayman, B., Wilkes, L., Halcomb, E. J., & Jackson, D. (2015). Lesbian women choosing motherhood: The journey to conception. *Journal of GLBT Family Studies, 11*(4), 395–409.

Hequembourg, A. (2004). Unscripted motherhood: Lesbian mothers negotiating incompletely institutionalized family relationships. *Journal of Social and Personal Relationships, 21*(6), 739–762.

Hollingsworth, L., & Ruffin, V. M. (2002). Why are so many U. S. families adopting internationally? A social exchange perspective. *Journal of Human Behavior in the Social Environment, 6,* 81–97.

Hutchinson, M. K., Thompson, A. C., & Cederbaum, J. A. (2006). Multisystem factors contributing to disparities in preventive health care among lesbian women. *Journal of Obstetric, Gynecologic, and Neonatal Nursing, 35*(3), 393–402.

Jadwin-Cakmak, L. A., Pingel, E. S., Harper, G. W., & Bauermeister, J. A. (2015). Coming out to dad: Young gay and bisexual men's experiences disclosing same-sex attraction to their fathers. *American Journal of Men's Health, 9*(4), 274–288.

Jennings, S., Mellish, L., Tasker, F., Lamb, M., & Golombok, S. (2014). Why adoption? Gay, lesbian, and heterosexual adoptive parents' reproductive experiences and reasons for adoption. *Adoption Quarterly, 17*(3), 205–226.

Johnson, S. M., & O'Connor, E. (2002). *The gay baby boom: The psychology of gay parenthood.* New York, NY: New York University Press.

Kail, B. L., Acosta, K. L., & Wright, E. R. (2015). State-level marriage equality and the health of same-sex couples. *American Journal of Public Health, 105*(6), 1101–1105.

Kimberly, C., & Moore, A. (2015). Attitudes to practice: National survey of adoption obstacles faced by gay and lesbian prospective parents. *Journal of Gay and Lesbian Social Services, 27*(4), 436–456.

Kinkler, L. A., & Goldberg, A. E. (2011). Working with what we've got: Perceptions of barriers and supports among same-sex adopting couples in non-metropolitan areas. *Family Relations, 60,* 387–403.

Kosciw, J. G., & Diaz, E. M. (2008). *Involved, invisible, ignored: The experiences of lesbian, gay, bisexual, and transgender parents and their children in our nation's K-12 schools.* New York, NY: Gay, Lesbian and Straight Education Network.

Kurdek, L. (2001). Differences between heterosexual-nonparent couples and gay, lesbian, and heterosexual-parent couples. *Journal of Family Issues, 22,* 727–754.

Kurdek, L. A. (2006). Differences between partners from heterosexual, gay, and lesbian cohabiting couples. *Journal of Marriage and Family, 68,* 509–528.

Kurdek, L. A. (2007). The allocation of household labor by partners in gay and lesbian couples. *Journal of Family Issues, 28,* 132–148.

Lannutti, P. J. (2011). Security, recognition, and misgivings: Exploring older same-sex couples' experiences of legally recognized same-sex marriage. *Journal of Social & Personal Relationships, 28,* 64–82.

Lavner, J. A., Waterman, J., & Peplau, L. A. (2012). Can gay and lesbian parents promote healthy development in high-risk children adopted from foster care? *American Journal of Orthopsychiatry, 82*(4), 465–472.

Legate, N., Ryan, R., & Weinstein, N. (2012). Is coming out always a 'good thing'? Exploring the relations of autonomy support, outness, and wellness for lesbian, gay, and bisexual individuals. *Social Psychology & Personality Science, 3,* 145–152.

Malebranche, D. J., Fields, E. L., Bryant, L. O., & Harper, S. R. (2009). Masculine socialization and sexual risk behaviors among Black men who have sex with men: A qualitative exploration. *Men and Masculinities, 12,* 90–112.

Malmquist, A., & Nelson, K. Z. (2014). Efforts to maintain a "just great" story: Lesbian parents' talk about encounters with professionals in fertility clinics and maternal and child health care services. *Feminism and Psychology, 24*(1), 56–73.

McCarn, S. R., & Fassinger, R. E. (1996). Revisioning sexual minority identity formation: A New model of lesbian identity and its implications for counseling and research. *The Counseling Psychologist, 24,* 508–534.

McDermott, E. (2006). Surviving in dangerous places: Lesbian identity performances in the workplace, social class, and psychological health. *Feminism & Psychology, 16,* 193–211.

Mendez, S. N., Holman, E. G., Oswald, R. F., & Izenstark, D. (2016). Minority stress in the context of rural economic hardship: One lesbian mother's story. *Journal of GLBT Family Studies, 12*(5), 491–511.

Merighi, J. R., & Grimes, M. D. (2000). Coming out to families in a multicultural context. *Families in Society, 81,* 32–41.

Meuwly, N., Feinstein, B., Davila, J., Nunez, D., Garcia, D., & Bodenmann, G. (2013). Relationship quality among Swiss women in opposite-sex versus same-sex romantic relationships. *Swiss Journal of Psychology, 72,* 229–233.

Meyer, I. (2003). Prejudice, social stress, and mental health in lesbian, gay, and bisexual populations: Conceptual issues and research evidence. *Psychological Bulletin, 129,* 674–697.

Moore, M. R. (2011). *Invisible families: Gay identities, relationships, and motherhood among Black women.* Berkeley: University of California Press.

Moreau, J. (2019). Anti-LGBTQ adoption bills "snowballing" in state legislatures, rights group says. Retrieved from https://www.nbcnews.com/feature/nbc-out/anti-lgbtq-adoption-bills-snowballing-state-legislatures-rights-group-says-n991156

Movement Advancement Project. (2019). *Equality maps: Health care laws and policies.* Retrieved from http://www.lgbtmap.org/equality-maps/health care_laws_and_policies

Nadal, K. L., & Corpus, M. J. H. (2013). "Tomboys" and "baklas": Experiences of lesbian and gay Filipino Americans. *Asian American Journal of Psychology, 4*(3), 166–175.

Nicol, P., Chapman, R., Watkins, R., Young, J., & Shields, L. (2013). Tertiary paediatric hospital health professionals' attitudes to lesbian, gay, bisexual and transgender parents seeking health care for their children. *Journal of Clinical Nursing, 22*(23/24), 3396–3405.

Office for Civil Rights. (2019). *Protecting statutory conscience rights in health care; Delegations of authority* (Pub. L. No. 84 FR 23170, 103). Department of Health and Human Services. Retrieved from https://www.federalregister.gov/documents/2019/05/21/2019-09667/protecting-statutory-conscience-rights-in-health-care-delegations-of-authority

Ogolsky, B. G., Monk, J. K., Rice, T. K. M., & Oswald, R. F. (2019). Personal well-being across the transition to marriage equality: A longitudinal analysis. *Journal of Family Psychology, 33*(4), 422–432.

Orne, J. (2011). "You will always have to 'out' yourself": Reconsidering coming out through strategic outness. *Sexualities, 14,* 681–703.

Patterson, C. J., Hurt, S., & Mason, C. D. (1998). Families of the lesbian baby boom: Children's contact with grandparents and other adults. *American Journal of Orthopsychiatry, 68,* 390–399.

Peplau, L. A., & Fingerhut, A. W. (2007). The close relationships of lesbians and gay men. *Annual Review of Psychology, 58,* 373–408.

Perrin, E. C., Hurley, S. M., Mattern, K., Flavin, L., & Pinderhughes, E. E. (2019). Barriers and stigma experienced by gay fathers and their children. *Pediatrics, 143*(2), e20180683.

Perrin, E. C., Pinderhughes, E. E., Mattern, K., Hurley, S. M., & Newman, R. A. (2016). Experiences of children with gay fathers. *Clinical Pediatrics, 55*(14), 1305–1317.

Potter, D. (2012). Same-sex parent families and children's academic achievement. *Journal of Marriage and Family, 74,* 556–571.

Potter, E., & Allen, K. R. (2016). Agency and access: How gay fathers secure health insurance for their families. *Journal of GLBT Family Studies, 12*(3), 300–317.

Priddle, H. (2015). How well are lesbians treated in UK fertility clinics? *Human Fertility, 18*(3), 194–199.

Riggs, D.W. (2011). Australian lesbian and gay foster carers negotiating the child protection system: Strengths and challenges. *Sexuality Research and Social Policy, 8,* 215–226.

Rosenfeld, M. J. (2010). Nontraditional families and childhood progress through school. *Demography, 47,* 755–775.

Rosenthal, L., & Starks, T. J. (2015). Relationship stigma and relationship outcomes in interracial and same-sex relationships: Examination of sources and buffers. *Journal of Family Psychology, 29*(6), 818–830.

Ross, L. E., Dobinson, C., & Eady, A. (2010). Perceived determinants of mental health for bisexual people: A qualitative examination. *American Journal of Public Health, 100,* 496–502.

Rostosky, S. S., & Riggle, E. D. B. (2019). What makes same-sex relationships endure? In A. E. Goldberg & A. P. Romero (Eds.), *LGBTQ divorce and relationship dissolution: Psychological and legal perspectives and implications for practice* (pp. 49–69). New York, NY: Oxford University Press.

Rostosky, S. S., Riggle, E. D. B., Savage, T. A., Roberts, S. D., & Singletary, G. (2008). Interracial same-sex couples' perceptions of stress and coping: An exploratory study. *Journal of GLBT Family Studies, 4,* 277–299.

Russell, G. M., & Richards, J. A. (2003). Stressor and resilience factors for lesbians, gay men, and bisexuals confronting antigay politics. *American Journal of Community Psychology, 31,* 313–328.

Sabin, J. A., Riskind, R. G., & Nosek, B. A. (2015). Health care providers' implicit and explicit attitudes toward lesbian women and gay men. *American Journal of Public Health, 105*(9), 1831–1841.

Scout, Lombardi, E., & White, B. (2010). To the Editors. *Journal of Gay & Lesbian Mental Health, 14*(3), 257–258.

Shapiro, J. (2013). The law governing LGBT-parent families. In A. E. Goldberg & K. R. Allen (Eds.), *LGBT-parent families: Innovations in research and implications for practice* (pp. 291–304). New York, NY: Springer.

Shulman, J., Gotta, G., & Green, R.-J. (2012). Will marriage matter? Effects of marriage anticipated by same-sex couples. *Journal of Family Issues, 33,* 158–181.

Solomon, S. E., Rothblum, E. D., & Balsam, K. F. (2005). Money, housework, sex, and conflict: Same-sex couples in civil unions, those not in civil unions, and heterosexual married siblings. *Sex Roles, 52,* 561–575.

Spidsberg, B. D. (2007). Vulnerable and strong: Lesbian women encountering maternity care. *Journal of Advanced Nursing, 60,* 478–486.

Steinbugler, A. C. (2005). Visibility as privilege and danger: Heterosexual and same-sex interracial intimacy in the 21st century. *Sexualities, 8,* 425–443.

Sumontha, J., Farr, R. H., & Patterson, C. J. (2016). Social support and coparenting among lesbian, gay, and heterosexual adoptive parents. *Journal of Family Psychology, 30*(8), 987–996.

Tasker, F. L. (2013). Lesbian and gay parenting post-heterosexual divorce and separation. In A. E. Goldberg & K. R. Allen (Eds.), *LGBT-parent families: Innovations in research and implications for practice* (pp. 3–20). New York, NY: Springer.

Titlestad, A., & Robinson, K. (2019). Navigating parenthood as two women; The positive aspects and strengths of female same-sex parenting. *Journal of GLBT Family Studies, 15*(2), 186–209.

Tornello, S. L., Kruczkowski, S. M., & Patterson, C. J. (2015). Division of labor and relationship quality among male same-sex couples who became fathers via surrogacy. *Journal of GLBT Family Studies, 11*(4), 375–394.

Totenhagen, C. J., Randall, A. K., & Lloyd, K. (2018). Stress and relationship functioning in same-sex couples: The vulnerabilities of internalized homophobia and outness. *Family Relations*, 67(3), 399–413.

Twist, M. L. C., Bergdall, M. K., Belous, C. K., & Maier, C. A. (2017). Electronic visibility management of lesbian, gay, and bisexual identities and relationships in young adulthood. *Journal of Couple and Relationship Therapy*, 16(4), 271–285.

United States Department of Health & Human Services: Office on Women's Health. (2000). *Lesbian health fact sheet*. Retrieved from https://permanent.access.gpo.gov/lps38813/Lesbian%20Health.pdf

van Gelderen, L., Bos, H. M. W., Gartrell, N. K., Hermanns, J., & Perrin, E. C. (2012). Quality of life of adolescents raised from birth by lesbian mothers: The US National Longitudinal Lesbian Family Study. *Journal of Developmental & Behavioral Pediatrics, 33,* 1–7.

Vaughan, M. D. & Waehler, C. A. (2010). Coming out growth: Conceptualizing and measuring stress-related growth associated with coming out to others as a sexual minority. *Journal of Adult Development, 17,* 94–109.

Vencill, J. A., Carlson, S., Iantaffi, A., & Miner, M. (2017). Mental health, relationships, and sex: Exploring patterns among bisexual individuals in mixed orientation relationships. *Sexual and Relationship Therapy, 33*(1/2), 14–33.

Wainright J. L., Russell, S. T., & Patterson, C. J. (2004). Psychosocial adjustment, school outcomes, and romantic relationships of adolescents with same-sex parents. *Child Development*, 75(6),1886–1898.Webster,C. R.,&Telingator,C. J. (2016). Lesbian, gay, bisexual, and transgender families. *Pediatric Clinics of North America*, 63(6), 1107–1119.

Wells, M. B., & Lang, S. N. (2016). Supporting same-sex mothers in the Nordic child health field: A systematic literature review and meta-synthesis of the most gender equal countries. *Journal of Clinical Nursing*, 25(23/24), 3469–3483.

Whitchurch, G. G., & Constantine, L. L. (1993). Systems theory. In P. G. Boss, W. J., Doherty, R., LaRossa, W. R. Schumm, & S. K. Steinmetz (Eds.), *Sourcebook of family theories and methods: A contextual approach* (pp. 325–352). New York, NY: Plenum.

Willis, P. (2011). Laboring in silence: Young lesbian, gay, bisexual, and queer-identifying workers' negotiations of the workplace closet in Australian organizations. *Youth and Society, 43*(3), 957–981.

Wojnar, D. M., & Katzenmeyer, A. (2014). Experiences of preconception, pregnancy, and new motherhood for lesbian nonbiological mothers. *Journal of Obstetric, Gynecologic, and Neonatal Nursing, 43*(1), 50–60.

Wood, K. (2016). "It's all a bit pantomime": An exploratory study of gay and lesbian adopters and foster-carers in England and Wales. *British Journal of Social Work, 46*(6), 1708–1723.

Yon Leau, C., & Muñoz-Laboy, M. (2010). "I don't like to say that I'm anything": Sexuality politics and cultural critique among sexual-minority Latino youth. *Sexuality Research and Social Policy, 7*(2), 105–117.

CHAPTER 7

Stress and Coping in Later Life

Áine M. Humble

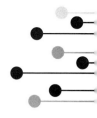

Vignette

Alfonso and Malena Gomez live in a small town, and their two children, Carmen and Eduardo, and four grand-children live nearby. Alfonso, 68, retired from construction, and Malena, 61, retired from teaching. Although they both retired this year, Malena would have preferred to keep working a few more years. Alfonso loves to fish and take long walks when the weather is good. Malena reads and does crossword puzzles and draws strength from her religious faith. Alfonso has big plans for retirement; he wants to travel in a newly purchased RV and go fishing as often as he can. They feel they are healthy; however, Alfonso has macular degeneration and difficulty sleeping, and Malena has arthritis. In recent years, she has also showed some short-term memory loss. Carmen has been pushing to get her mother's memory checked, but Alfonso is resistant. He is afraid of what they may find, and being a caregiver for his wife is not something he wants to consider. Carmen provides most of the assistance to her parents and knows this will only increase. She feels frustrated that Eduardo is not "stepping up to the plate" and doing more to help out their parents. Because Carmen works full time and has a family of her own, she also worries her responsibilities will eventually overwhelm her and negatively affect her marriage or employment.

As illustrated in the vignette, aging takes place within the context of families. Yet, it is often viewed primarily from a human development perspective, with little recognition given to the importance of family relationships or the impact that family roles and responsibilities have on the aging process. In response to this situation, the field of *family gerontology* emerged to draw attention to the intersection between aging, family systems, and the life course (Roberto, Blieszner, & Allen, 2006). This intersection can be conceptualized from the perspective of the aging individual or from the family system, with emphasis on the experiences of older family members (Blieszner & Bedford, 2012). A bidirectional approach enables researchers and practitioners to consider the influences that family members have on individual responses to the processes of aging as well as older adults' impacts on their families.

In this chapter, I discuss individual and family challenges that can coincide with aging. I emphasize the concept of the "aging family" as it pertains to later life family relationships, transitions, and the social support networks of older family members. I discuss the demographic changes taking place in the United States that have profoundly affected the structure of American society. Using both ecological systems theory (Bronfenbrenner, 1979) and family stress and resilience theory (Allen & Henderson, 2017), I explore stressful events commonly associated with aging, focusing on retirement, caregiving, elder abuse, and skipped generation families. Finally, models of coping and adaptation applied in later life are reviewed.

The Aging Family

From a family development perspective, an *aging family* consists of primary members who are middle age (at least 40 years old) and older (Silverstein & Giarrusso, 2010) and who are experiencing later-life events and transitions such as retirement, widowhood, later-life divorce (Wu, 2017) or marriage, grandparenthood, caregiving, and end-of-life issues. The study of aging families pertains to entire family systems, with emphasis on relationships, transitions, and social support networks of older family members.

Everyone ages within a family context, regardless of family size or whether all members are biologically related. Not all older adults, however, follow a traditional life course (i.e., marry, have children, launch children, retire). Factors such as high divorce rates; increased cohabitation, remarriage, and same-sex marriage later in life; and reduced fertility "have altered the microcontext in which intergenerational, spousal, and sibling relationships function" (Silverstein & Giarrusso, 2010, p. 1039). Additionally, a new and increasing kind of partnership occurring later in life is one in which two heterosexual individuals maintain separate households but are committed to each other in a long-term relationship (this is new only for heterosexual couples because same-sex couples have been in these kind of relationships for years due to not being able to marry; Connidis & Barnett, 2019). Such configurations are called "LLATs" (living apart together later in life) and they are more common in European countries than in the United States (Connidis, Borell, & Karlsson, 2017). Because of the family diversity in the United States and worldwide, scholars need to recognize the many types of families that impact individual aging experiences. In this chapter, I employ a broad definition of family, recognizing the diversity that exists, and focus on aging family systems rather than individual aging family members.

Aging families can vary in ways such as family size and structure, emotional connection, geographic distance, and family roles. Aging families include opposite-sex and same-sex couples in cohabiting, common-law, or long-term marriages, with or without children; and those who are newly married (e.g., Humble, 2013), divorced, or widowed. Some have four or more living generations, whereas others have only one or two generations. Some families have emotionally close ties with members interacting on a regular basis, whereas others display conflicted interaction styles, feelings of ambivalence, or infrequent interaction due to personal reasons (e.g., estrangement; Agllias, 2016) or geographic distance. Regardless of such differences, however, many face similar later-life transitions and age-related changes, and it is by focusing on these similarities that scholars can better understand how aging families function.

Two factors set aging families apart from younger families. The first factor relates to the extended family history that members share. How members of aging families communicate with one another and how they respond to anticipated changes (e.g., retirement) or family crises, for example, are influenced by interactional patterns and coping strategies established in earlier years (Connidis & Barnett, 2019). A long family history can be a source of strength for family members or, alternatively, a painful barrier difficult to overcome.

Another factor that sets aging families apart from families earlier in their development is the likelihood that they will experience coinciding joyful and painful events. At no other life stage is the family system more likely to encounter growth and loss in such close proximity. For example, the loss of a spouse or partner can have a profound impact on the well-being of the surviving individual as well as challenge the stability and functioning of an entire family system. At the same time, a grandchild's birth can be an opportunity for increased family cohesion. Both normative and nonnormative later-life transitions and events can contribute to both joyful and painful emotions, making for complex and bittersweet family dynamics. In fact, *ambivalence*—the "simultaneously held opposing feelings or emotions that are due in part to countervailing expectations about how individuals should act" (Connidis & McMullin, 2002, p. 558)—can be a common response to transitions and complex intergenerational relationships occurring later in life (Silverstein & Giarrusso, 2010). For example, older rural parents in China can show ambivalence toward their children—in particular, sons—when the adult children do not achieve the parents' desired level of upward mobility (Guo, Chi, & Silverstein, 2013). Sociological ambivalence is also present in heterosexual LLATs, when older couples negotiate gender in a different way than expected and also reject societal expectations that they must live with their intimate partners in the same household (Connidis et al., 2017; Connidis & Barnett, 2019).

Demographic Trends

Families exist within a larger social and cultural context, and scholars can gain a better understanding of aging families by recognizing the many demographic changes that are currently taking place in the United States and globally. These shifting trends directly affect how aging families evolve and respond to the demands of later life. For example, at the international level, "vast economic, technological, legal, and political changes" (Zoekler & Silverstein, 2016, p. 169) affect how individuals work (e.g., at what age they retire or whether they move to another country for employment) and, in turn, affect their families.

Demographic changes that took place in the United States during the 20th century have had profound effects on the structure of American society. The average life expectancy of an infant born in the United States, for example, increased from 47.3 years in 1900 to 78.7 years in 2010 (U.S. Census Bureau, 2014). This is the greatest increase in longevity ever documented in human history, and it has resulted in the rapid growth of the older adult population. Given these dramatic changes in longevity combined with the aging of the baby boom population (individuals born between 1946 and 1964), growth in the older adult population is predicted to continue at a relatively rapid rate. In 2016, 49.2 million Americans were over the age of 65 (Roberts, Ogunwole, Blakeslee, & Rabe, 2018), and the older population (65+) will make up 20% of the U.S. population by 2029, the time at which all baby boomers will be 65 years or older (Colby & Ortman, 2014).

Gerontologists frequently differentiate individuals over 65 years old into three categories: *young-old* (65 to 74), *middle-old* (75 to 84), and *oldest-old* (85 and above) (Hooyman & Kiyak, 2011). Those in the oldest-old population have been the fastest growing segment of older adults, increasing from under 4% between the years of 1900 and 1940 to 13.6% of the aging population in 2010 (U.S. Census Bureau, 2014). This group is more likely than younger elders to have health or mobility limitations (Roberts et al., 2018), experience the death of a spouse, or require instrumental assistance. It was expected, however, that this percentage would decline for the decade following 2010 and then remain below 2010 rates when increasing numbers of baby boomers turn 65 (U.S. Census Bureau, 2014).

In addition to cohort differences in the older adult population, gender differences also exist with regard to longevity, marital status, and living situation. Life expectancy for a female child born in 2010 in the United States is estimated at 81 years; for a male child it is 76 years (U.S. Census Bureau, 2014). Due to men's higher mortality rates across the life span and "differences in attitudes, behaviors, social roles and biological risks between men and women," women outnumber men in later life (He, Sengupta, Velkoff, & DeBarros, 2005, p. 36). In the oldest age group (85 and older), women outnumber men at a ratio of about 2 to 1 (Roberts et al., 2018). However, as American women increasingly enter the workforce, experience higher stress levels, and adopt unhealthy lifestyle habits, it is expected they will lose their longevity advantage over men (U.S. Census Bureau, 2014). Related to longevity is the common experience of widowhood in later life; particularly for heterosexual women who frequently outlive their spouses. Higher widowhood rates for older women contribute significantly to the likelihood they will live alone. In fact, in 2010, of those 65 and over living alone, 71% were women (U.S. Census Bureau, 2014).

The older adult population in the United States is racially and ethnically diverse and the level of diversity in this group is predicted to increase (Ortman,

Velkoff, & Hogan, 2014), including immigrants—a group that includes both foreign-born older adults who have lived in the United States for many years as well as those who recently migrated to the United States to join family or were admitted as refugees (Leach, 2009). The Hispanic population is expected to grow the most dramatically, increasing from 7% of the total aging population in 2010 to 18% by 2050. Minority groups will also increase in the oldest-old group, although they are less represented in this group compared to their proportion of the general population (Roberts et al., 2018). Race and ethnicity have an impact on life expectancy (Medina, Sabo, & Vespa, 2019).

Finally, it is difficult to estimate the number of older LGBTQ (lesbian, gay, bisexual, transgender, and queer) individuals in the United States primarily due to their reluctance to self-identify for fear of rejection or retribution. However, an estimated 2.7 million individuals 50 years and older identify as LGBTQ, and by 2060 this may exceed 5 million (Fredriksen-Goldsen, Kim, Bryan, Shiu, & Emlet, 2017).

Stress In Later Life

Scholars recognize the different types of stressful experiences older adults encounter, such as chronic role strains, daily hassles, and lifetime trauma (Krause, 2007), and they emphasize the effects of such stress on health and well-being (Aldwin, Yancura, & Boeninger, 2007). Research often focuses on the coping strategies of aging individuals rather than how aging families experience and adapt to later life challenges, yet these stressors are often experienced within the context of a family system with multiple generations affected.

In accordance with ecological systems theory (Bronfenbrenner, 1979), aging individuals and their families confront stressors at multiple systemic levels. At the *macrosystem* level (i.e., the cultural contexts influencing how people live), families must deal with government policies, economic realities, and social expectations surrounding care. "Isms" such as ageism, racism, sexism, and heterosexism and political ideologies are also examples of macrosystem factors. At the *exosystem* level, formalized health care, insurance companies, care facilities, and other professional agencies are involved. At the *meso-* and *microsystem* levels respectively, aging families manage their home environments, neighborhood resources, transportation accessibility, and renegotiate family roles and responsibilities.

Stressors encountered during the young-old years can differ significantly from those encountered during the middle-old years and oldest-old years. During the young-old years, a majority of seniors are making their own decisions, engaging with family and community activities, and experiencing anticipated and normative life events (e.g., retirement). These transitions can be stressful because they involve role changes and family adjustments, but they also offer opportunities for growth and development. In later life, seniors often face changes that take place within a context of physical decline and the contraction of social and family interaction patterns, and many relationships can change at this stage in a person's life (Scott, Jackson, & Bergman, 2011). Moreover, decisions can be more difficult because they relate to relinquishing power and changing levels of independence. Examples of these later life decisions can include accepting assistance from family or service professionals, relocating to a new city to be closer to one's adult children, placing a spouse in a nursing home, or relinquishing one's driver's license. However, as age increases, the likelihood of an individual encountering events related to physical frailty, disability, and cognitive impairment increase. As a result, stressors experienced in late life, especially age 85 and beyond, are associated with greater stress. It is important to note, however, that some stress occurring later in life may be cumulative, having developed over a long period of time (Scott et al., 2011)—change over time, or the *chronosystem*, is also a part of the ecological model.

Family stress and resilience theory combines several theories to examine the inevitable stressors that families face over the life course and how they cope with them (Allen & Henderson, 2017). A central component of this theory is the Double ABC-X model of family stress, which looks at how a stressor event (the A factor) interacts with resources (the B factor) and families' perceptions of the event as stressful (the C factor) to result in a crisis (the X factor), and what happens postcrisis. The *perception* of the event is the most powerful variable in explaining family stress (Allen & Henderson, 2017; Henry, Morris, & Harrist, 2015). Thus, it is critical that scholars understand what both older adults *and* their families identify as stressful life events. Older adults report experiences in three stressor areas: (a) health and physical functioning, (b) personal and social problems, and (c) difficulties faced by family members (Aldwin, 1990; Aldwin, Sutton, Chiara, & Spiro, 1996). Events that appeared to cause the highest stress ratings included the death of a child, institutionalization of a spouse, or death of a spouse. Least stressful life events were a spouse's retirement, the individual's own retirement, and an increase in paid or volunteer responsibilities. A common assumption is that the circumstances individuals identify as stressful are those that affect them directly. However, research indicates that older adults spend considerable time worrying about other people's problems (e.g., a spouse's health, an adult child's marriage, a grandchild's life choices). Aldwin (1990) and others refer to this as *nonegocentric stress* (Sutin, Costa, Wethington, & Eaton, 2010).

There are competing perceptions regarding how much stress is experienced in old age. On one hand, seniors encounter fewer life events and transitions than do younger adults (Aldwin et al., 2007; Stawski, Sliwinski, Almeida, & Smyth, 2008). Later life is frequently characterized as a time of fewer responsibilities than young adulthood, less salient social roles, decreased time demands, and therefore greater flexibility and freedom. On the other hand, aging can be considered a stressful life process (Lawrence & Schigelone, 2002). One study found that more than 4 out of 5 individuals over the age of 60 had experienced a *major life-event* stressor in the past 12 months—the most frequently reported events were a family member or friend's death, financial difficulties, and declining health (Bellingtier, Neupert, & Kotter-Grühn, 2017). Stressors may also be characterized as *daily stressors*, such as a family's concerns about and strategies related to their aging parent's ability to take their medication, how to help that person get to their medical appointment amid other responsibilities, or a frail senior's struggles with taking their dog for a walk.

Although many stressors associated with aging may be challenging, aging itself is not only about decline and disability. Getting older can involve personal growth and development, a sense of satisfaction with one's accomplishments, and enthusiasm for new experiences and transitions. Researchers use the terms *stress-related growth* and *posttraumatic growth* (Aldwin & Igarashi, 2012) to refer to positive outcomes emerging from stress such as resilience. Resilience is not just an individual characteristic, however. It is embedded in and supported by relationships rather than simply a person's internal sense of hardiness (Walsh, 2006). Additionally, the family resilience approach incorporates ecological concepts by recognizing the important role that communities and broader contexts play in supporting families (Henry et al., 2015). Aldwin and Igarashi (2012) point out that these external systems "do not *cause* individual resilience; rather, they provide an *opportunity* to use resources" (p. 118).

Stressful Events In Later Life

Many later-life events can test the adaptability and coping resources of aging families. Two major transitions that can be stressful are retirement and caregiving. Elder abuse and unanticipated caring for grandchildren (skipped-generation families) are other stressful experiences that can happen to a minority of older adults. In this section, I briefly discuss these four stressors and the implications they have for aging families.

Retirement

Retirement traditionally refers to a person's withdrawal from the paid labor force. It is currently experienced by the majority of older adults, both men and women. It can be a long-anticipated event that provides new opportunities for personal growth and development (Fehr, 2012), the discovery of new interests and relationships, and a release from demanding time constraints. At the same time, it can pose unique challenges, including the loss of a work role identity, decreased social contact with peers, a reduced sense of personal achievement, and loss of economic stability (Szinovacz, 2003). There are a variety of outcomes with regard to retirement well-being. Data from the longitudinal U.S. Health and Retirement Study show that in between 1998 and 2012, fewer people report being very satisfied (a decline from 60.4% to 48.6%) and more people report being not at all satisfied (an increase from 7.9% to 10.5%) (Banerjee, 2016). The increase of people moderately satisfied had increased from 31.7% to 40.9% during that same time.

Financial stress is a key consideration for retirees, not only in terms of one's eligibility to retire but also in relation to one's future economic security. Many retirees may return to work for financial reasons, and the fact that many people still work "in retirement" raises the question of whether the traditional definition of retirement still makes sense. In the past, retirement typically meant leaving a full-time job and no longer working for pay, but there is increasing diversity in how people view and experience retirement (Denton & Spencer, 2009) and deal with the associated stressors. New definitions of retirement reflect the multiple pathways individuals now choose, such as transitioning to a new job or career, reducing employment hours but continuing to work, or finding recreational employment that is less stressful and more enjoyable. Further, people can "unre-tire" by reentering the workforce or "reretire" by choosing to retire more than once (Shultz & Wang, 2011). In addition to financial preparation, individuals must also be psychologically prepared for retirement, and they benefit from having a purpose in their lives as well as having support from their families (Asebedo & Seay, 2014).

Retirement is a significant life transition, and it affects not only the individual but also the entire family system, including one's spouse or partner, children, and extended kin (van Solinge & Henkens, 2005; Szinovacz & Davey, 2005). With regard to marriage, retirement may reinforce preretirement marital quality. That is, those with good marriages prior to retirement will experience increased marital quality, whereas those in unhappy marriages will experience a decline in marital quality (Dew & Yorgason, 2010). For couples who jointly retire, especially those who share mutual interests and have effective communication skills, retirement can be a time of increased marital satisfaction and renewed intimacy. For other couples, however, extended free hours together with limited structure can result in greater conflict or may reveal an indisputable lack of common interests.

Retirement may impact spouses or partners differently as well, depending on the timing. When heterosexual couples experience *dysynchronized retirement* (retiring at different times), retirement satisfaction can be negatively affected; this is particularly true when wives continue to be employed after their husbands retire (Davey & Szinovacz, 2004). However, women who are pressured by their husbands to retire at the same time as their husbands and before they are ready to retire—such as Malena Gomez in the vignette at the start of this chapter—can experience difficulties (Zimmerman, Mitchell, Wister, & Gutman, 2000). Little research is carried out on same-sex couples and sexual minority individuals with regard to retirement (Mock & Schryer, 2017).

Caregiving

Chronic illness or disability is associated with advanced age, and such changes create increased needs for caregiving and major familial adjustments. The impact of a stroke, for example, creates stressors such as immediate physical and cogni-tive changes in a family member that need to be addressed, as well as ongoing uncertainty about how that person will recuperate from the stroke and how long a caregiving role will last (Hesamzadeh, Dalvandi, Maddah, Khoshknab, & Ahmadi, 2015).

A *caregiver* provides unpaid assistance to someone physically or psychologically impaired and therefore dependent on others (in contrast, *care providers* are individuals who are *paid* to assist a person). Approximately 39 million Americans were caregivers to an adult over 50 (National Alliance for Caregiving & AARP, 2015). The typical age of a caregiver is 49 years (but 1 in 10 is 75 years or older) and two-thirds are women. In about 10% of cases, the person is caring for their spouse.

Caregiving takes the form of different types of assistance. *Instrumental support* (hands-on assistance with daily functioning) and *emotional support* (actions and gestures expressing affection and encouragement) are two general types of assistance that researchers have frequently explored (Pearlin, Aneshensel, Mullan, & Whitlatch, 1995). *Care management* (e.g., arranging for paid care and seeking out information and resources) is a care activity seldom studied (Sadak, Wright, & Borson, 2016) but increasingly experienced, particularly for individuals providing assistance from a distance.

Family caregiving is provided by spouses and partners, adult children, extended family members, and fictive kin, and the motivation to provide care is what sets it apart from assistance supplied by paid sources. Individuals assist the aging family member because of feelings of love and affection or filial responsibility (Silverstein, Gans, & Yang, 2006). However, in some cases, care is provided because of family pressure to do so or because there is no one else to do it—more than half of caregivers report that they had no choice but to take on the caregiving role (National Alliance for Caregiving & AARP, 2015). Moreover, ambivalence can also be present even when a person chooses to take on a caregiving role (Pitzer, Fingerman, & Lefkowitz, 2011).

Many other factors influence who becomes a caregiver, with gender at the forefront. As with the Gomez family, featured in this chapter's vignette, caregiving responsibilities frequently fall to the women in families. Although increasing numbers of men have become caregivers in recent years, most families follow a gendered family pattern in which women are more likely than men to take on caregiving roles (e.g., if a wife is not available, a daughter or daughter-in-law takes over, rather than a son; Lai, Luk, & Andruske, 2007; Uhlenberg & Cheuk, 2008). The extent of the disability, potential caregivers' geographic proximity to the care recipient, work schedule flexibility, physical health, and available resources influence who will provide care. The relationship history between family members is important; for instance, stepfamilies and divorce may make intergenerational support to aging parents less certain (Silverstein & Giarrusso, 2010). Finally, culture also influences how families approach caregiving responsibilities; *familismo* in Latinx families and *filial piety* in Asian cultures encourage dedication and loyalty to one's family, thus encouraging family caregiving (Lai et al., 2007; Radina, Gibbons, & Li, 2009).

Caregiving can bring emotional closeness with a care recipient, a sense of accomplishment or purpose, and increased family cohesion (Coon, 2012). However, caregivers often face extensive demands on their time and difficulties that test their physical and mental endurance, referred to as *caregiver burden*. Caregiver burden is a "multidimensional response to the negative appraisal and perceived stress resulting from taking care of an ill individual, [and it] threatens the physical, psychological, emotional, and function health of caregivers" (Kim, Chang, Rose, & Kim, 2011, p. 864). Emotions commonly associated with caregiver burden are depression, loneliness, anger, and guilt. Caregivers frequently exhibit higher levels of depression, physical fatigue, and social isolation, compared to noncaregivers (Johnson, 2008). Having a strong sense of filial piety does not exempt people from experiencing caregiver burden (Lai et al., 2007).

Those caring for loved ones with dementia experience the most severe stress because of challenges specific to cognitive decline—that is, behavior problems, the need for constant supervision, progressive deterioration, and lack of reciprocal expressions of affection and gratitude (Pinquart & Sörensen, 2003). Many people taking care of individuals with dementia indicate that they are not confident in their care management skills and that they are not receiving enough help from care practitioners (Sadak et al., 2018). Dementia caregivers may also experience "dementia grief," which is "characterized by *ambiguous loss* [emphasis added]" (Blandin & Pepin, 2017, p. 70). The ambiguous loss is felt when a person with dementia eventually becomes psychologically absent (e.g., not remembering who their loved ones are) even though they are still physically present. This type of partial loss can be very difficult for caregivers who witness the gradual cognitive disappearance of their loved one on a daily basis.

As experienced by Carmen in the opening vignette, negotiating caregiving with other responsibilities can also be another source of caregiver stress. Similar to many caregiving adult children, Carmen is balancing her responsibilities to her parents with caring for her own family and working full time. Eventually caregivers may become physically exhausted and emotionally drained, experiencing *role overload* as they try to manage multiple roles, which can increase their sense of caregiver burden. At this stage, caregivers must make critical decisions about seeking assistance from others, scaling back their caregiving involvement, or reducing other commitments. Employed caregivers may be forced to reduce their hours or leave work entirely before they are financially and psychologically ready to do so (Johnson, 2008). Moderate caregiving demands (10 to 15 hours a week) are associated with middle-age women reducing their working hours whereas high caregiving demands (more than 20 hours a week) are associated with exiting the paid labor force (Moussa, 2019). Unfortunately, most caregivers wait until a crisis before asking for help. Moving a loved one into a long-term care facility may reduce some responsibilities, but it remains a stressful event in terms of locating optimal care, negotiating family involvement, or battling feelings of guilt (Caron, Ducharme, & Griffith, 2006). Moreover, such a move does not necessarily remove care-related stress. Care management is still required, and even more so if there is concern about unsatisfactory institutional care.

The stress associated with family caregiving goes beyond that experienced by caregivers. Although there is typically a primary caregiver, the entire family system may have to make accommodations and adjustments. Various family members may feel neglected by the caregiver, and feelings of inequity and conflict may emerge among siblings as they negotiate their contributions to care (Connidis & Barnett, 2019). Additionally, care recipients (i.e., the aging family members) encounter unique stressors related to their illness and increased dependence. Reduced self-esteem, frustration at their lack of autonomy, dealing with chronic or terminal illnesses, and institutionalization can result in considerable stress and depression for the care recipient (Brown, 2007). Further, most caregiving situations are inequitable in that care recipients receive more support than they are able to reciprocate. This inequity contributes to reduced well-being as they experience feelings of being a burden to others (Brown, 2007).

Recall that, according to the Double ABC-X model of family stress, available resources (e.g., a family's own coping strategies and support services) are significant in influencing families' stress levels. In recognition of the stress associated with caregiving, numerous agencies and organizations at the exo and macrolevels have developed interventions, such as support groups, respite care services, adult daycare services, and educational and resource information. These resources can assist families in dealing with stressful situations as well as provide valuable information about local, state, and federal resources.

It is important to note, however, that not all people, as they age, will have caregivers who can assist them, and this creates a source of stress for the aging person, themselves. "Unbefriended" adults have nobody to help them with care, and they may be assigned a public guardian (Chamberlain, Baik, & Estabrooks, 2018). LGBTQ individuals who are estranged or distant from their families or without a partner, for example, experience difficulties with regard to chronic health-care needs and end-of-care preparations (de Vries et al., 2019).

Elder Abuse

Elder abuse is an unfortunate situation experienced by a minority of older adults that only recently has received increased attention (Mysyuk, Westendorp, & Lindenberg, 2013). According to the World Health Organization, *elder abuse* refers to "a single, or repeated act, or lack of appropriate action, occurring within any relationship where there is an expectation of trust which causes harm or distress to an older person" (World Health Organization [WHO], 2002, pp. 126–127). It is important to emphasize that elder abuse occurs within a *trust relationship* in which another person is responsible toward an older person (Goergen & Beaulieu, 2013); as such, it cannot be carried out by a stranger. In approximately 90% of elder abuse cases, family members are the perpetrators (Eisokovits, Koren, &

Band-Winterstein, 2013; Mysyuk et al., 2013). Not surprisingly, perpetrators often live with the elder they are abusing, and this is particularly true for older women (Amstadter et al., 2011). Paid caregivers in institutions, also in positions of trust toward frail older individuals and responsible for their well-being, can be perpetrators (as well as residents), but little empirical research has been carried out in this area (Yon, Ramiro-Gonzalez, Mikton, Huber, & Sethi, 2019).

Five types of elder abuse are typically recognized: (a) *physical* (e.g., hitting, choking, pinching, shaking, or using restraints); (b) *emotional* (e.g., isolating, insulting, humiliating, threatening, infantilizing, overprotecting, maliciously outing an older LGBTQ person); (c) *financial* (e.g., illegal or improper use of an elder's funds, property, or assets); (d) *sexual* (e.g., unwanted touching); and (e) intentional or unintentional *neglect* (e.g., failure to provide food, water, or medication, or leaving them alone for long periods of time; WHO, 2002).

A meta-analysis of 52 studies by Yon, Mikton, Gassoumis, and Wilber (2017) suggests that 1 in 6 adults over the age of 60 worldwide have been affected by elder abuse but also noticed considerable geographic variation. Prevalence rates in countries such as the United States, Canada, and Great Britain range from 1% to 10% (Mysyuk et al., 2013), and rates differ based on the type of elder abuse being examined. Psychological abuse is the most common form of elder abuse in both community and institutional settings (Yon et al., 2017, Yon et al., 2019).

Available data from adult protective services agencies in the United States emphasize that despite an increase in the reporting of elder abuse, it is suspected that a substantial number of elder abuse cases go undetected and untreated each year (Jirik & Sanders, 2014). Abusive actions occurring within family homes are underreported because what happens in a home is considered private. Older individuals may face difficult decisions regarding whether or not to openly report elder abuse (for those who are cognitively and physically able to do so), considering the costs and rewards. On one hand, for example, reporting the abuse could stop it; on the other hand, it might remove a person from their lives who still was important to them and change the older person's life in unanticipated ways (e.g., he or she might now have to move into a long-term care facility if an important source of support is lost). Older individuals are more likely than young adults (university students) to think that reporting an abusive situation would make matters worse and to want to keep the situation private (Aday, Wallace, & Scott, 2017). Reporting elder abuse is not just the responsibility of family members though. Health practitioners and other professionals who can also report may erroneously think they need more evidence than is needed (Dong, 2015).

Typical factors associated with an elder's vulnerability are "age, sex, race and ethnicity, socioeconomic status, cognitive impairment, physical disability, depressive symptoms, social network, and social participation" (Dong & Simon, 2014, p. 10). For example, individuals who are over age 80, female, African American, have more than two health issues, or have little social support are at a high risk of elder abuse. Those with dementia (particularly late-stage dementia) are also at a much higher risk compared to the general population of older adults due to their greater dependence (Dong, Chen, & Simon, 2014). Older individuals with five or more risk factors are 26 times more likely to experience elder abuse compared to those with two or less risk factors (Dong & Simon, 2014).

Many people assume that elder abuse emerges out of caregiver burden—a person caring for the dependent older person becomes too stressed with their responsibilities (lacking personal, family, and community-level resources to cope) and thus lashes out in some way at the older person. This can certainly be the situation in some cases; however, this explanation has its limitations (Brandl & Raymond, 2012; Harbison et al., 2012). Specifically, this justification for abuse places blame on the older person (e.g., if they were easier to care for the caregiver would not feel overwhelmed) and attempts to excuse the abuser (Brandl & Raymond, 2012). Instead of the care receiver's dependency on the caregiver being a risk factor, some have argued that it is the caregiver's dependency on the care receiver for things such as housing and income that leads to the abuse (Brandl & Raymond, 2012). Additionally, substance abuse and mental illnesses may be contributing factors (Pickering & Phillips, 2014). Abuse in caregiving contexts may be the result of many interlocking factors (WHO, 2002), and Lowenstein (2010) argues that ambivalence also plays a role.

Family dynamics are important to examine, as families can have complicated patterns of interaction influencing how they cope with challenges later in life (Eisokovits et al., 2013). Subscribing strongly to *familism* may put older adults at greater risk of abuse since their abusers know they are unlikely to report them. Older Latinx immigrants and other groups, particularly those who live with their abusers, may hide such mistreatment because they want to protect their families or avoid shame (DeLiema, Gassoumis, Homeier, & Wilber, 2012). Cultures promoting harmony, such as Japanese, Korean, and Chinese cultures, may "sacrifice" individuals' well-being for the greater good of the group (family) (WHO, 2002). Gao, Sun, and Hodge (2019) suggest that "bi-cultural" identities in older adults can help in Chinese American families. Such dual identities can promote cultural beliefs in families such as filial piety that protect older adults, as well as encourage acculturation to the United States, which may include greater awareness of adult protection services and awareness of what constitutes adult abuse. English language difficulties, citizenship status, and fear or mistrust of authorities may further decrease the likelihood that older Latinx (and other groups) report abuse (DeLiema et al., 2012).

Additionally, because in many cases elder abuse may be an extension of earlier abusive patterns (McDonald & Thomas, 2013), reaching out for assistance within a dysfunctional family system is unlikely. Pickering and Phillips (2014) criticize many theories of elder abuse for ignoring the fact that psychological and verbal patterns of abuse by adult children toward cognitively intact parents, for example, may be long-standing interactional patterns that have simply persisted into later life.

To fully understand and prevent elder abuse, an ecological approach is necessary. Multiple intervention opportunities (e.g., substance abuse treatment programs and caregiver respite programs) can contribute to strengthening family systems in the long term. Researchers, practitioners, and policy makers must also go beyond immediate family contexts and community resources to examine how factors such as societal values about aging and who is expected to take on unpaid caregiving in families play a role in elder abuse. Cultural values influencing family dynamics (Yon et al., 2017) and broader societal and economic changes that have eroded family and community connections for older adults (WHO, 2002) also need to be examined. Worldwide, many countries have been slow in developing elder abuse prevention initiatives, such as public information campaigns to increase awareness of elder abuse (WHO, 2014).

Skipped Generation Families

Skipped generation families refer to families in which children are being raised solely by their grandparents rather than their parents. Other terms used are *custodial grandparents* and *grandfamilies* (Hayslip, Fruhauf, & Doblin-MacNab, 2019). Attempting to determine the degree to which this is a phenomenon is difficult, as grandfamilies come in different formats. For example, some may be formal situations (e.g., a child has been placed in "foster care" rather than with nonrelatives), whereas others may be informal arrangements. Grandfamilies may also differ in their permanency (Hayslip et al., 2019)—some may be temporary while a family gets through a particular crisis, whereas other situations may continue indefinitely. However, it is estimated that over 1.7 million children in the United States are being raised by their grandparents (U.S. Census Bureau, 2017), and this number has increased in recent years (Anderson, 2019; Backhouse & Graham, 2012). Interestingly, the parents are still often present in these households (Anderson, 2019) or may visit regularly (Pilkauskas & Dunifon, 2016). The 2012 American Community study found that the average child living with a grandparent was around 10 years old and had lived with their grandparent for over 5½ years. Most of the grandparents expected that the grandchildren would stay with them until they were adults (Pilkauskas & Dunifon, 2016).

The reasons why children come to be cared for by their grandparent are complex. Addiction is a major factor (Backhouse & Graham, 2012; Gordon, 2018), such as the opioid crisis (Anderson, 2019), but this problem rarely exists on its own. Other related factors are "incarceration, mental health problems, HIV/AIDS, child abuse and neglect, as well as the trend by welfare authorities toward placing children at risk into kinship care rather than foster care" (Backhouse & Graham, 2012, p. 307). Another factor is migration, which is influenced by broader global issues related to chronic poverty or other living conditions in people's homelands, and further complicated by migration policies in the country to which they have migrated (Yarris, 2017). A typical migration example is one in which a parent moves to another country to secure employment. For example, when Nicaraguan mothers migrate to other countries to support their children financially, grandmothers back home show their *solidaridad* (solidarity) and support through caring for the children left in the home country (Yarris, 2017). Skipped-generation families may also result when parents are deported (Beltran & Cooper, 2018). A less often considered scenario is one in which *floating grandparents* leave their rural hometowns and lives behind to migrate to urban areas *with* their adult child to provide childcare (Qi, 2018).

Cultural characteristics increase the odds that a grandparent will be a primary caregiver for their grandchild. Data from the 2000 Census of Population, for example, showed that approximately 10% of AIAN (American Indian/Alaska Native) or African American grandparents were raising their grandchildren—a higher percentage than non-Hispanic White, Latinx, or Asian grandparents (Mutchler, Baker, & Lee, 2007). The cultural context of skipped-generation families is important to consider, given that those who are non-White, rural, or living in poverty may be particularly disadvantaged (Hayslip et al., 2019).

Skipped-generation families typically occur because a parent is experiencing challenges raising their child; therefore, these families start with various stressors. However, new stressors can also develop, which results in a *stressor pileup* (Anderson & Henderson, 2017). A common initial stressor is a grandchild's emotional or behavioral problems due to factors such as neglect, abuse, or a parent's addiction, which a grandparent then needs to manage (Gordon, 2018; Hayslip et al., 2019; Pilkaushas & Dunifron, 2016). Even though grandparents are primary caregivers, parents may still be in the child's life, and further stressors may result from children acting out after parental visits (Gordon, 2018). The grandparent and their child may also have conflicting ideas about how to raise the child (Hayslip et al., 2019). Moreover, the grandparent may have a mixture of conflicting and complex emotions about the changed living environment. Caring for a grandchild can be rewarding and grandparents take satisfaction in knowing that they are having a positive impact on their grandchild (Qi, 2018). Also present, however, can be concern for the adult child, shame about having somehow failed as a parent, anger and resentment about the situation and a longing for their past lives, and ambiguity about their roles (Beltran & Cooper, 2018; Hayslip et al., 2019). Financial, legal, and health concerns are also outcomes (Backhouse & Graham, 2012; Beltran & Cooper, 2018; Gordon, 2018; Hayslip et al., 2019; Qi, 2018). Additional complications occur if the grandparent and their adult child are estranged (Hayslip et al., 2019) or if the grandparent initiated the process of having their adult child declared unfit (Beltran & Cooper, 2018).

It is not just the actual stressor events that create stress though. Smith, Cichy, and Montoro-Rodriguez (2015) note that the perception that social support is present is associated with better health outcomes for grandparents (Smith et al., 2015), pointing to the importance of the definition of the situation, and so are the type of coping skills used (resources). In their parenting roles, grandparents will interact with many different ecological environments such as school, legal, and welfare systems (Backhouse & Graham, 2012) and housing and health services (Gordon, 2018), thus informal and formal support are key. Beltran and Cooper (2018) provide a number of suggestions about how to better support immigrant grandfamilies, including those in which the grandparents "lack lawful immigration status" (p. 107) (i.e., are undocumented). Having translators and translating documents into different languages is one suggestion.

Models of Coping and Adaptation

Because older individuals frequently experience simultaneous multiple stressors (i.e., failing health, increased dependence, and reduced resources), their coping methods (and the coping methods of those around them) are critical to their adjustment. Older adults often employ creative approaches to adapt to the social and functional limitations they encounter as they age. One example is the resourcefulness and positive cognitive appraisal strategies that custodial grandparents in skipped-generation families demonstrate (Hayslip et al., 2019), which are associated with better health for grandmothers in particular (Smith et al., 2015).

Problem-focused coping (an active strategy) occurs when individuals attempt to establish a semblance of control within an uncontrollable situation, by identifying specific and attainable goals they can reach. Older persons worried about their driving, for example, may decide to only drive during the day time, avoid driving on busy streets, or seek rides from family members and friends (Choi, Adams, & Mezuk, 2012).

In contrast, *emotion-focused coping* involves a more cognitive response to stress through the reinterpretation of events, application of humor or religious or spiritual faith, or through detachment or denial. Denial of a problem, however, is a passive and destructive coping strategy. Related to emotional regulation is the coping process of *positive reappraisal*. In this type of coping, the older individual reframes a stressful situation to "minimize negative feelings, ignore unpleasant events, and process emotions less deeply" (Labouvie-Vief, 2005, cited in Tschanz et al., 2013, pp. 826–827) as well as focus on positive characteristics of the situation. Family members in skipped-generation families could focus on the benefits to a child being raised in a more stable environment rather than the losses associated with the parent's opioid addiction or incarceration. With regard to driving, such coping may involve an acceptance of the inevitability of having to reduce or stop one's driving, or it could involve denial of the problem (Choi et al., 2012).

Individuals close to the older person also engage in similar active or passive coping strategies, and their responses have considerable influence on older adults' adaptations to age-related changes and their responses to stress. Families' positive influences usually take the form of social support. Three key types of behaviors constitute social support: aid, affect, and affirmation (Antonucci, 2001). *Aid* consists of tangible types of assistance, such as transportation, help with personal care tasks, or direction regarding where to obtain information about elder abuse. *Affect* refers to emotional support, provided through expressions of care and concern for an aging family member. Finally, *affirmation* involves the sharing of values and the affirmation of the aging family member's importance and the decisions they make, such as the decision to stop driving.

In keeping with a relational approach to resilience (Walsh, 2006), most social support scholars view social relationships as critical to how older adults cope with the challenges of aging (Antonucci, Jackson, & Biggs, 2007; Silverstein et al., 2006). In fact, much research supports the assertion that social support has a positive influence on the health and well-being of older adults. The presence of social support, and even the anticipation of future support, appears to have a buffering effect on stress, mitigating its negative impacts. Anticipated support (believing that support will be provided in the future if needed) also appears to have a more significant impact on health and well-being than support already received or the frequency of contact with others (Antonucci et al., 2007). This finding emphasizes the importance of the perception of one's support situation (the C factor in the Double ABC-X model) in addition to the actual amount or quality of support available (the B factor) within a family. Accessing one's social support network in times of need, however, may depend on the type of stressor as well as the maintenance of quality relationships (Birditt, Antonucci, & Tighe, 2012).

Once again, from an ecological standpoint (Bronfenbrenner, 1979), it is important to recognize that larger social systems play a role in affecting aging individuals' and families' responses to stress. For example, at the macrolevel, many government and social policies contribute to the circumstances of individuals' retirements such as what retirement benefits and resources are available and when they are available (Calasanti, 2000). Prohibitive immigration policies change the nature of transnational families, resulting in more grandparents taking on unexpected parenting roles with their grandchildren (Yarris, 2017). Federal work plans such as the United States National Alzheimer's Project (U.S. Department of Health and Human Services, 2018), which was created in 2012 and updated every year, can set guidelines for how all government levels can support individuals with dementia and their caregivers. Exosystem features such as flex time, family leave time, and shared jobs can assist employed caregivers to remain at work. Finally, at the microlevel, family members, friends, and other individuals can significantly influence how older adult members cope with age-associated changes in terms of interaction patterns and support provided.

Conclusion

Demographic changes that have taken place over the past century have significantly affected the structure, nature, and resources of aging families in the United States and around the world. Later life is frequently associated with stressful life events and transitions, and given our expanding aging populations and the implications of this growth, it is important for researchers and practitioners to understand the strategies that older adults use to cope effectively and the role of families and other systems in the positive adjustment of older adults. Due to the heterogeneity that exists among older adults and their families, perceptions of particular events and how individuals and families cope with these changes will continue to vary. Researchers documenting aging families' adaptive strategies may benefit from exploring more fully the inherent ability of seniors to grow and develop despite advancing age as well as characteristics of the broader environment that help to facilitate such resilience.

DISCUSSION QUESTIONS

1. Caregiving is a gendered phenomenon, but in heterosexual LLATs, women feel "less obliged to honor traditional gender roles as they preserve some separateness and pursue personal interests" (Connidis & Barnett, 2019, p. 156). What happens, then, when an older woman's long-term male partner who lives in another household requires increased care, and does that woman's adult children—if present—feel any obligations to assist with that care?

2. What are examples of conflicting ideas that grandparents and their children might have

about how best to raise the grand children? Could there be different levels or sources of conflict in various skipped-generation families based on factors such as age, race/ethnicity, and migration status of the grandparent? Explain.

3. What contemporary factors at the macro level have affected individuals' decisions about retirement (e.g., how to retire, when to retire, how much savings they have, etc.)?

REFERENCES

Aday, R.H., Wallace, B., & Scott, S.J. (2017). Generational differences in knowledge, recognition, and perceptions of elder abuse reporting. *Educational Gerontology, 43*, 568–581.

Agllias, K. (2016). Disconnection and decision-making: Adult children explain their reasons for estranging from parents. *Australian Social Work, 69*, 92–104.

Aldwin, C. M. (1990). The elders life stress inventory: Egocentric and nonegocentric stress. In M. A. P. Stephens, J. H. Crowther, S. E. Hobfoll, &

D. L. Tennenbaum (Eds.), *Stress and coping in later-life families* (pp. 49–69). New York, NY: Hemisphere.

Aldwin, C. M., & Igarashi, H. (2012). An ecological model of resilience in later life. *Annual Review of Gerontology & Geriatrics, 32,* 115–130.

Aldwin, C. M., Sutton, K. J., Chiara, G., & Spiro, A., III. (1996). Age differences in stress, coping, and appraisal: Findings from the normative aging study. *Journal of Gerontology: Psychological Sciences, 51B,* 179–188.

Aldwin, C. M., Yancura, L. A., & Boeninger, D. K. (2007). Coping, health, and aging. In C.M. Aldwin, C. L. Park, & A. Spiro III (Eds.), *Handbook of health psychology and aging* (pp. 210–226). New York. NY: Guilford Press.

Allen, K. R., & Henderson, A. C. (2017). *Family theories: Foundations and applications*. Malden, MA: Wiley Blackwell.

Amstadter, A. B., Cisler, J. M., McCauley, J. L., Hernandez, M. A., Muzzy, W., & Acierno, R. (2011). Do incident and perpetrator characteristics of elder mistreatment differ by gender of the victim? Results from the National Elder Mistreatment Study. *Journal of Elder Abuse & Neglect, 23,* 43–57.

Anderson, L. (2019, April 12). The opioid prescribing rate and grandparents raising grandchildren: State and county level analysis (SEHSD Working Paper 2019-24). Retrieved from https://www.census.gov/library/working-papers/2019/demo/SEHSD-WP2019-04.html

Antonucci, T. C. (2001). Social relations: An examination of social networks, social support, and sense of control. In J. E. Birren & K. W. Schaie (Eds.), *Handbook of the psychology of aging* (5th ed., pp. 427–453). San Diego, CA: Academic.

Antonucci, T. C., Jackson, J. S., & Biggs, S. (2007). Intergenerational relations: Theory, research, and policy. *Journal of Social Issues, 63,* 679–693.

Asebedo, S. D., & Seay, M. C. (2014). Positive psychological attributes and retirement satisfaction. *Journal of Financial Counseling and Planning, 25,* 161–173.

Backhouse, J., & Graham, A. (2012). Grandparents raising grandchildren: Negotiating the complexities of role-identity conflict. *Child & Family Social Work, 17,* 306–315.

Banerjee, S. (2016, April). *Trends in retirement satisfaction in the United States: Fewer having a great time*. Washington, DC: Employee Benefit Research Institute. Retrieved from https://papers.ssrn.com/sol3/papers.cfm?abstract_id=2772072

Bellingtier, J. A., Neupert, S. D., & Kotter-Grühn, D. (2017). The combined effects of daily stressors and major life events on daily subjective ages. *Journals of Gerontology: Psychological Sciences, 72,* 613–621.

Beltran, A., & Cooper, C. R. (2018). Promising practices and policies to support grandparents that include immigrants. *Child Welfare, 96,* 103–125.

Birditt, K. S., Antonucci, T. C., & Tighe, L. (2012). Enacted support during stressful life events in middle and older adulthood: An examination of the interpersonal context. *Psychology and Aging, 27,* 728–741. https://doi.org/10.1037/a0026967

Blieszner, R., & Bedford, V. H. (2012). The family context of aging. In R. Blieszner & V. H. Bedford (Eds.), *Handbook of aging and the family* (2nd ed., pp. 3–8). Santa Barbara, CA: ABC-CLIO.

Blandin, K., & Pepin, R. (2017). Dementia grief: A theoretical model of a unique grief experience. *Dementia, 16,* 67–78.

Brandl, B., & Raymond, J. A. (2012). Policy implications of recognizing that caregiver stress is *not* the primary cause of elder abuse. *Generations, 36*(3), 32–39.

Bronfenbrenner, U. (1979). *The ecology of human development*. Cambridge, MA: Harvard University Press.

Brown, E. (2007). Care recipients' psychological well-being: The role of sense of control and caregiver type. *Aging & Mental Health, 11,* 405–414.

Calasanti, T. M. (2000). Incorporating diversity. In E. W. Markson & L. A. Hollis-Sawyer (Eds.), *Intersections of aging* (pp. 188–202). Los Angeles, CA: Roxbury.

Caron, C. D., Ducharme, F., & Griffith, J. (2006). Deciding on institutionalization for a relative with dementia: The most difficult decision for caregivers. *Canadian Journal on Aging, 25,* 193–205.

Chamberlain, S., Baik, S., & Estabrooks, C. (2018). Going it alone: A scoping review of unbefriended older adults. *Canadian Journal on Aging, 37,* 1–11.

Choi, M., Adams, K. B., & Mezuk, B. (2012). Examining the aging process through the stress-coping framework: Application to driving cessation later in life. *Aging & Mental Health, 16,* 75–83.

Colby, S. L., & Ortman, J. M. (2014). *The baby boom cohort in the United States: 2012 to 2060. Current Population Reports.* Washington, DC: U.S. Bureau of the Census. Retrieved from https://www.census.gov/library/publications/2014/demo/p25-1141.html

Connidis, I. A., & Barnett, A. E. (2019). *Family ties & aging* (3rd ed.). Los Angeles, CA: SAGE.

Connidis, I. A., Borell, K., Karlsson, S. G. (2017). Ambivalence and living apart together in later life: A critical research proposal. *Journal of Marriage and Family, 79,* 1404–1418.

Connidis, I. A., & McMullin, J. A. (2002). Sociological ambivalence and family ties: A critical perspective. *Journal of Marriage and Family, 64,* 558–567.

Coon, D. W. (2012). Resilience and family caregiving. In B. Hayslip & C. G. Smith (Eds.), *Annual Review of Gerontology and Geriatrics: Emerging perspectives on resilience in adulthood and later life* (pp. 231–249). New York, NY: Springer.

Davey, A., & Szinovacz, M. E. (2004). Dimensions of marital quality and retirement. *Journal of Family Issues, 25,* 431–464.

DeLiema, M., Gassoumis, Z. D., Homeier, D. C., & Wilber, K. H. (2012). Determining prevalence and correlates of elder abuse using *promotores*: Low-income immigrant Latinos report high rates of abuse and neglect. *Journal of the American Geriatrics Society, 60,* 1333–1339.

Denton, F. T., & Spencer, B. G. (2009). What is retirement? A review and assessment of alternative concepts and measures. *Canadian Journal on Aging, 28,* 63–76.

de Vries, B., Gutman, G., Humble, A. M., Gahagan, J., Chamberland, L., Aubert, P., Fast, J., & Mock, S. (2019). End-of-life preparations among LGBT older Canadian adults: The missing conversation. *International Journal of Aging and Human Development, 88,* 358–379.

Dew, J., & Yorgason, J. (2010). Economic pressure and marital conflict in retirement-aged couples. *Journal of Family Issues, 31,* 164–188.

Dong, X. Q. (2015). Elder abuse: Systematic review and implications for practice. *Journal of the American Geriatrics Society, 63,* 1214–1238.

Dong, X. Q., Chen, R., & Simon, M. A. (2014). Elder abuse and dementia: A review of the research and health policy. *Health Affairs, 33,* 642–649.

Dong, X. Q., & Simon, M. A. (2014). Vulnerability risk index profile for elder abuse in a community-dwelling population. *Journal of the American Geriatrics Society, 62,* 10–15.

Eisokovits, Z., Koren, C., & Band-Winterstein, T. (2013). The social construction of social problems: The case of elder abuse and neglect. *International Psychogeriatrics, 25,* 1291–1298.

Fehr, R. (2012). Is retirement always stressful? The potential impact of creativity. *American Psychologist, 67,* 76–77.

Fredriksen-Goldsen, K. I., Kim, H.-J., Bryan, A. E. B., Shiu, C., & Emlet, C. A. (2017). The cascading effects of marginalization and pathways of resilience in attaining good health among LGBT older adults. *Gerontologist, 57,* S72–S83.

Goergen, T., & Beaulieu, M. (2013). Critical concepts in elder abuse research. *International Psychogeriatrics, 25,* 1217–1228.

Gao, X., Sun, F., & Hodge, D. R. (2019). Elder mistreatment among Chinese American families: Do acculturation and traditionalism matter? *Journals of Gerontology: Social Sciences, 74,* 465–473.

Gordon, L. (2018). "My granddaughter is a drug addict": Grandparents caring for the children of addicted parents. *Kōtuitui: New Zealand Journal of Social Sciences Online, 13*(1), 39–54.

Guo, M., Chi, I., & Silverstein, M. (2013). Sources of older parents' ambivalent feelings toward their adult children: The case of rural China. *The Journals of Gerontology, Series B: Psychological Sciences and Social Sciences, 68,* 420–430.

Harbison, J., Couglan, S., Beaulieu, M., Karabonow, J., vanderPlaat, M., Wildeman, S., & Wexler, E. (2012). Understanding "elder abuse and neglect": A critique of assumptions underpinning responses to the mistreatment and neglect of older people. *Journal of Elder Abuse & Neglect, 24,* 88–103.

Hayslip, B. Jr, Fruhauf, C.A., & Doblin-MacNab, M.L. (2019). Grandparents raising grandchildren: What have we learned over the past decade? *The Gerontologist, 59,* e152–e163.

He, W., Sengupta, M., Velkoff, V. A., & DeBarros, K. A. (2005, December). *65+ in the United States: 2005. Current Population Reports.* Washington, DC: U.S. Bureau of the Census. Retrieved from http://www.census.gov/prod/2006pubs/p23-209.pdf

Henry, C. S., Morris, A. S., & Harrist, A. W. (2015). Family resilience: Moving into the third wave. *Family Relations, 64,* 22–43.

Hesamzadeh, A., Dalvandi, A., Maddah, S. B., Khoshknab, M. F., & Ahmadi, F. (2015). Family adaptation to stroke: A metasynthesis of qualitative research based on Double ABCX model. *Asian Nursing Research, 9,* 177–184.

Hooyman, N. R., & Kiyak, H. A. (2011). *Social gerontology: A multidisciplinary perspective* (9th ed.). Boston, MA: Pearson.

Humble, A. M. (2013). Moving from ambivalence to certainty: Older same-sex couples marry in Canada. *Canadian Journal on Aging, 32,* 131–144.

Jirik, S., & Sanders, S. (2014). Analysis of elder abuse statutes across the United States, 2011–2012. *Journal of Gerontological Social Work, 57,* 478–497.

Johnson, R. W. (2008). Choosing between paid elder care and unpaid help from adult children: The role of relative prices in the care decision. In M. E. Szinovacz & A. Davey (Eds.), *Caregiving contexts: Cultural, familial, and societal implications* (pp. 35–69). New York, NY: Springer.

Kim, H., Chang, M., Rose, K., & Kim, S. (2011). Predictors of caregiver burden in caregivers of individuals with dementia. *Journal of Advanced Nursing, 68,* 846–855.

Krause, N. (2007). Evaluating the stress-buffering function of meaning in life among older people. *Journal of Aging and Health, 19,* 792–812.

Lai, D. W. L., Luk, P. K. F., & Andruske, C. L. (2007). Gender differences in caregiving: A case in Chinese Canadian caregivers. *Journal of Women & Aging, 19,* 161–178.

Lawrence, A. R., & Schigelone, A. R. S. (2002). Reciprocity beyond dyadic relationships. *Research on Aging, 24,* 684–704.

Leach, M. (2009). America's older immigrants: A profile. *Generations, 32,* 343–349.

Lowenstein, A. (2010). Caregiving and elder abuse and neglect: Developing a new conceptual perspective. *Ageing International, 35,* 215–227.

McDonald, L., & Thomas, C. (2013). Elder abuse through a life course lens. *International Psychogeriatrics, 25,* 1235–1243.

Medina, L., Sabo, S., & Vespa, J. (2019, April). *Living longer: Historical and projected gains to life expectancy, 1960–2060.* Poster presented at the Annual Meeting of the Population Association of America, Austin, Texas.

Moussa, M. M. (2019). The relationship between elder care-giving and labour force participation in the context of policies addressing population ageing: A review of empirical studies published between 2006 and 2016. *Ageing & Society, 39,* 1281–1310.

Mock, S. E., & Schryer, E. (2017). Perceived support and the retirement expectations of sexual minority adults. *Canadian Journal on Aging, 36,* 170–177.

Mutchler, J. E., Baker, L. A., & Lee, S.-A. (2007). Grandparents responsible for grandchildren in Native-American families. *Social Science Quarterly, 88,* 990–1009.

Mysyuk, Y., Westendorp, R. G., & Lindenberg, J. (2013). Added value of elder abuse definitions: A review. *Aging Research Reviews, 12,* 50–57.

National Alliance for Caregiving & AARP. (2015). *2015 report: Caregiving in the U.S.* Washington, DC: Author. Retrieved from https://www.caregiving .org/wp-content/uploads/2015/05/2015_Care givingintheUS_Final-Report-June-4_WEB.pdf

Ortman, J. M., Velkoff, V. A., & Hogan, H. (2014). *An aging nation: The older population in the United States. Current Population Reports.* Washington, DC: U.S. Bureau of the Census. Retrieved from http://www.census.gov/prod/2014pubs/p25-1140.pdf

Pearlin, L. I., Aneshensel, C. S., Mullan, J. T., & Whitlatch, C. J. (1995). Caregiving and its social support. In R. H. Binstock & L. K. George (Eds.), *Handbook of aging and the social sciences* (4th ed., pp. 283–302). San Diego, CA: Academic.

Pickering, C. E. Z., & Phillips, L. R. (2014). Development of a causal model for elder mistreatment. *Public Health Nursing, 31,* 363–372.

Pilkauskas, N. V., & Dunifon, R. E. (2016). Understanding grandfamilies: Characteristics of grandparents, nonresident parents, and children. *Journal of Marriage and Family, 78,* 623–633.

Pinquart, M., & Sörensen, S. (2003). Differences between caregivers and noncaregivers in psychological health and physical health: A meta-analysis. *Psychology and Aging, 18,* 250–267.

Pitzer, L., Fingerman, K. L., & Lefkowitz, E. S. (2011). Development of the parent adult relationships questionnaire (PARQ). *International Journal of Aging and Human Development, 72,* 111–135.

Qi, X. (2018). Floating grandparents: Rethinking family obligation and intergenerational support. *International Sociology, 33,* 761–777.

Radina, M. E., Gibbons, H. M., & Li, J.-Y. (2009). Explicit versus implicit family decision-making strategies among Mexican American caregiving adult children. *Marriage & Family Review, 45,* 392–411.

Roberto, K. A., Blieszner, R., & Allen, K. R. (2006). Theorizing in family gerontology: New opportunities for research and practice. *Family Relations, 55,* 513–525.

Roberts, A. W., Ogunwole, S. U., Blakeslee, L., & Rabe, M. A. (2018, October). The population 65 years and older in the United States: 2016. *American Community Survey Reports, ACS-38.* Washington, DC: U.S. Census Bureau.

Sadak, T., Wright, J., & Borson, S. (2018). Managing your loved one's health: Development of a new care management measure for dementia family caregivers. *Journal of Applied Gerontology, 37,* 620–643.

Scott, S. B., Jackson, B. R., & Bergman, C. S. (2011). What contributes to perceived stress in later life? A recursive partitioning approach. *Psychology and Aging, 26,* 830–843.

Shultz, K. S., & Wang, M. (2011). Psychological perspectives on the changing nature of retirement. *American Psychologist, 66,* 170–179.

Silverstein, M., Gans, D., & Yang, F. M. (2006). Intergenerational support to aging parents: The role of norms and needs. *Journal of Family Issues, 27,* 1068–1084.

Silverstein, M., & Giarrusso, R. (2010). Aging and family life: A decade review. *Journal of Marriage and Family, 72,* 1039–1058.

Smith, G. C., Cichy, K. E., & Montoro-Rodriguez, J. (2015). Impact of coping resources on the well-being of custodial grandmothers and grandchildren. *Family Relations, 64,* 378–392.

Stawski, R. S., Sliwinski, M. J., Almeida, D. M., & Smyth, J. M. (2008). Reported exposure and emotional reactivity to daily stressors: The roles of adult age and global perceived stress. *Psychology and Aging, 23,* 52–61.

Sutin, A. R., Costa, P. T., Jr., Wethington, E., & Eaton, W. (2010). Turning points and lessons learned: Stressful life events and personality trait development across middle adulthood. *Psychology and Aging, 25,* 524–533.

Szinovacz, M. (2003). Contexts and pathways: Retirement as institution, process, and experience. In G. A. Adams & T. A. Beehr (Eds.), *Retirement: Reasons, processes, and results* (pp. 6–52). New York, NY: Springer.

Szinovacz, M., & Davey, A. (2005). Retirement and marital decision making: Effects on retirement satisfaction. *Journal of Marriage and Family, 67,* 387–398.

Tschanz, J. T., Pfister, R., Wanzek, J., Corcoran, C., Smith, K., Tschanz, B. T., Steffens, D. C., Østbye, T., Welsh-Bohmer, K.A., & Norton, M.C. (2013). Stressful life events and cognitive decline in late life: Moderation by education and age. The Cache County Study. *International Journal of Geriatric Psychiatry, 28,* 821–830.

Uhlenberg, P., & Cheuk, M. (2008). Demographic change and the future of informal caregiving. In M. E. Szinovacz & A. Davey (Eds.), *Caregiving contexts: Cultural, familial, and societal implications* (pp. 9–33). New York, NY: Springer.

U.S. Department of Health and Human Services. (2018). *National plan to address Alzheimer's Disease: 2018 update.* Retrieved from https://aspe.hhs.gov/system/files/pdf/259581/NatPlan2018.pdf

U.S. Census Bureau. (2014). *65+ in the United States: 2010* (P23-212). Washington, DC: U.S. Government Printing Office.

U.S. Census Bureau. (2017). *S1002: Grandparents, American Community Survey, 2016 1-year estimates.* Retrieved from https://data.census.gov/cedsci/all?q=Grandparents,%20American%20Community%20Survey,%202016%201-year%20estimates.%20&hidePreview=false&tid=ACSDT1Y2016.B10063&t=Counts,%20Estimates,%20and%20Projections%3AGrandparents%20and%20Grandchildren&y=2016

van Solinge, H., & Henkens, K. (2005). Couples' adjustment to retirement: A multi-actor panel study. *Journals of Gerontology: Social Sciences, 60B,* S11–S20. https://doi.org/10.1093/geronb/60.1.S11

Walsh, F. (2006). *Strengthening family resilience* (2nd ed.). New York, NY: Guilford Press.

World Health Organization. (2002). *World report on violence and health.* Geneva. Retrieved from https://www.who.int/violence_injury_prevention/violence/world_report/en

World Health Organization. (2014). *Global status report on violence prevention 2014.* Geneva. Retrieved from https://www.who.int/violence_injury_prevention/violence/status_report/2014/en/

Wu, H. (2017). Age variation in the divorce rate, 1990–2015. *Family Profiles,* FP-17-20. Bowling Green, OH: National Center for Family and Marriage Research. https://doi.org/10.25035/ncfmr/fp-17-20

Yarris, K. E. (2017). *Care across generations: Solidarity and sacrifice in transnational families.* Stanford, CA: Stanford University Press.

Yon, Y., Ramiro-Gonzalez, M., Mikton, C. R., Huber, M., & Sethi, D. (2019). The prevalence of elder abuse in institutional settings: A systematic review and meta-analysis. *The European Journal of Public Health, 29,* 58–67.

Yon, Y., Mikton, C. R., Gassoumis, Z. D., & Wilber, K. H. (2017). Elder abuse prevalence in community settings: A systematic review and meta-analysis. *Lancet Global Health, 5,* e147–e156.

Zimmerman, L., Mitchell, B., Wister, A., & Gutman, G. (2000). Unanticipated consequences: A comparison of expected and actual retirement timing among older women. *Journal of Women & Aging, 12,* 109–128.

Zoekler, J. M., & Silverstein, M. (2016). Work and retirement. In M. H. Meyer & E. A. Daniele (Eds.), *Gerontology: Changes, challenges, and solutions* (Vol 1, pp. 161–190). Santa Barbara, CA: Praeger.

Stressful Family Transitions

CHAPTER 8

Divorce
Variation and Fluidity

David H. Demo, Mark A. Fine, and
Savannah Sommers

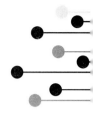

The word *divorce* conjures up images of divided families, vulnerable children, failed marriages, unmet or unfulfilled commitments, long and expensive legal battles, resentment, hostility, bitterness, and economic hardship. It is understandable that people do not think positively about divorce. Adults do not marry with the expectation, and certainly not the hope, that their marriages will one day be dissolved, nor do most children hope that their parents will divorce and live apart. Nevertheless, large proportions of American families have experienced or are experiencing parental divorce, a phenomenon that cuts across racial and ethnic groups, albeit to varying degrees.

In the past century, there have been drastic changes in marriage and divorce across all social and demographic groups; couples have delayed marriage, divorce rates have increased, and nonmarital cohabitation has become more common (Raley, Sweeney, & Wondra, 2015). Data from the 2008–2012 American Community Survey demonstrated that at almost every age, divorce rates are the lowest among Asian and foreign-born Hispanic women, and highest for African American and American Indian women (Raley et al., 2015). Further, these racial and ethnic gaps in divorce are expected to continue to grow (Raley et al., 2015). Partly because of the prevalence of divorce, but also because of other factors such as increases in cohabitation, many children and adolescents do not live with two parents.

In this chapter, we provide an overview of what we know about divorce, the consequences it has on family members, and interventions designed to help those who are experiencing this family stressor. To accomplish these goals, we first provide a theoretical model that illuminates processes and outcomes relevant to divorce, with an emphasis on factors contributing to variation and fluidity in how individuals experience divorce (Demo & Fine, 2010). Second, to illuminate the context in which the model is embedded, we describe historical trends and patterns that place recent trends into context. Third, we present information on factors that predict and that may cause divorce. Fourth, using our theoretical model as a foundation, we review the literature on the consequences of divorce for parents and children, emphasizing risk and protective factors that predict how family members will adjust to this stressor. Finally, we describe and evaluate interventions that may facilitate divorce adjustment, focusing on parenting education for divorcing parents and divorce mediation.

Note: The authors acknowledge the important contributions of Lawrence H. Ganong on previous versions of this chapter.

Theoretical Perspective

The divorce variation and fluidity model (DVFM; Demo & Fine, 2010), illustrated in Figure 8.1, highlights two central features of the divorce process: (1) there is considerable *variability* in how family members experience and adjust to divorce; and (2) children's and adults' adjustment during and following divorce is typically *fluid*, or changes over time. Although divorce is generally associated with stresses and compromised adjustment among both children and adults, as we describe in more detail below, there is extensive variability. Some children and adults suffer dramatic setbacks to their well-being during and following divorce; some experience relatively minor or short-term deficits; some retain their predivorce adjustment level; and still others rebound quickly from divorce with improved adjustment. Which factors account for this variation? Why do some adults feel relieved and function quite well following divorce while others feel defeated and

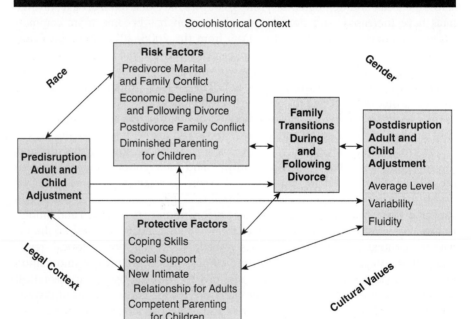

Figure 8.1   Divorce Variation and Fluidity Model

Source: Demo, D. H., & Fine, M. A. (2010). *Beyond the average divorce.* Thousand Oaks, CA: SAGE.

depressed? Similarly, why do some children and adolescents adjust successfully to parental divorce, reduced contact with one or more parents, and other changes accompanying marital disruption, while some of their peers are devastated?

In examining these questions, we also direct attention to the related issue of change over time, or fluidity, in individual adjustment. As the divorce process unfolds, both children and adults experience ebbs and flows in their adjustment, which are related to changes in residence, neighborhoods, schools, jobs, family relationships, friends, and standard of living. The DVFM is an integrative process model that outlines key factors influencing child and adult adjustment to divorce. The model is designed to be illustrative rather than exhaustive, and it is intended to demonstrate the highly dynamic nature of the divorce process. Divorce does not occur in a vacuum but is embedded within a complex set of interrelated contexts identified in the outer margins of Figure 8.1, including the legal climate, economic conditions, cultural values, gender, race, and sociohistorical context.

At the far left side of Figure 8.1, predisruption levels of adult and child adjustment are posited to influence how the divorce process unfolds. Individuals who are functioning well prior to family disruption are posited to be better prepared for, or even protected from, some of the stresses associated with divorce, whereas individuals with lower adjustment levels prior to divorce are more vulnerable to subsequent risks and transitions. Longitudinal studies indicate that children and adults who are better adjusted prior to divorce have better outcomes following divorce (Arkes, 2015; van der Wal, Finkenauer, & Visser, 2019), particularly for children in families that had higher incomes before the divorce and children whose mothers engaged in more sensitive (Weaver & Schofield, 2015) and supportive (Rappaport, 2013) parenting before the divorce.

The two large boxes in the center of Figure 8.1 illuminate the mediating influence of risk factors and protective factors in understanding resilience to divorce. Risk factors increase the likelihood of negative outcomes, whereas protective factors increase the chances of positive outcomes. Thus, resilience, which is enhanced by a higher ratio of protective factors to risk factors, refers to processes by which an individual (or group) overcomes difficult circumstances, "bounces back" from adversity, and becomes stronger in the face of a crisis (Walsh, 2002). The risk and resilience framework addresses why some parents and children in divorced families cope relatively well with this transition, whereas others do not adapt as successfully. For example, factors that increase the risk of negative divorce outcomes include child maladjustment before the divorce, financial difficulties, conflict between the ex-spouses, and reduced involvement by the nonresidential parent (Demo & Buehler, 2013). By contrast, resilience is thought to be enhanced by such factors as family members receiving support from close friends, children not blaming themselves for their parents' divorce, and family members retaining an optimistic stance toward the changes that they will experience following divorce (Demo & Buehler, 2013).

The DVFM places the research focus on understanding *variation* in responses to the challenges posed by divorce and life in a single-parent household. For example, research has suggested that experiencing parental divorce increases the risk of children experiencing social, emotional, academic, or behavioral problems (Amato & Anthony, 2014). For example, Hetherington and Kelly (2002) found that the risk of children experiencing socioemotional and behavioral problems was approximately 20% for those who experienced divorce compared to 10% for those whose parents remained married. Although this suggests a heightened risk, this finding also indicates that *most* children in divorced families do *not* develop such problems. The DVFM attempts to identify factors that account for these differential outcomes to the same stressor.

In this framework, outcomes depend on the interplay among risk and protective factors and mechanisms (Margolin, Oliver, & Medina, 2001). Risk factors increase the likelihood of undesirable outcomes, whereas risk mechanisms are the processes by which a particular stressor (e.g., parental divorce) leads to adjustment difficulties. Protective factors are characteristics that promote adaptation to difficult circumstances, as well as family and contextual factors that buffer the effects of severe risk. Protective mechanisms are the ways in which protective factors have their positive effects. One type of protective factor—coping resources—refers to the social, economic, psychological, emotional, and physical assets on which family members can draw (Ahrons, 1994). Adaptation is facilitated to the extent that there are protective factors that are strong enough to help individuals and families cope with the risks that accompany stressors such as divorce.

Borrowing from the life-course perspective (Elder, 1998), the DVFM recognizes that family transitions during and following divorce play a critical role in shaping life trajectories, developmental change, and postdivorce adjustment. Family transitions refer to changes in family structure or household living arrangements associated with beginning or ending cohabiting, marital, or remarital relationships. For example, parents or other adults may move into or out of the household following divorce, thereby forming or disrupting relationships with children. Some adults pursue new romantic relationships but remain single, while others cohabit or remarry, perhaps multiple times, and many form stepfamilies. The DVFM directs attention to these transitions and the timing, duration, and quality of these relationships in moderating the impact of divorce on individual adjustment.

History and Context

Although it is commonly believed that the divorce rate was low through the 1950s and then soared in recent decades, the divorce rate actually increased steadily from the mid-19th century through the 1970s (Teachman, Tedrow, & Hall, 2006). The divorce rate then stabilized at a high level in the early 1980s and declined modestly since then (Amato, 2014; Cherlin, 2017). Further, in 2014, the crude divorce rate in the United States declined to 3.2, which was the lowest this rate has been since 1969 (Cherlin, 2017). Given these changes, there is currently approximately a 40% lifetime risk of divorce in the United States (Cherlin, 2017), meaning that there is a 40% probability that individuals in their first marriages will experience divorce in their lifetimes.

Why did divorce rates rise substantially until the early 1980s? The cultural climate in the United States during the 1960s and 1970s featured an increasing emphasis on individualism (Cherlin, 2009). From the late 1950s to the late 1980s, singlehood, cohabitation, childlessness, and nonmarital sexual relations became more acceptable, while opposition to abortion and divorce weakened (Amato, 2004; Demo & Fine, 2010). For many, concerns with self-fulfillment and career development diminished their commitment to family, rendering marriage and other intimate relationships vulnerable.

Economic factors also contributed to rising divorce rates. Changing work patterns, diminished occupational opportunities, men's declining labor force involvement, stagnant wages for White men and declining wages for African American men, and massive underemployment for millions of lower income wage earners created domestic turmoil for many families (Perelli-Harris, Berrington, Gassen, Galezewska, & Holland, 2017). Although women earn less than men for the same work, their reduced economic dependence on men made divorce a more acceptable alternative for women in unhappy marriages.

Many observers have argued that higher divorce rates until the 1980s were a result of declining levels of marital satisfaction (Birditt, Brown, Orbuch, & McIlvane, 2010). However, although overall levels of marital satisfaction have declined, there is little evidence that this decline led to an increase in the divorce rate (Stanley, 2019). Perhaps a more plausible explanation of the increase in the divorce rate in the late 1960s and 1970s is that many individuals, especially women, recognized that marriage was not meeting their personal needs (Amato, 2004; Cherlin, 2004). In this context, it is perhaps not surprising that women initiate divorce more often than men (Amato, 2014).

Other factors serve to undermine marital stability. Individuals often have unrealistic, idealistic, and romanticized notions about marriage. These conditions—personal fulfillment being strongly valued, lofty expectations not being satisfied, declines in marital satisfaction, and the perception that acceptable alternatives are available—increase the probability of divorce. Because it is unlikely that there will be substantial changes in these conditions in the near future, the divorce rate in the United States is likely to remain at or near current levels.

Factors that Predict and Cause Divorce

The divorce variation and fluidity model encourages us to explore which factors are predictive of some couples staying together while others dissolve their relationship and the causal mechanisms underlying *why* these factors are predictive of marital (in)stability. There is consistent evidence that several demographic, individual difference, and relationship variables contribute to a higher probability of divorce (i.e., they constitute risk factors) (Amato, 2010; Hawkins, Willoughby, & Doherty, 2012). Unfortunately, we know much less about how relationship processes relate to the likelihood of divorce than we do about the influence of demographic and individual difference factors (Amato, 2004; Rodrigues, Hall, & Fincham, 2006).

Demographic risks include (a) being African American; (b) living in the western and southern parts of the United States; (c) living in an urban area; (d) cohabiting premaritally, especially with a partner whom one does not later marry; (e) having a premarital birth; (f) being young at the time of marriage; (g) having less education; (h) being married for a shorter amount of time; (i) being remarried; (j) having divorced parents; and (k) being less religious. In terms of individual difference variables, divorce risk is positively related to neuroticism (i.e., a generalized tendency to experience negative emotions, such as sadness, anger, guilt, fear, and embarrassment), psychopathology, thinking of divorce, and higher levels of self-monitoring (i.e., the ability and motivation to control one's presentation to others). Finally, with respect to relationship variables, divorce risk is related to dissatisfaction with marriage, lower levels of commitment to the relationship, frequent conflict, domestic violence, fewer investments in the relationship, and more negativity than positivity in marital interactions (Amato, 2010; Rodrigues et al., 2006).

Identifying risk factors is considerably easier to do than identifying the *causes* of divorce. Determining the causes of relationship dissolution is extremely difficult because there are important distinctions between what people report to be the cause of their break-up and what may have *actually* caused the break-up (Powell & Fine, 2009). Hopper (1993, 2001) has suggested that people who are going through a divorce typically construct a public account of what happened in their relationship that led to its termination. These narrative accounts often present the individual in a positive light, minimizing their role and attributing the dissolution to either one's ex-spouse or partner or to circumstances beyond one's control. Thus, these stories may be both incomplete and inaccurate with respect to how the events surrounding the divorce actually unfolded. In addition, individuals may come to actually believe their stories, even if they were distortions of the "truth."

By contrast, researchers attempt to identify the causes of divorce when they look for regularities in factors that lead to divorce across a population. Whereas the divorced individual's perspective identifies their subjective view of what caused the dissolution of the relationship, the researcher's perspective uses empirical investigations to identify factors that seem to account for divorce in the general population. However, it is important to keep in mind that, like with much of social science research, some of the most effective and strongest tools for determining causation—such as the use of experimental designs—cannot be used in the study of relationship outcomes (e.g., researchers cannot ethically or even logistically randomly assign 50% of their participants to a divorce group and 50% to a still-married group!). Despite such limitations, some of the standard ways for testing causation *are* available to divorce researchers, such as the use of longitudinal designs and statistically controlling for extraneous variables. Thus, the divorced individual's account and the researcher's perspective have different goals, sometimes complementary strengths and limitations, and may reach seemingly divergent conclusions. For example, many individuals blame the termination of their relationship on infidelity (Powell & Fine, 2009). However, because many relationships survive instances of infidelity, the researcher perspective suggests that infidelity is seldom the primary cause of dissolution. Therefore, each perspective taps a different, but important, aspect of the complex picture of why dissolution occurs.

What do ex-spouses typically report when asked "What went wrong?" in their marriages? Wives report more dissatisfaction with marriage than do husbands (Amato, Johnson, Booth, & Rogers, 2003). Common complaints by ex-wives include husbands' authoritarianism, mental cruelty, verbal and physical abuse, excessive drinking, lack of love, neglect of children, emotional and personality problems, and extramarital sex. Men describe their former wives as nagging, whining, faultfinding, and immature (Hetherington & Kelly, 2002). It is common for women and men to share the views that communication problems, unhappiness, and incompatibility led to the divorce (Hawkins et al., 2012). Former spouses' descriptions of their marriages underscore that traditional gender scripts and power imbalances in marriage, work, and parenthood often have undesirable, even harsh, consequences for family members. However, as Hopper's work suggests, partners' accounts of the end of their romantic relationships are socially constructed to create a story that is acceptable to themselves as well as to those in their family and social networks. Thus, such accounts should be interpreted cautiously, as they may not accurately portray the events as they actually occurred.

Divorce and Its Aftermath

Research using large and representative samples has found moderate, mostly short-term effects on adult (Amato, 2014) and child adjustment (Amato & Anthony, 2014). Regarding children, Emery (1999) concluded that (a) divorce is a stressful experience; (b) divorce leads to higher levels of clinically significant adjustment and mental health problems; (c) most children are resilient and adjust well to divorce over time; (d) children whose parents divorce report considerable pain, unhappy memories, and continued distress; and (e) postdivorce family interaction patterns greatly influence adjustment following divorce. Emery's inferences are helpful because they can help make sense of seemingly disparate conclusions in the literature. For example, whereas some researchers have focused on the high levels of pain and distress that children of divorce experience (Emery's fourth point above), others (e.g., Hetherington) have targeted the higher levels of adjustment problems that such children experience at least in the short term (Emery's second point above).

There is also considerable variability in the nature of adjustment to divorce (Amato & Anthony, 2014; Demo & Fine, 2010). Individuals differ, sometimes considerably, in how they respond to divorce and in their *perceptions* of their adjustment to divorce. As feminist researchers emphasize, family life is perceived, defined, and experienced differently by each family member (Few-Demo, Lloyd, & Allen, 2014). Rather than a unitary or "core" family reality, there are multiple and sometimes conflicting realities. Understanding divorce requires us to understand the perspectives of all family members regarding their predivorce and postdivorce family histories, relationships, and experiences.

It is important to note that adjustment to divorce occurs within a society that typically has held negative views of divorce. Although public disapproval of divorce has softened, divorced individuals still confront stigma and members of single-parent families continue to feel deficient (Zartler, 2014). In response, as noted earlier, divorced individuals develop elaborate accounts that help them view their role in the divorce in a more positive light to themselves and others (Hopper, 1993, 2001).

The circumstances associated with social disapproval are different for women than for men. Gerstel (1990) found that, compared to childless women, divorced mothers experienced harsher disapproval, particularly if they had young children, whereas divorced men did not perceive any differences in social reactions based on whether or not they were parents. Men who had been sexually involved outside the marriage prior to separation reported experiencing greater disapproval from others than did other men. Gerstel concluded that the processes associated with social rejection and stigma reflect "a gender-based ideology of divorce—and marriage" (1990, p. 464). More recent research has indicated that the stigma associated with being divorced has declined for both men and women, but Gerstel's work is still valuable in highlighting that men and women experience *different types* of social disapproval in ways that are consistent with a gender-based perspective of marriage and divorce.

With this in mind, we now consider the specific consequences of divorce in several important life domains. To illustrate some key points, we present brief vignettes from interviews with college students who have experienced parental divorce (Harvey & Fine, 2011). The vignettes are not designed to be representative, but to highlight variability in children's responses.

Economic Consequences

Women are more likely to be economically disadvantaged after divorce than are men. Of course, some women and men fare better financially than others; having a high predivorce standard of living is a protective factor that lessens the negative economic impact of divorce. Nevertheless, despite this individual variation, a clear pattern is that the economic well-being of divorced women and their children plunges in comparison to predivorce levels, while divorced men often enjoy a *better* financial situation postdivorce (Tach & Eads, 2015). Tach and Eads (2015), however, noted that the disadvantage in women's economic well-being relative to men's has declined over time (42% lower in the 1980s vs. 33% lower by 2000).

The economic costs of divorce are greater for women because most marriages and divorces involve children, and mothers continue to devote substantially more time and money than fathers to caring for children (Altintas & Sullivan, 2016). The time women invest in childcare and other unpaid family labor restricts not only their income, but also their educational and occupational opportunities. Women are less likely to work if they have young children, and family demands prompt many employed women to reduce time spent in paid work (Maume, 2016). Another major reason why women suffer more financially after divorce than men is that many fathers do not comply fully with child support awards. Many mothers receive irregular or incomplete child support payments, and a substantial minority receives nothing (Ha, Cancian, & Meyer, 2011). Even when fathers comply fully, child support awards are typically too low to meet the costs of raising children, and they are often not indexed for inflation. One college student described the changes this way:

> Before the divorce, we were fairly well off, living in a nice house and getting most of what we wanted. After the divorce, my mother, my sister, and I moved into a small 2-bedroom apartment that was not even close to as nice as our former house. My parents argued a lot about the financial aspects of the divorce settlement and many of these arguments were in front of me. As a result, I became more aware than I wanted to of how child support was determined in Missouri. After the settlement, both my parents felt that they had been treated unfairly and both claimed to be "poor." All I cared about was that it seemed that there wasn't any money to buy things with and this was all that much harder to deal with because, before the divorce, I had gotten used to getting what I wanted. The biggest changes I noticed following divorce were in the kind of place we lived in and the lack of having enough money to go around. (Harvey & Fine, 2011, p. 43)

Institutionalized sexism and gender discrimination in the wage workplace also contribute to women's sustained postdivorce economic decline. Most employment opportunities for women are in low-paying or temporary work, which offers little opportunity for advancement. Women's lower earnings relative to men's, when combined with the inadequacies of child support payments and the lack of affordable child care, doom many women and their families to long periods of economic hardship following divorce.

Psychological Adjustment

In some cases, it is fairly straightforward to think of changes associated with divorce as *consequences* of divorce, such as changes in the size or composition of friendship networks or income. But some changes may predate the divorce, and the timing of other changes is more difficult to assess. For example, how do we determine whether an adult's postdivorce adjustment problems are attributable to chronic strains associated with single-parenting, to long-term mental or physical health problems, to family conflict or abuse that occurred prior to the divorce, or to some combination of these (and perhaps other) factors? It is extremely difficult to tease apart these varying possibilities.

Although several studies have examined the course of adult psychological adjustment following divorce, many have involved cross-sectional designs, have relied on clinical or convenience samples, or have failed to include comparison groups. Still, there are some consistent findings. As reviewed in Demo and Fine (2010), longitudinal studies have consistently shown that an important predictor of both women's and men's postdivorce psychological adjustment was their *pre*divorce adjustment. For both sexes, better coping and emotional functioning prior to divorce were associated with more effective coping and less anger and emotional distress after divorce. Preseparation communication and shared decision-making regarding childrearing also were associated with more cooperative involvement between parents after divorce. It should be noted, however, that individuals from ethnic/racial minority groups are underrepresented in the samples of these longitudinal (and other) studies.

There are interesting similarities and differences in the ways that women and men respond to family experiences preceding and following divorce. Both divorced women and divorced men who are involved in relationships with new partners adjust better psychologically and emotionally than others without such relationships (i.e., having a new romantic relationship served as a protective factor) (Amato, 2014). Yet women appear to be bothered more by pre- and postdivorce family issues, tensions, and conflicts. For men, "new relationships were able to undo, with surprising rapidity, the narcissistic injury engendered by the divorce" (Coysh et al., 1989, p. 68). In contrast, "women appear to be more affected by the residual hostility from the past marriage and problematic relations between partners and children in their new marriages or relationships" (p. 68). A 22 year-old woman described her mother's struggles during and following divorce:

> While this was going on, my mother's self-esteem plummeted as she slipped into a deep depression. This was probably the most difficult part. For various reasons, all of her friends deserted her at once. This simply increased her feeling of loneliness and anger, and isolation. Because we were around, we bore most of my mom's frustrations. My mother would become angry and lash out at us. As the oldest child and the one with the shortest fuse, I caught the worst. . . . She was going through a period of regression, acting like a teenager with her newfound freedom. I felt the need to let her know that her immature, reckless behavior was not acceptable with me. (Harvey & Fine, 2011, p. 46)

There are a number of possible explanations for gender differences in post-divorce adjustment. Women, in general, are more deeply committed to marriage, parenthood, and family life than men are; women devote substantially more time and energy to these activities than men do; and women are better attuned than men to family members' needs, the emotional climate of the marriage, and marital problems (Roman & Cortina, 2016). Having invested more in the relationship, it is reasonable that the dissolution of the relationship would inflict greater emotional pain on women than on men. Other factors certainly contribute to women's postdivorce distress, including their worsened economic position and the chronic stresses associated with coordinating employment and single parenting (Tach & Eads, 2015).

As bleak a picture as this paints for many divorced women, there is considerable evidence to suggest that divorce is a short-term crisis, with stress increasing as the divorce approaches, then subsiding postdivorce as life is reorganized and individuals adjust to new routines and lifestyles (Demo & Fine, 2010). Many divorced women may feel that even with the demands placed on them following divorce, they prefer their current situation to the lives they had when they were married.

The evidence on race differences in adjustment to divorce is limited, but it appears that compared to their white counterparts, African American women receive more social support postdivorce (Brown, Orbuch, & Maharaj, 2010). Kitson (1992) suggested that, although African Americans view divorce as regrettable, the higher divorce rate among African Americans prompts greater acceptance and less stigma. Social, emotional, and financial adjustment to divorce appear to be very similar among Whites and African Americans (Lawson & Satti, 2016).

Children's Adjustment

Perhaps no issue surrounding divorce generates more concern or stirs more controversy than children's adjustment to divorce, and the research literature on the subject is voluminous (e.g., see Amato, 2010). Here, we briefly summarize what we know about how children are influenced by processes associated with divorce, highlight the variability found in children's ability to adapt to divorce, and offer some explanations for these patterns.

As is the case for most adults, the evidence suggests that most children and adolescents experience adjustment difficulties (but not necessarily at *clinical* levels) for 1 to 2 years during the period leading up to and immediately following parental separation and divorce (Hetherington & Kelly, 2002). This is usually the period when marital and family conflicts intensify, when legal battles are fought, and when relationships with residential and nonresidential parents are restructured and renegotiated. On average, however, the adjustment of children and adolescents following divorce is only moderately lower than that of their counterparts in continuously intact first-marriage families (Demo & Fine, 2010). Recent analyses of two national samples reported "a substantial degree of variability in children's outcomes following parental divorce, with some children declining, others improving, and most not changing at all" (Amato & Anthony, 2014, p. 370).

Factors that are protective of children's postdivorce adjustment are the provision of economic resources; having positive, nurturing relationships with both parents; low levels of interparental and family conflict (Amato, 2014; Demo & Fine, 2010; Elam, Sandler, Wolchik, Tein, & Rogers, 2019); and higher levels of predivorce adjustment (Strohschein, 2012). It is widely speculated that reduced involvement with nonresidential parents is damaging to children's well-being. Heightening this concern are studies showing that in many cases, paternal involvement following divorce is infrequent (McNamee, Amato, & King, 2014) and that fathers' contact typically diminishes over time (Cheadle, Amato, & King, 2010). A 20 year-old woman described how her relationship with her father deteriorated:

> Eventually he "became too busy," according to my father, to take our visits any longer. He still sent us birthday and Christmas cards with money enclosed and stopped by every once in a while. Then everything stopped for a few years. Neither my brother nor I had any contact with him, and he never saw us. The next time that I did see him I was probably 15 or 16 years old and was with my friends at the supermarket. I ran into him in the parking lot and all he could say was things to belittle me. He asked if I was pregnant, if I was still working fast food, or if I had flunked out of school by now. He made me feel about one inch tall and embarrassed me so much in front of my friends. He wasn't even happy to see me. Luckily, my friends stuck up for me and told him to "fuck off" and took me away from him.

> The next time I saw him was at Walmart my junior year in college, where I endured the same treatment. This time, though, I had a lot more to say for myself and told him exactly what had gone on in my life concerning college, and my career just to prove to him that I was going somewhere in life. Both times I've run into him at the store, he was buying beer. So much for AA. (Harvey & Fine, 2011, p. 95)

But the broader picture on children's relationships with parents following divorce is both more complex and more encouraging. Children live in a wide variety of family situations postdivorce, including arrangements in which non-residential fathers (especially African American fathers) maintain regular contact with their children (Cheadle et al., 2010). Many children change residences (some several times) to live with a different parent (Brown, 2010). children living with their fathers typically have relatively frequent contact with nonresidential mothers (Stewart, 2010), and most children and adolescents adapt well to diverse forms of postdivorce family life (Demo & Fine, 2010). These patterns demonstrate that traditional definitions of family structure (e.g., father present or father absent) and broad generalizations of postdivorce parenting (e.g., "deadbeat dads") obscure substantial temporal and cultural variation in residential and visitation processes (Cherlin, 2010).

Following divorce, the *quality* of children's relationships with both parents affects their adjustment to divorce (Sigal, Sandler, Wolchik, & Braver, 2011). There is also consistent evidence that children's adjustment is enhanced if they have a good relationship with at least one (but not necessarily both) of their parents (Vanassche, Sodermans, Matthijs, & Swicegood, 2014). Following divorce, conflicts between parents may lessen in frequency and intensity, and children benefit most when parents insulate children from these tensions, as this 20 year-old woman describes:

> Although I was very upset when my parents told me that they were getting a divorce, after a few years I knew that it was for the best. In fact, I couldn't even imagine how my parents had been able to get along as good as they did. After the divorce, my parents really tried to keep me out of the middle. I know that they were angry with each other, particularly my father being mad at my mom, but they always seemed to be able to put aside their differences so that they could do what was best for me. In fact, in the past few years, they have even become sort of like friends again. I don't want to put my kids through a divorce, but if it has to happen, I hope I can put their needs first like my parents did for me. (Harvey & Fine, 2011, p. 63)

A serious problem confronting many children following divorce is prolonged economic hardship. Although children's postdivorce residential arrangements are variable and change over time, roughly 4 out of 5 children live with their mother, 10% live with their father, and the remainder have dual residences or live in other arrangements (Bjarnason & Arnarsson, 2011). As we have seen, most women and children experience a sharp, long-term decline in their standard of living following divorce. Economic hardship is associated with lowered parental well-being, less effective and less supportive parenting, inconsistent and harsh discipline, and distressed and impaired socioemotional functioning in children (Neppl, Senia, & Donnellan, 2016). It should be clear, however, that these adverse effects are products of chronic financial stress and can be experienced by children in divorced and nondivorced families alike.

Multiple Family Transitions and Children's and Parents' Adjustment

Although research indicates that most children and adolescents who experience their parents' divorce score in the normal (or nonclinical) range on measures of adjustment, a small but growing minority may be at prolonged risk because of multiple transitions in family living arrangements. Transitions in family living arrangements refer to changes in family structure, marital status, or household living arrangements that mark the beginning or the end of cohabiting, marital, or remarried relationships. As children age, the likelihood increases that they will experience family structure change, as does the probability that they will experience more than one family transition. According to Cavanagh and Huston (2008), more than 1 in 4 children in the NICHD Study of Early Child Care and Youth Development experienced two or more family transitions by the end of fourth grade. Recent data suggest that the percentage of children experiencing multiple transitions has increased (Fomby & Osborne, 2017).

Consequences for Children

What effects do multiple family transitions have on children? Each family structure transition can be emotionally stressful, so there is the potential that the cumulative effect of multiple transitions across childhood and adolescence may be quite harmful (Johnston, Fine, Crosby, & Willse, 2019). When parents and their romantic partners move into and out of the household, there are disruptions in adult sources of support, nurturance, supervision, and discipline. Changes in parenting behaviors, family routines, and emotional attachments are often accompanied by changes in residences, schools, neighborhoods, and peer groups. The changes can be confusing and bothersome to children, especially at the beginning, but over time many children and parents report happier relationships. An illustration of how these complex family structures can improve is described by a 22-year-old man:

> Eventually both of my parents remarried around the time of my preteen and young teenage years. I definitely had a hard time accepting these remarriages, especially my mom's. When I was in seventh grade, I had to move to Indiana with my mom because my stepdad had trouble finding a job in Chicago where both my mom and dad lived. I was angry and bitter that I was essentially being taken away from my dad, my friends, and my hometown. My relationship with my stepdad struggled for a long time after the move. My real dad and I had always had a close relationship and so the distance between us was extremely hard on both of us and suffered in the long run. My dad remarried last although he had dated my stepmom for many years beforehand. Even though I only saw my dad and stepmom on alternating holidays and for a month each summer, my stepmom and I also had a rocky relationship. Looking back, I was jealous and bitter at my two stepparents for altering the life that I had gotten used to after the divorce.

> The main positive aspect that I gained from my stepparents though was my stepsiblings whom I now consider my own brothers and sisters. I was an only child and since it wasn't possible anymore to have biological siblings, stepsiblings were the next best thing. I have four older siblings on my mom's side and two younger siblings on my dad's side now. I love them all

very much and have a unique and special relationship with each of them. Another advantage of my parents' divorce and remarriages, besides the gain of family, would be all the friends and people that I have met. They have each had a strong impact in my life and will remain friends for life. I am very thankful for their presence in my life. Another positive aspect of the remarriages is of course my parents' happiness. They are both very happy with their new partners and have each been married for over a decade now. I seriously doubt that either one will divorce again, which of course pleases me. (Harvey & Fine, 2011, p. 68)

Analyses of data from five waves of the Fragile Families Study found that the frequency of mothers' partnership transitions was negatively associated with children's socioemotional, cognitive, and behavioral outcomes (Fomby & Osborne, 2017). The pattern of accumulating effects of multiple transitions was obtained across White, Black, and Hispanic children. However, it is important to note that family context attenuated this association. Thus, while the number of family transitions experienced may be a risk in itself, there are other family processes that can serve as risk or protective factors for children during these transitions (e.g., parenting style, communication, routines, and household chaos).

In addition, also using the Fragile Families data set, Johnston et al. (2019) found that the number of family structure transitions were directly related to *teachers' reports*, but not *maternal reports*, of modest, although significant, changes in children's internalizing and externalizing behavior problems. Also, for both teachers' and maternal reports of children's outcomes, maternal depression mediated the effects of cumulative family structure transitions on children's externalizing and internalizing behaviors, suggesting that family processes, in addition to family structure changes, affect the trajectories of children's behavior problems over time.

The Johnston et al. (2019) study also examined racial/ethnic differences in the number of parenting transitions, as well as in the effects of cumulative parenting transitions on children across African American, White, and Latinx children. First, Johnston et al. found that African American children and White children experienced similar total numbers of parenting transitions, whereas Latinx children experienced fewer transitions than did children in the other two racial/ethnic groups (Fine & Johnston, in press). This finding may reflect the relatively lower divorce rates among Latinx couples, which would result in smaller numbers of parenting transitions for these children.

Second, Fine and Johnston (in press) found that the number of parenting transitions was inversely related to children's well-being at age 9 for African American and White children. For African American children, larger numbers of parenting transitions were related to less cooperation and self-control skills and more externalizing problems at age 9. Thus, the aggregation of these transitions has an overall negative, although modest, impact later in the child's life. It should be noted that the number of significant effects was relatively small (less than 50% of the path coefficients were statistically significant for both groups) and, for those that were significant, the effect sizes were generally small.

Some have suggested that African American children are less detrimentally affected by divorce, remarriage, and cohabitation than are children in other racial and ethnic groups because of higher levels of extended family support, greater stress in their daily lives, and less stigma associated with these transitions. However, the Fine and Johnston (in press) findings suggest that there are no racial and ethnic differences in both the number of parenting transitions and the effects of these transitions on children's development. Clearly, more research is needed on the extent to which race moderates the relations between the number of parenting transitions and children's outcomes.

Consequences for Adults

For adults, given the relatively high divorce rates for first marriages and the even higher dissolution rates for subsequent marriages, multiple divorces continue to be quite common (Aughinbaugh, Robles, & Sun, 2013), although this rate may have gone down slightly in the last decade because of slightly declining marriage rates, increases in cohabitation, and modest declines in the divorce rate since 1980 (Guzzo, 2014). Furthermore, there is some evidence that the frequency of family transitions (i.e., marriage, divorce, cohabitation, singlehood) is related to higher levels of depression for women (Cavanagh & Fomby, 2019).

In sum, multiple family structure transitions have modest detrimental effects for women, and perhaps men, but these negative consequences for adults are smaller in magnitude than are the comparable effects for children. Perhaps the effects on adults are smaller because adults (to varying degrees) choose to make these transitions whereas children's transitions are often decided for them because many adults have more sophisticated and effective coping skills than children, or because some adults may become more accustomed to divorce stressors (and presumably less affected by them) with each subsequent divorce.

Interventions

In this section, we consider two types of interventions that attempt to improve the lives of those who have experienced divorce: parenting education for divorcing parents and family mediation. These two were selected because they have become institutionalized in the "divorce industry," have achieved a high level of popularity, have already affected large numbers of divorced families, and involve some degree of collaboration between legal and nonlegal professionals.

Parenting Education for Divorcing Parents

One arena in which the divorce industry is very apparent is parenting education for divorcing parents. Partly because of an increased awareness of the stresses that divorce places on children, attention has been focused on helping children adjust more effectively to divorce. In recent years, the most frequent way this has been addressed is through educational programs that prepare parents to help their children cope with divorce. Parent education for separated and divorced parents is available in the vast majority of the states (46 as of 2008; Pollett & Lombreglia, 2008), and most of these programs are court mandated (Emery, Rowen, & Dinescu, 2014). However, there is often a disconnect between being mandated by a judge to attend these programs and actual attendance (deLusé & Braver, 2015). These programs are offered in schools, universities, community agencies, and family courts, and they range widely in length and number of sessions, instructional methods, and educational goals. In general, these programs address child-focused, parent-focused, or court-focused content, including (a) postdivorce reactions of children and parents, (b) children's needs and reactions to divorce at different ages, (c) the benefits of cooperative postdivorce parenting, and (d) the emotional costs of placing children in the middle of parental disputes (Blaisure & Geasler, 2006).

The quality of the evaluations of these programs has lagged far behind programmatic development (Sigal et al., 2011). When evaluations of these programs are conducted, they have primarily consisted of "consumer satisfaction" questionnaires that ask participants how satisfied they were with various aspects of the program (Blaisure & Geasler, 2006). Results from these questionnaires typically show that consumers are very satisfied with the programs (Schramm & Calix, 2011), which is not surprising given that clients usually report having positive experiences with a wide range of interventions. However, emerging methodological techniques have begun to utilize person-centered analyses to better evaluate program effectiveness based on typologies (Galovan & Schramm, 2017). Findings from Galovan and Schramm (2017) suggest that parenting education programs should consider tailoring their content and teaching approaches to parents with different types of coparenting styles (e.g., highly conflictual vs. cooperative) to maximize program effectiveness.

However, client satisfaction does not necessarily mean that the programs are successful in achieving their primary goal—fostering behavioral change. Unfortunately, we know relatively little about the short- and long-term effectiveness of these parenting education programs in affecting behavior change. The few studies examining such change have generally found positive effects when program participants are compared to controls who have not participated in any structured program (Galovan & Schramm, 2017). Some have reported that compared to parents who do not attend such programs, parents in divorce education programs were more willing to seek outside help, litigated less often, engaged in less conflict with coparents, and had improved child and parent well-being (deLusé & Braver, 2015; Fackrell, Hawkins, & Kay, 2011; Sigal et al., 2011).

Further, research on the long-term effectiveness of parenting education classes is lacking, and what does exist has continued to focus on participant satisfaction rather than actual skills or outcomes (Salem, Sandler, & Wolchik, 2013;

Schramm & Calix, 2011). There is some evidence that these programs may have immediate benefits, but these benefits may subside within a few months (Schramm & Calix, 2011), further supporting the need for evaluation of long-term effectiveness (Fackrell et al., 2011). Although there has been some improvement in the quality of and frequency of program evaluations of these programs, there is still a great deal of work to do before we can conclude with confidence that the benefits of these programs endure for several years.

These educational programs have political and intuitive appeal, so the absence of supportive evidence of effectiveness has not deterred their widespread use and dissemination. However, without sound evaluation findings, courts and legislatures will find it increasingly difficult to justify mandating such programs. Thus, evaluations of these programs that extend beyond consumer satisfaction are very much needed. Some families also face numerous cultural, structural, and resource challenges that make it difficult to continue these programs for extended periods of time (Pruett & Cornett, 2017). The University of Denver attempted to combat these obstacles by forming the Resource Center for Separating and Divorcing Families (RCSDF) that used a community-based rather than court-based model to assist with the divorce process (Pruett & Cornett, 2017). Community-based educational programs have become increasingly popular because of their ability to offer an array of services, such as educational and mental health services, while reducing the amount of time and money that is required (Pruett & Cornett, 2017; Salem et al., 2013).

Given that the primary targets of parent education for divorcing parents are *children*, one might wonder why children themselves are not the direct recipients of intervention. There are a number of reasons why parents are the direct recipients of these educational sessions, including that (a) they are more amenable to such interventions, (b) they perhaps have the insight and motivation to benefit from the material presented, and (c) it is logistically easier to require adults than children to attend such a session. Nevertheless, there are a number of programs developed for children whose parents are divorced or divorcing (e.g., Pedro-Carroll, 1997). Many of these are school-based programs that focus on helping children adapt socially and emotionally; becoming aware of their feelings about themselves, their parents, and the divorce; expressing feelings in appropriate ways; learning to cope with frustration; learning to get along with others; and enhancing self-esteem. There is some evidence that these group interventions are effective (fewer symptoms of depression, anxiety, and anger) (Esmaeilian, Dehghani, Dehghani, & Lee, 2018), but few programs have been adequately evaluated in controlled studies, and findings from the evaluation studies that have been conducted are not consistent or clear-cut.

Divorce Mediation

Mediation is one of a class of alternative dispute resolution approaches; they are considered "alternative" because they are less adversarial than traditional legal procedures and seek to reach agreements in a more cooperative manner. Divorce mediation consists of an impartial third party helping a divorcing or divorced couple identify, discuss, and, hopefully, resolve disagreements related to the divorce. Mediation has grown rapidly and is mandated in several states (Emery et al., 2014). Mediation usually addresses some or all of five areas of potential conflict: (1) property division, (2) spousal support, (3) child support, (4) custody, and (5) visitation (Shaw, 2010). Successful mediation allows the divorcing couple to maintain control of decisions in these domains and results in each party feeling some ownership over the divorce agreement (Shaw, 2010).

Mediation is based on the principle of cooperative negotiation, which is unlike the typically adversarial nature of the U.S. legal system, which views the parties as disputants who compete with each other for limited resources. In contrast to psychotherapy, mediation targets more specific, pragmatic, concrete, and immediate issues. Emery (1999) described the core of mediation as "renegotiating family relationships" (p. 379). The negotiation of relationships is not achieved by exploring psychological issues, but rather by helping the (ex)partners agree on issues regarding child rearing. Although mediation is a popular alternative to traditional legal procedures, there have been scarce amounts of research that have examined its effectiveness (Ballard, Holtzworth-Munroe, Applegate, D'Onofrio, & Bates, 2013). Considering the limited research in this area, there is room for improvement of mediation strategies, including the involvement of children or incorporating children's thoughts and feelings into negotiations (Ballard et al., 2013).

Although early evidence was promising, subsequent research has led to less optimistic conclusions. Several studies suggested that mediation was associated with better quality co-parenting than were more traditional adversarial approaches, but that there were no short-term differences between the two approaches in enhancing psychological well-being (McIntosh & Tan, 2017). The lack of positive short-term effects of mediation on some dimensions may be due to overly high expectations about what a brief intervention such as mediation can reasonably accomplish or a lack of measures that are sensitive to the nuanced ways that mediation may be helpful.

Nevertheless, mediation has been shown to be effective on some dimensions. In the Charlottesville Mediation Study (Sbarra & Emery, 2006), one of only three major mediation studies that were included in the Shaw (2010) meta-analysis, parents consistently preferred mediation over litigation in terms of both the process (e.g., feeling understood) and perceived outcomes (e.g., one's rights being protected) of the intervention. Furthermore, in a long-term (12-year) follow-up, nonresidential parents who went through mediation had considerably more contact (both face to face and by telephone) with their children than did those who had litigated settlements (Sbarra & Emery, 2006). However, a potential drawback of this additional contact is that ex-partners reported being more attached to each other than partners who went through litigation.

Mediation has its critics. First, almost 30 years ago, Menzel (1991) expressed concern that men's greater power places women at a disadvantage in negotiating and that mediators do not take these power differentials into account. Clearly, the potentially negative consequences of such power differentials are still present. On the other hand, noting that women are more satisfied than are men with both litigated and mediated settlements, Emery (1995) suggested that it is not that women are disadvantaged in mediation, but rather that men are disadvantaged in litigation. Thus, according to this view, men have more to gain in mediation than they often do in litigation, which leads them to be more satisfied with mediated agreements.

Second, mediation is not an appropriate strategy for some couples. Spouses who cannot communicate and problem solve with each other, whether because one or both spouses have personality characteristics that prohibit cooperative problem solving or because the couple has dysfunctional interactional patterns, are inappropriate candidates for mediation.

Third, there has been controversy regarding who can be effective mediators. Mediators generally fall into one of two groups: lawyers and (nonlegally trained) mental health professionals. Some have argued that lawyers are best suited to be mediators because of their knowledge of the law, whereas others have suggested that mental health professionals have greater knowledge of the psychological and emotional aspects of how children, parents, and families cope with divorce. Consistent with Emery's (1995) prediction, mediation has not and probably will not become a separate profession, but it has developed within both the mental health and legal professions.

Finally, there is some controversy pertaining to whether mediation should be mandated, used only in select cases, or voluntary. As Sbarra and Emery (2006) and Beck, Walsh, Mechanic, and Taylor (2010) noted, there are some cases when mediation may be inappropriate, such as when a child or a spouse has been abused. Nevertheless, because mandating mediation typically requires that a couple attend and participate in a session but not necessarily reach a settlement, there are strong reasons to require mediation except in selected cases.

Conclusions

Divorce has become almost a normative experience in the 21st century. Although there is considerable variation in children's and adults' emotional adjustment to divorce (see Demo & Fine, 2010), most children and adults adapt well to a variety of postdivorce family forms and function in the normal ranges of adjustment. Among the small percentage who experience lingering difficulties, the problems can often be traced to poor adjustment preceding the divorce; predivorce family tension, stress, conflict, and hostility; postdivorce economic decline; postdivorce conflict between the ex-spouses; and multiple transitions in family living arrangements.

Divorce is more widely accepted and less stigmatized today than in the past, but it still tends to be viewed negatively and is often blamed for many individual and societal problems. Opposition to divorce also has legal and political implications as, from time to time, there have been efforts to make it more difficult for married couples to obtain divorces, such as longer waiting periods and requiring participation in counseling before the divorce is granted. The evidence reviewed in this chapter suggests that divorce is a prevalent (and sometimes even necessary) aspect of family life, and we believe that little is likely to be gained by restricting divorce and further stigmatizing it. Our position is that it makes more sense for family researchers, practitioners, and policymakers to focus attention and resources on identifying risk and protective factors and processes that are related to how effectively people adjust to divorce. For example, what can be done to help parents keep their children out of the middle of their conflicts? What are the best ways for parents to communicate their impending divorce to their children? How do support networks facilitate the adjustment of divorcing parents? In our opinion, exploring these and other issues from research, practice, and policy perspectives will be more helpful than devoting resources to trying to prevent the occurrence of divorce itself.

With specific reference to interventions, attention also needs to be devoted to designing programs that better prepare and educate divorcing adults—parents and nonparents alike—for the financial, coparenting, and personal stresses, transitions, and challenges they will face in a variety of postdivorce family forms. Client satisfaction with educational programs for divorcing parents is impressive, but little research has evaluated the short- and long-term impact of these programs on parenting effectiveness, parent–child relationships, or child well-being. Additional programs, with appropriate levels of pretesting, designed specifically for children are also needed. Finally, while there is a growing body of evidence suggesting that divorce mediation has numerous advantages over conventional adversarial divorces, more research is needed that evaluates when mediation is most effective and for which groups it is particularly well-suited. The challenge will be to explore these and other interventions as ways of normalizing divorce and facilitating healthy adjustment to this stressor.

DISCUSSION QUESTIONS

1. According to the DVFM, what are some factors that help to explain variability in family members' adjustment to divorce? What are some reasons that account for fluidity in parents' and children's adjustment to divorce?

2. Describe several demographic, individual difference, and relationship variables that contribute to a higher probability of divorce. Select one variable from each category and explain why the variable has the effect of increasing the likelihood of divorce.

3. What are some common consequences for parents and children who experience multiple family transitions?

4. Two interventions—parent education and divorce mediation—are described in the chapter. For each intervention, explain the rationale for why it is expected to be helpful, the benefits each intervention is expected to generate, and questions that so far have yet to be resolved regarding each intervention.

REFERENCES

Ahrons, C. (1994). *The good divorce: Keeping your family together when your marriage comes apart.* New York, NY: Harper Collins.

Altintas, E., & Sullivan, O. (2016). Fifty years of change updated: Cross-national gender convergence in housework. *Demographic Research, 35,* 455–469.

Amato, P. R. (2004). Divorce in social and historical context: Changing scientific perspectives on children and marital dissolution. In M. Coleman & L. Ganong (Eds.), *Handbook of contemporary families: Considering the past, contemplating the future* (pp. 265–281). Thousand Oaks, CA: SAGE.

Amato, P. R. (2010). Research on divorce: Continuing trends and new developments. *Journal of Marriage and Family, 72,* 650–666.

Amato, P. R. (2014). The consequences of divorce for adults and children: An update. *Društvena istraživanja: časopis za opća društvena pitanja [Social Research: A Journal for General Social Issues], 23*(1), 5–24.

Amato, P. R., & Anthony, C. J. (2014). Estimating the effects of parental divorce and death with fixed effects models. *Journal of Marriage and Family, 76,* 370–386.

Amato, P. R., Johnson, D., Booth, A., & Rogers, S. (2003). Continuity and change in marital quality between 1980 and 2000. *Journal of Marriage and Family, 65,* 1–22.

Arkes, J. (2015). The temporal effects of divorces and separations on children's academic achievement and problem behavior. *Journal of Divorce & Remarriage, 56,* 25–42.

Aughinbaugh, A., Robles, O., & Sun, H. (2013). Marriage and divorce: Patterns by gender, race, and educational attainment. *Monthly Labor Review, 136*(10), 1–19.

Ballard, R. H., Holtzworth-Munroe, A., Applegate, A. G., D'Onofrio, B. M., & Bates, J. E. (2013). A randomized controlled trial of child-informed mediation. *Psychology, Public Policy, and Law, 19*(3), 271.

Beck, C. J. A., Walsh, M. E., Mechanic, M. B., & Taylor, C. S. (2010). Mediator assessment, documentation, and disposition of child custody cases involving intimate partner abuse: A naturalistic evaluation of one county's practices. *Law and Human Behavior, 34,* 227–240.

Birditt, K. S., Brown, E., Orbuch, T. L., & McIlvane, J. M. (2010). Marital conflict behaviors and implications for divorce over 16 years. *Journal of Marriage and Family, 72*(5), 1188–1204.

Bjarnason, T., & Arnarsson, A. M. (2011). Joint physical custody and communication with parents: a cross-national study of children in 36 western countries. *Journal of Comparative Family Studies, 42*(6), 871–890.

Blaisure, K. R., & Geasler, M. J. (2006). Educational interventions for separating and divorcing parents. In M. A. Fine & J. H. Harvey (Eds.), *Handbook of divorce and relationship dissolution* (pp. 575–602). Mahwah, NJ: Erlbaum.

Brown, S. L. (2010). Marriage and child well-being: Research and policy perspectives. *Journal of Marriage and Family*, 72(5), 1059–1077.

Brown, E., Orbuch, T. L., & Maharaj, A. (2010). Social networks and marital stability among Black American and White American couples. In K. T. Sullivan & J. Davila (Eds.), *Support processes in intimate relationships* (pp. 318–334). New York, NY: Oxford University Press.

Cavanagh, S. E., & Fomby, P. (2019). Family instability in the lives of American children. *Annual Review of Sociology*, 45, 493–513.

Cavanagh, S. E., & Huston, A. C. (2008). The timing of family instability and children's social development. *Journal of Marriage and Family*, 70, 1258–1270.

Cheadle, J. E., Amato, P. R., & King, V. (2010). Patterns of nonresident father contact. *Demography*, 47, 205–225.

Cherlin, A. J. (2004). The deinstitutionalization of American marriage. *Journal of Marriage and Family*, 66, 848–861.

Cherlin, A. J. (2009). *The marriage-go-round*. New York, NY: Vintage.

Cherlin, A. J. (2010). Demographic trends in the United States: A review of research in the 2000s. *Journal of Marriage and Family* 72(3), 402–419. doi:10.1111/j.1741-3737.2010.00710.x.

Cherlin, A. J. (2017). Introduction to the special collection on separation, divorce, repartnering, and remarriage around the world. *Demographic Research*, 37, 1275–1296.

Coysh, W. S., Johnston, J. R., Tschann, J. M., Wallerstein, J. S., & Kline, M. (1989). Parental postdivorce adjustment in joint and sole physical custody families. *Journal of Family Issues*, 10, 52–71.

deLusé, S. R., & Braver, S. L. (2015). A rigorous quasi-experimental design to evaluate the causal effect of a mandatory divorce education program. *Family Court Review*, 53(1), 66–78.

Demo, D., H., & Buehler, C. (2013). Theoretical approaches to studying divorce. In M. A. Fine & F. D. Fincham (Eds.), *Handbook of family theories: A content-based approach* (pp. 263–279). New York, NY: Taylor and Francis.

Demo, D. H., & Fine, M. A. (2010). *Beyond the average divorce*. Thousand Oaks, CA: SAGE.

Elder, G. H., Jr. (1998). The life course as developmental theory. *Child Development*, 69, 1–12.

Elam, K. K., Sandler, I., Wolchik, S. A., Tein, J. Y., & Rogers, A. (2019). Latent profiles of postdivorce parenting time, conflict, and quality: Children's adjustment associations. *Journal of Family Psychology*, 33, 499–510.

Emery, R. E. (1995). Divorce mediation: Negotiating agreements and renegotiating relationships. *Family Relations*, 44, 377–383.

Emery, R. E. (1999). *Marriage, divorce, and children's adjustment* (2nd ed.). Thousand Oaks, CA: SAGE.

Emery, R. E., Rowen, J., & Dinescu, D. (2014). New roles for family therapists in the courts: An overview with a focus on custody dispute resolution. *Family Process*, 53(3), 500–515.

Esmaeilian, N., Dehghani, M., Dehghani, Z., & Lee, J. (2018). Mindfulness-based cognitive therapy enhances emotional resiliency in children with divorced parents. *Mindfulness*, 9(4), 1052–1062

Fackrell, T. A., Hawkins, A. J., & Kay, N. M. (2011). How effective are court-affiliated divorcing parents education programs? A meta-analytic study. *Family Court Review*, 49(1), 107–119.

Few-Demo, A. L., Lloyd, S. A., & Allen, K. R. (2014). It's all about power: Integrating feminist family studies and family communication. *Journal of Family Communication*, 14(2), 85–94.

Fine, M. A., & Johnston, C. (in press). Marriage, divorce, and remarriage. In A. J. James, Jr. (Ed.), *Black families: A systems approach.*

Fomby, P., & Osborne, C. (2017). Family instability, multipartner fertility, and behavior in middle childhood. *Journal of Marriage and Family, 79*(1), 75–93.

Galovan, A. M., & Schramm, D. G. (2017). Initial coparenting patterns and postdivorce parent education programming: A latent class analysis. *Journal of Divorce & Remarriage, 58*(3), 212–226.

Gerstel, N. (1990). Divorce and stigma. In C. Carlson (Ed.), *Perspectives on the family: History, class, and feminism* (pp. 460–478). Belmont, CA: Wadsworth.

Guzzo, K. J. (2014). Trends in cohabitation outcomes: Compositional changes and engagement among never married young adults. *Journal of Marriage and Family, 76,* 826–842.

Ha, Y., Cancian, M., & Meyer, D. R. (2011). The regularity of child support and its contribution to the regularity of income. *Social Service Review, 85*(3), 401–419.

Harvey, J. H., & Fine, M. A. (2011). *Children of divorce: Stories of loss and growth.* Routledge.

Hawkins, A. J., Willoughby, B. J., & Doherty, W. J. (2012). Reasons for divorce and openness to marital reconciliation. *Journal of Divorce & Remarriage, 53*(6), 453–463.

Hetherington, E. M., & Kelly, J. (2002). *For better or for worse.* New York, NY: Norton.

Hopper, J. (1993). The rhetoric of motives in divorce. *Journal of Marriage and the Family, 55,* 801–813.

Hopper, J. (2001). The symbolic origins of conflict in divorce. *Journal of Marriage and Family, 63,* 430–445.

Johnston, C., Fine, M. A., Crosby, D., & Willse, J. (2019). *Multiple family transitions and children's externalizing and internalizing behaviors.* Manuscript submitted for publication.

Kitson, G. C. (1992). *Portrait of divorce: Adjustment to marital breakdown.* New York, NY: Guilford Press.

Lawson, E. J., & Satti, F. (2016). The aftermath of divorce: Postdivorce adjustment strategies of South Asian, black, and white women in the United States. *Journal of Divorce & Remarriage, 57*(6), 411–431.

Margolin, G., Oliver, P. H., & Medina, A. M. (2001). Conceptual issues in understanding the relation between interparental conflict and child adjustment. In J. H. Grych & F. D. Fincham (Eds.), *Interparental conflict and child development* (pp. 9–38). Cambridge, England: Cambridge University Press.

Maume, D. J. (2016). Can men make time for family? Paid work, care work, work-family reconciliation policies, and gender equality. *Social Currents, 3*(1), 43–63.

McIntosh, J. E., & Tan, E. S. (2017). Young children in divorce and separation: Pilot study of a mediation-based co-parenting intervention. *Family Court Review, 55*(3), 329–344.

McNamee, C. B., Amato, P. R., & King, V. (2014). Nonresident father involvement with children and divorced women's likelihood of remarriage. *Journal of Marriage and Family, 76,* 862–874.

Menzel, K. E. (1991). Judging the fairness of mediation: A critical framework. *Mediation Quarterly, 9,* 3–20.

Neppl, T. K., Senia, J. M., & Donnellan, M. B. (2016). Effects of economic hardship: Testing the family stress model over time. *Journal of Family Psychology, 30*(1), 12.

Pedro-Carroll, J. (1997). The Children of Divorce Intervention Program: Fostering resilient outcomes for school-aged children. In G. W. Albee &

T. P. Gullotta (Eds.), *Primary prevention works* (pp. 213–238). Thousand Oaks, CA: SAGE.

Perelli-Harris, B., Berrington, A., Gassen, N. S., Galezewska, P., & Holland, J. A. (2017). The rise in divorce and cohabitation: Is there a link? *Population and Development Review, 43*(2), 303.

Pollet, S. L., & Lombreglia, M. (2008). A nationwide survey of mandatory parent education. *Family Court Review, 46*, 375–394.

Powell, D., & Fine, M. A. (2009). Relationship dissolution, causes. In H. T. Reis & S. Sprecher (Eds.), *Encyclopedia of human relationships*. Thousand Oaks, CA: SAGE.

Pruett, M. K., & Cornett, L. (2017). Evaluation of the University of Denver's Center for Separating and Divorcing Families: The First Out-of-Court Divorce Option 1. *Family Court Review, 55*(3), 375–389.

Raley, R. K., Sweeney, M. M., & Wondra, D. (2015). The growing racial and ethnic divide in U.S. marriage patterns. *Future Child, 25*(2), 89–109.

Rappaport, S. R. (2013). Deconstructing the impact of divorce on children. *Family Law Quarterly, 47*, 353.

Rodrigues, A. E., Hall, J. H., & Fincham, F. D. (2006). What predicts divorce and relationship dissolution. In M. A. Fine & J. H. Harvey (Eds.), *Handbook of divorce and relationship dissolution* (pp. 85–112). Mahwah, NJ: Erlbaum.

Roman, J. G., & Cortina, C. (2016). Family time of couples with children: Shortening gender differences in parenting? *Review of Economics of the Household, 14*(4), 921–940.

Salem, P., Sandler, I., & Wolchik, S. (2013). Taking stock of parent education in the family courts: Envisioning a public health approach. *Family Court Review, 51*(1), 131–148.

Sbarra, D. A., & Emery, R. E. (2006). In the presence of grief: The role of cognitive emotional adaptation in contemporary divorce mediation. In M. A. Fine & J. H. Harvey (Eds.), *Handbook of divorce and relationship dissolution* (pp. 553–573). Mahwah, NJ: Erlbaum.

Schramm, D. G., & Calix, S. (2011). Focus on kids: Evaluation of a research-based divorce education program. *Journal of Divorce & Remarriage, 52*(7), 529–549.

Shaw, L. A. (2010). Divorce mediation outcome research: A meta-analysis. *Conflict Resolution Quarterly, 27*(4), 447–467.

Sigal, A., Sandler, I., Wolchik, S., & Braver, S. (2011). Do parent education programs promote healthy postdivorce parenting? Critical distinctions and a review of the evidence. *Family Court Review, 49*(1), 120–139.

Stanley, S. (2019, July 9). *Cruising at altitude: Reconciling a high divorce rate with high marital satisfaction ratings* [Web log post]. Institute for Family Studies. https://ifstudies.org/blog/cruising-at-altitude-reconciling-a-high-divorce-rate-with-high-marital-satisfaction-ratings

Stewart, S. D. (2010). Children with nonresident parents: Living arrangements, visitation, and child support. *Journal of Marriage and Family, 72*(5), 1078–1091.

Strohschein, L. (2012). Parental divorce and child mental health: Accounting for predisruption differences. *Journal of Divorce & Remarriage, 53*(6), 489–502.

Tach, L. M., & Eads, A. (2015). Trends in the economic consequences of marital and cohabitation dissolution in the United States. *Demography, 52*(2), 401–432.

Teachman, J. D., Tedrow, L., & Hall, M. (2006). The demographic future of divorce. In M. A. Fine & J. H. Harvey (Eds.), *Handbook of divorce and relationship dissolution* (pp. 59–82). Mahwah, NJ: Erlbaum.

Vanassche, S., Sodermans, A. K., Matthijs, K., & Swicegood, G. (2014). The effects of family type, family relationships and parental role models on delinquency and alcohol use among Flemish adolescents. *Journal of Child and Family Studies, 23*(1), 128–143.

van der Wal, R. C., Finkenauer, C., & Visser, M. M. (2019). Reconciling mixed findings on children's adjustment following high-conflict divorce. *Journal of Child and Family Studies, 28*(2), 468–478.

Walsh, F. (2002). A family resilience framework: Innovative practice applications. *Family Relations, 51*, 130–137.

Weaver, J. M., & Schofield, T. J. (2015). Mediation and moderation of divorce effects on children's behavior problems. *Journal of Family Psychology, 29*, 39–48.

Zartler, U. (2014). How to deal with moral tales: Constructions and strategies of single-parent families. *Journal of Marriage and Family, 76*, 604–619.

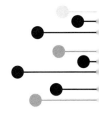

CHAPTER 9

Stress and Resilience in Stepfamilies Today

Chelsea Garneau-Rosner and
Braquel Egginton

Vignette

Nick was single when he met Adina and gave little thought to how her 10-year-old son, Jared, would affect their relationship. When they married a year later, they had never discussed his role in their new stepfamily. Nick expected the transition would be smooth, and he would act like a "regular father" after the marriage, partly because Jared's father had not been around for 9 years. It soon became clear, however, that neither Jared nor Adina shared this expectation. Nick and Jared had screaming matches every time Nick enforced a household rule or told Jared what to do. Frequently, Adina came to the defense of her son. Over time, Nick began to feel like he did not have a place in the family and felt betrayed by Adina's loyalty to her son. Often, when the three of them were together, it ended in a fight or in silence.

Stepfamilies have long been the focus of research (see Ganong & Coleman, 2017) with an emphasis on traditionally defined *stepfamilies*—families in which at least one adult was remarried and brought children from a prior union into the current one. A majority of these families were formed following divorce rather than the death of spouse. However, much has changed in family life, and scholars are now more inclusive in defining stepfamilies to reflect the diversity of pathways that lead to them. For example, although stepfamilies consistently include children from prior unions, we also recognize those formed when never-married individuals with children go on to cohabit with or marry a partner who is not their child's biological parent. The typical pathway continues to be from one marriage to another marriage; however, stepfamilies are also recognized as forming after the dissolution and repartnering of nonmarital relationships involving both same-sex and heterosexual pairings. It is the children that link prior and current unions, regardless of whether these unions result from marriages.

The labels used to describe stepfamilies have also evolved over time. For example, earlier research and scholarly writing on stepfamilies frequently used terms such as *reconstituted* or *merged* families, whereas *blended* is a more common label. Other current terms reflect the diversity in pathways to stepfamilies and their structure by distinguishing between *married* and *cohabiting*, or unmarried, stepfamilies and those that are *simple* versus *complex*. A simple stepfamily includes two adults of which only one is a parent, whereas a complex stepfamily includes two adults who are both parents, regardless of where the children reside. Recently, some researchers have proposed the *hybrid* stepfamily, where at least one shared child is born in the stepfamily who is biologically related to both parents, creating a half-sibling relationship to any stepchildren in the family (Harcourt, Adler-Baeder, Erath, & Pettit, 2015). The terms *resident* and *nonresident* account for whether the stepfamily household is the primary home of the child, which is often determined by residing in the home at least half of the time. It is important to note that although attempts have been made more recently to recognize various aspects of stepfamily diversity, much of what is known about stepfamily relationships continues to be based primarily on research with samples of married, resident stepfather families.

We begin this chapter by addressing the prevalence and demographic characteristics of stepfamilies in general. Then we discuss stepfamily stress from a family systems perspective to identify sources of stress within the various subsystems and the most common characteristics of resilient stepfamilies. We end with a brief description of psychoeducational and clinical approaches to easing stepfamily adjustment.

Prevalence and Demographic Characteristics of Stepfamilies

Estimates of the prevalence of stepfamilies in the United States today are often drawn from national surveys, such as the U.S. Census or the American Community Survey (ACS), and the results may vary (see Kreider & Lofquist, 2014, for a discussion). Some estimates focus on children of the householder (e.g., Census), whereas other estimates reference children by the type of relationship to both coresident parents (e.g., Current Population Reports [CPR]). However, all sources typically underestimate the number of stepfamilies by excluding (a) stepchildren who are nonresident and live elsewhere (often with a single parent and are counted as children in single-parent families) and (b) resident and nonresident children who are 18 years and older. Regardless of these and other limitations, we draw upon these data in addition to data from large, nationally representative datasets which together provide the most current and accurate picture of stepfamilies in the United States.

The most recent estimates using nationally representative samples, show that 36% to 43% of cohabiting couples and 27% to 43% of married couples are stepfamilies (Cohen, 2011; Guzzo, 2017). Related to an overall increase in cohabitation and decrease in marriage (Cherlin, 2010), stepfamilies are less likely than in the past to be formed through remarriage (only 38% of all stepfamilies in 2013 compared to 66% in 1988), with almost a quarter formed through the cohabitation of two never-married adults (Guzzo, 2017). Children are most likely to reside in one of two types of stepfamilies. One type is a simple stepfamily that consists of the biological mother and a stepfather, as in the case of Nick, Adina, and Jared. Another type is a complex stepfamily, where children live with their mother and a stepfather, and the mother is a nonresident stepmother to her husband's children. In recent work, researchers have begun to emphasize the need to better acknowledge the complexity of stepfamilies by defining stepfamilies by sibling relationships as well as by parent–child relationships. As mentioned earlier, a third type of stepfamily has been proposed which is labeled the *hybrid* stepfamily (Harcourt et al., 2015). This type of stepfamily is characterized by the presence of a half-sibling, or in other words a shared biological child in addition to step- and biological children.

More information comes from examining children's living arrangements. The most recent and comprehensive data come from the 2018 Current Population survey and are compiled in a report on children's well-being by the Federal Interagency Forum on Child and Family Statistics (2019). Estimates are that about 9.5% of children under 18 live with a stepparent, including 5% in married and 4.5% in cohabiting stepfamilies. Recall that children who reside with a single parent (usually a mother) and whose nonresident parent has repartnered or remarried are omitted from these numbers. The ages of stepchildren vary across married and cohabiting stepfamilies. Among children living with a married stepparent, roughly 9% are 5 years or younger, 61% are between 6 and 14 years and 30% are between 15 and 17 years. Comparatively, children living with a cohabiting stepparent tend to be younger, with 29% being 5 years and under, 53% between 6 and 14 years, and 18% between 15 and 17 years. Unfortunately, these data do not allow us to know how many of these stepparents also have children living elsewhere, but our best estimates suggest that about half of stepfather families do. The majority of children in stepfamilies are White (52%), 26% are Hispanic, and 12.5% are African American—this is similar to children in nonstepfamily households. Stepchildren are more likely to live in poverty than children living with two biological parents, whether married or cohabiting.

Compared with married stepfamilies, the adults in cohabiting stepfamilies are younger, more likely African American or Hispanic, and have lower incomes and education with both adults in the labor force and more children from prior partnerships (Kreider & Lofquist, 2014). Cohabiting stepfamilies are less stable than those formed through remarriage.

A Family Systems Approach to Stress and Resilience in Stepfamilies

The unique family dynamics and potential sources of stress in stepfamilies are best understood and examined from a family systems perspective (Cox & Paley, 1997). This theoretical approach considers families as complex operating systems of individuals and groups of individuals, or subsystems (i.e., relationships among individuals within a family, such as the couple subsystem, parenting subsystem or sibling subsystem). Importantly, when an individual or subsystem experiences stress, other individuals or subsystems within the family are affected and vice versa, and this is often referred to as the "ripple effect." Subsystems are an appropriate unit of analysis for understanding stepfamilies, because stress in these families results from highly complex processes that cannot be thoroughly understood by focusing on the perspective of a single member.

Stress in the Larger Family System

The complexities of stepfamily relationships put them at greater risk for more family-level stress compared to traditional two-biological-parent families. Generally, common sources of stress in stepfamilies include more family transitions and instability, less clarity regarding member roles and family boundaries, and unrealistic expectations based on comparisons to the traditional two-biological-parent model. These sources of stress result primarily from the complex stepfamily structure and, thus, are unique to these families. The development of a stepfamily involves many transitions for all family members, and these can lead to significant family stress. Transitions include changes in household membership, residence (often motivated by needing a "fresh start" and new home to call their own), neighborhoods and schools, children's friendships, and adult relationships, as well as familiar routines. Stepfamilies must also decide how to distribute resources within the new family structure, including resources of money, space, time, and even affection. Particularly for children who previously lived with a single parent, the addition of a stepparent can mean an increase in financial resources in the family, but new stepsiblings can mean having to share a bedroom and making space throughout the house for more toys and belongings. Parents must find time to spend with their children and a new partner or spouse and, in some cases, devote energy to developing a relationship with new stepchildren.

In the face of multiple transitions and changes, stepfamilies must negotiate new expectations, roles, rules, routines, and rituals which meet the needs of all family members. Basic patterns of family interaction may be interrupted when roles in the family change. For example, an oldest child may be displaced by an older stepsibling, which can lead to role confusion for someone who has always been seen as the leader or most responsible sibling in the family due to their birth order. Expectations regarding daily family patterns, such as understanding how and when chores should be completed or who decides what to watch on television, are no longer a given and must be discussed or renegotiated. Different subsystems of biologically related family members may have family rituals that conflict with each other. For example, for the parent and child subsystem Friday night is considered "family movie night," whereas for the stepparent and child subsystem Fridays are "family game night."

Although adjusting to new roles may be difficult, stepparents especially struggle to determine their place in the new family system. Compared to parenting biological children, stepparenting lacks clear guidelines or social norms, and many stepparents at least initially experience ambivalence about interacting with stepchildren. Expectations may vary from doing little in child-rearing to playing primary disciplinarian and nurturing roles similar to a parent. The resulting role ambiguity is a source of stress for several reasons. First, with uncertainty and the resulting frustration stepparents often experience another layer of ambiguity at the family level, where other members hold different expectations for them (Ganong & Coleman, 2017). Stepfamilies in which family members are unable to agree on the stepparent's role tend to be more poorly adjusted, and when they are unable to meet the role expectations, stepparents report poorer individual adjustment. Stepmothers report feelings of isolation, along with a lack of preparation and general frustration with the roles they are expected to fulfil (Riness & Sailor, 2015).

Like role ambiguity, boundaries are less clear in stepfamilies than nonstepfamilies. Clear boundaries are important to healthy family functioning according to family systems theory, as internal boundaries help to better define stepparent roles in relation to other family members, and external boundaries allow families to establish their family identity. In stepfamilies, internal boundary ambiguity results in role ambiguity, as is evident in the case of Nick's confusion regarding how to enforce household rules. Also, external boundary ambiguity often results in disagreements within families over who is and is not a member, especially when nonresident parents are actively involved with children. Findings from one study indicate that mothers and their adolescents disagreed on their family structure, and those in more complex family structures (e.g., stepfamilies) are less clear about who constitutes a legitimate family member (Brown & Manning, 2009). In fact, nonresident stepmothers were likely to use a biological definition of family and frequently excluded stepchildren when defining their families (Doodson & Morley, 2006). Other research (Stewart, 2005) reported that greater boundary ambiguity was linked with living in a nonresident stepfamily, adolescent reports of lower family closeness and connectedness, and women reporting more spousal disagreement and greater risk for separation. Stepchildren are more likely to consider stepparents as family members when they receive encouragement from biological parents, view the stepparent as a replacement or substitute for an absent biological parent, when they use labels that indicate a more traditional parent–child relationships (e.g. Dad Dave or Mama Michelle), and when they have resided together with their stepparent or were younger at the time of stepfamily formation (Ganong, Coleman, Chapman, & Jamison, 2018).

The final family-level source of stress in stepfamilies comes from holding unrealistic or stereotypically negative expectations for stepfamily life (Garneau, Higginbotham, & Adler-Baeder, 2015). Stepfamily scholars suggest that holding misguided beliefs or expectations can be harmful to family relationships, and evidence supports this assertion. Frequently stepfamily members turn to the familiar rules and roles of traditional two-biological-parent models, only to experience even greater distress when their attempts to implement similar rules and roles backfire (e.g., Ganong & Coleman, 2017). Many stepfamilies fall prey to the "social stigma perspective," which identifies stepfamilies as inferior to the traditional two-biological-parent family model and as an undesirable family form. Tied into this social stigma is "wicked stepmother" ideology and the view that stepparents cannot be loving and nurturing to stepchildren (Miller, Cartwright, & Gibson, 2018). On the other end of the range of expectations lies the unrealistic belief that adjustment will occur quickly following remarriage or cohabitation, and family members will easily develop close relationships resembling those in two-biological-parent families. As Nick learned in the opening vignette, overly optimistic expectations can increase stress in stepfamilies due to frustration and conflict once the realities of stepfamily life set in. Although many stepfamilies are able to successfully adjust to their new family and build strong, satisfying relationships, the process often takes time, and relationships must be allowed to develop differently than expected in nonstepfamilies.

Stress in the Couple Subsystem

Within stepfamilies, parents and stepparents belong to two related but distinct subsystems, the couple subsystem and the coparenting subsystem, each with unique opportunities for stress. The couple subsystem is particularly vulnerable due to the stress originating in other family subsystems (e.g., stepparent–stepchild), the continued presence of former partners (i.e., children's other biological parent), and lingering relational concerns from previous marriages or relationships. Importantly, many stepcouples also lack the strong couple bond or conflict management skills necessary to effectively overcome this stress.

Research shows that remarriages are at greater risk for dissolution than first marriages, and that cohabiting partnerships are at even greater risk for dissolution than marriages (Sassler, 2010). Although little is known about the source of this risk, there is some support for a selectivity hypothesis: Persons who divorce and remarry forming stepfamilies have unique characteristics that predispose them to dissolution (e.g., history of divorce in their family of origin; Jensen, Shafer, Guo, & Larson, 2017). There is evidence that the presence of children from a previous relationship is a primary source of stress and associated with greater likelihood of divorce (Teachman, 2008), and that stepfamilies with complex structures (e.g., his/hers/ours) are more prone to dramatic declines in marital quality (Slattery, Bruce, Halford, & Nicholson, 2011), which is linked with dissolution. Couple relationship quality in both married and cohabiting stepfamilies has also recently been identified as an important predictor of parenting and stepparenting quality (e.g., Jensen, Lombardi, & Larson, 2015). Still other research shows that the quality of the couple relationship is affected by the quality of the stepparent–stepchild relationship rather than the reverse which is true in two-biological-parent families. In fact, clinical stepfamily experts have long emphasized the importance of building strong couple bonds (see Browning & Artelt, 2012). The parent–child relationship precedes that of the stepcouple, meaning couple or spousal relationships must develop concurrently with stepparent–stepchild relationships. Because the children's needs take precedence over adults' needs, the stepcouple relationship is often neglected due to the demands of fostering relationships with stepchildren. Juggling these competing relationship demands can be stressful and negatively affect relationship quality (Slattery et al., 2011).

Lingering influences of a previous marriage and divorce can also be a source of stress for many stepcouples. Divorced adults may be coping with feelings of loss related to the dissolution of the prior marriage or unresolved emotional problems from the relationship. As such, partners may approach the new relationship with greater caution or anxiety, especially following divorce from a long-term relationship, and it is common to hold high expectations for the new partner to be "perfect." Thus, new stepcouples often experience pressure to meet high expectations while handling the competing demands of fostering multiple new stepfamily relationships. Findings from one study suggest that individuals who have unresolved issues from their previous marriage may put less effort into their remarriage, which in turn is linked with lower relationship satisfaction and greater risk for instability (Shafer, Jensen, Pace, & Larson, 2013).

Some have posited that stepcouples experience greater conflict and are less likely to use effective conflict management strategies than couples in nonstepfamilies; however, research findings are mixed. Although they likely experience more opportunities for conflict due to their complex family relationships, some evidence suggests that stepcouples experience both less positive and less negative interactions (Halford, Nicholson, & Sanders, 2007). Stepcouples also report more open expressions of anger, irritation, and criticism during conflict. However, these potentially negative behaviors appear to be diminished by other demonstrations of spousal support and use of affirming communication strategies (e.g., Brown & Robinson, 2012), such as communicating respect and acceptance.

Much less is known about couple relationships involving nonresident parents and stepparents, and many such couples must also negotiate living as a part-time stepfamily household with the associated stress. Overall, nonresident stepcouples tend to be more couple focused and formed with the primary goal of fulfilling the parent's desire for a partner with less emphasis on the new partner's role of stepparent (Ganong & Coleman, 2017). However, these couples still report tension in their relationship, as well as the parent–child and stepparent–stepchild relationships. Among other sources, some of this tension results from loyalty binds, or feeling caught between one's love and commitment to a child and one's love and commitment to a new partner. In a small sample of nonresident stepmothers, a lack of control over matters involving the stepchild led to feelings of powerlessness and combined with anger and resentment had a negative impact on the marital relationship (Henry & McCue, 2009). Other results found that nonresident stepcouples have no more difficulty with triangulation and developing clear boundaries within the family or with increased exclusion of the stepparent than do resident stepcouples (Gosseline & David, 2007). Regardless of residence status, stepcouple relationship quality overall is lower when there are problems in the stepparent–stepchild relationship.

Stress in the Stepcouple Coparenting Subsystem

In addition to the couple or spousal subsystem, stepcouples also relate to one another as coparents. Few clear social norms regarding stepparenting leave stepcouples with the complicated task of determining how to best parent the children together. Similar to Nick and Adina, few stepcouples discuss issues of coparenting prior to cohabiting (e.g., Cartwright, 2010). Evidence shows, however, that when stepcouples are unable to come to an agreement or gain clarity regarding the stepparents' role, stepparent well-being suffers (Felker, Fromme, Arnaut, & Stoll, 2002). Because one of the greatest sources of stress within stepfamilies is conflict in the stepparent–stepchild relationship, this often spills over into the stepcouple-coparenting relationship. In fact, the functioning of the stepparent–stepchild subsystem may be more important to stepcouple relationship stability than is the functioning of their subsystem. Couples in stepfamilies report greater tension and more disagreement than those in two-biological-parent families with child-rearing being one of the most frequent topics of conflict (Hetherington & Kelly, 2002). In fact, child-rearing is the most common topic of conflict in remarried families with finances ranking second compared to the reverse ranking of these two topics in first marriages (Stanley, Markman, & Whitton, 2002). Also, the structure of stepfamilies is such that at least one biological parent–child subsystem comes into the newly formed stepfamily with established family rules, routines, and culture. As coparents, stepcouples must come to terms with possible differences in their parenting styles and expectations for household rules and management, and this negotiation process can be a significant source of stress, particularly when differences are large and the couple struggles to compromise.

Because the structure of a stepfamily creates opportunities for loyalty binds, or situations where one family member feels torn between the competing wants and needs of two or more family members, they can be a significant source of stress in the coparenting subsystem. Adina felt torn between a desire to defend Jared when conflict arose between him and Nick; yet, she simultaneously wished to avoid conflict with Nick and to support his stepparenting. When asked about coparenting in stepfamilies, mothers reported viewing themselves as the captains in their coparenting teams (Ganong, Coleman, Jamison, & Feistman, 2015). Weaver and Coleman (2010) interviewed biological mothers in stepfamilies and found that they often try to negotiate the relationship between their children and new spouse, more frequently siding with their children when conflict intensified, using four primary strategies. *Defenders* protected their children and perceived stepparent–stepchild conflict as a result of the stepparent's "attacks." *Gatekeepers* protected their children by controlling and limiting the development of a close stepparent–stepchild relationship, either resulting from a lack of trust that the relationship would be stable or in an attempt to separate their roles as mothers and wives. *Mediators* aimed to reduce stepparent–stepchild conflict and foster relationship development by stepping in to help solve problems, increasing stress for many mothers. Lastly, some mothers were *interpreters*, interrupting disagreements and conflict and using detailed explanations to help stepparents and children better understand one another. When mothers see stepfathers as good caregivers and fathers as good parents and when they have more cooperative coparenting relationships with fathers, they tend to facilitate more active coparenting roles for stepfathers (Ganong et al., 2015). As was the case with Nick, loyalty binds can cause stepparents to feel that their needs come last, and the resulting sense of exclusion can negatively affect the couple relationship. Because stepchildren often continue their contact with a nonresident parent, usually their father, they can experience loyalty binds feeling torn between their love and commitment to the nonresident parent and the resident parent or stepparent. Thus, the coparenting that occurs across households and involves resident parents, nonresident parents, and stepparents is also a source of stress and requires negotiation of child-related issues and financial concerns.

Given the frequency of child- and finance-related conflict, child support issues are particularly difficult to manage (Gold, 2009). Such issues suggest that decisions related to money management are complicated in these families. Money is more likely to be managed separately in stepfamilies than in nonstepfamilies, often with each partner taking primary financial responsibility for their own children (e.g., Raijas, 2011). The numerous transitions that often precede stepfamily formation (e.g., separation or divorce, establishing child support, moving residences, cohabitation with a new partner) are accompanied by financial transitions, which can increase financial stress going into the new stepfamily. Research indicates that remarried women who manage their money jointly tend to be more financially secure than those who manage a portion of their finances separately (van Eeden-Moorefield, Pasley, Dolan, & Engel, 2007), and this is linked with better child outcomes. Other research shows that the decision to pool financial resources is considered by some stepfamily members to be symbolic of greater commitment to the new family and more family cohesion (Burgoyne & Morrison, 1997).

Stress in the Parent–Child Subsystem

In stepfamilies, the biological parent–child subsystem has the longest duration or shared history together. Even so, numerous opportunities for stress are present in this subsystem due to shifts in the parent's time and attention that result from the addition of new stepmembers and the increased complexities of family interactions.

Roughly 86% of mothers begin dating within two years of divorcing, 45% are in a "serious" monogamous relationship (Langlais, Anderson, & Greene, 2015), and the majority go on to repartner or remarry quickly. Little is known about the dating processes of postdivorce parents, particularly fathers; however, their courtship can be a significant source of stress for both parents and children. For example, Anderson and Greene (2005) identified nine transitions couples and families experience as part of the repartnering process leading to remarriage. These included the initiation of dating, introducing the new partner to the children, identifying the relationship as "serious," sleeping over when the child is present, cohabitation, break-up of the relationship, nonmarital pregnancy, engagement, and remarriage. These transitions can be stressful in part because there are few social norms on how best to handle them. When a parent begins dating, children who have been holding out hope for their parents' reconciliation may experience a renewed sense of loss, although for some this may not come until one parent remarries. The introduction of a new dating partner can cause even greater stress for children who spent a significant amount of time in a single-parent household or who developed a close relationship as the parent's confidant, as the introduction of a new partner or stepparent means a loss of time and attention from the biological parent. In families with multiple children, older siblings may take on some of the caretaking responsibilities over their younger siblings, which is also likely to be renegotiated when a new adult joins the household.

Opportunities for conflict also increase in the parent–child relationship when stepfamilies form, especially when children are adolescents—a period often marked by more intensive parent–child conflict (Hetherington & Kelly 2002). Although parents tend to side with their children, children may experience a coalition or agreement between parent and stepparent as lack of parental support or a threat to the parent–child bond. Additionally, parent–child relationships are especially difficult when stepchildren resist accepting the stepparent into the family. Overall, findings show that a mother's parenting stress increases when she moves in with a stepfather more so than when a previously single mother moves in with a child's biological father (Cooper, McLanahan, Meadows, & Brooks-Gunn, 2009), suggesting that increase in stress is related to the more complex nature of the parent–child–stepparent triadic relationship wherein stepparents are the outsider to an already established parent–child relationship.

Stress in the Stepparent–Stepchild Subsystem

The stepparent–stepchild relationship is perhaps the most fragile of subsystems in the new family, partly because it has the shortest shared history and experience. Thus, it is not surprising that this relationship is considered the greatest source of stress in stepfamilies. Two primary sources of stress in this subsystem are disagreement regarding the stepparent's role and stepchildren's loyalty to their other biological parent.

Research in this area is limited in that most of what is known about stepparent–stepchild relationships comes from research of resident stepfathers and stepchildren. Findings show that, on average, stepchildren's relationships with resident stepfathers are more strongly associated with aspects of their well-being than their relationships with nonresident biological fathers (e.g.,

Amato, King, & Thorsen, 2016). Developing a relationship with a stepchild often does not come easy for stepparents, and it is even more difficult when the stepparent lacks a clear understanding of what their role should be. Often, stepparents and parents expect the stepparent to play a more active parenting role unlike stepchildren, who are seeking more of a "friendship-like" relationship with stepparents (Ganong & Coleman, 2017). Overwhelmingly, research suggests that stress is greater in stepfamilies when stepparents attempt to adopt a disciplinary role with stepchildren too quickly, and these relationships are more positive when stepparents engage in more one-on-one affinity-seeking strategies early on, such as engaging in fun activities, communicating, and completing other tasks (e.g., chores or homework; see Jensen & Howard, 2015). Affinity-seeking behaviors not only lower stepfather–stepchild conflict, but also result in closer stepcouple relationships and stronger stepfamily ties (Ganong, Jensen, Sanner, Russell, & Coleman, 2019). Mothers often play an important role in the development of stepfather–stepchild relationships. Some mothers help to encourage and facilitate the development of closer relationships, whereas others discourage stepfathers from adopting an active stepparenting role. In general, and at least early on, opportunities for stress and conflict in the stepparent–stepchild relationship tend to be greater and opportunities for bonding fewer when spending time in the context of the whole family.

Stepchildren also play an important role in the development of relationships with stepparents, engaging in various behaviors that influence how stepparents attempt to relate to them. Stepchildren make intentional choices to express their love and affection for stepparents, to accept their influence, and have fun with them. For many children, the decision to accept a new stepparent is complicated by feelings of loyalty toward the biological parent of the same gender. They worry that becoming close to their stepfather will diminish their closeness with their father. In high conflict stepfamilies, the parent may reinforce or encourage these concerns to thwart the development of the stepparent–stepchild relationship. What is clear here is that the stress associated with stepfamily development increases significantly for children who are placed in the middle of adult conflict.

The stress experienced in the stepparent–stepchild relationship depends on a variety of factors (see van Eeden-Moorefield & Pasley, 2012). For example, younger children are more accepting of a stepparent than are older children. Also, because relationships take time to develop, stepparent–stepchild relationships of shorter duration are often less positive than those of longer duration, and they are more positive in resident compared to nonresident stepfamilies. Gender also makes a difference, such that stepfathers and stepsons adjust better than stepfathers and stepdaughters. Still other research shows that child temperament and adjustment affect the nature of the stepparent–stepchild relationship; specifically, stepfathers express more warmth toward stepchildren who are more active and sociable rather than those less active and shy, and children's adjustment prior to stepfamily formation is a positive predictor of closer stepfather–stepchild relationships. Finally, compared to simple stepfamilies, in complex stepfamilies, stepparents may have greater difficulty determining how to engage as stepparents in ways that are different from their roles as parents to their children.

Stress in the Sibling Subsystem

Of the primary subsystems in stepfamilies, the sibling subsystem is perhaps the least understood. The composition of this subsystem can be exceedingly complex, with a variety of combinations of full, half-, and stepsibling relationships. More complex sibling constellations may increase opportunities for stress in stepfamilies, as alliances and loyalties can develop with biological relatedness as a dividing factor. The presence of shared children, who are born within the stepfamily and biological children of both parents, tends to increase efforts in the stepfamily to appear to conform to nuclear family norms (Sanner, Ganong, & Coleman, 2019). Such efforts can lead to strict boundaries that stifle open communication about complex stepfamily issues and increase stress. Conflict among siblings in stepfamilies is also a source of potential stress, but surprisingly little research attention has been paid to these relationship dynamics.

Some findings indicate that stepsiblings tend to have the lowest levels of negativity compared to half-siblings and full siblings within and outside of stepfamilies (Anderson, 1999). However, stress may be present even when levels of overt conflict or negativity are low, because relationships among half-siblings and stepsiblings are influenced by differential parenting along biological lines. Parents tend to feel closest to their own children, so they practice differential parenting, which is more common in stepfamilies than nonstepfamilies (O'Connor, Dunn, Jenkins, & Rashbash, 2006). By design, half-sibling relationships involve an older sibling who is a stepchild and a younger sibling who is a shared biological child of the parent and stepparent. Differential parenting and the fact that stepchildren's family histories are marked by comparatively more instability and loss than their half-siblings, can lead to issues of guilt and resentment in their relationships (Sanner et al., 2019). The birth of a half-sibling into a stepfamily can also lead to the feelings of displacement among school-age stepchildren, yet this is not unlike children in two-biological-parent families.

Stress in the Binuclear Family Context

Stepfamilies are often formed in the context of a shared custody arrangement between former partners (and continuing relationships with extended family members especially paternal grandparents), which results in children having membership in at least two households. The level of stress associated with interactions across households varies greatly according to the quality of coparenting relationships. High levels of postdivorce or separation conflict between former partners likely spills over into the coparenting relationship, increasing stress in other subsystems and ultimately putting children at greater risk for poor outcomes.

Although 50/50 joint custody arrangements are becoming more common today, most children in stepfamilies spend more time in one parent's household than the other (Cancian, Meyer, Brown, & Cook, 2014). In stepfamilies where one parent maintains primary residential custody, it is not uncommon for this parent to try to control child-rearing practices when the child is in the other parent's care; this is often not well received by the nonresident parent.

In the stepfamily context, "coparenting teams" become more complex, as the adults must not only negotiate the parenting roles of each biological parent but also the role that the stepparent will play in child-rearing. Mothers have been found to play complex roles in fostering family cohesion through simultaneously managing active coparenting relationships with their children's nonresident biological fathers and stepfathers (Favez, Widmer, Doan, & Tissot, 2015). Children suffer when parents are unable to develop a cooperative coparenting relationship following the end of their relationship (Dunn, O'Connor, & Cheng, 2005), as parents may send messages through the child, exposing them to undesirable information and negativity, so a child's relationship with a nonresident parent is another possible source of stress.

Stepfamily Resilience

Vignette

Vanessa and David moved in together 6 months ago, along with Vanessa's two teenage daughters, Elle (13) and Kate (15), from her previous marriage, and David's son, Wes (6), who lives with them every other week. The couple started dating a year earlier, soon after David's divorce was finalized and 5 years after Vanessa's divorce. Both David and Vanessa experienced difficult divorces and were aware of the impact it had on their children. From the beginning, they spent a lot of time discussing concerns about how their relationship would affect their children and even sought support from friends and Vanessa's pastor. When they decided to remarry, their expectations were realistic. They knew that they would have to create new family rituals and traditions with a lot of input from their children. The couple also decided early on that they would not play a disciplinary role with each other's children but would support each other in the efforts to discipline their own children. Vanessa's daughters enjoy having a younger brother in the house, and everyone looks forward to family movie night when Wes is present.

As is evident in this vignette, many stepfamilies adjust well to their new life and demonstrate resilience to confronting what are common sources of stress. Here we address the characteristics of these resilient stepfamilies.

1. **Realistic and positive expectations.** Like Vanessa and David, stepfamilies who identify as "successful" report having realistic

expectations for their family relationships. For example, some individuals expect immediate feelings of love and affection among family members; however, stepfamily relationships become closer overtime when allowed to develop more slowly and naturally (van Eeden-Moorefield & Pasley, 2012). Also, beliefs that finances should be pooled and that adjustment should not come quickly are associated with reports of more family cohesion (Higginbotham & Agee, 2013) and higher marital quality and positive couple interaction (Garneau, Higginbotham, & Adler-Baeder, 2015).

2. **Clear roles and boundaries.** Stepfamilies adjust better when roles and boundaries are clear (Brown & Robinson, 2012). David and Vanessa established guidelines for their roles as parents and stepparents, allowing each to carry out their expected duties without fear of being undermined by the other. Everyone in the family understands and agrees upon their relationships, as well as the expected rules and roles that accompany these relationships.

3. **Open, clear communication and empathy.** Schrodt (2006) identified five different types of stepfamilies based on their ability to communicate effectively. Overall, those in stepfamilies with more involvement, flexibility, and expressiveness, and less dissension and avoidance were closer, reported greater family cohesion and had more positive stepparent–stepchild relationships. When the decision to cohabit or remarry is discussed openly with children, and they are given the opportunity to express their concerns or feelings, an easier transition with greater acceptance results (Cartwright, 2012). Successful stepfamilies use affirming communication strategies and communicate respect and acceptance (e.g., Brown & Robinson, 2012). Clear communication between partners in the stepcouple is an influential factor in alleviating the relationship tension that may surface as a result of stepparent–stepchild issues (Pace, Shafer, Jensen, & Larsen, 2015). This includes communicating anything from extreme concerns to small everyday matters. Also, stepfamilies tend to fare better when stepchildren are able to express themselves and communicate openly with both resident parents and stepparents, which results in stepchildren feeling like they are in a "real family" (Baxter, Braithwaite, & Bryant, 2006). They also feel closer to their stepfathers when they can talk about them with their mothers and when the mother and stepfather agree more on parenting and argue less (Jensen & Shafer, 2013).

4. **Flexibility.** Resilient stepfamilies are able to adapt and adjust to the numerous changes that accompany stepfamily formation (Brown & Robinson, 2012). They can renegotiate family boundaries to accept new members and develop relationships. Successful stepfamilies create an environment that allows members to adjust to their new roles and are

open to revising old routines and rituals and establishing new ones. David and Vanessa and their children were open-minded when it came to merging their two family cultures, and each family member contributed to the development of new family rituals and traditions. Forgiveness can also be a key to fostering flexibility in stepfamily relationships, as it encourages mutual perspective-taking and creates opportunities to change maladaptive relationship patterns (Waldron, Braithwaite, Oliver, Kloeber, & Marsh, 2018).

5. **Bonding and relationship building.** Well-adjusted stepfamilies emphasize the importance of spending time together as a family (Brown & Robinson, 2012) and use family activities and routines to promote bonding. Spending quality time together increases feeling like a family, and closer relationships within the resident stepfamily are linked with less stress for stepchildren as the family is forming. Importantly, recommendations for successful relationship building in stepfamilies are to start slowly and spend more time getting to know one another in dyads rather than as a whole family initially (Metts et al., 2013). When stepparents and stepchildren reside together, they are more likely to develop trust in their relationship, which increases the likelihood of stepchildren considering stepfathers as "family." Vanessa and David's new family established a family movie night ritual, which helped build a sense of togetherness on the weekends when Wes was present.

6. **Strong social support systems.** Social support from multiple sources is a key to adjustment in stepfamilies, and this can come from former spouses, friends, relatives, and the broader community. For example, when stepparents and nonresident parents have more supportive relationships, stepparents are more satisfied with their partners (Schrodt, 2010). Social support in the community context may be especially important for the well-being of the stepfamily adults (van Eeden-Moorefield & Pasley, 2012).

7. **Positive coparenting relationships.** More cooperative coparenting both within and across households is an important sources of resilience in stepfamilies. Supportive coparenting relationships across households decrease stepchildren's sense of being torn between competing loyalties to biological parents (Schrodt, 2016), a factor that can negatively impact stepchildren's well-being and parent–child relationship quality. Even when positive coparenting strategies are difficult to implement, stepchildren fare better when biological parents at least engage in fewer negative coparenting behaviors. Within the stepfamily household, lower levels of coparenting conflict are associated with higher quality couple relationships (Favez et al., 2015), and improvements in coparenting agreement are related to concurrent improvements in stepparent's feelings of parenting efficacy (Garneau & Adler-Baeder, 2015).

Working Professionally with Stepfamilies

In recent years, more focus has been directed toward prevention and intervention strategies that reduce stress and increase stepfamily resilience. This focus has taken primarily two forms: the design, implementation, and evaluation of psychoeducation/relationship education programs and clinical interventions directed to the specific needs of stepfamilies.

Psychoeducation/Relationship Education

Clinical scholarship on the effectiveness of education-based interventions for stepfamilies began in the late 1970s, but attempts to develop empirically based programs are more recent (see Whitton, Nicholson, & Markman, 2008). Since 2000, efforts have increased to adapt psychoeducational interventions and develop new ones specifically targeting the needs of individuals and couples in complex family structures, such as stepfamilies. Although a variety of in-person and online programs are available to stepfamilies, many are sold commercially, are self-led, and have not been empirically evaluated.

Focusing on the strengths of stepfamilies as a unique family structure instead of "broken" families, Adler-Baeder, Robertson, and Schramm (2010) outlined a conceptual model to aid in the evaluation of existing programs and the development of new relationship education programs for stepfamilies. Key to this model is a combination of psychoeducation and skills-based activities that address aspects of family functioning unique to stepfamilies and the core relationship skills essential to any healthy couple relationship. Several educational programs for stepfamilies have been evaluated using rigorous methodology (e.g., inclusion of control or comparison groups) and are shown to improve various aspects of stepfamily well-being (e.g., effective parenting/stepparenting, coparenting, family cohesion, and marital quality) (e.g., Garneau & Adler-Baeder, 2015; Lucier-Greer, Adler-Baeder, Harcourt, & Gregson, 2014). Importantly, general relationship education programs targeting basic but not stepfamily-specific interpersonal skills also are effective in improving individual-, couple-, and family-level well-being in stepfamilies (see Lucier-Greer, Adler-Baeder, Ketring, Harcourt, & Smith, 2012). However, qualitative findings indicate that participants in a stepfamily-specific program following Adler-Baeder and colleagues' (2010) proposed model report specific benefits from normalizing common stepfamily challenges and learning effective solutions to manage unique challenges in stepfamilies (Skogrand, Torres, & Higginbotham, 2010).

Clinical Intervention

For some stepfamilies, psychoeducational interventions may be enough to improve family functioning, whereas others may require a more focused intervention by a trained mental health professional. Much of the early published work on the complex relationship dynamics of stepfamilies came from scholars who drew heavily upon their own experiences working with stepfamilies in clinical settings. Over time, many of the assertions and recommendations made by these scholars were supported by research findings. As a result, strategies for addressing the unique challenges facing stepfamilies who seek help through counseling and family therapy were refined into a 10-step clinical approach to stepfamily therapy (Browning & Artelt, 2012).

As with psychoeducational interventions, clinical strategies for working with stepfamilies stem from the idea that issues are primarily rooted in their complex structure, and that stepfamilies' needs and relationship dynamics are different from those in nonstepfamilies. However, many of the strategies that developed were based on the functioning in biological-two-parent families and needed to be adjusted or avoided when working with stepfamilies. Browning and Artelt's (2012) model identifies steps for stepfamily therapy organized into three phases. First, *diagnostic steps* guide clinicians to more effectively identify the structure, subsystems, and concerns of the family within the unique context of their stepfamily dynamics. Next, *primary clinical interventions* are used to help normalize the stepfamily's experiences, increase empathy, and use a subsystems approach to help the family begin to understand issues of miscommunication and adjust their systemic functioning. Finally, during the *stepfamily integration* phase, practitioners help strengthen the coparenting relationships in the stepfamily, improve communication, and better integrate the various subsystems into the stepfamily. This proposed model is helpful in addressing the needs of stepfamilies in clinical settings as it combines the use of psychoeducation about normal, healthy stepfamily functioning with a systems approach to family therapy.

Conclusion

The information we presented here suggests that although stepfamilies are likely to experience greater stress than traditional, two-biological-parent families, there is also evidence that many of these families overcome or successfully cope with stress and adapt well to their more complicated family lives. Using a family systems approach, we have discussed some of the unique stresses that are part of living in a stepfamily while emphasizing the diversity across them. There is much variation in the nature of family life and the various relationships among family members. Much of the variations stems from the complexity of the family configurations and the linkages with those outside the immediate household, including nonresident parents and their spouses or partners and the broader social context in which they are embedded. Inherent in any discussion of stress is the opportunity for stepfamilies to demonstrate resilience, and we ended with a presentation of the characteristics of stepfamilies which lend themselves to success.

DISCUSSION QUESTIONS

1. Based on your own experiences, do you think that most people are aware of the unique challenges of stepfamilies compared to nonstepfamilies? Identify three things that you did not know prior to reading this chapter that family members should understand and consider before forming a new stepfamily to ease their transition.

2. Consider Vanessa and David's stepfamily in the second vignette. Describe how each child's stepfamily experience and relationship with their stepparent may differ based on their age, gender, and how much time they spend in the home.

3. Two years after they marry, Nick and Adina decide to have a child together.
   a. How might the introduction of a shared child into their stepfamily impact each of the subsystems differently?
   b. Considering the seven key characteristics of resilient stepfamilies discussed in this chapter, what recommendations would you have for Nick and Adina to help them reduce additional stress and increase resilience?

REFERENCES

Adler-Baeder, F., Robertson, A., & Schramm, D. G. (2010). Conceptual framework for marriage education programs for stepfamily couples with consideration for socioeconomic context. *Marriage & Family Review, 46*, 300–322.

Amato, P. R., King, V., & Thorsen, M. L. (2016). Parent–child relationships in stepfather families and adolescent adjustment: A latent class analysis. *Journal of Marriage and Family, 78*(2), 482–497.

Anderson, E. R. (1999). Sibling, half sibling, and stepsibling relationships in remarried families. *Monographs of the Society for Research in Child Development, 64*, 101–126.

Anderson, E. R., & Green, S. M. (2005). Transitions in parental repartnering after divorce. *Journal of Divorce & Remarriage, 4*(3/4), 47–62.

Baxter, L. A., Braithwaite, D. O., & Bryant, L. E. (2006). Types of communication triads perceived by young-adult stepchildren in established stepfamilies. *Communication Studies, 57*, 381–400.

Brown, S. L., & Manning, W. D. (2009). Family boundary ambiguity and the measurement of family structure: The significance of cohabitation. *Demography, 46*, 85–101.

Brown, O., & Robinson, J. (2012). Resilience in remarried families. *South African Journal of Psychology, 42*, 114–126.

Browning, S., & Artelt, E. (2012). *Stepfamily therapy: A 10-step clinical approach.* Washington, DC: American Psychological Association.

Burgoyne, C. B., & Morrison, V. (1997). Money in remarriage: Keeping things simple—and separate. *The Sociological Review, 45*, 364–395.

Cancian, M., Meyer, D. R., Brown, P. R., & Cook, S. T. (2014). Who gets custody now? Dramatic changes in children's living arrangements after divorce. *Demography, 51*, 1381–1396.

Cartwright, C. (2010). Preparing to repartner and live in a stepfamily: An exploratory investigation. *Journal of Family Studies, 16*, 237–250.

Cartwright, C. (2012). The challenges of being a mother in a stepfamily. *Journal of Divorce & Remarriage, 53*, 503–513.

Cherlin, A. J. (2010). Demographic trends in the United States: A review of research in the 2000s. *Journal of Marriage and Family, 72*, 403–419.

Cohen, J. A. (2011). Children in cohabiting unions. (FP-11-07). National Center for Family & Marriage Research. Retrieved from http://ncfmr. bgsu.edu/pdf/ family_profiles/ file101018.pdf

Cooper, C. E., McLanahan, S. S., Meadows, S. O., & Brooks-Gunn, J. (2009). Family structure transitions and parenting stress. *Journal of Marriage and Family, 71*, 558–574.

Cox, M. J., & Paley, B. (1997). Families as systems. *Annual Review of Psychology, 48*, 243–267.

Doodson, L., & Morley, D. (2006). Understanding the roles of non-residential stepmothers. *Journal of Divorce & Remarriage, 45*(3/4), 109–126.

Dunn, J., O'Connor, T. G., & Cheng, H. (2005). Children's responses to conflict between their different parents: Mothers, stepfathers, nonresident fathers, and nonresident stepmothers. *Journal of Clinical Child and Adolescent Psychology, 34*, 223–234.

Federal Interagency Forum on Child and Family Statistics. (2019). Table FAM1.B: Family Structure and Children's Living Arrangements: Detailed Living Arrangements of Children by Gender, Race and Hispanic Origin, Age, Parent's Education, and Poverty Status, 2018. *America's Children: Key National Indicators of Well-Being, 2019*. Retrieved from https://www.childstats.gov/americaschildren /tables/fam1b.asp

Felker, J. A., Fromme, D. K., Arnaut, G. L., & Stoll, B. M. (2002). A qualitative analysis of stepfamilies. *Journal of Divorce & Remarriage, 38*, 125–142.

Favez, N., Widmer, E. D., Doan, M. T., & Tissot, H. (2015). Coparenting in stepfamilies: Maternal promotion of family cohesiveness with partner and with father. *Journal of Child and family Studies, 24*, 3268–3278.

Ganong, L. H., & Coleman, M. (2017). *Stepfamily relationships: Development, dynamics, and interventions* (2nd ed.). New York, NY: Springer.

Ganong, L. H., Coleman, M., Chapman, A., & Jamison, T. (2018). Stepchildren claiming stepparents. *Journal of Family Issues, 39*(6), 1712–1736.

Ganong, L. H., Coleman, M., Jamison, T., & Feistman, R. (2015). Divorced mothers' coparental boundary maintenance after parents repartner. *Journal of Family Psychology, 29*, 221–231.

Ganong, L. H., Jensen, T., Sanner, C., Russell, L., & Coleman, M. (2019). Stepfathers' affinity-seeking with stepchildren, stepfather-stepchild relationship quality, marital quality, and stepfamily cohesion among stepfathers and mothers. *Journal of Family Psychology, 33*(5), 521–531.

Garneau, C. L., & Adler-Baeder, F. (2015). Changes in stepparents' coparenting and parenting following participation in a community-based relationship education program. *Family Process, 54*(4), 590–599.

Garneau, C. L., Higginbotham, B., & Adler-Baeder, F. (2015). Remarriage beliefs as predictors of marital quality and positive interaction in stepcouples: An actor-partner interdependence model. *Family Process, 54*, 730–745.

Gold, J. M. (2009). Negotiating the financial concerns of stepfamilies: Directions for family counselors. *The Family Journal, 17*(2), 185–188.

Gosseline, J., & David, H. (2007). Risk and resilience factors linked with the psychosocial adjustment of adolescents, stepparents and biological parents. *Journal of Divorce & Remarriage, 48*, 29–51.

Guzzo, K. B. (2017). Shifts in higher-order unions and stepfamilies among currently cohabiting and married women of childbearing age. *Journal of Family Issues, 38,* 1775–1799.

Halford, K., Nicholson, J., & Sanders, M. (2007). Couple communication in stepfamilies. *Family Process, 46,* 471–783.

Harcourt, K. T., Adler-Baeder, F., Erath, S., & Pettit, G. S. (2015). Examining family structure and half-sibling influence on adolescent well-being. *Journal of Family Issues, 36,* 250–272.

Henry, P. J., & McCue, J. (2009). The experience of nonresidential stepmothers. *Journal of Divorce & Remarriage, 50,* 185–205.

Hetherington, E. M., & Kelly, J. (2002). *For better or worse: Divorce reconsidered.* New York, NY: Norton.

Higginbotham, B., & Agee, L. (2013). Endorsement of remarriage beliefs, spousal consistency, and remarital adjustment. *Marriage & Family Review, 49,* 177–190.

Jensen, T. M., & Howard, M. O. (2015). Perceived stepparent–child relationship quality: A systematic review of stepchildren's perspectives. *Marriage & Family Review, 51,* 99–153.

Jensen, T. M., Lombardi, B. M., & Larson, J. H. (2015). Adult attachment and stepparenting issues: Couple relationship quality as a mediating factor. *Journal of Divorce & Remarriage, 56*(1), 80–94.

Jensen, T. M., & Shafer, K. (2013). Stepfamily functioning and closeness: Children's views on second marriages and stepfather relationships. *Social Work, 58,* 127–136.

Jensen, T. M., Shafer, K., Guo, S., & Larson, J. H. (2017). Differences in relationship stability between individuals in first and second marriages: A propensity score analysis. *Journal of Family Issues, 38,* 406–432.

Kreider, R., & Lofquist, D. A. (2014). *Adopted children and stepchildren: 2010* (Current Population Reports, P220–572). Washington, DC: U.S. Government Printing Office.

Langlais, M. R., Anderson, E. R., & Greene, S. M. (2015) Characterizing mother's dating after divorce. *Journal of Divorce & Remarriage, 56*(3), 180–198.

Lucier-Greer, M., Adler-Baeder, F., Harcourt, K. T., & Gregson, K. D. (2014). Relationship education for stepcouples reporting relationship instability—Evaluation of the Smart Steps: Embrace the Journey curriculum. *Journal of Marital & Family Therapy, 40,* 454–469.

Lucier-Greer, M., Adler-Baeder, F., Ketring, S.A., Harcourt, K.T., & Smith, T. (2012). Comparing the experiences of couples in first marriages and remarriages in couple and relationship education. *Journal of Divorce & Remarriage, 53,* 55–75.

Metts, S., Braithwaite, D. O., Schrodt, P., Wang, T. R., Holman, A. J., Nuru, A. K., & Abetz, J. S. (2013). The experience and expression of stepchildren's emotions at critical events in stepfamily life. *Journal of Divorce & Remarriage, 54,* 414–437.

Miller, A., Cartwright, C., & Gibson, K. (2018). Stepmothers' perceptions and experiences of the wicked stepmother stereotype. *Journal of Family Issues, 39,* 1984–2006.

O'Connor, T. G., Dunn, J., Jenkins, J. M., Rashbash, J. (2006). Predictors of between-family and within-family variation in parent-child relationships. *Journal of Child Psychology and Psychiatry, 47,* 498–510.

Pace, G. T., Shafer, K., Jensen, T. M., & Larson, J. H. (2015). Stepparenting issues and relationship quality: The role of clear communication. *Journal of Social Work, 15,* 24–44.

Raijas, A. (2011). Money management in blended and nuclear families. *Journal of Economic Psychology, 32,* 556–563.

Riness, L. S., & Sailor, J. L. (2015). An exploration of the lived experience of step-motherhood. *Journal of Divorce & Remarriage, 56*(3), 171–179.

Sanner, C., Ganong, L., & Coleman, M. (2019). Shared children in stepfamilies: Experiences living in a hybrid family structure. *Journal of Marriage and Family.* doi: 10.1111/jomf.12631

Sassler, S. (2010). Partnering across the life course: Sex, relationships and mate selection. *Journal of Marriage and Family, 72,* 557–575.

Schrodt, P. (2006). A typological examination of communication competence and mental health in stepchildren. *Communication Monographs, 73,* 309–333.

Schrodt, P. (2010). Coparental communication with nonresidential parents as a predictor of couples' relational satisfaction and mental health in stepfamilies. *Western Journal of Communication, 74,* 484–503.

Schrodt, P. (2016). Coparental communication with nonresidential parents as a predictor of children's feelings of being caught in stepfamilies. *Communication Reports, 29,* 63–74.

Shafer, K., Jensen, T. M., Pace, G. T., & Larson, J. H. (2013). Former spouse ties and postdivorce relationship quality: Relationship effect as a mediator. *Journal of Social Service Research, 39,* 629–645.

Skogrand, L., Torres, E., & Higginbotham, B. J. (2010). Stepfamily education: Benefits of a group-formatted intervention. *The Family Journal, 18,* 234–240.

Slattery, M. E., Bruce, V., Halford, W. K., & Nicholson, J. M. (2011). Predicting married and cohabitation couples' futures from their descriptions of stepfamily life. *Journal of Family Psychology, 25,* 560–569.

Stanley, S. M., Markman, H. J., & Whitton, S. W. (2002). Communication, conflict, and commitment: Insights on the foundations of relationship success from a national survey. *Family Process, 41,* 659–675.

Stewart, S. D. (2005). Boundary ambiguity in stepfamilies. *Journal of Family Issues, 26,* 1002–1029.

Teachman, J. (2008). Complex life course patterns and the risk of divorce in second marriages. *Journal of Marriage and Family, 70,* 294–305.

van Eeden-Moorefield, B., & Pasley, K. (2012). Remarriage and stepfamilies. In G. Peterson & K. R. Bush (Eds.), *Handbook of marriage and the family* (3rd ed., pp. 517–547). New York, NY: Springer.

van Eeden-Moorefield, B., Pasley, K., Dolan, E. M., & Engel, M. (2007). From divorce to remarriage. *Journal of Divorce & Remarriage, 47*(3/4), 21–42.

Weaver, S. E., & Coleman, M. (2010). Caught in the middle: Mothers in stepfamilies. *Journal of Social and Personal Relationships, 27,* 305–326.

Waldron, V. R., Braithwaite, D. O., Oliver, B. M., Kloeber, D. N., & Marsh, J. (2018). Discourses of forgiveness and resilience in stepchild–stepparent relationships. *Journal of Applied Communication Research, 46,* 561–582.

Whitton, S. W., Nicholson, J. M., & Markman, H. J. (2008). Research on interventions for stepfamily couples: The state of the field. In J. Pryor (Ed.), *The international handbook of stepfamilies: Policy and practice in legal, research, and clinical environments* (pp. 455–484). New York, NY: Wiley.

CHAPTER 10

Immigrant Families
Resilience Through Adversity

Bertranna A. Muruthi, Hyoun K. Kim,
James Muruthi, and Jaehee Kim

There are more than 44.5 million immigrants residing in the United States (Zong, Batalova, & Burrows, 2019). South or East Asia is the single largest source region (26.9%) followed by Mexico (26.8%). Other regions accounting for significant shares are Europe and Canada (13.5%), the Caribbean (9.6%) and Central America (7.9%) (Department of Homeland Security, 2017). Immigrants migrate to the United States for various reasons. First, economic mobility is the most prominent reason for immigration to the United States (Thomas, 2012). Families with limited opportunities to support their basic necessities treat immigration as their only hope (Deere et. al., 1990). Such families are pulled to the United States by better economic opportunities, thus increasing their probabilities for better social status and upward mobility. However, these families are often vulnerable to separation because limited resources do not allow for migration of the entire family unit (Chioneso, 2008). Second, the Immigration Reform and Nationality Act of 1965 has created favorable conditions for individuals to migrate to the United States for family reunification. This reform in immigration legislation has been beneficial to immigrant families because it allowed close relatives of U.S. citizens and permanent residents to immigrate to the country (Thomas, 2012). Third, a growing number of families immigrate because of humanitarian reasons (e.g., wars, political or religious persecution, internal conflicts, and natural disasters).

Throughout the relocation and resettlement experience, immigrants in the United States face unique experiences that deserve nuanced understanding. Although studies have shown evidence of resilience (e.g., Goodman, Vesely, Letiecq, & Cleaveland, 2017), many immigrants experience a wide variety of challenges and stressors such as poverty, discrimination, social isolation, and language barriers. Within the context of transitions and change, family plays a pivotal role in the individual immigrant's adjustment to life in the United States. The family provides resources and the socialization of individuals, but also influences the development of its members (Bronfenbrenner, 1986). Immigration has a direct impact on family factors such as marriage, structure, and parenting practices among immigrant families (Thomas, 2012). In this chapter, we address stressors and adaptation among immigrant families. We included a vignette to provide examples throughout the chapter.

Abigail went to Philadelphia with her two children Annabel (9 mos.) and Jack (2), to visit her sister Judith. Annabel obtained a visa from the Ghanaian embassy to visit the United States for 6 months and had to return home before it expired. Abigail's husband passed away 2 months ago and she was living with her mother and her four children. Abigail is also currently 3 months pregnant. Abigail wanted a visa that would allow her mother and all her children to come with her to the United States but was only able to obtain a visa for herself and her two younger children. Abigail had limited resources and opportunities for her family in Ghana, she worked at a factory and was unable to support her family without her husband's income.

Abigail's sister Judith migrated 5 years prior and obtained her U.S. residency (green card) by marrying her husband Jacob who was born in Philadelphia. Abigail was happy to be in the United States with her sister, but felt concerned for her two older children who she had to leave in Ghana with her mother. Abigail was supposed to leave the United States 4 months ago but she decided to stay in the United States so that her children could have better opportunities. Abigail also gave birth to her daughter Emma while in the United States. Abigail did not know when she would be able to see her other children because she and her two children where now undocumented and unable to travel back to Ghana.

The Family Resilience Framework

The family resilience framework (Walsh, 2003) can be most helpful in understanding immigrant families' adjustment. Although immigrant families inevitably undergo myriad challenges and stressful situations, many of them arise from such difficult experiences and successfully maneuver their new lives in the United States. While some immigrant families struggle and are chronically exposed to adversities, others recover from short-term setbacks and successfully respond to challenges. According to Walsh's (2003) conceptualization, successful family adjustment can be viewed as an interplay of multiple strengths and limitations within the family, individuals, and larger communities. This framework also underlines that in facing adverse experiences, families and individuals can acquire coping skills which promote growth.

Studies have focused on individual resilience to explain variations in individual outcomes or on how family dynamics and processes serve to influence individuals' resilience (Goodman et al., 2017). However, these early studies based on the resilience perspective have defined and measured strength-based individual and family processes without much consideration of broader ecosystemic contexts (Goodman et al., 2017). More recent perspectives have been expanded to capture the fact that substantial aspects of immigrant family life are heavily regulated by external influences beyond individuals and family, such as immigration policies, regulations regarding housing and employment, and education systems (Vesely, Letiecq, & Goodman, 2017).

This newer approach places immigrant families within the macro-level socio-structural context to "include structural stressors, social inequalities, institutionalized racism, discrimination, bias, and structural violence" (Vesely et al., 2017, p. 94) and seeks to delineate how these macro-level factors interact to influence resilience among immigrant families. This theoretical shift has in part been necessitated by the increasingly diverse immigrant demographic. In particular, the rising number of undocumented families, unaccompanied minors, and refugees in recent years has led to a hostile and anti-immigrant environment, which is likely to render poor adjustment outcomes in immigrant families. Therefore, it would be difficult to understand immigrant families' resilient processes without considering how various sociostructural factors beyond the level of individual and family interpose immigrant families' daily lives.

Family processes such as belief systems, organizational patterns and communication patterns interact with broader sociostructural factors and influence immigrant families' adaption processes. These three key processes have been emphasized in contribution to the resilience of immigrant families when they encounter a challenge or crisis. *Challenges* are defined as "short-term situations that require adaptation," while *crisis* are identified as "chronic situations that require adjustment" (Simon, Murphy, & Smith, 2005, p. 427). Walsh's three key processes have promoted the family functioning and resilience of immigrant families by mediating the "impacts of stress for all members and their relationships" (Walsh, 2006, p. 26).

Family Belief Systems

Walsh (2006) refers to beliefs as being "at the very heart of who we are and how we understand and make sense of our experience" (p. 49). Belief systems are very important to resilience at the individual and familial level, especially for immigrant families. These belief systems are rooted in traditional and "cultural values" (p. 50) that have often been passed down from generation to generation. For example, religiosity and spirituality are also factors that increase likeliness of resilience at individual and family levels. Valdez and colleagues (2013), noted that undocumented Mexican families who participate in "spiritual, folk, and cultural rituals and traditions" (p. 383) are better able to connect with their family members by reinforcing family cultural heritage. A family's outlook plays a large role in determining whether or not they will be successful in overcoming adversity. According to Walsh (2006), "a positive outlook has been found to be vitally important for resilience" (p. 65). When individuals have hope and are optimistic, they can focus on their strengths and achieve their maximum potential. Positive illusions help buffer stress, promote strong mental health, and lead to adaptive coping (Walsh, 2006, p. 67).

Organizational Patterns

Although some may refer to the idea of resilience as having the ability to bounce back from adversity, Walsh (2006) refers to family resilience as *bouncing forward*, (p. 84) referring to the family's progression in the future. Families must be able to adapt when presented with change in order to be successful and resilient. When facing adverse situations, it is imperative for families to remain united in order to overcome their challenges as a functional family unit. According to Hancock (2005), family is identified as a "survival net for its members" (p. 693). By valuing the relationships among family members and the success of the family unit over individual needs, families can focus on becoming resilient as a family when faced with a crisis.

Communication and Communal Problem Solving

Clear and direct communication is fundamental to the success and functioning of relationships between family members. According to Walsh (2006), "communication in healthy families is direct, clear, specific, and honest," (p. 107) regardless of cultural differences. In order to keep family equilibrium or homeostasis, it is necessary to have clear family roles so all the needs of a family are met. Family members who know their roles will be more conscious of the role and position they can take to help the family overcome an adverse situation as a whole. According to Walsh (2006), family resilience is distinguished by a family's "ability to manage conflict and address problems collaboratively" (p. 116).

Vignette

Abigail's sister Judith is excited to help her sister, and her niece and nephew, but she and her husband are having financial difficulties and both work two jobs. This makes it difficult for Abigail to work because she has two very young children and cannot afford childcare outside of her sister and brother-in law. Judith attends a small church within her community that many other Ghanaian families attend as well as migrants from other African countries. Abigail also begins to attend the church and is able to meet other women who have small children in her community. Abigail continues to have issues finding a job because of her undocumented status and because of her lack of childcare, but finds herself babysitting children for women in the church for extra money. Abigail is also developing anxiety over her undocumented status and uses the church and her faith as a way to cope with her fears. Abigail continues to lean on her sister and her husband for support but also finds that she is able to use the church for other resources to help her family.

Complexities of Legality

Immigrant families are often viewed as one dimensional yet they may face a variety of complex experiences and needs issues. Many immigrant families are mixed status families, meaning that members of the family have a variety of immigration statuses. For example, Abigail and her children are currently undocumented but her sister and brother-in-law are legal in the United States. Abigail's newborn child is a U.S. citizen with an undocumented parent and undocumented siblings.

Liminal Legality

Working with Salvadoran and Guatemalan mothers who held Temporary Protected Status (TPS), Menjivar (2006) conceptualized liminal legality. This conceptualization encompassed Victor Turner's (1969) idea of liminality meaning "neither here, nor there" and Susan Coutin's (2000) work on "legal nonexistence." Liminal legality has been defined in research as a period of "in-between" where an individual's status lies somewhere between documented and undocumented statuses (Cebulko, 2014; Chacon, 2015). Individuals who may fall into the liminal legality category include those who have partial documentation, like a work permit, social security number, or a driver's license, but do not have the same rights afforded to them as U.S. citizens. The concept of liminal legality gives scholars and clinicians a framework for working with quasi-legal persons who face legal barriers without access to full citizenship (Cebulko, 2014; Chacon 2015; Menjivar, 2006).

Undocumented Families

There are 11.3 million undocumented immigrants living in the United States, including those without any legal documents and those who overstayed their visas (Rosenblum & McCabe, 2014). Between 2003 and 2013, 3.7 million undocumented immigrants were deported from the United States (Rosenblum & McCabe, 2014). Of those almost 4 million people, 91% were from Mexico and Central America (Rosenblum & McCabe, 2014). It is predicted that deportation-related separations are likely to increase rapidly with the growing rates of anti-immigrant sentiment in the United States (Cervantes, Ullrich, & Mathhews, 2018).

Undocumented immigrants face a myriad of challenges due to their undocumented status, including discrimination, marginalization, limited access to health care, challenges with transportation, language barriers, and lack of employment benefits (Raffaelli, Tran, Wiley, Galarza-Heras, Lazarevic, 2012). Undocumented individuals are less likely to use community and governmental resources in an effort to reduce their exposure to authorities and decrease their chances of being detained or deported (Chavez, Lopez, Englebrecht, & Viramontez Anguiano, 2012).

Many undocumented Latinx parents have faced discrimination and marginalization in employment opportunities (Hall, Greenman, & Farkas, 2010). Due to anti-immigrant legislation, it is legal for employers to demand proof of documentation from their employees (Brabeck, Lykes, & Hershberg, 2011). When employees cannot present legal documents or fail background checks, they may lose their employment and the main, or only, source of income for their families (Philbin, Flake, Hatzenbuehler, & Hirsch, 2018). Without legal status, Latinx immigrants are often left with lower paying or physically demanding jobs, such as construction, landscaping, or janitorial work (Yoshikawa, 2011). De Genova (2002) posits that the potential risk of being detained or deported is a marginalizing force for undocumented immigrants because it often leads to hypervigilance and exclusion from social events (Menjivar, 2011). The media attention on raids and detention centers has increased the fear of family separation for mixed-status Latinx families (Dreby, 2010).

Citizen Children

Much of the existing research has focused on children with undocumented parents. Research has found that citizen children in mixed-status families experience high levels of fear of having an undocumented parent detained or deported (Chavez et al., 2012; Rodriguez, 2019). This daily fear can lead to severe emotional, behavioral, and developmental issues (Dreby, 2010), including severe anxiety and depression (Rodriguez, 2019). Chaudry et al. (2010) found that after a parent is deported, children experienced changes in their sleeping and eating patterns and an increase in fear, crying, and anxiety expressed as aggression, clinginess, or withdrawal.

While citizen children may be eligible to access services and benefits in the community, their undocumented parents may refrain from using these services to decrease their potential of being detained or deported (Dreby, 2015; Hagan, Rodriguez, Capps, & Kabiri, 2003; Huang, Yu, & Ledsky, 2006). Abigail's daughter Emma qualified for benefits, but Abigail was so afraid that she or her other children would be deported she did not sign up for the support.

Refugees

Globally there are 25.9 million refugees who have been forcibly removed from their homes (Blizzard & Batalova, 2019). In 2018, 22,491 refugees arrived in the United States. The top sending countries included the Democratic Republic of Congo (35%), Burma (17.4%), and Ukraine (12.3%) (Blizzard & Batalova, 2019). While refugee families have some similarities to immigrant families, it is important to recognize the unique experiences of refugee families. Within refugee populations, PTSD, depression, and anxiety are the most commonly diagnosed mental health disorders (Sapthiang, Van Gordon, Shonin, & Griffiths, 2019). While we often see these mental health challenges within refugee communities, only a small amount of research has been done to ensure that we are screening, diagnosing, and treating refugees accurately (Morina & Sterr, 2019).

The strength of family relationships and family cohesiveness is consistently found to be a resiliency factor in refugee families and contributes to overall levels of well-being (Copolov, Knowles, & Meyer, 2018; Marley & Mauki, 2018; Stark et al., 2019). Family relationships may be especially significant for adolescent and child refugees (Marely & Mauki, 2018; Stark et al., 2019). It is important to note that while having family members physically present in their host country is a significant predictor of overall well-being (Copolov et al., 2018), close family relationships with those who they were forced to leave behind in their home country may also predict levels of distress (Gangamma & Shipman, 2017). Refugees who settle in a host country often worry about their family members and friends left behind in their home countries, which often works to inhibit refugees' ability to create a new home and community in their host country (Gangamma & Shipman, 2017). In addition to family relationships, there is also strong evidence to suggest that levels of acculturation and the maintenance of a cultural identity are strong predictors of personal well-being for refugees (Copolov et al., 2018; Marley & Mauki, 2018).

Staying Connected

The separation of families due to immigration and deportation has created the development of transnational family interactions, meaning that immigrant families remain financially and emotionally connected across borders. A common practice for transnational families is remittances. *Remittances* are defined as an exchange of goods and resources across borders by people in a host country and their counterparts in their country of origin (Portes & Celaya, 2013). Often, family members in the receiving country rely on remittances for their economic well-being and governments appreciate the opportunity for foreign exchange (Zontini & Reynolds, 2007). Remittances can be informal, a family member hand-delivering money, or formal, a family member transferring money through a mobile banking app (Social Science Research Council 2009). Informal remittances are more common, making it difficult to assess the exact monetary rate of such exchanges (Sander, 2003). Abigail is unable to visit her children in Ghana but she frequently calls and stays connected through social media. She also sends money to her mother every month to help support her family. Abigail is unsure about when she will be able to see her mother and her children again but her transnational behaviors keep her connected to them and help to decrease her worry.

Acculturation

Acculturation refers to the level which people adapt to their host culture socially and psychologically (Berry, 1997, 2005). The word *acculturation* is used in the literature to describe the contextual and individual processes that occur as people adjust to a new culture (Berry, 2005). The word implies that all people live in

As Jack and Annabel get older, they begin to attend school in the United States and are exposed to more American norms and culture. Abigail worries about her children and does not want them to forget their Ghanaian heritage. She notices that Jack is no longer interested in speaking their language, Twi, in the home. Annabel on the other hand has grown very interested in learning more about Ghana and asks her mom questions about the culture and her family back in Ghana. Emma has not attended school yet, but speaks Twi fluently and knows only some English words. What Abigail is seeing in her children is the acculturation process as they begin to adapt to the United States.

societies with multiple cultural influences, promoting exchanges between minority and majority groups (Berry, 1997, 2005).

What complicates this idea is that majority cultural groups have the power to engage in or reject cultural exchanges with minority groups (Berry, 1997). For immigrants, there is a constant negotiation between maintaining their native culture and engaging with their host culture (Berry, 1997). There are four categories of acculturation based on this process: assimilation, integration, separation, and marginalization. *Assimilation* is defined as individuals abandoning their native culture to immerse themselves in the norms of the dominant culture. *Integration* is engaging with the norms of the dominant culture while maintaining one's native culture. *Separation* is maintaining one's own culture while completely rejecting the host culture. Lastly, *marginalization* is a rejection of both the native and host cultures (Berry, 2005). These four categories depend not only on the choices of the individual, but also on the levels of acceptance or rejection of the host culture. For example, for integration to occur, the dominant culture must accept the notion that culturally different people can be accepted and respected in society at large (Berry, 1997, 2009).

Immigrants face the challenge of maintaining their native culture while also creating connections with their host culture (Berry, 2005; Berry, Phinney, Sam & Vedder, 2006). Berry (1997) found that a "fit" may be realized when an immigrant group's efforts to integrate are accepted by the dominant cultural group. If this "fit" does not occur, immigrants may be marginalized by or segregated from the dominant group. For instance, Caribbean families often struggle choosing between their traditional values and cultural practices in the United States. They may respond by assimilating into the dominant culture by adopting new cultural practices or by separating themselves from the dominant culture by creating or joining exclusive cultural enclaves (Chaney, 2010). When this happens, conflict may emerge, resulting in acculturative stress or psychopathology in immigrant families, such as feelings of marginalization or heightened psychosomatic symptoms (Berry, 1997).

The bidirectionality of acculturation receives little attention in the literature. Berry (1997) notes that acculturation affects immigrant groups, but also influences the cultural practices of the host culture. When the dominant cultural group enforces certain practices, it limits the choices available to nondominant groups and individuals, which then limits how they are able to acculturate (Berry, 1997). These limitations may push immigrant groups to either assimilate or become marginalized.

Immigrant Children and Youth

Children of immigrant families are the fastest growing segment of the U.S. population (Portes & Rivas, 2011; Tienda & Haskins, 2011). Children of immigrants comprise more than 1 in 4 of all U.S. children under the age of 5 (Park & Katsiaficas, 2019). As such, how these children fare will have significant long-lasting implications for our nation's social and economic future (Portes & Rivas, 2011; Shields & Behrman, 2004). While children of immigrant families often encounter multiple challenges, it is also true that many of them are from families with many strengths such as supportive families and cohesive ethnic communities of fellow immigrants, all of which serves to protect them against potentially negative outcomes (Shields & Behrman, 2004). Therefore, it is important to understand immigrant children's adjustment within the context of these families' unique strengths and challenges.

Portes and Rivas (2011) have argued that healthy intact families, strong work ethic and aspirations, and cohesive ethnic communities are the major strengths that characterize many immigrant families. Overall, children of immigrant families are born healthier with lower rates of infant mortality and low birth weights and experience fewer health problems (e.g., injuries, physical impairments, infectious diseases), than those from U.S.-born parents (Shields & Behrman, 2004). Further, immigrant children are more likely to live with two parents and with a large extended family than are children in U.S.-born families (Hernandez, Denton, & Blanchard, 2011; Shields & Behrman, 2004). Another strength of immigrant families that is crucial in understanding immigrant children's adjustment is their strong work ethic and high aspirations (Shields & Behrman, 2004). Immigrant parents come to the United States mainly to improve their quality of living and tend to have high expectations of children. Children of immigrant families often develop a strong sense of family obligation and understand the importance of education; thus these children tend to have high educational aspirations and are less likely to engage in health-risk behaviors such as substance use, early health-risking sexual behaviors, and delinquent behaviors (Hernandez & Darke, 1999). Furthermore, ethnic communities in which many immigrant families settle when they first arrive in the United States also play a significant role in facilitating children's psychosocial and academic adjustment (e.g., finding a job, helping navigate school system) by reinforcing cultural values and by buffering them from the negative influences of mainstream society (Garcia-Coll & Szalacha, 2004).

On the other hand, children of immigrant families must manage unique challenges (Shields & Behrman, 2004). Children in immigrant families are more likely than those in U.S.-born families to have parents who have not graduated from high school. For instance, immigrant parents of young children are more than twice as likely as native-born parents to have less than a high school diploma or equivalent, representing 45% of all parents of young children who have limited education (Park & McHugh, 2014). Abigail graduated from high school in Ghana but her diploma was not recognized by the board of education in Philadelphia. With the support of her family, Abigail was able to obtain her GED.

The low level of parents' education in immigrant families, along with limited language skills can have significant implications for their children's adjustment because these parents are less able to help navigate school systems and educational processes in mainstream society. Another challenge that many children in immigrant families have to endure is poverty (Borjas, 2011; Tienda & Haskins, 2011). Almost half of children from immigrant families live in households that qualify for some type of U.S. government aid, compared to one-third of children with U.S.-born parents (Borjas, 2011). This may be due mainly to the fact that immigrant parents are overrepresented among manual workers with very low wages and limited benefits (Shields & Behrman, 2004). Furthermore, they are more likely than U.S.-born workers to have only part-time work and less likely to have health insurance for their children (Shields & Behrman, 2004). This suggests that children in immigrant families are likely to be at risk for poor health and academic achievement over time. In addition, children in immigrant families must navigate discrimination and racism at school (Garcia-Coll & Szalacha, 2004), which leads them to develop negative attitudes toward teachers, peers, and scholastic achievement over time (Shields & Behrman, 2004). In sum, much evidence has suggested that many children in immigrant families experience multiple risk factors due to these challenges and that effects of these multiple risk factors are closely linked to the adjustment of children in immigrant families.

Adjustment of Children of Immigrant Families

One aspect that uniquely characterizes and influences children of immigrant families is parentification (Godsall, Jurkovic, Emshoff, Anderson, & Stanwyck, 2004; Kuperminc, Wilkins, Jurkovic & Perilla, 2013; Winton, 2003). Parentification refers to "when a child assumes typical parental responsibility for caregiving to siblings or to parents or both" (Weisskirch, 2010, p. 77). The children of immigrant families often have better language and life skills than their foreign-born parents (e.g., driving, Internet use); thus children "serve as translators, chauffeurs, and liaisons between the parents and the outside world" (Weisskirch, 2010, p. 77). Although there is no doubt that parentification is closely associated with children's adjustment and parent–child relationships, specific findings are rather inconsistent. For instance, Latinx youth were found to report distressful feelings when engaging in language brokering for parents, which was then associated with problematic family relationships, suggesting maladaptive effects of parentification (Peris, Goeke-Morey, Cumming, & Emery, 2008; Weisskirch, 2007). Similarly, immigrant parents from the former Soviet Union to Israel reported negative feelings associated with loss of status for having their children speak on their behalf, which led to low self-esteem and self-efficacy in youth (Oznobishin & Kurman, 2009). Studies that have found maladaptive aspects of parentification tend to highlight the overburden in children, which leads to problematic adjustment among these children (Burton, 2007). Abigail spoke English, but found it difficult to understand the dialect in the United States and was often confused. Abigail's son Jack was often tasked with helping his mother interpret paperwork and bills that she received in the mail. Jack felt burdened by his role as interpreter, but felt obligated to help his family. As Jack got older, he would omit information that his mother received from school if it reported any of his bad behavior. Jack's teacher began to notice this discrepancy and began to invite Jack's mother to the school for one-on-one meetings.

However, some other studies report adaptive effects of parentification in children of immigrant families (Dorner, Orellana, & Jiménez, 2008; Winton, 2003). For instance, in Bajaj's (2008) study, Asian Pacific American youth reported that language brokering provided opportunities to talk with their parents and to participate in family decision making. Vietnamese youth also reported that the amount of cultural brokering was associated with family adaptability, although it was unassociated with family satisfaction or cohesion (Trickett & Jones, 2007). These findings suggest that parentification may facilitate family coping in the new environment and positively influence children's development by increasing connectedness, loyalty, cooperation and kinship ties within the family (Esparza & Sanchez, 2008). In fact, empirical studies found that parentification promoted the child's self-concepts, ethnic identify, competence, positive social relationships, and academic achievement (Kuperminc, Wilkins, Roche & Alvarez-Jimenez, 2009; Kuperminc et al., 2013; Pomerantz, Qin, Wang, & Chen, 2011; Weisskirch, 2005). These studies have argued that for many children of immigrant families, parentification such as language brokering is considered part of normative family assisting behaviors that occur routinely in the household (Orellana, 2001, 2003) and that such family assistance promotes the child's sense of role fulfillment, and subsequently helps them cope with challenges they face in mainstream society (Fuligni & Flook, 2005).

Although children of immigrant families share unique strengths, the benefits of these strengths tend to be lessened for those whose parents have limited English, are not authorized to live and work in the United States, and have low earnings (Tienda & Haskins, 2011). These issues seriously undermine children's academic achievement, educational attainment, and subsequently their long-term economic prospects. Findings indicate that children from families in which English is not spoken tend to have lower levels of reading and math achievement (Schneider,

Martinez, & Owens, 2006). In particular, when children of immigrant families begin kindergarten with limited oral English proficiency, their reading skills fall behind native speakers, leading to a significant achievement gap by fifth grade (Kieffer, 2008). This suggests that these children can benefit from participating in center-based early childhood care and education (ECE) programs before they transition to school. However, access to such nonparental ECE programs is limited for many immigrant families because of multiple barriers (e.g., language barriers, complexity of the system, and undocumented status) (Karoly & Gonzalez, 2011).

Interparental Conflict and Parent–Child Conflict

Challenges that many immigrant families must navigate can place a strain on their family relationships. Stress from unemployment and disadvantageous economic and social situations are likely to affect family stability and these families are more likely to experience conflict, compared to other families (Chung & Fuligni, 2009). Studies on violence against immigrant women and children indicated that in East and Middle Eastern communities with traditional gender roles (e.g., Indian, Chinese, Japanese, Korean, Iraqi), isolation from family and social support, economic insecurity, and alcohol use of males were significantly associated with increased violence in immigrant families and vulnerability of women and children in these families (Fontes, 2002; Lee, 2007; Raj & Silverman, 2002). In a study of adolescents from Latin American, Asian, and European backgrounds, Chung and Fuligni (2009) found that adolescents of Asian backgrounds tended to report the least frequent parental conflict but they were more vulnerable to interparental conflict than their European and Latin American peers. The findings also indicated that the parent–adolescent conflict mediated the association between interparental conflict and emotional distress. Other studies also found that marital quality in Latinx families was significantly and negatively associated with children's outcome (Formoso, Gonzales, Barrera, & Dumka, 2007; Leidy, Parke, Cladis, Coltrane & Duffy, 2009). Studies have noted that given Latinx families' high emphasis on the collective family as a whole, the interparental relationship quality is likely to be particularly salient for children's adjustment.

Aging Immigrants and Families

The U.S. population is becoming more diverse and ethnically diverse, in particular. A major reason for the ethnic diversity is faster rates of growth of foreign-born individuals than native-born individuals. The fastest growing foreign-born ethnic group is the Asian population, whose growth is projected to increase by 100% over the next 4 decades (U.S. Census Bureau, 2014). The Hispanic population is also projected to experience one of the fastest rates of growth over the same period, with an expected increase from 253 million in 2020 to 275 million in

2060 (U.S. Census Bureau, 2014). Vespa, Armstrong, and Medina (2018) argue that the causes of this population growth between these groups are different. They suggest that Hispanic groups are increasing in numbers due to high fertility rates while international migration is the biggest driver for high increases among Asian groups. The faster rate of growth among foreign-born individuals will also be reflected among people 65 years and older. The causes of this growth are two pronged: Long-term immigrants are aging with the rest of the native population and recent family reunification policies have allowed aging immigrants, especially parents, to join their relatives in the United States (Carr & Tienda, 2013).

Compared to long-term immigrants, recent aging immigrants are disproportionately at a socioeconomic disadvantage. Literature shows that recent older immigrants are (1) more vulnerable due to limited English language proficiency, (2) less educated, (3) more likely to live in poverty, (4) likely to live in isolation and, (5) dependent on family for support (Treas, 2009; Treas & Batalova, 2009). We believe that in addition to macro-level issues, it is critical to understand the roles of informal social structures (such as families) because it gives a clearer picture of the mediating effects of culture on immigrant aging and well-being.

Familial Unity and Reciprocity

Recent immigrants' sending (native) cultures promote close family ties. Comparatively, the cultural traditions of the United States emphasizes independence. Referred to in the literature as *familism*, recent Hispanic immigrants observe a close commitment and loyalty to close and extended family members (Katiria Perez & Cruess, 2014). Filial obligation is a typical aspect of family relationships. The support bank model metaphor (Antonucci, 1990) suggests that parents invest time, resources, and emotional capital in their young children, and the expectation is for the children to reciprocate in kind when the parents need assistance in old age. Adult Hispanic children are expected, and feel obliged to care for their recently immigrated parents. Chinese children also face similar expectations due to Confucian norms, filial piety precisely, of eldercare and reverence (Yee, Debaryshe, Yuen, Kim, & McCubbin, 2007). However, a study on filial expectations between Chinese adult children and their aging parents revealed that the children had higher filial expectations for themselves than their parents' expectations on the younger cohorts (Guo, Byram, & Dong, 2019). This study also revealed that low educational attainment, poorer health, lower rates of acculturation, and closer relationships with adult children were related to higher filial expectations among older Chinese parents.

While these are traditional expectations, it is important to note that the collectivist behavior is crucial for the late-life immigrants because family support is essential for their survival (especially the less acculturated late-life immigrants) in the United States. On one end, studies have shown that most late-life immigrants rely on their adult children to navigate language, financial, and cultural challenges of living in the American culture. For example, in a study of Cambodian refugee families in the United States, Muruthi and Lewis (2017) revealed that immigration stressors often forced late-life immigrant parents to cohabit with their children. Following a common trend in the literature, this study also showed that different interpretations of cultural norms of family collectivism often led to intergenerational ambivalence between the younger and older cohorts. In some cases, this ambivalence can manifest as feelings of caregiving burden and open disrespect toward the elders (Mui & Kang, 2006). Cohabiting parents have also reported feeling powerless and defaulting to their adult-children's wishes in all family matters (Treas & Mazumdar, 2002).

On the flip side, late-life immigrants are also critical contributors in their families. Precisely, aging immigrants are custodians of native cultures, they preserve food ways, and offer childcare for their families (Barer & Johnson, 2003; Treas & Mazumdar, 2002). These traits often improve the well-being of their families in more than one way. For example, aging Korean parents reported using ethnic food as a means to frequently bring the family together (Yoo & Zippay, 2012). These parents revealed that sharing native foods (such as kimchi) was their alternative to providing financial assistance to their adult children. Beyond buffering the cost of childcare for their extended families, late-life immigrants who care for their children also allow the middle generation (especially women) to return to work (Hu, 2018).

Social Isolation

Despite the communal family values, some late-life immigrants have reported feelings of loneliness. In a study of transnational elders, Treas and Mazumdar (2002) discovered that loneliness was a common theme in their responses. According to these authors, widows, very old and sick individuals were more likely to report feeling lonely. English language inefficiency is also a key contributor to social isolation because late-life immigrants often lack the language skills to navigate public infrastructure, such as transportation (Gentry, 2010). In addition, the reliance on adult children for socialization and companionship often fails the older generation when work and nuclear family responsibilities demand most of the adult children's time (Muruthi & Lewis, 2017; Treas & Mazumdar, 2002). Late-life immigrants who mourn the loss of their previous socioeconomic status in sending countries have also reported feelings of social isolation (Muruthi & Lewis, 2017).

However, some late-life immigrants mitigate the loss of social networks by creating new networks in the United States. Creating new networks can be facilitated through living in or near ethnic communities or enclaves. Examples of cities with large ethnic enclaves include Miami, South Bronx, Los Angeles, and cities such as Washington D.C. and New York with Chinatown neighborhoods. They often move to neighborhoods with people of similar native backgrounds. Also known as immigrant ethnic enclaves, such neighborhoods help late-life immigrants acclimate easier because of the geographic proximity to other immigrants who not only speak the same language, but who also follow similar cultural practices (Mazumdar, Mazumdar, Docuyanan, & McLaughlin, 2000) or by participating in religious and cultural activities (Yang & Ebaugh, 2001). In line with Berry's (1997) bidirectional model of acculturation, ethnic enclaves ultimately help late-life immigrants retain their heritage culture. Despite the collectivist benefits implied here, it should be underlined that late-life immigrants often maintain a small group (of between two to three members, often kin-based) of trusted connections (Viruell-Fuentes & Schulz, 2009).

Immigrant Families Physical and Mental Health

A recent study based on eight national data systems including the National Vital Statistics System (NVSS), National Health Interview Survey (NHIS), National Survey of Children's Health, National Longitudinal Mortality Study, and American Community Survey have found that immigrants tended to show lower levels of disability and mortality and higher life expectancy than the U.S. born (National Center for Health Statistics, 2012). For instance, U.S.-born adults were more likely to be obese (23% vs. 16%), to smoke (24% vs. 14%), and to have hypertension (24% vs. 20%) than their immigrant counterparts, although the overall prevalence of these chronic diseases tend to vary with significantly higher prevalence rates among U.S.-born Black adults than Asian, Hispanic and White adults.

Similarly, foreign-born non-Hispanic Black and Hispanic immigrant adults often report fewer psychological symptoms compared with their U.S.-born counterparts (Dey, Lucas & Division of Health Interview Statistics, 2006; Hajat, Lucas & Kington, 2000). Again, evidence has consistently suggested significant differences in physical and mental health among U.S.-born and foreign-born immigrants (Dey et al., 2006; Leong, Park & Kalibatseva, 2013). Although many foreign-born immigrants tend to have inadequate resources and limited access to health-care systems, they report better health outcomes than their U.S.-born counterparts on many health measures (Dey et al., 2006). The "healthy immigrant effect" or "positive immigrant selectivity" hypothesis posits that those who chose to immigrate tend to be healthier than those who remain in their countries of origin. Evidence has suggested that immigrants tend to have lower levels of health risking behaviors (e.g., smoking and drinking) and higher levels of social support, compared to their native-born counterparts which then leads to better health outcomes. However, such (physical) health patterns appear to vary across racial/ethnic groups. In particular, the level of acculturation plays a significant role in shaping characteristics of health among immigrants, especially for Hispanic immigrants. In terms of self-reported health status, White immigrant adults who lived in the United States for 5 years or more were more likely to report good health, compared to other immigrant counterparts such as Black immigrant adults. Such difference might be associated with social interaction, such as lower educational opportunities, poverty, discrimination, and being unstable in status. Non-White immigrants are more likely to experience these negative contexts as they live longer periods of time in United States and subsequently experience poor health.

Aging Immigrant Health

While acculturation and premigration stressors have been shown to negatively impact the health of aging immigrants, studies have shown that perceived support from close relatives and living in cohesive neighborhoods buffers the effects of immigration-related factors on health (Raffaelli et al., 2013). The underlying assumption in explaining this buffering effect is that at the individual level, social support is able to "provide a sense of attachment; facilitate access to tangible resources; and position individuals within the context of a social group that offers normative social influence" (Viruell-Fuentes, Morenoff, Williams, & House, 2013, p. 3).

On the one end, the literature shows that family support is negatively associated with health problems among aging immigrants. For example, a study on older Korean immigrants revealed that belonging to a large social network and staying in regular contact with family (and friends) was associated with less reports of depression (Lee, Crittenden, & Yu, 1996). In fact, a more recent study on the same population highlighted that among highly acculturated older Koreans, those with high social support exhibited lower levels of depression (Kim, Sangalang, & Kihl, 2012). Other studies have nuanced both the types of family relationships and support while investigating how they impact older immigrants' health. For instance, Muruthi and Lewis (2017) conducted a longitudinal study to investigate whether positive spousal support (among other indicators) was a significant predictor of depressive symptoms among older Hispanic adults. They discovered that positive spousal support (together with depressive symptoms and chronic conditions at baseline) was negatively associated with depressive symptoms. On the other end, several studies have indicated that overreliance on family support and homoethnic neighborhoods can induce psychological stress among older cohorts (Mui & Kang, 2006) and shelter them from transitioning into neighborhoods with higher social and health capital (Cook, Alegría, Lin, & Guo, 2009) respectively.

Considerations for Intervention

Immigration processes can create implications for immigrant families in the United States. Therefore, it is paramount that clinical evaluations of this group should consider contexts of migration, duration of family separation and changing family dynamics. These changes should be treated as normal but stressful parts of the migration process. This work proposes that therapists, and other clinicians, should employ culturally responsive treatments that explore issues from multiple perspectives. Peer-based interventions, school–family–community partnerships, and psychoeducational approaches have proven to be the most successful intervention strategies when working with immigrant communities (Mitchell & Bryan, 2007; Thomas, Clarke, & Kroliczak, 2008).

Peer-based Intervention

Peer-based interventions use peers to provide information regarding treatment options, adherence to care, accessing health and other support services, as well as support to the individual (Pivnick, Jacobson, Blank, & Villegas, 2010; Thomas et al., 2008). This type of intervention is particularly useful in scenarios where participants from impoverished communities need more support and are no longer in regular contact with their peers because of geographic separation (Pfeiffer et al., 2012). In this model, peer and professional facilitators work together for optimal levels of support for targeted immigrants. This intervention relies on the assumption that individuals in need are more likely to relate with people in similar peer groups. Peer support increases immigrants' ability to overcome immigration stressors in the host country by providing the necessary psychosocial assistance for individuals in need (Pottinger, Stair, & Brown, 2008).

The disadvantages of this method include fear of disclosure and lack of peer consultants to implement programming. In a study about the efficiency of a peer intervention within a Caribbean community, Thomas and colleagues (2008) uncovered that participants could not open up during interventions because of living in close proximity to their peers. This challenge brings about issues regarding confidentiality and trust during clinical treatments (Greenidge, 2007). It is also important to consider that peer networks are also more successful if individuals and their peers have a preexisting trusting relationship (Pfeiffer et al., 2012).

School–family–community Partnership

School–family–community partnerships provide valuable system support services that help school counselors bridge cultural gaps among the featured communities, build educational resilience in children, and empower families in dealing with immigration stressors (Bryan & Holcomb-McCoy, 2007). Bryan and Henry (2012) assert that effective partnerships are built on a foundation of shared principles or values that enable a healthy collaboration process among partners. This relationship can lead to improved success and access for students and their families, especially those who come from disadvantaged backgrounds (Bryan & Henry, 2012). Even though educational attainment is emphasized among most immigrant families, accessing educational facilities can be a challenge because of an intersection of factors such as lack of childcare, transportation, long work hours, multiple jobs, language barriers, and unfamiliarity with the American school system (Mitchell & Bryan, 2007).

Psychoeducational Approach

A psychoeducational approach disseminates information in a more informal way. For example, putting prevention pamphlets in a church brochure disseminates information to the community without putting unwanted pressure on the recipients. This also allows for the spreading of information to a wide cross-section of people in a short period of time (Pottinger et al., 2008). The psychoeducational intervention is feasible, and cost effective to implement (Navidian, Kermansaravi, & Rigi, 2012). Organizations such as parents and teachers' associations, and churches form readily available groups where therapists and social service providers could present information about migration issues and these groups can serve as possible sources of support (Pottinger et al., 2008).

Conclusion

The family unit plays an important role in the provision of resources and the socialization of individuals, but also influences the development of its members (Bronfenbrenner, 1986). Immigration has a direct impact on family factors such as marriage, structure, and parenting practices among immigrant people (Thomas, 2012). Family support has been recorded to be the backbone of immigrant families' survival because the exchange of resources buffers the impact of immigration stressors (Chioneso, 2008). Members of immigrant families are also more likely to feel increased impacts of stress and anxiety provoked by the process of immigration because of limited family support networks (Glasgow & Gouse-Shees, 1995). Reduced family support can therefore lead to increased risks of developing somatic complications and illnesses (Reynolds, 2005). In addition, disjointed family relationships reduce opportunities for intergenerational transfer of cultural beliefs and practices, a process that is vital in the preservation of culture (Chamberlain, 2003).

The family resilience framework which encompasses the complexity of socio-structural factors in immigrant families' adjustment processes can be useful to inform efforts to better serve immigrant families. In particular, this perspective highlights the need to develop programs that address factors at multiple levels for immigrant families. The family resilience framework is especially suited for the study of immigrant families because of its focus on family belief systems, family organization, and the capacity for problem solving, which align with the core experiences of families in transition.

DISCUSSION QUESTIONS

1. What are some contextual factors that may negatively impact immigrant families as they try to resettle in the United States? Explain how family resilience may be able to buffer some of these factors.

2. Abigail and her two oldest children in the United States are undocumented. What are some possible ways that the children's undocumented status might impact their future? How might the families undocumented status impact the youngest

child who was born in the United States, and therefore is a U.S. citizen?

3. Explain advantages and disadvantages of the various intervention types presented in the chapter, and which intervention would likely work best for Abigail's family and why?

REFERENCES

Antonucci, T. (1990). Social supports and social relationships. In R. H. Binstock & L. K. George (Eds.), *Handbook of aging and the social sciences* (3rd ed., pp. 205–226). New York, NY: Academic Press.

Bajaj, R. (2008, September). *Recording voices: Stories of Asian Pacific American youth as language brokers in New York City* (Policy Brief). New York, NY: Coalition for Asian American Children and Families.

Barer, B. M., & Johnson, C. L. (2003). Problems and problem solving among aging White and Black Americans. *Journal of Aging Studies, 17*(3), 323–340.

Berry, J. W. (1997). Immigration, acculturation, and adaption. *Applied Psychology, 46*(1), 5–34.

Berry, J. W. (2005). Acculturation: Living successfully in two cultures. *International Journal of Intercultural Relations, 29*(6), 697–712. doi: 10.1016/j.iijintrel.2005.07.013

Berry, J. W. (2009). A critique of critical acculturation. *International Journal of Intercultural Relations, 33*(5), 361–371.

Berry, J. W., Phinney, J. S., Sam, D. L., & Vedder, P. (2006). Immigrant youth: Acculturation, identity, and adaptation. *Applied Psychology: An International Review, 55*(3), 303–332.

Blizzard, B., & Batalova, J. (2019). *Refugee and asylees in the United States*. Washington, DC: Migration Policy Institute. Retrieved from https://www.migrationpolicy.org/article/refugees-and-asylees-united-states#Refugee_Arrivals_and_Countries_of_Origin

Borjas, G. J. (2011). Poverty and program participation among immigrant children. *The Future of Children, 21*(1), 247–266.

Brabeck, K. M., Lykes, M. B., & Hershberg, R. (2011). Framing immigration to and deportation from the United States: Guatemalan and Salvadoran families make meaning of their experiences. *Community, Work & Family, 14*(3), 1–22.

Bronfenbrenner, U. (1986). Ecology of the family as a context for human development: Research perspectives. *Developmental Psychology, 22*, 6, 723–742.

Bryan, J., & Henry, L. (2012). A model for building school–family–community partnerships: Principles and process. *Journal of Counseling & Development, 90*(4), 408–420.

Bryan, J., & Holcomb-McCoy, C. (2007). An examination of school counselor involvement in school–family–community Partnerships. *Professional School Counseling, 10*(5), 441–454.

Burton, L. (2007). Childhood adultification in economically disadvantaged families: A conceptual model. *Family Relations, 56*(4), 329–345.

Carr, S., & Tienda, M. (2013). Family sponsorship and late-age immigration in aging America: Revised and expanded estimates of chained migration. *Population Research and Policy Review., 32*(6), 825–849.

Cebulko, K. (2014) Documented, undocumented, and liminally legal: Legal status during the transition to adulthood for 1.5-generation Brazilian immigrants. *The Sociological Quarterly*, 55(1), 143–167.

Cervantes, W., Ullrich, R., & Matthews, H. (2018) *Our children's fear: Immigration policy's effects on young children*. Washington, DC: Center for Law and Social Policy.

Chacon, J. M. (2015) Producing liminal legality. *Denver University Law Review*, 92(4), 709–767.

Chamberlain, M. (2003). Rethinking Caribbean families: Extending the links. *Community, Work & Family*, 6(1), 63–76.

Chaney, J. (2010). The formation of a Hispanic enclave in Nashville, Tennessee. *Southeastern Geographer*, 50(1), 17–38.

Chaudry, A., Capps, R., Pedroza, J., Castaneda, R. M., Santos, R., & Scott, M. M. (2010). *Facing our future: Children in the aftermath of immigration enforcement*. Washington, DC: Urban Institute. Retrieved from http://www.urban.org/UploadedPDF/412020_FacingOurFuture_final.pdf

Chavez, J. M., Lopez, A., Englebrecht, C. M., & Viramontez Anguiano, R. P. (2012). Sufren los niños: Exploring the impact of unauthorized immigration status on children's well-being. *Family Court Review*, 50(4), 638–649.

Chung, G. H., & Fuligni, A. J. (2009). Daily family conflict and emotional distress among adolescents from Latin American, Asian, and European backgrounds. *Developmental Psychology*, 45(5), 1406–1415.

Chioneso, N. A. (2008). (Re)Expressions of African/Caribbean cultural roots in Canada. *Journal of Black Studies*, 39(1), 69–84.

Cook, B., Alegría, M., Lin, J. Y., & Guo, J. (2009). Pathways and correlates connecting Latinos' mental health with exposure to the United States. *American Journal of Public Health*, 99(12), 2247–2254.

Copolov, C., Knowles, A., & Meyer, D. (2018). Exploring the predictors and mediators of personal wellbeing for young Hazaras with refugee backgrounds in Australia. *Australian Journal of Psychology*, 70(2), 122–130.

Coutin, S. B. (2000) Denationalization, inclusion, and exclusion: Negotiating the boundaries of belonging. *Indiana Journal of Global Legal Studies*, 7(2), 585–593.

De Genova, N. P. (2002) Migrant "illegality" and deportability in everyday life. *Annual Review of Anthropology*, 31, 419–447.

Department of Homeland Security. (2017). *Yearbook of Immigration Statistics 2017*. Washington, DC: Author. Retrieved from https://www.dhs.gov/immigration-statistics/yearbook/2017

Deere, C., Antrobus, P., Bolles, L., Melendez, E., Phillips, P., Rivera, M., & Safa, H. (1990). *Shadows of the sun: Caribbean development and US policy*. San Francisco, CA: Westview Press.

Dey, A. N., Lucas, J. W., & Division of Health Interview Statistics. (2006). *Physical and mental health characteristics of U. S.- and foreign-born adults: United States, 1998–2003*. Hyattsville, MD: U.S. Department of Health and Human Services, Centers for Disease Control and Prevention, National Center for Health Statistics. Retrieved from https://www.cdc.gov/nchs/data/ad/ad369.pdf

Dorner, L. M., Orellana, M. F., & Jiménez, R. (2008). It's one of those things that you do to help the family: Language brokering and the development of immigrant adolescents. *Journal of Adolescent Research*, 23(5), 515–543.

Dreby, J. (2010). *Divided by borders: Mexican migrants and their children*. Berkeley: University of California Press.

Dreby, J. (2015). U.S. immigration policy and family separation: The consequences for children's well-being. *Social Science & Medicine, 132,* 245–251.

Esparza, P., & Sanchez, B. (2008). The role of attitudinal familism in academic outcomes: A study of urban, Latino high school seniors. *Cultural Diversity and Ethnic Minority Psychology, 14*(3), 193–200.

Fontes, L. A. (2002). Child discipline and physical abuse in immigrant Latino families: Reducing violence and misunderstandings. *Journal of Counseling & Development, 80*(1), 31–40.

Formoso, D., Gonzales, N. A., Barrera, M., & Dumka, L. E. (2007). Interparental relations, maternal employment, and fathering in Mexican American families. *Journal of Marriage and Family, 69*(1), 26–39.

Fuligni, A. J., & Flook, L. (2005). A social identity approach to ethnic differences in family relationships during adolescence. In R. Kail (Ed.), *Advances in child development and behavior* (pp. 125–152). New York, NY: Academic Press.

Gangamma, R., & Shipman, D. (2017). Transnational intersectionality as a framework for working with resettled refugees. *Journal of Marital and Family Therapy, 44,* 206–219. doi: 10.1111/jmft12267

Garcia-Coll, C., & Szalacha, L. A. (2004). The multiple context of middle childhood. *Children of Immigrant Families, 14*(2), 81–97.

Gentry, M. (2010). Challenges of elderly immigrants. *Human Services Today, 6*(2), 1–4.

Glasgow, G. F., & Gouse-Sheese, J. (1995). Themes of rejection and abandonment in group work with Caribbean adolescents. *Social Work with Groups, 17, 4,* 3–27.

Godsall, R. E., Jurkovic, G. J., Emshoff, J., Anderson, L., & Stanwyck, D. (2004). Why some kids do well in bad situations: Relation of parental alcohol misuse and parentification to children's self-concept. *Substance Use & Misuse, 39*(5), 789–809.

Goodman, R. D., Vesely, C. K., Letiecq, B., & Cleaveland, C. L. (2017). Trauma and resilience among refugee and undocumented immigrant women. *Journal of Counseling & Development, 95*(3), 309–321.

Greenidge, W. L. (2007). *Attitudes towards seeking professional counseling: The role of outcome expectation and emotional openness in English-speaking Caribbean college students in the U.S. and the Caribbean* (Doctoral dissertation). University of Central Florida, Electronic Theses and Dissertations, 3179. Retrieved from https://stars.library.ucf.edu/etd/3179

Guo, M., Byram, E., & Dong, X. (2019). Filial expectation among Chinese immigrants in the United States of America: A cohort comparison. *Ageing and Society,* 1–21. doi.org/10.1017/S0144686X1900059X

Hagan, J., Rodriguez, N., Capps, R., & Kabiri, N. (2003). The effects of recent welfare and immigration reforms on immigrants' access to health care. *International Migration Review, 37*(2), 444–463.

Hajat, A., Lucas, J. B., & Kington, R. (2000). *Health outcomes among Hispanic subgroups: Data from the National Health Interview Survey, 1992–95* (No. 310). Hyattsville, MD: US Department of Health and Human Services, Centers for Disease Control and Prevention, National Center for Health Statistics.

Hall, M., Greenman, E., & Farkas, G. (2010) Legal status and wage disparities for Mexican immigrants. *Social Forces, 89*(2), 491–513.

Hancock, T. U. (2005) Cultural competence in the assessment of poor Mexican families in the rural southeastern united states. *Child Welfare, 84*(5), 689–711.

Hernandez, D. J., & Darke, K. (1999). Socioeconomic and demographic risk factors and resources among children in immigrant and native-born families: 1910, 1960, and 1990. In Committee on the Health and Adjustment of Immigrant Children and Families (Ed.), *Children of immigrants: Health, adjustment, and public assistance* (pp. 19–125). Washington, DC: National Academies Press.

Hernandez, D. J., Denton, N. A., & Blanchard, V. L. (2011). Children in the United States of America: A statistical portrait by race-ethnicity, immigrant origins, and language. *The ANNALS of the American Academy of Political and Social Science*, 633(1), 102–127.

Hu, X. (2018). Filling the niche: The role of the parents of immigrants in the United States. *RSF: The Russell SAGE Foundation Journal of the Social Sciences*, 4(1), 96–114.

Huang, Z. J., Yu, S. M., & Ledsky, R. (2006). Health status and health service access and use among children in the U.S. immigrant families. *American Journal of Public Health*, 96(4), 634–640.

Katiria Perez, G., & Cruess, D. (2014). The impact of familism on physical and mental health among Hispanics in the United States. *Health Psychology Review*, 8(1), 95–127.

Karoly, L. A., & Gonzalez, G. C. (2011). Early care and education for children in immigrant families. *The Future of Children*, 21, 71–101.

Kieffer, M. J. (2008). Catching up or falling behind? Initial English proficiency, concentrated poverty, and the reading growth of language minority learners in the United States. *Journal of Educational Psychology*, 100(4), 851–868.

Kim, B. J., Sangalang, C. C., & Kihl, T. (2012). Effects of acculturation and social network support on depression among elderly Korean immigrants. *Aging & Mental Health*, 16(6), 787–794.

Kuperminc, G. P., Wilkins, N. J., Roche, C., & Alvarez-Jimenez, A. (2009). Risk, resilience, and positive development among Latino youth. In F. A. Villarruel, G. Carlo, J. M. Grau, M. Azmitia, N. J. Cabrera, & T. Chahin (Eds.), *Handbook of U.S. Latino psychology: Developmental and community-based perspectives* (pp. 213–233). Thousand Oaks, CA: SAGE.

Kuperminc, G. P., Wilkins, N. J., Jurkovic, G. J., & Perilla, J. L. (2013). Filial responsibility, perceived fairness, and psychological functioning of Latino youth from immigrant families. *Journal of Family Psychology*, 27(2), 173–182.

Lee, E. (2007). Domestic violence and risk factors among Korean immigrant women in the United States. *Journal of Violence*, 22(3), 141–149.

Lee, M. S., Crittenden, K. S., & Yu, E. (1996). Social support and depression among elderly Korean immigrants in the United States. *International Journal of Aging and Human Development*, 42, 313–327.

Leidy, M. S., Parke, R. D., Cladis, M., Coltrane, S., & Duffy, S. (2009). Positive marital quality, acculturative stress, and child outcomes among Mexican Americans. *Journal of Marriage and Family*, 71(4), 833–847.

Leong, F., Park, Y. S., & Kalibatseva, Z. (2013). Disentangling immigrant status in mental health: Psychological protective and risk factors among Latino and Asian American immigrant. *American Journal of Orthopsychiatry*, 83(2/3), 361–371.

Marley, C., & Mauki, B. (2018). Resilience and protective factors among refugee children post-migration to high-income countries: A systematic review. *European Journal of public Health*, 29(4), 706–713. doi: https://doi.org/10.1093/eurpub/cky232

Mazumdar, S., Mazumdar, S., Docuyanan, F., & McLaughlin, C. M. (2000). Creating a sense of place: The Vietnamese-Americans and Little Saigon. *Journal Of Environmental Psychology*, 20(4), 319–333.

Menjivar, C. (2006). Liminal legality: Salvadoran and Guatemalan immigrants' lives in the United States. *American Journal of Sociology*, 111(4), 999–1037.

Menjivar, C. (2011). The power of the law: Central American's legality and everyday life in Phoenix, Arizona. *Latino Studies, 9*(4), 377–395.

Mitchell, N. A., & Bryan, J. A. (2007). School–family–community partnerships: Strategies for school counselors working with Caribbean immigrant families. *Professional School Counseling, 10*(4), 399–409.

Morina, N., & Sterr, T. N. (2019). Lack of evidence for the efficacy of psychotherapies for PTSD and depression in child and adolescent refugees. *World Psychiatry, 18*(1), 107–108.

Mui, A. C., & Kang, S. Y. (2006). Acculturation stress and depression among Asian immigrant elders. *Social Work, 51*, 243–255.

Muruthi, J. R., & Lewis, D. C. (2017). Cambodian refugee families: Impacts of immigration-related stressors on intergenerational relationships. *Journal of Intergenerational Relationships, 15*(2), 125–142.

National Center for Health Statistics. (2012). *Health, United States, 2011 with special feature on socioeconomic status and health.* Hyattsville, MD: US Department of Health and Human Services. Retrieved from https://www.ncbi.nlm.nih.gov/pubmed/22812021

Navidian, A., Kermansaravi, F., & Rigi, S. N. (2012). The effectiveness of a group psycho-educational program on family caregiver burden of patients with mental disorders. *BMC Research Notes, 5*(1), 399.

Orellana, M. F. (2001). The work kids do: Mexican and Central American immigrant children's contribution to households and school in California. *Harvard Educational Review, 71*(3), 366–389.

Orellana, M. F. (2003). Responsibilities of children in Latino immigrant homes. *New Directions for Youth Development, 100*, 25–39.

Oznobishin, O., & Kurman, J. (2009). Parent–child role reversal and psychological adjustment among immigrant youth in Israel. *Journal of Family Psychology, 23*(3), 405–415.

Peris, T. S., Goeke-Morey, M. C., Cumming, M. E., & Emery, R. E. (2008). Marital conflict and support seeking by parents in adolescence: Empirical support for the parentification construct. *Journal of Family Psychology, 22*(4), 633–642.

Park, M., & McHugh, M. (2014). *Immigrant parents and early childhood programs: Addressing barriers of literacy, culture, and systems knowledge.* Washington, DC: Migration Policy Institute. Retrieved from www.migrationpolicy.org/research/immigrant-parents-early-childhood-programs-barriers

Park, M., & Katsiaficas, C. (2019). *Mitigating the effects of trauma among young children of immigrants and refugees: The role of early childhood programs.* Washington, DC. Migration Policy Institute. Retrieved from https://www.migrationpolicy.org/research/mitigating-effects-trauma-young-children-immigrants-refugees

Pfeiffer, P. N., Blow, A. J., Miller, E., Forman, J., Dalack, G. W., & Valenstein, M. (2012). Peers and peer-based interventions in supporting reintegration and mental health among National Guard soldiers: A qualitative study. *Military Medicine, 177*, 12, 1471–1476.

Philbin, M. M., Flake, M., Hatzenbuehler, M. L., & Hirsch, J. S. (2018) State-level immigration and immigrant-focused policies as drivers of Latino health disparities in the United States. *Social Science and Medicine, 199*, 29–38.

Pivnick, A., Jacobson, A., Blank, A., & Villegas, M. (2010). Accessing primary care: HIV+ Caribbean immigrants in the Bronx. *Journal of Immigrant & Minority Health, 12*(4), 496–505.

Pomerantz, E. M., Qin, L. L., Wang, Q., & Chen, H. C. (2011). Changes in early adolescents' sense of responsibility to their parents in the United States and China: Implications for academic functioning. *Child Development, 82*(4), 1136–1151.

Portes, A., & Celaya, A. (2013) Modernization for emigration: Determinants & consequences of the brain drain. *Daedalus, 142*(3), 170–184.

Portes, A., & Rivas, A. (2011). The adaptation of migrant children. *The Future of Children, 21,* 219–246.

Pottinger, A. M., Stair, A. G., & Brown, S. W. (2008). A counselling framework for Caribbean children and families who have experienced migratory separation and reunion. *International Journal for the Advancement of Counselling, 30*(1), 15–24.

Raffaelli, M., Tran, S. P., Wiley, A. R., Galarza-Heras, M., & Lazarevic, V. (2012) Risk and resilience in rural communities: The experiences of immigrant Latina mothers. *Family Relations, 61*(4), 559–570.

Raj, A., & Silverman, J. (2002). Violence against immigrant women: The roles of culture, context, and legal immigrant status on intimate partner violence. *Violence Against Women, 8*(3), 367–398.

Reynolds, T. (2005). *Caribbean mothers: Identity and experience in the U.K.* London, England: Tufnell Press.

Rodriguez, C. (2019). Latino/a citizen children of undocumented parents negotiating illegality. *Journal of Marriage and Family, 81*(3), 713–728.

Rosenblum, M., & McCabe, K. (2014). Deportation and discretion: Reviewing the record and options for change. Washington, DC: Migration Policy Institute. Retrieved from www .migrationpolicy.org/research/deportation-and -discretionreviewing-record-and-options-change

Sander, C. (2003). *Migrant remittances to developing countries. A scoping study: Overview and introduction to issues for pro-poor financial services.* Report prepared for UK Department for International Development, London, England.

Sapthiang, S., Van Gordon, W., Shonin, E., & Griffiths, M. D. (2019). The mental health needs of child and adolescent refugee and asylum seekers entering Europe. *Social Health and Behavior, 2*(1), 13–16.

Schneider, B., Martinez, S., & Owens, A. (2006). Barriers to education opportunities for Hispanics in the United States. In M. Tienda & F. Mitchell (Eds.), *Hispanics and the future of America* (pp. 179–227), Washington, DC: The National Academic Press.

Shields, M. K., & Behrman, R. E. (2004). Children of immigrant families: Analysis and recommendations. *The Future of Children, 14*(2), 4–15.

Simon, J. B., Murphy, J. J., & Smith, S. M. (2005) Understanding and fostering family resilience. *The Family Journal, 13*(4), 427–436.

Social Science Research Council. (2009). *Formal vs. informal remittances.* Brooklyn, NY: Social Science Research Council.

Stark, M. D., Quinn, B. P., Hennessey, K. A., Rutledge, A. A., Hunter, A. K., & Gordillo, P. K. (2019). Examining resiliency in adolescent refugees through the tree of life activity. *Journal of Youth Development, 14*(2), 130–152.

Thomas, L., Clarke, T., & Kroliczak, A. (2008). Implementation of peer support demonstration project for HIV+ Caribbean immigrants: A descriptive paper. *Journal of Immigrant & Refugee Studies, 6*(4), 526–544.

Thomas, K. J. A. (2012). *A demographic profile of Black Caribbean immigrants in the United States.* Washington DC: Migration Policy Institute.

Tienda, M., & Haskins, R. (2011). Immigrant children: Introducing the issue. *The Future of Children, 21,* 3–18.

Treas, J. (2009). Age in standards and standards for age: Institutionalizing chronological age as biographical necessity. In M. Lampland & S. L. Star (Eds.), *Standards and their stories: How quantifying, classifying, and formalizing practices shape everyday life* (pp. 65–87). Ithaca, NY: Cornell University Press.

Treas, J., & Batalova, J. (2009). Immigrants and aging. In P. Uhlenberg (Ed.), *International handbook of population aging* (pp. 365–394). New York, NY: Springer.

Treas, J., & Mazumdar, S. (2002). Older people in America's immigrant families: Dilemmas of dependence, integration, and isolation. *Journal of Aging Studies*, 16(3), 243–258.

Trickett, E. J., & Jones, C. J. (2007). Adolescent culture brokering and family functioning: A study of families from Vietnam. *Cultural Diversity and Ethnic Minority Psychology*, 13(2), 143–150.

Turner, V. (1969). Liminality and communitas. In V. Turner, *The ritual process: Structure and anti-structure*, 94–130. New York, NY: Routledge.

Valdez, C. R., Abegglen, J., & Hauser, C. T. (2013). Fortalezas Familiares Program: Building sociocultural and family strengths in Latina women with depression and their families. *Family Process*, 52(3), 378–393.

Vesely, C. K., Letiecq, B. L., & Goodman, R. D. (2017). Immigrant family resilience in context: Using a community-based approach to build a new conceptual model. *Journal of Family Theory & Review*, 9(1), 93–110.

Vespa, J., Armstrong, D. M., & Medina, L. (2018). *Demographic turning points for the United States: Population projections for 2020 to 2060.* Washington, DC: US Department of Commerce, Economics and Statistics Administration, US Census Bureau.

Viruell-Fuentes, E. A., Morenoff, J. D., Williams, D. R., & House, J. S. (2013). Contextualizing nativity status, Latino social ties, and ethnic enclaves: An examination of the "immigrant social ties hypothesis." *Ethnicity & Health*, 18(6), 586–609.

Viruell-Fuentes, E. A., & Schulz, A. J. (2009). Toward a dynamic conceptualization of social ties and context: Implications for understanding immigrant and Latino health. *American Journal of Public Health*, 99(12), 2167–2175.

Walsh, F. (2003). Family resilience: A framework for clinical practice. *Family Process*, 42(1), 1–18.

Walsh, F. (2006). *Strengthening family resilience* (2nd ed.). New York, NY: Guilford Press.

Weisskirch, S. A. (2005). The relationship of language brokering to ethnic identity for Latino early adolescents. *Hispanic Journal of Behavioral Sciences*, 27(3), 286–299.

Weisskirch, R. S. (2010). Child language brokers in immigrant families: An overview of family dynamics. *MediAzioni*, 10, 68–87. Retrieved from http://mediazioni.sitlec.unibo.it/images/stories/PDF_folder/document-pdf/monografia2010CLB/04%20weisskirch%20pp68_87.pdf

Weisskirch, R. S. (2007). Feelings about language brokering and family relations among Mexican American early adolescents. *The Journal of Early Adolescence*, 27(4), 545–561.

Winton, C. A. (2003). *Children as caregivers: Parental and parentified children.* Boston, MA: Allyn & Bacon.

Yang, F., & Ebaugh, H. R. (2001). Transformations in new immigrant religions and their global implications. *American Sociological Review*, 66(2), 269–288.

Yee, B. W. K., Debaryshe, B. D., Yuen, S., Kim, S. Y., & McCubbin, H. I. (2007). Asian American and Pacific Islander families: Resiliency and life-span socialization in a cultural context. In F. T. L. Leong, A. Inman, A. Ebreo, L. H. Yang, L. M. Kinoshita, & M. Fu (Eds.), *Handbook of Asian American psychology* (2nd ed., pp. 69–86). Thousand Oaks, CA: SAGE.

Yoshikawa, H. (2011). *Immigrants raising citizens: Undocumented parents and their young children.* New York, NY: Russell SAGE Foundation.

Yoo, J., & Zippay, A. (2012). Social networks among lower income Korean elderly immigrants in the U.S. *Journal of Aging Studies.,26*(3), 368–376.

Zong, J., Batalova, J., & Burrows, M. (2019). *Frequently requested statistics on immigrants and immigration in the United States.* Washington, DC: Migration Policy Institute.

Zontini, E., & Reynolds, T. (2007) Ethnicity, families, and social capital: Caring relationships across Italian and Caribbean transnational families. *International Review of Sociology, 17*(2), 257–277.

Contextual Influences on Family Stress

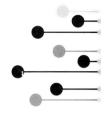

CHAPTER 11

Economic Stress and Families

Suzanne Bartholomae and
Jonathan Fox

Vignette

Daniel Greene, 53, was recently part of a mass layoff at a high-tech firm. Daniel was always a hardworking, dedicated employee who cared about his job. Daniel has been married to Erica for 11 years. They have three children. He made $60,000 a year and was the major breadwinner of the family. Daniel receives a weekly unemployment check, but it isn't enough to cover his family's expenses, and unemployment benefits stop after 26 weeks. Daniel and Erica didn't have an emergency savings account, so they had to borrow some money from Erica's mother. Their credit cards have also made up for some of the shortfall in income, and they may soon tap into the retirement savings Daniel accumulated while working. Daniel is becoming more and more withdrawn socially. Last week, he ran into a former colleague at the park who suggested he consider some short-term work for Uber to make some quick cash. He told Erica how awkward the conversation was when he was asked what he has been up to; he said he felt like a "total loser." He doesn't sleep at night and seems to be irritable most of the time. He snaps at Erica and the children. Daniel's oldest daughter has been acting out at school, Erica received a call from the school counselor. Erica feels bad for Daniel, but she is losing patience and just hopes that something good will happen soon.

Daniel and Erica's difficulties are similar to the financial struggles experienced by many families. In this chapter, we start by discussing ways that economic stress is measured and defined by family scientists, followed by an overview of current economic conditions of the American family. We then review measures of family economic well-being such as employment instability and insecurity, and how these measures relate to economic stress and threaten family welfare. We then use the family stress model (FSM) as a framework (Conger, Conger, & Martin, 2010; Conger & Elder, 1994) and discuss the outcomes associated with economic stress, including a review of the research on economic stress and its interaction with resources and problem solving. Finally, using a family economic life cycle, we discuss coping strategies to combat negative economic events.

As family scientists, we have long examined the link between adverse economic conditions and family processes and outcomes. A longitudinal study of children of the Great Depression published in the 1970s linked economic hardship to the reorganization of family roles and responsibilities (Elder, 1974). Similarly, rural farm families who experienced a severe economic downturn in the 1980s were the focus of several studies, showing the link between economic pressure and elevated depression, hostility, and marital distress (Conger & Conger, 2002; Conger & Elder, 1994). Several recent studies examined the effect of the Great Recession on families, providing a living laboratory to study economic stress (e.g., Glei, Goldman, & Weinstein, 2019; Stewart, Dew, & Lee, 2017). Taken together, there is a body of work that captures the importance of explaining how economic stress and financial problems influence family life.

Defining and Measuring Economic Stress

Economic stress can be the by-product of conditions in the national, regional, or local economy, as seen during the Great Recession. Economic stress can be described as either *normative* (resulting from expected milestones in the family life cycle, such as marriage or birth of a child) or *situational/nonnormative* (stemming from unexpected events, such as divorce, retirement, or illness). In addition, economic stress associated with life events may be *temporary* (e.g., a short-term drop in income due to job loss) or *chronic* (e.g., a long-term income loss because of a permanent work-limiting disability) (Voydanoff, 1983). Daniel's economic stress began with his layoff and would be considered temporary if he quickly rebounded by finding gainful employment. His stress is considered chronic if he continues to be unemployed.

Family researchers often use the term *economic* or *financial stress* interchangeably with such terms as *economic* or *financial distress, hardship, pressure, and strain*. The concept of economic stress can be decomposed into employment and income-related stressors that can be described objectively (e.g., a lack of regular work and income) or subjectively (e.g., worrying about possible unemployment; Voydanoff & Donnelly, 1988). To assess objective economic stress, researchers examine patterns of employment and changes in income over time, for example, by comparing various individual, couple, and family outcomes (e.g., depression, marital satisfaction, and parenting) by employed versus unemployed status.

Financial strain represents the subjective, psychological aspects of economic stress and is thought to be related to but independent of one's income. *Subjective measurement* of economic strain or pressure can be defined as "the perceived adequacy of financial resources, financial concerns and worries, and expectations regarding one's future economic situation" (Voydanoff & Donnelly, 1988, p. 98). Families of similar income levels can have considerably different experiences with financial strain and well-being based on their access to and management of economic resources like home ownership and characteristics like family size and number of dependents. Researchers have generally assessed levels of financial strain by asking individuals to rate how often they worry about their finances, how satisfied they are with their financial situation, their level of difficulty paying bills, and whether they have enough money to meet necessities or have money left over at the end of the month. The Consumer Financial Protection Bureau (CFPB), the federal agency created by the Dodd-Frank Wall Street Reform and Consumer Protection Act that was a result of the financial crisis in 2008, coalesced stakeholders around defining, measuring, and addressing the concept of financial well-being, and introduced a scale in 2015. The CFPB's definition of financial well-being is "a state of being wherein a person can fully meet current and ongoing financial obligations, can feel secure in their financial future, and is able to make choices that allow enjoyment of life" (Consumer Financial Protection Bureau [CFPB], 2017, p. 13). The components of economic stress are unique to each individual and family system, particularly the perception of the event. For Daniel and Erica, they had some resources to draw from and were able to make some adjustments; however, this combination is unique for each family.

Economic Conditions of the American Family

In the last decade, the American economy has experienced a steady recovery from one of the longest and most severe economic downturns in American history, the Great Recession. During the Great Recession (December 2007 to June 2009), families sustained severe job losses, high unemployment, record-breaking long-term unemployment, significant job shortages, large declines in income, and a substantial rise in poverty (Bernstein, 2014; Rothstein, 2017). Research shows that during an economic recession, marriage, divorce, and fertility rates tend to decline and rates of family violence and suicide increase; when the economy is thriving, these indicators tend to work in the opposite direction (Blair, 2012). Some economic metrics, such as historically low unemployment, paint a rosy picture for American families; however, metrics of financial security examined more closely at the individual, family, and household level depict a different scenario. Several family economic indicators have not returned to prerecession levels and the hardships of the Great Recession are still being felt by families (Dolan, 2016; Kirsch, Love, Radler, & Ryff, 2019).

The United States is long heralded as one of the most affluent countries, with most families historically benefiting from a strong and prosperous economy. This distinction no longer holds. The American dream, previously achieved by hard work and self-reliance, has become out of reach for many (Lamont, 2019). Relative to other nations, recent data show a decline in the number of Americans in the middle class, stagnant middle-class wages, a rise in income inequality, and the American middle class is no longer the world's wealthiest (Krause & Sawhill, 2018). Currently families cannot keep up with the rising costs of being in the middle class and maintaining a middle-class standard of living. A recent study notes, "Even with the economy approaching full employment, nearly 40% of adults reported that they or their families had trouble meeting at least one basic need for food, health care, housing, or utilities in 2017" (Karpman, Zuckerman, & Gonzalez, 2018). Economic security is at the core of being middle class. Whether measured objectively or subjectively, many families, regardless of income level, are experiencing economic stress and financial pressures (Karpman, et al., 2018; Wiedrich & Newville, 2019), with economic stress varying by a person's education, race, and neighborhood (Board of Governors of the Federal Reserve System, 2019).

Measures of Family Economic Well-Being

For many families it takes just one crisis, such as a divorce or job loss, to devastate their economic well-being. Most measures of economic well-being vary substantially by demographic characteristics (e.g., gender, education, marital status, minority group status). We present a variety of economic indicators that family scientists use to measure and estimate the prevalence of economic stress in families. Studies by family scientists have documented the critical role economic resources play in the quality of family functioning (Masarik & Conger, 2017; Shelleby, 2018).

Employment Instability and Insecurity: A Threat to Family Life

The economic stressor most frequently studied by family researchers relates to employment—both job insecurity and unemployment. Job insecurity is the real or perceived threat of losing one's job. Both job insecurity and unemployment have been associated with poor physical health, high depressive symptoms, and lower life satisfaction (De Witte, Pienaar, & De Cuyper, 2016; Urbanaviciute, De Witte, & Rossier, 2019). Symptoms commonly associated with unemployment and job loss include a sense of helplessness, insecurity, depression, emotional exhaustion, anxiety, substance abuse, drinking-related problems, strained family relationships, role anxiety, damaged self-esteem, suicidal behaviors, and depletion of financial resources (De Witte et al., 2016).

Unemployment might result from job dismissal, factory closing, or forced early retirement. Single-earner families, like Daniel and Erica's, are more vulnerable financially, in the case of illness or job loss, they have no safety net from a backup earner. On the other hand, with a two-income family budget where both paychecks are needed where to meet financial obligations, job loss or illness is potentially more serious than for a one-earner family where the other person can enter the labor market to make up for an income loss. With Daniel's job loss came new constraints, disruptions, and stressors. The impact to his family was similar to what the research demonstrates—family relationships were strained and children experienced behavioral changes not previously seen such as conduct disorders, adolescent drinking, literacy issues, and poor physical health (Masarik & Conger, 2017; Shelleby, 2018). For Daniel, there were also nonfinancial impacts, such as a loss of structure to his day, loss of social status associated with his job, disrupted social networks, reduced opportunities for social contact, and reduced goals and task demands (Creed & Klisch, 2005).

When the economy and labor market are healthy, families typically prosper. However, measures of the economy no longer provide an accurate measure of the experiences of families (Wiedrich & Newville, 2019). The unemployment rate is close to a 50-year low in the United States at 3.7% (U.S. Bureau of Labor Statistics, 2019), however more than one-fifth (22.5%) of jobs are in a low-wage occupation (Wiedrich & Newville, 2019). The U.S. labor market had one of the worst records of job growth and sustained the most severe job loss in 7 decades at the start of the Great Recession (Mishel, Bivens, Gould, & Shierholz, 2012), with well-paying industries, such as construction and manufacturing, hit the hardest (Rothstein, 2017). The quality of jobs available and the precariousness of work is a source of economic stress (Blustein, 2019). The past decade has seen a rise in the gig economy (e.g., Uber drivers), from 10% in 2005 to about 16% in 2015 (Katz & Krueger, 2016). Gig work is freelance, independent work that pays a person by a task or project (e.g., housekeeping, selling goods online) rather than an hourly wage or salary. About 1 in 4 Americans reported wages from the gig economy (Smith, 2016), some rely on gig work as their main source of income, others as a supplement (Board of Governors of the Federal Reserve System, 2019). Gig work provides less security and fewer protections and benefits (e.g., health insurance or paid leave) than traditional work (Blustein, 2019). These labor market conditions have dismantled the financial security of many families, increasing feelings of stress.

Income: Family Livelihood

An important indicator used to measure family economic well-being is income. Income represents the flow of financial resources into a household at a particular time, allowing families to pay their mortgage, utility, and groceries bills and allowing parents to invest in their children's upbringing and education. Daniel and Erica had a steady income prior to his layoff. During tough economic times like a recession, income can ward off stress. Studies show a negative relationship between income and financial stress, with higher levels of income associated with lower economic stress (French & Vigne, 2019; Valentino, Moore, Cleveland, Greenberg, & Tan, 2014). According to the U.S. Financial Health Pulse survey, almost half of Americans reported that in the past 12 months their spending equaled or surpassed their income (Garon, Dunn, Golvala, & Wilson, 2018). One reason is that families are more often experiencing dips and spikes in income. Termed *income volatility*, about one-fifth of households (20.1%) experienced a moderate to severe fluctuation in income on a month-to-month basis (Wiedrich & Newville, 2019). Studies show that families that spend beyond their income are more likely to be in financial distress (Chalise & Anong, 2017). Income has both a direct and indirect effect on marital outcomes, including an increase in conflict, problems, and thoughts of divorce, as well as lower marital happiness and interaction (Dew, 2009; Wheeler, Kerpelman, & Yorgason, 2019). Stable income has been associated with greater marital satisfaction (Wong & Goodwin, 2009).

In the past several decades, income growth has been stagnant for families in the middle class (Krause & Sawhill, 2018). In 2017, family household median income before taxes was $77,713, only recently rebounding from the Great Recession (Fontenot, Semega, & Kollar, 2018). Median income for all household types was $61,372 in 2017, with married couple households having the highest median income ($90,386), followed by male-headed family households with no wife present ($60,843; Fontenot, et al., 2018). Most recent estimates show that wives earned more than husbands in 29% of dual-earner marriages, an increase from 23% in the 1990s and 16% in 1980s (U.S. Census Bureau, 2012). Family households that were maintained by women with no husband present had the lowest income, $41,703 (Fontenot et al., 2018). Middle-income families were the majority 4 decades ago (62%), however, they have lost ground (43%) as of 2015 (Pew Research Center, 2015). In 2017, households in the 90th percentile had incomes of $179,077, over seven times more than households in the 20th percentile (Fontenot, et al., 2018).

Median household income is an imperfect measure of financial security because it only counts cash benefits and does not include the value of non-cash benefits from employers (e.g., retirement plan contributions), food stamps (Supplemental Nutrition Assistance Program, known as SNAP), health insurance (Medicare, Medicaid), public housing, or other income-support programs (DeNavas-Walt & Proctor, 2014). Household income or poverty level determines one's eligibility for benefits from public programs. Based on 2017 U.S. Census data, the poverty rate for families was 9.3%, and approximately 7.8 million families were in poverty; female-headed households represented the largest proportion (25.7%; Fontenot et al., 2018). Many of the basics that most of us take for granted, families in poverty live without, including safe and quality living conditions, a healthy diet, and medical care.

Net Worth: A Measure of Family Wealth

Net worth is a tremendously important indicator of family economic well-being. Higher net worth denotes greater financial security and independence when times are tough, increased opportunities to further education and employment, and one's ability to move upward in terms of economic mobility and social class (McKernan, Ratcliffe, Steuerle, & Zhang, 2013). Net worth consists of a family's total assets (money accumulated in savings, checking, and retirement accounts including 401(k) plans and individual retirement accounts; real estate including home equity; stock holdings; and other assets such as cars and furniture) minus total liabilities (money owed on debts such as mortgages, credit cards, student loans). Net worth can be negative or positive, and in most cases, a negative net worth would be a reliable indicator of economic stress. Net worth typically increases with income (the strongest association), age (net worth increases until about age 60), education, housing status (home ownership accounts for the largest piece of net worth among middle-class families), gender (men's net worth is typically higher than women's), and marital status (marriage leads to increased net worth, but not in all cases) and is associated with a variety of outcomes such as greater occupational attainment, greater educational and cognitive achievement of children, and increased likelihood of enrolling in college and completing a college degree (Killewald, Pfeffer, & Schachner, 2017; Wolff, 2017).

Median household net worth of all families was $97,300, and mean net worth was $692,100 in 2016 (Bricker et al., 2017). Net worth plunged and inequality rose quickly after the Great Recession and has rebounded in the past few years (Wolff, 2017). Inequality is strikingly evident in the distribution of net worth; the lowest income households (<20 percentile) had a median net worth of $7,000 compared to $296,900 (80–89.9 percentile) and $1,161,000 (90–100 percentile) for households in the highest percentiles (Bricker et al., 2017). There is alarming disparity in net worth levels among ethnic minority groups. In 2016, White-only households had a median net worth of $146,400 compared to net worth of $13,600 for Black or African American non-Hispanic and $14,200 for Hispanic households (Bricker et al., 2017). The types of assets held vary by household wealth and contribute to wealth disparity. Financial assets, such as bank accounts, stocks, bonds, and retirement accounts, tend to be held by wealthier households whereas lower and middle-income households hold most of their wealth in home equity through home ownership (Schuetz, 2019; Wolff, 2017). Borrowing on credit cards and dipping into retirement savings will erode the value of Daniel and Erica's net worth.

Home Ownership: The American Dream

Families continue to maintain the American dream of home ownership though this opportunity has been somewhat stagnant. Since the 1960s, homeownership rates for the United States have ranged between 63% and 69%, with about 64.1% of families owning their primary residence in 2019 (U.S. Census Bureau, 2019). A lack of affordability in the housing market has historically been a challenge for low-income families, but middle-income families now face the same affordability issue (Schuetz, 2019). In 2016, the average home equity was $197,500, and the median home value was $185,000 (Bricker et al., 2017). Home ownership rates vary by family income—in 2016, the home ownership rate was 46.9% for families in the bottom half of the income distribution compared to 91.4% for families in the top 10% (Bricker et al., 2017).

For American families, building home equity is fundamental to building wealth. Home equity—the value of a home less the amount owed on the mortgage—constitutes a family's greatest financial asset and share of net worth. Several studies demonstrate the benefits of homeownership to individuals (e.g., better mental and physical health), children (e.g., greater educational attainment), and the community (higher civic engagement and social involvement) (Lindblad & Quercia, 2014; Schuetz, 2019). Home ownership is typically the largest budget item for families, more than double food or transportation costs (Schuetz, 2019). If a family overcommits resources to their housing payments, it can create economic stress.

Household Debt and Families: Borrowing Against the Future

Debt is a financial instrument that can be used to create wealth and opportunities for families. In 2016, 77% of families held some type of debt, the top three types were credit card debt, mortgages, and education loans (Bricker et al., 2017). Not all household debt is bad, secured debts, loans that are guaranteed by a specific asset, are typically planned debts and increase family wealth whereas unsecured debt is any type of debt that require no collateral and is not protected such as credit card debt, medical bills, and utility bills. For example, a mortgage is a secured debt where collateral (e.g., a house) is secured against the amount owed. A mortgage provides an opportunity for home ownership, which in turn contributes to increased wealth when families accumulate equity (the value of savings attained by making monthly mortgage payments). Student loan debt is another example of debt that helps create wealth and has long-term returns by investing in a person's human capital.

The most threatening type of debt to the long-term financial well-being of families is unsecured consumer credit—typically used to purchase items and services that do not last longer than the payment period, require interest payments to the lender, and yield no economic return while being held. In other words, this debt adds no personal assets to a family, and instead creates a burden of repayment. Unsecured debt has been found to cause greater stress for individuals compared to unsecured debt (Dunn & Mirzaie, 2016). Among adults, the relationship between unsecured debt and self-rated health, obesity, depression, substance use, and suicide is well established (Richardson, Elliott, & Roberts, 2013). Berger and Houle (2016) found that higher levels of secured debt were associated with greater socioemotional well-being in children whereas higher levels of unsecured debt were associated with declines in children's socioemotional well-being, highlighting the differential impact of debt type.

A prerequisite for debt is access to credit. In 2018, about one-third of American adults applied for some type of credit, and about seven in ten were granted it. Denial for credit access is most commonly experienced by low-income households, and regardless of income, individuals of color more frequently report being denied credit (Board of Governors of the Federal Reserve, 2019). In 2016, about 43.9% of all family households carried a balance on their credit card, and the average family carried $5,700 in credit card debt (Bricker et al., 2014). Credit card debt has been found to negatively impact perceived emotional and financial well-being (Bell et al., 2014; Hunter & Heath, 2017); physical health conditions (Turunen & Hiilamo, 2014); and increased symptoms of depression, anxiety, and anger (Berger, Collins, & Cuesta, 2016; Zurlo, Yoon, & Kim, 2014).

Household debt becomes problematic when large amounts of unsecured debt are assumed and other financial obligations cannot be met. Daniel and Erica will be in trouble if they continue to rack up credit card debt. One-third of Americans reported that they have more debt than they can manage, with debt loads ranging between $19,000 and $25,000, excluding mortgage and home equity lines of credit (Garon et al., 2018). Stress from debt is exacerbated when a collection agency is involved (Dunn & Mirzaie, 2016). Indebtedness has serious health effects including associations with depression, overall well-being, health, health-related behavior, and suicidal ideation (Turunen & Hiilamo, 2014). Among married couples, consumer debt predicted more frequent marital conflict (Dew, 2008) and the likelihood of marital dissolution or divorce (Dew, 2011). In comparison, couples whose home mortgage was paid off, reported greater marital satisfaction (Nelson, Delgadillo, & Dew, 2013). Couples may recognize that consumer debt constrains future choices and may resent the time and money required to make debt payments (Dew, 2008). If Daniel and Erica's debt becomes unmanageable, there will be negative ramifications for them as individuals, as previously noted, and may impact their relationship.

When a family's debt becomes overwhelming, personal bankruptcy is an option. With bankruptcy, a person files a petition in federal court to declare their inability to repay their debts and files either a Chapter 7, when they sell off their assets to repay their debts, or a Chapter 13, when they structure a plan to repay debt. The majority of bankruptcy filings occur because of reasons beyond the control of the family, such as job loss, divorce, or illness coupled with a lack of health insurance. Bankruptcy is a substantial indicator of a family experiencing severe economic stress, and it comes with long-term consequences. For example, a family's ability to secure credit, or low-cost loans for housing and education are greatly diminished after filing for bankruptcy. Between 2005 and 2017, there were 12.8 million bankruptcy filings, 68% were Chapter 7 filings and 32% were Chapter 13 (United States Courts, 2018). Around 750,000 households filed for bankruptcy during a 12-month period ending March 31, 2019 (U.S. Bankruptcy Courts, 2019). Families largely file due to unmanageable consumer debt, with unpaid medical bills being the primary cause of bankruptcy (Himmelstein, Lawless, Thorne, Foohey, & Woolhandler, 2019).

Savings: Family Safety Net

Families who have excess money after paying their household expenses can build savings that provide a cushion for emergencies and unexpected expenses or use it to build wealth. When income exceeds expenses, a family has positive cash flow, which is a key to reducing economic stress and increasing financial security over the long term (Aspen Institute, 2019). The personal savings rate of Americans is 6.1%, which is the percentage that a person sets aside from income for savings (U.S. Bureau of Economic Analysis, 2019). In 2016, the proportion of American families who reported saving over the past year was 55.4% (Bricker et al., 2017). Americans typically save their money for big purchases, like buying a house or car, retirement, education, travel, and emergency savings. The median percentage of income saved by Americans was 2%, about 25% reported that they did not have any retirement savings (Board of Governors of the Federal Reserve System, 2019). Daniel is upset about the possibility of dipping into his retirement savings and not being able to save money toward a college savings fund for his children.

The importance of savings is greater than ever because families are receiving fewer health and pension or retirement benefits from private employers (Weller, 2014). Families who maintain a cash reserve in an emergency savings account create a financial safety net that can help to avoid a financial crisis and enable them to meet financial obligations. Financial professionals recommend a 3- to 6-month emergency savings fund in the case of unexpected job loss or work-limiting disability. Half of Americans have an emergency or rainy-day fund set aside to cover 3 months of expenses if they lost a job. Expenses on a smaller scale are challenging for 40% of adults who report they would have difficulty covering an unexpected expense of $400, such as a car repair (Board of Governors of the Federal Reserve System, 2019). With no safety net, like in Daniel's situation, many American families are not prepared to face a financial disruption.

The Family Economic Stress Model

The family economic stress model attributed to Conger and Elder (1994) predicts that economic hardship will lead to child and family outcomes through adverse changes in personal mental health, marital quality, and parenting. The process begins with external economic pressures such as involuntary job separation or a general countrywide economic downturn, such as the Great Recession, that lead to financial strains. These pressures result in declines in parental mental health, such as increased depression, which challenges both marital quality and parenting practices. Finally, compromised parenting yields negative family outcomes most often observed in child mental health and behavior. Now referred to as simply, the family stress model, the model has been applied to models of family and child outcomes in diverse economic systems and cultures (for reviews see Conger et al., 2010; Masarik & Conger, 2017); performing equally well in Finland's welfare state (Solantaus, Leinonen, & Punamaki, 2004), communist China (Shek, 2003), and capitalist economies such as the United States (Conger & Elder, 1994).

Economic stress in the family manifests itself directly by influencing individual well-being and indirectly by influencing family interaction (Neppl, Senia, & Donnellan, 2016). Economic factors (e.g., unemployment, low income, excessive debt levels) have negative effects on the mental health and well-being of individuals (Frasquilho et al., 2015; French & Vigne, 2019; Zurlo et al., 2014). Researchers have identified a relationship between economic stress and individual distress, such as increased levels of anger, hostility, depression, anxiety, somatic complaints, poor physical health, and suicidal behaviors (De Witte et al., 2016; Urbanaviciute et al., 2019). In Daniel's case, his ego and self-esteem have been greatly damaged by the layoff, so he feels depressed and irritable.

The adverse effect of economic stress on family functioning and family relationships is well documented (Neppl et al., 2016; White, Liu, Nair, & Tein, 2015). Studies show economic stress linked to decreased family satisfaction and cohesion (Blom, Kraaykamp, & Verbakel, 2019; Voydanoff, 1990), forcing family members to adapt their roles and responsibilities. In Daniel's case, Erica is seeking work after being a stay-at-home mom, just as research shows, when a family experiences an income decline because of one member's job loss, other family members may be required to contribute to household resources by finding employment (Elder & Caspi, 1988). Economic stress can also lead to diminished relationship quality in the family through the strain and disruption caused by changes in social activities as well as changes in the support provided by social networks (Voydanoff, 1990). For example, Daniel and Erica are considering cutting back on the children's extracurricular activities because the added expense is causing stress.

The marital relationship is altered by economic stress, and studies support the family stress model with respect to marital outcomes (Dew, 2007; Laxman, Higginbotham, MacArthur, & Plummer Lee, 2019). Specifically, a couple's adverse economic circumstances (e.g., loss of income), increases financial strain, which increases individual psychological distress, which in turn negatively impacts marital stability and adjustment (Fonseca, Cunha, Crespo, & Relvas, 2016; Kelley, LeBaron, & Hill, 2018). This process results in increased financial disputes and thus greater marital tension and discord (Dew, 2007, 2008; Wheeler et al., 2019), increases husbands' hostility and explosiveness and decreases their supportiveness and warmth (Conger et al., 1990; Neppl et al., 2016), and the overall quality of the marital relationship declines (Dew, 2008; Fonseca et al., 2016; Kelley et at., 2018).

Families facing economic stress often find the quality of their parental well-being suffers, resulting in elevated anxiety, psychological distress, hostility, general life stress, depressive symptoms, somatization, and decreased feelings of efficacy (Kavanaugh, Neppl, & Melby, 2018; Neppl et al., 2016). Further, economic stress has been shown to affect parenting practices by reducing warmth and affective support (Mistry, Lowe, Benner, & Chien, 2008; White et al., 2015); reducing levels of sensitive, supportive behavior (Newland, Crnic, Cox, & Mills-Koonce, 2013); increasing inconsistent, controlling, and punitive discipline (Mistry et al., 2008); and lowering levels of parent involvement and supportiveness (Conger & Conger, 2002; Kavanaugh et al., 2018). Levels of maternal warmth and social support and the provision of child learning experiences in the home are also affected negatively by economic stress (Klebanov, Brooks-Gunn, & Duncan, 1994).

Short- and long-term child outcomes have been associated with economic stress. Children who experience economic stress have been found to exhibit greater levels of depression, psychological distress, anxiety (Frasquilho et al., 2016; Newland et al., 2013); psychosomatic symptoms and chronic illness (Moustgaard, Avendano, & Martikainen, 2018; Pederson, Madsen, & Kohler, 2005); more externalizing aggressive and antisocial problem behavior (Ponnet, 2014; Neppl et al., 2016); decreased levels of self-esteem, self-efficacy, mastery, life satisfaction, and resourcefulness (Maserik & Conger, 2017; Mistry, Benner, Tan, & Kim, 2009); diminished school performance (Gilbert, Spears Brown, & Mistry, 2017) and increased substance abuse and psychiatric morbidity (Shek, 2003). A father's negativity resulting from economic pressure has been found to increase children's risk of depression and aggression (Elder, Conger, Foster, & Ardelt, 1992), whereas maternal financial stress has been shown to decrease the quality of the mother–child relationship, resulting in greater levels of depression and loneliness (Lempers & Clark-Lempers, 1997). Greater financial strain also reduces positive parent–adolescent relations—measured as shared activities and supportiveness—and increases negative parent–adolescent relations—measured as frequency of conflict and aggressive interactions such as shouting or acting angry (Gutman, McLoyd, & Tokoyawa, 2005).

Coping with Economic Stress

The characteristics of financially challenged families—such as adaptability, cohesion, and communication patterns—that are in place both prior to and during a stressor event have an important role in the relationship between the event (such as unemployment and its associated hardships) and individual and family reactions. Families experiencing economic stress from their financial situation can draw on individual (e.g., education), psychological (e.g., self-efficacy), social (e.g., social support), relational (e.g., marital relationship), and financial (e.g., savings) resources to cope with their situation (Bartholomae & Fox, 2017; Valentino et al., 2014).

Individuals with positive self-evaluations, such as high self-esteem or self-worth and a strong sense of personal control or mastery over their situation, are better prepared to manage their economic adversities and financial difficulties (Kim, Basset, So, & Voisin, 2019; Prawitz, Kalkowski, & Cohart, 2014). As such, these qualities can weaken the link between financial stress and mental health outcomes (McKee-Ryan, Song, Wanberg, & Kinicki, 2005; Zurlo et al., 2014). For example, self-efficacy and locus of control has been found to be an effective moderator in the context of economic stress (Prawitz et al., 2014), influencing how an individual reacts to a given stressor event. Studies of unemployment have found that high self-efficacy successfully predicts reemployment (McKee-Ryan et al., 2005) as does an individual's sense of employability (De Cuyper, Mäkikangas, Kinnunen, Mauno, & De Witte, 2012), hope, optimism, and resilience (Chen & Lim, 2012). In Daniel's case, being laid off was unexpected and quite damaging to his self-esteem. He is relying on financial resources, such as savings and unemployment compensation, which are also important in mediating the effect economic stress has on individual and family outcomes (Dew, 2007; Rothwell & Han, 2010). The impact of job loss can be alleviated by income, liquid assets (e.g., money in bank accounts), public assistance (Mistry et al., 2008; McKee-Ryan et al., 2005), as well as the continuation of fringe benefits such as health insurance, severance pay, and pensions (Voydanoff, 1983).

As outlined in the family stress model, some social resources such as integration into family and social networks and quality of one's interpersonal relationships are weakened by financial strain. According to Elder and Caspi (1988), families respond to economic loss by restructuring resources and relationships. Restructuring may relieve the situation without improving it, or it may be an adaptive coping strategy. For those struggling with chronic economic issues, several coping strategies have been identified as effective in breaking the links established in the family stress model. For example, coping strategies such as problem solving, social support, acceptance of the situation, positive thinking, and distraction have been associated with fewer somatic complaints as well as anxious and depressive symptoms among families suffering from chronic economic stress (Wadsworth & Santiago, 2008).

Family Financial Planning as a Coping Resource

Family financial planning can alleviate the psychological and social damage caused by economic stress, family vulnerability, and exposure to economic stress. The family life cycle model developed by Ando and Modigliani (1963) is a common framework for understanding saving and consumption (spending) behavior of families. Over the family life cycle, spending is expected to be smooth and stable as the family maintains a standard of living with the use of savings during low-income periods. However, actual consumption patterns are often affected by changing family needs and wants, situational stressors, and significant historical events (Fox, 1995). When it comes to family's saving and spending behavior, it is important to consider temptation, self-control, and other psychological aspects that effects decision-making over the life cycle (Shefrin & Thaler, 1988). Part of the gap between the theory of household resource allocation over time and actual resource allocation is also explained by the nonnormative factors that are so prevalent among American families, including unanticipated unemployment, divorce, casualty losses, and unanticipated health-care expenses.

The family economic life cycle is comprised of three key phases, identified by the relationship between expenditure and earning levels that define the life-cycle savings hypothesis. These phases, which we discuss in turn below, can serve as guidelines for addressing economic stress. When families employ systematic money management strategies, they can reduce or eliminate conflict during tough financial times. For example, research has shown that couples have fewer finance-related arguments when they use financial management strategies such as tracking spending, record keeping, goal-setting practices, and saving (Godwin, 1994). Couples under economic pressure who use effective problem-solving skills and positive communication patterns (e.g., using humor, being affirming, and acknowledging couple interdependence) reduce marital conflict and thus marital distress (Afifi et al., 2018; Conger et al., 1990).

Phase I. Family Formation: Starting a Credit and Debt Management Program

In the family formation phase, a family is expected to accumulate significant amounts of debt through the use of installment and consumer credit, largely as a result of the purchase of a home and expenses of child-rearing for families with children. Planning for payment against this debt and worrying about possible default can easily become a source of stress within a family; however, by creating and following a debt management plan, stress can be reduced. To make such a plan, the family needs to (a) establish credit goals or debt limits; (b) explore, understand, and make good choices among the various sources of credit; and (c) make fair comparisons between the costs of different types of credit (Garman & Forgue, 2018). Once family members have set their goals and tolerable debt levels, they can study their formal (banks or bank-like institutions) and informal (relatives and friends) credit options. Determining the actual cost of credit (the interest rate) should be salient in the family's credit decision. Saving current income is a primary mechanism through which families achieve financial goals and prepare for financial emergencies. Saving provides a sense of economic control and serves as a safeguard or a coping resource in the event of economic stress (e.g., unemployment).

Phase II. Repaying Debt and Saving for Retirement

In the second phase of the family economic life cycle, the time at which most household heads reach their peak earning years, many families plan to accumulate wealth in anticipation of a substantial decrease in earned income in retirement. During this phase, families reduce or stabilize living expenses so they do not exceed income. As income increases with workplace experience, and household formation nears completion, immediate financial demands are expected to subside, and the family has an opportunity to accumulate savings and pay off debt accumulated in the formation stage. However, during these peak earning years, many families are challenged by the repayment of accumulated debt, college education expenses, and deferral of the proper amount of consumption until retirement, when reduced earnings are anticipated.

Families use tax planning, investment, and asset protection strategies to move assets from one point in the life cycle to another. Unfortunately, the complexity of these financial strategies can often become a source of additional economic stress in families (Aldana & Liljenquist, 1998). As a result, many families now seek the help of family financial managers to retire the debt accumulated in the previous phase and invest any surplus in financial assets. The most important action a family can take in this phase is to accurately determine their debt. Once the amount of debt is clear, they can allocate savings toward debt repayment, retire loans with the highest interest first, thus "investing" in the highest return assets earlier. This method of thinking about debt repayment, in similar terms as saving for future financial goals, helps financial managers justify an emphasis on debt repayment early in the economic life cycle, potentially relieving some of the stress involved in delaying savings for retirement and longer range financial goals.

Nonprofit organizations, such as Consumer Credit Counseling Services, have been established to assist families with the debt management process. Typically, such an organization will help a family reestablish more manageable payment terms for debt. The counseling service commonly collects a lump sum payment from the family and redistributes the money to the creditors, thus relieving family members of the stress involved in direct contact with creditors. Research findings suggest that working with credit counselors can have positive impacts on individuals' financial well-being and health (Kim, Garman, & Sorhaindo, 2003; O'Neill, Sorhaindo, Xiao, & Garman, 2005). Clients who participated in a debt management program have reported improved debt levels and liquidity (Roll & Moulton, 2016), and those reporting improved health outcomes were more likely to engage in positive financial behaviors (O'Neill et al., 2005). However, using such a debt management system can also have significant drawbacks. The process itself is often reported as a negative event in credit bureau files, and participants must agree to discontinue any use of credit during the debt management process.

As families struggle to retire the debt, they have accumulated in the formation stage, families with children may encounter significant additional educational expenses as offspring approach college age. Educational spending pressures have risen steadily in the United States as tuition increases have consistently outpaced increases in wages. The widespread perception of the hopelessness of this situation is expressed in most families' unwillingness to plan for or begin saving for their children's education. A recent study found that parents plan to cover about 62% (down from 70% two years earlier) of their children's total college costs but are on track to save only 28% of that goal (Fidelity Investments, 2018). Other surveys show that half of parents with college-bound children are taking advantage of plans, like Coverdell Savings Accounts or 529 plans, to save for their children's education, up from 24% almost a decade earlier (College Savings Foundation, 2010, 2019). Parents of college students face competing pressures, whether to save for their retirement or their children's education goals; the percentage of families who use retirement assets to pay for college expenses ranges from 7% to 25% (Brandon, 2014).

Studies consistently find that American families are underfinancing their retirement, and most agree that retirement preparation is stressful (Employee Benefit Research Institute, 2019). These families will either need to increase their savings or reduce their living standards below expected levels upon retirement. In a recent poll of Americans, the number one financial worry was adequately saving for retirement (Newport, 2018). Among Americans still working, about one-quarter indicate they have no savings for retirement or a pension, and 13% of those still working who are age 60 or older have not saved for retirement (Board of Governors of the Federal Reserve System, 2019). An estimated 41% of American households headed by adults between ages 35 and 64 are predicted to fall short of money in retirement (VanDerhei, 2019), showing they are likely not on track for retirement at their household's preretirement consumption level.

Retirement planning is a daunting process for most families. Garman and Forgue (2018) outline the formal process of retirement planning; families can use their guidelines to determine the levels of savings they need to meet their retirement spending needs. As with all financial planning prescriptions, the process begins with goal setting. Goals are set based on income needs in retirement. Someone anticipating retirement will evaluate the income needed to maintain the household's current lifestyle or anticipated lifestyle in retirement. Many Americans say they are uncertain about what their retirement looks like (Scott, 2018). A rule of thumb is to plan on retirement income equal to about 70% to 80% of preretirement income (this is referred to as replacement rate), but some sources suggest families plan on needing a replacement rate of 100%.

Anticipated retirement resources are then evaluated, subtracted from retirement needs, and a savings gap is estimated. Additional annual contributions needed to fill this gap are then calculated, and investment decisions are made to match individual investor risk-tolerance levels and specific financial goals in retirement. In this final part of the retirement planning and saving process, a wide range of tax, investment, and insurance planning tools are available to families.

It is at this point that many families rely on financial managers to cope with the complexities of the financial planning process. In fact, the sheer breadth of the field of financial planning appears to be a source of economic stress in families. One study found the lack of financial education and understanding about financial matters is a significant determinant of financial strain (Aldana & Liljenquist, 1998). Families who receive professional advice about finances and retirement have been found to be more satisfied with their current financial situation than families who do not receive such advice (Kim et al., 2003). About two-thirds of Americans are confident that their efforts to save for retirement and their knowledge about how much they should be saving to maintain their preretirement lifestyle are adequate, yet only 42% have actually estimated the exact amount of money they will need (Employee Benefit Research Institute, 2019). Due to concerns about a lack of preparedness and lack of saving for retirement, many resources exist from government entities and organizations.

Phase III. Living in Retirement and Planning for Intergenerational Transfers

In the third phase of the family economic life cycle, consumption expenditures are expected to outpace earnings as families tap savings and investment income for expenditures in retirement. At this end of the life cycle, some families face the problem of living on reduced incomes whereas others need to distribute excess assets among family members or favorite charities. These wealth transfers, and planning for them, can easily become an additional source of family stress and conflict through competition for assets. Many Americans report that they need to work as long as possible because they could not afford to retire, with 65% reporting they "probably" or "definitely" would work past 65, and more than half of Americans predicting they will probably or definitely retire after 65 years of age (Scott, 2018).

The quality of the retirement experience relies on financial security. The average life expectancy for those reaching age 65 is 83 for males and 85.6 for females (Administration for Community Living, 2018). Thus, most Americans can expect to spend about 20 years of their life in retirement. The uncertainty of Social Security, fewer employer-sponsored pension plans, and economic conditions like the Great Recession are among the reasons for delayed expected retirement (Scott, 2018). When Americans say they will retire, a key factor is the value of their investments, followed by their health, the cost of health care, and inflation (Newport, 2018).

In the simplest form of the family life-cycle savings model, families are assumed to hold no bequest motives, with every dollar spent during the lifetimes of the immediate family members. Clearly, an important extension of this life-cycle framework is consideration of the impact and process of passing wealth between generations (Modigliani, 1988). Stress resulting from the estate planning or intergenerational transfer portion of a family financial plan likely comes directly from (a) perceived legal complexities associated with asset transfers before and after death and (b) changing roles of family members in the financial management process. The goal of estate planning is to maximize compliance with the decedent's wants while minimizing the erosion of wealth through taxes and transaction costs.

Conclusion

Economic stress exacts social and psychological costs on the quality of family life, and family scientists are just beginning to uncover the toll the Great Recession had on family functioning. Families vary significantly in their vulnerability to changing economic events. Differing levels of resources and adoption of coping strategies explain family resilience under economic stress. In this chapter, we have offered the process of family financial planning over distinct life-cycle stages as a general preventive strategy, to help families reduce the social and psychological costs associated with economic stress. A robust literature supports the family stress model, however, further research investigating the strategies and coping mechanisms that help ameliorate the impact of economic stress on individuals and family relationships would benefit policy makers and practitioners.

Note: We want to express our gratitude to Naomi Meinertz for her research and editorial assistance.

DISCUSSION QUESTIONS ●——————————————

1. How does the economy affect families?

2. From the family stress model perspective, how does economic stress influence the family?

3. How has economic stress affected your family?

4. Describe some strategies that families can implement during tough economic times.

REFERENCES ——————————————

Administration for Community Living. (2018). *2017 profile of older Americans*. Washington, DC: U.S. Department of Health and Human Services.

Afifi, T. D., Davis, S., Merrill, A. F., Coveleski, S., Denes, A., & Shahnazi, A. F. (2018). Couples' communication about financial uncertainty following the Great Recession and its association with stress, mental health and divorce proneness. *Journal of Family and Economic Issues, 39*(2), 205–219. doi:10.1007/s10834-017-9560-5

Aldana, S. G., & Liljenquist, W. (1998). Validity and reliability of a financial strain survey. *Financial Counseling and Planning, 9*(2), 11–18. Retrieved from http://citeseerx.ist.psu.edu/viewdoc/download?doi=10.1.1.539.5100&rep=rep1&type=pdf

Ando, A., & Modigliani, F. (1963). The "Life Cycle" hypothesis of saving: Aggregate implications and tests. *American Economic Review, 53*(1), 55–84. Retrieved from https://www.jstor.org/stable/1817129

Aspen Institute. (2019). *Short-term financial stability: A foundation for security and well-being*. Washington, DC: Financial Security Program. Retrieved from https://www.aspeninstitute.org/publications/short-term-financial-stability-a-foundation-for-security-and-well-being/

Bartholomae, S., & Fox, J. (2017). Coping with economic stress: A test of deterioration and stress-suppressing models. *Journal of Financial Therapy, 8*(1), 6. doi:10.4148/1944-9771.1134

Bell, M. M., Nelson, J. S., Spann, S. M., Molloy, C. J., Britt, S. L., & Goff, B. N. (2014). The impact of financial resources on soldiers' well-being. *Journal of Financial Counseling and Planning, 25*(1), 41–52.

Berger, L. M., & Houle, J. N. (2016). Parental debt and children's socioemotional well-being. *Pediatrics, 137*(2), e20153059. doi:10.1542/peds.2015-3059

Berger, L. M., Collins, J. M., & Cuesta, L. (2016). Household debt and adult depressive symptoms in the United States. *Journal of Family and Economic Issues, 37*(1), 42–57. doi:10.1007/s10834-015-9443-6

Bernstein, J. (2014). *Testimony of Jared Bernstein, senior fellow, Center on Budget and Policy Priorities, before the Joint Economic Committee*. Retrieved from http://www.cbpp.org/cms/?fa=view&id=4164

Blair, S. L. (2012). Economic stress and the family. *Contemporary perspectives in family research* (Vol. 6). Bingley, England: Emerald Group.

Blom, N., Kraaykamp, G., & Verbakel, E. (2019). Current and expected economic hardship and satisfaction with family life in Europe. *Journal of Family Issues, 40*(1), 3–32. doi:10.1177/0192513X18802328

Blustein, D. L. (2019). *The importance of work in an age of uncertainty: The eroding work experience in America*. New York, NY: Oxford University Press.

Board of Governors of the Federal Reserve System. (2019). *Household economic well-being. Report on the economic well-being of U.S. households in 2018.* Retrieved from https://www.federalreserve.gov/publications/files/2018-report-economic-well-being-us-households-201905.pdf

Brandon, E. (2014). *More parents use retirement accounts to pay for college.* Retrieved from http://money.usnews.com/money/retirement/articles/2014/09/02/more-parents-use-retirement-accounts-to-pay-for-college

Bricker, J., Dettling, L. J., Henriques, A., Hsu, J. W., Jacobs, L., Moore, K. B., . . . & Windle, R. A. (2017). Changes in U.S. family finances from 2013 to 2016: Evidence from the Survey of Consumer Finances. *Federal Reserve Bulletin, 103*(3), 1–41.

Bricker, J., Dettling, L. J., Henriques, A., Hsu, J. W., Moore, K. B., Sabelhaus, J., . . . & Windle, R. A. (2014). Changes in U.S. family finances from 2010 to 2013: Evidence from the survey of consumer finances. *Federal Reserve Bulletin, 100*(4), 1–41. Retrieved from https://www.federalreserve.gov/pubs/bulletin/2014/pdf/scf14.pdf

Chalise, L., & Anong, S. (2017). Spending behavior change and financial distress during the Great Recession. *Journal of Financial Counseling and Planning, 28*(1), 49–61. doi:10.1891/1052-3073.28.1.49

Chen, D. J. Q., & Lim, V. K. G. (2012). Strength in adversity: The influence of psychological capital on job search. *Journal of Organizational Behavior, 33*(6), 811–839. doi:10.1002/job.1814

College Savings Foundation. (2010). *State of College Saving Survey.* Retrieved from https://www.collegesavingsfoundation.org/wp-content/uploads/2016/06/CSF-2010-State-of-College-Savings-Survey-Results.pdf

College Savings Foundation. (2019). *2018 Parent Survey.* Retrieved from https://www.collegesavingsfoundation.org/industry-research/2018-parents-survey/

Conger, R. D., & Conger, K. J. (2002). Resilience in Midwestern families: Selected findings from the first decade of a prospective, longitudinal study. *Journal of Marriage and Family, 64*(2), 361–373. https://www.jstor.org/stable/3600110

Conger, R. D., Conger, K. J., & Martin, M. J. (2010). Socioeconomic status, family processes, and individual development. *Journal of Marriage and Family, 72*(3), 685–704. doi:10.1111/j.1741-3737.2010.00725

Conger, R. D., & Elder, G. H., Jr., (1994). *Families in troubled times: Adapting to change in rural America.* New York, NY: Aldine.

Conger, R. D., Elder, G. H., Jr., Lorenz, F. O., Conger, K. J., Simons, R. L., Whitbeck, L. B., . . . & Melby, J. N. (1990). Linking economic hardship to marital quality and instability. *Journal of Marriage and the Family, 52*(3), 643–656. doi:10.2307/352931

Conger, R. D., Rueter, M., & Elder, G. Jr. (1999). Couple resilience to economic pressure. *Journal of Personality and Social Psychology, 76*(1), 54–71. doi:10.1037/0022-3514.76.1.54

Consumer Financial Protection Bureau. (2017). *Financial well-being in America.* Washington, DC: Author. Retrieved from https://files.consumerfinance.gov/f/documents/201709_cfpb_financial-well-being-in-America.pdf

Creed, P. A., & Klisch, J. (2005). Future outlook and financial strain: Testing the personal agency and latent deprivation models of unemployment and well-being. *Journal of Occupational Healthy Psychology, 10*(3), 251–260. doi:10.1037/1076-8998.10.3.251

De Cuyper, N., Mäkikangas, A., Kinnunen, U., Mauno, S., & De Witte, H. (2012). Cross-lagged associations between perceived external employability, job insecurity, and exhaustion: Testing gain and loss spirals according to the conservation of resources theory. *Journal of Organizational Behavior, 33*(6), 770–788. doi:10.1002/job.1800

DeNavas-Walt, C., & Proctor, B. D. (2014). *Income and poverty in the United States, 2013: Current population reports* (P60-249). Washington, DC.: U.S. Government Printing Office.

Dew, J. (2007). Two sides of the same coin? The differing roles of assets and consumer debt in marriage. *Journal of Family and Economic Issues, 28*(1), 89–104. doi:10.1007/s10834-006-9051-6

Dew, J. (2008). Debt change and marital satisfaction change in recently married couples. *Family Relations, 57*(1), 60–71. Retrieved from https://www.jstor.org/stable/40005368

Dew, J. (2009). Thrifty couples are the happiest. In W. B. Wilcox (Ed.), *The state of our unions* (pp. 23–30). Charlottesville, VA: The National Marriage Project.

Dew, J. (2011). The association between consumer debt and the likelihood of divorce. *Journal of Family and Economic Issues, 32*(4), 554–565. doi:10.1007/s10834-011-9274-z

De Witte, H., Pienaar, J., & De Cuyper, N. (2016). Review of 30 years of longitudinal studies on the association between job insecurity and health and well-being: Is there causal evidence? *Australian Psychologist, 51*(1), 18–31. doi:10.1111/ap.12176

Dolan, E. M. (2016). Uneven recoveries from the Great Recession. *Journal of Economic and Family Issues, 37*(3), 331–332. doi:10.1007/s10834-016-9504-5

Dunn, L. F., & Mirzaie, I. A. (2016). Consumer debt stress, changes in household debt, and the Great Recession. *Economic Inquiry, 54*(1), 201–214. doi:10.1111/ecin.12218

Employee Benefit Research Institute. (2019). *2019 retirement confidence survey: Summary report.* Retrieved from https://www.ebri.org/docs/default-source/rcs/2019-rcs/2019-rcs-short-report.pdf

Elder, G. H., Jr. (1974). *Children of the Great Depression: Social change in life experience.* Chicago, IL: University of Chicago Press.

Elder, G. H., Jr., & Caspi, A. (1988). Economic stress in lives: Developmental perspectives. *Journal of Social Issues, 44*(2), 25–45. doi:10.1111/j.1540-4560.1988.tb02090.x

Elder, G. H., Jr., Conger, R. D., Foster, E. M., & Ardelt, M. (1992). Families under economic pressure. *Journal of Family Issues, 13*(1), 5–37. doi:10.1177/019251392013001002

Fidelity Investments. (2018). *2018 College savings indicator.* Retrieved from https://www.fidelity.com/bin-public/060_www_fidelity_com/documents/PR/CSI-2018-Executive-Summary.pdf

Fonseca, G., Cunha, D., Crespo, C., & Relvas, A. P. (2016). Families in the context of macroeconomic crises: A systematic review. *Journal of Family Psychology, 30*(6), 687–697. doi:10.1037/fam0000230

Fontenot, K., Semega, J., & Kollar, M. (2018). *Income and Poverty in the United States: 2017* (Current Population Reports, P60-263). Washington, DC: U.S. Census Bureau.

Fox, J. J. (1995). Household demand system analysis: Implications of unit root econometrics for modeling, testing and policy analysis. *Consumer Interests Annual, 41,* 195–201.

Frasquilho, D., de Matos, M. G., Marques, A., Neville, F. G., Gaspar, T., & Caldas-de-Almeida, J. M. (2016). Unemployment, parental distress and youth emotional well-being: The moderation roles of parent–youth relationship and financial deprivation. *Child Psychiatry & Human Development, 47*(5), 751–758. doi:10.1007/s10578-015-0610-7

Frasquilho, D., Matos, M. G., Salonna, F., Guerreiro, D., Storti, C. C., Gaspar, T., & Caldas-de-Almeida, J. M. (2015). Mental health outcomes in times of economic recession: A systematic literature review. *BMC Public Health, 16*(1), 115. doi:10.1186/s12889-016-2720-y

French, D., & Vigne, S. (2019). The causes and consequences of household financial strain:

A systematic review. *International Review of Financial Analysis, 62,* 150–156. doi:10.1016/j.irfa.2018.09.008

Garman, E. T., & Forgue, R. E. (2018). *Personal finance* (13th ed.). Boston, MA: Houghton Mifflin.

Garon, T., Dunn, A., Golvala, K., & Wilson, E. (2018). *U.S. Financial Health Pulse: 2018 Baseline Survey Results.* Washington, DC: Center for Financial Services Innovation. Retrieved from https://s3.amazonaws.com/cfsi-innovation-files-2018/wp-content/uploads/2018/11/20213012/Pulse-2018-Baseline-Survey-Results-11-16.18.pdf

Glei, D. A., Goldman, N., & Weinstein, M. (2019). A growing socioeconomic divide: Effects of the Great Recession on perceived economic distress in the United States. *PloS One, 14*(4), e0214947. doi:10.1371/journal.pone.0214947

Gilbert, L. R., Spears Brown, C., & Mistry, R. S. (2017). Latino immigrant parents' financial stress, depression, and academic involvement predicting child academic success. *Psychology in the Schools, 54*(9), 1202–1215. doi:10.1002/pits.22067

Godwin, D. D. (1994). Antecedents and consequences of newlyweds' cash flow management. *Financial Counseling and Planning, 5*(4), 161–190.

Gutman, L. M., McLoyd, V. C., & Tokoyawa, T. (2005). Financial strain, neighborhood stress, parenting behaviors, and adolescent adjustment in urban African American families. *Journal of Research on Adolescence, 15*(4), 425–449. doi:10.1111/j.1532-7795.2005.00106.x

Himmelstein, D. U., Lawless, R. M., Thorne, D., Foohey, P., & Woolhandler, S. (2019). Medical bankruptcy: Still common despite the Affordable Care Act. *American Journal of Public Health, 109*(3), 431–433. doi:10.2105/AJPH.2018.304901

Hunter, J. I.., & Heath, C. J. (2017). The relationship between credit card use behavior and household well-being during the Great Recession: Implications for the ethics of credit use. *Journal of*

Financial Counseling and Planning, 28(2), 213–224. doi:10.1891/1052-3073.28.2.213

Karpman, M., Zuckerman, S., & Gonzalez, D. (2018). *Material hardship among nonelderly adults and their families in 2017: Implications for the safety net.* Washington, DC: Urban Institute. Retrieved from https://www.urban.org/sites/default/files/publication/98918/material_hardship_among_nonelderly_adults_and_their_families_in_2017.pdf

Katz, L., & Krueger, A. (2016). *The rise and nature of alternative work arrangements in the United States, 1995–2015.* (NBER No. 22667). Cambridge, MA. National Bureau of Economic Research. Retrieved from https://www.nber.org/papers/w22667

Kavanaugh, S. A., Neppl, T. K., & Melby, J. N. (2018). Economic pressure and depressive symptoms: Testing the family stress model from adolescence to adulthood. *Journal of Family Psychology, 32*(7), 957–965. doi:10.1037/fam0000462

Kelley, H. H., LeBaron, A. B., & Hill, E. J. (2018). Financial stress and marital quality: The moderating influence of couple communication. *Journal of Financial Therapy, 9*(2), 3. doi:10.4148/1944-9771.1176

Kim, D. H., Bassett, S. M., So, S., & Voisin, D. R. (2019). Family stress and youth mental health problems: Self-efficacy and future orientation mediation. *American Journal of Orthopsychiatry, 89*(2), 125–133. doi:10.1037/ort0000371

Kim, J., Garman, E. T., & Sorhaindo, S. (2003). Relationships among credit counseling clients' financial well-being, financial behaviors, financial stressor events, and health. *Financial Counseling and Planning, 14*(2), 75–87.

Killewald, A., Pfeffer, F. T., & Schachner, J. N. (2017). Wealth inequality and accumulation. *Annual Review of Sociology, 43,* 379–404. doi:10.1146/annurev-soc-060116-053331

Kirsch, J. A., Love, G. D., Radler, B. T., & Ryff, C. D. (2019). Scientific imperatives vis-à-vis growing inequality in America. *American Psychologist,* 74(7), 764–777. doi:10.1037/amp0000481

Klebanov, P. K., Brooks-Gunn, J., & Duncan, G. J. (1994). Does neighborhood and family poverty affect mothers' parenting, mental health, and social support? *Journal of Marriage and the Family, 56*(2), 441–455. doi:10.2307/353111

Krause, E., & Sawhill, I. V. (2018). Seven reasons to worry about the American middle class. Washington, DC: Brookings Institute. Retrieved from https://www.brookings.edu/blog/social-mobility-memos/2018/06/05/seven-reasons-to-worry-about-the-american-middle-class/

Lamont, M. (2019). From "having" to "being": Self-worth and the current crisis of American society. *The British Journal of Sociology, 70*(3), 660–707. doi:10.1111/1468-4446.12667

Laxman, D. J., Higginbotham, B. J., MacArthur, S. S., & Plummer Lee, C. (2019). A test of the family stress model using a remarriage sample. *Journal of Divorce & Remarriage*, 1–19. doi:10.1080/10502556.2019.1586230

Lempers, J. D., & Clark-Lempers, D. S. (1997). Economic hardship, family relationships, and adolescent distress: An evaluation of a stress-distress mediation model in mother-daughter and mother-son dyads. *Adolescence, 32*(126), 339–356.

Lindblad, M. R., & Quercia, R. G. (2014). Why is homeownership associated with nonfinancial benefits? A path analysis of competing mechanisms. *Housing Policy Debate, 25*(2), 263–288. doi:10.1080/10511482.2014.956776

Masarik, A. S., & Conger, R. D. (2017). Stress and child development: A review of the family stress model. *Current Opinion in Psychology, 13*, 85–90. doi:10.1016/j.copsyc.2016.05.008

Mckee-Ryan, F. M., Song, Z., Wanberg, C. R., & Kinicki, A. J. (2005). Psychological and physical well-being during unemployment: A meta-analytic study. *Journal of Applied Psychology, 90*(1) 53–76. doi:10.1037/0021-9010.90.1.53

McKernan, S. M., Ratcliffe, C., Steuerle, E., & Zhang, S. (2013). *Less than equal: Racial disparities in wealth accumulation.* Urban Institute. Retrieved from http://www.urban.org/uploadedpdf/412802-less-than-equal-racial-disparities-in-wealth-accumulation.pdf

Mishel, L., Bivens. J., Gould. E., & Shierholz. H. (2012). *The state of working America* (12th ed.). Ithaca, NY: Cornell University Press.

Mistry, R. S., Benner, A. D., Tan, C. S., & Kim, S. Y. (2009). Family economic stress and academic well-being among Chinese-American youth: The influence of adolescents' perceptions of economic strain. *Journal of Family Psychology, 23*(3), 279–290. doi:10.1037/a0015403

Mistry, R. S., Lowe, E. D., Benner, A. D., & Chien, N. (2008). Expanding the family economic stress model: Insights from a mixed-methods approach. *Journal of Marriage & Family, 70*(1), 196–209. Retrieved from https://www.jstor.org/stable/40056262

Modigliani, F. (1988). The role of intergenerational transfers and life cycle saving in the accumulation of wealth. *Journal of Economic Perspectives, 2*(2), 15–40. Retrieved from https://www.jstor.org/stable/1942847

Moustgaard, H., Avendano, M., & Martikainen, P. (2018). Parental unemployment and offspring psychotropic medication purchases: A longitudinal fixed-effects analysis of 138,644 adolescents. *American Journal of Epidemiology, 187*(9), 1880–1888. doi:10.1093/aje/kwy084

Nelson, S., Delgadillo, L., & Dew, J. (2013). Housing and marital satisfaction. *Marriage & Family Review, 49*(6), 546–561. doi:10.1080/01494929.2013.789460

Neppl, T. K., Senia, J. M., & Donnellan, M. B. (2016). Effects of economic hardship: Testing the family stress model over time. *Journal of Family Psychology, 30*(1), 12–21. doi:10.1037/fam0000168

Newland, R. P., Crnic, K. A., Cox, M. J., & Mills-Koonce, R. W. (2013). The family model stress and maternal psychological symptoms: Mediated pathways from economic hardship to parenting. *Journal of Family Psychology, 27*(1), 96–105. doi:10.1037/a0031112

Newport, F. (2018). *Update: Americans' concerns about retirement persist*. Retrieved from https://news.gallup.com/poll/233861/update-americans-concerns-retirement-persist.aspx

O'Neill, B., Sorhaindo, B., Xiao, J. J., & Garman, E. T. (2005). Financially distressed consumers: Their financial practices, financial well-being, and health. *Journal of Financial Counseling and Planning, 16*(1), 73–87.

Pederson, R. C., Madsen, M., & Kohler, L. (2005). Does financial strain explain the association between children's morbidity and parental non-employment? *Journal of Epidemiology and Community Health, 59*(4), 316–321. doi:10.1136/jech.2003.013839

Pew Research Center. (2015). The American middle class is losing ground: No longer the majority and falling behind financially. Washington, D.C. Retrieved from https://www.pewsocialtrends.org/2015/12/09/the-american-middle-class-is-losing-ground/

Ponnet, K. (2014). Financial stress, parent functioning and adolescent problem behavior: An actor–partner interdependence approach to family stress processes in low-, middle-, and high-income families. *Journal of Youth and Adolescence, 43*(10), 1752–1769. doi:10.1007/s10964-014-0159-y

Prawitz, A. D., Kalkowski, J. C., & Cohart, J. (2014). Responses to economic pressure by low-income families: Financial distress and hopefulness. *Journal of Family and Economic Issues, 34*(1), 29–40. doi:10.1007/s10834-012-9288-1

Richardson, T., Elliott, P., & Roberts, R. (2013). The relationship between personal unsecured debt and mental and physical health: A systematic review and meta-analysis. *Clinical Psychology Review, 33*(8), 1148–1162.

Roll, S., & Moulton, S. (2016). The NFCC's Sharpen Your Financial Focus Initiative Impact Evaluation: Final report. Retrieved from https://sharpen.nfcc.org/wp-content/uploads/2016/07/SharpenYourFinancialFocusEvaluation-Report.pdf

Rothstein, J. (2017). The Great Recession and its aftermath: What role for structural changes? *RSF: The Russell SAGE Foundation Journal of the Social Sciences, 3*(3), 22–49. doi:10.7758/rsf.2017.3.3.02

Rothwell, D. W., & Han, C. K. (2010). Exploring the relationship between assets and family stress among low-income families. *Family Relations, 59*(4), 396–407. doi:10.1111/j. 1741-3729.2010

Schuetz, J. (2019). *Cost, crowding, or commuting? Housing stress on the middle class*. Washington DC. Brookings Institute. Retrieved from https://www.brookings.edu/research/cost-crowding-or-commuting-housing-stress-on-the-middle-class/

Scott, J. (2018). *When do American plan to retire? How workers envision their futures*. Washington, DC: Pew Charitable Trusts. Retrieved from https://www.pewtrusts.org/en/research-and-analysis/issue-briefs/2018/11/when-do-americans-plan-to-retire

Shek, D. T. L. (2003). Economic stress, psychological well-being and problem behavior in Chinese adolescents with economic disadvantage. *Journal of Youth and Adolescence, 32*(4), 259–266. doi:10.1023/A:1023080826557

Shelleby, E. C. (2018). Economic stress in fragile families: Pathways to parent and child maladjustment. *Journal of Child and Family Studies, 27*(12), 3877–3886. Retrieved from https://link.springer.com/article/10.1007/s10826-018-1232-z

Shefrin, H. M., & Thaler, R. H. (1988). The behavioral life-cycle hypothesis. *Economic Inquiry,*

26(4), 609–643. doi:10.1111/j.1465-7295.1988.tb01520.x

Smith, A. (2016). *Gig work, online selling and home sharing*. Washington, DC: Pew Research Center. Retrieved from https://www.pewinternet.org/2016/11/17/gig-work-online-selling-and-home-sharing/

Solantaus, T., Leinonen, J., & Punamaki, R. L. (2004). Children's mental health in times of economic recession: Replication and extension of the family economic stress model in Finland. *Developmental Psychology, 40*(3), 412–429. doi:10.1037/0012-1649.40.3.412

Stewart, R. C., Dew, J. P., & Lee, Y. G. (2017). The association between employment and housing-related financial stressors and marital outcomes during the 2007–2009 recession. *Journal of Financial Therapy, 8*(1), 4. doi:10.4148/1944-9771.1125

Turunen, E., & Hiilamo, H. (2014). Health effects of indebtedness: A systematic review. *BMC Public Health, 14*(1), 489. doi:10.1186/1471-2458-14-489

U.S. Bankruptcy Courts. (2019). *Table F-2. U.S. Bankruptcy Courts—business and nonbusiness cases commenced, by chapter of the bankruptcy code, during the 12-month period ending March 31, 2019*. Retrieved from https://www.uscourts.gov/sites/default/files/bf_f2_0331.2019.pdf

U.S. Bureau of Economic Analysis. (2019). *Personal saving rate [PSAVERT]*. Federal Reserve Bank of St. Louis. Retrieved from https://fred.stlouisfed.org/series/PSAVERT

U.S. Bureau of Labor Statistics. (2019). *Civilian unemployment rate [UNRATE]*. Federal Reserve Bank of St. Louis. Retrieved from https://fred.stlouisfed.org/series/UNRATE

U.S. Census Bureau. (2019). *Current population survey/Housing vacancy survey, April 4, 2019*. Retrieved from https://www.census.gov/housing/hvs/data/q219ind.html

U.S. Census Bureau. (2012). *Table F-22, Married-couple families with wives' earnings greater than husbands' earnings: 1988 to 2012. Income-Families*. Retrieved from https://www.census.gov/data/tables/time-series/demo/income-poverty/historical-income-families.html

United States Courts. (2018). *Just the facts: Consumer bankruptcy filings, 2006–2017*. Retrieved from https://www.uscourts.gov/news/2018/03/07/just-facts-consumer-bankruptcy-filings-2006-2017

Urbanaviciute, I., De Witte, H., & Rossier, J. (2019). Perceived job insecurity and self-rated health: Testing reciprocal relationships in a five-wave study. *Social Science & Medicine, 233*(2), 201–207. doi:10.1016/j.socscimed.2019.05.039

Valentino, S. W., Moore, J. E., Cleveland, M. J., Greenberg, M. T., & Tan, X. (2014). Profiles of financial stress over time using subgroup analysis. *Journal of Family and Economic Issues, 35*(1), 51–64.

VanDerhei, J. (2019). *Retirement savings shortfalls: Evidence from EBRI's 2019 retirement security projection model*. Washington, DC: Employee Benefit Research Institute. Retrieved from https://www.ebri.org/content/retirement-savings-shortfalls-evidence-from-ebri-s-2019-retirement-security-projection-model

Voydanoff, P. (1983). Unemployment: Family strategies for adaptation. In C. R. Figley & H. I. McCubbin (Eds.), *Stress in the family: Vol. 2. Coping with catastrophe* (pp. 90–102). New York, NY: Brunner/Mazel.

Voydanoff, P. (1990). Economic distress and family relations: A review of the eighties. *Journal of Marriage and the Family, 52*(4), 1099–1115. doi:10.2307/353321

Voydanoff, P., & Donnelly, B. W. (1988). Economic distress, family coping, and quality of family life. In P. Voydanoff & L. C. Majka (Eds.), *Families and economic distress: Coping strategies and social policies* (pp. 97–116). Newbury Park, CA: SAGE.

Wadsworth, M. E., & Santiago, C. D. (2008). Risk and resiliency processes in ethnically diverse families in poverty. *Journal of Family Psychology, 22*(3), 399–410. doi:10.1037/0893-3200.22.3.399

Weller, C. E. (2014). *Economic snapshot: September 2014*. Retrieved from http://cdn.americanprogress .org/wp-content/uploads/2014/09/Sept14-econ snapshot.pdf

Wheeler, B. E., Kerpelman, J. L., & Yorgason, J. B. (2019). Economic hardship, financial distress, and marital quality: The role of relational aggression. *Journal of Family and Economic Issues, 40*(4), 658–672. doi:10.1007/s10834-019-09632-4

White, R. M. B., Liu, Y., Nair, R. L., & Tein, J.-Y. (2015). Longitudinal and integrative tests of family stress model effects on Mexican origin adolescents. *Developmental Psychology, 51*(5), 649–662. doi:10.1037/a0038993

Wiedrich, K., & Newville, D. (2019). *Vulnerability in the face of economic uncertainty: Key findings from the 2019 Prosperity Now Scorecard*. Washington, DC: Prosperity Now. Retrieved from https:// prosperitynow.org/sites/default/files/resources /2019_Scorecard_Key_Findings.pdf

Wolff, E. N. (2017). *Household wealth trends in the United States, 1962 to 2016: Has middle class wealth recovered?* (NBER Working Paper No. 24085). National Bureau of Economic Research. doi:10.3386/w24085

Wong, S., & Goodwin, R. (2009). Experiencing marital satisfaction across three cultures: A qualitative study. *Journal of Social and Personal Relationships, 26*(8), 1011–1028. doi:10.1177 /0265407509347938

Zurlo, K. A., Yoon, W., & Kim, H. (2014). Unsecured consumer debt and mental health outcomes in middle-aged and older Americans. *Journals of Gerontology, Series B: Psychological Sciences and Social Sciences, 69*(3), 461–469.

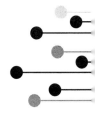

CHAPTER 12

Race, Ethnicity, and Family Stress

Anthony G. James, Veronica R. Barrios, Roudi Roy, and Soyoung Lee

Introduction

Little to no debate exists regarding whether families experience stress and stressors. This assumption applies to all families, regardless of context. Such assumptions can, unfortunately, manifest beliefs of families experiencing stress and stressors, and responses to them, in a uniform fashion. Certainly there exists some overlap in stress and stressors that families face; there can also be drastically different stress-related experience or responses across different racial and cultural groups. This chapter hopefully brings to rest such fallacious thinking by addressing two questions. First, what are the common stress and stressors facing ethnic minority groups in the United States (i.e., African American, Asian American, Latinx American)? Secondly, how do these groups respond to such stress and stressors?

We address these questions by first providing a brief review (see Price, Bush, Price, & McKenry, Chapter 1 in this volume) of mainstream theoretical models (ABC-X, Double ABC-X, vulnerability-stress-adaptation model) used to describe and explain family stress, as well as other key constructs related to stress (chronic vs. acute). We also apply a newer model that provides scholars with the ability to describe and explain context-specific stress (sociocultural family stress model). Finally, we apply these models to the three largest ethnic minority groups in America, to better equip scholars with mechanisms for describing and explaining family stress across specific groups in the United States.

Of note, because we are discussing ethnic and racial groups in this chapter, it is important to clearly conceptualize what we mean by these terms to not insinuate shared meaning. By *race*, we are referring to categories assigned to individuals based on shared phenotypic characteristics (e.g., skin color). By *ethnicity*, we refer to groups of people that share common origin and culture. These definitions allow for complexity such as people of the same racial group (e.g., Black Americans) having different ethnicities (e.g., African Americans born in Jamaica vs. in the United States). Importantly, these ethnic and racial differences greatly influence stress experienced by a given group, and how they respond to such experiences.

Overview of Family Stress Theories and Frameworks

Source of stress can derive from the many interactions between persons and families and the environments in which they are embedded. One key individual feature is a person's race or ethnicity and how those features or characteristics match up with environmental demands. Moreover, several models and frameworks in family science literature can be used to examine the stressors families face and how they respond to them, particularly how these factors relate to their race or their ethnicity. We briefly review each, with a particular focus on how they can promote understanding family stress in relation to race or ethnicity.

ABC-X Model

Two of the more prominent theories of family stress are the ABC-X and Double ABC-X theories (Hill, 1958; McCubbin & Patterson, 1983), both of which explain processes of how families respond to stress they experience (See Chapter 1). Briefly, A represents the stress event, B represents family resources to respond to the event, C represents the family's perception of the event, and X represents the crisis the family experiences as a result of the original stress event. The major limitation of this theory is the assumption that families only experience one crisis at a time. McCubbin and Patterson's adaptation to the Double ABC-X theory addressed this by accounting for the multiple stressors families experience over time (i.e., stress pile up).

To be sure this theory has been applied to a wide variety of stressors that families can experience (e.g., a parent losing a job; McKee-Ryan & Maitoza, 2018), but less so to better understand how race or ethnicity can be a source of family stress in a given environment. For this reason, McNeil Smith and Landor (2018) offer the sociocultural family stress (SFS) model to more fully capture the contextualized stressful experiences facing racially and ethnically diverse families.

SFS Model

The SFS model is an extension of the ABC-X model in that it includes the contextual model of family stress (CMFS; Boss, 2002; Boss, Bryant, & Mancini, 2016) and the mundane everyday environmental stress (MEES; Carroll, 1998) frameworks within it. The SFS model provides scholars a mechanism for examining context-specific stressful events that impact families. For the purposes of this chapter, we use ethnicity and race as sources for said context-specific stressful events, or how families may respond as a result of their unique characteristics. Specific examples of family stress among families of color can include how a particular group is positioned within a given society (e.g., how resources are distributed in a given society and the ease to which one group has access to said resource relative to other groups; Pearlin, 1989), how families are structured (e.g., going from largely two-parent to single-parent structures; James, Coard, Fine, & Rudy, 2018), or even the intersecting of multiple identities that combined produce unique stressors (e.g., being a single-parent Asian American woman; McNeil Smith & Landor, 2018).

This chapter applies the ABC-X model, and its adaptations, to explore unique experiences of stress among the three largest U.S. ethnic minority groups. It is first important to discuss why this is even necessary. Most would agree that there is a seemingly innumerable number of factors, or some combination of them, that cause family stress but sometimes family stress is context specific. This chapter examines the factors of ethnicity and race of a family. Moreover, different groups of families may experience similar stressful events but race or culture may result in families experiencing the same event in different ways. Below, we explore cases to help explain how race and ethnicity influence family stress processes, across different groups in the United States.

Stress in Asian American Families

Parenting is a culturally sensitive, multidimensional family process, yet the complexity and heterogeneity in Asian American parenting experiences have not been explored in depth. Additionally, despite ongoing, conscientious efforts of enculturation and acculturation, many Asian American parents still face unique challenges while parenting under the influence of the two major stereotypes toward their families: (1) the perpetual foreigner stereotype and (2) the model minority myth or stereotype (Hou, Kim, & Wang, 2016; Juang, Yoo & Atkin, 2017). For example, Asian American parenting is often represented as a product of hierarchical, authoritarian, and collectivistic cultural values with a high emphasis on academic success. A controversial discussion of "tiger mothering" reiterates the prevalence of an overgeneralized, stereotypical view toward Asian American parenting in the United States (Choi, 2017; Duncan & Wong, 2014; Shih, Chang, & Chen, 2019). However, recent studies have challenged the strict application of Baumrind's (1978) parenting style typologies to Asian American parenting. The meaning of authoritarian parenting in Asian American families is somewhat different from European American perspectives, focusing more on socializing children with family interdependence and recognition, obligation and humility, and emotional controls, grounded in collectivistic cultural aspects (Chao & Kaeochinda, 2010; Choi, 2017; Russell, Crocket, & Chao, 2010). Asian American youths do not always experience negative outcomes in Asian familial cultural contexts that mirror Eurocentric defined authoritarian parenting styles (Choi, 2017; Hou et al., 2016; Russell et al., 2010). Here, we apply the ABC-X theory to Asian American parenting in the context of the aforementioned stereotypes.

Case 1: Parenting Expectations and Practices Against the Perpetual Foreigner Stereotype

Many Asian Americans are often asked "Where are you from?" followed by "Where are you *really* from?" (Duncan & Wong, 2014). These seemingly innocent questions explicitly or implicitly deny Asian Americans their full citizenship and a sense of national belonging. Such questions also express a sentiment that Asian Americans are expected to return to their *real* home countries. These experiences can produce stress in families, despite the fact that many are native-born Americans (Duncan & Wong, 2014), hence becoming "forever foreigners" (Shih et al., 2019) across family generations in the United States.

The A in this case example would be the perpetual foreigner stereotype toward Asian American families. *Perpetual foreigner stereotype* is defined as being mistaken as a foreigner even though individuals were born in the United States or multigenerations of their families have resided in the United States. Many Asian Americans are often assumed to be from other countries and are often frowned upon for using their own ethnic languages rather than English (Hou et al., 2016; Juang et al., 2017). Any ethnic or racial groups can experience those racialized views, yet it is most commonly reported by Asian Americans (Hou et al. 2016; Leong, Park, & Kalibatseva, 2013), in particular among East Asian Americans (Duncan & Wong, 2014).

The B in this case would be strong commitments toward families that many Asian American families maintain and technology that helps Asian American families utilize their transnational resources.

Family Obligations and Parenting Expectations

Many Asian Americans share strong values toward interdependence among family members and strong parenting expectations, though variation across ethnic and cultural groups exist (Choi, 2017; Paik, Rahman, Kula, Saito, & Witenstein, 2017a, 2017b; Russell et al., 2010). For example, Confucian family ideology is prevalent in many Korean and Chinese families (Jang, Lee, Sung, & Lee, 2016; Paik et al., 2017a; Russell et al., 2010), which emphasizes an obligation between parents and children. Providing instrumental and strategic support for their children's social achievements and betterment is an important parenting expectation over extended periods, such as *nae ri sa rang* (i.e., parent generations often have stronger affection toward their children than the other way around) (Jang et al., 2016). Through filial piety, children are responsible for their parents' physical and emotional well-being by respecting, honoring, and caring for their parents in order to repay such parents' endless love, devotion, and sacrifice (Chao & Kaeochinda, 2010; Jang et al., 2016). These mutual parent–child investments build strong bonds among Korean and Chinese families, such as *qin* (Chao & Kaeochinda, 2010) in Chinese culture. Similarly, parents transfer core family values through cultural specific family socialization processes, such as *ga jung kyo yuk* (i.e., informal education and socialization process at home in Korean families; Choi, Park, Lee, Kim, & Tan, 2017), or *chiao shu* and *guan* (i.e., parental training and love in a highly involved, supportive, and caring manner in Chinese families; Russell et al., 2010). However, these family processes are often simply categorized as an authoritarian parenting style, and its cultural specific meanings are not correctly understood within Eurocentric parenting perspectives (Chao & Kaeochinda, 2010; Choi et al., 2017).

Filipino families have multicultural backgrounds based on Catholicism and multiple colonization throughout their histories, different from Korean and Chinese families. Yet, Filipino families also emphasize mutual obligations among family members (*utan ng loob*), harmonious interpersonal relations (*pakikisama*), and *hiya* (sense of propriety or saving face) (Russell et al., 2010), similar to Chinese families (Chao & Kaeochinda, 2010), even more so than Korean families (Choi et al., 2017). Filipino families also emphasize parental sacrifices as part of normative parental roles and expectations (Chao & Kaeochinda, 2010; Choi et al., 2017). The strong parent–child commitment to mutually obligatory relationships in many Asian American families can promote academic success, and buffering the risks of their children's maladjustments, and protecting them from racial discrimination.

Technology and Transnationalism

With drastic changes in technology, social media can be critical in immigrant or transnational family life. Using various social media, many immigrant families are able to connect with nonimmigrant families residing in their ethnic homeland. As a result, Bacigalupe and Cámara (2012) argued for the importance of understanding how nonimmigrant family continually impact immigrant families' decision-making processes through technologies. Additionally, those who have limited English proficiency can get access to better resources, information, and networking systems for parenting, provided with their own ethnic languages through the Internet and other social media platforms (Lee, Bai, & You, 2016). For example, breastfeeding is one of the first parenting decisions that many families experience. During this family process, Korean American mothers were able to retrieve helpful breastfeeding information and resources through Korean books, TV, and websites as well as web communications with other Korean mothers. Technology was helpful not only to those uncomfortable using English but also to those fluent in English while discussing culturally sensitive issues regarding breastfeeding (Lee et al., 2016), particularly regarding health-care-related terminology.

The C in this case example would be parents' understanding the explicit and implicit impacts of the perpetual foreigner stereotype on their parenting experiences. Many Asian American parents are first-generation immigrants who experience ongoing battles of negotiation between enculturation and acculturation (Choi, 2017; Russell et al., 2010). Approximately 66% of Asian Americans are foreign born, which is almost twice as high as Latinx group (34%) (Asian

Americans Advancing Justice, 2019). Those exhibiting low English proficiency are more likely to report bicultural management difficulty (Choi, 2017; Hou et al., 2016). Additionally, their children experience more racially charged bullying or discrimination relative to peers from other ethnic groups (Leong et al., 2013), even though many of them are American born or came to the United States at a young age (Choi, 2017).

Unfortunately, Filipino children have to navigate additional racial discrimination due to their darker skin colors from both within and outside Asian American groups, in addition to typical racial discrimination toward Asian Americans (Choi et al., 2017). Of note, this issue also reflects the SFS model in that skin-tone differences unique within a group produce sociocultural interactions that produce more or less stress within the group for certain features or characteristics (McNeil Smith & Landor, 2018). As part of parental coping strategies, Filipino American parents often practice stronger behavioral controls to protect their children from such negative experiences (Choi et al., 2017). Chinese families who experience racial discrimination employ various coping strategies, such as increasing family time and being an emotional and physical safety net for their children (Kiang & Witkow, 2017). Among lower SES families, strong family ties and support from their co-ethnic communities helps in preventing children's lower educational achievement (Hou et al., 2016; Paik et al. 2017b).

The X in this case example would be various types of parenting stress experienced by Asian American parents and children across family generations. The perpetual foreigner and the model minority myth are often manifested to microaggressions or overtly discriminatory actions toward Asian Americans, impacting the lives of Asian Americans families (Choi, 2017; Hou et al., 2016; Juang et al., 2017). Asian Americans who have experienced these stereotypes are more likely to report higher levels of parenting stress, identity malformation, acculturative stress, family conflicts, gender discrimination, mental health issues, and limited access to social support and resources (Choi, 2017; Duncan & Wong, 2014; Hou et al., 2016; Leong et al., 2013; Shih et al., 2019; Russell et al., 2010).

More specifically, Hou et al. (2016) found that Chinese American parents who have experienced perpetual foreigner stereotypes and bicultural maintenance difficulties are more likely to experience marital and parent–child conflicts, resulting in children's negative psychological, behavioral and academic adjustment. This implies that Asian American children's struggles do not merely result from Asian Americans' tiger-parenting styles or their inability to be acculturated to the host society. The fundamental trigger of Asian American youths' maladjustment can stem from persistent stereotypes toward Asian Americans, such as model minorities and perpetual foreigners, in the United States. Therefore, Asian American parents must understand how these stereotypes and discriminatory experiences impact them and their children. Second or further generations suffer more due to their conflicting identities as Americans and Asians. This also impels parents to engage in balanced racial and ethnic socialization of children that help them adapt to a racialized society (Hughes, Witherspoon, Rivas-Drake, & West-Bey,

2009). Though excessive racial socialization can build up to exaggerated mistrusts of the mainstream society, ignoring existence or impacts of these stereotypes is harmful and irresponsible for the well-being of children and families.

Case 2: Parental Involvement in Education Against the Model Minority Myth

The complexity and the diaspora of familial, ethnic, cultural, and social characteristics have produced different educational outcomes within and between Asian American groups (Keo, 2019; Shih et al., 2019). For example, most East and South Asian Americans have higher levels of accomplishments at both K–12 and postsecondary level education. Although Vietnamese and Filipinos experience diverse educational achievements, South East Asian Americans generally display lower achievement relative to East and South Asian American groups (Paik et al., 2017a, 2017b). Some Asian American parents are scolded for their lack of parental involvement as the main cause of their children's lower educational outcomes. However, these parents may not be equipped with appropriate resources. Reflecting the SFS model, culturally, some Asian American parents believe that strict removal of themselves from the educational authorities (e.g., teachers, schools) shows their respect toward them (Chiang, Fisher, Collins, & Ting, 2015; Keo, 2019; Shih et al., 2019), resulting in low involvement at schools.

The A in this case would be the model minority myth toward Asian Americans in general, and families. The model minority myth (MMM) explicitly describes Asian Americans as high-achieving, hardworking, and rule-following model minorities, mainly based on high overall income and education and lower utilization of social welfare programs (Juang et al., 2017; Shih et al., 2019). However, Asian Americans as a group also have many within group differences, intersecting with their immigration histories, resettlement experiences, language proficiencies, occupations, religions, co-ethnic social capitals and networks, and other various factors surrounding individual Asian Americans and their families (Choi, 2017; Paik et al., 2017a; Shih et al., 2019). The MMM often overlooks these differences and various needs within Asian Americans, resulting in further underrepresenting of those most in need and marginalizing them from gaining access to appropriate public and governmental support (Lee et al., 2017; Paik et al., 2017a, 2017b; Shih et al., 2019), which create family stress. Further, the MMM can cause political and racial frictions between Asian Americans and other ethnic groups (Chow, 2017; Shih et al., 2019), preventing Asian Americans from advancing their political and social movements toward social justice (Chow, 2017; Juang et al., 2017).

The B in this case example would be ethnic networks and social capitals that various Asian American groups create, maintain, and distribute to their own ethnic group members. Using the cultural and structural co-ethnic model, Paik et al. (2017a, 2017b) explained how cultural (e.g., heritage values, beliefs, and behaviors) and structural (e.g., socioeconomic and educational status, immigration context and selectivity) factors of each ethnic group actively interact within co-ethnic social structures (e.g., ethnic programs, schools, faith-based institutions, community organizations) and create social capitals for their own ethnic group members. Strong co-ethnic groups further provide economic opportunities, information, or resources for their own members, whereas weak or dispersed ethnic groups are less dependent on each other and do not have power to generate such social capitals. For example, many East Asians, Asian Indians, Vietnamese, and Filipinos hold managerial, professional, and entrepreneurial types of occupations, resulting in being categorized as middle- and upper class families. In particular, co-ethnic social networks among Chinese, Koreans, and Vietnamese are more structured and well-resourced due to their longer immigration histories and strong ties through business associations, religious organizations, and co-ethnic neighborhoods. These strong co-ethnic ties and resources are helpful to further mobilize social capitals within their co-ethnic groups and boost their co-ethnic group members' education and business. Conversely, larger portions of Bangladeshis, Pakistanis, and many South East Asians derive from working-class or lower income families. The co-ethnic social networks and capitals of these groups are not strong enough to provide economic opportunities of social upward mobility for newcomers and the next generations of their own ethnic group. Weak or disperse social networks are often linked with lower educational achievement and parental involvement in education among South East Asians (Paik et al., 2017a, 2017b), which can result in lowered resources and increased stress.

The C in this case would be the internal pressure and the invisibility that Asian American families experience due to the MMM. Under the influence of the model minority stereotype, many Asian Americans have constantly felt pressured to prove themselves or live up to unrealistic expectations, yet become stuck as middlemen who are less prominent in leadership positions (Juang et al., 2017). Moreover, their social activism to eradicate or reduce such oppressive stereotypes also become less visible despite a long history of active participation in social justice (Choi, 2017; Duncan & Wong, 2014).

The X in this case would be the inequality and the marginalization among underrepresented Asian American families. As discussed, under the scope of MMM, the large in-group differences are overlooked and many view Asian American families as being free from problems. For example, East Asian Americans are also often categorized as an educationally high achieving group, yet some of their lower SES working-class families are more likely to display lower educational achievement or involvement, and higher anxiety and other mental health issues, compared to their upper and middle-class counterparts (Shih et al., 2019). Finally, several families under the Asian American moniker (e.g., Hmong, Cambodian, and Vietnamese) clearly understand the importance of education, but are constrained by factors that hinder their ability to provide equitable opportunities for their children (e.g., ignorance of formal U.S. education systems, lower English proficiency, lower SES, long working hours, and refugee and immigrant resettlement). However, under the MMM, the lack of visibility of these families limit their access to appropriate resources and social support, worsening the inequality in education (Chiang et al.,

2015; Dao, 2019; Keo, 2019; Lee et al., 2017). In short, the stress induced by racial and ethnic minority status in the United States places great burdens on many Asian American families, severely limiting their ability to thrive, particularly as it relates to the rearing of their children.

Stress in Latinx Families

Case 1: The Family With Children of Different "Races"

Latinx families experience discrimination on the basis of skin color regularly, albeit they themselves may not have awareness of their lower status within society if they were not born in the United States (Viruell-Fuentes, 2007). Latinx families may have a varied racial ancestry, which causes unique discriminatory experiences for members within the family. For example, Latinx families may have nuclear members that are of African, White, Asian, or of Indigenous ancestry differing from other racial groups when attempting to racially categorize themselves (Parker, Horowitz, Morin, & Lopez, 2015). As a result, skin color and phenotypic appearances vary and create diverse lived experiences for individuals and their families. Discrimination that favors the light-skinned members over the dark-skinned members is called *colorism* (Hunter, 2007). Colorism demonstrates the inculcation within members of society that lighter skin is somehow better and therefore more desired. This belief persists even when families have mixed racial composition (Hunter, 2007). This has implications for Latinx members and their families because members who are racially non-White are more likely to experience discrimination and negative well-being (Chavez-Dueñas, Adames, & Organista, 2014), a finding that has been supported in the literature over many decades (e.g., Cota-Robles Suarez, 1971; Fergus, 2017). Skin color and phenotypic expression create such varied experiences that the lumping of all Latinx families into one homogenous ethnic group erases different family-lived experiences based on race. As previously noted, the SFS model explicitly demonstrates how skin tone differences within groups produce variation in lived experience and family processes, stress in this case (McNeil Smith & Landor, 2018).

The A in this case example is a family with two or more children with different racial compositions. As a Latinx family navigates highly racialized social structures, parents must enact varying socialization practices based on differences in how their children are viewed. A particular Latinx family may have a child that presents as White and another that presents as Black. While parents may be inclined to parent them similarly, the reality that their children may be treated differently due to their race creates the need for differential parenting. Parental desires of equal socialization do not align with the reality that the child presenting as White will more than likely have experiences that provide privilege more often than oppression (Hunter, 2007), with the reverse being for the

Black child. Choosing to not differentiate parenting runs the risk of their children being ill-prepared for racialized social experiences and responding in an adaptive manner.

The B in this case example would be the amount of parenting resources available to the family regarding discriminatory practices and raising children in a racialized society. As parents raising children from two or more distinct racial groups, they need resources to enable them to learn about how to raise their children to be aware and safe within society. Lacking such knowledge can affect adjustment within youth and academic achievement (Varner et al., 2018). There is a need for parental awareness regarding implicit prejudices and the intergenerational transmission of implicit prejudices, particularly how their children may enact prejudice between each other and toward other children (Pirchio, Passiatore, Panno, Maricchiolo, & Carrus, 2018). Similarly, some studies show that Latinx youth may be unaware of their "lower" racial status until they interact within social settings (Dulin-Keita, Hannon, Fernandez, & Cockerham, 2011; Viruell-Fuentes, 2007), yet within this family, the Black Latinx child will be aware of their race well before their White Latinx sibling. Thus, Latinx families must be aware of their social status as Latinx members but also as a member of whatever racial group they may belong to. Resources regarding the treatment of Latinx member within the United States as well as the treatment of different racial groups in the United States could provide the foundation to parenting their children about race and ethnicity within the United States.

The C in this example is the Latinx family's, including individual member's, perception of race. As stated earlier, colorism can be found not only within society but also within families. Yet not all members within the Latinx community understand race the same way other groups in our society may (Viruell-Fuentes, 2007). Nonetheless, Latinx members who are of lighter tone are perceived to hold a more favorable status both outside and within the home (Chavez-Dueñas et al., 2014; Hunter, 2007). Perhaps the lighter skinned child within this family receives more positive attention (i.e., told how beautiful they are), while the darker skinned child within this family receives negative attention (i.e., reprimanded more). Between the sibling dyad, the White child may not perceive benefits attributed to their skin tone while the Black child may point out the differential treatment their sibling receives. The children's perceptions of discrimination inevitably differ based on sociocultural values. Outside the home, discriminatory behaviors may also manifest. The parents' perception as to whether such experiences are occurring, and whether or not they believe they themselves are contributing to preferential treatment on the basis skin color (e.g., praising one child more based on their image), affects family dynamics.

The X in this case example is the crisis created from the discrimination the darker skinned child is experiencing. The crisis within this multiracial family (A) may be avoided if the parents have access to resources and knowledge (B) about discrimination based on ethnicity and race within the United States. Their perceptions (C) may differ in favor of protecting and educating their children to be aware of such discriminatory practices and how to navigate racialized spaces. They may also learn to parent in a manner that does not create preferences on the basis of race or encourage protective interactions between their children rather than divisive interactions based in race. However, if the parents are unaware of discriminatory practices based in race and ethnicity, then a crisis may ensue while parents try to navigate discrimination and its impact on their children and family.

Case 2: ¿Y Mami? Transnational Families

Another source of stress that may be present in Latinx families within the United States is sustaining their transnational family. Transnationalism refers to families that live in separate countries thus causing fragmentation or disruption in composition, dynamics, and communication, between the members who leave for a new country and the members who remain in the country of origin (Rodríguez Martin, 2011). A transnational family may have various formations, for example, parent(s), child(ren), or extended family may exist in different dyads while also living in two or more separate countries, thus making them a transnational family. These transnational families maintain contact through sending money, traveling back and forth, and communicating through phone or social networks (Waldinger, 2007). There is so much contact within some transnational families that they have been called "virtual migrant families" (Sandoval Forero, 2011). These unique family processes create additional stressors for families. The A in this case example is a U.S.-based Latinx family with members in other countries abroad. A U.S.-based Latinx family consisting of a father and his two daughters are navigating a transnational family formation. The mother and wife of this family still resides in their Latinx country of origin. The father emigrated to the United States first and began his citizenship, later claiming his daughters, who were offered the opportunity to legally join their father. The mother is unable to join the family in the United States per immigration policies. The family is still closely tied to their mother–wife as well as their extended family (i.e. grandparents, aunts, uncles, cousins) back in their home country. This aligns with most transnational families who find a way to remain in contact with family, even if they are in a different country (Waldinger, 2007).

The B in this case example are the resources for communication that the family uses to allow for continued family functioning although all family members are not in the same location. Resources necessary for such families include the technological means for regular communication. Transnational families rely on video-chatting or texting, social media, and other methods of technology to remain in contact with one another (Bacigalupe & Cámara, 2012), which requires that members in both countries have access to the technology necessary to maintain contact. In addition to access, technology infrastructure (e.g., electricity, cell phone towers, Internet) and operational knowledge (e.g., operation of advanced communication such as smartphones, phone applications [apps], computers) are necessary to sustain such communication. Thus, several constraints to communications exists for transnational families.

The C in this case example would be the family's perception of continued communication with members outside the household. It is possible that members feel that they are maintaining communication, yet actual contact can vary across different family subsystems. For example, perhaps the parents maintain contact, but the daughters have less contact with their mother or other members. Variations can be due to several factors such as one daughter seeks her mother more relative to other children or the father reaches out to his parents with more frequency than his wife. As communication patterns manifest, what's important is that as family members feel less contact or connection, their perception of their own or other members' importance within the family may also fluctuate. Naturally, fluctuations in connection and communication among members in distinct countries can create stress and conflict in the family. The father desires to focus on maintaining his wife's status as a mother to his daughters, thus engaging his wife in family decisions. Yet, the daughters may feel that the absence of their mother means her opinion matter less. Perhaps, the daughters also want to maintain their mother's role as a wife and therefore become sensitive and over vigilant of their father's relationships with other females, reporting to their mother about their father's relationships. The family may experience an infinite number of examples of conflict or stress due to the perceived inability to maintain their transnational family, or due to different perceptions of frequency and need for communication.

The X in this example is the crisis that ensues from maintaining (or lack thereof) the transnational family. The transnational family communication (A) in this scenario, seeks technological means (B) to maintain contact with one another, in order to still perceive, feel, and function like family (C), and when this contact and connection is not possible, a crisis in family structure (X) results. If the family successfully uses technology and maintains continuous contact across family members, then a virtual relationship may partially fulfill the otherwise missing in-person interaction. The mother maintains her status as "mom" to her daughters and as "wife" to her husband. If she is unsuccessful in continually being integrated and counted on as a family member, then the family may experience the crisis of one of their integral family members no longer forming part of the family. The family structure is altered due to her absence.

Transnational Latinx families may be similar to other immigrant groups in their experiences of transnationalism. However, current political attitudes affect Latinx families differently than some other groups (i.e., White Europeans). The level of contact between transnational families is often a reflection of the sociopolitical climate in the host country (i.e. Latinx who have legal U.S. documentation can travel more frequently; Tamaki, 2011) and the level of attachment to the United States as a host country (Waldinger, 2007; i.e., those Latinx with high levels of contact associated with lower levels of attachment to the United States), although the last point is disputed in the literature (Tamaki, 2011). Policies such as "zero tolerance" can affect how Latinx families are able to maintain contact across borders, often limiting in-person contact. Similarly, with family members detained and families separated without knowledge of where members are, communication between family members can be severely limited.

Stress in African American Families

The contemporary structure of African American families has resulted in an amalgamation of problems that produce stress for African American families. Similarly, the stress of living as a racial minority family in the United States also produces family processes unique to African American families. Each situation is examined, using ABC-X and SFS models, below.

Case 1: The Single-Mother Experience With an Infant

The occurrence of single-parent households is not unique to the African American family experience. According to the 2017 American Community Survey, roughly 34% of children under the age of 18 live in single-parent homes, 26% of which live in single-mother households and 8% live in single-father households (McFarland et al., 2019). Among African American families, however, a total of 64% of children under the age of 18 live in homes with a single parent, accounting for the highest percentage of single-parent household across race/ethnicity groups in the United States. The majority of African American children in single-parent households live with their single mother at roughly 86%, and the other 14% live with their single fathers (McFarland et al., 2019). Perhaps what is unique to the African American family experience is the fact that almost 70% of children born to African American mothers in 2017 were born to single mothers (Martin, Hamilton, Osterman, Driscoll, & Drake, 2018), a 5% decline from a decade earlier. The experience of motherhood for a single parent undoubtedly increases the experience of stress. The heterogeneity that exist among single-mother families in term of level of education, income, self-efficacy, and availability of social support can impact just how much the stress is experienced by an individual parent (Murry, Bynum, Brody, Willert, & Stephens, 2001). For example, among African American families, the stress of single parenthood can be alleviated by support from family members; but it can also be escalated by a lack of resources and access that exist in underserved communities in which many single mothers reside (Kotchick, Dorsey & Heller, 2005). Using the ABC-X model we evaluate factors that can contribute to an African American mothers overall experience of crisis.

The A in this case example would be the experience of single parenthood with an infant. Single mothers experience numerous hardships related to economic, work-related and family difficulties, (Murry et al., 2001), particularly mothers of infants who are highly dependent and require care 24 hours a day (Roy, Schumm & Britt, 2014). Aside from the childcare responsibilities, there are other household tasks (e.g., household labor, finding source of income). Further, childcare presents stress through issues such as being employed and securing affordable quality childcare, or being unemployed and not needing external childcare but struggling with securing costly items such as diapers, clothes, breastfeeding items or formula.

The B in this case example is resources available to a single parent. An essential resource that a new parent requires is support, particularly family support (Roy et al., 2014), which among single Black mothers acts as an important buffer against greater psychological distress (Kotchick et al., 2005). In fact, social support positively impacts parenting behaviors (Degarmo, Patras, & Eap, 2008). Among African American families, the extended family, which is an extension of the nuclear family, is an important source of support. This support can be instrumental (i.e., a service or tangible goods, such as help with childcare or providing clothes) or expressive (i.e., emotional support such as advice giving or simply conversing about daily problems; Miller-Cribbs & Farber, 2008). Depending on factors of proximity, family support is linked with type of support available, how to provide or access financial support, or means of expressing emotional support.

Among African American mothers', childcare is the primary type of support received by extended family members followed by financial support and emotional support (Jayakody, Chatters, & Taylor, 1993). African American families have long been recognized for their strong extended family support systems (Billingsley, 1992; Hill, 2003; McAdoo, 1997). However, residential proximity can influence patterns of support (Miller-Cribbs & Farber, 2008). For example, the further kin are geographically, the less they are able to participate in various types of resource exchange. Proximity may not affect financial or emotional support but it can limit the amount of childcare support received, the most prevalent support to African American mothers (Jayakody et al., 1994). This notion of isolation may be more problematic for African American families who depend heavily on these various forms of support.

The C in this example would be the single-mother's perception of her situation. A single-mother's perception of control over her situation and self-efficacy in her success, greatly impact her ability to cope as a single parent (Respler-Herman, Mowder, Yasik, & Shamah, 2012). Mothers with greater self-efficacy, much like those with greater social support, demonstrate less parental stress (Jackson, 2000). Yet it can be difficult to maintain a positive perception while in poverty. More so for single mothers who are at greater risk for experiencing poverty, hence the term "the feminization of poverty" (Pearce, 1978). Yet poverty and the social conditions experienced by African American families may result from macro-level stressors (e.g., institutional racism) that penetrate the African American family experience (Murry, Butler-Barnes, Mayo-Gamble, & Inniss-Thompson, 2018). Such macro stressors influence employment opportunities available to African American men impacting the economic imbalance socially enforced on African American men and women.

Although single African American fathers' households are increasing and these men tend to be more financially secure than their female counterparts (Blow, 2015), societal perceptions of African American fathers, and mothers as uneducated, unengaged and ill-equipped to parent continually feeds the misconception that Black families are broken. This also represents differential levels of stress, for sociocultural and gendered reasons, across varying structures of African American families.

The X in this example would then be the crisis that is created from the event of becoming a single parent. Single-parent households are disadvantaged in numerous ways, especially the economic disadvantage created from being a single-source-income household. Social scientists have repeatedly demonstrated the negative consequences living in poverty has on children (Barnett, 2008). Thus, the disadvantages experienced by children in African American single-mother households creates a continuous cycle of poverty that can only be broken when young men are afforded the same opportunities as their White male counterparts. Some of the stressful realities of poverty impacting African American families, particularly single mothers, stem from the institutionalization of systemic racism, in our schools and our criminal justice system.

Case 2: Differential Approach to Interactions With Law Enforcement

All families engage with law enforcement in America at some point but there's a unique history about these interactions that produces unique and chronic stress for African Americans. We argue that race and ethnic differences serve as moderating factors when considering how families respond to the stress of interactions with law enforcement.

The A in this case example is interacting with a law enforcement agent or the possibility of interacting with such agents. The history of African American individuals, families, and community interactions with law enforcement has been described as one of terror (Hawkins & Thomas, 2013; Stevenson, 2015). That perspective argues that Black Americans and African Americans had a particular place in the racial order (i.e., beneath that of White Americans), and to reify a racial order and according behavior. Community- and state-sanctioned force was used to produce a fear of behavior that violated the said racial order. Tactics used across levels of law enforcement and militia groups ranged on a scale of severity from fatal to nonbodily injurious tactics (e.g., chasing a person with a vehicle). These historical practices produced conditions whereby Black Americans created narratives about the extent to which (or lack thereof) law enforcement protected any rights they had or even the extent to which those agents were empathic to their humanity. This produced family processes that ranged from using "green books" (i.e., a guide book used to inform readers of locations safe to drive or be as a Black person in America; Ramsey & Strauss, 2010) or "driving while black" socialization practices that warned youth of appropriate behavior during interactions with law enforcement while driving (Panebianco, 2009).

The B in this case includes resources families have to cope with the stress. Families cope with stressful events in many ways. Formal coping include filing a complaint through the law enforcement agency or court. However, if fears of retaliation, or apathy about reconciliatory responses would follow such complaints, manifest, it is unlikely that such strategies will reduce the stress of such events. Informal coping strategies can include avoiding law enforcement at all costs, socialize children and youth to take certain actions if they engage with law enforcement (e.g., don't argue, keep hands visible, don't run, memorize badge numbers or names, limit the number of youth of color in a car at one time). While such actions may bring some relief to parents, it may have little to no effect on law enforcement practices.

The C is the perception that the family has of the event (ABC-X) and perception of the event as a result of prior events (Double ABC-X). Prior negative interactions with law enforcement over time has created narratives that can shape both the perceptions of, and family processes within, Black families (James et al., 2018). Additionally, the perceptions and processes have been fueled by negative (even fatal) interactions between African Americans and law enforcement agents in an age where social media can quickly disseminate such events. Incidents such as the deaths of Sandra Bland, Michael Brown, and Trayvon Martin, among several others, by direct force or while in law enforcement custody, played out on social media and strengthen many beliefs about the potential harms to African Americans through law enforcement interactions. Notably, perceptions by African American families prevail even in misalignment with data. For instance, the net number of fatal interactions by law enforcement officials is higher among White Americans relative to Black Americans, but Blacks are more likely to be killed at disproportionately higher rates, regardless of the race or ethnicity of the police officer (Edwards, Lee, & Esposito, 2019; Menifield, Shin, & Strother, 2019). However, given those empirical facts, the stress and strain of being victim of an injurious, or fatal, interaction, the video evidence in conjunction with family narratives create perceptions that have real implications for the stress experienced by African American individuals, families, and communities (Turner & Richardson, 2016).

The X is the crisis created from the event, or events (Double ABC-X), have several consequences for families. African American families feel the constant need to socialize their children to race and racism (James et al., 2018). Unfortunately, consistently preparing children for such bias in society can have adverse effects on the socioemotional health of African American youth (Dotterer & James, 2018; Hughes et al., 2009). At a macro scale, many families that exist in communities that are highly policed may continually live with the fear of having a negative interaction with law enforcement. Considering such contexts, the fear of living in such a state has made the stress of such a negative interaction with law enforcement a chronic stressor for African American families, while such stress may be an acute stressor in other communities. This creates one aspect of the MEES that Peters and Massey (1983) referred to about the stressful lives of African Americans. Further, race creates in this instance a contextually specific type of stress for African American families (McNeil Smith & Landor, 2018), even though most or all families have to interact with law enforcement at some level.

Conclusion

Some may read this chapter and conclude that family stress is solely the fault of a given family. However, this would be a misunderstanding of our arguments. Let us state unequivocally, that families are not solely responsible for the stress they experience, or even how they respond to the stressors. As Pearlin (1989) noted, how families are positioned in society, and their access to resources, what counts as a stressful event (A), the resources the family has at their disposal to address said life happening (B), or how they perceive the event (C) can influence resultant family stress (X). Such situations are going to depend upon the stratification of social systems (e.g., race and ethnicity).

A general aim of this chapter is to equip readers with an ability to understand and explain cross-group confusions regarding how a family responds to life's happenings. For instance, it is common to hear non-African American persons say, "I just don't understand why they always bring up race when it comes to law enforcement." What such comments suggest is that this person share life experiences with someone from a different ethnic or racial group, yet how they perceive the event, or have and utilize resources to navigate it, can vary. An SFS approach possibly aids this person's understanding that the same event has different meanings and perceptions tied to certain events given the history of interactions a particular group has had with the institution in question. Though the event is the same, its impact and response vary on the grounds of race and ethnicity, which can impact family processes such as preparing children to safely interact with law enforcement. This stressor is a part of their mundane everyday environmental stress (MEES) and while it is the case that White individuals have negative interactions with law enforcement (Pegues, 2017), African Americans are disproportionately represented among those experiencing fatal interactions with law enforcement (Strother, Menifield, & Shin, 2018).

Considering Asian American families, what is considered good parenting is a culturally sensitive matter. Therefore, a simple dichotomous judgement toward certain parenting practices that are not consistent with mainstream practices or expectations is dangerous. The in-depth understanding of the cultural meaning of different parenting practices, variations of it, and the impacts of parenting expectations and practices in the contexts of active and complex enculturation and acculturation processes is much needed. Further support for Asian American parents' efforts to overcome the major stereotypes in the United States through various aspects of family processes, including racial, ethnic, and cultural socialization, for the next generation of Asian Americans, is also strongly required.

DISCUSSION QUESTIONS

1. Describe how race or ethnicity impacts whether a given stressor is differentially categorized as chronic or acute stress across different families.

2. How does the SFS model enhance understanding of family stress in racial or ethnic families?

3. In what ways does colorism impact family processes in Latinx families?

4. Explain why emotional closeness in transnational families can take on a different form or function compared to families where all members live in the same household.

5. How do we parent our children as Asian Americans (or as any other ethnic/cultural groups) when facing racially charged stereotypes in daily lives?

6. How do we further understand parenting experiences among underrepresented Asian American families (or for any other ethnic/cultural groups)?

REFERENCES

Asian Americans Advancing Justice. (2019). *Immigration and immigrant rights*. Retrieved from https://advancingjustice-aajc.org/index.php/immigration-and-immigrant-rights

Bacigalupe, G., & Cámara, M. (2012). Transnational families and social technologies: Reassessing immigration psychology. *Journal of Ethnic & Migration Studies, 38*(9), 1425–1438. doi:10.1080/1369183X.2012.698211

Barnett M. A. (2008). Economic disadvantage in complex family systems: Expansion of family stress models. *Clinical Child and Family Psychology Review, 11*(3), 145–161. doi:10.1007/s10567-008-0034-z

Baumrind, D. (1978). Parental disciplinary patterns and social competence in children. *Youth and Society, 9*, 239–275.

Billingsley, A. (1992). *Climbing Jacob's Ladder: The enduring legacy of African-American families*. New York, NY: Simon & Schuster.

Blow, C. (2015, June 8). Black dads are doing best of all. The New York Times Retrieved from https://www.nytimes.com/2015/06/08/opinion/charles-blow-black-dads-are-doing-the-best-of-all.html

Boss, P. G. (2002). *Family stress management*. Thousand Oaks, CA: SAGE.

Boss, P. G., Bryant, C., & Mancini, J. (2016). *Family stress management: A contextual approach* (3rd ed.). Thousand Oaks, CA: SAGE.

Carroll, G. (1998). Mundane extreme environmental stress and African American families: A case for recognizing different realities. *Journal of Comparative Family Studies,29*(2), 271–284.

Chavez-Dueñas, N. Y., Adames, H. Y., & Organista, K. C. (2014). Skin-color prejudice and within-group racial discrimination: Historical and current impact on Latino/a populations. *Hispanic Journal of Behavioral Sciences, 36*(1), 3–26. doi:10.1177/0739986313511306

Chao, R. K., & Kaeochinda, K. F. (2010). Parental sacrifice and acceptance as distinct dimensions of parental support among Chinese and Filipino American adolescent. In S. T. Russell, L. J. Crockett, & R. K. Chao (Eds.), *Asian American parenting and* parent–adolescent relationships (pp. 61–78). New York, NY: Springer Science+Business Media.

Chiang, A., Fisher, J., Collins, W., & Ting, M. (2015). (Mis)Labeled: The challenge of academic capital formation of Hmong American high school student in an urban setting. *Journal of Southeast Asian American Education and Advancement, 10*(1), Article 4.

Choi, Y. (2017). Introduction: Rising challenges and opportunities of uncertain times for Asian American families. In Y. Choi & Hahm, Y. C. (Eds.), *Asian American parenting: Family process and intervention* (pp. 1–10). Cham, Switzerland: Springer International.

Choi, Y., Park, M., Lee, J. P., Kim, T. Y., & Tan, K. (2017). Culture and family process: Examination of culture-specific family process via development of new parenting measures among Filipino and Korean American families with adolescents. In Y. Choi & Hahm, Y. C. (Eds.), *Asian American parenting: Family process and intervention* (pp. 37–68). Cham, Switzerland: Springer International.

Chow, K. (2017, April). "Model minority" myth again used as a racial wedge between Asians and Blacks. *Code Switch: Race and identity, remixed.* Retrieved from https://www.npr.org/sections /codeswitch/2017/04/19/524571669/model -minority-myth again-used-as-a-racial-wedge-be tween-asians-and-blacks

Cota-Robles Suarez, C. (1971). Skin color as a factor in racial identification and preference of young Chicano children. *Atzlan, 2*(1), 107–150.

Dao, N. (2019). Transnational Vietnamese: Language practices, new literacies, and redefinition of the "American Dream." *Journal of Southeast Asian American Education and Advancement, 14*(1), doi:10.7771/2153-8999.1175

Degarmo, D. S., Patras, J., & Eap, S. (2008). Social support for divorced fathers' parenting: Testing a stress-buffering model. *Family Relations, 57,* 35–48.

Dotterer, A. M., & James, A. (2018). Can parenting microprotections buffer against adolescents' experiences of racial discrimination? *Journal of Youth and Adolescence, 47*(1), 38–50.

Dulin-Keita, A., Hannon, L., Fernandez, J. R., & Cockerham, W. C. (2011). The defining moment: Children's conceptualization of race and experiences with racial discrimination. *Ethnic and Racial Studies, 34*(4), 662–682. doi:10.1080/01419870. 2011.535906

Duncan, P., & Wong, G. (2014). Introduction: Contextualizing and politicizing mothering in East Asian communities. In P. Duncan & G. Wong (Eds.), *Mothering in East Asian communities: Politics and practices* (pp. 1–27). Ontario, Canada: Demeter Press.

Edwards, F., Lee, H., & Esposito, M. (2019). Risk of being killed by police use of force in the United States by age, race–ethnicity, and sex. *Proceedings of the National Academy of Sciences, 116*(34), 16793–16798.

Fergus, E. (2017). "Because I'm light skin . . . they think I'm Italian": Mexican students' experiences of racialization in predominantly White schools. *Urban Education, 52*(4), 460–490. doi:10.1177/0042085916666931

Hawkins, H., & Thomas, R. (2013). White policing of black populations: A history of race and social control in America. In E. Cashmore & E. McLaughlin (Eds.), *Out of Order: Policing Black People* (pp. 65–86). New York, NY: Routledge.

Hill, R. B. (2003). *The strengths of Black families* (2nd ed.). New York, NY: University Press of America.

Hill, R. (1958). Generic features of families under stress, *Social Casework 49,* 139–150.

Hou, Y., Kim, S. Y., & Wang, Y. (2016). Parental acculturative stressors and adolescent adjustment through interparental and parent–child relationships in Chinese American families. *Journal of Youth Adolescence, 45,* 1466–1481.

Hughes, D., Witherspoon, D., Rivas-Drake, D., & West-Bey, N. (2009). Received ethnic–racial socialization messages and youths' academic and behavioral outcomes: Examining the mediating role of ethnic identity and self-esteem. *Cultural Diversity and Ethnic Minority Psychology, 15*(2), 112–124. doi: 10.1037/a0015509

Hunter, M. (2007). The persistent problem of colorism: Skin tone, status, and inequality. *Sociology Compass, 1,* 237–254. doi:10.1111/j.1751-9020 .2007.00006.x

Jackson, A. P. (2000). Maternal self-efficacy and children's influence on stress and parenting among single black mothers in poverty. *Journal of Family Issues, 21*(1), 3–16.

James, A. G., Coard, S. I., Fine, M. A., & Rudy, D. (2018). The central roles of race and racism in reframing family systems theory: A consideration of choice and time. *Journal of Family Theory & Review, 10*(2), 419–433. https://doi.org/10.1111 /jftr.12262

Jang, J., Lee, S., Sung, M., & Lee, J. (2016). Family relationships and communication in Korea. In G. Jian & G. Ray (Eds.), *Communication and human relationships in East Asian cultures* (pp. 165–196). Dubuque, IA: Kendall Hunt.

Jayakody, R., Chatters, L. M., & Taylor, R. J. (1993). Family support to single and married African American mothers: The provision of financial, emotional and child care assistance. *Journal of Marriage and Family, 55,* 261–276.

Juang, L. P., Yoo, H. C., & Atkin, A. (2017). A critical race perspective on an empirical review of Asian American parental racial-ethnic socialization. In Y. Choi & Hahm, Y. C. (Eds.), *Asian American parenting: Family process and intervention* (pp.11–36). Cham, Switzerland: Springer International.

Keo, P. T. (2019). Cambodian American views of partnerships in public education. *Journal of Southeast Asian American Education and Advancement, 14*(1), Article 1. doi: 10.7771/2153 8999.1158.

Kiang, L., & Witkow, M. R. (2017). Daily associations between adolescents' race-related experiences and family processes. In Y. Choi & Hahm, Y. C. (Eds.), *Asian American parenting: Family process and intervention* (pp. 117–142). Cham, Switzerland: Springer International.

Kotchick, B. A., Dorsey, S., & Heller, L. (2005). Predictors of parenting among African American single mothers: Personal and contextual factors. *Journal of Marriage and Family, 67*(2), 448–460. doi: 10.1111/j.0022-2445.2005.00127.x

Lee, S., Bai, Y. K., & You, S.-B. (2018). Ecological factors influencing breastfeeding decisions among Korean immigrant mothers in America. *Journal of Child and Family Studies, 27,* 928–943.

Lee, D. M., Duesbery, L., Han, P. P., Tashi, T., Her, C. S., & Ooka Pang, V. (2017). Academic needs and family factors in the education of Southeast Asian American students: Dismantling the model minority myth. *Journal of Southeast Asian American Education and Advancement, 12*(2), Article 2. doi: 10.7771/2153-8999.1154

Leong, F., Park, Y. S., & Kalibatseva, Z. (2013). Disentangling immigrant status in mental health: Psychological protective and risk factors among Latino and Asian American immigrants. *American Journal of Orthopsychiatry, 83,* 361–371. https:// www.vox.com/identities/2016/8/13/17938186 /police-shootings-killings-racism racial-disparities

Martin, J. A., Hamilton, B. E, Osterman, M. J. K., Driscoll, A. K., & Drake, P. (2018). Births: Final data for 2017. *National Vital Statistics Reports, 67*(8). Hyattsville, MD: National Center for Health Statistics. Retrieved from https://www.cdc.gov /nchs/data/nvsr/nvsr67/nvsr67_08-508.pdf

McAdoo, H. (1997). *Black families* (3rd ed.). Thousand Oaks, CA: SAGE

McCubbin, H. I., & Patterson, J. M. (1983). The family stress process: The Double ABC-X model of adjustment and adaptation. *Marriage & Family Review, 6*(1/2), 7–37.

Menifield, C. E., Shin, G., & Strother, L. (2019). Do White law enforcement officers target minority suspects? *Public Administration Review, 79*(1), 56–68.

McFarland, J., Hussar, B., Zhang, J., Wang, X., Wang, K., Hein, S., . . . & Barmer, A. (2019). *The condition of education 2019* (NCES 2019-144). U.S. Department of Education. Washington, D.C.: National Center for Education Statistics. Retrieved from https://nces.ed.gov/pubs2019/2019144.pdf

McKee-Ryan, F. M., & Maitoza, R. (2018). Job loss, unemployment, and families. In U. C. Klehe & E. A. van Hooft (Eds.), *Oxford handbook of job loss and job search* (pp. 87–98). New York, NY: Oxford University Press.

McNeil Smith, S., & Landor, A. M. (2018). Toward a better understanding of African American families: Development of the sociocultural family stress model. *Journal of Family Theory & Review, 10*(2), 434–450.

Miller-Cribbs, J. E., & Farber, N. B. (2008). Kin networks and poverty among African Americans: Past and present. *Social Work, 53*(1), 43–51.

Murry, V. M., Butler-Barnes, S. T., Mayo-Gamble, T. L., & Inniss-Thompson, M. N. (2018). Excavating new constructs for family stress theories in the context of everyday life experiences of Black American families. *Journal of Family Theory & Review, 10*(2), 384–405.

Murry, V. M., Smith Bynum, M., Brody, G. H., Willert, A., & Stephens, D. (2001). African American single mother and children in context: A review of studies on risk and resilience. *Clinical Child and Family Psychology Review,4*(2), 133–155. https://doi.org/10.1023/A:1011381114782

Paik, S. J., Rahman, Z., Kula, S. M., Saito, E., & Witenstein, M. A. (2017a). Diverse Asian American families and communities: Culture, structure, and education (Part 1: Why they differ). *School Community Journal, 27*(2), 35–66. Retrieved from http://www.adi.org/journal/2017fw/PaikEtAlPart1Fall2017.pdf

Paik, S. J., Rahman, Z., Kula, S. M., Saito, E., & Witenstein, M. A. (2017b). Ethnic afterschool programs and language schools in diverse Asian American communities: Varying resources, opportunities, and educational experiences (Part 2: How they differ). *School Community Journal, 27*(2), 67–97. Retrieved from http://www.adi.org/journal/2017fw/PaikEtAlPart2Fall2017.pdf

Panebianco, F. (2009, April). "Driving While Black": A theory for interethnic integration and evolution of prejudice. *University Ca'Foscari of Venice, Dept. of Economics Research Paper Series No. 10/WP/2009.* Available at SSRN, https://ssrn.com/abstract=1396675

Parker, K. Horowitz, J. M, Morin, R., & Lopez, M. H. (2015). Multiracial in America: Proud, diverse and growing in numbers. Washington, DC: Pew Research Center. Retrieved from https://www.pewsocialtrends.org/2015/06/11/chapter-7-the-many-dimensions-of-hispanic-racial-identity/

Pearce, D. (1978). The feminization of poverty: Women, work and welfare. *Urban and Social Change Review, 11*(1/2), 28–36.

Pegues, J. (2017). *Black and blue: Inside the divide between the police and black America.* Amherst, NY: Prometheus Books.

Peters, M., & Massey G. (1983). Mundane extreme environmental stress in family stress theories: The case of Black families in White America. *Marriage and Family Review, 6*, 193–218.

Pirchio, S., Passiatore, Y., Panno, A., Maricchiolo, F., & Carrus, G. (2018). A chip off the old block: Parents' subtle ethnic prejudice predicts children's implicit prejudice. *Frontiers in Psychology, 9*(110), 1–9. doi:10.3389/fpsyg.2018.00110

Ramsey, C. A., & Strauss, G. (2010). *Ruth and the green book*. Minneapolis, MN: Carolrhoda Books.

Respler-Herman, M. Mowder, B. A., Yasik, A. E, & Shamah, R. (2012). Parenting beliefs, parental stress, and social support relationships. *Journal of Child and Family Studies.*, 21(2), 190–198. https://doi.org/10.1007/s10826-011-9462-3

Rodríguez Martín, L. I. (2011). Siempre estamos conectados: Así sé que me quiere mucho. Comunicaciones en familias transnacionales a través de internet. *Revista Latinoamericana de Estudios de Familia, 3*, 50–64.

Roy, R. N., Schumm, W. R., & Britt, S. L. (2014). *Transition to parenthood*. New York, NY: Springer-Verlag.

Russell, S. T., Crockett, L. J., & Chao, R. K. (2010). Introduction: Asian American parenting and parent–adolescent relationships. In S. T. Russell, L. J. Crockett, & R. K. Chao (Eds.), *Asian American parenting and parent–adolescent relationships* (pp. 1–16). New York, NY: Springer Science+Business Media.

Sandoval Forero, E. A. (2011). La etnografia virtual para el studio de familias transnacionales en México y Estados Unidos. *Revista Latinoamericana de Estudios de Familia, 3*, 85–104.

Shih, K. Y., Chang, T.-F., & Chen, S.-Y. (2019). Impacts of the model minority myth on Asian American individuals and families: Social justice and critical race feminist perspectives. *Journal of Family Theory & Review, 11*, 412–428.

Stevenson, B. (2015). *Just mercy: A story of justice and redemption*. New York, NY: Spiegel & Grau.

Strother, L., Menifield, C., & Shin, G. (2018, August). We gathered data on every confirmed line-of-duty police killing of a civilian in 2014 and 2015. *The Washington Post*. Retrieved from https://www.washingtonpost.com/news/monkey-cage/wp/2018/08/29/we gathered-data-on-every-confirmed-line-of-duty-police-killing-of-a-civilian-in-2014-and 2015-heres-what-we-found/?noredirect=on

Tamaki, E. (2011). Transnational home engagement among Latino and Asian Americans: Resources and motivation. *The International Migration Review, 45*(1), 148–173.

Turner, E. A., & Richardson, J. (2016). Racial trauma is real: The impact of police shootings on African Americans. *Psychology Benefits Blog of the American Psychological Association*. Retrieved from https://psychologybenefits.org/2016/07/14/racial-trauma-police-shootings-on-african-americans/

Varner, F. A., Hou, Y., Hodzic, T., Hurd, N. M., Butler-Barnes, S. T., & Rowley, S. J. (2018). Racial discrimination experiences and African American youth adjustment: The role of parenting profiles based on racial socialization and involved-vigilant parenting. *Cultural Diversity & Ethnic Minority Psychology, 24*(2), 173–186. doi:10.1037/cdp0000180

Waldinger, R. (2007). *Between here and there: How attached are Latino immigrants to their native country?* Retrieved from http://pewrsr.ch/1OOHwEH

Viruell-Fuentes, E. A. (2007). Beyond acculturation: immigration, discrimination, and health research among Mexicans in the United States. *Social Science & Medicine, 65*(7), 1524–1535. https://doi.org/10.1016/j.socscimed.2007.05.010

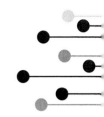

CHAPTER 13

The Newest Generation of U.S. Veterans and Their Families

Kyung-Hee Lee and
Shelley MacDermid Wadsworth

More than 2.77 million U.S. service members deployed between 2001 and 2015, creating a new generation of veterans (Wenger, O'Connell, & Cottrell, 2018). This chapter discusses challenges these new veterans and their families may face, guided by the life course perspective, which conceptualizes human development as unfolding over time, shaped by the choices and actions of individuals within constraints imposed by historical and social contexts. The chapter first situates the current wars and veterans in historical context (historical time). Next, individual transitions and challenges for veterans, their spouses, and their children are discussed, followed by a discussion of family transitions (linked lives). Finally, three interventions targeting challenges facing veterans and their families are introduced.

The Newest Generation of Veterans and Their Families

More than 2.77 million service members have been deployed to Iraq or Afghanistan between 2001 and 2015 (Wenger et al., 2018). As the military operations for these conflicts wind down and the U.S. military shrinks, this new generation of combat-exposed veterans is joining veterans of previous wars in U.S. society. The experiences of recent veterans differ from those of previous wars in many ways. For example, all recent veterans served in an all-volunteer force. In addition, many experienced multiple deployments with little time at home between (Chandra et al., 2010). The nature of combat in Iraq and Afghanistan also differed, resulting in distinct injury profiles relative to previous wars. Thus, the challenges experienced in the aftermath of war are also likely to be somewhat different for this generation than for veterans of previous wars.

Most U.S. military members—slightly more than 80%—serve in enlisted ranks, are White (31.3% active component, 26.1% reserve component) and male (83.8% active component, 80.4% reserve component). About half (49%) are married, and 38.4% and 41.5% of the members of the active and reserve components, respectively, have children (Office of the Deputy Assistant Secretary of Defense [ODASD, MC&FP], 2018). Along with service members, family members also are influenced by wars and deployments. In this chapter, we discuss the challenges faced by Operation Enduring Freedom (OEF)/Operation Iraqi Freedom (OIF)/ Operation New Dawn (OND) veterans and their families after deployments and during the transition into civilian life, using life course perspectives (Wilmoth &

London, 2013). We begin by discussing the experiences of individual family members, followed by the experiences of families as a whole. Finally, information regarding policy and prevention programs for military and veteran families is provided. It is important that we acknowledge that this chapter has an important bias: We focus almost exclusively on family challenges and problems, even though most veteran families do NOT experience long-term negative consequences (National Academies of Sciences, Engineering, and Medicine, 2019). We do this because readers of this text are likely to enter helping professions where they may encounter families struggling with challenges.

Theoretical Framework: Life Course

Vignette

Alvaro Ramos is a 27-year-old Hispanic male with a wife, Victoria (age 27), and a 3-year-old son, Jesus. After 4 years in the military and two deployments to Iraq as a medical specialist, he decided not to re-enlist. Upon entering civilian life, he wanted to stay in the medical field both for job security and his passion for the field. He decided to go to a vocational college and get a stable job as a licensed nurse as soon as possible. They moved close to Alvaro's school away from the military base. His wife who had stayed at home taking care of their son while he was deployed agreed to take a job at a floral shop to help support the family while he was in school. Still, he needed to find a part-time job to make ends meet and work in the evenings and some weekends. Jesus started going to day care during the day.

Life-course perspectives (Wilmoth & London, 2013) provide very useful concepts such as historical time, transitions, timing, and linked lives that help us to understand veterans and their family lives. Life-course perspectives conceptualize human development as comprising processes that unfold over time and emphasize that individuals shape their own life course through the choices they make and actions they take, within constraints imposed by historical and social contexts. The concept of *historical time* helps us understand events in larger contexts. For example, as discussed briefly above, veterans' experiences of the most recent conflicts are very different from those during the Vietnam War, and as a consequence, the new generation of veterans and their families may face different challenges in the future. Thus, it is important to consider historical time in understanding each generation of veterans and their families.

Individual and family lives are marked by both minor and major *transitions*. Some transitions are very common and experienced by most people, such as starting school or retiring, while other transitions are rare, such as being deployed to a combat zone or experiencing the sudden death of a family member. Transitions bring changes in roles and statuses to the individuals involved, such as when a job transition for one spouse means that the other becomes the primary economic provider for the family. Common transitions are usually easier to cope with than rare ones because people generally are more likely to have prior knowledge of or experience with similar transitions and thus know what to expect in their new roles. Another important aspect of transitions is when they occur (the *timing* of the transition). Even common transitions can cause negative stress when they happen unexpectedly or at a time in life that does not conform to societal expectations. For example, in the vignette above, Alvaro is a veteran and older than the traditional college student. He also has family responsibilities that many single students do not. Thus, his college experience differs from that of a young student right out of high school, and he may experience some challenges as a result.

Life-course perspectives also emphasize the importance of *linked lives*. The concept of linked lives refers to connections people have not only to one another but also to larger contexts such as other generations in their family, other people in the society, and historical events. The concept of linked lives helps to explain why and how a service member's experiences during combat deployment are connected to historic timing of the war, and social and military support for the war. For example, many individuals joined the U.S. military in the aftermath of September 11, 2001. The concept of linked lives also helps to explain how service members' family members are affected by military service and deployments because it emphasizes the connections between the transitions of one family member and the experiences of other family members. In the Ramos family's case, Alvaro's decision to separate from the military changed many aspects of his family's life. Individually, Alvaro started a school and a job, and Victoria now has a new job, which means Jesus has to start going to a childcare facility during the day. Moreover, the move was a transition for the family as a whole.

Historical Time: The New Context

Placing the recent wars into the context of historical time helps us to understand the experiences of OEF/OIF/OND veterans and their families. The recent conflict differs from previous wars in many ways. First, all military forces are now volunteers, unlike most of the veterans of prior conflicts, most of whom were drafted. This means that service members are now more likely to be married or have children while still serving, and likely to serve for longer periods. Second, due to the long duration of the conflicts, OEF/OIF/OND veterans tend to have experienced higher numbers of deployments and longer cumulative durations of deployments than veterans of previous wars (Chandra et al., 2010). Between 2001 and 2015, 2.77 million service members completed 5.4 million deployments, with 40% deployed more than once. Over half (56.8%) had family responsibilities to spouses (56.8%) or children (45.3%). (Wenger, 2018). Thus, service members experienced longer separations from their families and greater risk of exposure to combat and injuries. Third, despite the large number of OEF/OIF/OND veterans, the proportion of them in the general population is smaller than veterans of previous wars. For example, only 12% of male and 3% of female Americans under the age of 35 are OEF/OIF/OND veterans compared to 50% of male and 15% female Americans under the age of 35 in the post–World War II veteran population (Castro & Kintzle, 2014). The implication is that OEF/OIF/OND veterans have entered predominantly civilian communities where there may be limited familiarity with their experiences and as a result may not be able to find the support they need. Fourth, due to the nature of combat and advances in protective equipment and medical treatment during the recent wars, the types and prognoses of injuries differ from prior conflicts. For example, the estimated survival rate from injuries in the recent wars is 90% (Klocek, 2008), compared to 70% during the Vietnam War. Injuries sustained in the recent wars are most often due to explosives (75%), which tend to cause multiple injuries, especially in the head and neck regions of the body. In contrast, most injuries during the Vietnam war were due to gunshots (Belmont et al., 2010).

Individual Transitions: Veterans

For most service members, military service incorporates a series of transitions, from one rank or role to another, as well as deployments and, eventually, separation from military service. Many veterans pursue further education following deployments or military service, or enter or return to the civilian labor force. Others may return home with wounds or injuries. In this section, some of the transitions and related challenges veterans may experience are discussed, including education, employment, and wounds or injuries.

Education

After returning from deployment or completing military service, many veterans enter or return to colleges or universities to continue their education. Historically, veterans have been successful in pursuing higher education. For example, almost 8 million World War II veterans earned degrees in postsecondary schools or finished vocational training (Greenberg, 1997). In 2005, 65.7% of male veterans between the ages of 25 and 64 who were in the labor force had at least some college or an associate's degree, compared to 58% of nonveterans. The difference was larger for female veterans (79.8% vs. 64.9%; Holder, 2007).

The educational benefits of the various versions of the GI Bill are aimed at increasing educational attainment of OEF/OIF/OND veterans. In fact, almost 1 million OEF/OIF/OND veterans had used GI bill benefits for education by 2015 (Cate, Lyon, Schmeling, & Bogue, 2017). Student veterans may encounter a variety of challenges, including navigating benefit procedures, adjusting to the non-military environment (e.g., managing their own schedule and duties), being older than other students, and coping with the insensitivities of others to war-related issues (Barry, Whiteman & MacDermid Wadsworth, 2014). Combat exposure and PTSD symptoms are also negatively related to the educational performance and social functioning of student veterans (Barry et al., 2014). Compared to civilian students, student veterans tend to engage in more risky behaviors such as use of alcohol and drugs, and violence than nonveteran students (Widome, Laska, Gulden, Fu, & Lust, 2011). Evidence regarding GPAs is mixed, with large studies finding both lower (Durdella & Kim, 2012), and higher (Cate et al., 2017) levels relative to civilian students, likely due to the analyses of possible confounding variables. How well universities are prepared to help student veterans deal with the challenges is largely unknown (Barry et al., 2014).

Employment

In general, the employment situations of veterans have compared favorably to those of their civilian counterparts. According to the Bureau of Labor Statistics (2019), the unemployment rate of all veterans in 2018 was 3.5%, compared to 3.8% for nonveterans. The unemployment rates of male OEF/OIF/OND veterans have been higher, however, than those of nonveterans, in 2018 at 3.9% compared to 3.8% for male nonveterans, but for female veterans, the difference was larger and in the opposite direction (3.5% vs. 3.7%). Unemployment rates among OIF/OEF veterans in 2018 were considerably lower than at their peak in 2011, when the rate was 12.1% compared to 8.3% for all veterans and 8.2% for nonveterans (Bureau of Labor Statistics, 2012, 2019). When examined by ethnicity, veterans of all ethnicity groups except Black veterans had higher unemployment rates than their counterpart nonveterans. The differences between OEF/OIF/OND veterans and nonveterans seemed to be driven also by the unemployment rates of younger veterans. For example, the unemployment rates of OEF/OIF/OND veterans between 18 and 24 years (10.6%), 25 to 34 years (4.1%), and 35 to 44 (3.5%) were higher than similarly aged male nonveterans (8.0%, 3.9%, and 3.0% respectively) while the unemployment rates for male veterans and nonveterans ages 35 and older were lower than those of nonveterans (2.4% vs. 2.8% for ages 45 to 54; 2.3% vs. 2.9% for ages 55 to 64; and 3.0% vs. 3.2% for ages 65 years and older; Bureau of Labor Statistics, 2019).

Job performance and employment can be hindered by physical and psychological injuries related to military service. For example, PTSD has been related to deterioration in work functioning, and job loss (Institute of Medicine, 2013). Moreover, employers may hesitate to hire veterans with possible psychological problems such as PTSD (Institute of Medicine, 2013). Governmental efforts to increase employment of veterans such as tax credits for employers have been in place, but research about their effectiveness is lacking at this point.

Military service can be related to veterans' earnings in the civilian job market. Historically, veterans of World War II outperformed nonveterans in education attainment and earnings, while Vietnam War veterans did not do as well as their civilian counterparts (MacLean & Elder, 2007). The 2016 VA Profile of Veterans

(National Center for Veterans Analysis and Statistics, 2018), which is based on data from the American Community Survey, reported that median earnings were higher for veterans than nonveterans, both for males ($49,994 vs. $39,985) and females ($38,709 vs. $29,974).

Injuries

Over, 50,000 service members were injured in OIF/OEF/OND (Fischer, 2015). The most common injuries were from explosives (75%). Injuries to extremities were the most common location of physical injuries (51.9%), followed by head and neck (28.1%), abdomen (10.1%), and thorax (9.9%) (Belmont, McCriskin, Sieg, Burks, & Schoenfeld, 2012). Traumatic brain injury (TBI) accounted for 327,299 injuries during the recent conflicts (Fischer, 2015). TBI is defined by the Department of Defense as structural injury and/or physiological disruption of brain function caused by an external force (Institute of Medicine, 2013). TBI severity is determined by the extent of loss of consciousness and posttraumatic amnesia; over 90% of TBIs in OEF/OIF/OND veterans are classified as mild (Institute of Medicine, 2013). The long-term outcomes of TBI are related to impairment in cognitive functioning such as attention, concentration, reaction time, memory, processing speed, and decision-making (Institute of Medicine, 2013). People with mild or moderate TBIs typically recover fully from the cognitive impairment within 6 months, but impairment from severe TBIs lasts longer. Long-term prognosis of TBI is complicated because veterans with a TBI have a higher risk of having other psychological problems such as PTSD, depression, or anxiety, which can delay recovery and make it difficult to isolate the effects of TBI. In particular, veterans with a TBI have greater risks of depression, which increase with the severity of the TBI. TBI is also related to increase in aggressive behaviors, unemployment, and relationship problems.

Mental health problems such as PTSD and depression among veterans have received considerable media attention. The estimated prevalence rate of PTSD in OEF/OIF/OND veterans ranges from 5% to 20% (Institute of Medicine, 2013) compared to 6.8% in the general population (Kessler et al., 2005). The rate is higher in service members with combat experience, severe injuries, and military sexual trauma. Symptoms of PTSD include intrusive memories, emotional numbing, avoidance of cues, and hyperarousal (Institute of Medicine, 2013). Combat veterans can show symptoms of PTSD 40 years after their service (Spiro, Schnurr, & Aldwin, 1994). Moreover, PTSD is related to other mental disorders such as depression and psychosocial problems such as relationship problems, legal problems, and violence. The prevalence rate of major depression among OEF/OIF/OND veterans ranges from 5% to 37% and the chance of being diagnosed with major depression increases with combat exposure (Institute of Medicine, 2013). In the general population, the rate is 18.4% or more (Kessler et al., 2005). Resilience—individuals' ability to adapt to changes and stress—and social support have been identified as protective factors for both PTSD and depression (Institute of Medicine, 2013).

Suicide

Suicide is the third-leading cause of death among U.S. military members and has been rising (Armed Forces Health Surveillance Center, 2012). Before 2001, military suicide rates were 20% lower than those among civilians (Eaton, Messer, Wilson, & Hoge, 2006). According to the Department of Defense Suicide Event Report (Pruitt et al., 2019), however, by 2017 the suicide rate was 21.9 per 100,000 for those serving on active duty, 25.7 per 100,000 for those in the Reserves, and 29.1 per 100,000 in the National Guard, all much higher than the rate of 17.4 per 100,000 individuals ages 17 to 59 in the general population in the same year. Firearms were the most frequently used method of suicide (Pruitt et al., 2019). The suicide rate among veterans was even higher in 2017, at 27.7 per 100,000 (Office of Mental Health and Suicide Prevention, 2019). Risk factors include mental health problems including PTSD and substance abuse, exposure to adversities during childhood, and stressful life experiences, while protective factors include social support, and optimism (Institute of Medicine, 2013). However, the importance of risk factors seems to change over the life course of veterans. For example, Kaplan and colleagues (2012) found that for younger veterans (ages 18 to 34) who committed suicide, relationship problems and alcohol use were more common than for middle-age veterans (ages 35 to 44 and 45 to 64), for whom mental health problems were more common (Kaplan, McFarland, Huguet, & Valenstein, 2012).

Recent research suggests that veterans of OEF/OIF/OND are at greater risk of suicide than other veterans (Bruce, 2010). Unique aspects of the OEF/OIF/OND conflicts may contribute to the elevated levels of risk. First, as discussed above, TBI is more common among OEF/OIF/OND veterans than others, and TBI is a risk factor for suicide in military populations (Institute of Medicine, 2013). Second, due to the volunteer nature of the current military force, new generations of veterans may enter a general population in which only a small percentage of members has served in the military, possibly resulting in a lack of deep understanding and shared experience of the wars (Castro & Kintzle, 2014). As a result, veterans may not find the social and community support they need. Third, OEF/OIF/OND veterans tend to have experienced more and longer deployments than veterans of previous wars (Institute of Medicine, 2013); and prolonged combat experiences are related to suicide risk (Bruce, 2010).

The military population is always changing, and lesbian, gay and bisexual service members are an increasingly visible subgroup. Much remains to be learned about the experiences of these service members but existing evidence suggests that they experience challenges similar to those of others, as well as an additional set of challenges related to their minority status, such as harassment (Ramirez & Bloeser, 2018).

Individual Transitions: Spouses

Vignette

Steve Mosier (age 37) came back from his last deployment with a severe traumatic brain injury (TBI) from a roadside bomb in Afghanistan. He also suffers from posttraumatic stress disorder (PTSD). Although Steve has made significant progress in his cognitive functioning, he still has problems with memory, concentration, and fatigue after a year of treatment. These symptoms, combined with symptoms of PTSD, make it hard for him to hold a steady job. His wife, Dana (age 37), manages most of the household and parenting responsibilities, Steve's medical and rehabilitation appointments, and her part-time job with help from their teenage son, Kevin (age 15). Dana often reports being overwhelmed with all the responsibilities and feeling depressed. Kevin misses the time spent with his dad before the injury. They used to build model planes together, which is harder now because his dad gets tired very quickly and has trouble concentrating on things. Their 10-year-old daughter, Tina, does not feel really close to Steve because Steve had been in and out of her life due to three deployments. Most of the time, she avoids interacting with him.

Military service can dictate many aspects of families' lives. For example, many military families move frequently and experience many separations, both short and long, for training or deployments. The demands of military life on families of service members fall heavily on spouses. For example, frequent relocations have negative impacts on the careers of military spouses. Compared to civilian wives, military wives in one large national study were 9% less likely to be employed and, when employed, tended to earn 14% less than civilian wives of similar background between 2005 and 2011 (Hosek & MacDermid Wadsworth, 2013).

Deployments pose additional challenges to spouses of service members. During deployment, spouses assume additional household and parenting responsibilities, and may constantly worry about the safety of deployed service members while also trying to maintain intimate connections with them (National Academies of Sciences, Engineering, and Medicine, 2019). Thus, it is not surprising to find that during deployment, spouses have been found to experience depression (12.2%) and anxiety disorders (17.4%) at rates similar to service members after deployment (depression 14.2%–14.7% and anxiety 15.7%–17.5%; Eaton et al., 2008) and rates higher than spouses not experiencing deployment (23.7% vs. 19.1% for depression and 13.6% vs. 10.8% for anxiety; Mansfield et al., 2010).

After service members return from deployment, new challenges can arise for spouses. Family tasks minor and major, from taking out the garbage to disciplining children need to be redefined, renegotiated, and redistributed. Some spouses may find it difficult to relinquish their newly acquired autonomy to make decisions (Institute of Medicine, 2013). In addition, some couples struggle to reconnect and communicate with each other following deployment (Knobloch & Theiss, 2012), and some spouses report depression, anxiety, PTSD, and relationship difficulties during the reunion period (Institute of Medicine, 2013). These patterns are less evident, however, in tightly controlled longitudinal comparisons with matched spouses not experiencing deployment; there, group differences shrink or disappear (Meadows, Tanielian, & Karney, 2016). The challenges are greater for spouses of injured service members (National Academies of Sciences, Engineering, and Medicine, 2019); these will be discussed later.

Deployments may have additional negative implications for spouses' employment. In the 2017 Military Lifestyle survey by Blue Star Families, the top barriers to employment reported by spouses were the demands of military jobs, problems finding childcare, and family responsibilities (Shiffer et al., 2017). Juggling work and family while functioning as a single parent during deployment can be difficult, and earnings may not be enough to cover increased childcare expenses. Thus, some spouses leave paid employment during deployment (Institute of Medicine, 2013). Some spouses report that employers are hesitant to hire them because they know that the military may order their family to move at any time (Castaneda & Harrell, 2008).

In summary, military spouses share many aspects of military transitions with service members. Often, military spouses must shoulder the bulk of family responsibilities with limited help from service members. The challenges of the military lifestyle may become more intense during and after deployments, sometimes with negative implications for the psychological well-being of military spouses. Disruption in military spouses' employment while service members are in the military may have long-lasting effects on their career trajectories.

Individual Transitions: Children

Military children are similar to civilian children in many respects. For example, research in the 1990s indicated that military children reported similar rates of psychological and physical health problems as civilian children (Jeffereys & Leitzel, 2000). More recent data indicate that military and civilian adolescents are similar in the likelihood of using alcohol (MacDermid Wadsworth, Bailey, & Coppola, 2017). Military life brings several benefits to children in the form of access to health care, housing, subsidized childcare, and parental income (MacDermid Wadsworth et al., 2017). Military life also poses challenges, however, such as rates of relocation two to three times those of civilian children (Institute of Medicine, 2013).

Many studies report negative impacts of parental deployment on children. Similar to spouses, children's well-being is negatively related to cumulative duration of deployments (Chandra et al., 2010). A meta-analysis of 16 studies concluded that deployment had small negative effects ($r = .08$) on children's overall adjustment and academic performance (Cunitz et al., 2019) that varied by age. The negative effects were strongest during middle childhood (6 to 11 years,

r = 16 to 22) and weakest for adolescents (12 to 18 years). In national Youth Risk Behavior Survey data, military adolescents appear to be more likely to have had suicidal thoughts, to have used cigarettes or other substances, and to have had more experiences of violence and harassment (MacDermid Wadsworth et al., 2017).

Research findings consistently demonstrate that children's emotional, social, and academic problems in the context of deployment and reintegration depend on the well-being of the nondeployed parent. When nondeployed parents experience higher levels of distress, their children often do exhibit more social and emotional problems (Lester & Flake, 2013).

New challenges after deployed parents return home include fitting the returning parent back into the family routine, re-establishing closeness in the parents' relationship, dealing with returning parents' mood changes, and reconnecting with the returning parent (Chandra et al., 2010). In Tina's case in the second vignette, her dad had been gone for a great portion of her life, thus missing a chance to establish a secure relationship with her. Tina was having a harder time connecting with her dad than her brother, who had developed a secure bond with his dad before the deployments started. There is also evidence that older children have more difficulties during reintegration (Chandra et al., 2010).

In summary, there is evidence that parental deployments have negative effects on children's outcomes. However, most research on the effects of parental deployments on children has mostly examined short-term outcomes (Lester & Flake, 2013). The lack of evidence on long-term consequences makes it hard to determine how parental deployments during childhood influence trajectories of educational achievement or well-being over the life course. Moreover, it is important to note that military children have many protective factors, including health care, housing, and high-quality childcare provided by the military.

Linked Lives: Family Transitions

In previous sections, we have discussed the experiences of individual family members as a function of deployment-related transitions. Available evidence suggests that military service has positive long-term effects on families, especially ethnic minority families (National Academies of Sciences, Engineering, and Medicine, 2019). However, wartime deployments and subsequent combat exposure may have negative impacts on some families. In the following sections, we discuss some transitions that affect family relationships.

Couple Relationships

Military service and deployment present challenges to couple relationships. During deployments, spouses at home have to deal with daily family and parenting responsibilities with limited help from their spouse, as well as loneliness and worries about the safety of the service member (National Academies of Sciences,

Engineering, and Medicine, 2019). Both at-home spouses and service members report challenges of maintaining connections with each other and experiencing uncertainty about their relationship during deployment (Wilson et al., 2018). Service members' return home also poses challenges, such as renegotiating roles and responsibilities (Baptist et al., 2011).

The relationship between deployment and marital quality is complex, and deployment does not affect every marriage in the same way. For example, a retrospective study of wives whose husbands had been deployed found five different trajectories of marital satisfaction across the deployment cycle (steady, decreasing, increasing, turbulent, and dipped) (Parcell & Maguire, 2014). Recent evidence suggests that it may not be deployment alone that is associated with lower relationship quality, but also exposure to traumatic experiences and symptoms of posttraumatic stress. Some evidence suggests that the first deployment may be especially important for couple relationships (Karney & Trail, 2017). Regarding the nature of marriages, marital quality prior to deployment, the ability to exchange mutual support during deployment, and religious beliefs seem important to marital relationships after deployment (Baptist et al., 2011).

Communication during and after deployment also impacts marital relationships (Baptist et al., 2011; Wilson et al., 2018). During deployment, both spouses and service members struggle between the need to communicate to feel connected and the need to limit information they share with their spouse in order to protect the other from worrying (Baptist et al., 2011). A study of wives of deployed service members who limited information sharing to protect their husbands showed that they reported lower physical and mental health, whereas wives who disclosed stressful situations to their husband reported higher marital satisfaction after deployment (Joseph & Afifi, 2010).

Some studies examined frequencies and methods of communication during deployment in order to determine which are most beneficial to postdeployment adjustment. Ponder and Aguirre (2012) found that service members who communicated daily with their spouses reported higher marital satisfaction after deployment than those who communicated with their spouses less than once per week. They also found that use of traditional mail was related to higher marital satisfaction compared to other methods of communication. However, the benefits of frequent communication also depend on marital quality prior to deployment.

Findings about the impact of deployment on divorce are not yet conclusive. Using data from the Defense Manpower Data Center (DMDC) that depict service members' marital and deployment histories, Karney and Crown (2007) examined divorce trends between 2002 and 2005 among service members who married during that period and found that longer deployments were related to lower risk of divorce. However, in another study, also using the data from the DMDC, Negrusa and colleagues (2014) expanded the time frame to between 1999 and 2008 and found that longer cumulative months of deployments were related to increased risk of divorce. The predicted divorce rate within 2 years of marriage for service members returning from 6-month deployments was 1.4%, increasing to 1.5%, 1.8%, and above 2% with each 6-month increase. So, for example, by 3 years beyond the start of their marriages, 12.4% of couples who had experienced 6 months of deployment had divorced, compared to 8.4% of couples who had not experienced deployment (Negrusa, Negrusa, & Hosek, 2014). Both studies (Karney & Crown, 2007; Negrusa et al., 2014) found, however, that the negative impact of deployment on divorce risk was stronger for female service members. Possibly due in part to military policies emphasizing marriage, the likelihood of divorce appears to be somewhat less likely among service members than in the general population, but more likely overall, particularly in the first 2 years following military service (Routon, 2017).

Child Maltreatment

The rate of documented child maltreatment in military families in 2017 was 5.0 unduplicated cases per 1,000 children (Department of Defense, 2018), which was less than the 9.1 per 1,000 children in the U. S. civilian population (Department of Health & Human Services, 2018). The rate of child maltreatment in the military has fluctuated, however. Specifically, rates steadily increased from 5.8 cases per 1,000 in 2001 to 6.4 in 2004, followed by a decrease to 4.3 in 2009. Current rates do not differ significantly from the 10-year average.

Parental deployment is a significant risk factor for child maltreatment. Service members' departures to, as well as return from, deployments have been found to be related to increases in military child maltreatment, neglect in particular (Cozza et al., 2018; Rentz et al., 2007). In a recent study of Air Force families where maltreatment had previously occurred, there were more maltreatment cases by deploying parents prior to than following deployment (Thomsen et al., 2014), and the rate of child maltreatment by at-home parents was highest during deployment (McCarthy et al., 2013). These findings illustrate how the transition-related stressors may influence family members differently.

Families of Injured Veterans

As described previously, veterans' injuries vary in their nature, severity, and prognosis. Service members' injuries may have significant effects on family relationships, and family members may need to adjust their lives to the changing needs of the injured veterans. In most cases, like in the Mosier family of Vignette 2, family members are the primary sources of practical support (e.g., managing doctors' appointments and household tasks, assisting the injured veteran with daily activities) and emotional support. Many military family caregivers face unique challenges such as dealing with multiple injuries, navigating complex care systems, caring for mental and physiological injuries, and providing round-the-clock care, sometimes for many years (National Academies of Sciences, Engineering, and Medicine, 2019). In the Mosier family, Dana takes on all these responsibilities herself while managing her part-time job and caring for the children.

Spouses of injured veterans often become the primary caregiver, placing them at risk for caregiver burden, which refers to diverse stresses (e.g., physical, emotional, financial) related to providing care (Bastawrous, 2013). In general, spouses of injured veterans, like Dana, report higher levels of distress (Calhoun, Beckham, & Bosworth, 2002) and, in the cases of PTSD especially, physical and psychological intimate partner violence (Taft, Watkins, Stafford, Street, & Monson, 2011).

Service members' injuries also have direct and indirect impacts on children. Some injuries prevent service members from actively participating in parenting or joining certain family activities, thus spending less time with their children (National Academies of Sciences, Engineering, and Medicine, 2019). Some service members may return home substantially changed by their experiences. Many mental disorders such as depression, PTSD, and TBI are related to changes in mood, personality, or cognitive function. In these cases, children may feel uncertain about their parents or even avoid them, as Tina in the Mosier family does. When changes are drastic or permanent, children have to deal with the loss of the parents they used to know. Children also may experience sadness or confusion over the changes. The effects of parental injury differ based on the developmental status of the children. Younger children may exhibit behavior problems or revert to behaviors they have outgrown (e.g., sucking a thumb) while teenagers may withdraw from the family. Older children, like Kevin in the Mosier family in the vignette, also may need to help taking care of the injured parent, resulting in caregiving challenges for themselves (National Academies of Sciences, Engineering, and Medicine, 2019).

As discussed previously, children are very susceptible to their parents' distress. Family life disruptions including disturbances in routines, changes in discipline, and reduced time spent with children have been related to higher distress in children (Cozza et al., 2010). In the Mosier family, Steve's participation in family and parenting activities is limited, and Dana's caregiver burden and stress levels are high, potentially making their children more vulnerable to distress.

Families Coping with Loss

As of September 2014, more than 6,800 service members had died as a result of injuries acquired during OEF, OIF, and OND (DeBruyne, 2018), and the suicide rate among members of the Armed Forces also had increased substantially. Although many scholars agree that the grieving processes in military families are similar to those in civilian families, Cohen and Mannarino (2004) identified some aspects unique to military death which may make grief more complicated. First, death by injury or suicide may occur during as well as following deployment. Second, during a deployment, families are constantly aware of the danger service members are facing and hopeful that they will never receive an unexpected knock on the door, notifying them of injury or death of their loved ones. Third, with combat death, there are chances that the family may recover only parts of the remains or may not have remains at all. Fourth, with the death of the service member, families who were living in military installations may have to move away from their friends and social support. Military families do receive some supports after the injury or death of a service member, such as a military funeral, financial support, and health care, depending upon their service member's status and military rules regarding family eligibility (i.e., spouses and children are more likely to receive supports than parents or adult siblings). Some family members take great pride and attribute great meaning to their loved one's combat death (National Academies of Sciences, Engineering, and Medicine, 2019). The grieving process of spouses or partners of deceased service members is important for themselves as well as for their children. Children seem to adjust better after service member parents' death when the surviving parent is doing better and parenting more effectively.

In summary, some family transitions after deployment are very challenging for military families. Although it will be some time before we fully understand the long-term effects of the current wars on family trajectories, some of the transitions we have discussed have the potential to alter veteran families' lives enormously. For this reason, it may be important to identify more vulnerable families and their needs in order to be able to provide appropriate support.

Prevention and Intervention

There are many prevention and intervention programs available to military families, made possible by the efforts of government and military leaders, employers, universities, philanthropic organizations, and others. The G.I. Bill is a government and military effort with a long history. The Veteran Jobs Mission is led by civilian employers. Families Overcoming Under Stress (FOCUS) is a partnership between military organizations and a university.

GI Bill

Military service can interrupt or delay service members' pursuit of higher education because most service members join the military when they otherwise could have pursued higher education. Since the end of World War II, a series of "GI Bills" have addressed these interruptions or delays by providing financial support for the pursuit of higher education. For example, approximately 7.8 million World War II veterans and 3 million Korean War veterans have used GI Bill benefits for education, and these veterans have higher levels of education and earnings than those who did not use GI Bill benefits (Stanley, 2003).

Over 1 million OEF/OIF/OND veterans have used a GI Bill since 2001, 51.7% of whom earned a degree or certificate within 8 years, a rate similar to nonveteran students, and higher than that of returning adult students (Cate et al., 2017). Student veterans also have higher grade point averages than other students (Cate et al., 2017). The 2009 Post-9/11 GI Bill provides more financial aid for education than its predecessors and also allows veterans to transfer their benefits to their spouses or children (U.S. Department of Veterans Affairs, 2014).

Veteran Jobs Mission

The Veteran Jobs Mission (www.veteranjobsmission.com) is an effort led by civilian employers to help veterans successfully reintegrate into civilian society. In 2011, 11 large companies formed a coalition with the goal of hiring 100,000 veterans by 2020. They also committed to sharing information regarding quarterly hiring numbers and best practices. By 2014, they had hired 190,046 veterans and the coalition had grown to include more than 170 companies. After exceeding their original goal, they set a new goal of hiring 200,000 by 2020, and as of 2019 had hired 500,000. The 100,000 Jobs Mission website serves as a place where veterans and employers can connect by providing resources and tools for both veterans and employers, including job listings, interview tips, and best practices.

Families Overcoming Under Stress (FOCUS)

FOCUS was originally developed by the University of California, Los Angeles (UCLA) and Harvard Medical School to help children dealing with high stress and their families. Since being adapted for military families dealing with deployment, FOCUS has been implemented at military installations of all military branches, led by the U.S. Navy. Responding to diverse family needs, FOCUS now has been adapted for families with children between the ages of 3 and 5, families without children, and families dealing with wounds and injuries (Lester et al., 2016).

FOCUS is an evidence-based and standardized prevention program for families. The training focuses on psychoeducation, emotional regulation skills, goal setting and problem-solving skills, techniques for managing traumatic stress reminders, and family communication skills (Lester et al., 2016). An evaluation of the effectiveness of FOCUS (Lester et al., 2016) found significant improvement in psychological distress of both service members and nonservice member parents, family functioning, children's behavioral problems and prosocial behaviors, and children's use of positive coping strategies.

Conclusion

Despite the challenges that deployments and separating from the military pose for families, research suggests that most families successfully adjust to these transitions and changes. However, research also finds that some challenges are more stressful than others and some individuals and families are at higher risk than others. Therefore, individual challenges and adjustments need to be understood in their historical and relational contexts. When comparing veterans of the current wars to veterans of previous wars, there are both similarities (e.g., education attainment) and differences (e.g., unemployment rate and suicide rate). Furthermore, veterans' deployment history and adjustment are related to the adjustment of spouses and children. It is still too early to draw conclusions about the effects of recent deployments on military families. Some challenges such as physical and psychological injuries may have long-term consequences. Thus, more longitudinal research is needed to determine how, if any, deployments change life trajectories of veteran families over time and why some families adjust better after deployment than others.

DISCUSSION QUESTIONS ●

1. Many factors can help to "protect" members of military families, some of which are provided by the Department of Defense. Identify personal or family characteristics and resources or factors outside the family that might serve as "protective factors."

2. This chapter makes the point that military families have had different experiences during the most recent versus earlier

conflicts. Identify specific ways that their experiences have differed. What reasons does the chapter offer for why this might be the case, and what do you think?

3. Deployments vary widely in their characteristics. Which characteristics of deployments does the chapter suggest might be most likely to lead to difficulties for families?

REFERENCES

Armed Forces Health Surveillance Center. (2012). Death by suicide while on active duty, active and reserve components, US Armed Forces, 1998–2011. *Medical Surveillance Monthly Report, 19*(6), 2–11.

Baptist, J. A., Amanor-Boadu, Y., Garrett, K., Goff, B. S. N., Collum, J., Gamble, P., . . . & Wick, S. (2011). Military marriages: The aftermath of Operation Iraqi Freedom (OIF) and Operation Enduring Freedom (OEF) deployments. *Contemporary Family Therapy, 33*(3), 199–214.

Barry, A. E., Whiteman, S. D., & MacDermid Wadsworth, S. (2014). Student service members/veterans in higher education: A systematic review. *Journal of Student Affairs Research and Practice, 51*(1), 30–42.

Bastawrous, M. (2013). Caregiver burden—A critical discussion. *International Journal of Nursing Studies, 50*(3), 431–441.

Belmont, P. J., Goodman, G. P., Zacchilli, M., Posner, M., Evans, C., & Owens, B. D. (2010). Incidence and epidemiology of combat injuries sustained during "the surge" portion of Operation Iraqi Freedom by a U.S. Army brigade combat team. *The Journal of Trauma: Injury, Infection, and Critical Care, 68*(1), 204–210.

Belmont, P. J., McCriskin, B. J., Sieg, R. N., Burks, R., & Schoenfeld, A. J. (2012). Combat wounds in Iraq and Afghanistan from 2005 to 2009. *Journal of Trauma and Acute Care Surgery, 73*(1), 3–12.

Bruce, M. L. (2010). Suicide risk and prevention in veteran populations. *Annals of the New York Academy of Sciences, 1208*(1), 98–103.

Bureau of Labor Statistics. (2019). *Employment situation of veterans 2018.* Retrieved from https://www.bls.gov/news.release/vet.nr0.htm

Bureau of Labor Statistics. (2012). *Employment situation of veterans 2011*. Retrieved from https://www.bls.gov/ted/2012/ted_20120323_data.htm

Calhoun, P. S., Beckham, J. C., & Bosworth, H. B. (2002). Caregiver burden and psychological distress in partners of veterans with chronic post-traumatic stress disorder. *Journal of Traumatic Stress, 15*(3), 205–212.

Castaneda, L. W., & Harrell, M. C. (2008). Military spouse employment a grounded theory approach to experiences and perceptions. *Armed Forces & Society, 34*(3), 389–412.

Castro, C. A., & Kintzle, S. (2014). Suicides in the military: The post-modern combat veteran and the Hemingway effect. *Current Psychiatry Reports, 16*(8), 1–9.

Cate, C. A., Lyon, J. S., Schmeling, J., & Bogue, B. Y. (2017). *National Veteran Education Success Tracker: A report on the academic success of student veterans using the post-9/11 GI Bill*. Washington, DC: Student Veterans of America.

Chandra, A., Lara-Cinisomo, S., Jaycox, L. H., Tanielian, T., Burns, R. M., Ruder, T., & Han, B. (2010). Children on the homefront: The experience of children from military families. *Pediatrics, 125*(1), 16–25.

Cohen, J. A., & Mannarino, A. P. (2004). Treatment of childhood traumatic grief. *Journal of Clinical Child & Adolescent Psychology, 33*(4), 819–831.

Cozza, S. J., Guimond, J. M., McKibben, J. B. A., Chun, R. S., Arata-Maiers, T. L., Schneider, B., . . . & Ursano, R. J. (2010). Combat-injured service members and their families: The relationship of child distress and spouse-perceived family distress and disruption. *Journal of Traumatic Stress, 23*(1), 112–115.

Cozza, S. J., Whaley, G. L., Fisher, J. E., Zhou, J., Ortiz, C. D., McCarroll, J. E., . . . & Ursano, R. J. (2018). Deployment status and child neglect types in the U.S. Army. *Child Maltreatment, 23*(1), 25–33.

Cunitz, K., Dölitzsch, C., Kösters, M., Willmund, G., Zimmermann, P., Bühler, A. H., . . . & Kölch, M. (2019). Parental military deployment as risk factor for children's mental health: A meta-analytical review. *Child and Adolescent Psychiatry and Mental Health, 13*. https://doi.org/10.1186/s13034-019-0287-y

DeBruyne, N. F. (2018). *American war and military operations casualties: Lists and statistics*. Washington, DC: Congressional Research Service.

Department of Defense. (2018). *Report on child abuse and neglect and domestic abuse in the military for fiscal year 2017*. Washington, DC: Author. Retrieved from http://download.militaryonesource.mil/12038/MOS/Reports/FAP-FY17-DoD-Report.pdf

Department of Health & Human Services Children's Bureau. (2018). *Child maltreatment 2017*. Washington, DC: Author.

Durdella, N. R., & Kim, Y. K. (2012). Understanding patterns of college outcomes among student veterans. *Journal of Studies in Education, 2*(2), 109–129.

Eaton, K. M., Hoge, C. W., Messer, S. C., Whitt, A. A., Cabrera, O. A., McGurk, D., . . . & Castro, C. A. (2008). Prevalence of mental health problems, treatment need, and barriers to care among primary care-seeking spouses of military service members involved in Iraq and Afghanistan deployments. *Military Medicine, 173*(11), 1051–1056.

Eaton, K. M., Messer, S. C., Wilson, A. L. G., & Hoge, C. W. (2006). Strengthening the validity of population-based suicide rate comparisons: An illustration using U.S. military and civilian data. *Suicide and Life-Threatening Behavior, 36*(2), 182–191.

Fischer, H. (2015). *A guide to U.S. military casualty statistics: Operation Freedom's Sentinel, Operation*

Inherent Resolve, Operation New Dawn, Operation Iraqi Freedom, and Operation Enduring Freedom. Washington, DC: Congressional Research Service.

Greenberg, M. (1997). *The GI Bill: The law that changed America*. West Palm Beach, FL: Lickle.

Holder, K. A. (2007). *Exploring the veteran-nonveteran earnings differential in the 2005 American Community Survey*. Paper presented at the annual meeting of the American Sociological Association, New York, NY.

Hosek, J., & MacDermid Wadsworth, S. (2013). Economic conditions of military families. *The Future of Children, 23*(2) 41–59.

Institute of Medicine. (2013). *Returning home from Iraq and Afghanistan: Assessment of readjustment needs of veterans, service members, and their families*. Washington, DC: The National Academies Press.

Jeffereys, D. J., & Leitzel, J. D. (2000). The strengths and vulnerabilities of adolescents in military families. In J. A. Martin, L. N. Rosen, & L. R. Sparacino (Eds.), *The military family: A practice guide for human service providers* (pp. 225–240). Westport, CT: Praeger.

Joseph, A. L., & Afifi, T. D. (2010). Military wives' stressful disclosures to their deployed husbands: The role of protective buffering. *Journal of Applied Communication Research, 38*(4), 412–434.

Kaplan, M. S., McFarland, B. H., Huguet, N., & Valenstein, M. (2012). Suicide risk and precipitating circumstances among young, middle-aged, and older male veterans. *American Journal of Public Health, 102*(S1), S131–S137.

Karney, B. R., & Crown, J. S. (2007). *Families under stress: An assessment of data, theory, and research on marriage and divorce in the military* (Vol. 599). Santa Monica, CA: RAND.

Karney, B. R., & Trail, T. E. (2017). Associations between prior deployments and marital satisfaction among Army couples. *Journal of Marriage and Family, 79*, 147–160.

Kessler, R. C., Berglund, P., Demler, O., Jin, R., Merikangas, K. R., & Walters, E. E. (2005). Lifetime prevalence and age-of-onset distributions of DSM-IV disorders in the national comorbidity survey replication. *Archives of General Psychiatry, 62*(6), 593–602.

Klocek, J. W. (2008). The physical and psychological impact of your injury and disability. In N. D. Ainspan & W. E. Park (Eds.), *Returning wars' wounded, injured, and ill: A reference handbook* (pp. 50–66). Westport, CT: Praeger.

Knobloch, L. K., & Theiss, J. A. (2012). Experiences of US military couples during the post-deployment transition: Applying the relational turbulence model. *Journal of Social and Personal Relationships, 29*(4), 423–450.

Lester, P., & Flake, E. (2013). How wartime military service affects children and families. *Future of Children. 23*(2), 121–141.

Lester, P., Liang, L.-J., Milburn, N., Mogil, C., Kirsten Woodward, K., Nash, W., . . . & Saltzman, W. (2016). Evaluation of a family-centered preventive intervention for military families: Parent and child longitudinal outcomes. *Journal of the American Academy of Child & Adolescent Psychiatry, 55*, 14–24.

MacDermid Wadsworth, S., Bailey, K. M., & Coppola, E. C. (2017). U.S. military children and the wartime deployments of family members. *Child Development Perspectives, 1*, 23–28.

MacLean, A., & Elder, G. H. (2007). Military service in the life course. *Annual Review of Sociology, 33*(1), 175–196.

Mansfield, A. J., Kaufman, J. S., Marshall, S. W., Gaynes, B. N., Morrissey, J. P., & Engel, C. C. (2010). Deployment and the use of mental health services among U.S. Army wives. *New England Journal of Medicine, 362*(2), 101–109.

McCarthy, R. J., Rabenhorst, M. M., Thomsen, C. J., Milner, J. S., Travis, W. J., Copeland, C. W., & Foster, R. E. (2013). Child maltreatment among civilian parents before, during, and after deployment in United States Air Force Families. *Psychology of Violence, 5*(1), 26–34. http://dx.doi.org/10.1037/a0035433

Meadows, S. O., Tanielian, T., & Karney, B. R., (Eds.). (2016). *The Deployment Life Study: Longitudinal analysis of military families across the deployment cycle.* Santa Monica, CA: RAND.

National Academies of Sciences, Engineering, and Medicine. (2019). *Strengthening the Military Family Readiness System for a changing American society.* Washington, DC: The National Academies Press.

National Center for Veterans Analysis and Statistics. (2018). *Profile of veterans: 2016.* Washington, DC: Department of Veterans Affairs.

Negrusa, S., Negrusa, B., & Hosek, J. (2014). Gone to war: Have deployments increased divorces? *Journal of Population Economics, 27*(2), 473–496.

Office of the Deputy Assistant Secretary of Defense for Military Community and Family Policy (ODASD [MC&FP]). (2018). *2017 Demographics: Profile of the military community.* Arlington, VA: Department of Defense.

Office of Mental Health and Suicide Prevention. (2019). *2019 National Veteran Suicide Prevention Report.* Washington, DC: Department of Veterans Affairs.

Parcell, E. S., & Maguire, K. C. (2014). Turning points and trajectories in military deployment. *Journal of Family Communication, 14*(2), 129–148.

Ponder, W. N., & Aguirre, R. T. P. (2012). Internet-based spousal communication during deployment: Does it increase post-deployment marital satisfaction? *Advances in Social Work, 13*(1), 216–228.

Ramirez, H., & Bloeser, K. (2018). Risk and resilience: A review of the health literature of veterans who identify as LGBT. In E. C. Ritchie, J. E. Wise, & B. Pyle (Eds.), *Gay mental healthcare providers and patients in the military* (pp. 9–24). Cham, Switzerland: Springer.

Rentz, E. D., Marshall, S. W., Loomis, D., Casteel, C., Martin, S. L., & Gibbs, D. A. (2007). Effect of deployment on the occurrence of child maltreatment in military and nonmilitary families. *American Journal of Epidemiology, 165*(10), 1199–1206.

Routon, P. W. (2017). Military service and marital dissolution: A trajectory analysis. *Review of Economics of the Household, 15*, 335–355.

Shiffer, C. O., Maury, R. V., Sonethavilay, H., Hurwitz, J. L., Lee, H. C., Linsner, R. K., & Mehta, M. S. (2017). *2017 Blue Star Families Military Family Lifestyle Survey.* Encinitas, CA: Blue Star Families.

Pruitt, L. D., Smolenski, D. J., Tucker, J., Issa, F., Chodacki, J., McGraw, K., & Kennedy, C. H. (2019). *Department of Defense Suicide Event Report (DoDSER) Calendar Year 2017 Annual Report.* Arlington, VA: Defense Health Agency.

Spiro, A., Schnurr, P. P., & Aldwin, C. M. (1994). Combat-related posttraumatic stress disorder symptoms in older men. *Psychology and Aging, 9*(1), 17–26.

Stanley, M. (2003). College education and the midcentury GI bills. *The Quarterly Journal of Economics, 118*(2), 671–708.

Taft, C. T., Watkins, L. E., Stafford, J., Street, A. E., & Monson, C. M. (2011). Posttraumatic stress disorder and intimate relationship problems: A meta-analysis. *Journal of Consulting and Clinical Psychology, 79*(1), 22–33.

Thomsen, C. J., Rabenhorst, M. M., McCarthy, R. J., Milner, J. S., Travis, W. J., Foster, R. E., & Copeland, C. W. (2014). Child maltreatment before and after combat-related deployment among active-duty United States Air Force maltreating parents. *Psychology of Violence, 4*(2), 143–155.

U.S. Department of Veterans Affairs. (2014). *Education and training*. Retrieved from http://www.benefits.va.gov/gibill/

Wenger, J. W., O'Connell, C., & Cottrell, L. (2018). *Examination of recent deployment experiences across the services and components*. Santa Monica, CA: RAND.

Widome, R., Laska, M. N., Gulden, A., Fu, S. S., & Lust, K. (2011). Health risk behaviors of Afghanistan and Iraq War veterans attending college. *American Journal of Health Promotion, 26*(2), 101–108.

Wilmoth, J. M., & London, A. S. (Eds.). (2013). *Life course perspectives on military service*. New York, NY: Routledge.

Wilson, S. R., Marini, C. M., Franks, M. M., Whiteman, S. D., Topp, D., & MacDermid Wadsworth, S. (2018). Communication and connection during deployment: A daily-diary study from the perspective of at-home partners. *Journal of Family Psychology, 32*(1), 42–44.

Stress Relating to Family and Community Violence

CHAPTER 14

Promoting Pathways to Resilient Outcomes for Maltreated Children

Margaret O'Dougherty Wright and
Lucy Allbaugh

Decades of research have clearly demonstrated the negative and enduring consequences of child abuse and neglect on cognitive, emotional, behavioral, social, and physical health outcomes for children over the course of their lives (Cicchetti & Toth, 2005; Jaffee, 2017). However, while past research often neglected to study heterogeneity in outcomes among maltreated children, there has been growing interest in examining the processes that underlie resilience for some members of this high-risk group (Cicchetti, 2013; Haskett, Nears, Ward, & McPherson, 2006; Jaffee, Caspi, Moffitt, Polo-Tomas, & Taylor, 2007). To gain a better understanding of what might predict these divergent life pathways, this chapter focuses on data from longitudinal studies that have examined a wide range of developmental outcomes. The chapter highlights what is known about factors that heighten risk for psychopathology and behavioral dysfunction following child maltreatment, as well as factors that promote positive adaptation and that protect or mitigate against adverse, enduring effects. Promising interventions to foster resilience and recovery following child maltreatment are also reviewed.

Resilience following child maltreatment is conceptualized as a dynamic, multilevel process, potentially changing over time depending on a variety of contextual factors and relational transactions. Since resilience is typically considered to be a multidetermined process, its presence is inferred in research studies, not measured directly, based on an assessment of both exposure to a risk condition or traumatic experience and subsequent positive adaptation. Our conceptualization of resilience is informed by ecological (Bronfenbrenner, 1979; Cicchetti & Lynch, 1993; Ungar, Ghazinour, & Richter, 2013); family systems (Goldenberg & Goldenberg, 2013; Walsh, 2006); and developmental, organizational, and attachment perspectives (Cicchetti, 2013; Masten, 2014; Sroufe, Egeland, Carlson, & Collins, 2005; Wright, Masten, & Narayan, 2013). We embrace a relational and developmental systems perspective, using the definition of *resilience* provided by Masten: "the capacity of a dynamic system to adapt successfully to disturbances that threaten system function, viability, or development" (2014, p. 10).

We view this capacity to adapt as influenced by many interactions within biological and psychological processes within the individual, to the levels of family, community, physical environment, and the broader cultural group in which the individual is embedded (Wright & Masten, 2015). As a result of these dynamic interactions, an individual's adaptive capacity for responding successfully to threat or challenge also depends on other systems' responses to the individual. This is the essence of a dynamic systems model of development. All adaptive (and maladaptive) behavior emerges from continual interactions of systems within the individual (e.g., genes, physiological, and psychological functioning) with systems in the environment, including other people (e.g., family members, extended kin, peers, teachers) and contexts (e.g., physical ecology, educational system, spiritual community, employment opportunities for the family, health-care resources). This complexity highlights the importance of adopting an ecological, transactional, life span perspective.

Because of this dynamic interplay between multiple systemic levels, there are many challenges in conducting research on resilience following child maltreatment. Notably, since resilient outcomes reflect dynamic transactions between a person and their familial and community support systems, an individual's capacity for resilience can change over time with changing circumstances, the emergence of new threats and challenges, and alterations in access to and availability of social and organizational support (Masten, 2014; Wright & Masten, 2015). Consequently, longitudinal study of adjustment over time is critical in identifying the processes that help to maintain or that disrupt resilient functioning. In addition, given the multidimensional nature of resilience, it is critical to assess a range of outcomes across a variety of domains (e.g., cognitive, emotional, behavioral, social, and health). An individual may be resilient with respect to some adaptive outcomes and not to others and may be more affected by particular types of stressors and challenges than others. How resilient outcomes are defined and the threshold for determining resilience that is used (e.g., the comparison sample and cut-off scores employed) also needs to be stated explicitly so that findings across studies can be compared. For example, Cicchetti and Rogosch (1997) determined resilience for their maltreated sample in comparison to the functioning assessed in their full sample of at-risk and maltreated individuals. Other studies have assessed success in meeting developmental tasks (Farber & Egeland, 1987) or used normed measures of psychopathology and/or positive adjustment (Kaufman, Cook, Arny, Jones, & Pittinsky, 1994; Sagy & Dotan, 2001). Such methodological differences can significantly impact reported rates of resilience (Haskett et al., 2006). Finally, it would be particularly helpful if studies documented whether the child or family had access to and used interventions that might have significantly altered the family's functioning. This would help to identify important protective influences altering the child's or family's trajectory in a positive direction that might account for some of the diversity in adjustment observed within the group.

Rates of Resilience Among Maltreated Children

Longitudinal studies that have examined resilience following severe maltreatment have found evidence for adaptive functioning for some individuals across specific domains of functioning, but unfortunately only a small proportion of individuals consistently demonstrate resilience across a wide range of domains. Rates of resilience vary considerably depending on the definition of resilience, specific assessment measures, and breadth of domains assessed. In a prospective study of a nationally representative sample of children who had been involved with child protective services, Jaffee and Gallop (2007) reported that between 37% and 49% of the children demonstrated resilience in at least one domain (i.e., obtained an average score on a normed measure of mental health, social functioning, or academic achievement) over a 3-year assessment period. However, only 11% to 14% of children were resilient across all three domains at any point in time, and only 2% were consistently resilient across all domains at all assessment periods. These findings are similar to others obtained using longitudinal designs, multiple indicators of resilience, and samples with significant maltreatment histories. Utilizing such comprehensive criteria, only 10% to 22% of children with maltreatment histories are typically classified as resilient (e.g., Cicchetti & Rogosch, 1997; DuMont, Widom, & Czaja, 2007; Egeland, Carlson, & Sroufe, 1993; Herrenkohl, Herrenkohl, & Egolf, 1994; Topitzes, Mersky, Dezen, & Reynolds, 2013). In summary, when a high threshold for resilient functioning is used (e.g., global competence across multiple domains across multiple time periods), a low proportion of maltreated children typically meet the criteria (Jaffee & Gallop, 2007; Topitzes et al., 2013). Many children with severe maltreatment histories, while able to function well in some domains, typically struggle in others and often demonstrate fluctuations in functioning over time and across domains. Of note, rates of resilience in maltreated children tend to be lower than those for children who have experienced other types of family adversity such as parental drug abuse (35%; Luthar, D'Avanzo, & Hites, 2003) and poverty (40%; Owens & Shaw, 2003). Since child maltreatment often occurs in the context of both of these types of family stress, the very low rates of resilience in maltreated children may be related to their cumulative exposure to adversity.

There are many reasons why stability in resilient functioning may be difficult to achieve for children with severe maltreatment histories. Their abuse or neglect is often characterized by an early onset and enduring nature, which heightens negative consequences (Cicchetti & Toth, 2005). Child maltreatment often occurs in the context of an ongoing relationship, which, particularly in cases of family members, typically continues following the incident, allowing for further instances of abuse and neglect. Maltreatment by family members who are supposed to love, protect, and care for you is particularly difficult to understand and assimilate. Such treatment is antithetical to widely held societal values that the family should be a safe, dependable, and nurturing place (Centers for Disease Control [CDC], 2014). Prior research has shown that familial child maltreatment can significantly disrupt the development of secure attachment (Bernard et al., 2012). In such families, the child's source of safety and protection is also a source of danger and distress (Charuvastra & Cloitre, 2008), which can lead to difficulty regulating emotions and internalizing secure expectations of support and assistance (Bowlby, 1988; Sroufe, 2005). In describing the challenges to successful adjustment a child in a maltreating family faces, Cicchetti (2013) highlights how dramatically such a home departs from the "average expectable environment" a child needs:

> Child maltreatment constitutes a severe, if not the most severe, environmental hazard to children's adaptive and healthy development. Deprived of many of the experiences believed to promote adaptive functioning across the lifespan, maltreated children traverse a probabilistic pathway characterized by an increased likelihood for a compromised resolution of stage-salient developmental tasks. (pp. 402–403)

In addition, children who experience maltreatment can also be confronted with multiple stressful life experiences, rather than an isolated instance of abuse or neglect. Research suggests that it is this cumulative exposure to risk that most strongly predicts negative outcomes (Evans, Li, & Whipple, 2013). For example, a child who is abused or neglected by their parents might also live in poverty, reside with a parent who struggles with significant psychopathology or addiction, live in substandard housing in a dangerous neighborhood, attend a school with inadequate resources and inexperienced teachers, have poor access to medical care, and have limited support outside their family. Each of these risk factors might impact different aspects of the child's physical health, psychological well-being, educational achievement, social relationships, and behavioral functioning or may interact in a nonadditive fashion to account for the uneven pattern of adaptation often observed in survivors of child maltreatment. This highlights the importance of assessing intensity, timing, and pattern of multiple risk exposure in determining developmental outcomes (Evans et al., 2013).

Another reason resilience may be rare among maltreated children is an absence of protective factors. Access to and ability to draw from resources, assets, and protective factors within themselves, their relationships, and their connections to other adaptive systems (Masten, 2014; Wright et al., 2013) are critical in understanding variability in adaptive outcomes following maltreatment. The availability of such resources can significantly influence, ameliorate, or alter the impact of maltreatment. Promotive influences (i.e., factors with equally beneficial effects regardless of risk level) and protective factors (i.e., variables that play a special role when risk or adversity is high) that have empirical evidence of acting as either a correlate, mediator, or moderator of resilience following maltreatment are listed in Table 14.1.

It is important to note that, typically as the number of risk factors rise, assets or resources decline (Cicchetti, Rogosch, Lynch, & Holt, 1993; Masten, 2014). This reflects the fact that risk factors and resources are often inversely related to each other and in some cases are on opposite ends of the same continuum (e.g., low and high IQ; poor and high quality parenting; Wright & Masten, 2015). Below, a case example from our longitudinal study (Wright, Allbaugh, Kaufman, Folger, & Noll, 2019) of girls with significant maltreatment histories illustrates the importance of understanding multiple risk and protective factors that might be influential in determining outcome.

Table 14.1 Factors Related to Resilience Following Child Maltreatment

Child Factors

Positive emotion and good self-regulatory ability
High self-esteem and feelings of self-worth
Internal perceptions of control
Interpersonal reserve and self-reliance
Good cognitive ability and reading skills
Academic engagement and motivation
Active coping skills and ability to process the traumatic experiences
Good social problem-solving ability
Abuse-specific attributions that are not blaming of self, shaming of self, or excessively
    hostile toward other peers

Parent Factors

Strong and positive parent–child attachment with at least one parental figure
Positive parental perceptions of the child
Parent knowledge of child development, parental competence
High levels of positive parenting
Belief of child's disclosure and support following disclosure
No continuation of abuse behaviors, abuse incident time limited
Absence of parental psychopathology

Family Factors

Positive family communication and problem solving
Adequate conflict resolution skills
Adaptability, flexibility, stability, and cohesion
Affective involvement and family engagement
Adequate income

Peer and Community Factors

Presence of a close reciprocal friendship
Presence of at least one supportive adult
Stable love relationship history
Strong educational system available
Opportunities for parental employment
Safe neighborhood housing and recreational areas
Availability of and access to good medical and mental health care
Social and organizational support available to the family

Janelle (a pseudonym) endured sexual abuse by her stepfather, which began when she was 5 years old and continued until she disclosed the abuse at age 13. She lived with her mother, stepfather, and three siblings, and does not believe that others in her family were aware of the abuse until it was revealed to a younger sister and then her mother. To Janelle's relief, her mother was immediately supportive, fully believed the details of the abuse, and quickly alerted the authorities. These parental responses represent significant protective factors that may have helped to ameliorate Janelle's internalization of self-blame, shame, or feelings of powerlessness. Despite her fear, Janelle spoke with police and provided them with the information necessary to arrest her stepfather and send him to jail. She spoke with a counselor shortly after disclosure, and this further helped her understand that the abuse was not her fault. Her siblings supported her by distancing themselves from their stepfather. Janelle later faced additional stressors, including the death of extended family members, violence in her neighborhood, and an adolescent pregnancy. Despite the traumas she endured, she graduated from high school, is currently enrolled in college, and has not struggled with significant psychopathology. She has significant concerns about her daughter becoming a victim of abuse but has developed a range of strategies for keeping her child safe and managing her own anxiety to avoid becoming overwhelmed. While she has struggled at times with maintaining developmentally appropriate expectations of her child, they appear to have a warm, secure bond.

Longitudinal Studies Examining Resilient Outcomes for Maltreated Children

Most of the existing research has identified correlates of resilience as opposed to processes involved in resilience. Because we view resilience as a dynamic, transactional process, we believe that longitudinal studies have the greatest potential for identifying protective and mitigating influences, as well as the interactions between individual and environment factors that foster or impede resilience. Protective factors likely vary depending on the child's age and developmental stage, with different variables predicting resilience over time (Haskett et al., 2006). There has also been little attention paid to processes that lead to sustained resilience over time, which can only be accomplished through longitudinal research. Consequently, in this section, we will focus primarily, although not exclusively, on studies that examine resilience in maltreated children over time and use an ecological multisystems approach. For clarity, we will highlight factors that have been identified within the maltreated child, as well as features of the family environment and factors within the broader social context and community (see Table 14.1 for an overview). Wherever possible, interactions across these systems will be reviewed since the manner in which the child responds to and interacts with risk and protective factors at each level of the ecology is what accounts for the diversity in outcomes found among maltreated children.

Characteristics of the Child That Predict Resilience

The child's personal characteristics have been among the most frequently examined factors in research attempting to account for later resilience following child maltreatment (e.g., in Janelle's case, her patience and easy temperament fostered positive coping following additional ongoing stressors). Of note, self-system processes and personality characteristics have often emerged as more central factors in predicting resilient outcomes for maltreated children than have the relationship variables that have been assessed (Cicchetti, 2013). Whereas these latter factors (e.g., perceived emotional availability of mother) have been critical in predicting resilient outcomes in matched comparison samples of nonmaltreated children, they have not always been as salient for children with significant maltreatment histories. In part, this may relate to the large proportion of maltreated children who develop insecure or disorganized attachment relationships with their caregivers (Cyr, Euser, Bakermans-Kranenburg, & Van IJzendoorn, 2010). Consequently, these children might not trust that they can turn to caregivers for support and assistance and so develop alternative, independent means of coping. In other words, while relationships are protective when they are stable and nurturing, many maltreated children lack such relationships and, in these cases, individual-level factors may emerge as more salient predictors of later resilience (Holmes, Soon, Voith, Kobulsky, & Steigerwald, 2015).

Personality factors that have emerged as significantly related to later resilience include self-reliance, self-confidence and high self-esteem, ego-control and a more reserved way of interacting with others, and ego-resilience characterized by flexible use of problem-solving strategies (Cicchetti & Rogosch, 1997; Kim & Cicchetti, 2003; Wright, Turanovic, O'Neal, Morse, & Booth, 2019). Upon reflection, it is not so surprising that these personal characteristics might be more adaptive in the context of a high stress, maltreating home environment where staying attuned to danger, not being demanding, and being cautious and interpersonally reserved might help protect the child from being the target of continued abuse (Cicchetti et al., 1993; Cicchetti & Rogosch, 1997). In a longitudinal investigation exploring personality characteristics associated with resilience, Rogosch and Cicchetti (2004) found two distinct adaptive personality patterns that they labeled "gregarious" and "reserved." Children who had been maltreated, as well as comparison children, who were characterized by these patterns had more adaptive peer relationships than those who were characterized as "dysphoric," "undercontrolled," or "overcontrolled." These findings highlighted the importance of understanding the psychological and biological underpinnings of positive emotion and self-regulation, which have been consistent correlates of resilient outcomes (Cicchetti, 2013; Curtis & Cicchetti, 2007).

Prolonged stress, which often results when child maltreatment is severe and chronic, has been related to increased allostatic load, characterized by dysregulated physiological functioning across multiple biological systems. Current research is examining how the regulation of physiological stress response systems is disrupted by abuse and neglect, resulting in vulnerability in other stress sensitive systems (e.g., the sympathetic nervous system, limbic and endocrine systems, and the immune system; Charney, 2004; Cicchetti & Rogosch, 2012). Though specific research on the range of potential physiological, genetic, and neurobiological predictors of resilience is nascent (McEwen, Gray, & Nasca, 2015), there is evidence for markers that may indicate a resilient trajectory for maltreated children. For example, a meta-analysis found support for a variant of the *MAOA* gene as a buffer against later antisocial behavior among men exposed to child maltreatment (Byrd & Manuck, 2014). With respect to neurobiological predictors, short-term longitudinal findings suggest reward processing in the basal ganglia may be important for emotional well-being. Specifically, among adolescents with child maltreatment histories, reward reactivity (i.e., response time on a behavioral reward-processing task, activation of relevant areas of the basal ganglia) may moderate the link between child maltreatment and adolescent depression, with greater reward reactivity serving a protective function (Dennison et al., 2016). This remains a critical area of research, as a better understanding of physiological, genetic, and neurobiological markers of resilience may be critical for more precise targeting of early intervention efforts.

Many children who have experienced maltreatment have difficulties in school and with peers (Jaffee & Gallop, 2007; Shonk & Cicchetti, 2001; Topitzes et al., 2013). Consequently, cognitive ability and social problem-solving skills have been explored as factors that might be associated with resilient outcomes. There has been inconsistency in the findings and stability of the effects over time with respect to measures of cognitive ability, with some studies not finding IQ or receptive vocabulary assessments predictive of later resilience (Cicchetti et al., 1993; Flores, Cicchetti, & Rogosch, 2005). However, success in school and strong academic motivation can provide a protective buffer for maltreated children and have been correlated with high self-esteem, feelings of self-efficacy, and vocational success (Shonk & Cicchetti, 2001). Traditional indicators of school success, such as high IQ and good receptive vocabulary skills, as well as academic engagement and motivation, help children to function successfully in the school environment (Shonk & Cicchetti, 2001). In the Lehigh Longitudinal Study (Herrenkohl, Herrenkohl, Rupert, Egolf, & Lutz, 1995), maltreated children with higher cognitive functioning in elementary school were more likely to be successful at high school follow-up, although IQ was a less powerful predictor than socioeconomic status (SES) or parenting behaviors. In the Chicago Longitudinal Study, which followed low-income minority participants for 24 years, reading achievement scores in eighth grade were significant mediators of adult resilience (Topitzes et al., 2013). Lower cognitive functioning in maltreated children has been linked with subsequent antisocial behavior and mental health difficulties (Topitzes, Mersky, & Reynolds, 2011). Similarly, college attendance and graduation predict lower rates of violent offending in adulthood, particularly for those exposed to high-frequency child physical abuse (Wright et al., 2019). Such findings suggest that cognitive strengths or impairments might impact later resilience through noncognitive domains, in a cascading effect (Masten et al., 2005). Research in this area has also highlighted the importance of interactions between cognitive ability and other contextual influences. For example, in DuMont and colleagues' study (2007), a significant interaction occurred between the maltreated child's cognitive ability and the level of advantage in the child's neighborhood of origin in predicting adult resilience. Participants who had high cognitive ability and also grew up in advantaged neighborhoods were three times more likely to be resilient than those from the same type of neighborhood who had lower cognitive ability. However, in less advantaged neighborhoods, these variables were not related.

In Jaffee and colleagues' (Jaffee et al., 2007) longitudinal study, child strengths at ages 5 and 7 played a more important role in distinguishing resilient from non-resilient outcomes for boys than for girls. Boys, but not girls, who demonstrated high IQ had a greater probability of being resilient. The authors speculated that bright boys who were sociable and well-controlled might elicit more positive attention from teachers and other adults than girls with similar strengths, as such behaviors may be less expected in boys, particularly those who come from difficult home environments (Jaffee et al., 2007). However, other research exploring gender differences in adult resilience among abused children has revealed that more women met criteria for resilience, across more domains of functioning, than did men (DuMont et al., 2007). The factors impacting the trajectory of resilience are likely complex and context dependent and influenced by a variety of family and social factors discussed below. How these dynamics change over time for men and women and impact their trajectories has received little attention.

Social competence and good social problem-solving skills also enhance the likelihood that a maltreated child will be successful in forming close peer relationships, an important contributor to a resilient outcome. Child characteristics such as good emotion regulation and high sociability (e.g., extraversion) likely help in the formation and continuation of supportive relationships with both peers and other adult mentors (Herrenkohl, 2013; Holmes et al., 2015). In the Chicago Longitudinal Study (Topitzes et al., 2013), peer social skills directly mediated later adult resilience, and the absence of positive peer social skills, coupled with acting out behaviors at ages 10 to 13, were strong contributors to later juvenile delinquency in adolescence and negative adjustment in adulthood. Other work has found that child prosocial skills, along with fewer internalizing symptoms, predicted lower rates of clinically significant aggressive behavior at 6-year follow-up (Holmes et al., 2015).

In addition, children's internalized schemas, or internal working models, regarding evaluations of the self, others, and expectations for future events and interactions also likely contribute to their adjustment and to the quality of their relationships with others. When children have been exposed to a family environment in which their needs are met, they are more likely to develop positive self-regard and positive expectations of others, while negative evaluations of themselves, others, and the future are more likely in the context of a maltreating environment (see Cicchetti & Lynch, 1995). Evidence has demonstrated the relationship between social-information processing biases and both internalizing symptoms and externalizing behavioral problems (Dodge, 1993; Price & Landsverk, 1998). Processing patterns that reflect biased, hostile, inaccurate, or inept ways of perceiving the social world have been related to peer rejection, aggression, and other psychopathology (Dodge, 1993; Dodge & Coie, 1987).

The social cognitive processes that have received the most research attention have been attributional style and generation of adaptive social response strategies. Research that examined attributions of self-blame for the abuse experience found that self-blaming and self-shaming attributions do contribute unique variance to internalizing problems, even when controlling for abuse severity (McGee, Wolfe, & Wilson, 1997). In Janelle's case, support from her mother and siblings enabled her to access appropriate legal and mental health services. Their support and these resources may have helped her to process and understand these experiences, decreasing the likelihood of internalized self-blame for the sexual abuse. Brown and Kolko (1999) also examined the relationship between physical abuse experiences; global and abuse-specific attributions; and level of anxiety, depression, and behavior problems. Both global and abuse specific attributional assessments accounted for significant variance in outcome, beyond that accounted for by abusive parenting. These findings highlight the salience of attributions, which may be as important as the abuse experience itself, in accounting for the development of psychopathology. Price and Landsverk (1998) found that caregiver report of the child's social competence, but not general degree of behavioral problems, was predicted by the degree to which children attributed hostile intent to peer behavior. Maltreated children who processed social information in an unbiased and competent manner were more likely to develop adaptive and competent forms of social responses than children who processed the information in a more biased manner. In contrast to the Brown and Kolko study, Price and Landsverk (1998) found that social problem-solving skills were predictive of both social competence and behavioral problems. Seeking adult assistance, ineffective strategies, and aggressive responses were related to externalizing problems, and ineffective problem-solving strategies predicted internalizing problems. Overall, the findings across these studies suggest the importance of examining attributional style and social problem-solving responses as potential mediating mechanisms linked to later functioning. If attributions and subsequent social responses are a driving force for positive or adverse outcomes for maltreated children, treatment approaches should emphasize social information processing, social problem-solving skills, and cognitive restructuring of attributions as key treatment intervention targets.

Protective Factors Within the Family Environment

While individual child factors have been widely explored with respect to fostering resilience, there are robust findings regarding the importance of parenting practices, the parent–child relationship, individual parent characteristics, and factors related to the larger family context. Interaction between individual child characteristics and the family context are also crucial to consider, as individual level protective factors may function differently within the context of certain family dynamics or parenting practices. A strong longitudinal study (Jaffee et al., 2007) examined individual factors in the context of cumulative life stress (a variable comprised of a range of stressful parenting, family, and community factors). Findings revealed that having fewer stressors differentiated resilient from nonresilient maltreated children with respect to antisocial symptoms, and that individual strengths (i.e., high IQ) predicted increased resilience only in the context of few (less than four) cumulative stressors. With a high number of stressors, these same strengths actually detracted from later resilience. Thus, it is of utmost importance to understand not only parent and family factors that may promote resilience but also how they interact with individual and contextual factors.

The importance of the parent–child relationship has been widely studied, and it is critical that a child have a strong attachment relationship with at least one stable parental figure (Banyard, Williams, Siegel, & West, 2002; Herrenkohl et al., 1994; Oshiri, Topple, & Carlson, 2017; Siegel, 2000). In Janelle's case, support from her mother and siblings was a key factor in determining her resilient outcome. Strong attachment by child sexual abuse (CSA) survivors to a nonmaltreating mother predicted lower rates of abuse in adult relationships (Siegel, 2000) and higher scores on a multidimensional measure of resilience (Banyard et al., 2002). Presence of an affectionate and supportive nonabusing parent was associated with better school achievement among adolescent survivors of child physical abuse (Herrenkohl et al., 1994), and caregiver closeness was found to predict trajectories of competence in social skills among maltreated youth (Oshiri et al., 2017). It is important to note that seemingly contradictory findings suggest that acknowledging a parent's rejection and seeking alternative sources of support and affection also promotes resilience (Herrenkohl et al., 1994). This highlights the importance of distinguishing between a bond with a parent who is and one who is not capable of providing warmth and support. In some cases, seeking alternative relationships may be a better strategy for meeting emotional and developmental needs. Those who are able to recognize and accept their situation and feelings, or are more self-reliant generally, may be better poised to seek alternative stable attachment relationships (Cicchetti & Rogosch, 1997).

A range of positive parenting factors are associated with increased rates of resilience, likely because they strengthen the attachment bond between parent and child. One such factor is the extent to which the parent holds positive perceptions of and expectations for the child. Such perceptions may include accurate knowledge of child developmental milestones and needs or accurate expectations of the child with respect to both successes and limitations. In particular, the expectation that the child be capable of self-sufficiency was associated with goal setting, determination, and ultimately academic achievement in one small sample longitudinal study (Herrenkohl et al., 1994). Smith Slep and O'Leary (2007) found realistic expectations to be correlated with, though not predictive of, a broad measure of child resilience. Attributing blame to the child and use of overly negative discipline strategies has also been associated with aggression by both mothers and fathers (Smith Slep & O'Leary, 2007), which is itself associated with less resilient outcomes.

Ongoing parental aggression, particularly ongoing abuse, or any abuse that occurs when the child is relatively older, is related to lower rates of resilience in adult romantic relationships and risk for revictimization (Banyard et al., 2002) and poorer school achievement (Herrenkohl et al., 1994). Such findings highlight the importance of positive rather than harsh or aggressive parenting strategies. Emotionally responsive caregiving in particular is a salient protective factor (Egeland et al., 1993). A crucial parenting response for nonmaltreating parents is support following disclosure of the abuse, which includes belief in the child's experiences, not blaming the child, and nonjudgment (Elliott & Carnes, 2001). A longitudinal study of female CSA survivors has established that blame, punishment, or disbelief following disclosure of abuse is associated with later dissociative symptoms (Banyard et al., 2002). Children whose parents react with blame to their disclosure of abuse may have a more difficult time coping with their experience and may also have a more difficult time accessing other necessary resources, such as legal intervention, medical, or mental health services. However, having a parent who is supportive and believes the child (as Janelle's mother did) and who can be a secure base from which they can embark on recovery, is a significant protective factor. Research findings have indicated that parent support following disclosure may be a better predictor of the child's later adjustment than the specific nature of the abuse experience (Tremblay, Hébert, & Piché, 1999).

With respect to individual parent characteristics, lower rates of parental psychopathology have been associated with greater resilience among maltreated children. Longitudinal data have indicated that parents with fewer antisocial personality traits (Jaffee et al., 2007) and absence of substance use disorders (Banyard et al., 2002; Jaffee et al., 2007) were more able to provide stability to their children, which fostered resilience. However, it is important to note that findings regarding parental antisocial personality traits in the Jaffee and colleagues' (2007) study were only significant among maltreated boys; girls' resilience was somewhat surprisingly not impacted by parents' antisocial symptoms. This highlights the importance of child–environment fit and emphasizes the differential impact that parent and family factors can have on individual children. Other factors, including parent education, occupation, and socioeconomic status, may promote resilience for some survivors. Mersky and Topitzes (2010) found that lower utilization of government assistance predicted high school completion and college attendance among maltreated children. Conversely, among female sexual abuse survivors,

Banyard and colleagues (2002) did not find that family income predicted resilience, again highlighting that such factors are far from universal.

Factors related to the overall family environment are also widely implicated in the development of resilience. In Banyard and colleagues' (2002) longitudinal study of female CSA survivors, family of origin difficulty was associated with revictimization in adulthood. Positive family communication, conflict resolution, and problem-solving skills can foster a safer and more stable environment, and overall stability and cohesion of the family unit is important for promoting later well-being in a range of domains (Banyard et al., 2002). Affective involvement of the parents and overall family engagement can be crucial. Physical stability is also important. More frequent moves or changes in foster care placement have predicted lower resilience in adolescence and, although it did not directly predict adult resilience, this type of stability also predicted stability of resilience from adolescence to adulthood (DuMont et al., 2007). Fewer placements predicted resilience among adult CSA survivors (Banyard et al., 2002), and the presence of at least one stable caretaker throughout childhood was protective for some adolescents with physical abuse histories; those with stable caretakers and fewer foster care placements were more likely to complete school and less likely to have serious mental health problems (Herrenkohl et al., 1994).

Quality and stability of parenting is also critical when assessing the effectiveness of out-of-home placement. One study of children placed in either kinship or foster care found rather surprisingly high rates of behavioral (64.2%) and emotional (58.6%) resilience. Positive parenting, less need for treatment, and fewer children in the home predicted a resilient trajectory for children with conduct problems over a 4-year period (Bell, Romano, & Flynn, 2015). Emotional resilience predictors included fewer changes in caregiver, older age at first placement, and less need for treatment. For both types of resilience, the child's internal assets, such as higher academic motivation and engagement, more positive values, better social competence, higher self-esteem, and stronger sense of purpose were predictive (Bell et al., 2015). Similarly, positive parenting by foster parents has been associated with less negative affect among maltreated children exhibiting problematic sexual behaviors (Leon, Ragsdale, Miller, & Spacarelli, 2008). Leon and colleagues (2008) also identified, however, that the impact of parenting on sexual behaviors was moderated by parent-perceived supportiveness of the foster care agency; children whose foster parents felt more supported had less sexual rumination as compared to those whose foster parents did not feel supported. These findings underscore the importance of positive parenting in foster care, but understanding how individual, dyadic, and systemic factors interact with this relational dynamic is also critical.

Protective Factors Within the Broader Community Context

Unfortunately, significantly less research has focused on community-level factors. One area that has emerged as significant focuses on the nature of relationships outside the family, particularly with peers and with supportive adult mentors, teachers, or camp counselors. High quality, positive, and reciprocal relationships with peers emerged as a protective factor bolstering self-esteem for maltreated children in the Virginia Longitudinal Study (Bolger, Patterson, & Kupersmidt, 1998). Maltreated children who had a reciprocal friendship were three times more likely to be classified as resilient, and this was particularly the case for children whose maltreatment was chronic and involved physical abuse. Peer acceptance and friendships have been linked to lower engagement in externalizing behaviors among children exposed to domestic violence and harsh discipline practices in the context of ecological disadvantage (Criss, Pettit, Bates, Dodge, & Lapp, 2002). Among maltreated youth, resilience reflected by social skills competencies was associated with lower rates of delinquency and substance use, fewer symptoms of psychopathology, better health and life skills, higher grades, and more optimistic expectations for the future (Oshiri et al, 2017). More extensive peer friendships were also protective against later peer victimization for children exposed to harsh, punitive, and hostile family environments (Schwartz, Dodge, Pettit, Bates, 2000). Similarly, adolescents who experienced maltreatment early in their life but had positive peer relationships were also more resilient (Collishaw et al., 2007; Perkins & Jones, 2004). Such friendships might enhance maltreated children's sense of emotional security and provide a much needed context in which to both learn and practice social skills and receive support and affection from others. This opportunity might be especially valuable for maltreated children whose families lack a consistent setting for positive interactions and affirmations of self-worth. However, other research has revealed that close friends might not always be protective and, in some circumstances, might be associated with increased risk for negative outcomes. It is critical to assess the characteristics of the peers and whether they engage in predominantly prosocial or deviant behaviors. Interactions with peers can provide opportunities for learning antisocial behavior. For example, Perkins and Jones (2004) found that having close friends who engaged in risky behaviors was associated with poorer adjustment, which is consistent with other research indicating the influence of peer group norms on engaging in deviant behavior (Gifford-Smith, Dodge, Dishion, & McCord, 2005).

Evidence of the protective influence of supportive relationships with adults outside the context of the immediate family is also mixed. In work by Cicchetti and colleagues (Cicchetti & Rogosch, 1997; Flores et al., 2005), the ability to form a relationship with a camp counselor was associated with later resilience, but interpersonal relationship features were stronger predictors of resilience for similarly disadvantaged but not maltreated comparison children. Their research suggested that one of the deleterious effects of maltreatment might be difficulty in making use of relationships with other adults to surmount challenges. In the Perkins and Jones (2004) study, support from other adults acted contrary to predictions. Having a close relationship with an adult outside the family increased the maltreated child's risk of engaging in five risky behaviors (i.e., alcohol use, drug use, tobacco use, risky sexual behavior, and suicide) and was surprisingly associated with lower school success. Paralleling the findings obtained with peers, this suggests that for some maltreated individuals, the type of adult that is sought out when support is not available from the family may not provide adaptive guidance or foster success in meeting developmental goals.

However, other research has provided support for the role of outside adults in fostering resilience. In Banyard and colleagues' (2002) study of African American CSA survivors, receiving support from a special relationship in the women's lives was an important protective factor. Similarly, maltreated individuals involved with highly supportive partners were more likely to be resilient in young adulthood than those without such relationships (DuMont et al., 2007), and, in adulthood, married survivors of high-frequency child physical abuse were less likely to be violent offenders than their unmarried counterparts (Wright et al., 2019). Finally, survivors report the subjective importance of such supportive relationships with adults; in the Minnesota Parent–Child Interaction Project (Pianta, Egeland, & Erickson, 1989), women with histories of maltreatment who were functioning adequately as mothers did report that having had a supportive, caring, and nurturing adult present during their own development was beneficial.

In reflecting on these inconsistent and at times counterintuitive findings, what stands out is that these relationships (i.e., with parents, peers, partners, other adults) have often been studied in relative isolation and not in interaction with each other over time. The various capacities required to develop well-functioning social relationships and willingness to rely on others for support likely draw upon the individual's entire history of relational experiences. This includes early attachment and closeness to caregivers, the quality and reliability of ongoing parental and nonparental support, and one's history of social competence with peers (Sroufe et al., 2005). Surprisingly, how these different aspects of the maltreated child's relational history work together has received little attention. Future longitudinal research focusing on how a secure or insecure attachment history specifically impacts subsequent engagement, closeness, and willingness to rely on others would be very helpful in understanding how best to support adaptive pathways to resilient outcomes for these children.

Community-level protective factors that have been studied in other high-risk contexts (e.g., poverty) typically focus on the roles of high-quality schools, availability of extracurricular activities, safe neighborhoods, employment opportunities for parents, participation in religious organizations, and access to good medical and mental health services (Masten, 2014; Wright & Masten, 2015). Since success in school is a strong predictor of positive vocational and mental health outcomes generally, access to high-quality schools and positive school climate has received attention with respect to later resilience for maltreated children. Perkins and Jones (2004) found positive school climate to be associated with lower engagement in six of seven risky behaviors. Moreover, Sagy and Dotan (2001) found that sense of school membership and support from adults in the school and community were associated with greater competence and less psychological distress for mal-treated children. However, counter to predictions, Perkins and Jones (2004) found that engagement in extracurricular activities was associated with more antisocial behaviors in their sample. In a similar vein, Oshiri and colleagues (2017) found that, while more school engagement was related to resilient trajectories in social skills competencies, it was also linked to a breakdown of social skills over time. Similar to findings on friendships, the characteristics of the peers engaging in the extracurricular activities (e.g., aggressive and substance abusing vs. conscientious and supportive), and other characteristics of the school environment itself may be key to understanding whether participation will lead to problematic or prosocial behaviors.

Not surprisingly, children living in neighborhoods with high crime, low social cohesion, and low social control are less likely to be resilient, especially when also living within a maltreating family (Jaffee et al., 2007). In addition, cumulative risk models have been strong negative predictors of resilience and outweigh any single risk or protective factor in a number of studies (DuMont et al., 2007; Jaffee et al., 2007). In DuMont and colleagues' (2007) study, those who were continu-ously resilient over a 25-year period were more likely to be female, had lived with both parents or in a long-term placement as a child, had a supportive partner relationship, and, critically, had experienced a low number of additional stressful life events. Across studies in this area, when children faced multiple family and neighborhood stressors in addition to maltreatment, even the presence of individ-ual strengths was not sufficient to protect against later difficulties. These findings support multisystemic interventions that target multiple levels within the child's ecology. As Ungar (2005) suggests, "Protective processes are not one dimensional, but interact with the settings in which they appear" (p. xxv). The longitudinal research on resilience in maltreated children to date has advanced a more contex-tually relevant, transactional understanding of resilience. However, there is still much work to be done to understand how to foster resilience over time. In the next section, we highlight clinical interventions that attempt to foster recovery for children and families who have experienced maltreatment and that aim to prevent the intergenerational continuity of maltreatment.

How Interventions Can Foster Resilience in Maltreated Children

An ecological, transactional theory of resilience has also provided a way of think-ing about interventions to foster recovery and promote resilience for maltreated children and their families (Asawa, Hansen, & Flood, 2008; Barlow, Simkiss, & Stewart-Brown, 2006; MacMillan et al., 2009). While the target(s) of intervention may differ, these programs typically focus on factors amenable to change that have been linked to later positive outcomes in empirical research and attempt to avoid decontextualized approaches that often have poor long-term outcomes. Because risk and resilience are determined by dynamic contexts and reciprocal relationships between the children and their environment, intervention models have been designed to intervene at the level of the individual (i.e., individual therapy with the child as the primary target of services), the parent–child dyad (i.e., therapy with the child and parents), or the child's community (i.e., the school). Each of these types of intervention will be described, and existing evidence of their efficacy will be briefly reviewed. We begin with a case study of a highly vulnerable participant from our project (Wright et al., 2019) and highlight key areas of intervention that might serve to alter her high-risk trajectory.

Vignette

Ashley (a pseudonym) grew up in a chaotic and neglectful household in which violent fights between her often-intoxicated parents, emotional abuse from her father, hunger, and intermittent homelessness were common. She had multiple foster placements but always ended up back home in neighborhoods with high levels of poverty and violence. She also became pregnant as a teen, which interfered with high school graduation. She had two children with a partner who eventually left her to raise the children on her own. She had a series of low-paying jobs before being recently fired for unreliability and conflict with others. With nowhere to live and no income, Ashley was forced to choose between moving back with her father, still an active drug user and emotionally abusive, or surrendering her children to foster care. Unable to face such a separation, she moved in with her father who frequently threatened to file false reports of child abuse if she did not give him her meager earnings so that he could purchase drugs. A dearth of protective factors in her life has resulted in ongoing struggles for Ashley as a young adult. She alternately feels emotionally overwhelmed and numb and has frequent panic attacks. She relies on her daughter for emotional support, despite the child's very young age. Though she objects to harsh discipline, she has resorted to shouting at and spanking her children to keep them quiet for fear of eviction. Ashley is struggling significantly, both personally and as a parent. Given the precariousness of her own mental health, her significant current life stress, continuing emotionally abusive treatment by her father, and a limited repertoire of coping skills, she may be at risk for abuse or neglect of her own children. There are several promising comprehensive interventions that could help her and that might alter her very high-risk trajectory. In addition to working to improve her access to resources, individual therapy might be particularly beneficial in helping Ashely cope with distress related to her profound childhood neglect, abuse, and exposure to parental violence and may provide strategies for coping with significant emotion dysregulation. She might also benefit from an intervention that addresses the multiple aspects of her life that are overwhelming and provides assistance in addressing housing and employment needs. Finally, Ashely and her children might particularly benefit from a parent–child intervention program that bolsters her parenting skills, supports her children's development, and improves overall family functioning.

Interventions at Specific Levels of the Ecosystem

Trauma-Focused Cognitive Behavioral Therapy (TF-CBT)

TF-CBT is a cognitive-behavioral intervention for children ages 3 to 18 with emotional problems following significant traumatic experiences, such as child maltreatment. While nonoffending parents are typically involved, the primary target of services is the individual child. Through a series of modules, children learn skills for processing thoughts, feelings, and behaviors related to the event itself. Parents are simultaneously instructed in specific parenting skills aimed at enhancing safety and improving family communication (e.g., Deblinger, Mannarino, Cohen, Runyon, & Steer, 2011). An extensive literature demonstrates the effectiveness of TF-CBT for reducing child PTSD symptomatology, improving parent emotional well-being, and increasing positive parenting practices (e.g., Cohen, Deblinger, Mannarino, & Steer, 2005), and evidence suggests that gains are maintained through 2-year follow-up (Deblinger, Steer, & Lippman, 1999); including among ethnically and socioeconomically diverse samples (e.g., Cohen et al., 2005).

Alternative for Families: A Cognitive Behavioral Therapy (AF-CBT)

Like TF-CBT, AF-CBT is a cognitive-behavioral intervention involving the child and parent(s). While TF-CBT considers the child as the target of services and involves primarily nonoffending parents, AF-CBT is an adult-focused, family-centered therapy for reducing child maltreatment by changing parent behavior through teaching skills and changing the overall family environment by addressing family communication and parent symptomatology (e.g., Kolko, Iselin, & Gully 2011). Importantly, AF-CBT has been widely used with ethnically diverse samples of at-risk and maltreating families (Kolko et al., 2011). Both the CBT and family therapy (FT) components of AF-CBT have been found to be associated with reduced parent-to-child and child-to-parent violence; reduced parent child abuse potential, physical discipline, threats, and anger; fewer overall family problems; improved child social competence; and reduced child symptomatology (Kolko et al., 2011).

Child-Parent Psychotherapy (CPP)

Also known as Infant–Parent Psychotherapy (IPP), Toddler–Parent–Psychotherapy (TPP), and Preschooler–Parent Psychotherapy (PPP), depending on the age of the child, CPP is an intervention based on attachment theory that considers the parent–child relationship as the main focus of therapeutic services. Through nondirective, nondidactic relational interactions with the parent and child, the therapist models use of reflective functioning, provides psychoeducation about child development, and explores the parent's own maltreatment history (e.g., Lieberman, Van Horn, & Ghosh Ippen, 2005). Given Ashley's significant history of abuse and neglect and continued exposure to very disturbed family of origin relational patterns, this type of intervention might be particularly beneficial for her and her children. It could help Ashely better understand and support her children's developmental needs, reduce her reliance on them to meet her pressing emotional needs, and provide the personal support and guidance to her that has been missing in her life. Other attachment-based, dyadic interventions have been developed, many of which are similar to CPP with respect to the provision of services and the proposed mechanisms of change (e.g., Bernard et al., 2012; Marvin, Cooper, Hoffman, & Powell, 2002). Extensive evidence among racially and socioeconomically diverse samples suggests that CPP can improve attachment security and organization (Stronach, Toth, Rogosch, & Cicchetti, 2013), reduce child internalizing and externalizing behaviors (Dozier et al., 2006; Lieberman et al., 2005), reduce parent distress (Lieberman et al., 2005), and reduce maltreatment recidivism (Osofsky et al., 2007).

Parent–Child Interaction Therapy (PCIT)

PCIT is another intervention that considers the parent–child dyad as the target of clinical services and includes any important caregivers. PCIT is based on social learning theory, and clinicians teach parents alternative discipline and reward strategies that will help them bond with their child and shape the child's behavior without resorting to aggression or violence (e.g., Chaffin et al., 2004; Eyberg, 1988). This type of intervention might be very helpful to Ashley in teaching positive parenting responses and more effective discipline techniques. PCIT is typically provided in a clinic environment, and parents are asked to practice skills at home between sessions (Timmer et al., 2006; Chaffin et al., 2004). Extensive evidence suggests PCIT as an effective strategy for teaching positive parenting behaviors; reducing observed problematic parenting strategies (Chaffin et al., 2004; Hakman, Chaffin, Funderburk, & Silovsky, 2009), increasing parent emotional well-being (Timmer et al., 2006), and decreasing children's observed problem behaviors such as internalizing and externalizing symptoms (e.g., Chaffin et al., 2004; Hakman et al., 2009). PCIT has been found to reduce maltreatment recidivism (Chaffin, Funderburk, Bard, Valle, & Gurwitch 2011; Chaffin et al., 2004), however, when explored separately, this effect was only found for physical abuse and not neglect (Chaffin et al., 2004).

Nurse–Family Partnership (NFP)

NFP is a home-visitation model, based in attachment theory, targeting the parent–child dyad. It has demonstrated efficacy with individuals whose life circumstances are similar to those of Ashley. It also incorporates self-efficacy theory and an ecological model to conceptualize child developmental needs. Nurses visit first-time moms and their infants in their homes weekly starting during pregnancy and continue until the child is 2 years of age; fathers and other caregivers are included whenever possible. Nurses provide information and guidance on child development, maternal mental health, and the parent–child bond, and help support the family in pursuing their educational and occupational goals and facilitate connection with case management (Olds et al., 1997). While NFP was not developed specifically to address maltreatment, it is routinely offered to maltreating and at-risk families. Extensive research has linked NFP to a range of improved outcomes among this population including reductions in child abuse and neglect; improved parent financial stability, romantic partner stability, and child academic functioning; and fewer child injuries due to preventable causes (Olds et al., 2007). Outcomes at 12-years postintervention also revealed reduced likelihood of youth substance use and internalizing symptoms and increased educational success (Kitzman et al., 2010). Such robust findings have been obtained among racially and socioeconomically diverse samples (Olds et al., 2007).

Incredible Years (IY)

The Incredible Years (IY) series is a set of programs aimed at children, parents, and teachers, that seeks to support child social, emotional, and behavioral development (Webster-Stratton, 1981). Implemented primarily in schools to target classroom behaviors, IY was not designed to intervene specifically with maltreating or at-risk families. However, IY targets emotional problems that are commonly the outcome of maltreatment and promotes positive parenting behaviors that can take the place of harsh or violent discipline. Thus, such services can be of huge potential benefit to maltreated children. According to a meta-analytic study of IY trials, IY is associated with reduced disruptive and problem behaviors and with increased prosocial behaviors (Menting, Orobio de Castro, & Matthys, 2013). The program has also been associated with reduced harsh or physical discipline by parents, increased family communication, parenting confidence, decreased parent psychopathology, and teacher positive verbalizations (Webster-Stratton & Reid, 2010). More recently, IY has been studied in maltreating and at-risk families with promising results including improved parenting practices (i.e., decreased harsh and physical discipline and increased positive verbalizations), improved parent perceptions of the child (Letarte, Normandeau, & Allard, 2010), and improved child behaviors (Hurlburt, Nguyen, Reid, Webster-Stratton, & Zhang, 2013).

Interventions Targeting Multiple Systems

Multisystemic Therapy (MST)

As the name implies, MST is an intervention that targets multiple ecological systems, including the family, school, and other community groups. MST is based on a socioecological framework in which all stakeholders (i.e., the child, family members, case workers) are involved in goal setting, selection of specific interventions to address identified target behaviors, and ongoing assessment of progress (e.g., Henggeler, Schoenwald, Borduin, Rowland, & Cunningham, 2009). An adaptation of MST specifically for maltreating and at-risk families (MST for Child Abuse and Neglect; MST-CAN) has been developed which incorporates expanded availability of on-call therapists, ongoing analysis of abuse, and development of a family safety plan (Swenson, Penman, Henggeler, & Rowland, 2010). MST was developed for use with adolescents and is thus a much-needed intervention to address the needs of somewhat older maltreatment survivors. It might have been a particularly helpful intervention for Ashley's family of origin. In trials of MST-CAN with physical abuse survivors (ages ranging 10 to 17), those in MST experienced a more significant decline in PTSD, internalizing, and dissociative symptoms (Schaeffer, Swenson, Tuerk, & Henggeler, 2013; Swenson, Schaeffer, Henggeler, Faldowski, & Mayhew, 2010). Reductions in parent distress and substance use have also been reported (Schaeffer et al., 2013; Swenson, Schaeffer et al., 2010). Importantly, decreased physical and emotional abuse and neglect have been reported by youths (Swenson, Schaeffer et al., 2010) and reflected in child welfare records (Schaeffer et al., 2013) following MST.

Positive Parenting Program (Triple P)

Triple P is another intervention that targets multiple ecological systems including the family, school, and wider community and is a tiered system of programs designed to support families and to prevent and treat child behavioral and emotional problems (e.g., Foster, Prinz, Sanders, & Shapiro, 2008). The first tier focuses on intervention at the community level; information about typical child developmental difficulties and intervention options is disseminated widely, and parenting discussion groups are formed. Depending on the family's needs, family therapy may be recommended and may include individual, group, or online sessions. Triple P is a program for families of children up to 12 years of age and Teen Triple P is available for children ages 12 to 16. Triple P has been extensively researched, and a robust body of literature suggests that it can impact a wide variety of outcomes for a range of families. However, comparatively less work has been done with maltreating and at-risk families. Because of the importance of community level implementation, population-level data is perhaps the best way to assess the effects of this program. Such findings suggest that counties in which the Triple P system was implemented had fewer cases of substantiated child maltreatment and fewer hospital staff reports of maltreatment-related injuries (Prinz, Sanders, Shapiro, Whitaker, & Lutzker, 2009).

Conclusion

The case examples of Janelle and Ashley highlight the importance of a comprehensive assessment of risk and protective factors at multiple levels of the child's ecology in order to understand what influences each person's developmental trajectory and how to best intervene. Reflecting on Ashley's specific situation, in order to effectively alter her trajectory in a positive direction, it is critically important to reduce the risk for continued abuse in her living situation. Finding safe alternative housing; assisting in addressing her current mental health, parenting, and employment needs; and helping her to find ways to increase her resources and develop new protective systems and other forms of support stand out as potential points of intervention. Such a multilevel, ecologically informed perspective could be critical in maximizing Ashley's chances for a resilient outcome. Janelle's case study reveals the importance of a key turning point in a maltreated child's life—the response to disclosure of abuse. Her mother believed her and took immediate legal action which resulted in cessation of the sexual abuse and prosecution of the stepfather. Janelle's siblings were also very supportive, and mental health services were provided to help Janelle and her family cope successfully with the aftermath of this traumatic experience. Each example illustrates how resilience is dynamic and is negotiated over time, with many possible turning points that can result in significant alterations in the developmental trajectory.

While we typically think of resilience as "bouncing back" from a crisis and resuming our "normal" life before the crisis, Walsh perceptively notes that it is also important to understand the process as "bouncing forward," which involves constructing a new sense of oneself in relation to others and the world (Walsh, 2002, p. 35). Future research should attend more closely to this dynamic process unfolding over time and provide a fine-grained analysis of the complex and interconnected factors (within the person, family, and community) that foster or limit the individual's response to adversity and that influence hopes, expectations, and opportunities for the future. Qualitative research can be invaluable in revealing these complex interactions between child and environment and in identifying important protective influences. In particular, far greater attention needs to be paid to the interactions between the child's personal characteristics (e.g., gender, ability, temperament and personality, coping style) and specific family and community risks, resources, and supports. The potential protective role of schools and other community contexts (e.g., religious institutions, parent support groups, hospitals, social service agencies) needs much more research attention as well. While it seems safe to assume that our intervention efforts might be more successful if they addressed multiple levels of the child's ecology, at the present time, significantly less is known about how to intervene effectively at the ecosystem level, such as family–school partnerships or other collaborative relationships that might promote resilient child and family outcomes (Haskett et al., 2006).

Our review of longitudinal research examining rates of resilience in maltreated children revealed that only a small percentage of children was consistently identified as resilient over time, particularly when resilience was defined across a variety of domains of functioning. While disturbing, this low rate of resilience was not unexpected as the maltreatment experiences were often associated with a variety of other significant adversities (e.g., poverty, living in a high-crime area) and significant life stressors (e.g., living with an antisocial, depressed, or substance-abusing parent, experiencing the violent death of a family member). Findings highlighted the enduring and pervasive effects of child maltreatment and revealed that the majority of maltreated children did have a difficult time recovering from the cumulative adversity they had faced. In addition to the impact of maltreatment on overall mental health, significant physical health concerns, heightened risk of engaging in delinquent and criminal behavior, lower educational and occupational attainment, reduced competence as a parent, and an elevated risk of intergenerational continuity of abuse have been documented in their adult lives (DuMont et al., 2007; Topitzes et al., 2013; Trickett, Noll, & Putnam, 2011).

These findings emphasize the importance of effective prevention and intervention efforts. While the interventions described need more rigorous evaluation, examination across diverse cultural groups, and a longer term follow-up period to document continued effectiveness, they represent promising avenues for intervening in the lives of these vulnerable children and their families. These approaches may offer new interventions that can be disseminated more widely at the community level. It would be very helpful for future research to explore the specific time points that are the most sensitive for effective intervention and to examine what resources are most culturally relevant for specific groups to foster resilient trajectories (Panter-Brick, 2015). There has been relatively little research on how patterns of coping with child maltreatment might differ across cultures and limited focus as well on cultural protective factors and processes (Theron, Liebenberg, & Unger, 2015). Such research is critically needed to advance our understanding of how to maximize resilient outcomes over time.

A key factor identified as very important, is intervening early in the child's life to reduce cumulative risk exposure. This can also create opportunities for the child to develop important emotional, social, academic, and behavioral competencies that can foster personal protective resources. Early intervention with maltreating parents might also result in the creation of a more stable, responsive, and caring home environment (CDC, 2014) and provide a context for positive parent–child interactions. Intervention research to date supports the importance of transactional, dyadic models of intervention and highlights the need to address negative bidirectional parent–child interactions that increase risk for negative outcomes (Chaffin et al., 2004). A shift to a multilevel dynamic systems model of risk and resilience will provide a powerful direction for future research on intervention and help to tailor our interventions to the specific needs of each child and family. Due to the dynamic nature of development, there is much that we can do to promote resilience and help to alter life-course trajectories in a positive direction. Our challenge is to discover what combination of support and resources are needed for each family we work with and how these factors work together to promote and maintain the family's well-being over the long term.

DISCUSSION QUESTIONS

1. How adequately are we measuring resilience following child maltreatment? What types of assessments might be more informative and guide intervention more successfully?

2. As parents with more than one child typically know, children often respond differently to the same situation and parents often respond differently to each of their children. How can this knowledge guide our interventions following an episode of child maltreatment?

3. What protective factors seem to be most malleable? How might this knowledge be applied to intervention programs to promote resilience in maltreated children?

REFERENCES

Asawa, L. E., Hansen, D. J., & Flood, M. F. (2008). Early childhood intervention programs: Opportunities and challenges for preventing child maltreatment. *Education & Treatment of Children, 31,* 73–110.

Banyard, V. L., Williams, L. M., Siegel, J. A., & West, C. M. (2002). Childhood sexual abuse in the lives of Black women: Risk and resilience in a longitudinal study. *Women & Therapy, 25(3/4),* 45–58.

Barlow, J., Simkiss, D., & Stewart-Brown, S. (2006). Interventions to prevent or ameliorate child physical abuse and neglect: Findings from a systematic review. *Journal of Children's Services, 1,* 6–28.

Bell, T., Romano, E., & Flynn, R. J. (2015). Profiles and predictors of behavioural resilience among children in child welfare. *Child Abuse & Neglect, 48,* 92–103.

Bernard, K., Dozier, M., Bick, J., Lewis-Morrarty, E., Lindhiem, O., & Carlson, E. (2012). Enhancing attachment organization among maltreated children: Results of a randomized clinical trial. *Child Development, 83,* 623–636.

Bolger, K. E., Patterson, C. J., & Kupersmidt, J. B. (1998). Peer relationships and self-esteem among children who have been maltreated. *Child Development, 69(4),* 1171–1197.

Bowlby, J. (1988). *A secure base.* New York, NY: Basic Books.

Bronfenbrenner, U. (1979). *The ecology of human development: Experiments by nature and design.* Cambridge, MA: Harvard University Press.

Brown, E. J., & Kolko, D. J. (1999). Child victims' attributions about being physically abused: An examination of factors associated with symptom severity. *Journal of Abnormal Child Psychology, 27,* 311–322.

Byrd, A. L., & Manuck, S. B. (2014). MAOA, childhood maltreatment, and antisocial behaviors: Meta-analysis of a gene-environment interaction. *Biological Psychiatry, 75(1),* 9–17.

Centers for Disease Control. (2014). *Promoting safe, stable and nurturing relationships: A strategic direction for child maltreatment prevention.* Retrieved from http://www.cdc.gov/violenceprevention/pdf/cm_strategic_direction--long-a.pdf.

Chaffin, M., Funderburk, B., Bard, D., Valle, L.A., & Gurwitch, R. (2011). A combined motivation And Parent–Child Interaction Therapy package reduces child welfare recidivism in a randomized dismantling field trial. *Journal of Consulting and Clinical Psychology, 79,* 84–95.

Chaffin, M., Silovsky, J. F., Funderburk, B., Valle, L. A., Brestan, E. V., Balachova, T., . . . &

Bonner, B. L. (2004). Parent–Child Interaction Therapy with physically abusive parents: Efficacy for reducing future abuse reports. *Journal of Consulting and Clinical Psychology, 72*, 500–510.

Charney, D. S. (2004). Psychobiological mechanisms of resilience and vulnerability. *American Journal of Psychiatry, 161*, 195–216.

Charuvastra, A., & Cloitre, M. (2008). Social bonds and posttraumatic stress disorder. *Annual Review of Psychology, 59*, 301–328.

Cicchetti, D. (2013). Annual research review: Resilient functioning in maltreated children—past, present, and future perspectives. *The Journal of Child Psychology and Psychiatry, 54*, 402–422.

Cicchetti, D., & Lynch, M. (1993). Toward an ecological/transactional model of community violence and child maltreatment: Consequences for children's development. *Psychiatry, 56*, 96–117.

Cicchetti, D., & Lynch, M. (1995). Failures in the expectable environment and their impact on individual development: The case of child maltreatment. In D. Cicchetti, & D. J. Cohen (Eds.), *Developmental psychopathology, Vol 2: Risk, disorder, and adaptation* (pp. 32–71). Oxford, England: Wiley.

Cicchetti, D., & Rogosch, F. A. (1997). The role of self-organization in the promotion of resilience in maltreated children. *Development and Psychopathology, 9*, 797–815.

Cicchetti, D., & Rogosch, F. A. (2012). Gene × Environment interaction and resilience: Effects of child maltreatment and serotonin, corticotropin releasing hormone, dopamine, and oxytocin genes. *Development and Psychopathology, 24*, 411–427.

Cicchetti, D., Rogosch, F. A., Lynch, M., & Holt, K. D. (1993). Resilience in maltreated children: Processes leading to adaptive outcome. *Development and Psychopathology, 5*, 629–647.

Cicchetti, D., & Toth, S. L. (2005). Child maltreatment. *Annual Review of Clinical Psychology, 1*, 409–438.

Cohen, J. A., Deblinger, E, Mannarino, A. P., & Steer, R. A. (2005). A multisite, randomized controlled trial for children with sexual abuse-related PTSD symptoms. *Journal of the American Academy of Child and Adolescent Psychiatry, 43*, 393–402.

Collishaw, S., Pickles, A., Messer, J., Rutter, M., Shearer, C., & Maughan, B. (2007). Resilience to adult psychopathology following childhood maltreatment: Evidence from a community sample. *Child Abuse & Neglect, 31*, 211–229.

Criss, M. M., Pettit, G. S., Bates, J. E., Dodge, K. A., & Lapp, A. L. (2002). Family adversity, positive peer relationships, and children's externalizing behavior: A longitudinal perspective on risk and resilience. *Child Development, 73*, 1220–1237.

Curtis, W. J., & Cicchetti, D. (2007). Emotion and resilience: A multilevel investigation of hemispheric electroencephalogram asymmetry and emotion regulation in maltreated and nonmaltreated children. *Development and Psychopathology, 19*, 811–840.

Cyr, C., Euser, E. M., Bakermans-Kranenburg, M. J., & Van IJzendoorn, M. H. (2010). Attachment security and disorganization in maltreating and high-risk families: A series of meta-analyses. *Development and Psychopathology, 22*, 87–108.

Deblinger, E., Mannarino, A. P., Cohen, J. A., Runyon, M. K., & Steer, R. A. (2011). Trauma-focused cognitive behavioral therapy for children: Impact of the trauma narrative and treatment length. *Depression and Anxiety, 28*, 67–75.

Deblinger, E., Steer, R., Lippmann, J. (1999). Two-year follow-up study of cognitive behavioral therapy for sexually abused children suffering posttraumatic stress symptoms. *Child Abuse & Neglect, 23*, 1371–1378.

Dennison, M. J., Sheridan, M. A., Busso, D. S., Jenness, J. L., Peverill, M., Rosen, M. L., & McLaughlin, K. A. (2016). Neurobehavioral markers of resilience to depression among adolescents exposed to child abuse. *Journal of Abnormal Psychology, 125,* 1201–1212.

Dodge, K. A. (1993). Social-cognitive mechanisms in the development of conduct disorder and depression. *Annual Review of Psychology, 44,* 559–584.

Dodge, K. A., & Coie, J. D. (1987). Social-information-processing factors in reactive and proactive aggression in children's peer groups. *Journal of Personality and Social Psychology, 53*(6), 1146–1158.

Dozier, M., Peloso, E., Lindhiem, O., Gordon, M. K., Manni, M., Sepulveda, S., Ackerman, J., Bernier, A., & Levine, S. (2006). Developing evidence-based interventions for foster children: An example of a randomized clinical trial with infants and toddlers. *Journal of Social Issues, 62,* 767–785.

DuMont, K. A., Widom, C. S., & Czaja, S. J. (2007). Predictors of resilience in abused and neglected children grown-up: The role of individual and neighborhood characteristics. *Child Abuse & Neglect, 31,* 255–274.

Egeland, B., Carlson, E., & Sroufe, L. A. (1993). Resilience as process. *Development and Psychopathology, 5,* 517–528.

Elliott, A. N., & Carnes, C. N. (2001). Reactions of nonoffending parents to the sexual abuse of their child: A review of the literature. *Child Maltreatment, 6,* 314–331.

Evans, G. W., Li, D., & Whipple, S. S. (2013). Cumulative risk and child development. *Psychological Bulletin, 139,* 1342–1396.

Eyberg, S.M. (1988). Parent–Child Interaction Therapy: Integration of traditional and behavioral concerns. *Child & Family Behavior Therapy, 10,* 33–46.

Farber, E. A., & Egeland, B. (1987). Invulnerability among abused and neglected children. In E. J. Anthony & B. Cohen (Eds.), *The invulnerable child* (pp. 253–288). New York, NY: Guilford Press.

Flores, E., Cicchetti, D., & Rogosch, F. A. (2005). Predictors of resilience in maltreated and nonmaltreated Latino children. *Developmental Psychology, 41,* 338–351.

Foster, E. M., Prinz, R. J., Sanders, M. R., & Shapiro, C. J. (2008). The costs of a public health infrastructure for delivering parenting and family support. *Children and Youth Services Review, 30,* 493–501.

Gifford-Smith, M., Dodge, K. A., Dishion, T. J., & McCord, J. (2005). Peer influence in children and adolescents: Crossing the bridge from developmental to intervention science. *Journal of Abnormal Child Psychology, 33,* 255–265.

Goldenberg, H., & Goldenberg, I. (2013). *Family therapy: An overview* (8th ed.). Belmont, CA: Brooks/Cole.

Hakman, M., Chaffin, M., Funderburk, B., & Silovsky, J. F. (2009). Change trajectories for parent-child interaction sequences during Parent-Child Interaction Therapy for child physical abuse. *Child Abuse & Neglect, 33,* 461–470.

Haskett, M. E., Nears, K., Ward, C. S., & McPherson, A. V. (2006). Diversity in adjustment of maltreated children: Factors associated with resilient functioning. *Clinical Psychology Review, 26,* 796–812.

Henggeler, S. W., Schoenwald, S. K., Borduin, C. M., Rowland, M. D., & Cunningham, P. B. (2009). *Multisystemic therapy for antisocial behavior in children and adolescents.* New York, NY: Guilford Press.

Herrenkohl, E. C., Herrenkohl, R. C., & Egolf, B. (1994). Resilient early school-age children from maltreating homes: Outcomes in late adolescence. *American Journal of Orthopsychiatry, 64,* 301–309.

Herrenkohl, E. C., Herrenkohl, R. C., Rupert, L. J., Egolf, B. P., & Lutz, J. G. (1995). Risk factors for behavioral dysfunction: The relative impact of maltreatment, SES, physical health problems, cognitive ability, and quality of parent-child interaction. *Child Abuse & Neglect, 19*, 191–203.

Herrenkohl, T. I. (2013). Person-environment interactions and the shaping of resilience. *Trauma, Violence, & Abuse, 14*, 191–194.

Holmes, M. R., Yoon, S., Voith, L. A., Kobulsky, J. M., & Steigerwald, S. (2015). Resilience in physically abused children: Protective factors for aggression. *Behavioral Science, 5*, 176–189.

Hurlburt, M., Nguyen, K., Reid, J., Webster-Stratton, C., & Zhang, J. (2013). Efficacy of the Incredible Years group parent program with families in Head Start who self-reported a history of child maltreatment. *Child Abuse & Neglect, 37*, 531–543.

Jaffee, S. R. (2017). Child maltreatment and risk for psychopathology in childhood and adulthood. *Annual Review of Clinical Psychology, 13*, 525–551.

Jaffee, S. R., Caspi, A., Moffitt, T. E., Polo-Tomas, M., & Taylor, A. (2007). Individual, family, and neighborhood factors distinguish resilient from non-resilient maltreated children: A cumulative stressors model. *Child Abuse & Neglect, 31*, 231–253.

Jaffee, S. R., & Gallop, R. (2007). Social, emotional, and academic competence among children who have had contact with child protective services: Prevalence and stability estimates. *Journal of the American Academy of Child and Adolescent Psychiatry, 46*, 757–765.

Kaufman, J., Cook, A., Arny, L., Jones, B., & Pittinsky, T. (1994). Problems defining resiliency: Illustrations from the study of maltreated children. *Development and Psychopathology, 6*, 215–229.

Kim, J., & Cicchetti, D. (2003). Social self-efficacy and behavior problems in maltreated and nonmaltreated children. *Journal of Clinical Child & Adolescent Psychology, 32*, 106–117.

Kitzman, H. J., Olds, D. L., Cole, R. E., Hanks, C. A., Anson, E. A., Arcoleo, K. J., . . . & Holmberg, J. R. (2010). Enduring effects of prenatal and infancy home visiting by nurses on children: Follow-up of a randomized trial among children at age 12 years. *Archives of Pediatrics & Adolescent Medicine, 164*, 412–418.

Kolko, D. J., Iselin, A. M., & Gully, K. J. (2011). Evaluation of the sustainability and clinical outcome of Alternatives for Families: A Cognitive-Behavioral Therapy (AF-CBT) in a child protection center. *Child Abuse & Neglect, 35*, 105–116.

Leon, S. C., Ragsdale, B., Miller, S. A., & Spacarelli, S. (2008). Trauma resilience among youth in substitute care demonstrating sexual behavioral problems. *Child Abuse & Neglect, 32*, 67–81.

Letarte, M. J., Normandeau, S., & Allard, J. (2010). Effectiveness of a parent training program "Incredible Years" in a child protection program. *Child Abuse & Neglect, 34*, 253–261.

Lieberman, A. F., Van Horn, P., & Ghosh Ippen, C. (2005). Toward evidence-based treatment: Child-parent psychotherapy with preschoolers exposed to marital violence. *Journal of the American Academy of Child and Adolescent Psychiatry, 44*, 1241–1248.

Luthar, S. S., D'Avanzo, K., & Hites, S. (2003). Maternal drug abuse versus other psychological disturbances. In S. Luthar (Ed.), *Resilience and vulnerability: Adaptation in the context of childhood adversities* (pp. 104–130). New York, NY: Cambridge University Press.

MacMillan, H., Wathen, C. N., Barlow, J., Fergusson, D. M., Leventhal, J. M., & Taussig, H. N. (2009). Interventions to prevent child maltreatment and associated impairment. *Lancet, 373*, 250–266.

Marvin, R., Cooper, G., Hoffman, K., & Powell, B. (2002). The Circle of Security Project:

Attachment-based intervention with caregiver-pre-school child dyads. *Attachment & Human Development, 4,* 107–124.

Masten, A. S. (2014). *Ordinary magic: Resilience in development.* New York, NY: Guilford Press.

Masten, A. S., Roisman, G. I., Long, J. D., Burt, K. B., Obradović, J., Riley, J. R., . . . & Tellegen, A. (2005). Developmental cascades: Linking academic achievement and externalizing and internalizing symptoms over 20 years. *Developmental Psychology, 41,* 733–746.

McEwen, B. S., Gray, J. D., & Nasca, C. (2015). Recognizing resilience: Learning from the effects of stress on the brain. *Neurobiology of Stress, 1(2015),* 1–11.

McGee, R. A., Wolfe, D. A., & Wilson, S. K. (1997). Multiple maltreatment experiences and adolescent behavior problems: Adolescents' perspectives. *Development and Psychopathology, 9,* 131–149.

Menting, A. T. A., Orobio de Castro, B., & Matthys, W. (2013). Effectiveness of the Incredible Years parent training to modify disruptive and prosocial child behavior: A meta-analytic review. *Clinical Psychology Review, 33,* 901–913.

Mersky, J. P., & Topitzes, J. (2010). Comparing early adult outcomes of maltreated and non-maltreated children: A prospective longitudinal investigation. *Children and Youth Services Review, 32,* 1086–1096.

Olds, D., Eckenrode, J., Henderson, C., Kitzman, H., Powers, J., Cole, R., . . . & Luckey, D. (1997). Long-term effects of home visitation on maternal life course and child abuse and neglect: A 15-year follow-up of a randomized trial. *Journal of the American Medical Association, 278,* 637–643.

Olds, D. L., Kitzman, H., Hanks, C., Cole, R., Anson, E., Sidora-Arcoleo, K., . . . & Bondy, J. (2007). Effects of nurse home visiting on maternal

and child functioning: Age-9 follow-up of a randomized trial. *Pediatrics, 120,* e832–e845.

Oshiri, A., Topple, T. A., & Carlson, M. W. (2017). Positive youth development and resilience: Growth patterns of social skills among youth investigated for maltreatment. *Child Development, 88,* 1087–1099.

Osofsky, J. D., Kronenberg, M., Hammer, J. H., Lederman, C., Katz, L., Adams, S., . . . & Hogan, A. (2007). The development and evaluation of the intervention model for the Florida Infant Mental Health Pilot Program. *Infant Mental Health Journal, 28,* 259–280.

Owens, E. B., & Shaw, D. S. (2003). Predicting growth curves of externalizing behavior across the preschool years. *Journal of Abnormal Child Psychology, 31,* 575–590.

Panter-Brick, C. (2015). Culture and resilience: Next steps for theory and practice. In L. C. Theron, L. Liebenberg, & M. Ungar (Eds.), *Youth resilience and culture: Commonalities and complexities* (pp. 233–244). New York, NY: Springer.

Perkins, D. F., & Jones, K. R. (2004). Risk behaviors and resiliency within physically abused adolescents. *Child Abuse & Neglect, 28,* 547–563.

Pianta, R., Egeland, B., & Erickson, M. F. (1989). The antecedents of maltreatment: Results of the mother–child interaction research project. In D. Cicchetti & V. Carlson (Eds.) *Child maltreatment: Theory and research on the causes and consequences of child abuse and neglect* (pp. 203–253). New York, NY: Cambridge University Press.

Price, J. M., & Landsverk, J. (1998). Social information-processing patterns as predictors of social adaptation and behavior problems among maltreated children in foster care. *Child Abuse & Neglect, 22,* 845–858.

Prinz, R. J., Sanders, M. R., Shapiro, C. J., Whitaker, D. J., & Lutzker, J. R. (2009). Population-based prevention of child maltreatment: The

U.S. Triple P system population trial. *Prevention Science, 10,* 1–12.

Rogosch, F. A., & Cicchetti, D. (2004). Child maltreatment and emergent personality organization: Perspectives from the five-factor model. *Journal of Abnormal Psychology, 32,* 123–145.

Sagy, S., & Dotan, N. (2001). Coping resources of maltreated children in the family: A salutogenic approach. *Child Abuse & Neglect, 25,* 1463–1480.

Schaeffer, C. M., Swenson, C. C., Tuerk, E. H., & Henggeler, S. W. (2013). Comprehensive treatment for co-occurring child maltreatment and parental substance abuse: Outcomes from a 24-month pilot study of the MST-Building Stronger Families program. *Child Abuse & Neglect, 37,* 596–607.

Schwartz, D., Dodge, K. A., Pettit, G. S., & Bates, J. E. (2000). Friendship as a moderating factor in the pathway between early harsh home environment and later victimization in the peer group. *Developmental Psychology, 36,* 646–662.

Shonk, S. M., & Cicchetti, D. (2001). Maltreatment, competency deficits, and risk for academic and behavioral maladjustment. *Developmental Psychology, 37,* 3–17.

Siegel, J. A. (2000). Aggressive behavior among women sexually abused as children. *Violence and Victims, 15,* 235–255.

Smith Slep, A. M., & O'Leary, S. G. (2007). Multivariate models of mothers' and fathers' aggression toward their children. *Journal of Consulting and Clinical Psychology, 75,* 739.

Sroufe, L. A. (2005). Attachment and development: A prospective, longitudinal study from birth to adulthood. *Attachment & Human Development, 7,* 349–367.

Sroufe, L. A., Egeland, B., Carlson, E. A., & Collins, W. A. (2005). *The development of the person: The Minnesota study of risk and adaptation from birth to adulthood.* New York, NY: Guilford Press.

Stronach, E. P., Toth, S. L., Rogosch, F., & Cicchetti, D. (2013). Preventive interventions and sustained attachment security in maltreated children. *Development and Psychopathology, 25,* 919–930.

Swenson, C. C., Penman, J., Henggeler, S. W., & Rowland, M. D. (2010). *Multisystemic therapy for child abuse and neglect.* Charleston, SC: Family Services Research Center, MUSC.

Swenson, C. C., Schaeffer, C. M., Henggeler, S. W., Faldowski, R., & Mayhew, A. M. (2010). Multisystemic therapy for child abuse and neglect: A randomized effectiveness trial. *Journal of Family Psychology, 24,* 497–507.

Theron, L. C., Liebenberg, L., & Ungar, M. (Eds.). (2015). *Youth resilience and culture: Commonalities and complexities.* New York, NY: Springer.

Timmer, S. G., Urquiza, A. J., Herschell, A. D., McGrath, J. M., Zebell, N. M., Porter, A. L., & Vargas, E. C. (2006). Parent–Child Interaction Therapy: Application of an empirically supported treatment to maltreated children in foster care. *Child Welfare, 85*(6), 919–939.

Topitzes, J., Mersky, J. P., Dezen, K., & Reynolds, A. J. (2013). Adult resilience among maltreated children: A prospective investigation of main effect and mediating models. *Child and Youth Services Review, 35,* 937–949.

Topitzes, J., Mersky, J. P., & Reynolds, A. J. (2011). Child maltreatment and offending behavior: Gender specific effects and pathways. *Criminal Justice & Behavior, 38,* 492–510.

Tremblay, C., Hébert, M., & Piché, C. (1999). Coping strategies and social support as mediators of consequences in child sexual abuse victims. *Child Abuse & Neglect, 23,* 929–945.

Trickett, P. K., Noll, J. G., & Putnam, F. W. (2011). The impact of sexual abuse on female development: Lessons from a multigenerational, longitudinal research study. *Development and Psychopathology, 23,* 453–476.

Ungar, M. (2005). Introduction: Resilience across cultures and contexts. In M. Ungar (Eds.) *Handbook for working with children and youth: Pathways to resilience across cultures and contexts* (pp. xv–xxxix). Thousand Oaks, CA: SAGE.

Ungar, M., Ghazinour, M., & Richter, J. (2013). Annual review of research: What is resilience within the social ecology of human development? *Journal of Child Psychology and Psychiatry, 54,* 348–366.

Walsh, F. (2002). Bouncing forward: Resilience in the aftermath of September 11. *Family Process, 41,* 34–36.

Walsh, F. (2006). *Strengthening family resilience* (2nd ed.). New York, NY: Guilford Press.

Webster-Stratton, C. (1981). Modification of mothers' behaviors and attitudes through videotape modeling group discussion program. *Behavior Therapy, 12,* 634–642.

Webster-Stratton, C., & Reid, M. (2010). Adapting the Incredible Years, an evidence-based parenting programme, for families involved in the child welfare system. *Journal of Children's Services, 5,* 25–42.

Wright, M. O., Allbaugh, L. J., Kaufman, J., Folger, S. F., & Noll, J. G. (2019). *Understanding lives in context: The challenges and triumphs of teen mothers with a history of child maltreatment.* Manuscript in preparation.

Wright, M. O., & Masten, A. S. (2015). Pathways to resilience in context. In L. C. Theron, L. Liebenberg, & M. Ungar (Eds.), *Youth resilience and culture: Commonalities and complexities* (pp. 3–22). New York, NY: Springer.

Wright, M. O., Masten, A. S., & Narayan, A. J. (2013). Resilience processes in development: Four waves of research on positive adaptation in the context of adversity. In S. Goldstein & R. B. Brooks (Eds.), *Handbook of resilience in children* (pp. 15–37). New York, NY: Springer

Wright, K. A., Turanovic, J. J., O'Neal, E. N., Morse, S. J., & Booth, E. T. (2019). The cycle of violence revisited: Childhood revictimization, resilience, and future violence. *Journal of Interpersonal Violence, 34,* 1261–1286.

CHAPTER 15

Stress and Coping With Intimate Partner Violence

Lyndal Khaw

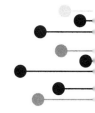

Vignette

Lucy met Dylan through a mutual friend at a party. They instantly hit it off. From the start, Dylan had many qualities that attracted Lucy; he was charming, smart, and witty. After a few months of dating, the couple moved in together. This is when Lucy began to notice some changes in Dylan's demeanor. He grew easily agitated and often blamed her when something went wrong. When Lucy accidentally burnt his toast one morning, he shattered a plate on the floor and shouted, "Only an idiot would burn toast!" One evening, after Lucy came home late from dinner with friends, Dylan demanded to know why she was late and who she was with. Lucy tried to leave but Dylan grabbed her arm, shoved her against the wall, and hit her in the face. Feeling shaken and frightened, Lucy heard him say, "Next time I'll do more than punch your pretty face."

Every day, thousands of people like Lucy experience physical, sexual, or psychological abuse by their current or former intimate partners. The Centers for Disease Control (CDC) describes intimate partner violence (IPV) as a serious, preventable health problem in America (2018), a far departure from what was once considered a private family matter. According to the National Intimate Partner and Sexual Violence Survey (NISVS), more than a third (36.4%) of women in the United States have reported being raped, physically abused, or stalked by an intimate partner at some point in their lives, and nearly half of all men and women have experienced some form of psychological aggression by an intimate partner (Smith et al., 2018). IPV affects individuals and families of every race, age, socioeconomic class, gender, and sexual orientation. Because of its far-reaching impact, IPV poses a high economic cost to the United States, exceeding $9.3 billion in 2017 dollars—most of which entails medical care costs and work productivity losses (Institute for Women's Policy Research, 2017). Considering the social and financial costs involved, it is not surprising that IPV is a major physical, psychological, and economic stressor to individuals and families.

Types of Intimate Partner Violence

As a family stressor, IPV comes in multiple forms and generates a wide range of effects on families and individuals. Boss (2002) describes the gravity of this stressor succinctly when she described IPV as a "terrorist at work inside the family who overpowers . . . and erodes the self-esteem of family members, produces feelings of helplessness and inadequacy in them, and shatters their assumption of fairness in the world" (p. 165). Although both men and women perpetrate and experience IPV, research overwhelmingly suggests greater prevalence and injury rates of IPV among female victims compared to males (Smith et al., 2018). For ease of reading, this chapter mostly refers to heterosexual females as victims or survivors (e.g., Lucy in the vignette above), but this should *not* be misconstrued as only females are impacted by IPV.

Physical and Sexual Abuse

Also known as battering, the CDC defines *physical abuse* as the intentional use of physical force to inflict harm or injury to an intimate partner (2018). Physical abuse includes a wide range of abusive behaviors such as hitting, kicking, slapping, shoving, choking, stabbing, and intimate partner homicide. News and other media outlets focus their reporting on physical abuse because its effects are more visible, making it the most recognizable form of IPV. For example, in 2014, Baltimore Ravens running back Ray Rice was arrested for punching and knocking out his current fiancée Janay Palmer in an elevator. Pictures and videos of Janay's unconscious body being dragged out of the elevator surfaced in the news and went viral through social media, highlighting the traumatic injuries one may endure from physical IPV.

Another recognizable form of IPV is sexual abuse, which in many cases, also results in serious physical trauma to victims. While some inconsistencies exist in defining *sexual abuse*, this type of violence generally constitutes "forcing or attempting to force a partner to take part in a sex act, sexual touching, or a non-physical sexual event when the partner does not or cannot consent" (CDC, 2018). Some researchers extend the definition of sexual abuse in relationships to include an abuser's control over a survivors' reproductive rights and decision making (e.g., reproductive coercion; Lévesque & Rousseau, 2019). This expanded definition is timely given recent changes to state laws that may further restrict women's access to abortions or affordable birth control (see National Women's Law Center, 2019). Sexual abuse in relationships (e.g., marital rape) is deemed overlooked and trivialized—as a matter of secrecy, fear, and personal shame often keep survivors from disclosing sexual abuse (Barker, Stewart, & Vigod, 2019).

Worldwide, approximately 16% to 65% of women across various nations report experiencing physical or sexual violence by a current or former male intimate partner in their lifetime (Devries et al., 2013). This trend, however, does not fully reflect dynamics in queer relationships. Compared to heterosexual men and women, sexual minority men and women (e.g., gay, lesbian) are more likely to be physically assaulted by all groups of perpetrators, including intimate partners (Tjaden, Thoennes, & Allison, 1999). However, gay men seem to perpetrate IPV at higher rates compared to lesbian women. Recent work suggests that, compared to heterosexual and lesbian women, bisexual women experience the highest rates of IPV, with a majority of perpetrators reported being male partners (Addington & Dixon, 2019). These trends lend support to the notion that men are still the primary perpetrators of IPV, regardless of sexual orientation (Tjaden et al., 1999).

Physical abuse victimization seems to differ along racial lines, with higher rates reported among non-White women (Stockman, Hayashi, & Campbell, 2015). For example, the 2010 NISVS reveals the highest prevalence rates for physical IPV were among multiracial women, followed by non-Hispanic Black, and American Indian or Native Alaskan women (Black et al., 2011). Lower prevalence rates were reported for Hispanic and non-Hispanic White women, as well as Asian or Pacific Islanders. However, because victims and perpetrators often underreport IPV, these rates are likely underestimated (Barnett, Miller-Perrin, & Perrin, 2011).

The list of both short- and long-term effects of physical IPV is exhaustive. A study comparing 201 physically abused and 240 never-abused women found that physically abused women have a 50% to 70% chance of increased gynecological (e.g., vaginal infections), central nervous (e.g., persisting headaches), chronic stress-related (e.g., back pain, digestive problems), and overall health problems (Campbell et al., 2002). Effects are greater for women who have been sexually abused, with or without the presence of physical IPV. Similarly, Bonomi, Anderson, Rivara, and Thompson (2007) reported deleterious health effects for women experiencing both physical and sexual IPV, such as higher rates of depression, compared to those experiencing no IPV or physical IPV only. These effects are compounded for ethnic minority women (Stockman et al., 2015). For mothers, experiences of physical IPV before or during a pregnancy is also linked to a host of maternal and infant health risks, including high blood pressure, increased hospital visits, preterm delivery, and low birth weight (Alhusen, Ray, Sharps, & Bullock, 2015). Finally, physical IPV can and often does result in death. Data from the National Violent Death Reporting System show that 80% of IPV-related homicide victims were killed by intimate partners; 77% of these victims were women (Smith, Fowler, & Niolon, 2014). The remaining 20% were corollary victims, killed because they were in the wrong place at the wrong time. Many of these victims were the target victims' own children (Smith et al., 2014).

Psychological Aggression

Psychological aggression is the "use of verbal and nonverbal communication with the intent to harm another person mentally or emotionally or exert control" (CDC, 2018). This type of IPV may include humiliation, coercive control, isolation, and degradation of an intimate partner, as well as economic abuse and psychological destabilization (i.e., making someone feel crazy; Tolman, 1989). Among nonheterosexual couples, threats to disclose a partner's sexuality (i.e., to "out" someone) may be used to further isolate victims from their family and friends (Calton, Cattaneo, & Gebhard, 2016). Recently, stalking is also regarded as a form of psychological aggression. Specifically, harassment and threats through unwanted calls, visits, or e-mails can exude a serious mental and psychological toll on victims (Diette, Goldsmith, Hamilton, Darity, & McFarland, 2014).

It was previously thought that psychological aggression only occurred when physical abuse was present. However, IPV researchers now claim that in many cases, psychological aggression occurs independently of physical IPV, and there is evidence to suggest that psychological aggression alone may be far more damaging than physical IPV (Lawrence, Yoon, Langer, & Ro, 2009). Psychological aggression is the most common form of IPV, with approximately 43 million women and 38 million men reporting having experienced it in their lifetime (Smith et al., 2018). In a review of 204 studies, Carney and Barner (2012) indicate the average prevalence rate of psychological aggression and control is about 80%. However, the prevalence rates varied greatly, ranging from 4% to over 90%. This wide range may be due to the inconsistencies in how researchers define and measure psychological aggression and controlling behaviors in general (Barnett et al., 2011).

Just like physical IPV, psychological aggression produces a host of short- and long-term physical, emotional, and psychological effects that are well documented. For example, Coker, Davis et al. (2002) found that both men and women who report severe forms of psychological abuse are at increased risk of poor physical health and depressive symptoms, compared to those who reported physical IPV alone. Higher risk of substance abuse use is also reported among psychologically abused survivors (Lacey et al., 2013). Diette et al. (2014) found that stalked women between ages 23 and 29 are 265% more likely to have mental health issues than women who have not been victims of stalking. Chronic exposure to psychological aggression also strongly predicts posttraumatic stress disorder (PTSD) experiences (Arias & Pape, 1999) and accelerated cellular aging, indicative of poorer health or greater morbidity (Humphreys et al., 2012). Psychological aggression also interferes with effective strategies to cope with IPV. Coping difficulties may explain why victims of psychological IPV are less likely to leave their abusers (Arias & Pape, 1999) and more likely to have suicidal thoughts or attempt suicide (Pico-Alfonso et al., 2006).

Types of IPV: Making Distinctions

Another issue IPV researchers cannot seem to agree on is the issue of gender differences in IPV. Using findings from hundreds of studies, some IPV experts have argued that men are just as likely as women to be victimized, and that women are just as, if not *more*, violent than men (i.e., the notion of gender symmetry; Archer, 2000). This perspective is commonly known as the *family violence perspective.*

Conversely, many IPV scholars and women's advocates, who support the feminist perspective, reject these conclusions, citing methodological flaws in the gender symmetry studies (Kimmel, 2002). Rather, they contend women are consistently victimized at greater rates compared to men (i.e., gender asymmetry).

To reconcile these opposing sides, Johnson (1995, 2006) proposed an important view suggesting that conclusions made by both the family violence and feminist perspectives were neither totally right nor wrong. Due largely to the inconsistencies in how IPV is measured and how participants are recruited, Johnson suggests that studies from both perspectives were actually measuring different types of IPV. Johnson proposed five types of IPV: coercive controlling violence (formerly known as patriarchal terrorism), situational couple violence (formerly known as common couple violence), violent resistance, separation-instigated violence, and mutual violent control (Johnson, 2006). In this chapter, we will not discuss mutual violent control (i.e., in which both partners are exerting coercive control on each other) as it is not fully understood (Kelly & Johnson, 2008) and lacks empirical work.

Coercive Controlling Violence

According to Kelly and Johnson (2008), the term *coercive controlling violence* (CCV) describes "a pattern of emotionally abusive intimidation, coercion, and control coupled with physical violence against partners" (p. 478). The deliberate use of coercive control tactics (e.g., threats, economic control, isolation) is central in these relationships. In his 1995 review and in subsequent work, Johnson notes that most victims of CCV are women abused by men, consistent with the feminist perspective of gender asymmetry in IPV (Johnson, 2006). Higher rates of CCV are shown in agency samples (e.g., shelters, courts, hospitals) that often report more frequent and severe experiences of violence. Johnson argues that the frequency and severity of IPV may prompt victims to seek help from these agencies in the first place. It is common for survivors of CCV to report greater negative impact from experiencing psychological aggression over physical violence (Kelly & Johnson, 2008).

Situational Couple Violence

In contrast, *situational couple violence* (SCV) is the type of IPV where a pattern of control is generally absent from the relationship. Rather, violence is situation based; it escalates and erupts when couples are facing a conflict (Johnson, 1995), which makes it more common than CCV. Johnson (2006) reported that perpetrators of SCV were roughly equal in terms of gender (56% men vs. 44% women), which is more aligned with the family violence perspective of gender symmetry. Individuals who experience this type of IPV are more likely to be found in community samples (e.g., general surveys) rather than agency samples. Because SCV is conflict provoked, contact with formal help-seeking agencies (e.g., shelters) may not be as frequent or necessary, compared to a CCV case (Kelly & Johnson, 2008).

Violent Resistance

Commonly known in legal circles as *self-defense*, violent resistance is most frequently reported in cases where the survivor is using violence to protect themselves or others from harm inflicted by their abusive partners who perpetrate CCV (Miller & Meloy, 2006). It is important to note that violent resistance is not used by the survivor to gain control over their partners (Bair-Merritt, et al., 2010). As with any type of IPV, perpetrators may be of any gender; however, most who have used violent resistance are women. According to Kelly and Johnson (2008), violent resistance is more reactive, immediate, and "short-lived" (p. 484) in nature, thus does not usually lead to interactions with formal help-seeking systems (e.g., police).

Separation-Intigated Violence

Another type of violence that is not motivated by coercive control is *separation-instigated violence*, which may occur only after a couple separates. This particular type of IPV is unique in that there is usually no prior indication or threat of abusive behaviors while the couple was still together. Perpetrated symmetrically by both men and women, Kelly and Johnson (2008) posit that the violence emerges due to extreme psychological shock or surprise resulting from the separation (e.g. being served divorce papers unexpectedly), and in many cases, the perpetrator later expresses regret for lashing out in anger.

Explaining Violence by an Intimate Partner

On November 27, 2018, *The New York Times* published an article with the headline, "Most Dangerous Place for Women is the Home, U.N. Report Finds" (Zraick, 2018). They were referring to findings from a worldwide study conducted by the United Nations Office of Drugs and Crime, which investigated homicides rates of women in 2017. Of the 87,000 reported cases, roughly 50,000 female victims were intentionally murdered by an intimate partner or a family member (U.N. Office of Drugs and Crime, 2018). Indeed, every day in the United States and worldwide, a woman is more likely to be abused or killed by her current or former husband or boyfriend than by an acquaintance or stranger. Why are some intimate partners violent? There are no definitive answers, but three possible explanations focusing on social learning theory, abusers' individual characteristics, and patriarchal structures will be discussed.

Social Learning Theory: *"His Dad Was Abusive, Too"*

According to social learning theory, almost all forms of human behavior can be mimicked or modeled by observing and interacting with others in an environment.

Some researchers believe that perpetrators of IPV ultimately learned violent behaviors from watching others. In 1961, psychologist Alfred Bandura found that when children as young as 3, watch an adult behave aggressively toward an inflatable doll (famously known as the "Bobo Doll") they are likely to imitate these aggressive acts themselves (Bandura, Ross, & Ross, 1961). Interestingly, boys appeared to use more aggression toward the doll especially if their observed adult was also male, suggesting the effects of same-sex modeling behaviors.

Bandura's groundbreaking work pioneered the way for researchers to continue exploring the strong link between exposure to violence (e.g., through video games and media) and aggressive thoughts and behaviors among children and young adults. When it comes to IPV, the notion of perpetrating violence as a learned behavior is also supported by research. In an extensive review of the literature, Delsol and Margolin (2004) found that approximately 60% of abusive men (vs. only 20% of nonabusive men) reported being exposed to some form of violence while they were growing up. Also, known as the *intergenerational transmission of violence*, there is considerable evidence suggesting that men raised in violent homes (e.g., where they may have witnessed or experienced abuse) are more likely to use violence in their intimate relationships, compared to men raised in nonviolent homes (Herrenkohl & Rousson, 2018).

Abusers' Individual Characteristics: *"She Always Had an Anger Problem"*

Another body of research has pointed specifically at abusers' individual characteristics to explain their violent behaviors, for example, anger. For years, studies have shown that abusers have higher levels of anger and hostility compared to nonviolent individuals, with abusers committing more severe violence and reporting more anger and hostility than those committing less severe violence (Norlander & Eckhardt, 2005). Because anger is an emotion, it is believed that IPV abusers lack emotion regulation skills and, thus, seem to have more difficulty controlling their anger (Gardner, Moore, & Dettore, 2014). Nevertheless, some studies find intervention programs that focus on anger management for IPV perpetrators have little to no effect on their behaviors, as many men continue to use violence beyond completion of the program (Babcock, Green, & Robie, 2004). Thus, while anger and hostility are characteristics of some IPV abusers, the functional role of anger in an IPV relationship is not yet fully understood (Norlander & Eckhardt, 2005).

Abusers' drug and alcohol usage and its connection to IPV have also been vastly researched. For example, Caetano, Schafer, and Cunradi (2001) reported that 30% to 40% of male abusers and 27% to 34% of female perpetrators had been drinking at the time of abuse. An abuser is 11 times more likely to be violent on a day that he has been drinking (Fals-Stewart, 2003) and tends to use more severe violence while abusing drugs or alcohol (Thomas, Bennett, & Stoops, 2013). While IPV and substance abuse use are *connected*, we must refrain from assuming cause and effect. Research has determined that drugs and alcohol do not *cause* people to use violence. Indeed, the majority of heavy drinkers are not violent and the majority of IPV perpetrators are not under the influence of substances at the time of abuse (Caetano et al., 2001). Rather, abusers who already have violent tendencies may exhibit more severe behaviors when under the influence.

Patriarchal Structure: *"He Was the King of the Castle"*

Much of the IPV literature centers on gender as a factor to explain why intimate partners may become violent. Feminist researchers have long argued that the root of IPV lies in a heterosexist-patriarchal system where women are deemed inferior to men, and therefore are at greater risk of being victims of IPV. Historically, marriage itself was seen as an institution that oppressed women; men were socially prescribed the role as "head of households" and held social and economic power in the family. For example, it was a common expectation for women to honor and obey their husbands (think of traditional wedding vows still used today that convey this expectation). In the United States, men were legally allowed to hit their wives until 1920; however, IPV was mostly seen as a private family affair and not a social problem, up until the 1970s when the battered women's movement gained momentum (Barnett et al., 2011). Even so, marital rape was still legal in some parts of the United States until 1993, thus exonerating men who raped their wives from legal prosecution (Erez, 2002). Although the United States has made leaps in enacting laws to eradicate violence and protect survivors, the Violence Against Women Act (VAWA) was not signed into law by Congress until 1994 and explicit protections for gay, lesbian, and transgender individuals were added only in 2013. Unfortunately, VAWA was not reauthorized by the current U.S. Congress and expired in February 2019, which means these federal protections are no longer available to IPV survivors, most of whom are women. This example clearly illustrates how laws can further reinforce patriarchal systems that are still very much present today.

As with laws, cultures and cultural beliefs also play an extraordinary role in sustaining patriarchy. Outside of the United States, a study with Palestinian husbands revealed a tendency to justify wife beating as acceptable including blaming the victim for the violence (Haj-Yahia, 1998). Similarly, Zakar, Zakar, and Kraemer (2013) reported how the notion of an ideal wife among Pakistani men includes being docile and "subject to control, discipline and violent punishment" (p. 246). Many women in these cultures also share these beliefs; in one study of 1,854 married Jordanian women, 98% reported being subjected to at least one form of IPV and 93% of the women also believed that wives must oblige their husbands (Al-Badayneh, 2012). Likewise, Chinese women who strongly accept traditional gender roles in justifying IPV are more vulnerable to experiencing IPV (Lin, Sun, Liu, & Chen, 2018).

Having set the stage for the types, effects, and explanations for IPV, let us now explore how IPV affects individuals and families as a stressor. Guided by Boss's (2002) contextual model of family stress, we discuss various stress factors using relevant information from IPV studies.

Contextual Model of Family Stress

In 1958, Hill proposed the ABC-X model of family stress, which is considered the basis of all family stress theories. The contextual model of family stress (CMFS) is a heuristic extension of the ABC-X model that includes internal and external contexts surrounding the family (see Boss, 2002). A simplified version of the CMFS is adapted for this chapter—in the core, sits the classic ABC-X stress model factors, surrounded by the family's external context. Each factor is further explicated below. See Figure 15.1 for a representation of the simplified model.

The ABC-X Model

Stressor Event (A)

The A-factor is the stressor event, or the incident or situation that has the *potential* to invoke change in the family system. Although the label implies that the

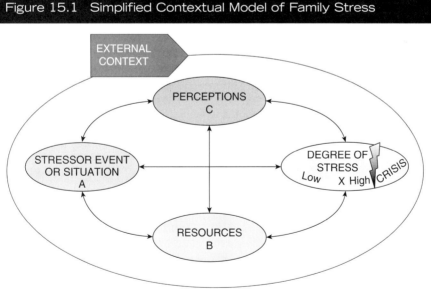

Figure 15.1   Simplified Contextual Model of Family Stress

Source: Simplified Contextual Model of Family Stress. Adapted from Boss, P. G. (2002). *Family stress management: A contextual approach* (2nd Ed.). Thousand Oaks, CA: SAGE.

event "produces" stress, Boss cautions that not all stressor events are stress induc-
ing since what is perceived as stressful in one family may not be so in another.
With numerous physical, psychological, and emotional effects that are well
documented in research, it is clear that IPV is stressful to most families. However,
the degree of stress produced in each family could vary, depending on the *source*
(e.g., internal vs. external), *type* (e.g., normative/predictable vs. catastrophic/
unexpected), *duration* (e.g., chronic vs. acute), and *density* (e.g., cumulative vs.
isolated) of the stressor event. Theoretically, a woman who is physically abused by
her husband for the first time after 5 years of marriage, would likely perceive IPV
differently from another woman who has been physically abused consistently for
the past 5 years of her marriage.

Research suggests that the severity and type of abuse does influence a victim's
response and help-seeking behaviors. Generally, the more severe and frequent the
violence, the more likely IPV victims are to seek help (Duterte et al., 2008). For
example, when IPV reaches a dangerous and potentially life-threatening point,
physically and psychologically abused women most often seek help from legal
and medical support systems such as the police or their family doctor (Vatnar &
Bjørkly, 2013). Comparatively, victims of psychological or stalking-related IPV are
more likely to disclose the violence to their informal support systems, such as
family and friends (Sylaska & Edwards, 2014). These findings appear consistent
with Johnson's types of IPV discussed earlier. Leone, Johnson, and Cohan (2007)
found that women experiencing CCV relied more heavily on formal support systems whereas women experiencing SCV frequently sought help from friends and
neighbors. Indeed, the nature of the stressor event has a strong influence on the
remaining factors in the model.

Resources (B)

The B-factor represents an individual's or a family's assets used to respond to
or deal with the stressor event. Resources range from economic and tangible assets
(e.g., money, education, social support), to emotional and psychological ones (e.g.,
coping skills). The absence or lack of resources may jeopardize a families' ability
to manage the stressor event, placing them at risk for experiencing high levels of
stress or crisis. IPV research has consistently identified the role of social support
as a protective factor in mitigating the harmful mental health effects of IPV (e.g.,
depression) and helping them engage in leaving their partners (Beeble, Bybee,
Sullivan, & Adams, 2009; Zapor, Wolford-Clevenger, & Johnson, 2018). Economic
resources also play a similar role. Higher rates of IPV are reported among low-
income and poor families, and effects are compounded among women of color
(e.g., Black women; Gillum, 2019). Goodman, Smyth, Borges, and Singer (2009)
theorized that when IPV and poverty intersect, the combination of stress, powerlessness, and social isolation puts victims at greater risk of developing emotional
difficulties such as PTSD and depression. The lack of resources and the resulting

social and structural conditions seem central in proliferating the cycle of IPV for individuals in poverty.

Of course, IPV also occurs in high-income families, albeit at slightly lower rates. For these families, having economic resources does not guarantee an active response to the stressor event, as each individual perceives and utilizes resources in different ways (Boss, 2002). Faced with the social pressure to preserve their family status, a high-income survivor may see wealth as a barrier, rather than a resource, to cope with IPV. Consequently, she may be left relying on other available resources, as shown in the findings reported in Haselschwerdt and Hardesty's (2017) qualitative study of affluent IPV survivors. Specifically, themes of materialism, perfectionism, and maintenance of status played a role in these survivors' decision to remain in their relationships. In the end, what seemed most helpful to them in coping with IPV was not their family's wealth, but their formal and informal support systems.

Perception (C)

The C-factor is defined as the individual or collective assessment of the stressor event or situation and is hailed the most important factor in the CMFS by Boss (2002). How an individual or family perceives the stressor event can ultimately determine the degree of stress experienced by the family and subsequently, determine the outcome. Consider again the vignette at the start of this chapter: If Lucy believed that Dylan's actions were abusive and wrong, her subsequent response may be vastly different than if she blamed herself for his abusive outburst. Perceptions of reality can be distorted (Boss, 2002), which is why so many victims' initial response to IPV is to deny its existence. Because relationships are viewed through rose-colored glasses, victims are able to minimize IPV and disengage from the reality of their situation (Shir, 1999). However, as Boss puts it, "when even one family member begins to see things differently . . . change is on the way," (2002, p. 61). For example, in a study conducted with 25 abused mothers, once the mothers shifted their perception from prioritizing the family unity to prioritizing the safety of their children, they stopped efforts to keep the relationship together and focused on leaving safely instead (Khaw & Hardesty, 2015).

Stress or Crisis (X)

As shown in Figure 15.1, Boss (2002) modified the X-factor in the CMFS to illustrate low to high degrees of family stress, a construct that is distinct from family crisis. Family stress is considered as any kind of pressure, disturbance, or change to the family's equilibrium or state of stability. In many cases, individuals and families employ coping mechanisms to manage their lives so that the stress becomes tolerable. Such mechanisms are well illustrated in IPV research. Survivor theory contends that IPV victims actively engage in strategies to keep themselves safe in their relationships (Gondolf & Fisher, 1988). For example, to prevent violent episodes, survivors may use placating strategies like avoiding the abuser, keeping the kids quiet when the abuser is home, and asking the abuser to calm down or seek counseling (Goodkind, Sullivan, & Bybee, 2004). Abused women also use personal strategies like relying on religion for strength and guidance (Brabeck & Guzman, 2008). For a host of personal, interpersonal, and societal reasons, IPV victims may use these strategies to tolerate the abuse for a long time before ever defining the abuse as unacceptable or intolerable (Liang, Goodman, Tummala-Narra, & Weintraub, 2005).

When the level of stress (and the abuse) becomes too overwhelming for the family, it could lead to a crisis. Boss (2002) describes family crisis as a state of "acute disequilibrium" (p. 67), where the family system hits a breaking point and is believed to have become dysfunctional. Qualitative studies of IPV suggest that the turning point from stress to crisis may be marked by an event or a series of events that lead to the realization the situation will never get better (Khaw & Hardesty, 2007). Some documented events include an escalation in IPV severity or frequency (e.g., abuser attempts to kill the victim), a major violation of trust (e.g., abuser commits infidelity), or a direct effect of IPV on children (e.g., abuser abuses the children). Once again, individual and family perception of this triggering situation may vary and could determine the tipping point at which family stress actually becomes a crisis.

External Context

The external context surrounding the individual or family is one over which they have little control. According to the CMFS, external contexts consist of any historical, cultural, economic, developmental, and hereditary or biological components that provide a "setting" within which families operate and manage stressor events (Boss, 2002). When exploring IPV, the external contexts of individuals and families must be considered, as perceptions of and responses to IPV depend on these settings. To illustrate, we once again consider the vignette at the start of this chapter. From the description, we know that Lucy is a heterosexual, young female victim of IPV by a male partner. But what if the context of this abuse was a lesbian couple, or a man abused by a female partner? Would perceptions of IPV change? The answer is yes, and we briefly explore the external contexts affecting two distinct groups afflicted by IPV.

IPV in the Context of Queer Relationships

Compared to heterosexual relationships, IPV in same-sex or bisexual relationships is relatively understudied. Dubbing them as "invisible victims," a study by Messinger (2011) found that being gay, lesbian, or bisexual increases the likelihood of experiencing all forms of IPV. Rohrbaugh's (2006) review of same-sex IPV studies over 3 decades suggests that IPV occurs in approximately 12% of all same-sex relationships. Gay, lesbian, or bisexual IPV victims experience violence within the cultural and historical context of heterosexism, a social belief system of privilege that favors and assumes heterosexuality. An example of heterosexism is the default perception that in any given relationship, the abuser is always male and the victim is always female. Coupled with homophobia (i.e., a negative prejudice toward queer populations) gay, lesbian, and bisexual individuals and their families who experience IPV find their experiences minimized, ignored, or even used against them. In the United States, shelters designated for queer survivors are uncommon, thus explaining the notably low number of same-sex or bisexual IPV victims who seek help from formal agencies (National Coalition of Anti-Violence Programs, 2013).

Another important external context to consider is the historical (and legal) context of same-sex partnerships in the United States. Because of heterosexism, the rights for same-sex couples to legally marry and have children have historically been limited. Even though the Supreme Court passed marriage equality in the United States in June 2015, technically granting civil protection to IPV victims in same-sex marriages, there are still state-by-state variations in how IPV among queer individuals is perceived and attended to. For example, as of August 2019, all states have employed gender-neutral domestic violence statutes except for North Carolina (Network for Public Health Law, 2019). Given precarious legal standings, queer survivors may mistrust formal support systems and cope with IPV on their own (Hardesty, Oswald, Khaw, & Fonseca, 2011).

IPV in the Context of Male Victimization

The growing body of research on male victims of IPV suggests that the experiences of men and their responses to IPV occur within the sociocultural confines of rigid gender roles and expectations (Kimmel, 2002). In particular, our society assumes that men, being the physically larger sex, should have the ability to defend themselves in an IPV situation and thus, should not be victims. As Howard and Hollander (1996) surmised, "victimization, particularly in relation to physical abuse, seems so deeply coded as a female experience in contemporary Western society that a man who finds himself victimized is literally 'feminized' . . ." (p. 86). Indeed, male IPV victims are socially isolated, stigmatized, and perceived as weak, vulnerable, or effeminate (Allen-Collinson, 2010).

Research suggests that these cultural and biological contexts play an important role in men's help-seeking patterns. For example, Tsui, Cheung, and Leung (2010) found that male IPV victims generally hide their victim identity and very few use formal support resources because they do not meet male survivors' needs (e.g., most shelters still primarily serve only female clients). Consistent with the social stigma of being a male victim, men often cite shame and embarrassment as a prominent reason for not seeking help (Tsui et al., 2010). Studies also reveal the legal barriers to help-seeking for male IPV victims. In a review of the criminal justice literature, Shuler (2010) noted male victims' experiences of unfair treatment by heterosexist law enforcement and court systems, including being arrested for IPV, facing disbelief of their abuse allegations, and female abusers receiving lenient sentences or case dismissals by judges.

Leaving Abusive Partners and Postseparation Coping

In the final part of this chapter, I highlight the strength and resilience of IPV survivors in leaving their abusive relationships and maintaining separation from their former partners. I also briefly discuss research on the process of leaving, followed by the coping strategies used by survivors to manage abusers' intrusion and maintain safety beyond separation. The chapter concludes with an overview of key interventions with abused IPV individuals and their families.

Leaving as a Process

Research suggests that most victims do eventually leave their abusers, often over multiple attempts (Khaw & Hardesty, 2015). This process is emotionally and physically exhausting, making it a stressor that potentially creates stress or incites a family crisis. Consistent with Boss's (2002) interpretation of the CMFS, external (e.g., cultural context) and internal stressors (e.g., fear of abusers) interact with coping resources to moderate and predict responses in the process of leaving (Anderson & Saunders, 2003). Leaving may also lead to crisis, for example, about two in five women report that IPV became worse when they tried to end the relationship (Goodkind et al., 2004) and the risk of intimate partner homicide increases at this point (Campbell et al., 2003). Over time, however, leaving an abusive partner is associated with better psychological wellbeing (Anderson & Saunders, 2003); as survivors regain a sense of agency and self-worth, they generally report better health outcomes compared to women who remain in IPV relationships (Campbell & Soeken, 1999).

Leaving an abusive partner is a process that involves multiple stages, rather than a single isolated event (Khaw & Hardesty, 2007). As shown in Table 15.1, a number of qualitative studies have found that the experience of leaving an abusive partner frequently takes place within a stage-based process. The first stage(s) usually consists of survivors initially coping with IPV by tolerating or denying the violence and trying to appease abusers (Landenburger, 1989). However, once they recognize the abuse or see the effects of IPV on their family, they begin to emotionally and physically separate from their partners and the relationship (Merritt-Gray & Wuest, 1995; Moss, Pitula, Campbell, & Halstead, 1997). In postseparation, they attempt to carry on by actively maintaining separation from their former partners (Taylor, 2002).

Table 15.1 Research on the Process of Leaving

Research on the Process of Leaving (adapted from Khaw & Hardesty, 2007)

Study	Stages of Leaving	Description of Women's Responses
Landenburger (1989)	Binding Enduring Disengaging Recovering	Tries to make things work and appease abuser Tolerates abuse and self-blames Labels her situation as abusive and leaves Remains separated from the abuser
Merritt-Gray & Wuest (1995)	Counteracting Abuse Breaking Free Not Going Back Moving On	Refuses to leave Leaves the abuser and becomes a survivor Remains separated from the abuser Removed from the abuse but continues reclaiming self and her identity
Moss, Pitula, Campbell, & Halstead (1997)	Being In Getting Out Going On	Endures the abuse using several coping mechanisms (e.g., denial) Recognizes the abuse and leaves Grieves the loss of identities, relationships, and trust in others
Taylor (2002)	Defining Moments Moving Away Moving On	Disengages from the abuse and leaves Distances herself from the abuser Maintains separation from the abuser

Source: Adapted from Khaw, L., & Hardesty, J. L. (2007). Theorizing the process of leaving: Turning points and trajectories in the stages of change model. *Family Relations, 56*(4), 413–425.

Postseparation Coping

One common misconception is that after women leave their abusive partners, the abuse ends. Research shows this is *not* the case; even in postseparation, abused women are still at high risk for IPV (see Walker, Logan, Jordan, and Campbell, 2004). Fleury, Sullivan, and Bybee (2000) noted that 1 in 3 women in their study experienced an assault at least once by their ex-partner after leaving; about 72% of these assaults were severe and lethal, such as being kicked, choked, raped, or stabbed. Stalking is another tactic used by abusers during separation, especially when more severe IPV was experienced during the relationship (Senkans, McEwan, & Ogloff, 2017). Indeed, IPV may in fact escalate after separation (Fleury et al., 2000).

Coping with the aftermath of IPV and with the process of leaving can be a significant challenge. Quite often, abusers maintain a presence in survivors' lives because of coparenting (Walker et al., 2004). In a study involving 19 mothers who divorced their abusive husbands, Hardesty and Ganong (2006) found that fear of the abuser, pragmatic reasons (e.g., financial demands), and family ideology (e.g., belief that their children needed a father) drove mothers to settle for dual custody arrangements that allowed abusers to remain involved in family life. As a result, these abusers continued to exert control over their former partners. Other studies, such as Wuest, Ford-Gilboe, Merritt-Gray, and Berman (2003) and Khaw and Hardesty (2015) report parallel observations of abusers controlling women's lives postseparation, either through direct (e.g., verbally abusing mothers while exchanging children for visitations) or indirect behaviors (e.g., making false allegations of mothers abusing their children in court). Wuest and colleagues (2003) identify this type of unwanted presence as intrusion, which interferes with mothers and children's physical, psychological, and mental health. Intrusion also impedes coping and hinders women's plans to move on and gain closure from their past (Khaw & Hardesty, 2015).

To manage and resist abusers' postseparation intrusion, women initiate strategies that center on either setting rigid family boundaries or renegotiating new ones. One strategy is to set rigid boundaries and exclude ex-partners from their new lives (Khaw & Hardesty, 2015). Specifically, these women reinforce physical limitations (e.g., telling the abuser to stay away), seek protective orders, and use third parties to avoid direct contact with ex-partners. However, many mothers view father involvement as important for children's development and thus, continue to coparent with their ex-partners. In these cases, family boundaries were renegotiated by women so that ex-partners continued to be a part of their children's lives, but did not overlap with theirs (e.g., having two separate birthday parties for a child; Khaw & Hardesty, 2015). Either way, efforts to renegotiate or set rigid boundaries help women regain a sense of control as they keep their former partners out of their lives as much as possible (Hardesty & Ganong, 2006).

Interventions for IPV

Given the scope and complexity of IPV, it is important to consider some key interventions that are available to victims and families. When an IPV victim seeks help from formal support systems, a domestic violence shelter is usually their first point of contact. According to the National Network to End Domestic Violence (2017), there were 1,873 shelters in the United States serving almost 72,245 victims (both adults and children) in *one* day. The need is great. Shelters not only provide safety and refuge from abusive homes, they also offer nonresidential services such as support and advocacy for legal cases, children's programs, and individual or group counseling. Research suggests that women who spend at least one night in a shelter and are exposed to ongoing advocacy and counseling services report less repeated IPV incidents and an improved quality of life (Wathen & McMillan, 2003). Further, interactions with other shelter residents provide survivors with valuable social support from other fellow survivors of IPV (Sullivan, 2018). Another important service commonly offered by shelters is safety-planning, where IPV victims get help in developing an individualized plan to keep themselves and their children safe (Murray & Graves, 2013; Sullivan, 2018).

In situations where victims must make a spontaneous decision to leave, quick and appropriate emergency responses by "front line" professionals (e.g., law enforcement and medical staff) are crucial to ensure the safety of victims and their families. In a nationwide study of over 14,000 law enforcement agencies, Townsend, Hunt, Kuck, and Baxter (2005) reported most police departments in the United States have established written protocols for responding to emergency IPV calls, and increasingly, more law enforcement offices are requiring officers and emergency dispatchers to receive specialized IPV training. However, the same report also notes that many police departments do not include same-sex or dating relationships in their written protocols, which invariably excludes some victims from getting the help or protection they need. Similarly, medical professionals are in a unique position to detect IPV and respond to patients' disclosure (Cronholm, Fogarty, Ambuel, & Harrison, 2011). Whether a victim goes in for a routine medical examination or to seek treatment for their IPV-related injuries, a physician or nurse may be the first person the victim has ever spoken to about IPV. In this scenario, it is critical that questioning and screening for IPV is performed in a nonjudgmental and respectful way, as an inappropriate response (or nonresponse) to disclosure may lead to victims' perpetual mistrust of formal support systems (Cronholm et al., 2011; Murray & Graves, 2013). A medical professional's nonresponse or lack of IPV screening can be viewed as a "missed opportunity" (p. 445) to document IPV and subsequently provide resources and support that can help survivors achieve safety (Coker, Bethea, Smith, Fadden, & Brandt, 2002).

While IPV interventions play a crucial role in keeping individuals and families safe, focusing on IPV *prevention* is also a valuable goal (CDC, 2018). As discussed earlier, violence may be a socially learned behavior. Therefore, promoting a healthy, respectful, and nonviolent model of intimate relationships through prevention education should theoretically reduce the occurrence of IPV over time. For example, research indicates that prevention programs that target adolescents who are most at risk for IPV (e.g., inner-city adolescents) are successful in reducing the rates of both IPV perpetration and victimization (Langhinrichsen-Rohling & Turner, 2012). When it comes to addressing a social problem like IPV, an ounce of prevention may indeed yield a pound of cure.

DISCUSSION QUESTIONS

1. The chapter discussed three possible explanations for why some intimate partners are violent: social learning, individual characteristics, and patriarchal structure. Using the contextual model of family stress (Figure 15.1), consider how each explanation may play a role in how a survivor perceives, and responds to the stressor event "A" (i.e., IPV).

2. What are some reasons why survivors of IPV stay in their relationships for a long time, sometimes even years?

3. Pretend that Lucy, in the vignette at the start of the chapter, is your best friend. She chose to confide in you about her abusive relationship with Dylan. How would you respond and what are some things you can do to support and empower Lucy?

REFERENCES

Addington, L., & Dixon, E. (2019). *Intimate partner violence involving lesbian, gay and bisexual individuals: A look at national data* [Webinar slides]. Retrieved from https://ncvc.dspacedirect.org/handle/20.500.11990/1278

Al-Badayneh, D. M. (2012). Violence against women in Jordan. *Journal of Family Violence, 27,* 369–379.

Alhusen, J. L., Ray, E., Sharps, P., & Bullock, L. (2015). Intimate partner violence during pregnancy: Maternal and neonatal outcomes. *Journal of Women's Health, 24*(1), 100–106.

Allen-Collinson, J. (2010). A marked man: Female-perpetrated intimate partner abuse. *International Journal of Men's Health, 8*(1), 22–40.

Anderson, D. K., & Saunders, D. G. (2003). Leaving an abusive partner: An empirical review of predictors, the process of leaving, and psychological well-being. *Trauma, Violence, & Abuse, 4*(2), 163–191.

Archer, J. (2000). Sex differences in aggression between heterosexual partners: A meta-analytic review. *Psychological Bulletin, 126,* 651–680.

Arias, I., & Pape, K. T. (1999). Psychological abuse: Implications for adjustment and commitment to leave violent partners. *Violence & Victims, 14*(1), 55–67.

Babcock, J. C., Green, C. E., & Robie, C. (2004). Does batterers' treatment work? A meta-analytic review of domestic violence treatment. *Clinical Psychology Review, 23,* 1023–1053.

Bair-Merritt, M. H., Shea Crowne, S., Thompson, D. A., Sibinga, E., Trent, M., & Campbell, J. (2010). Why do women use intimate partner violence? A systematic review of women's motivations. *Trauma, Violence, & Abuse, 11*(4), 178–189.

Bandura, A., Ross, D., & Ross, S. A. (1961). Transmission of aggression through imitation of aggressive models. *The Journal of Abnormal and Social Psychology, 63*(3), 575–582.

Barker, L. C., Stewart, D. E., & Vigod, S. N. (2019). Intimate partner sexual violence: An often overlooked problem. *Journal of Women's Health, 28*(3), 363–374.

Barnett, O. W., Miller-Perrin, C. L., & Perrin, R. D. (2011). *Family violence across the lifespan: An introduction* (3rd ed.). Thousand Oaks, CA: SAGE.

Beeble, M. L., Bybee, D., Sullivan, C. M., & Adams, A. E. (2009). Main, mediating, and moderating effects of social support on the well-being of survivors of intimate partner violence across 2 years. *Journal of Consulting and Clinical Psychology, 77*(4), 718–729.

Black, M. C., Basile, K. C., Breiding, M. J., Smith, S. G., Walters, M. L., Merrick, M. T., Chen, J., & Stevens, M. R. (2011). *The National Intimate Partner and Sexual Violence Survey (NISVS): 2010 summary report.* Atlanta, GA: Centers for Disease Control and Prevention.

Bonomi, A. E., Anderson, M. L., Rivara, F. P., & Thompson, R. S. (2007). Health outcomes in women with physical and sexual intimate partner violence exposure. *Journal of Women's Health, 16*(7), 987–997.

Boss, P. G. (2002). *Family stress management: A contextual approach* (2nd ed.). Thousand Oaks, CA: SAGE.

Brabeck, K. M., & Guzman, M. R. (2008). Frequency and perceived effectiveness of strategies to survive abuse employed by battered Mexican-origin women. *Violence Against Women, 14*(11), 1274–1294.

Caetano, R., Schafer, J., & Cunradi, C. B. (2001). Alcohol-related intimate partner violence among White, Black, and Hispanic couples in the United States. *Alcohol Research and Health, 25*(1), 58–65.

Calton, J. M., Cattaneo, L. B., & Gebhard, K. T. (2016). Barriers to help seeking for lesbian, gay, bisexual, transgender, and queer survivors of intimate partner violence. *Trauma, Violence, & Abuse, 17*(5), 585–600.

Campbell, J., Jones, A. S., Dienemann, J., Kub, J., Schollenberger, J., O'Campo, . . . & Wynne, C. (2002). Intimate partner violence and physical health consequences. *Archives of Internal Medicine, 162*(10), 1157–1163.

Campbell, J. C., & Soeken, K. L. (1999). Women's responses to battering over time: An analysis of change. *Journal of Interpersonal Violence, 14*(1), 21–40.

Campbell, J. C., Webster, D., Koziol-McLain, J., Block, C., Campbell, D., Curry, M. A., . . . & Laughon, K. (2003). Risk factors for femicide in abusive relationships: Results from a multisite case control study. *American Journal of Public Health, 93*(7), 1089–1097. http://dx.doi.org/10.2105/AJPH.93.7.1089

Carney, M. M., & Barner, J. R. (2012). Prevalence of partner abuse: Rates of emotional abuse and control. *Partner Abuse, 3*(3), 286–335.

Center for Disease Control and Prevention. (2018, October 23). *Intimate partner violence.* Retrieved from https://www.cdc.gov/violenceprevention/intimatepartnerviolence/index.html

Coker, A. L., Bethea, L., Smith, P. H., Fadden, M. K., & Brandt, H. M. (2002). Missed opportunities: Intimate partner violence in family practice settings. *Preventive Medicine, 34*(4), 445–454.

Coker, A. L., Davis, K. E., Arias, I., Desai, S., Sanderson, M., Brandt, H. M., & Smith, P. H. (2002). Physical and mental health effects of intimate partner violence for men and women. *American Journal of Preventive Medicine, 23*(4), 260–268.

Cronholm, P. F., Fogarty, C. T., Ambuel, B., & Harrison, S. L. (2011). Intimate partner violence. *American Family Physician, 83*(10), 1165–1172.

Delsol, C., & Margolin, G. (2004). The role of family-of-origin violence in men's marital violence perpetration. *Clinical Psychology Review, 24*(1), 99–122.

Devries, K. M., Mak, J. Y., Garcia-Moreno, C., Petzold, M., Child, J. C., Falder, G., . . . & Pallitto, C. (2013). The global prevalence of intimate partner violence against women. *Science, 340*(6140), 1527–1528.

Diette, T. M., Goldsmith, A. H., Hamilton, D., Darity, W., & McFarland, K. (2014), Stalking: Does it leave a psychological footprint? *Social Science Quarterly, 95*(2), 563–580.

Duterte, E. E., Bonomi, A. E., Kernic, M. A., Schiff, M. A., Thompson, R. S., & Rivara, F. P. (2008). Correlates of medical and legal help seeking among women reporting intimate partner violence. *Journal of Women's Health, 17*(1), 85–95.

Erez, E. (2002). Domestic violence and the criminal justice system: An overview. *Online Journal of Issues in Nursing, 7*(1). Retrieved from https://www.researchgate.net/publication/11329468_Domestic_violence_and_the_criminal_justice_system_An_overview

Fals-Stewart, W. (2003). The occurrence of partner physical aggression on days of alcohol consumption: A longitudinal diary study. *Journal of Consulting and Clinical Psychology, 71*(1), 41–52.

Fleury, R. E., Sullivan, C. M., & Bybee, D. I. (2000). When ending the relationship does not end the violence: Women's experiences of violence by former partners. *Violence Against Women, 6*(12), 1363–1383.

Gardner, F. L., Moore, Z. E., & Dettore, M. (2014). The relationship between anger, childhood maltreatment, and emotion regulation difficulties in intimate partner and non-intimate partner violence offenders. *Behavior Modification, 38*(4), 1–22.

Gillum, T. L. (2019). The intersection of intimate partner violence and poverty in Black communities. *Aggression and Violent Behavior, 46*, 37–44.

Gondolf, E. W., & Fisher, E. R. (1988). *Battered women as survivors: An alternative to treating learned helplessness.* Lexington, MA: Lexington Books.

Goodkind, J. R., Sullivan, C. M., & Bybee, D. I. (2004). A contextual analysis of battered women's safety planning. *Violence Against Women, 10*(5), 514–533.

Goodman, L. A., Smyth, K. F., Borges, A. M., & Singer, R. (2009). When crises collide: How intimate partner violence and poverty intersect to shape women's mental health and coping? *Trauma, Violence and Abuse, 10*(4), 306–329.

Haj-Yahia, M. M. (1998). Beliefs about wife beating among Palestinian women: The influence of their patriarchal ideology. *Violence Against Women, 4*(5), 533–558.

Hardesty, J. L., & Ganong, L. H. (2006). How women make custody decisions and manage co-parenting with abusive former husbands. *Journal of Social and Personal Relationships, 23*(4), 543–563.

Hardesty, J. L., Oswald, R. F., Khaw, L., & Fonseca, C. (2011). Lesbian/bisexual mothers and intimate partner violence: Help seeking in the context of social and legal vulnerability. *Violence Against Women, 17*(1), 28–46.

Haselschwerdt, M. L., & Hardesty, J. L. (2017). Managing secrecy and disclosure of domestic violence in affluent communities. *Journal of Marriage and Family, 79*(2), 556–570.

Herrenkohl, T. I., & Rousson, A. N. (2018). IPV and the intergenerational transmission of violence. *Family and Intimate Partner Violence Quarterly, 10*(4), 39–46.

Hill, R. (1958). Social stresses on the family: Generic features of families under stress. *Social Casework, 39*, 139–150.

Howard, J., & Hollander, J. (1996). *Gendered situations, gendered selves.* Thousand Oaks, CA: SAGE.

Humphreys, J., Epel, E. S., Cooper, B. A., Lin, J., Blackburn, E. H., & Lee, K. A. (2012). Telomere shortening in formerly abused and never abused women. *Biological Research for Nursing, 14*(2), 115–123.

Institute for Women's Policy Research. (2017, August 14). *The economic cost of intimate partner violence, sexual assault, and stalking* [Fact sheet]. Retrieved from https://iwpr.org/publications/economic-cost-intimate-partner-violence-sexual-assault-stalking/

Johnson, M. P. (1995). Patriarchal terrorism and common couple violence: Two forms of violence against women. *Journal of Marriage and the Family, 57*, 283–294.

Johnson, M. P. (2006). Conflict and control: Gender symmetry and asymmetry in domestic violence. *Violence Against Women, 12*(11), 1003–1018.

Kelly, J., & Johnson, M. P. (2008). Differentiation among types of intimate partner violence:

Research update and implications for interventions. *Family Court Review, 46*(3), 476–499.

Khaw, L., & Hardesty, J. L. (2007). Theorizing the process of leaving: Turning points and trajectories in the stages of change model. *Family Relations, 56*(4), 413–425.

Khaw, L., & Hardesty, J. L. (2015). Perceptions of boundary ambiguity in the process of leaving abusive partners. *Family Process, 54*(2), 327–343.

Kimmel, M. S. (2002). "Gender symmetry" in domestic violence: A substantive and methodological research review. *Violence Against Women, 8*(11), 1332–1363.

Lacey, K. K., McPherson, M. D., Samuel, P. S., Powell Scars, K., & Head, D. (2013). The impact of different types of intimate partner violence on the mental and physical health of women in different ethnic groups. *Journal of Interpersonal Violence, 28*(2), 359–385.

Landenburger, K. M. (1989). A process of entrapment and recovery from an abusive relationship. *Issues in Mental Health Nursing, 10*(3/4), 209–227.

Langhinrichsen-Rohling, J., & Turner, L. A. (2012). The efficacy of an intimate partner violence prevention program with high-risk adolescent girls: A preliminary test. *Prevention Science, 13*(4), 384–394.

Lawrence, E., Yoon, J., Langer, A., & Ro, E. (2009). Is psychological aggression as detrimental as physical aggression? The independent effects of psychological aggression on depression and anxiety symptoms. *Violence and Victims, 24*(1), 20–35.

Leone, J. M., Johnson, M. P., & Cohan, C. L. (2007). Victim help seeking: Differences between intimate terrorism and situational couple violence. *Family Relations, 56*(5), 427–439.

Lévesque, S., & Rousseau, C. (2019). Young women's acknowledgment of reproductive coercion: A qualitative analysis. *Journal of Interpersonal Violence.* Advance online publication. https://doi.org/10.1177/0886260519842169

Liang, B., Goodman, L., Tummala-Narra, P., & Weintraub, S. (2005). A theoretical framework for understanding help-seeking processes among survivors of intimate partner violence. *American Journal of Community Psychology, 36*(1/2), 71–84.

Lin, K., Sun, I. Y., Liu, J., & Chen, X. (2018). Chinese women's experience of intimate partner violence: Exploring factors affecting various types of IPV. *Violence Against Women, 24*(1), 66–84.

Merritt-Gray, M., & Wuest, J. (1995). Counteracting abuse and breaking free: The process of leaving revealed through women's voices. *Health Care for Women International, 16*(5), 399–412.

Messinger, A. M. (2011). Invisible victims: Same-sex IPV in the National Violence Against Women survey. *Journal of Interpersonal Violence, 26*(11), 2228–2243.

Miller, S. L., & Meloy, M. L. (2006). Women's use of force: Voices of women arrested for domestic violence. *Violence Against Women, 12*(1), 89–115.

Moss, V., Pitula, C., Campbell, J., & Halstead, L. (1997). The experiences of terminating an abusive relationship from an Anglo and African American perspective: A qualitative descriptive study. *Issues in Mental Health Nursing, 18*(5), 433–454.

Murray, C. E., & Graves, K. N. (2013). *Responding to family violence: A comprehensive, research-based guide for therapists.* New York, NY: Routledge.

National Coalition of Anti-Violence Programs. (2013). *Lesbian, gay, bisexual, transgender, queer, and HIV-affected intimate partner violence in 2012.* Atlanta, GA: Centers for Disease Control and Prevention.

National Network to End Domestic Violence (2017). *2017 Domestic Violence Counts National Summary.* Retrieved from https://nnedv.org/mdocs-posts/2017-national-summary/

National Women's Law Center. (2019). *Health care and reproductive rights.* Washington, DC.

Network for Public Health Law. (2019). *States of protection in the U.S. for victims of domestic violence in same-sex relationships.* Retrieved from https://www.networkforphl.org/resources/status-of-protections-in-the-u-s-for-victims-of-domestic-violence-in-same-sex-relationships/

Norlander, B., & Eckhardt, C. (2005). Anger, hostility, and male perpetrators of intimate partner violence: A meta-analytic review. *Clinical Psychology Review, 25*(2), 119–152.

Pico-Alfonso, M. A., Garcia-Linares, I., Celda-Navarro, N., Blasco-Ros, C., Echeburua, E., & Martinez, M. (2006). The impact of physical, psychological, and sexual intimate male partner violence on women's mental health: Depressive symptoms, posttraumatic stress disorder, state anxiety, and suicide. *Journal of Women's Health, 15*(5), 599–611.

Rohrbaugh, J. B. (2006). Domestic violence in same-gender relationships. *Family Court Review, 44*(2), 287–299.

Senkans, S., McEwan, T. E., & Ogloff, J. R. (2017). Assessing the link between intimate partner violence and postrelationship stalking: A gender-inclusive study. *Journal of Interpersonal Violence.* doi: 0886260517734859

Shir, J. S. (1999). Battered women's perceptions and expectations of their current and ideal marital relationship. *Journal of Family Violence, 14*(1), 71–82.

Shuler, A. C. (2010). Male victims of intimate partner violence in the United States: An examination of the review of literature through the critical theoretical perspective. *International Journal of Criminal Justice Sciences, 5*(1), 163–173.

Smith, S. G., Fowler, K. A., & Niolon, P. H. (2014). Intimate partner homicide and corollary victims in 16 states: National Violent Death Reporting System, 2003–2009. *American Journal of Public Health, 104*(3), 461–466.

Smith, S. G., Zhang, X., Basile, K. C., Merrick, M. T., Wang, J., Kresnow, M., & Chen, J. (2018). *The National Intimate Partner and Sexual Violence Survey (NISVS): 2015 data brief updated release.* Atlanta, GA: National Center for Injury Prevention and Control.

Stockman, J. K., Hayashi, H., & Campbell, J. C. (2015). Intimate partner violence and its health impact on ethnic minority women. *Journal of Women's Health, 24*(1), 62–79.

Sullivan, C. M. (2018). Understanding how domestic violence support services promote survivor well-being: A conceptual model. *Journal of Family Violence, 33*(2), 123–131.

Sylaska, K. M., & Edwards, K. M. (2014). Disclosure of intimate partner violence to informal social support network members: A review of the literature. *Trauma, Violence, & Abuse, 15*(1), 3–21.

Taylor, J. Y. (2002). "The straw that broke the camel's back": African American women's strategies for disengaging from abusive relationships. *Women & Therapy, 25*(3/4), 145–161.

Tjaden, P., Thoennes, N., & Allison, C. J. (1999). Comparing violence over the lifespan in samples of same-sex and opposite-sex cohabitants. *Violence and Victims, 14*(4), 413–425.

Thomas, M. D., Bennett, L. W., & Stoops, C. (2013). The treatment needs of substance abusing batters: A comparison of men who batter their female partners. *Journal of Family Violence, 28*(2), 121–129.

Tolman, R. M. (1989). The development of a measure of psychological maltreatment of women by their male partners. *Violence and Victims, 4*(3), 159–177.

Townsend, M., Hunt, D., Kuck, S., & Baxter, C. (2005). *Law enforcement response to domestic violence calls for service*. Washington, DC: U.S. Department of Justice.

Tsui, V., Cheung, M., & Leung, P. (2010). Help-seeking among male victims of partner abuse: Men's hard times. *Journal of Community Psychology, 38*(6), 769–780.

United Nations Office of Drugs and Crime. (2018). *Global study on homicide 2018*. Vienna, Austria: Author.

Vatnar, S. K. B., & Bjørkly, S. (2013). Lethal intimate partner violence: An interactional perspective on women's perceptions of lethal incidents. *Violence and Victims, 28*(5), 772–789.

Walker, R., Logan, T. K., Jordan, C. E., & Campbell, J. C. (2004). An integrative review of separation in the context of victimization: Consequences and implications for women. *Trauma, Violence, & Abuse, 5*(2), 143–193.

Wathen, C. N., & MacMillan, H. L. (2003). Interventions for violence against women: Scientific review. *JAMA, 289*(5), 589–600.

Wuest, J., Ford-Gilboe, M., Merritt-Gray, M., & Berman, H. (2003). Intrusion: The central problem for family health promotion among children and single mothers after leaving an abusive partner. *Qualitative Health Research, 13*(5), 597–622.

Zakar, R., Zakar, M. Z., & Kraemer, A. (2013). Men's beliefs and attitudes toward intimate partner violence against women in Pakistan. *Violence Against Women, 19*(2), 246–268.

Zapor, H., Wolford-Clevenger, C., & Johnson, D. M. (2018). The association between social support and stages of change in survivors of intimate partner violence. *Journal of Interpersonal Violence, 33*(7), 1051–1070.

Zraick, K. (2018, November 27). Most dangerous place for women is the home. *The New York Times*. Retrieved from https://www.nytimes.com/2018/11/27/world/female-homicide-gender-violence.html

Family Responses to School and Community Mass Violence

Amity Noltemeyer, Courtney L. McLaughlin, Mark R. McGowan, and Caitie Johnson

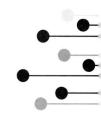

September 11th. Sandy Hook. The Boston Marathon bombing. Las Vegas. Parkland. El Paso. Whether directly or indirectly exposed, families are increasingly faced with the harsh reality associated with acts of mass violence in schools and communities. *Mass violence* refers to a variety of events including shootings, acts of terrorism, and other events that result in multiple fatalities and injuries (Fox & Levin, 2012; Substance Abuse and Mental Health Services Administration [SAMHSA], n.d.). Exposure to mass violence can contribute to short-term feelings of posttraumatic distress (Lowe & Galea, 2017) and long-term mental health and family functioning can also be significantly impaired (MacDermid Wadsworth, 2010). Although greater levels of exposure to an incident of mass violence have been associated with higher levels of posttraumatic symptoms (Lowe & Galea, 2017; Wilson, 2014), even those with no first-hand connection can report psychological sequelae in response to these events (e.g., Galea et al., 2002; Norris et al., 2002).

Despite the deleterious consequences of community and school violence, families' responses to these adverse situations are incredibly diverse. Some families demonstrate *resilience*, evidencing positive adaptation in the midst of tragedy. Considering the context in which families are situated, understanding how families respond to mass violence and how professionals can foster family resilience is important. In this chapter, we provide a hypothetical case study illustrating a family's experience with mass violence; describe the context of mass violence in the United States; delineate a theoretical framework to explain how it can impact families; and describe risk and protective factors that can influence family resilience, exploring implications for professionals working with families.

Hypothetical Case Study

Two weeks ago, a 16-year-old adolescent entered Rivertown High School with a gun and fatally shot two students and one teacher, injuring 26 others. Thirteen-year-old Rory Brown lives with her father, Mr. Brown, 20 minutes from Rivertown in Mountain Top, where Rory attends Mountain Top High School. Though the event did not occur in Rory's school, Mr. Brown and Rory are struggling

(Continued)

(Continued)

to cope and have many concerns and fears. Mr. Brown is concerned with providing the right supports for his daughter.

Immediately after the shooting, Rory's school, in collaboration with the Chamber of Commerce, mayor, community mental health agencies, hospital, and police, disseminated information to community members. They described how key agencies would communicate with community members and provided resources for support. Additionally, one of the documents was designed to help adults understand warning signs for children and adolescents who may be struggling to cope with the traumatic event. Finally, families were encouraged to reflect on services that their family has previously used as resources. Because they had previously used the support network at the Mountain Top Community Church, Mr. Brown reached out to church professionals for assistance in the family's coping process.

Although Mr. Brown felt that supports from his church were helpful in guiding him and Rory to make meaning out of the event, he still saw signs that Rory and he were struggling. Rory's teacher expressed similar concerns, stating that since the event Rory had been more argumentative, complained of frequent stomach aches, and displayed more inattention. This prompted Mr. Brown to contact the school psychologist at Mountain Top High School. The school psychologist met with Mr. Brown and discussed his pre-event and post-event parenting style as well as his family's routines and roles. Mr. Brown felt this conversation was helpful in recognizing the changes that occurred since the event. The school psychologist also recommended minimizing certain types of media exposure, since the family's repeated revisiting of the event via the television appeared to trigger anxiety. Finally, the school psychologist reminded Mr. Brown to continue to talk to Rory about the event and monitor signs of difficulty. At the end of the meeting, Mr. Brown was provided with a resource guide for additional supports that he and Rory might utilize. Mr. Brown planned to seek out family counseling services in order to assist him and Rory in answering questions about the event and renew their feelings of security and hope.

Mass Violence: the Context

Traumatic events, such as the shooting described in the case study, have a variety of social, psychological, physical, and economic consequences that disrupt numerous aspects of individual, family, and community functioning. In conceptualizing the impact of mass violence on our society, it is instructive to briefly explore the recent trends in violence. Incidences of mass violence take many forms in our communities and adopting a nuanced view of these differences holds important clinical implications for guiding prevention or intervention efforts. In this century, examples have included community shootings, school shootings, bombings, and coordinated airline hijackings. For the purposes of this discussion, we will differentiate between community and school violence more broadly. Although this differentiation is useful for exploring the impact of mass violence on families, many current understandings of individual and community responses to these events are derived from the broader trauma literature, which includes events such as natural disasters. For example, Norris et al. (2002) differentiated between disasters and mass violence in their meta-analysis of population outcomes, concluding that incidences of mass violence were significantly more likely to result in severe impairment than either technological (i.e., human-produced event without intention, such as an airplane crash) or natural disasters.

Regardless of the specific nature of the traumatizing event, the subsequent maladaptive or adaptive responses frequently form a common constellation of symptoms (Neria, Nandi, & Galea, 2007). Clinically, this presentation may manifest in individuals and families along a continuum ranging from mild distress to functionally limiting maladaptive responses resulting in the development of diagnosable psychiatric disorders (Galea, Nandi, & Vlahov, 2005; Galea & Resnick, 2005). In general, research has noted that exposure to a traumatic event is associated with increased rates of acute stress disorder, posttraumatic stress disorder (PTSD), major depression, panic disorder, generalized anxiety disorder, and substance use disorders (e.g., Norris et al., 2002; Schuster et al., 2001). However, the likelihood for maladaptive outcomes has been found to be influenced by certain conditions, including the directness of exposure to a traumatic experience, proximity to the trauma or threat, duration of exposure, fear response, premorbid functioning, prior trauma exposure, genetic predispositions, and other factors (Institute of Medicine, 2003; Ozer, Best, Lipsey, & Weiss, 2008). Familial maladaptive coping strategies may include denial, expressions of negative emotion, substance use, behavioral disengagement, and self-blame. Furthermore, familial responses to crisis may contribute to functional changes in the family system (Myer et al., 2014). In light of the literature concerning the particularly deleterious impact of mass violence, examples of these events will be reviewed to provide context for discussing both adaptive and maladaptive responses to these events.

Despite heightened public attention, mass shootings in either the community or school setting are rare. However, the malicious intent and unpredictable nature of these violent acts in our communities produces a disproportionately adverse impact on those directly and indirectly affected (Hughes et al., 2011; Norris et al., 2002). According to a 2014 Federal Bureau of Investigation (FBI) report, there have been 160 active shooter[1] incidents between 2000 and 2013 that resulted in 1,043 casualties (Blair & Schweit, 2014). These data seem to suggest an average of 11.4 incidents annually during this time period. However, the authors of the report note that these data illustrate an increasing trend over that time period, with an average of 6.4 incidents per year from 2000 to 2006 and an average of 16.4 incidences from 2007 to 2013 (see Figure 16.1). Among the 160 active shooter incidents during this period, approximately 45% occurred in commerce or business settings, 24% occurred in educational environments, and the remaining 30% occurred in areas such as open spaces, governmental properties,

---

[1] The term *active shooter* is defined as "an individual actively engaged in killing or attempting to kill people in a confined and populated area" with a firearm (Blair & Schweit, 2014, p. 5).

houses of worship, health-care facilities, and residences. When data from 2014 to 2018 are also taken into consideration, the notion that the United States is facing increasing prevalence rates for incidents involving active shooters is further supported. Between 2014 and 2017, there have been 90 active shooter incidents that have resulted in 1,174 casualties (Advanced Law Enforcement Rapid Response Training Center [ALERRT] & Federal Bureau of Investigation, 2018a; Schweit, 2016). The magnitude of harm associated with these incidences may also be intensifying, with the number of casualties during these 4 years exceeding the total number for the previous 14 years. The location of the incidents that occurred between 2014 and 2018 were similar to those that occurred between 2000 and 2013, with the majority occurring in commerce or business settings (38%) followed by educational environments (15%), open spaces (15%), governmental properties (15%), and other settings (15%; e.g. houses of worship, health-care facilities, and residences).

In 2018, a joint publication by the ALERRT Center and the FBI reported that there have been 27 active shooter incidents that resulted in 213 casualties (ALERRT Center & FBI, 2018b). The highest number of casualties in 2018 were reported in the Marjory Stoneman Douglas High School shooting (17 killed and 17 wounded) that occurred in Parkland, Florida. Similar to previous reports, the majority of incidents (60%) occurred in commerce- or business-related settings, with educational environments (19%) representing the next most common setting for active shooter incidents to occur.

In contrast to the increase in active shooter incidents recently, the prevalence rate for murder in the United States has been declining. Between the years of 1992 and 2017, the national murder rate dropped from 9.3 to 5.3 per 100,000 inhabitants (FBI, 2017). Consistent with national trends, the prevalence rate for violence in our nation's public schools has also demonstrated a decreasing trend since 1992 (Modzeleski et al., 2008). Further, with the exception of the 2012–2013 school year, these trends indicate that the student homicide rates have remained relatively stable since 2006 (Robers, Zhang, & Truman, 2012; Musu-Gillette et al., 2019). It is important to note that deviations in these trends are influenced by particularly deadly incidents of mass murder, such as the one that occurred at Sandy Hook Elementary School in Newtown, Connecticut, that claimed the lives of 20 first graders and six adults. It is also relevant to note that the homicide rate in school settings is notably higher when adults are also taken into account (see Figure 16.2). When the annual homicide rate for youth ages 5 to 18 is taken into consideration, however, the average number of school homicides accounts for less than 3% of these deaths (Musu-Gillette et al., 2019). In view of these data, the literature suggests that perceptions of public safety have been negatively biased by the media publicizing horrific events (Duwe, 2005; Van Dyke & Schroeder, 2006). It is important to keep in mind that, although active shooter incidents have increased, events like those described in the chapter case study are rare; general trends in the data reinforce the notion that schools remain a safe place for children. However, unlike prevalence rates for mass shootings in community settings

Active Shooter Incidents

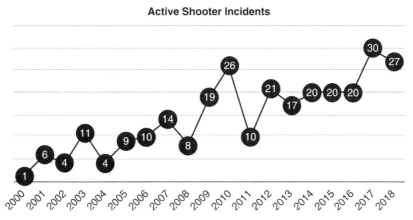

Source: Data obtained from the Active Shooter Incidents in the United States (Blair & Schweit, 2014; Schweit, 2016, ALERRT Center & Federal Bureau of Investigation, 2018a; ALERRT Center & FBI, 2018b).

Homicides at school from 1992-93 to 2015-16

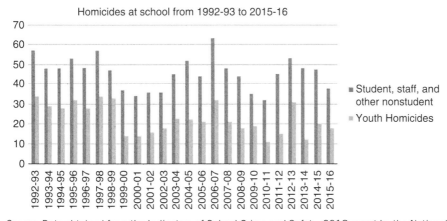

■ Student, staff, and other nonstudent

▪ Youth Homicides

Source: Data obtained from the Indicators of School Crime and Safety: 2018 report by the National Center for Education Statistics (Musu-Gillette et al., 2019).

(see Duwe, 2005), the current frequency of targeted violence in educational settings is a relatively recent phenomenon.

According to a joint report from the U.S. Secret Service and the Department of Education (Vossekuil, Fein, Reddy, Borum, & Modzeleski, 2002), there were three incidents of targeted school shootings in the 1970s, five in the 1980s, and twenty-eight in the 1990s. Between 2000 and 2018, there have been 54 incidents of targeted school shootings in educational settings (ALERRT Center & FBI, 2018a, 2018b; Blair & Schweit, 2014; Schweit, 2016). This evolving trend has fueled ongoing discussions concerning the psychological impact of these events on shaping our society's collective world view (Warnick, Johnson, & Rocha, 2010). Considering the important role perceptions play in psychological outcomes, it is reasonable to expect these trends to have implications for exposed individuals and families.

Research concerning the psychological impact of terrorism on perceptions of community safety also holds an increasingly important place when conceptualizing mass violence in this country. More specifically, when considering recent incidents of domestic terrorism, researchers have suggested that there is a new countrywide sense of vulnerability that contributes to increased levels of anxiety and stress concerning the possibility of another attack (Institute of Medicine, 2003). These psychological effects may be particularly strong for individuals who identify with groups targeted by hate-based violence, who may experience persistent fears for their safety and security in the aftermath of such attacks (Ghafoori et al., 2019).

It is relevant to note that the genesis of much of the professional literature on this topic in the United States began in response to the terrorist attacks on September 11, 2001. Media coverage of these attacks contributed significantly to the number of individuals exposed to the events as well as the duration of that exposure. Reactions of fear and horror can spread rapidly and are not limited to those experiencing the event directly. It also includes family members of victims and survivors, and people who are exposed through broadcast images (Institute of Medicine, 2003).

The psychological consequences of mass violence involve a range of cognitive, emotional, physical, and behavioral responses that occur in individuals and families as a result of exposure to, or threat of, a traumatic event (see Table 16.1). In the chapter case study, Rory was observed to have several of these responses—including physical symptoms, argumentativeness, and inattention. As noted, these consequences vary in terms of both severity and duration. Stress reactions immediately following a traumatic event are quite common and typically resolve rapidly. However, in instances where symptoms continue for more than three days, a formal diagnosis of acute stress disorder may be warranted (American Psychiatric Association, 2013).

Importantly, the family system has been demonstrated to play a critical role in mediating or buffering a child's vulnerability to maladaptive stress responses (Rutter, 1999). However, there is a reciprocal interaction between the child and

Table 16.1 Common Stress Reactions Following Traumatic Events

Physical	Cognitive	Emotional	Behavioral
Chest pain	Blaming others	Affective	Avoidance of triggers
Chills	Confusion	dysregulation	Antisocial acts
Difficulty breathing	Disorientation	Agitation	Changes in appetite
Dizziness	Heightened or lowered	Anxiety	Changes in social activity
Elevated blood	alertness	Apprehension	Exaggerated startle
pressure	Hypervigilance	Denial	response
Fatigue	Intrusive images	Depression	Restlessness
Headaches	Nightmares	Emotional numbing	Substance use
Muscle tremors	Poor attention	Fear	Withdrawal
Nausea	Poor concentration	Feeling overwhelmed	
Perspiration	Suspiciousness	Grief	
Rapid heart rate		Guilt	
Shock symptoms		Irritability	
Thirst		Panic	

family system to consider. For example, maladaptive responses to stressors may disrupt parenting practices by causing parents to be more irritable, controlling, and punitive. These maladaptive familial and parental responses may increase the likelihood that a child will experience negative behavioral and mental health outcomes (Han & Shaffer, 2014; Shaffer, Lindhiem, & Kolko, 2013; Webster-Stratton, 1990).

Theoretical Framework

The existence of mass violence in our society, and its unfavorable outcomes and correlates, is undeniable. However, individuals and families vary drastically in their responses to experienced or vicarious mass violence, with many demonstrating resilience. *Resilience* has been defined as ". . . patterns of desirable behavior in situations where adaptive functioning or development have been or currently are significantly threatened by adverse experiences . . ." (Masten, 1999, p. 283). Rather than referring to a within-individual trait or characteristic, current ecological conceptualizations of resilience recognize it as a dynamic and context-dependent process (e.g., Ungar, 2008). According to an interactive resilience model, resilience emerges for an individual when the relationship between an adversity and an unfavorable outcome is weakened by a protective factor (Masten, Cutuli, Herbers, & Reed, 2002). Two types of interaction effects can occur: (1) an always existing protective factor (e.g., individual temperament) moderates the impact of a risk (e.g., exposure to mass violence), and (2) a risk-activated protective factor (e.g., involvement in a support group following exposure to mass violence) moderates the impact of a risk. In both cases, the protective factor buffers the impact of mass violence on the development of psychopathology.

In addition to individual resilience, resilience processes also occur at the family level. Harrist, Henry, Liu, and Morris (2019) suggest that the concept of family resilience complements that of individual resilience but extends it by emphasizing the relational and meaning dynamics of family systems. Family resilience can be thought of as, "how family systems successfully navigate significant risk in ways that result in functioning as well or better than before the risk event" (Harrist, Henry, Liu, & Morris, 2019, p. 223). According to Walsh (2012, p. 15), it is necessary to build families' capacity for resilience because, "Major stresses can derail the functioning of a family system, with ripple effects for all members and their relationships. . . . When families suffer, their children suffer." Fortunately, the opposite can also be said when families resile, children flourish. For example, Bethell, Gombojav, and Whitaker (2019) demonstrated that a measure of family resilience positively predicts children flourishing in a graded fashion, with the strength of this relationship being similar across different levels of adversity exposure.

Integrating ecological and developmental perspectives, Walsh (2003) proposed a family resilience framework that recognizes three key processes for resilience: (1) family belief systems (e.g., making meaning of adversity, positive outlook, transcendence and spirituality), (2) organizational patterns (e.g., flexibility, connectedness, and social/economic resources), and (3) communication and problem solving (e.g., clarity, open emotional expression, and collaborative problem solving). This strength-based framework recognizes that adversity impacts the entire family, and family processes mediate adaptation of all members of the family and the family unit (Walsh, 2003, 2012). This model builds upon McCubbin and Patterson's (1983) Double ABC-X model—recognizing the importance of minimizing stressors, managing hardships, maintaining the family system morale, developing resources needed to meet demands, and developing structures to accommodate new demands (McCubbin & Patterson, 1983; Walsh, 1996)—but also extends it by proposing key processes within family belief systems, organizational patterns, and communication processes that contribute to resilience. Consistent with Walsh's (2003) focus on these three processes, Black and Lobo (2008) concluded that recurrent and prominent factors that defined resilient families include a positive outlook, spirituality or a shared value system, family member accord or cohesion, flexibility, harmonious family communication, sound financial management, family time, shared recreation, routines and rituals, and a support network. Harrist et al. (2019), in their family resilience model, also emphasize the importance of family adaptive systems in promoting resilience, placing a particular emphasis on the protective function of rituals and routines within family emotional, control, meaning, and maintenance adaptive systems.

Due to the interaction of individual and family processes in resilience, coupled with the limited empirical research on family resilience to mass violence specifically, we will next examine research on possible risk and protective factors that may impact both individual and family adaptation to the stress of mass violence.

Resilience in the Midst of Mass Violence

As previously mentioned, research has uncovered a variety of unfavorable outcomes associated with exposure to community and school mass violence. Only more recently, however, have investigations focused on adaptive responses—both within-individual and situational—that buffer the development of debilitating conditions such as PTSD and anxiety, and even have the potential to contribute to posttraumatic growth (PTG). While recognizing the diverse manifestations of mass violence, this review will focus on research regarding resilience following acts of terrorism and mass shootings in the United States.

Research on Individual Resilience Following Mass Violence

Research following the 9/11 attacks has furthered our understanding of situational factors that promote or impede resilience. For example, Silver, Holman, McIntosh, Poulin, and Gil-Rivas (2002) found that the degree of exposure (i.e., proximity to the attack sites, presence at a site, contact with a victim, and degree of watching events live on television) to the attacks significantly predicted subsequent psychological distress. In fact, degree of exposure was more predictive of distress than degree of loss. Further substantiating the exposure effect, Schlenger et al. (2002) found that the amount of time spent watching television coverage of the 9/11 attack predicted both PTSD symptomatology and general distress. Interestingly, Holman, Garfin, and Silver (2014) found that children who were exposed to daily media coverage of the Boston Marathon bombings (6 or more hours) had higher acute stress than children directly exposed to the bombing events. Together, these results suggest that television exposure to mass violence may increase individuals' risk for maladaptation. Regarding the chapter case study, these findings support the school psychologists' recommendation that Mr. Brown limit the amount of coverage he and Rory watched.

Surveying parents in New York City before and after 9/11, Stuber et al. (2005) also found that disaster experiences were associated with subsequent child behavior problems. Furthermore, family demographics (e.g., income, single-parent status, ethnicity) and parental reactions to the attacks were also related to behavioral problems. Parents who were unsure of how their child was responding to the attacks were also more likely to report behavior problems for that child following the attacks, and adolescents who observed a parent crying were more likely to evidence behavior problems 6 months following the attacks. Although youth may benefit from age-appropriate discussions about the attack, parental displays of distress may negatively impact child well-being in traumatic events when fear and uncertainty persist.

Bonanno, Galea, Bucciarelli, and Vlahov (2007) also studied resilience following the 9/11 attacks, with resilience being defined as having 1 or 0 posttraumatic stress symptoms along with lower levels of depression and substance use. The researchers found that demographic variables, resources, and additional life stressors predicted resilience among residents of the New York City area 6 months following the attacks. Being male, Asian, and over age 65 were demographic factors related to resilience. Furthermore, education was inversely related to resilience, suggesting education (or perhaps correlates of education such as work stress) hampered adaptation to the trauma in this sample. This finding contradicts some prior research, and may be unique to the 9/11 attacks or similar types of large-scale violence. Resources positively related to resilience were lack of income loss, presence of social support, and the absence of chronic disease. Finally, the absence of additional life stressors was found to be most strongly related to resilience; participants with no prior trauma, no recent stressful events, and additional traumatic events since 9/11 were more likely to be resilient.

Although research following 9/11 provided insights into risk and resilience processes following a high-profile act of mass violence, research on subsequent school and community mass shootings has also broadened our knowledge of factors contributing to psychosocial outcomes after mass violence. For example, in a synthesis of 11 studies on youth responses to six different school shootings between 2014 and 2017, Travers, McDonagh, and Elklit (2018) found that many youth exhibited resilience, demonstrating no long-term impairment. However, they found that risk for experiencing clinically significant outcomes was impacted by factors such as pretrauma functioning, degree of exposure to the shooting, degree of dissociation during the trauma, posttrauma emotion regulation, the flexibility of one's coping style, and social support.

Related to the importance of social support in promoting resilience, Hawdon, Räsänen, Oksanen, and Ryan (2012) studied three mass shootings and concluded that social solidarity emerging after the shootings decreased depressive symptoms and increased psychological well-being, even when controlling for other previously identified predictors of depression. Hawdon and Ryan's (2012) research following the Virginia Tech shooting further supports the importance of social connections with family and friends following a mass shooting. They found that social solidarity, engaging in community events, and face-to-face interactions with family members all significantly enhanced well-being 5 months after the mass shooting that occurred on campus. Furthermore, virtual interactions with friends and family members were found to be beneficial when paired with face-to-face interactions. Together, these results reveal the important protective function families can serve in individual adaptation. In the chapter case study, these findings suggest that Mr. Brown's ongoing supportive interactions with Rory were likely beneficial in her well-being.

In another study following the Virginia Tech shooting, Littleton, Axsom, and Grills-Taquechel (2009) analyzed the degree to which interpersonal (e.g., companionship, loyalty of friends) and intrapersonal (e.g., optimism, life direction) resource loss and gain following the shooting predicted subsequent psychological distress in a sample of female students at Virginia Tech. Results revealed that interpersonal and intrapersonal resource loss within the first 2 months following the shooting positively predicted greater psychological distress 6 months after the shooting. Furthermore, participants who experienced resource loss in the first 2 months after the shooting experienced an increased likelihood of further resource loss during the subsequent 4 months. Although resource gain was positively related to decreases in psychological distress, this relationship was weaker than it was between resource loss and psychological distress.

The impact of a secure attachment style on functioning after a school shooting has also been examined as an interpersonal resource that might mitigate the effects of trauma. Based on attachment theory, the manner in which an individual responds to a traumatic event, such as mass violence, may be rooted in that individual's attachment style that was established with the primary caregiver in infancy (Turunen, Haravuori, Punama, Suomalainen, & Marttunen, 2014). Turunen, Haravuori, Punama, Suomalainen, and Marttunen, (2014) studied the degree to which attachment style predicted PTSD and dissociative symptoms in a sample of survivors of a school shooting in Finland, and found that a secure attachment style provided the strongest protection against PTSD and dissociative symptoms. The more negative outcomes associated with the two insecure attachment types (avoidant and preoccupied) differed based on the amount of time since the shooting. The authors suggested that this finding could be explained in part by securely attached individuals' ability to recognize that other people are available for help and comfort, and to appraise their own situation and seek this help when needed. These findings suggest early caregiver–child relationships may play a role in subsequent responses to trauma.

Although the previously reviewed studies highlight several individual and contextual conditions that promote or impede resilience in the midst of mass violence, most did so by examining those factors associated with someone *not experiencing* the *negative outcomes* associated with mass violence exposure. In contrast, Tingey, McGuire, Stebbins, and Erickson (2019) recognized that some individuals do experience posttraumatic growth (PTG)—positive personal changes following a traumatic event. The researchers surveyed students, faculty, and staff attending a university in the United States where a shooting occurred that left one student dead and several others injured. They found that higher compassionate goals toward others predicted PTG, moral elevation (the emotion that occurs when witnessing acts of goodness) concurrently and prospectively predicted PTG, and moral elevation mediated the effects of others' compassionate goals on PTG. Their results suggest that we can identify factors that may buffer individuals from the negative impact of exposure to a traumatic act of mass violence, but so too can we perhaps identify and enhance factors associated with PTG.

Family Resilience and Mass Trauma

Whereas the preceding studies primarily focused on *individuals'* capacity for resilience, little research has focused on *family* processes as predictors or outcomes of resilience related to mass violence. However, drawing upon the broader traumatic loss literature, Walsh (2007) proposed that belief systems, organizational patterns, and communication processes can either serve as risk or protective factors for family resilience to trauma. For example, where shattered assumptions or a sense of hopelessness are risk factors for maladaptation, a belief system that can meaningfully manage the loss and maintain a positive outlook can serve to protect a family from negative outcomes. Related to organizational patterns, families should be supported to be flexible in roles to deal with the new challenges, yet provide security and stability to reduce chaos; they should also strive to remain connected and rely on family and community resources (Walsh, 2007). The latter is demonstrated in the chapter case study when Mr. Brown sought out community resources to help him and Rory cope with the trauma. Finally, communication processes should be characterized by clarity and consistency, and individual differences in emotional expression should be recognized (Walsh, 2007).

Gewirtz, Forgatch, and Wieling (2008) also drew from the mass trauma research to discuss the impact of parenting practices on child resilience. The researchers proposed that the quality of parenting subsequent to an instance of mass trauma mediates the relationship between the trauma and child adjustment. Gewirtz et al. proposed that exposure to mass trauma disrupts the family social system, and therefore recovery efforts after a traumatic event must strengthen parents' ability to promote positive family social interactions and draw upon available resources. For example, the authors suggested that parents who monitor, set limits, and problem solve after mass trauma are more likely have resilient children. Furthermore, the authors cited research suggesting that children use cues provided by parents to interpret whether a situation is safe or not; consequently, parental reactions to mass violence have the potential to influence child adaptation.

Benzies and Mychasiuk (2009) also conducted a review of research to identify risk and protective factors for family resilience at the individual, family, and community levels. At the individual level, malleable factors contributing to family resilience include an internal locus of control, an ability to regulate one's emotions, education, and coping skills. At the family level, being from a smaller family, having a mature mother, two-parent families, family cohesion, supportive parent–child interaction, social support, and stable or adequate income and housing have been shown to protect families from adversity. Finally, at the community level, involvement in the community, peer acceptance, supportive adult mentors, safe neighborhoods, and access to quality childcare and health care can be protective for families. Although family resilience represents a complex interplay between protective factors like these and risk factors, Benzies and Mychasiuk contend that these identified factors offer a starting point to inform family intervention.

Although these studies offer insights into factors that may help individuals and families adapt effectively, it is important to note that resilience is increasingly being viewed as a context- and culture-specific process (see James, Barrios, Roy & Lee, Chapter 4 in this volume). Therefore, factors that may contribute to the effective coping in one culture may not serve an equally protective role in another. For example, Clauss-Ehlers and Levi (2002) identified three cultural community resilience factors that may uniquely buffer community violence in Latinx communities: *familismo* (i.e., putting family needs first, an obligation to family)*, respeto* (i.e., acknowledging the authority of elders and people in positions of authority), and *personalismo* (i.e., recognizing the critical importance of positive relationships). Incorporating these values into support services could enhance psychosocial outcomes for Latinx families (Clauss-Ehlers & Levi, 2002), and is consistent with the ecological nature of Walsh's (2003) family resilience model.

Implications for Professionals Working with Families Exposed to Mass Violence Preparedness

If a violent event happened today, how ready is your family or community or school to respond? What are your family, community, or school's resources and skills to respond? Finally, does your family, community or school have the capacity to recover socially and emotionally? These three questions are the questions the National Child Traumatic Stress Network (2008) encourages professionals to ask to assess the community or school's readiness for a violent event. These questions are also a starting point for families and community leaders to assess their preparedness for a violent event.

Answers to these questions can serve as a foundation for the preparation work that is necessary to establish a comprehensive prevention and intervention plan for violent events. Preparation should involve education, practice, and planning (Jimerson, Brock, & Pletcher, 2005). In terms of education, there are a variety of crisis response trainings and resources available that provide appropriate models for families, communities, and schools to utilize. It is important that all members of the system are trained to respond within the specific family, community, or school environment. Furthermore, preventing mental health risk in the general population may help prevent future traumatic events. Mental Health First Aid (National Council for Behavioral Health, 2019) and QPR Suicide Triage Training (QPR Institute, 2019) are two examples of trainings that are designed to assist school professionals and parents in recognizing individual risk factors and connecting individuals to supports.

Enhancing protective factors is also key in the prevention of a traumatic event. Positive social relationships remain a protective factor that can be enhanced through prosocial activities that encourage the development of positive peer and adult relationships. Families, schools, and communities can directly promote these interactions through structured after-school programs (e.g., youth groups, athletics, art or music groups, clubs) or social gatherings. In the chapter case study, Mr. Brown reached out to his church network for social support that could be beneficial for him and Rory.

Beyond training and promoting prosocial relationships, professionals should work together to practice the application of their skills. Professionals (e.g., counselors, teachers, administrators) should consider exploring Triage Assessment System (Myer, 2001), Seven-Stage Model of Crisis Intervention (Roberts, 2000), the National Incident Management System (FEMA, 2020), or PREPaRE (Brock et al., 2009). These resources provide frameworks and tools for crisis prevention and support efforts after a crisis has occurred.

In addition to education and practice, professionals can plan ahead. For example, crisis response teams or interagency teams can be established to assist with response; a directory of resources can be created and maintained; methods for identifying and working with high-risk students can be identified; a caregiver training and information guide can be compiled; and an information dissemination system can be created (Jimerson et al., 2005). Several of these preventative strategies were utilized in the chapter case study. Planning may also entail establishing a tiered system of mental health support for families. Additionally, consideration for the anniversary may be included as a part of planning. Although the specific event and circumstances will dictate what is done, preparations may include collecting resources and ideas to assist in making key decisions about a memorial, rescreening families at risk, reactivating interagency supports, and so on. Table 16.2 contains resources to consider when planning.

Responding to Mass Violence: Enhancing Resilience

Individuals and families react differently to violent events, regardless if they are directly or indirectly involved. Therefore, professionals should prepare for a wide variety of familial needs. It is important for professionals to explore what resources an individual has previously accessed and to what extent those resources may be helpful to them as they begin the healing process (Walsh, 2007). For example, what connections does the individual have to family, community, cultural, and spiritual supports? Professionals must understand individuals' belief systems to assist them in understanding perceptions and coping strategies within the context of the family system. Furthermore, professionals should be equipped to intervene with the family system to assist in making meaningful changes through counseling that focuses on such things as couple relationships, parenting roles, and supports.

In terms of individual resilience, effective coping skills, belief systems, social support, emotional regulation, and internal loci of control have been found to be protective factors (Benzies & Mychasiuk, 2009; Bonanno, Galea, Bucciarelli, &

Table 16.2 Violent Event Resources for Communities and Schools

Organization	Resource Link	Description of Resource
Substance Abuse and Mental Health Services Administration (SAMHSA)	http://www.samhsa.gov/trauma-violence	Facts and resources
National Center for Crisis Management	http://www.nc-cm.org/index.htm	Membership and online training resources
The National Child Traumatic Stress Network	https://www.nctsn.org/resources/child-trauma-toolkit-educators	Child Trauma Toolkit for Educators
National Institute of Mental Health (NIMH)	https://www.nimh.nih.gov/health/publications/helping-children-and-adolescents-cope-with-disasters-and-other-traumatic-events/index.shtml	What Community Members Can Do
National Education Association Health Information Network	http://www.nea.org/assets/docs/NEA%20School%20Crisis%20Guide%202018.pdf	School Crisis Guide
Mental Health in School, UCLA Center	http://smhp.psych.ucla.edu/pdfdocs/crisis/crisis.pdf	Responding to Crisis at School
National Council for Behavioral Health; Mental Health First Aid USA	https://www.mentalhealthfirstaid.org/mental-health-resources/	Extensive list of specific resources by area of need or difficulty
Office of Homeland Security	http://www.dhs.gov/topics	Relevant topics include preventing terrorism and resiliency
National Incident Management System (NIMS)	http://www.fema.gov/national-incident-management-system	Information on a systematic framework for interagency management of threats or hazards

Vlahov, 2007). Therefore, professionals should consider preventatively encouraging individuals to develop effective coping skills, establish a belief system, maintain, or expand their social support system, practice healthy responses to life events, and recognize to what extent they believe they can control an event. Professionals may consider identifying families in need of individual supports by examining potentially vulnerable parenting subsystems (i.e., single parents, financially unstable families).

At the family level, supportive parent–child interaction including secure attachment styles, family cohesion, and stable and adequate income are examples of family protective factors (Benzies & Mychasiuk, 2009; Black & Lobo, 2008;

Turunen et al., 2014). Preventatively, professionals may consider offering education and intervention programs at both the family and community levels. Examples of preventative strategies may include improving relationships within the parenting subsystem (e.g., relationship between couples or single parent and their support system), parenting skills, family cohesion, community family events, and supports that encourage positive family interactions and cohesion. Community resilience, cohesion, and efficacy are essential factors in the prevention of maladaptive responses to a traumatic event. For example, safe neighborhoods, access to quality schools, childcare, health care, supportive mentors, and peer acceptance emerged as critical community protective factors within the literature (Benzies & Mychasiuk, 2009). Professionals may consider working with other community members to explore or enhance these factors within the community. Professionals may give consideration to utilizing a community climate survey or creating a mentor program in the community.

In addition to these general recommendations regarding promoting family resilience in the aftermath of mass violence, below are more specific recommendations to consider when working with families impacted by a violent event.

Mobilize Resources

Ideally, school and community teams will have engaged in planning prior to the occurrence of a violent event, including practice drills. If this has occurred, it is likely that teams have established connections with easily mobilizable agencies and have a mutual understanding of the system organization for family support. Mobilizing resources will likely involve a combination of emergency response for physical health (safe rooms, Kevlar blankets, etc.), basic resources (shelter, transportation, food), mental health supports, school and community agencies, and state and federal supports. Providing such resources is essential to counter the experience of loss often associated with a violent event (Hobfoll et al., 2007). It was evident in the chapter case study that Mr. Brown and Rory were within a prepared community that effectively mobilized resources after the traumatic event occurred.

Effective Parenting Style

Because violent events often create disruption to the family system, it is possible positive parenting within the family may be compromised. According to Gewirtz et al. (2008), recovery efforts after a traumatic event must strengthen parents' ability to promote positive family social interactions. Therefore, professionals should encourage parents to effectively provide support, monitor, set limits, and problem solve after the event (Gewirtz, Forgatch, & Wieling, 2008), just like the school psychologist did in the chapter case study. Counseling supports should continue to be considered as a part of the efforts made to enhance effective parenting, as described in the case study.

Organization and Communication

Professionals can support their clients to establish a way to organize their response to the violent event (Walsh, 2007). How will the family maintain or change their routines? Are there changes to familial roles? Are there changes to the rules the family previously followed? What levels of support will be most helpful to the family? Are they using all possible or needed supports? These questions relate to Walsh's (2012) notion of enhancing family organizational patterns. In the case study, Mr. Brown likely asked himself several of these questions as he engaged in effective organization and communication regarding his response to the violent event.

In addition to organization and communication within the family system, professionals must be aware of their own communication style. Hobfoll et al. (2007) cautions professionals against sharing rumors or "horror stories" as they are processing the event. Professionals may also consider supporting the community to prioritize efficient and accurate dissemination of information, which is helpful in supporting families with questions about their social support system (Hobfoll et al.). This step is critical because delays in linking individuals to their support networks have been found to increase the likelihood of symptoms associated with PTSD (Hobfoll et al.).

There are also unique communication issues to consider in the aftermath of targeted acts of hate-inspired mass violence. In these cases, it is important to reinforce appreciation for diversity, acknowledge that hateful words or actions will not be tolerated, reassure children and adolescents in targeted groups that adults will take care of them, and model and teach desired behavior (National Association of School Psychologists [NASP], 2018).

Media Exposure

Research has found that frequency and duration of media exposure of the violent event is associated with negative outcomes, even when controlling for factors such as prior mental health status and media exposure prior to the violent event (e.g., Holman, Garfin, & Silver, 2014). Social media has changed the way individuals are exposed to mass trauma. Information and misinformation spread faster, and images, sounds and commentary are produced immediately and sometimes even streamed live. Social media usage may impact exposure to a mass trauma event due to the increased frequency and duration social media users are exposed to content. Fletcher and Nielsen (2017) compared social media users to nonusers and found that in addition to using more online news sources, youth who use social media reported more of an influence from the news content they accessed via social media. In addition, adult and youth users of YouTube and Twitter reported greater impact than those who used Facebook (Fletcher & Nielsen). Families should consider limiting the amount of time exposed to the coverage of a mass traumatic event, which includes social media and other media outlets. Schlenger et al. (2002) recommended limiting television exposure because they found watching television coverage of the violent event predicted both PTSD symptomatology and general distress. Professionals are encouraged to help families examine all forms of media exposure which may include social media, television (including subscription services), text messages, e-mail, and virtual assistant devices, which may be programmed to report the news throughout the day. Professionals should also help parents consider the effects of event media exposure so that they can appropriately monitor exposure in themselves and their children. In the case study within this chapter, Mr. Brown recognized the need to set television limits.

Resilient Aspects to Social Media

Social media is a communication tool, which can also contribute to resiliency factors (e.g., when connecting with family and friends during and after a traumatic event). Many professional organizations also post resources on social media sites. For example, many of the resources listed in Table 16.2 have multiple social media sites (Facebook, Twitter, Instagram, etc.) that direct users to preventative and intervention tools. In addition, social media sites have support groups for postintervention supports. Therefore, clients may find several of these sites helpful for planning and intervention purposes. While social media has many helpful resources, consumers should always be cautious to access sites that are providing evidence-based information as the credibility of information on social media can vary.

Discover Meaning

Making meaning out of a violent event is considered an adaptive response because it promotes resiliency and healing by making the event more comprehensible and manageable (Walsh, 2007). Therefore, professionals should prepare to support their clients to discover meaning of the violent experience (Walsh, 2007). The examination of core beliefs is critical during this time as they provide people purpose and meaning in life (Walsh, 2007). Individuals may ask many "why" questions (i.e., "Why me?" "Why did this happen?" "Why did she do that?"). They may question their personal safety and the safety of their family, their personal legacy or mortality, the existence of a higher being such as God. (Walsh, 2007). Ultimately, professionals should aim to guide the client to explore these questions to promote positive coping and make meaning out of the experience for future events (Walsh, 2007). In the case study, Mr. Brown used mental health supports to help Rory and himself discover meaning.

Therapy-Based Interventions

Cognitive behavioral therapy (CBT) has been found to be effective with individuals and family systems who are struggling to cope with a violent event (Follette & Ruzek, 2006). Some hypothesize CBT is effective because it encourages the individual or family system to utilize problem-solving skills that enhance self-efficacy and internal locus of control (Follette & Ruzek, 2006). Often individuals struggling to cope with a violent event display symptoms of PTSD. There has been some evidence in the literature for utilizing exposure therapy or stress inoculation training with those struggling to cope with symptoms associated with PTSD (Hobfoll et al., 2007). As stated earlier, because the context of the violent event, and the population or culture impacted by it, are unique to each situation, the findings that are generalizable are limited.

Focus on Evidence-Based Practices

In the aftermath of an incident of mass violence, there may be a tendency to react with "quick fixes" or extreme solutions, but it is important to weigh the evidence supporting such solutions and their potential for harm. For example, the debate on arming teachers as a method of preventing mass violence in schools intensified in the aftermath of the Sandy Hook school shooting (Rostron, 2014). However, concerns have been raised about the lack of empirical evidence supporting this approach to preventing mass violence in schools and its potential to cause harm (e.g., NASP, 2018). In advocating for policies and practices to prevent mass violence, professionals should focus on those supported by evidence that have low risk of causing further harm.

Conclusion

Acts of mass violence are an unfortunate reality in our world. Although these events remain rare, they produce a range of unfavorable psychological consequences in exposed individuals and families. A resilience framework reveals preventative strategies and protective factors to promote adaptive functioning in the midst of posttraumatic stress and anxiety. Professionals working with families should consider their preparedness to respond to a violent event and should assist families in identifying and promoting prevention strategies and protective factors in the midst of posttraumatic stress. Although the recommendations outlined in this chapter may serve as a starting point for enhancing family functioning following an act of mass violence, resilience is a dynamic and context-dependent process; therefore, the type and intensity of the response should be adapted based on the unique characteristics of the family, event, and culture.

DISCUSSION QUESTIONS

1. After reviewing the case study in this chapter, discuss the strengths and weaknesses of the school's approach in responding to mass violence in their community. What did they do well? Could the school have done anything better? What additional considerations could support culturally diverse families in this school community?

2. Consider the actual prevalence rates of incidences of mass violence in schools as well as the high negative impacts of trauma through media exposure to events of mass violence. Discuss your thoughts related to media coverage of violent events in the 21st century.

3. Imagine that a parent or caregiver is approaching you for advice following an incident of mass violence in their community or school. Based on the research reviewed in this chapter, answer the following questions:

   a. What might you tell these caregivers to look out for as signs of trauma in their children?

   b. How may the student's reaction to trauma look different in different settings (for example, at school vs. at home)?

   c. What information would you give these caregivers about fostering resilience in their children following an event of mass violence?

   d. What information would you give them on fostering whole familial resilience?

REFERENCES

Advanced Law Enforcement Rapid Response Training (ALERRT) Center & Federal Bureau of Investigation, United States Department of Justice. (2018a). *Active shooter incidents in the United States in 2016 and 2017.* Retrieved from https://www.fbi .gov/file-repository/ active-shooter-incidents-us -2016-2017.pdf/view

Advanced Law Enforcement Rapid Response Training (ALERRT) Center & Federal Bureau of Investigation, United States Department of Justice. (2018b). *Active shooter incidents in the United States in 2018.* Retrieved from https://www.fbi.gov /file-repository/ active-shooter-incidents-in-the -us-2018-041019.pdf/view

American Psychiatric Association. (2013). *Diagnostic and statistical manual of mental disorders* (5th ed.). Washington, DC: Author.

Benzies, K., & Mychasiuk, R. (2009). Fostering family resiliency: A review of the key protective factors. *Child & Family Social Work, 14,* 103–114.

Bethell, C. D., Gombojav, N., & Whitaker, R. C. (2019). Family resilience and connection promote flourishing among US children, even among adversity. *Health Affairs, 38* (5), 729–737.

Black, K., & Lobo, M. (2008). A conceptual review of family resilience factors. *Journal of Family Nursing, 14*(1), 33–55.

Blair, J. P., & Schweit, K. W. (2014). *A study of active shooter incidents, 2000–2013.* Washington, DC: Texas State University and Federal Bureau of Investigation, U.S. Department of Justice.

Bonanno, G. A., Galea, S., Bucciarelli, A., & Vlahov, D. (2007). What predicts psychological resilience after disaster? The role of demographics, resources and life stress. *Journal of Consulting and Clinical Psychology, 75*(5), 671–682.

Brock, S. E., Lazarus, P. J., & Jimerson, S. R. (2002). *Best practices in school crisis prevention and intervention.* Bethesda, MD: National Association of School Psychologists Press.

Brock, S. E., Nickerson, A. B., Reeves, M. A., Jimerson, S. R., Lieberman, R. A., & Feinberg, T. A. (2009). *School crisis prevention and intervention: The PREPaRE model.* Bethesda, MD: National Association of School Psychologists.

Clauss-Ehlers, C. S., & Levi, L. L. (2002). Violence and community, terms in conflict: An ecological approach to resilience. *Journal of Social Distress and the Homeless, 11*(4), 265–278.

Duwe, G. (2005). A circle of distortion: The social construction of mass murder in the United States. *Western Criminology Review, 6*(1), 59–78.

Federal Bureau of Investigation. (2012). *Uniform crime reports: Crime in the United States 2011.* Retrieved from http://www.fbi.gov/about-us/cjis /ucr/crime-in-the-u.s/2011/crime-in-the-u.s .-2011/tables/table-1

Federal Bureau of Investigation. (2017). *Crime in the United States, 2017.* Retrieved from https://ucr .fbi.gov/crime-in-the-u.s/2017/crime-in-the-u.s .-2017

Federal Emergency Management Agency (FEMA). (2020). *National incident management system.* Retrieved from http://www.fema.gov/national -incident-management-system

Fletcher, R., & Nielsen, R. (2017). Are people incidentally exposed to news on social media? A comparative analysis. *News Media & Society, 20*(7), 2450–2088.

Follette, V. F., & Ruzek, J. I. (2006). *Cognitive-behavioral therapies for trauma* (2nd ed.). New York, NY: Guilford Press.

Fox, J. A., & Levin, J. (2012). *Extreme killing: Understanding serial and mass murder* (2nd ed.). Thousand Oaks, CA: SAGE.

Galea, S., Nandi, A., & Vlahov, D. (2005). The epidemiology of post-traumatic stress disorder after disasters. *Epidemiologic Reviews, 27,* 78–91.

Galea, S., Ahern, J., Resnick, H., Kilpatrick, D., Bucuvalas, M., Gold, J., & Vlahov, D. (2002). Psychological sequelae of the September 11 terrorist attacks in New York City. *New England Journal of Medicine, 246,* 982–987.

Galea, S., & Resnick, H. (2005). Posttraumatic stress disorder in the general population after mass terrorist incidents: Considerations about the nature of exposure. *CNS Spectrums, 10,* 107–115.

Gewirtz, A., Forgatch, M., & Wieling, E. (2008). Parenting practices as potential mechanisms for child adjustment following mass trauma. *Journal of Marital and Family Therapy, 34*(2), 177–192.

Ghafoori, B., Caspi, Y., Salgado, C., Allwood, M., Kreither, J., Tejada, J. L., . . . & Nadal, K. (2019). *Global perspectives on the trauma of hate-based violence: An International Society for Traumatic Stress Studies briefing paper.* Retrieved from www.istss .org/hate-based-violence

Han, Z., & Shaffer, A. (2014). Maternal expressed emotion in relation to child behavior problems: Differential and mediating effects. *Journal of Child & Family Studies, 23,* 1491–1500.

Harrist, A. W., Henry, C. S., Liu, C., & Morris, A. S. (2019). Family resilience: The power of rituals and routines in family adaptive systems. In B. H. Fiese (Ed.), *APA handbook of contemporary family psychology: Vol. 1* (pp. 223–239). Washington, DC: American Psychological Association.

Hawdon, J., Räsänen, P., Oksanen, A., & Ryan, J. (2012). Social solidarity and wellbeing after critical incidents: Three cases of mass shootings. *Journal of Critical Incident Analysis, 3,* 2–25.

Hawdon, J., & Ryan, J. (2012). Well-being after the Virginia Tech mass murder: The relative effectiveness of face-to-face and virtual interactions in providing support to survivors. *Traumatology, 18*(4), 3–12.

Hobfoll, S. E., Watson, P., Bell, C. C., Bryant, R. A., Brymer, M. J., Friedman, M. J., ... & Ursano, R. J. (2007). Five essential elements of immediate and mid-term mass trauma intervention: Empirical evidence. *Psychiatry, 70*(4), 283–315.

Holman, E. A., Garfin, D. R., & Silver, R. C. (2014). Media's role in broadcasting acute stress following the Boston Marathon bombings. *Proceedings of the National Academy of Sciences of the United States of America, 111*(1), 93–98.

Hughes, M., Brymer, M., Chiu, W. T., Fairbank, J. A., Jones, R. T., Pynoos, R. S., ... & Kessler, R. C. (2011). Posttraumatic stress among students after the shootings at Virginia Tech. *Psychological Trauma: Theory, Research, Practice, and Policy, 3*, 403–411.

Institute of Medicine. (2003). *Preparing for the psychological consequences of terrorism: A public health strategy*. Washington, DC: National Academic Press.

Jimerson, S. R., Brock, S. E., & Pletcher, S. W. (2005). An integrated model of school crisis preparedness and intervention: A shared foundation to facilitate international crisis intervention. *School Psychology International, 26*(3), 275–296.

Littleton, H. L., Axsom, D., & Grills-Taquechel, A. (2009). Adjustment following the mass shooting at Virginia Tech: The roles of resource loss and gain. *Psychological Trauma: Theory, Research, Practice and Policy, 1*(3), 206–219.

Lowe S. R., & Galea, S. (2017). The mental health consequences of mass shootings. *Trauma, Violence, & Abuse, 18* (1), 62–82.

MacDermid Wadsworth, S. M. (2010). Family risk and resilience in the context of war and terrorism. *Journal of Marriage and Family, 72*, 537–556.

Masten, A. S. (1999). Resilience comes of age: Reflections on the past and outlook for the next generation of research. In M. D. Glantz & J. L. Johnson (Eds.), *Resilience and development: Positive life adaptations* (pp. 281–296). New York, NY: Kluwer Academic/Plenum.

Masten, A. S., Cutuli, J. J., Herbers, J. E., & Reed, M. G. J. (2002). Resilience in development. In C. R. Snyder & S. J. Lopez (Eds.), *Handbook of positive psychology* (pp. 117–131). New York, NY: Oxford University Press.

Modzeleski, W., Feucht, T., Rand, M., Hall, J., Simon, T., & Butler, L., ... & Hertz, M. (2008). School-associated student homicides–United States, 1992–2006. *Morbidity and Mortality Weekly Report, 57*(2), 33–36.

Musu-Gillette, L., Zhang, A., Wang, K., Zhang, J., Kemp, J. Diliberti, M., & Oudekerk, B. A. (2018). *Indicators of school crime and safety: 2017* (NCES 2018-036/NCJ 251413). Washington, DC: National Center for Education Statistics, U.S. Department of Education, and Bureau of Justice Statistics, Office of Justice Programs, U.S. Department of Justice.

Myer, R. A. (2001). *Assessment for crisis intervention: A triage assessment model*. Pacific Grove, CA: Brooks/Cole.

Myer, R. A., Williams, R. C., Haley, M., Brownfield, J. N., McNicols, K. B., & Pribozie, N. (2014). Crisis intervention with families: Assessing changes in family characteristics. *Family Journal, 22*, 179–185.

National Association of School Psychologists. (2018). *NASP condemns hate speech and violence, calls on schools to reinforce safe, supportive school environments for all students*. Retrieved from www.nasponline.org

National Association of School Psychologists. (2018). *NASP opposes arming teachers*. Retrieved from www.nasponline.org

National Child Traumatic Stress Network Schools Committee. (2008). *Child trauma toolkit for educators*. Los Angeles, CA & Durham, NC: National Center for Child Traumatic Stress.

National Council for Behavioral Health. (2019). *Youth Mental Health First Aid*. Retrieved from http://www.mentalhealthfirstaid.org/cs/take-a-course/course-types/youth/

National Institute of Mental Health. (2006). *Helping children and adolescents with violence and disasters: What community members can do* (NIH Publication No. 07-3519). Retrieved from http://www.nimh.nih.gov/health/publications/helping-children-and-adolescents-cope-with-violence-and-disasters-community-members/helping-children-and-adolescents-cope-with-violence-and-disasters-what-community-members-can-do.pdf

Neria, Y., Nandi, A., & Galea, S. (2007). Posttraumatic stress disorder following disasters: A systematic review. *Psychological Medicine, 38*, 467–480.

Norris, F. H., Friedman, M. J., Watson, P. J., Byrne, C. M., Diaz E., & Kaniasty, K. (2002). 60,000 disaster victims speak: Part I. An empirical review of the empirical literature, 1981–2001. *Psychiatry, 65*, 207–239.

QPR Institute. (2019, July 8). *Question. Persuade. Refer.* Retrieved from https://qprinstitute.com/

Ozer, E. J., Best, S. R., Lipsey, T. L., & Weiss, D. S. (2008). Predictors of posttraumatic stress disorder and symptoms in adults: A meta-analysis. *Psychological Trauma: Theory, Research, Practice, and Policy, 129*(1), 3–36.

Robers, S., Zhang, J., & Truman, J. (2012). *Indicators of school crime and safety: 2011* (NCES 2012-002/NCJ 236021). Washington, DC: National Center for Education Statistics, U.S. Department of Education, & Bureau of Justice Statistics, Office of Justice Programs, U.S. Department of Justice.

Roberts, A. R. (Ed.). (2000). *Crisis intervention handbook: Assessment, treatment and research* (2nd ed.). New York, NY: Oxford University Press.

Rostron, A. (2014). School shootings and the legislative push to arm teachers. *University of Toledo Law Review, 45*, 439–455.

Schlenger, W. E., Caddell, J. M., Ebert, L., Jordan, B. K., Rourke, K. M., Wilson, D., . . . & Kulka, R. A. (2002). Psychological reactions to terrorist attacks: Findings from the National Study of Americans' Reactions to September 11. *Journal of the American Medical Association, 288*(5), 581–588.

Schuster, M. A., Stein, B. D., Jaycox, L., Collins, R. L., Marshall, G. N., Elliott, M. N., . . . & Berry, S. H. (2001). A national survey of stress reactions after the September 11, 2001, terrorist attacks. *New England Journal of Medicine, 345*(20), 1507–1512.

Schweit, K. W. (2016). *Active shooter incidents in the United States in 2014 and 2015*. Washington, DC: Federal Bureau of Investigation, U.S. Department of Justice.

Shaffer, A., Lindhiem, O., & Kolko, D. J. (2013). Treatment effects of a modular intervention for early-onset child behavior problems on family contextual outcomes. *Journal of Emotional and Behavioral Disorders, 21*, 277–288.

Silver, R. C., Holman, E. A., McIntosh, D. N., Poulin, M., & Gil-Rivas, V. (2002). Nationwide longitudinal study of psychological responses to September 11. *Journal of the American Medical Association, 288*(10), 1235–1244.

Stuber, J., Galea, S., Pfefferbaum, B., Vandivere, S., Moore, K., & Fairbrother, G. (2005). Behavior problems in New York City's children after the September 11, 2001, terrorist attacks. *American Journal of Orthopsychiatry, 7*(2), 190–200.

Substance Abuse and Mental Health Services Administration [SAMHSA]. (n.d.). *Incidents of mass violence*. Retrieved from http://www.disasterdistress

.samhsa.gov/disasters/incidents-of-mass-violence .aspx

Tingey, J. L., McGuire, A. P., Stebbins, O. L., & Erickson, T. M. (2019). Moral elevation and compassionate goals predict posttraumatic growth in the context of a college shooting. *The Journal of Positive Psychology, 14,* 261–270.

Travers, A. McDonagh, T., & Elklit, A. (2018). Youth responses to school shootings: A review. *Current Psychiatry Reports, 20,* 2–9.

Turunen, T., Haravuori, H., Punama, R., Suomalainen, L., & Marttunen, M. (2014). The role of attachment in recovery after a school-shooting trauma. *European Journal of Psychotraumatology, 5,* 1–10.

Ungar, M. (2008). Resilience across cultures. *British Journal of Social Work, 38,* 218–235.

Van Dyke, R. B., & Schroeder, J. L. (2006). Implementation of the Dallas Threat of Violence Risk Assessment. In S. R. Jimerson & M. J. Furlong (Eds.), *The handbook of school violence and school safety* (pp. 603–616). Mahwah, NJ: Erlbaum.

Vossekuil, B., Fein, R., Reddy, M., Borum, R., & Modzeleski, W. (2002). *The final report and findings of the safe school initiative: Implications for the prevention of school attacks in the United States.* Washington, DC: U.S. Department of Education, Office of Elementary and Secondary Education, Safe and Drug Free Schools Program, and U.S. Secret Service, National Threat Assessment Center.

Walsh, F. (1996). Family resilience: Crisis and Challenge. *Family Processes, 35,* 261–281.

Walsh, F. (2003). Family resilience: Strengths forged through adversity. In F. Walsh (Ed.), *Normal family processes* (3rd ed.) (pp. 399–423).

Walsh, F. (2007). Traumatic loss and major disasters: Strengthening family and community resilience. *Family Processes, 46*(2), 207–227.

Walsh, F. (2012). Facilitating family resilience: Relational resources for positive youth development in conditions of adversity. In M. Ungar (Ed.), *The social ecology of resilience: A handbook of theory and practice* (pp. 173–185). New York, NY: Springer.

Warnick, B. R., Johnson, B. A., & Rocha, S. (2010). Tragedy and the meaning of school shootings. *Educational Theory, 60,* 371–390.

Webster-Stratton, C. (1990). Stress: A potential disruptor of parent perceptions and family interactions. *Journal of Clinical Child Psychology, 19*(4), 302–312.

Wilson, L. C. (2014). Mass shootings: A meta-analysis of the dose-response relationship. *Journal of Traumatic Stress, 27,* 631–638.

Family Stress and Coping With Sickness and Death

CHAPTER 17

Physical Illness and Family Stress

Jeremy Yorgason, Stephanie Richardson, and Kevin Stott

In 2016, approximately 16% of adults in the United States reported having fair or poor self-rated health (Centers for Disease Control and Prevention, 2016). Furthermore, millions of Americans are diagnosed with some of the primary causes of disability and death, including heart disease, cancer, and diabetes (National Center for Chronic Disease Prevention and Health Promotion, 2019). While these statistics represent adult experiences within a given year, most families will face physical health challenges at some point across the life course. For some, physical illness is experienced in childhood or adolescence; others face these challenges during emerging adulthood or during midlife years. Still others face physical challenges associated with aging. Similar to the variety of stressors addressed in this book, physical illnesses typically occur within the context of family systems, where family relationships and health are seen as mutually influential. In this chapter, characteristics of physical illness are addressed; a theoretical model for examining health stressors and family resilience is presented; and using this model, research findings relating to three situations, including childhood physical illness, physical illness in marriage, and physical illness of aging parents, are discussed.

Illness Characteristics

Stressors associated with physical illnesses often involve a complex interplay of illness characteristics and circumstances. These factors often include (a) type of illness, (b) timing around diagnosis or illness phase, (c) life course timing of illness onset, (d) illness severity (e.g., level of pain, complications), (e) life threat, (f) illness uncertainty, and (g) projected duration of the illness (Rolland, 2019). To consider these characteristics, many studies on illness and families are carried out with small samples that are recruited with particular characteristics in mind, such as having a specific illness (which helps to control for illness intensity, threat, and projected duration to some degree; see Tully et al., 2019). Some studies recruit through medical arenas, allowing some uniformity in time since diagnosis (e.g., adolescents with type 1 diabetes; Kelly et al., 2019). Larger scale studies provide the benefit of tracking changes in health and family relationships across multiple years, with samples that generalize to larger populations (e.g., Waite, Laumann, Levinson, Lindau, & O'Muircheartaigh, 2019). This chapter includes findings from both small and larger scale studies, drawing upon the strengths of each approach.

Theoretical Framework

A broad range of theoretical frameworks has been applied to families and physical health. In this chapter, a combination of McCubbin and Patterson's Double ABC-X model (1982), Walsh's family resilience model (1998), and Karney and Bradbury's vulnerability-stress-adaptation model (1995) are presented. A representation integrating these approaches is shown in Figure 17.1.

Physical health stressors (Figure 17.1) are linked to *individual and family outcomes* through *adaptive processes*. Health stressors are sometimes due to chance (e.g., brain injury resulting from a car accident) and sometimes caused or influenced by stable characteristics or behaviors called *enduring vulnerabilities* or *enduring characteristics* (e.g., poor eating habits, lack of exercise, and genetic predisposition leading to type 2 diabetes). Health stressors and individual and family outcomes are also moderated by both positive and negative enduring characteristics. For example, when someone with the enduring vulnerability of depression experiences a physical health stressor (such as chronic back pain), the adaptive processes of the family can be different than if the person is not suffering from depression. Adaptive processes include family members' perceptions of the health stressors as well as their use of resources and the implementation of coping activities. The link between illness stressors and individual and family outcomes is also mediated by the adaptive processes that families undergo as they respond to stressors; that is, the ways that families adapt to illness stressors determine individual and family

Figure 17.1   Theoretical Model of Illness and Families Integrating Aspects of the Double ABC-X Model, Family Resilience, and the Vulnerability-Stress Adaptation Model

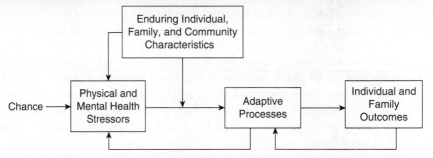

Source: Karney, B. R., & Bradbury, T. N. (1995). The longitudinal course of marital quality and stability: A review of theory, methods, and research. Psychological Bulletin, 118(1), 3–34.]

Note: Model adapted from Karney and Bradbury (1995). *Enduring characteristics* also called risk and protective factors in the resilience literature and family demands and family capabilities in the family stress literature (see Patterson, 2002).

outcomes to a greater extent than the actual stressors. For example, marital outcomes when a wife has cancer depend on the effectiveness of coping behaviors, perceptions of prognosis, and knowledge about the illness, rather than the sole fact of being diagnosed with cancer. In the model, circular patterns are shown where adaptive processes feed back into stressors and where individual and family outcomes feed back into adaptive processes. For example, if a husband who is diagnosed with anxiety communicates openly with his wife, receives support from her, and works together with her against the anxiety (positive adaptive processes), additional stressors will likely be managed. In contrast, if couples communicate poorly, are not supportive, and live separate lives (poor adaptive processes), additional stressors are more likely to pile up for the couple.

Resilience can be identified in various parts of the model. First, resilience could be examined by exploring enduring characteristics that lead to more positive family relationships or health outcomes. For example, cohesion may help families adapt more successfully to certain stressors. In this way, enduring characteristics are identified as risk and protective factors. Second, resilience could be identified in successful adaptive processes including an individual's or family's optimistic perceptions, helpful coping activities, and new resources that assist with family coping. Resilience could also be assessed by exploring various physical, psychological, and family relationship outcomes. As might be expected, resilience may reside in some family members but not in others.

When a Child Is Ill

This vignette provides an example of a potentially life-threatening and disabling circumstance (resulting from premature birth) that required intense and ongoing treatment. The Federal Interagency Forum on Child and Family Statistics (2018)

Vignette

Brandon and Carrie, twins, were born at 23 weeks gestation. The twins were delivered via C-section, and it took 13 minutes to revive Brandon due to the severe lack of lung development. Carrie weighed 1 lb. 9 oz., while Brandon weighed 1 lb. 7 oz. There was about an estimated 10% to 15% chance that either of them would live. Both babies spent 5 months in the neonatal intensive care unit (NICU). Carrie and Brandon each underwent multiple surgeries within the first year of their lives. Months went by full of wondering if the twins would pass away that day or if they would go on to live healthy lives. As would be expected, the transition to parenthood was extremely stressful for Carrie and Brandon's parents. Both twins survived the first 2 years of life and currently face only minimal developmental challenges. Despite the difficulties and unlikely odds that they faced as infants, they have been able to survive and even thrive.

reported that in 2016 approximately 11% of children between the ages of 5 and 17 had some functional limitation resulting from a chronic illness. The National Center for Health Statistics (2019) indicated that 18% of children 11 years and younger, and 27% of youth between 12 and 19 years of age (during 2015–2016) used prescription drugs within the past 30 days. These percentages may seem small, but with more than 74 million children under the age of 18 in the United States in 2017 (Federal Interagency Forum on Child and Family Statistics, 2018), they suggest a substantial number of affected children and families.

Health Stressors

Childhood illness can present various individual and family stressors that are sometimes unique to specific types of illnesses (Winter, Al Ghriwati, & Devine, 2019). To date, many studies have focused on specific illnesses, thereby providing details about illness characteristics including onset, duration, and ways that a particular illness can impact families. Illnesses that have been the focus of research include general health problems and chronic illness, asthma, autism, cancer, cerebral palsy, cystic fibrosis, diabetes, Down syndrome, obesity, and Rett syndrome.

Children with a chronic illness often encounter emotional and behavioral problems. For example, studies found that illness in many cases was associated with social problems (Case, Barber, & Starkey, 2015), financial strain (Kobylianskii et al., 2018), and sibling impact (Havill, Fleming, & Knafl, 2019). In contrast, Blackwell and colleagues (2019) found that although children with a chronic illness reported poorer general physical health, there were no differences in life satisfaction between children with and without a chronic illness.

Siblings of ill children can be affected by childhood illness in important ways (see Chapter 5 in this volume for discussion of siblings of children with intellectual and developmental disabilities). In a review of literature on how childhood chronic illness impacts siblings, Havill and colleagues (2019) found evidence that supported the creating a tenuous balance (CTB) theory. The CTB framework maps out how children with ill siblings experience the impact of childhood illness including (a) knowing something was seriously wrong, (b) figuring out the meaning of the disease, (c) adapting to changes in personal and family life, and (d) handling emotional reactions to the disease. These dimensions include important aspects of experiencing sibling illness including uncertainty around the illness diagnosis, thinking about mortality, assuming a parent-like role, and undergoing strong emotions. Some research suggests that healthy siblings fare better than ill children, yet parents may underestimate illness effects of one child on the health-related quality of life (HRQOL) of another child (Limbers & Skipper, 2014). In contrast, childhood illness may paradoxically be linked with greater sibling closeness, resulting in increased compassion and companionship (Sharpe & Rossiter, 2002).

Parents with a child who is chronically ill face stressors that are more intensive and pervasive than typical parental strains. Childhood illness can have pervasive negative effects on various aspects of the lives of family members, including their emotional well-being, social relationships, and financial well-being (Wightman, et al., 2019). In many cases, the compounded strains are so severe that parents experience symptoms common to posttraumatic stress (e.g., Wikman et al., 2017), and high levels of uncertainty (Mullins et al., 2015). In a mixed methods study of parenting when a child has a life-threatening illness, Mooney-Doyle, Deatrick, Ulrich, Meghani, and Feudtner (2018) found that although parents make every possible effort to meet the needs of both ill and healthy children, there are times when neither are met satisfactorily. Single parents likely face additional strain as they are often left to fill multiple roles alone.

Enduring Characteristics

Some characteristics of families protect them from or place them at an increased risk of experiencing illness stressors (e.g., socioeconomic status [SES], family structure, demographic factors). Studies indicate that the risk of children having a physical illness vary by gender, and race (Weisz & Quinn, 2018; Zhanga, De Lucab, Ohb, Liub, & Song, 2019). Further, Akosile, Chiazor, George, and Egharevba (2017) suggest that family structure (e.g., single-mother homes) is also predictive of increased risk, although this risk may simply be indicative of lower incomes.

Socioeconomic status (SES) can play an important role in relation to health and health-related stressors. Specifically, SES may be linked to health through a number of mechanisms including less access to health care, higher and ongoing environmental stress, and greater likelihood of childhood stress (Garrison & Rodgers, 2018). Although the effects of low SES on health across the lifespan appear pervasive and consistent, Johansson, Lingfors, Golsater, Kristenson, and Fransson (2019) found that participants in their study who had higher levels of physical activity also enjoyed good self-rated health, regardless of their SES. On a similarly positive note, Smith and colleagues (2019) found that children with a hearing loss receive the same level of care regardless of how the care was paid for (private insurance vs. Medicaid).

Following the reasoning of intersectionality theory (Few-Demo, 2014), SES often intersects with other characteristics, such as race, to impact health. For example, Latinx children are less likely to make preventative health-care visits, to have a family doctor they visit regularly, to visit a doctor, and are more likely to visit the emergency room (Langellier, Chen, Vargas-Bustamante, Inkelas, & Ortega, 2014). Disparities around Latinx health-care use may be linked to language barriers, not qualifying for governmental health-care assistance, and lower income (Langellier et al., 2014). Other race groups may experience disparities for a variety of reasons, and those who assist families with ill children need to be aware of the unique needs they may face.

Adaptive Processes

Adaptive processes among parents and siblings surrounding children's health involve coping behaviors, perceptions, and resources. Regarding coping behaviors, family actions can be related to various health, mental health, and relationship outcomes. A strong indicator of positive outcomes is "balanced coping" when illness demands are kept in perspective with other family needs. Balanced coping by parents becomes especially important in attending to the needs of both the ill child and healthy siblings (Mooney-Doyle, Deatrick, Ulrich, Meghani, & Feudtner, 2018). Other healthy family adaptive processes include (a) being actively engaged in problem-focused coping, (b) granting the child as much age-appropriate independence as they are capable of handling with the illness, and (c) receiving support from medical professionals (Heath, Farre, & Shaw, 2017; Zaidman-Zait et al., 2018). A number of programs have been developed to assist families dealing with the chronic illness of a child (e.g., Kieckhefer et al., 2014). Family treatment programs may be received best by families when they are tailored to meet the unique needs of the family system and are in relation to specific illnesses (see Hickey, Anderson, Hearps, & Jordan, 2018; West, Bell, Woodgate, & Moules, 2015).

Illness Perceptions

Perceptions of childhood physical health stressors often account for the link between illness and family resilience. However, perceptions likely differ over time and among family members (Andres et al., 2014; Pardo-Guijarro et al., 2015). Families' views of stress resulting from childhood illnesses likely evolve across diagnosis, treatment, and management phases. Before and shortly after diagnosis, for example, childhood illness may be especially ambiguous, leaving families to manage and live with an unknown future (Szulczewski et al., 2017; Tackett et al., 2015). Over time, childhood illness can present individuals with considerable life disruption, exposure to death and dying, changes to individual and family identity, and altered perceptions of time (e.g., focusing on the present while also recognizing the future and moving on with life; see Manning, Hemingway, & Redsell, 2017).

One demonstration of perceiving resilience is found in posttraumatic growth, or the ability to identify the benefits that result from a difficult experience. For example, in a study of 161 adults who experienced spinal cord injuries as children, January, Zebracki, Chlan, and Vogel (2015) found that most respondents identified at least one positive aspect of their life that resulted from their injury. They also found that posttraumatic growth was correlated with better cognitive and behavioral coping strategies among participants. Similarly, in a study of children with cancer and their parents, Wilson et al. (2016) reported that posttraumatic growth was associated with lower patient posttraumatic stress, with better parents' religious coping, and with stronger family and doctor relationships. From these studies, it appears that posttraumatic growth is more likely to occur when individuals, families, and their care providers manage a childhood illness in positive, unified, and even religious ways. Despite great physical or mental challenges, some families emerge stronger from their illness experiences.

Resources

A number of family resources have been linked to positive outcomes when childhood physical illness occurs. Some resources are specific to family functioning, such as positive parenting; maintaining clear boundaries; communicating effectively; being flexible with rules, roles, and expectations; being committed to the family; maintaining a healthy marriage relationship; and maintaining family rituals and routines (Duran, 2013; Ernst et al., 2019; Kars, Duijnstee, Pool, van Delden, & Grypdonck, 2008; Patterson, 1991). These family resources provide stability for families during times of crisis, ambiguity, and change. Other resources consist of networks outside the family, such as integration in a social system and having social support from family, friends, religious groups, the workplace, psychosocial interventions, and community agencies (McCubbin, Balling, Possin, Frierdich, & Bryne, 2002; Mullins et al., 2015). Further resources may involve whole-family treatments for illness of a child (see Kieckhefer et al., 2014).

Outcomes

Typical outcomes examined in studies of childhood illness include individual (child, parent, sibling) psychological distress, health changes for better or worse in the ill child, and individual child and family functioning (Patterson, 1991). For example, positive parenting behaviors have been linked with better type 1 diabetes treatment adherence (Goethals et al., 2017). Some research suggests that childhood illnesses can have a negative impact on the achievement of developmental milestones in young adulthood (Pinquart, 2014). On the negative side, ill children may be more isolated from social activities when the parents have high stress associated with their illness (Rani & Thomas, 2019). In contrast to individual outcomes, family functioning is more often viewed as part of the adaptive processes that feed into individual outcomes. In that study, family illness management styles were linked with levels of family and individual ill-child functioning. It is likely that these processes operate reciprocally.

When a Spouse or Partner Is Ill

Vignette

Juan and Marcela had been married for approximately 28 years when Juan started experiencing hand tremors and a weakened voice, symptoms that would later be identified as Parkinson's disease. Initially Juan downplayed the symptoms, which was a source of frustration to his wife who had a medical professional background. However, he eventually started visiting doctors to discuss his symptoms. Juan's case of Parkinson's was atypical and difficult to diagnose. Only after visiting multiple doctors over a number of years was a diagnosis made. A few years later, Juan started experiencing painful muscle spasms that impacted his sleep quality. He found himself wandering the house at night, looking for a place where he could be comfortable. Marcela felt that Juan was distancing himself from her by no longer sleeping close to her. Slowly, Marcela has begun to help with Juan's activities of daily living (ADL). Both are concerned about what the future may bring and how much this disease is going to further impact their marriage. Could they adapt their lives around this challenge in a way that their relationship would not only remain intact, but become stronger?

This vignette illustrates physical health challenges in the context of an intimate relationship that can influence relationship roles, routines, and interactions. Although many people have a family history of certain illnesses, these health challenges can still be unexpected, chronic, and sometimes progressive. Further, these and other age-related illnesses can significantly impact couple relationships, including marriage or committed partner relationships.

Studies examining the impact of a general decline in health indicate a minor yet significant decrease in marital quality (Badr & Acitelli, 2005; Booth & Johnson, 1994). Studies investigating the impact of specific health problems sometimes report marital quality declines, yet other times they offer a more complex pattern between illness and marriage. Specific illnesses that have been studied in relation to couple relationships include (but are not limited to) hemodialysis patients (Jiang et al., 2015), arthritis (Yorgason, Wheeler et al., 2019), multiple sclerosis (Neate et al., 2019), Parkinson's disease (Mavandadi et al., 2014), and diabetes (Burns, Fillo, Deschênes, & Schmitz, 2019).

Health Stressors

A growing body of literature examines the impact of physical illness within couple relationships (see Badr & Acitelli, 2017; Bookwala, 2016) and, in general, finds that the amount of stress varies by illness context. For example, among spousal dementia caregivers, daily burden has been shown to be a function of caregiving distress, psychological distress, and relationship quality (Pihet, Passini, &

Eicher, 2017). Stress among couples wherein one spouse was receiving hemodialysis was linked with lower marital satisfaction (Jiang et al., 2015). Although many couples develop aspects of resilience in their relationship when they face illness stressors, those facing greater levels of stress appear to experience stressor pileups, and do not necessarily develop greater resilience (Yorgason, Wheeler et al., 2019).

Although the stress associated with an illness can be difficult for a couple, illness can also have a positive influence on marital quality. Yorgason, Booth, and Johnson (2008) found that a health decline was related to a *decrease* in marital quality, yet the onset of a disability was related to an *increase* in marital quality. A decline in self-rated health likely represents initial changes in health, while the onset of a disability may represent health declines that occur well after health problems have been in process, allowing time for couples to adapt. Similar to this finding, studies of multiple sclerosis (Neate et al., 2019) and Parkinson's disease (Mavandadi et al., 2014) suggest that couples often make positive reappraisals of their relationship after facing serious health challenges. Neate and colleagues (2019) and Mavandadi and colleagues (2014) specifically reported that couples perceived benefits to their relationship, along with improved marital support and togetherness. Other couples report an increase in couple positivity during times of health-related stress (Lingard & Court, 2014). For these reasons, it is important to consider illness conditions when interpreting findings.

Timing of illness onset can also influence the amount of stress experienced by a couple. First, if illness onset is somewhat expected, such as in later life or where a clear pattern of family history provided forewarning, couples may adjust better than if it is completely unexpected. Likewise, prior knowledge of an illness before entering into marriage likely requires less adjustment. Finally, researchers have focused on stress at various points in the illness process, for example, at diagnosis, treatment, and during illness management (e.g. Varner et al., 2019).

Enduring Characteristics

The effects of physical illness challenges may be stronger for younger couples than older couples. The moderating effect of age is recognized in studies of couples dealing with illness during mid- and later life (Berg & Upchurch, 2007). For example, Yorgason and colleagues (2008) found that general health declines are more strongly related to lower marital happiness for young and midlife adults than for older adults. Given that many health problems are age related and perhaps anticipated, marital quality may act as a buffer to physical health concerns in later-life couples (Franks, Wehrspann, August, Rook, & Stephens, 2016). Despite this trend in the literature, studies describing the stressors of illness in both early and late marriage continue to emerge (see Monin et al., 2019; Nutting & Grafsky, 2017).

Whether the spouse is ill versus well, and female versus male are also important enduring characteristics. Studies indicate that marital quality is at greater risk for healthy spouses than for ill spouses (Burman & Margolin, 1992). Furthermore, patients and their partners may not always share the same appraisal of the illness.

For example, in a study of 199 couples where one spouse had type 1 diabetes, partners were more likely than patients to view the illness as shared, and when patient and partner illness appraisals were consistent, partner support was highest (Helgeson et al., 2019). In a study of couples where one received hemodialysis, external support was experienced differently for the ill versus well spouse (Jiang et al., 2015). Specifically, healthy spouses reported greater external support, and ill spouses reported lower external support when marital quality was higher. In relation to gender differences, in a study of couples where one spouse had a kidney transplant, Tkachenko, Franke, Peters, Schiffer, and Zimmermann (2019) found that female caregivers of male patients reported higher supportive dyadic coping than the male patients. They also found that female patients that had the kidney transplant reported higher stress communication, and higher dyadic coping across multiple subscales (supportive, positive, and overall dyadic coping) compared to male caregiver partners. In summary, it is important to consider how illness can impact patients and their partners differently, as well as how couples respond to illness differently when the male versus female is ill.

Additional enduring characteristics that can moderate the link between illness and adaptive processes include SES, religiosity, and social support. Socioeconomic status, as measured by income, access to health care, and education, often results in resources that lead to more adaptive processes. Alternatively, poverty is a risk factor for many illnesses and often presents barriers to optimal health care. Because of the Affordable Care Act, the number of Americans that have access to health care increased between 2013 and 2015 (Martinez & Ward, 2016). However, adults between ages 18 and 64 were less likely to seek medical care when they needed it, if they reported to be poor or near-poor (Martinez & Ward, 2016). Religiosity and spirituality have been associated with both lower levels of stress and higher levels of desirable outcomes within marriage (Ellison, Henderson, Glenn, & Harkrider, 2011; Yorgason, 2015). Benefits of religiosity are often attributed to the social support available through a faith community. Additionally, Clements and Ermakova (2012) showed that the religious construct of *surrender,* or self-denial for a divine purpose, can be an important stress buffer, which may indirectly have an impact on health.

Adaptive Processes and Outcomes

Adaptive processes that mediate the link between illness stressors and outcomes include illness mechanisms, illness-prompted resources, couple coping, and caregiving processes. *Illness mechanisms,* defined as life changes due to an illness, sometimes account for why illness is disruptive to families. Booth and Johnson (1994) reported that a decrease in finances, division of household labor, and marital problems account for some of the negative effects a health decline can have on marital happiness. Yorgason et al. (2008) also found that psychological distress was a consistent mediator between health decline and marital happiness.

Stress-prompted resources, defined as resources that emerge as a result of an illness, can also influence couple relationships and influence couple interactions.

In the case of diabetes, illness-prompted resources might include patient and spousal knowledge about the disease including how to manage it (Zajdel, Jelgeson, Seltman, Korytkowski, & Hausmann, 2018). Using that knowledge, activities such as meal planning and preparation, grocery shopping, having a shared diet plan, and the monitoring of blood sugar levels, when done together in a spirit of supportiveness and cooperation, have been shown to reduce stress and increase enjoyable marital interactions (August, Rook, Franks, & Parris Stephens, 2013). In other cases, medical professionals can provide knowledge that may help couples to prepare for caregiving roles (Henriksson, Årestedt, Benzein, Ternestedt, & Andershed, 2013).

Regarding couple adaptive processes, communication between spouses is paramount. Poor communication patterns, as illustrated by protective buffering (i.e., hiding negative feelings about the illness to avoid hurting the other spouse), can have negative consequences, such as lower life satisfaction and higher levels of depression and anxiety. In a study of 69 couples in which the wife had been diagnosed with early-stage breast cancer, protective buffering on a given day was associated with decreased relationship intimacy and with greater fear of cancer recurrence (Perndorfer Soriano, Siegel, & Laurenceau, 2019). In comparison, good couple communication and supportive interactions can facilitate positive outcomes. Positive problem solving has been associated with greater decreases in women's body mass index (BMI) during a diabetes treatment (Yorgason, Sandberg et al., 2019), and social-related coping efficacy has been linked with improved social or family well-being in persons with cancer (Merluzzi et al., 2019).

The supportive practices couples develop can represent some of the most important adaptive processes to illness. It is common that when an individual is ill, a spouse is called on to provide at least some care. It is important for the caregiver to balance caring behavior while allowing autonomy in the recipient. For example, gaining knowledge about an illness in order to provide support to an ill spouse can be done in either controlling or supportive ways (Houston-Barrett & Wilson, 2014). Revenson, Schiaffino, Majerovitz, and Gibofsky (1991) describe this continuum of supportive behavior as the double-edged sword of social support. They report that positive support predicts lower depression, and problematic support predicts higher depression among rheumatoid arthritis patients.

When Aging Parents Are Ill

Due to age-related declines in health, illness is common among older adults. Over 76% of adults over the age of 65 report to have at least one chronic disease (He et al., 2018). Some common illnesses among older adults include hypertension, type 2 diabetes, arthritis, chronic obstructive pulmonary disease, cancer, heart disease, and Alzheimer's disease (He et al., 2018; Tejada-Vera, 2019). It is estimated that 49% of caregivers are providing care for a parent or parent-in-law, making it the most common type of caregiving relationship (The National Alliance on

During the past 5 years, Diane has been caring for her mother, Thelma, who is diagnosed with Alzheimer's disease. Thelma also is bedridden due to hip problems that resulted from having multiple falls. As the primary caregiver, Diane has not been able to leave her mother's side for any extended amount of time. Diane's siblings are concerned because they have noticed that she is constantly tired and unusually anxious about future care options for her mother. Recently, Diane went to the emergency room to get help with irregular heart palpitations, which turned out to be an anxiety attack. Diane wonders how long she will be able to continue to provide this level of care for her mother.

Caregiving & AARP, 2015). Those providing care for a parent or parent-in-law frequently help with activities of daily living (ADLs). The ADLs with which those caregivers are most likely to assist include getting in and out of bed and chairs, and going to and from the toilet (The National Alliance on Caregiving & AARP, 2015).

Physical Health Stressors of Aging Parents

Physical health challenges in later life often lead to problems with ADLs. Thirty-two percent of the Medicare population experience functional impairment in at least one ADL (Statista, 2019), such as eating, bathing, dressing, toileting, oral care, and getting out of bed or chairs. Among persons in the United States over 65 years of age, many receive assistance with health-care needs through Medicare, a government subsidized insurance program (U.S. Centers for Medicare & Medicaid Services, n.d.). There are diverse pathways to becoming a caregiver for aging parents. For many, the process is gradual, with increasing care being linked to health deterioration and greater needs developing over time, for example, in cases of dementia. For others, becoming a caregiver occurs more rapidly due to a health crisis or emergency, such as with hospitalization due to having a stroke or being diagnosed with cancer. Regardless of how caregiving develops, physical health concerns of aging parents can present difficult challenges for those providing care.

Enduring Characteristics

Several factors moderate the link between stress resulting from caring for an ill parent and adaptive processes. Gender is an important moderating factor because women are more likely to be caregivers. The National Alliance on Caregiving and AARP (2015) report that 60% of caregivers are women, and that 62% of caregivers that spend over 20 hours per week in caregiving activities are women. Further, female caregivers often experience higher levels of distress and burden than male caregivers (Stewart et al., 2016).

Marital status and having siblings can also influence caregiving of ill parents by adult children. Unmarried adult children are more likely to coreside with a widowed mother (Seltzer & Friedman, 2014) and having a parent coreside with an adult child is linked to a lower likelihood of siblings becoming a caregiver (Pezzin, Pollak, & Schone, 2014). Some research suggests that aging parents with multiple children typically receive support from more than one child, although equality in the care provided tends to occur only when siblings have similar levels of other commitments (i.e., employment and marital status; Tolkacheva, van Groenou, & van Tilburg, 2014).

Ethnicity and culture may influence the likelihood of caregiving, associated stressors, and outcomes. On one hand, ethnic or cultural identity may increase the likelihood of an adult child wanting to provide care (Angel, Rote, Brown, Angel, & Markides, 2014). On the other hand, ethnic or cultural influences may decrease the likelihood of care-recipients using available formal services from which they might benefit (Brown, Friedemann, & Mauro, 2014). Culturally sensitive interventions for caregivers and aging care-recipients might enhance the quality of caregiving experiences of all involved. Although there are differences in what caregiving of older parents looks like among different cultures, some research has found that caregiving leads to similar outcomes across cultures, such as poor health of the caregiver (Mendez-Luck et al., 2016; National Alliance on Caregiving & AARP, 2015)

Adaptive Processes

Adaptive processes that mediate the link between caring for an aging parent and the amount of stress experienced include perceptions, resources, and coping activities. From a stress and coping paradigm (Lazarus & Folkman, 1984), the adult-child caregiver's appraisal of the situation will influence outcomes. Resources related to social support are strong indicators of resilience for caregivers and can be helpful by reducing stress, encouraging good health behaviors, and pursuing effective coping activities (Pinquart & Sörensen, 2007). Regarding resources, having a network of supports (Koehly, Ashida, Schafer, & Ludden, 2014), access to formal services (Danilovich, Xiang, & Pinto, 2017), assistance from siblings (Tolkacheva et al., 2014), and financial resources (Bouldin, Shaull, Andresen, Edwards, & McGuire, 2018) may be linked to better outcomes. In an intervention study of caregivers of family members with dementia, Czaja and colleagues (2018) found that a 6-month intervention involving information sessions and telephone support groups was linked with lower depressive symptoms and caregiver burden that were evident even 12 months postintervention.

Outcomes

Adult children report both strains and gains as caregivers (Lynch, Shuster, & Lobo, 2018). The most consistent findings suggest that caregivers experience various burdens brought on by the care they provide, including increased depression, health symptoms, outpatient doctor visits (Chan, Malhotra, Malhotra, Rush, & Østbye, 2013), and even increased mortality (Perkins et al., 2013). Such challenges may be partially due to having restrictions on normal activities, increased health symptoms (Smith, Williamson, Miller, & Schulz, 2011), changing role demands (e.g., work plus the demands of caregiving; Wang, Shyu, Chen, & Yang, 2011), chronic stress (Leggett, Zarit, Kim, Almeida, & Klein, 2014), financial strain (Lee, Tang, Kim, & Albert, 2014; Strauss, 2013), and repetitive health crises (Sims-Gould, Martin-Matthews, & Gignac, 2008). An early indicator of compassion fatigue among caregivers may involve behavioral disengagement (Lynch et al., 2018). In contrast, gains related to being an adult-child caregiver include personal and spiritual growth, enhanced feelings of mastery (Pope, 2013).

Conclusion

Commonalities between childhood, spousal, and parental physical illness provide a sense of what factors are most salient for families dealing with chronic health conditions. Despite the stress created by illness, many families are drawn closer together during the coping process. Furthermore, research suggests that families can experience strains and gains simultaneously.

Enduring characteristics can significantly influence the extent and duration of stress associated with illness and can be used as a target for intervention. Enduring characteristics that cannot be changed, such as gender, age, family structure, and ethnic background, often strongly influence the illness experience of all family members and should be considered when assisting families. For example, physical illness at any age is a challenge for families, although illness in later life may have less negative impact since it is more expected. Enduring characteristics that can be influenced, such as accessibility to health care, outside social support, and internal family interactions, also can be targeted by professionals as points of intervention. For instance, interacting in positive ways with the medical community and gaining knowledge about an illness can be important buffers to the stress associated with a specific illness. Finally, family patterns that are helpful when facing illness include effective family communication, "balanced" coping, family cohesion, and maintaining clear, yet flexible, boundaries.

Although perceptions of illness change with time, maintaining a positive outlook can be beneficial for individuals and families. This is not always easy, especially when an illness involves demanding or unrealistic expectations. Further, different family members may have diverse perceptions of the illness and the roles each family member is expected to carry out (i.e., parent, ill child, sibling). The outcomes of illness are often comorbid with or connected to psychological distress, indicating an important target for prevention and intervention.

Although a tremendous amount of research has been conducted in the areas reviewed in this chapter, there is much room for future study. While most researchers work to isolate the effects of individual illness, comorbidity, especially across physical health domains, needs further attention. From a methodological perspective, the study of illness in families includes a rich blend of qualitative and quantitative studies, yet future studies could use a mixed methods approach to explore resilience processes in greater depth. Many of the outcomes studied in research to date involve negative measures including psychological and relationship distress; hence, more measures of positive family functioning are needed. Although a growing number of studies are exploring illness longitudinally, the reality is that the windows of data collection often provide only a snapshot of the illness. Future research is needed to understand prediagnosis predictors of resilience, as well as family relationship processes across the different phases of illness. In addition, few studies have examined everyday physical illnesses in families, such as colds, the flu, a broken limb, mononucleosis, running a temperature, as well as fluctuations in depressive, anxious, and other psychological symptoms. More research is also needed to understand similarities in the effects of chronic illnesses in childhood, in adulthood, and in later life. Studies could be extended to examine illness management processes in families of diverse forms including blended families, multiple partner fertility, and so forth. Finally, literature exploring illness and families crosses many disciplines including nursing, medicine, and the social sciences. The influence of medical professionals interacting with families is such an integral aspect of experiencing illness that multidisciplinary research teams would enhance both the medical and social arenas.

Research exploring childhood illness, illness of a marriage partner, and caring for an ill parent has dramatically increased in recent decades. Findings indicate (a) an increasing knowledge of the stressors that individuals and families face, (b) the enduring characteristics that predispose families to experience illness and act as protective and risk factors once a chronic illness occurs, (c) adaptive processes families often use, (d) and positive and negative outcomes commonly experienced. Research that has been carried out provides a strong base for future work, yet further effort is needed to better understand illness experiences within families.

DISCUSSION QUESTIONS

1. How do different illness characteristics (illness type, severity, threat, duration, and diagnosis timing) relate differently to family stress depending on whether a child, spouse, or aging parent is ill?

2. What aspects of the three theoretical models used in this chapter (ABC-X model, the family resilience framework, and the vulnerability-stress-adaption model) overlap? Is there a common thread?

3. Using an example from a child, spouse, or aging parent that is ill, what adaptive process might be present given each of the dimensions found in Figure 17.1?

REFERENCES

Akosile, A. E., Chiazor, I. A., George, T. O., & Egharevba, M. E. (2017). Living alone: Exploring variations in single motherhood and child health in sub-Saharan Africa. *Gender & Behaviour, 15*(1), 8284–8300.

Andres, A. M., Alameda, A., Mayoral, O., Hernandez, F., Dominguez, E., Martinez Ojinaga, E., . . . & Tovar, J. A. (2014). Health-related quality of life in pediatric intestinal transplantation. *Pediatric Transplantation, 18*(7), 746–756.

Angel, J. L., Rote, S. M., Brown, D. C., Angel, R. J., & Markides, K. S. (2014). Nativity status and sources of care assistance among elderly Mexican-origin adults. *Journal of Cross-Cultural Gerontology, 29*(3), 243–258.

August, K. J., Rook, K. S., Franks, M. M., & Parris Stephens, M. A. (2013). Spouses' involvement in their partners' diabetes management: Associations with spouse stress and perceived marital quality. *Journal of Family Psychology, 27*(5), 712–721.

Badr, H., & Acitelli, L. K. (2005). Dyadic adjustment in chronic illness: Does relationship talk matter? *Journal of Family Psychology, 19*(3), 465–469.

Badr, H., & Acitelli, L. K. (2017). Re-thinking dyadic coping in the context of chronic illness. *Current Opinion in Psychology, 13*, 44–48.

Berg, C. A., & Upchurch, R. (2007). A developmental-contextual model of couples coping with chronic illness across the adult life span. *Psychological Bulletin, 133*(6), 920–954.

Blackwell, C. K., Elliott, A. J., Baniban, J., Herbstman, J., Hunt, K., Forrest, C.B., & Camargo, C. A., Jr. (2019). General health and life satisfaction in children with chronic illness. *Pediatrics, 143*(6), 1–8.

Bookwala, J. (Ed.). (2016). *Couple relationships in the middle and later years: Their nature, complexity, and role in health and illness.* Washington, DC: American Psychological Association.

Booth, A., & Johnson, D. R. (1994). Declining health and marital quality. *Journal of Marriage and the Family, 56*(1), 218–223.

Bouldin, E. D., Shaull, L., Andresen, E. M., Edwards, V. J., & McGuire, L. C. (2018). Financial and health barriers and caregiving-related difficulties among rural and urban caregivers. *The Journal of Rural Health, 34*(3), 263–274.

Brown, E. L., Friedemann, M. L., & Mauro, A. C. (2014). Use of adult day care service centers in an ethnically diverse sample of older adults. *Journal of Applied Gerontology, 33*(2), 189–206.

Burman, B., & Margolin, G. (1992). Analysis of the association between marital relationships and health problems: An interactional perspective. *Psychological Bulletin, 112*(1), 39–63.

Burns, R. J., Fillo, J., Deschênes, S. S., & Schmitz, N. (2019). Dyadic associations between physical activity and body mass index in couples in which one partner has diabetes: Results from the Lifelines cohort study. *Journal of Behavioral Medicine, 43*(1), 143–149.

Case, R. J. L., Barber, C. C., & Starkey, N. J. (2015). Psychosocial needs of parents and children accessing hospital outpatient paediatric services in New Zealand. *Journal of Paediatrics & Child Health, 51*(11), 1097–1102.

Caregiving in the U.S. (2015). *National Alliance for Caregiving and AARP.* Retrieved from https://www.aarp.org/content/dam/aarp/ppi/2015/caregiving-in-the-united-states-2015-report-revised.pdf

Centers for Disease Control and Prevention. (2016). *Chronic Disease Indicators* (CDI) Data [online]. Retrieved from https://www.cdc.gov/cdi/index.html

Chan, A., Malhotra, C., Malhotra, R., Rush, A. J., & Østbye, T. (2013). Health impacts of caregiving for older adults with functional limitations results from the Singapore Survey on Informal Caregiving. *Journal of Aging and Health, 25*(6), 998–1012.

Clements, A. D., & Ermakova, A. V. (2012). Surrender to God and stress: A possible link between religiosity and health. *Psychology of Religion and Spirituality, 4*(2), 93–107.

Czaja, S. J., Lee, C. C., Perdomo, D., Loewenstein, D., Bravo, M., Moxley, J. H., & Schulz, R. (2018). Community REACH: An implementation of an evidence-based caregiver program. *The Gerontologist, 58*(2), 130–137.

Danilovich, M., Xiang, X., & Pinto, D. (2017). Factors that influence self-reported health changes with caregiving. *Journal of Aging and Health, 29,* 1444–1458.

Duran, B. (2013). Posttraumatic growth as experienced by childhood cancer survivors and their families: A narrative synthesis of qualitative and quantitative research. *Journal of Pediatric Oncology Nursing, 30*(4), 179–197.

Ellison, C. G., Henderson, A. K., Glenn, N. D., & Harkrider, K. E. (2011). Sanctification, stress, and marital quality. *Family Relations: An Interdisciplinary Journal of Applied Family Studies, 60*(4), 404–420.

Ernst, M., Brähler, E., Klein, E. M., Jünger, C., Wild, P. S., Faber, J., . . . & Beutel, M. E. (2019). Parenting in the face of serious illness: Childhood cancer survivors remember different rearing behavior than the general population. *Psycho-Oncology, 28*(8), 1663–1670.

Federal Interagency Forum on Child and Family Statistics. (2018). *America's Children in Brief: Key National Indicators of Well-Being, 2018.* Retrieved from https://www.childstats.gov/pdf/ac2018/ac_18.pdf

Few-Demo,. A. L. (2014). Intersectionality as the "new" critical approach in feminist family studies: Evolving racial/ethnic feminisms and critical race theories. *Journal of Family Theory & Review, 6*(2), 169–183.

Franks, M. M., Wehrspann, E., August, K. J., Rook, K. S., & Parris Stephens, M. A. (2016). Chronic disease management in older couples: Spousal support versus control strategies. In J. Bookwala (Ed.), *Couple relationships in the middle and later years: Their nature, complexity, and role in health and illness.* (pp. 303–323). Washington, DC: American Psychological Association.

Garrison, S. M., & Rodgers, J. L. (2018). Decomposing the causes of the socioeconomic status-health gradient with biometrical modeling. *Journal of Personality and Social Psychology, 116*(6), 1030–1047.

Goethals, E. R., Oris, L., Soenens, B., Berg, C. A., Prikken, S., Van Broeck, N., . . . & Luyckx, K. (2017). Parenting and treatment adherence in type 1 diabetes throughout adolescence and emerging adulthood. *Journal of Pediatric Psychology, 42*(9), 922–932.

Havill, N., Fleming, L. K., & Knafl, K. (2019). Well siblings of children with chronic illness: A synthesis research study. *Research in Nursing & Health, 42*(5), 334–348.

He, Z., Bian, J., Carretta, H. J., Lee, J., Hogan, W. R., Shenkman, E., & Charness, N. (2018). Prevalence of multiple chronic conditions among older adults in Florida and the United States: Comparative analysis of the OneFlorida Data Trust and National Inpatient Sample. *Journal of Medical Internet research, 20*(4), 137.

Heath, G., Farre, A., & Shaw, K. (2017). Parenting a child with chronic illness as they transition into adulthood: A systematic review and thematic synthesis of parents' experiences. *Patient Education and Counseling, 100*(1), 76–92.

Helgeson, V. S., Van Vleet, M., Zajdel, M., Berg, C. A., Kelly, C. S., Tracy, E. L., & Litchman, M. L. (2019). Patient and partner illness appraisals and health among adults with type 1 diabetes. *Journal of Behavioral Medicine, 42*(3), 480–492.

Henriksson, A., Årestedt, K., Benzein, E., Ternestedt, B.-M., & Andershed, B. (2013). Effects of a support group programme for patients with life-threatening illness during ongoing palliative care. *Palliative Medicine, 27*(3), 257–264.

Hickey, L., Anderson, V., Hearps, S., & Jordan, B. (2018). Family appraisal of paediatric acquired brain injury: A social work clinical intervention trial. *Developmental Neurorehabilitation, 21*(7), 457–464.

Houston-Barrett, R. A., & Wilson, C. M. (2014). Couple's relationship with diabetes: Means and meanings for management success. *Journal of Marital and Family Therapy, 40*(1), 92–105.

Jiang, H., Wang, L., Zhang, Q., Liu, D., Ding, J., Lei, Z., . . . & Pan, F. (2015). Family functioning, marital satisfaction and social support in hemodialysis patients and their spouses. *Stress & Health: Journal of the International Society for the Investigation of Stress, 31*(2), 166–174.

January, A. M., Zebracki, K., Chlan, K. M., & Vogel, L. C. (2015). Understanding post-traumatic growth following pediatric-onset spinal cord injury: The critical role of coping strategies for facilitating positive psychological outcomes. *Developmental Medicine & Child Neurology, 57*(12), 1143–1149.

Johansson, L. M., Lingfors, H., Golsäter, M., Kristenson, M., & Fransson, E. I. (2019). Can physical activity compensate for low socioeconomic status with regard to poor self-rated health and low quality-of-life? *Health and Quality of Life Outcomes, 17*(1), 33.

Karney, B. R., & Bradbury, T. N. (1995). The longitudinal course of marital quality and stability: A review of theory, methods, and research. *Psychological Bulletin, 118*(1), 3–34.

Kars, M. C., Duijnstee, M. S. H., Pool, A., van Delden, J. J. M., & Grypdonck, M. H. F. (2008). Being there: Parenting the child with acute lymphoblastic leukaemia. *Journal of Clinical Nursing, 17*(12), 1553–1562.

Kelly, C. S., Berg, C. A., Lansing, A. H., Turner, S. L., Munion, A. K., Tracy, E. L., & Wiebe, D. J. (2019). Keeping parents connected in early emerging adulthood: Diabetes-related disclosure and solicitation. *Journal of Family Psychology, 33*(7), 809–818.

Kieckhefer, G. M., Trahms, C. M., Churchill, S. S., Kratz, L., Uding, N., & Villareale, N. (2014). A randomized clinical trial of the building on family strengths program: An education program for parents of children with chronic health conditions. *Maternal and Child Health Journal, 18*(3), 563–574.

Kobylianskii, A., Jegathesan, T., Young, E., Fung, K., Huber, J., & Minhas, R. S. (2018). Experiences of inner-city fathers of children with chronic illness. *Clinical Pediatrics, 57*(7), 792–801.

Koehly, L. M., Ashida, S., Schafer, E. J., & Ludden, A. (2014). Caregiving networks—Using a network approach to identify missed opportunities. *The Journals of Gerontology Series B: Psychological Sciences and Social Sciences, 70*, 143–154.

Langellier, B. A., Chen, J., Vargas-Bustamante, A., Inkelas, M., & Ortega, A. N. (2016). Understanding health-care access and utilization disparities among Latino children in the United States. *Journal of Child Health Care, 20*(2), 133–144.

Lazarus, R. S., & Folkman, S. (1984). *Stress, appraisal, and coping.* New York, NY: Springer.

Lee, Y., Tang, F., Kim, K. H., & Albert, S. M. (2014). The vicious cycle of parental caregiving and financial well-being: A longitudinal study of women. *The Journals of Gerontology Series B: Psychological Sciences and Social Sciences, 70*, 425–431.

Leggett, A. N., Zarit, S. H., Kim, K., Almeida, D. M., & Klein, L. C. (2014). Depressive mood, anger, and daily cortisol of caregivers on high- and low-stress days. *The Journals of Gerontology Series B: Psychological Sciences and Social Sciences, 70*, 820–829.

Limbers, C. A., & Skipper, S. (2014). Health-related quality of life measurement in siblings of children with physical chronic illness: A systematic review. *Families, Systems, & Health, 32*(4), 408–415.

Lingard, R. J., & Court, J. (2014). Can couples find a silver lining amid the dark cloud of ME/CFS: A pilot study. *The Family Journal, 22*(3), 304–310.

Lynch, S. H., Shuster, G., & Lobo, M. L. (2018). The family caregiver experience—Examining the positive and negative aspects of compassion satisfaction and compassion fatigue as caregiving outcomes. *Aging & Mental Health, 22*(11), 1424–1431.

Manning, J. C., Hemingway, P., & Redsell, S. A. (2017). Stories of survival: Children's narratives of psychosocial well-being following paediatric critical illness or injury. *Journal of Child Health Care, 21*(3), 236–252.

Martinez, M. E., & Ward, B. W. (2016). *Health care access and utilization among adults aged 18–64, by poverty level: United States, 2013–2015* (NCHS data brief, number 262). Hyattsville, MD: National Center for Health Statistics.

Mavandadi, S., Dobkin, R., Mamikonyan, E., Sayers, S., Ten Have, T., & Weintraub, D. (2014). Benefit finding and relationship quality in Parkinson's disease: A pilot dyadic analysis of husbands and wives. *Journal of Family Psychology, 28*(5), 728–734.

McCubbin, H. I., & Patterson, J. M. (1982). Family adaptation to crisis. In H. I. McCubbin, A. E. Cauble, & J. M. Patterson (Eds.), *Family stress, coping, and social support* (pp. 26–47). Springfield, IL: Thomas.

McCubbin, M., Balling, K., Possin, P., Frierdich, S., & Bryne, B. (2002). Family resiliency in childhood cancer. *Family Relations, 51*(2), 103–111.

Merluzzi, T. V., Serpentini, S., Philip, E. J., Yang, M., Salamanca, B. N., Heitzmann Ruhf, C. A., & Catarinella, A. (2019). Social relationship coping efficacy: A new construct in understanding social support and close personal relationships in persons with cancer. *Psycho-Oncology, 28*, 85–91.

Mendez-Luck, C. A., Geldhof, G. J., Anthony, K. P., Steers, W. N., Mangione, C. M., & Hays, R. D. (2016). Orientation to the caregiver role among Latinas of Mexican origin. *The Gerontologist, 56*(6), 99–108.

Mooney-Doyle, K., Deatrick, J. A., Ulrich, C. M., Meghani, S. H., & Feudtner, C. (2018). Parenting in childhood life-threatening illness: A mixed-methods study. *Journal of Palliative Medicine, 21*, 208–215.

Monin, J. K., Manigault, A., Levy, B. R., Schulz, R., Duker, A., Clark, M. S., . . . & Kershaw, T. (2019). Gender differences in short-term cardiovascular effects of giving and receiving support for health concerns in marriage. *Health Psychology, 38*(10), 936–947.

Mullins, L. L., Molzon, E. S., Suorsa, K. I., Tackett, A. P., Pai, A. L. H., & Chaney, J. M. (2015). Models of resilience: Developing psychosocial interventions for parents of children with chronic health conditions. *Family Relations, 64*(1), 176–189.

Neate, S. L., Taylor, K. L., Jelinek, G. A., De Livera, A. M., Simpson, J. S., Bevens, W., & Weiland, T. J. (2019). On the path together: Experiences of partners of people with multiple sclerosis of the impact of lifestyle modification on their relationship. *Health & Social Care in the Community, 27*(6), 1515–1524.

National Alliance on Caregiving & AARP. (2015). *Caregiving in the U.S.: 2015 report.* Retrieved from https://www.aarp.org/content/dam/aarp/ppi/2015/caregiving-in-the-united-states-2015-report-revised.pdf

National Center for Chronic Disease Prevention and Health Promotion. (2019). *About chronic diseases*. Retrieved from https://www.cdc.gov/chronicdisease/about/index.htm

National Center for Health Statistics. (2019). *Prescription drug use in the United States, 2015–2016* (NCHS Data Brief No. 334). Retrieved from https://www.cdc.gov/nchs/products/databriefs/db334.htm

Nutting, R., & Grafsky, E. L. (2017). Crohn's disease and the young couple: An interpretative phenomenological analysis. *Contemporary Family Therapy, 40*(2), 176–187.

Pardo-Guijarro, M. J., Martínez-Andrés, M., Notario-Pacheco, B., Solera-Martínez, M., Sánchez-López, M., & Martínez-Vizcaíno, V. (2015). Self-reports versus parental perceptions of health-related quality of life among deaf children and adolescents. *Journal of Deaf Studies and Deaf Education, 20*(3), 275–282.

Patterson, J. M. (1991). Family resilience to the challenge of a child's disability. *Pediatric Annals, 20*(9), 491–499.

Perkins, M., Howard, V. J., Wadley, V. G., Crowe, M., Safford, M. M., Haley, W. E., . . . & Roth, D. L. (2013). Caregiving strain and all-cause mortality: Evidence from the REGARDS study. *The Journals of Gerontology Series B: Psychological Sciences and Social Sciences, 68*(4), 504–512.

Perndorfer, C., Soriano, E. C., Siegel, S. D., & Laurenceau, J.-P. (2019). Everyday protective buffering predicts intimacy and fear of cancer recurrence in couples coping with early-stage breast cancer. *Psycho-Oncology, 28*(2), 317–323.

Pezzin, L. E., Pollak, R. A., & Schone, B. S. (2014). Bargaining power, parental caregiving, and intergenerational coresidence. *The Journals of Gerontology Series B: Psychological Sciences and Social Sciences, 70*, 969–980.

Pihet, S., Passini, C. M., & Eicher, M. (2017). Good and bad days: Fluctuations in the burden of informal dementia caregivers, an experience sampling study. *Nursing Research, 66*(6), 421–431.

Pinquart, M. (2014). Achievement of developmental milestones in emerging and young adults with and without pediatric chronic illness–A meta-analysis. *Journal of Pediatric Psychology, 39*(6), 577–587.

Pinquart, M., & Sörensen, S. (2007). Correlates of physical health of informal caregivers: A meta-analysis. *The Journals of Gerontology Series B: Psychological Sciences and Social Sciences, 62*(2), 126–137.

Pope, N. D. (2013). Views on aging: How caring for an aging parent influences adult daughters' perspectives on later life. *Journal of Adult Development, 20*(1), 46–56.

Rani, A., & Thomas, P. T. (2019). Stress and perceived stigma among parents of children with epilepsy. *Neurological Sciences: Official Journal of The Italian Neurological Society And Of The Italian Society Of Clinical Neurophysiology, 40*(7), 1363–1370.

Revenson, T. A., Schiaffino, K. M., Majerovitz, S.D., & Gibofsky, A. (1991). Social support as a double-edged sword: The relation of positive and problematic support to depression among rheumatoid arthritis patients. *Social Science & Medicine, 33*(7), 807–813.

Rolland, J. S. (2019). The family, chronic illness, and disability: An integrated practice model. In B. H. Fiese, M. Celano, K. Deater-Deckard, E. N. Jouriles, & M. A. Whisman (Eds.), *APA handbook of contemporary family psychology: Applications and broad impact of family psychology, Vol. 2* (pp. 85–102). Washington, DC: American Psychological Association.

Seltzer, J. A., & Friedman, E. M. (2014). Widowed mothers' coresidence with adult children.

The Journals of Gerontology Series B: Psychological Sciences and Social Sciences, 69B(1), 63–74.

Sharpe, D., & Rossiter, L. (2002). Siblings of children with a chronic illness: A meta-analysis. *Journal of Pediatric Psychology, 27*(8), 699–710.

Sims-Gould, J., Martin-Matthews, A., & Gignac, M. A. M. (2008). Episodic crises in the provision of care to elderly relatives. *Journal of Applied Gerontology, 27*(2), 123–140.

Smith, G. R., Williamson, G. M., Miller, L. S., & Schulz, R. (2011). Depression and quality of informal care: A longitudinal investigation of caregiving stressors. *Psychology and Aging, 26*(3), 584–591.

Smith, B., Zhang, J., Pham, G. N., Pakanati, K., Raol, N., Ongkasuwan, J., & Anne, S. (2019). Effects of socioeconomic status on children with hearing loss. *International Journal of Pediatric Otorhinolaryngology, 116*, 114–117.

Statista. (2019). *Characteristics of the Medicare population in 2019.* Retrieved from https://www.statista.com/statistics/246650/characteristics-of-the-us medicare-population/

Stewart, N. J., Morgan, D. G., Karunanayake, C. P., Wickenhauser, J. P., Cammer, A., Minish, D., . . . & Hayduk, L. A. (2016). Rural caregivers for a family member with dementia: Models of burden and distress differ for women and men. *Journal of Applied Gerontology, 35*(2), 150–178.

Strauss, J. R. (2013). Caregiving for parents and in-laws: Commonalities and differences. *Journal of Gerontological Social Work, 56*(1), 49–66.

Szulczewski, L., Mullins, L. L., Bidwell, S. L., Eddington, A. R., & Pai, A. L. H. (2017). Meta-analysis: Caregiver and youth uncertainty in pediatric chronic illness. *Journal of Pediatric Psychology, 42*(4), 395–421.

Tackett, A. P., Cushing, C. C., Suorsa, K. I., Mullins, A. J., Gamwell, K. L., Mayes, S., . . . & Mullins, L. L. (2015). Illness uncertainty, global psychological distress, and posttraumatic stress in pediatric cancer: A preliminary examination using a path analysis approach. *Journal of Pediatric Psychology, 41*(3), 309–318.

Talaei-Khoei, M., Fischerauer, S. F., Jha, R., Ring, D., Chen, N., & Vranceanu, A.-M. (2018). Bidirectional mediation of depression and pain intensity on their associations with upper extremity physical function. *Journal of Behavioral Medicine, 41*(3), 309–317.

Tejada-Vera B. (2019). *Leading Causes of Death: United States, 1999–2017.* National Center for Health Statistics.

Tkachenko, D., Franke, L., Peters, L., Schiffer, M., & Zimmermann, T. (2019). Dyadic coping of kidney transplant recipients and their partners: Sex and role differences. *Frontiers in Psychology, 10*, 397.

Tolkacheva, N., van Groenou, M. B., & van Tilburg, T. (2014). Sibling similarities and sharing the care of older parents. *Journal of Family Issues, 35*(3), 312–330.

Tully, C., Rose, M., Breen, S., Herrera, N., Shelef, D. Q., Streisand, R., & Teach, S. J. (2019). Relationship between parent mood and resilience and child health outcomes in pediatric asthma. *Families, Systems, & Health, 37*(2), 167–172.

U.S. Centers for Medicare & Medicaid Services. (n.d.). *What is Medicare?* Retrieved from https://www.medicare.gov/what-medicare-covers/your-medicare-coverage-choices/whats-medicare

Varner, S., Lloyd, G., Ranby, K. W., Callan, S., Robertson, C., & Lipkus, I. M. (2019). Illness uncertainty, partner support, and quality of life: A dyadic longitudinal investigation of couples facing prostate cancer. *Psychooncology, 28*(11), 2188–2194.

Walsh, F. (1998). *Strengthening family resilience.* New York, NY: Guilford Press.

Wang, Y.-N., Shyu, Y.-I. L., Chen, M.-C., & Yang, P.-S. (2011). Reconciling work and family caregiving among adult-child family caregivers of older people with dementia: Effects on role strain and depressive symptoms. *Journal of Advanced Nursing, 67*(4), 829–840.

Waite, L. J., Laumann, E. O., Levinson, W. S., Lindau, S. T., & O'Muircheartaigh, C. A. (2019). *National Social Life, Health, and Aging Project (NSHAP): Wave 1, [United States], 2005–2006.* Ann Arbor, MI: Inter-university Consortium for Political and Social Research.

Weisz, C., & Quinn, D. M. (2018). Stigmatized identities, psychological distress, and physical health: Intersections of homelessness and race. *Stigma and Health, 3*(3), 229–240.

West, C. H., Bell, J. M., Woodgate, R. L., & Moules, N. J. (2015). Waiting to return to normal: An exploration of family systems intervention in childhood cancer. *Journal of Family Nursing, 21*(2), 261–294.

Wightman, A., Taylor Zimmerman, C., Neul, S., Lepere, K., Cedars, K., & Opel, D. (2019). Caregiver experience in pediatric dialysis. *Pediatrics, 143*(2), e20182102.

Wikman, A., Ljungman, L., Pingel, R., Hagedoorn, M., Sanderman, R., von Essen, L., & Cernvall, M. (2017). The interdependence of posttraumatic stress symptoms in parental dyads during and after their child's treatment for cancer. *Acta Oncologica, 56*(12), 1698–1704.

Wilson, J. Z., Marin, D., Maxwell, K., Cumming, J., Berger, R., Saini, S., . . . & Chibnall, J. T. (2016). Association of posttraumatic growth and illness-related burden with psychosocial factors of patient, family, and provider in pediatric cancer survivors. *Journal of Traumatic Stress, 29*(5), 448–456.

Winter, M. A., Al Ghriwati, N., & Devine, K. A. (2019). Pediatric chronic health conditions: Adaptation within the family context. In B. H. Fiese (Ed.), *APA handbook of contemporary family psychology: Applications and broad impact of family psychology, Vol. 2* (pp. 69–84). Washington, DC: American Psychological Association.

Yorgason, J. B. (2015). Exploring daily religious/spiritual activities among older couples: Religious/spiritual influence moderating the effects of health symptoms on marital interactions. *Journal of Religion, Spirituality & Aging, 27,* 201–221.

Yorgason, J. B., Booth, A., & Johnson, D. (2008). Health, disability, and marital quality is the association different for younger versus older cohorts? *Research on Aging, 30*(6), 623–648.

Yorgason, J. B., Wheeler, B., Wong, J. D., Stott, K. L., Roper, S. O., & Christensen, K. D. N. (2019). Is higher stress associated with higher resilience? Exploring married couples' experiences managing comorbid diabetes and osteoarthritis. *Family Science Review, 23*(1), 122–140.

Yorgason, J. B., Sandberg, J. G., Weinstock, R. S., Trief, P. M., Fisher, L., & Hessler, D. (2019). The importance of relationship processes for lowering BMI over time in women with type 2 diabetes in a randomized controlled trial. *Obesity Research & Clinical Practice, 13*(6), 599–601.

Zajdel, M., Helgeson, V. S., Seltman, H. J., Korytkowski, M. T., & Hausmann, L. R. M. (2018). Daily communal coping in couples with type 2 diabetes: Links to mood and self-care. *Annals of Behavioral Medicine, 52*(3), 228–238.

Zaidman-Zait, A., Mirenda, P., Szatmari, P., Duku, E., Smith, I. M., Vaillancourt, T., . . . & Georgiades, S. (2018). Profiles of social and coping resources in families of children with autism spectrum disorder: Relations to parent and child outcomes. *Journal of Autism and Developmental Disorders, 48*(6), 2064–2076.

Zhanga, A., De Lucab, S., Ohb, S., Liub, C., & Song, X. (2019).The moderating effect of gender on the relationship between bullying victimization and adolescents' self–rated health: An exploratory study using the Fragile Families and Wellbeing Study. *Children & Youth Services Review, 96,* 155–162.

Family Socioeconomic Context and Mental Health in Parents and Children

A Heuristic Framework

Kandauda A. S. Wickrama, Catherine Walker O'Neal, and Tae Kyoung Lee

Research highlights the prevalence of psychological symptoms and disorders during adolescence and young adulthood, noting the continuity of symptoms from adolescence to young adulthood (Rutter, Kim-Cohen, & Maughan, 2006). At the same time, a growing body of literature suggests that midlife (40–60 years), a life stage when adults are often parenting adolescents or young adults, is also a sensitive period for the development of mental and physical health problems (Wickrama, Kwag, Lorenz, Conger, & Surjadi, 2010). Because parents and children are interdependent members of the same family system, it is essential to consider the prevalence and progression of both parents' and children's mental health together (i.e., family mental health) within a single theoretical framework. Specifically, understanding (a) the socioeconomic factors influencing family mental health; (b) change and continuity in family mental health; and (c) interindividual associations in family mental health can inform the formulation and implementation of health policies as well as intervention and prevention efforts, such as programming and counseling initiatives.

In the present focus on mental health outcomes of parents and children, we center our attention on psychopathology, particularly capturing the level (severity) of psychological symptoms, which can include various psychological problems such as depression, anxiety, hostility, and somatization. More specifically, we largely focus on depressive symptoms as a marker for distress. Research has shown that a global construct of general psychopathology underlies these multiple psychological symptoms (Derogatis & Melisaratos, 1983), and repeated and elevated levels of psychological symptoms may contribute to the onset of psychological disorders. Elevated levels of psychological symptoms or psychological disorders may continue over the life course within the same dimension (homotypic continuity) or across dimensions (heterotypic continuity; Rutter et al., 2006).

The association between adverse family socioeconomic conditions (hereafter termed *family socioeconomic risk*, FSR) and family mental health (i.e., parents' and offspring's mental health and the associations between family members mental health) is well established in the literature (c.f., Center on Social Determinants of Health, 2008). This association is evident in research rooted in numerous research traditions, including stress-health research, intergenerational and life-course research, relationship-focused research, and child and youth development research. Utilizing these various research traditions, researchers have identified different, but related, mechanisms that explain how FSR is linked to family mental health. Some of the most well-established mechanisms include direct stress exposure, destructive family processes, children's development problems, and early neurological and biological impairments (e.g., Conger, Conger, & Martin, 2010; Palacios-Barrios & Hanson, 2019; Seeman, Epel, Gruenewald, Karlamangla, & McEwen, 2010; Wickrama, O'Neal, & Lee, 2016a). Although these studies have supplied a large body of research on the effects of FSR, there is a general lack of integration across these research traditions, which is problematic for developing a comprehensive understanding of how FSR contributes to mental health for parents and children who are functioning in the same family system over a substantial period of their life course.

To this end, the current chapter provides a review of the mechanisms connecting FSR and family mental health for the purpose of developing a comprehensive integrated model drawing from multiple research traditions. The resulting integrated model, termed the *family socioeconomic risk and family mental health* (FSAMH) model was derived from our exploration of existing theoretical and empirical research including our own work and serves as a heuristic organizing framework providing a deeper understanding of the FSR–family mental health connection to guide future research, outreach, and policy initiatives.

The FSAMH model is primarily grounded in our understanding of the life-course perspective (Elder & Giele, 2009), stress theories (Lazarus, 1999; Pearlin, Schieman, Fazio, & Meersman, 2005), family systems perspective (Broderick, 1993; Cox & Paley, 1997), and particularly the family stress model, which sequentially combines relevant family and health constructs using important aspects of above theories and a developmental perspective (Conger et al., 2010). In addition, we draw from attachment theory (Bowlby, 1988) and self-regulation theory (Baumeister, 2002) as well as of previous biopsychosocial research to explain associations between constructs.

Before reviewing the FSAMH model in detail, particular life-course concepts that guided the creation of the FSAMH model warrant discussion. These include the importance of utilizing a "long view" to consider experiences over the life course, stress proliferation and the accrual of sequentially contingent stressors, cumulative influences over the life course, and the "linked lives" of family members (Elder & Giele, 2009). For instance, in utilizing a long view over the life course for both children (early life course) and parents (later life course), stressors associated with FSR, such as family economic hardship, continue over time *and* also proliferate into other domains, such as stressful family processes (Conger et al., 2010). This cascade, or *chain of risks* can have mental health consequences for children. In this manner, consistent with the life course *linked lives* notion and the interdependence tenet of family systems theory (Broderick, 1993; Cox & Paley, 1997), the FSAMH recognizes socioeconomic risk as a family-level characteristic with consequences for both parents and children. Fitting with these notions, the FSAMH framework also incorporates dynamic, dyadic mental health associations between (1) mothers and fathers and (2) parents and children over time.

FSAMH Model

The goal of this chapter is the development of a framework that aides in understanding the big picture of numerous pathways and mechanisms linking FSR and family mental health. Figure 18.1 illustrates the FSAMH model with three associated attributes (parents' mental health, family processes, and offspring development; Boxes 2, 3, 4) that directly and indirectly stem from FSR (Box 1) and continue over the life courses as trajectories to ultimately impact offspring mental health (Box 5) across childhood (<11 years) and adolescence (11–19 years) and into adulthood (19–40 years) acknowledging biological processes that are also at play (Boxes 6 and 7). In Figure 18.1, single-headed arrows depict unidirectional, additive influences, whereas double-headed arrows depict bidirectional dyadic associations that are often simultaneous. Double arrows depict moderating influences.

Figure 18.1   The Family Socioeconomic Risk and Mental Health (FSAMH) Model: A Heuristic Framework

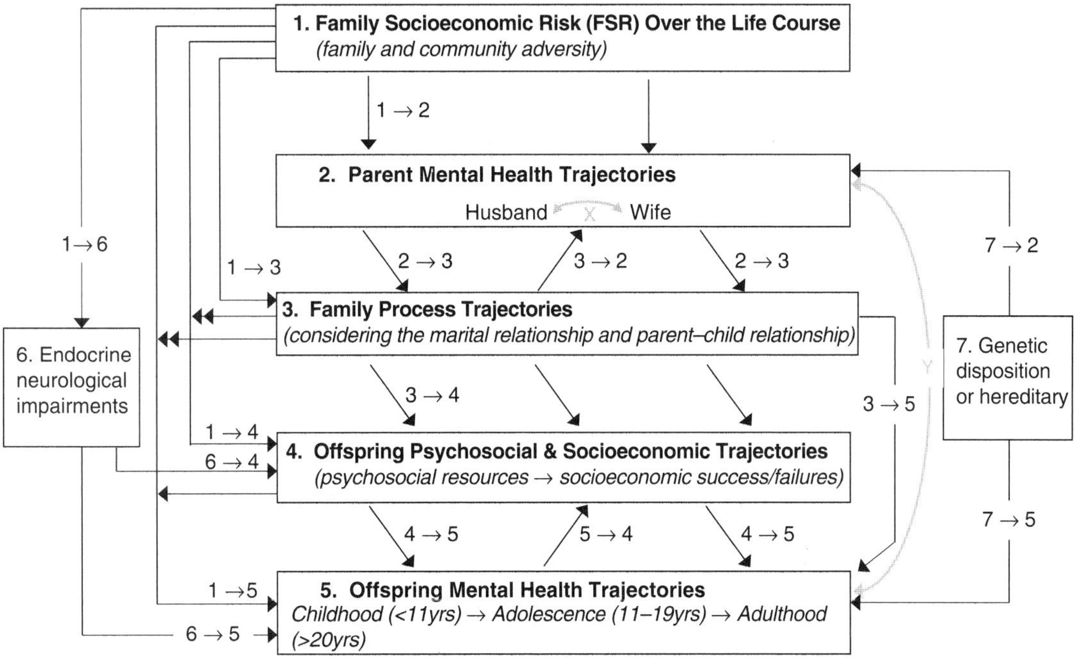

Note: Black arrows represent directional paths. Gray double-headed arrows represent bidirectional correlations. Double arrows represent moderating effects.

Beginning with FSR (Box 1), the figure depicts the influence of FSR on trajectories of parent mental health (Box 2), family processes (Box 3), offspring psychosocial and socioeconomic development (Box 4), and youth mental health (Box 5). Paths 2→3 and 3→2 depict the reciprocal influences between parents' mental health and family processes over time, particularly family processes related to the marital relationship. Path 3→4 represents the influence of family processes on youth psychosocial development and related socioeconomic trajectories. As illustrated in Box 4, the development of psychosocial and socioeconomic resources can also contribute to youth socioeconomic successes. Paths 4→5 and 5→4 depict reciprocal influences between youth socioeconomic trajectories and mental health trajectories.

We emphasize that Boxes 2 through 5 reflect parallel, longitudinal attributes as growth trajectories that change over time. As such, *trajectories* of attributes should be considered, accounting for their initial levels and change (slope) over time in order to utilize a long view to identify the continuity and changes in attributes over time. Also, they allow for the identification of both (1) associations between the levels of attributes and (2) associations between within-individual *changes* in attributes over the life course (e.g., interlocking trajectories of youth socioeconomic failures and depressive symptoms). These ideas are further incorporated in the FSAMH model through repeated and reciprocal arrows connecting boxes.

Meanwhile, Box 6 and associated paths depict the endocrine and neurological mediating influences, whereas Box 7 represents the role of genetic disposition including the hereditary connection between biological parents' mental health and their children's mental health. The moderating influences include family processes and youth developmental outcomes (e.g., psychosocial resources) as resilience factors that may modify the association between FSR and youth mental health outcomes (noted by double arrows in Figure 18.1). The curved arrow X notes the relational interdependence between husbands and wives, whereas the curved arrow Y notes the relational interdependence between parents and children. Figure 18.2 further illustrates these interdependencies to emphasize connections between family members' mental health over the life course by modeling dyadic and crossover influences (dependencies) involving parents and children.

We will discuss all the paths shown in FSAMH model (Figure 18.1) in the sections that follow beginning with defining and describing research that identifies specific FSR attributes and followed by an explanation of sequential mediation paths (Paths 1→2, 2→3, 3→4, 4→5) and reciprocal paths (Paths 3↔2 and 5 ↔ 4) resulting in youth mental health trajectories. We then describe (a) paths pertaining to endocrine and neurological impairments (Paths 1→6, 6→4, and 6→5), (b) the role of genetic disposition (Paths 7→2 and 7→5), (c) direct or "unpacked" paths (Paths 1→3, 1→4, 1→5, and 3→5), (d) dyadic associations X and Y, and (e) moderation or resilience as depicted by double-headed arrows.

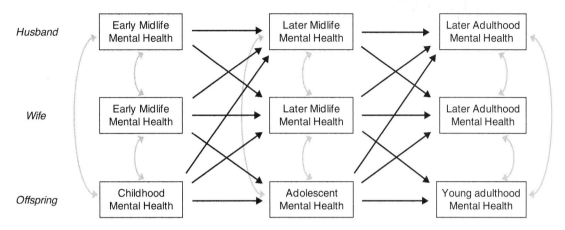

Figure 18.2   Mental Health Interdependence Among Family Members (Considering Husbands, Wives, and Offspring)

Note: Black arrows represent directional paths. Gray double-headed arrows represent bi-directional correlations. Double arrows represent moderating effects.

Family Socioeconomic Risk (FSR)

Family socioeconomic risk includes adverse socioeconomic conditions and related structural characteristics, such as family poverty, low parental education, adverse work conditions, unemployment (or under employment), minority status, and parents' marital status (Conger et al., 2010; Wickrama, Lee, O'Neal, & Kwon, 2015). Racial/ethnic minority status reflects a particularly unique risk given that it influences parents' and offspring's mental health through their experiences with systematic and day-to-day discrimination (Brody et al., 2013; Wickrama, Noh, & Bryant, 2005). Although race/ethnicity is related to socioeconomic status, mental health consequences associated with race/ethnicity should not be dismissed as a product of socioeconomic status (SES) entirely. Research has shown that the level of depressive symptoms are higher among African American youth compared to Caucasian youth after taking family socioeconomic characteristics into account (Wickrama et al., 2005).

In addition to family-level characteristics, adverse community characteristics in which the family resides also place families at risk for emotional problems. Examples of adverse community characteristics include structural and relational components of communities, such as high crime rates, poor housing, and high community unemployment rates along with a lack of physical or social resources and opportunities. For instance, studies have linked the deterioration of the physical, social, and normative community environments to residents' well-being (Cutrona et al., 2003; Wickrama et al., 2015). Through the ambient stress (i.e., community stress) that results from direct exposure to adverse community conditions, parents and children in adverse communities are predisposed to psychological symptoms (Ross & Mirowsky, 2009). Thus, both family and community socioeconomic adversities place parents and children at risk for poor mental health. As such, the FSAMH model incorporates both family and community socioeconomic adversity when conceptualizing socioeconomic risk factors (i.e., FSR) for poor mental health. Because FSR influences the mental health of parents *and* children, it can be considered as a common fate factor influencing family mental health (Ledermann & Kenny, 2012; Lee, Wickrama, & O'Neal, 2020).

Given that family and community adverse socioeconomic circumstances often co-occur, parents and children contend with constellations of socioeconomic stressors that serve as risk factors for poor mental health rather than isolated instances of socioeconomic adversity (Brody et al., 2013; Lee, Wickrama, & O'Neal, 2019). Although research notes robust findings related to the differential effects of both multiple and single risk factors (Sameroff, 2006), exposure to multiple socioeconomic adversities has generally been shown to result in more severe developmental and health consequences compared to exposure to single adverse socioeconomic experiences (Evans & Kim, 2010; Lee et al., 2019). For example, studies using composite measures to capture multiple indicators of FSR (e.g., current parent unemployment, single-parent family structure, inadequate income, and adverse community characteristics) demonstrate that, on average, youth who experience more socioeconomic risks average elevated psychological symptoms, less educational attainment, and more physical health problems than those who experience fewer socioeconomic risks (Brody et al., 2013; Wickrama, O'Neal, & Lee, 2016b). Drawing from these findings, there is a *cumulative* influence of socioeconomic adversity on developmental outcomes as well as physical and mental health outcomes of parents and children. That is, mental and physical health inequalities are, at least in part, explained by variation in exposure to cumulative socioeconomic adversity (Evans & Kim, 2010; Wickrama et al., 2016a, b). Consequently, the FSAMH model provides a framework for understanding how a specific socioeconomic risk factor (e.g., family poverty, minority status) or multiple socioeconomic risk factors come to influence the mental health of parents and children.

Family Socioeconomic Risk (FSR) and Parents' Mental Health (Path 1→2)

The central tenant of the family stress model is that the family economic pressure increases parents' distress, which has negative consequences for family well-being (Conger et al., 2010). Previous studies have documented that depressive symptoms can be both a direct and indirect reflection of family economic hardship as a prominent family stressor. Regarding the direct influence, stress researchers (e.g., Pearlin et al., 2005) posit that depression is one of the most observable reflections of stress, and experiences with economic hardship may directly generate depressive feelings. Consistent with stress appraisal theory (Lazarus, 1999), when an individual is exposed to a stressor (e.g., family economic hardship), they manage the stressor by subjectively appraising its threat and assessing available resources. Stress is thought to occur as a result of this stress-appraisal process. Negative effects of a stressor develop, in part, through the individual's excessive worry and related fear and sense of uncertainty (Nella, Panagopoulou, Galanis, Montgomery, & Benos, 2015), which often leads to increased psychological symptoms. In addition, the stress process theory (Pearlin et al., 2005) posits that chronic stressful conditions result in repeated and chronic negative emotions, which contribute to consistently elevated levels of psychological symptoms.

Depressive symptoms are also thought to be an indirect reflection of FSR, in part, because of the adverse material and health conditions associated with economic hardship. For example, studies have shown situations related to economic hardship, such as nutrient deficiency (Bodnar & Wisner, 2005) and poor housing conditions (Evans, Wells, & Moch, 2003), can have an adverse influence on mental health. Furthermore, as noted earlier, previous research also suggests that prolonged economic hardship more powerfully predicts depressive symptoms than acute stressful experiences, such as discrete stressful life events (Mossakowski, 2003). Thus, in addition to considering the *level* of economic hardship (i.e., severity) experienced, it is essential to consider the *length* of the hardship (i.e., acute or transient) (Yuan, 2008) and the amount of change in the hardship over time (Wickrama, O'Neal, & Lorenz, 2018b). Together, these considerations emphasize the importance of investigating longitudinal trajectories of economic hardship. Lorenz, Elder, Bao, Wickrama, and Conger (2000) found middle-age parents' income trajectories predicted their trajectories of family stressful life events, which, in turn, was implicated in husbands' and wives' trajectories of depressive symptoms.

Parents' Mental Health and Family Processes (Paths 2→3 and 3→2)

Numerous family studies have identified associations between family economic hardship and characteristics of the marital relationship, but spillover to other family relationships is also plausible, including the parent–child relationship. More specifically, chronic economic difficulties or stressful declines in economic well-being may lead to an accumulation of marital and parental disagreements and conflicts with long-term relational consequences (Path 2→3) (Conger, Rueter, & Elder, 1999). According to self-regulation theories, these spillover effects are largely explained by the depletion of self-regulatory resources (Baumeister, 2002). For example, stressful family economic conditions deplete spouses' energy and compromise their ability to manage relationship issues and conflicts, which ultimately results in destructive interactions between family members (Buck &

Neff, 2012). Previous family research has shown that in two-parent families at various life stages (e.g., middle-age mothers and fathers of adolescent children, couples in later adulthood), economic hardship results in distress including more expressions of hostility toward spouses and children and less warmth and supportive behaviors (Path 2→3) (Conger et al., 2010).

Although there is evidence that emotional distress impacts family processes, previous studies have shown that there is a reciprocal, often cyclical, effect as well. That is, stressful family processes also leads to emotional distress (Path 3→2) (Wickrama et al., 2018b; Wickrama, Bryant, & Wickrama, 2010). In addition to increasing negative interactions, such as marital hostility, emotional distress also deprives couples of spousal warmth and support, which is important in conceptualization of family processes because the romantic relationship serves as the most intimate psychological, emotional, and physical source of support available. As such, it is a large contributing factor to subsequent psychological well-being (Lorenz, Conger, Montague, & Wickrama, 1993). Because both feelings of distress and relational processes are continuous time-varying variables, examining parallel within-person changes in these variables (i.e., parallel trajectories) is essential for learning more about the association between these two variables (i.e., relational processes and psychological distress). Relatedly, previous studies have shown that spouses' individual trajectories of depressive symptoms are bidirectionally associated with their individual trajectories of marital quality (Davila, Karney, Hall, & Bradbury, 2003).

Beyond the marital relationship, marital conflicts are also consequential for parent–child relationships (Conger et al., 2010), in part as a spillover process where stress in one life domain or relationship "leaks" into other domains. As evidence of this, families with high marital conflict are often low on parental warmth and effective parent–child relations (Krishnakumar & Buehler, 2000).

Family Processes and Youth Psychosocial and Socioeconomic Development (Path 3→4)

As depicted by Path 3→4 and Box 4, family processes influence the development of youth psychosocial resources, which are essential for their later socioeconomic success. Attachment theory highlights the role of early affectional ties with parents in setting the stage for parents' continued influence over the child's life course as well as the development of psychosocial resources necessary for thriving at later life stages (Bowlby,1988). The central tenet in this theory is that the relationship with a caring and supportive parent (Box 3) allows children to develop a sense of security, which is considered to be the critical foundation for healthy socioemotional development (Box 4). A key component of an internal working model is the extent to which the individual perceives that they can influence the environment (i.e., sense of mastery or agency; Edwards, 2002). Thus, these parent–child relationships are hypothesized to be essential for the development of youth's psychosocial resources, including mastery.

Empirical research supports this theorizing. Conger, Williams, Little, Masyn, and Shebloski (2009) demonstrated how positive interactions among family members and negotiations that occur within the family foster the development of adolescents' psychosocial resources (psychosocial development), including mastery and self-regulation, and these psychosocial resources decrease the likelihood of socioeconomic developmental failures (e.g., the premature truncation of education attainment). Previous studies provide convincing evidence for the association between parent–child relationships and youth psychosocial development, as research has shown that the course of positive parent–child relations over time (i.e., trajectories) are associated with youth trajectories of psychosocial development (Choi, Hutchison, Lemberger, & Pope, 2012).

As shown in Box 4, time-varying psychosocial resources may contribute to parallel time-varying socioeconomic success or failures forming interlocking trajectories over adolescence and young adulthood. That is, psychosocial resources, are a key developmental resource in the early years with consequences for socioeconomic resources as offspring mature into emerging adulthood and beyond.

Youth Psychosocial and Socioeconomic Developmental Outcomes and Youth Mental Health (Paths 4→5 and 5→4)

A long history of social epidemiological research has shown that the lack of psychosocial resources and socioeconomic developmental failures are associated with emotional distress and discouragement (Path 4→5). Socioeconomic developmental failures can include educational failures (e.g., poor performance or lack of continued schooling), and these failures may proliferate over adolescence and young adulthood (Prawitz, Kalkowski, & Cohart, 2013). For instance, Ge, Lorenz, Conger, Elder, and Simons (1994) found that stressful life experiences increase offspring's sense of entrapment, feelings of anger, hopelessness, frustration, and other negative emotions, and trajectories of adolescent stressful life events are associated with trajectories of depressive symptoms. Conversely, developmental success, such as educational and occupational achievements, creates feelings of satisfaction and can further bolster mental health (Wickrama, Noh, & Elder, 2009).

Furthermore, when children or adolescents experience high levels of depressive symptoms early in their life, they are at increased risk for later depression (Keenan, Feng, Hipwell, & Klostermann, 2009). That is, the psychological repercussions of stressful life experiences in adolescence often persist into young adulthood creating depressive symptoms trajectories that continue over the early life course (Wickrama, Conger, Lorenz, & Jung, 2008). Additionally, because the behavior and social interactions of depressed individuals often result in further social rejection and avoidance from others (Rudolph, Flynn, Abaied, Groot, & Thompson, 2009), they may lack high-quality, fulfilling close relationships, and this lack of social support can have notable emotional consequences over time. These findings are in line with previous research documenting strong homotypic continuity in psychological symptoms over the early life course (Carballo et al.,

2011). Together, these studies provide evidence for the importance of considering mental health as a trajectory that exists over time rather than a discrete life circumstance.

As this trajectory of mental health unfolds over time, it can inform the psychosocial and socioeconomic trajectories. As such, the FSAMH model identifies a bidirectional relationship between psychosocial and socioeconomic developmental trajectories and depressive symptoms over adolescence and young adulthood (Paths 4→5 and 5→4). For example, research has shown that young adults' socioeconomic attainment mediates the relationship between early and later depressed mood (Wickrama et al., 2016a). Depressed youth may encounter difficulties developing the knowledge, psychological or cognitive capabilities, and skills necessary for successful educational and occupational attainment (Lewinsohn, Rhode, Seeley, Klein, & Gotlib, 2003). In addition, depressed individuals generally receive less social and family support than nondepressed persons, and social support is a key resource that can enhance individual success (Needham, 2009). For these reasons, mental health may contribute to impaired psychosocial characteristics such as lack of mastery and self-regulation, and socioeconomic developmental trajectories, including stressful work relationships, work instability, and decreased educational success. Moreover, failures in educational, economic, and work domains may produce chronically stressful life experiences that can perpetuate to a continued depressed mood. This view is consistent with the notion of a "kindling effect," which suggests that the consequences of depression increase the likelihood of recurring depression (Rudolph et al., 2009).

Neuroendocrine and Neurological Mediating Processes (Box 6)

Although the FSAMH model primarily focuses on environmental and social processes linking FSR to mental health trajectories over the life course, the role of biological processes cannot be overlooked (Paths 1→6, Path 6→4, and Path 6→5). Developmental studies suggest that biobehavioral system disruptions and, in turn, impaired psychosocial and cognitive functioning are consequential for youth development (Donnellan, Conger, McAdams, & Neppl, 2009; Whitbeck et al., 1991). More broadly, families experiencing FSR are, essentially, families under stress (Repetti, Taylor, & Seeman, 2002), and these stressful family environments strain family members', including children's, stress-responsive biological regulatory systems (Barker et al., 1993). These types of biobehavioral system disruptions are associated with childhood and adolescent neurocognitive, neurobehavioral, and physiological impairments (*biological programming*) (Repetti et al., 2002). These impaired psychophysiological and cognitive capacities result in the impaired development of psychosocial resources, such as cognitive processing, emotional regulation, mastery, self-esteem, and future orientation (e.g., Nam & Huang, 2009). These impairments may result in stressful educational and social failures, as well as mental health problems, and often continue into young adulthood (Repetti et al., 2002; Wickrama et al., 2016a).

Chronic stressful experiences may contribute to poor mental health through its influence on physiological regulatory systems. That is, stress indirectly influences mental health by causing deleterious effects on interconnected physiological mechanisms, which result in increased psychological symptoms (Lewinsohn, Clarke, Rohde, Hops, & Seely, 1996). Central physiological regulatory systems involved in this process include the sympathetic-adrenal-medullary (SAM) axis and the hypothalamic-pituitary-adrenal (HPA) axis (Seeman et al., 2010). These systems are activated by stress exposure, which results in their production of various neuroendocrine hormones (e.g., cortisol, epinephrine, and norepinephrine) that aid in productive short-term adaptations to stress. Although these responses are helpful in the moment, in the long-term, excessive physiological stress responses are contemporaneously and longitudinally associated with impaired psychosocial resources and, in turn, developmental failures and mental health problems (Seeman et al., 2010).

The excessive production of stress hormones (e.g., cortisol) can also structurally and functionally affect important brain regions and result in changes in memory formation and cognitive capacity (Gould, McEwen, Tanapat, Galea, & Fuchs, 1997). Research focused on children and adolescents has shown that stress hormones associated with early socioeconomic adversity is implicated in the functional connectivity among regions of the brain, which may have consequences for psychophysiological and cognitive capacities, particularly self-regulatory skills (Palacios-Barrios & Hanson, 2019), with poor regulation contributing to developmental failures and mental health problems.

Genetic Predisposition—Hereditary (Box 7)

As depicted by Box 7, children's gene structures are largely inherited from their biological parents. Variations in gene structures across individuals are referred to as polymorphisms, and each variant of a gene is an allele. Most existing molecular genetics research has examined variations in genetic disposition that play a role in the regulation of serotoninergic and dopaminergic neurotransmitter systems. Previous research has shown that certain polymorphisms (including candidate genes or single nucleotide polymorphisms, SNP) may be associated with developmental outcomes, including psychological vulnerability, academic and cognitive competency, and socioeconomic attainment as young adults. For example, 5-HTT is a key regulator of serotoninergic neurotransmission, and a polymorphism in the promoter region of this gene results in two variants. Research has shown that individuals with one or two copies of the 5-HTT short allele display more behavioral and psychological problems, including more depressive symptoms, than those with the long allele (Risch et al., 2009). Consequently, paths from Box 7 depict genetic influences on the mental health of parents and children (Paths 7→2 and 7→5, respectively).

Similarly, genes associated with dopamine functioning (DAT1, DRD2, and DRD4) and regulation of monamine levels (MAOA) have also been implicated in explaining variation in behaviors and psychological difficulties (e.g., Guo & Tillman, 2009). For instance, one study concluded that a SNP from an oxytocin receptor was associated with depressive symptoms (Saphire-Bernstein, Way, Kim, Sherman, & Taylor, 2011). Another study found evidence that specific variants of DRD2 and DRD4 were associated with higher levels of depression (Guo & Tillman, 2009).

Increasingly, genetic research has shown that, genetic influence for most phenotypes (e.g., behaviors, mental disorders and diseases) are polygenetic in nature. Multiple genes and SNPs have been shown to cumulatively influence an individual's behaviors and feelings (i.e., cumulative genetic influence or polygenetic effect) (Belsky & Beaver, 2011; Wickrama, Lee, & O'Neal, 2018a). Particularly, polygenetic indices made up of multiple genes and multiple SNP's have been shown to predict mental health outcomes.

Beyond direct effects of genetic variants, studies have found variants of genes can interact with environmental contexts to shape individuals' psychological vulnerability and developmental failures (termed *GxE influences*; Caspi & Moffitt, 2006). The stress-diathesis hypothesis posits that "risk alleles" or "vulnerability genes" make individuals more susceptible to stressful environments (e.g., FSR and/or adverse family processes) by triggering negative youth developmental and mental health outcomes (Shanahan & Boardman, 2009). Alternatively, the differential susceptibility hypothesis posits that genetic variants can have positive or negative effects depending on the environmental context, with certain genes resulting in positive outcomes under favorable conditions (e.g., positive family processes) and negative outcomes under stressful conditions (Belsky & Beaver, 2011). Other research suggests that GxE influences are life stage specific and may not appear until later in life because their salience varied by age, with salience generally increasing from childhood to young adulthood (Shanahan & Boardman, 2009). Thus, although not shown in Figure 18.1, a comprehensive consideration of how genetics contribute to parents' or children's mental health requires acknowledging potential interaction effects between the genetic disposition of parents or offspring and contextual factors (e.g., FSR and family process).

Direct Associations and Other Unpacked Mechanisms

FSR and Family Processes (Path 1→3)

As described above (Paths 1→2 and 2→3), much of the family and developmental research has documented parents' poor mental health as a central linking mechanism explaining why FSR is consequential for family processes. However, even after accounting for parents' mental health, there may be other explanations as to why FSR is implicated in adverse family processes. This is indicated in the FSAMH model as a "direct" link between FSR and family processes (Path 1→3).

For instance, other, unaccounted, mechanisms in operation may include material deprivation such as food, housing and transport. More generally, the spillover perspective is helpful for understanding and articulating how stressful experiences in one life domain (e.g., work or finances) can affect close relationships, particularly marital relationships but parent–child relationships as well (Whitbeck et al., 1997). Another example of this direct effect, or unpacked mechanism, (Path 1→3) between FSR and family processes is research documenting that lower SES parents who lack the necessary financial and material resources tend to utilize a harsher parenting style that is authoritarian and rejecting and engage in parental neglect and abuse (Conger & Donnellan, 2007). Similarly, lower parent education and disrupted or single parent households are other FSR factors that have been linked to ineffective parenting practices (Wickrama, Conger, Lorenz, & Elder, 1998).

Notably, these FSR-family process linkages are often complex processes driven by various factors. For instance, two plausible reasons for the association between parental education and parenting is that parents with less educational attainment are more likely to have work stress stemming from unfavorable job characteristics (e.g., low work control) at the same time that they are less likely to have access to the social and psychological resources, skills, and information that facilitate positive family processes (Clougherty, Souza, & Cullen, 2010). Regarding single parent families, stressful circumstances for single caregivers, combined with the absence of a caring and supportive co-parent, may increase the occurrence of ineffective parenting practices, such as parental rejection and a lack of parental warmth (Conger & Donnellan, 2007). These "unpacked" mechanisms are not isolated to the FSAMH model constructs of FSR and family processes. Consequently, "direct paths" are also incorporated from FSR to psychosocial and socioeconomic trajectories (Path 1→4) and mental health trajectories (Path 1→5).

FSR and Youth Socioeconomic Development (Path 1→4)

Youth exposure to early FSR also increases the likelihood that youth will encounter developmental failures (Path 1→4) (Attar, Guerra, & Tolan 1994). More specifically, longitudinal studies on youth development suggest that early cumulative socioeconomic adversity contributes to adolescents' difficulties with low educational performance and delinquent behaviors and young adults' struggles with low economic attainment and poor romantic relationship quality (Wickrama et al., 2008). These failures are thought to appear through a "chain of insults" that often begins with FSR and continues well into young adulthood. That is, in a successively contingent process, one stressful developmental failure may continue (e.g., poor academic performance) while another appears (e.g., delinquent behaviors), forming a cascading sequence of stress or risks (Hatch, 2005). This sequence of stressful experiences from adolescence to young adulthood is consistent with the life course "cascade model" (Brody, Chen, & Kogan, 2010), which provides a framework for understanding how risks proliferate and compound over adolescence and emerging adulthood as a life course process with multiple smaller effects combining over time to exert a cumulative effect (Hatch, 2005). Empirically, this proliferation has been demonstrated by recent work that found early cumulative socioeconomic experiences shaped life transition patterns from adolescence to young adulthood (Lee, Wickrama, O'Neal, & Prado, 2018). More specifically, youth who experienced more socioeconomic adversity were more likely to experience disrupted patterns of life transitions, characterized by school drop-out, early pregnancy, or early full-time employment before school completion.

FSR and Children's Mental Health (Path 1→5)

In addition to the factors outlined in the FSAMH model, other "unpacked factors" may cause children's psychological distress in response to FSR (Path 1→5). For instance, family socioeconomic adversity generally limits children's options for participating in extracurricular educational activities (Broh, 2002) and makes non-essentials, such as specific clothing and concert tickets, unattainable for youth whose families experience economic hardship, which may cause youth to perceive that they do not "fit in" (Orr, 2003). The lack of physical or social resources for these youth may, more generally, result in feeling trapped, angry, hopeless, and frustrated (Prawitz et al., 2013), increasing their susceptibility to more severe emotional and behavioral problems over time, including elevated levels of depressive symptoms (Kogan et al., 2010). Using growth mixture modeling, studies have shown that family socioeconomic characteristics influence youth's depressive, anxiety, and hostility symptoms as well as their more general psychopathology trajectories (Lee, Wickrama, O'Neal, & Lorenz, 2017; Wickrama et al., 2016a).

Structural elements, such as parents' marital status, may also be involved, given that children raised by divorced or single mothers are more likely to experience repeated economic hardship than children of consistently married parents (Sun & Li, 2001). Such risk factors become even more consequential for youth when they exist in combination with an adverse community context, such as a threatening community environment, poor housing, and related physical hazards as well as racial discrimination (Prawitz et al., 2013; Wickrama & Bryant, 2003).

Youth life stage at the time of FSR is also important to consider. For instance, socioeconomic adversity during adolescence occurs at a time when youth may already be experiencing an increase in life stress from biological changes (e.g., sexual maturation), changes in peer expectations, or changing roles within the family and other contexts. Moreover, these transitions vary in the degree to which they are within the adolescent's control, which can further exacerbate the stress experienced (Larson, Moneta, Richards, & Wilson, 2002). The stressful demands and circumstances stemming from these transitions have been shown to influence both the level and rate of change, or trajectory, of negative emotions including depressive symptoms across early and middle adolescence (Ge et al., 1994; Larson et al.,

2002). Thus, heightened distress is often a product of the combination of stressful biological, cognitive, and social changes that occur during adolescence, and this distress can be further heightened when they are accompanied by socioeconomic adversity (e.g., family cut-backs to make ends meet).

Family Process and Youth Mental Health (Path 3→5)

Two essential elements of ineffective parental practices involve (1) parental affect and (2) child management. Unhealthy parental affect refers to parental rejection, hostility, and lack of warmth, whereas poor child management encapsulates lack of supervision and inconsistent discipline (Conger & Donnellan 2007). Because it has been shown that the depressogenic effect of negative parental affect is stronger than that of poor child management, parents' unhealthy affect may operate as a primary stressor for children resulting in elevated depressive symptomatology (Path 3→5). Parental rejection, in particular, operates as a chronic stressor and can create a source of "identity disruption" (Thoits, 1995) for youth because children who suffer parental rejection are likely to feel worthless, disconnected from the family unit, hopeless, and unhappy. Providing evidence for the parallel association between within-individual changes in negative parenting and youth depressive symptoms, studies have shown that trajectories of negative parenting are associated with youth's trajectories of depressive symptoms over time (Wu, 2007).

Dyadic Associations in Mental Health (Paths X and Y)

Consistent with family systems theory (Cox & Paley, 1997) and the life course notion of "linked lives" (Elder & Giele, 2009), family members are interdependent parts of the family system, and members influence each other (i.e., interindividual influences). This view is depicted by Paths X and Y in Figure 18.1 and illustrated in Figure 18.2. Although the interdependent nature of husbands' and wives' lives is largely recognized, previous studies focused on FSR and mental health have generally not investigated these association in a dyadic context considering how spouses affect one another (Path X). Individual-level analyses (i.e., examining either husbands or wives, parents or children) without considering these interindividual associations (i.e., dependencies between spouses or parents or children) is not consistent with various theoretical perspectives and may also produce biased findings (Kenny, Kashy, & Cook, 2006).

Furthermore, it is also important to consider such interindividual effects over time. As previously noted, individuals who suffer from psychological symptoms, particularly depressive symptoms, are at risk for mental health symptoms at later life stages. However, considering the linked lives notion, spouses' depressive feelings may not only impact their future depressive symptoms (i.e., actor effect) but also their partners' depressive symptoms over time (i.e., partner effect).

For example, if one spouse experiences elevated feelings of distress, the spouse may experience an emotional response that can influence their subsequent distress feelings (Berscheid & Ammazzalorso, 2001). That is, longitudinal crossover, or partner effects, may exist because spouses' depressive feelings are interdependent and can be transmitted or spread between spouses forming parallel changes. This conceptualization is supported by past research which provides evidence of husbands' and wives' parallel trajectories of psychological symptoms over the life course (Kouros & Cummings, 2010) as well as mutual influences between spouses (Wickrama, King, O'Neal, & Lorenz, 2019). Moreover, as indicated by Path Y in Figure 18.1 and shown in Figure 18.2, we posit that similar contemporaneous correlations and actor and partner effects exist between parents' and children's mental health. Thus, empirical and conceptual research must consider husbands, wives, and children together as interdependent entities producing a web of interindividual influences over the life course.

One important caveat for future research to explore is the extent to which crossover influences between family members are comprised of different life course mechanisms depending on the length of time examined. For instance, in comparing short-term influences or stressors (e.g., acute illness) with long-term influences (e.g., chronic family economic hardship), crossover between family members may occur through different mechanisms. Moreover, there is the issue of life stage variation. Children are maturing at the same time as parents are aging. Therefore, interdependence between parents and children (and husbands and wives) may vary depending on the life stage (i.e., husband and wife interdependence in midlife compared to later adulthood or parent and child interdependence in midlife–childhood compared to later adulthood–young adulthood). As shown in Figure 18.2, a longitudinal framework accounting for multiple family members allows for an assessment of both long-term actor and partner effects involving depressive symptoms and the progression of psychological symptoms.

Resilience or Protective Factors

An important remaining question is why some youth are able to achieve developmental successes and better mental health despite stressful life experiences, such as family economic hardship. Developmental researchers contend that the availability of protective factors, including psychosocial resources, may counteract the adverse influence of risk factors. Drawing from a social psychological integrated model of simultaneous mediation and moderation (Muller, Judd, & Yzerbyt, 2005), this is illustrated in the FSAMH model, recognizing that offspring's psychosocial and socioeconomic resources (Box 4) can simultaneously mediate and moderate the association between FSR and youth developmental and mental health outcomes. Thus, psychosocial resources (e.g., self-regulation, self-esteem, mastery), which are influenced by family processes, can also serve as a source of resilience. These resources allow youth to thrive when they face adversity, or at least avoid more severe consequences of the hardship (Barker, Ornel, Verhulst, & Oldehinkel, 2011). For instance, FSR is likely to be less detrimental for offspring's mental health when they have sufficient psychosocial resources (Box 4).

In addition, supportive parenting (Box 3) may protect offspring from the adverse mental health influence of FSR. That is, effective family practices can operate both as mediators and moderators (i.e., protective factors) in this life course mental health process. Conversely, harsh and inconsistent parental practices may amplify the detrimental mental health effect of FSR.

Relationships with others outside of the family unit can also operate as resilient factors helping to develop offspring's positive psychological resources and bolster their mental health. For instance, researchers contend that low SES youth who are exposed to positive role models may develop healthy emotion regulation behaviors in the face of stress and adopt a favorable future orientation (i.e., thinking positively about their future and planning for success) because positive role models provide the stable attachment relationships necessary for promoting positive development (Chen & Miller, 2012). This contention is referred to as a "shift and persist" strategy because it allows youth to "shift" themselves in the face of immediate stressors in order to "persist" in the broader perspective of life.

Practical Implications

From a prevention perspective, identifying early, and chronic, predictors of increasing or continually high depressive symptoms is imperative given the high continuity of depressive symptoms over the life course for both parents and children (Keenan et al., 2009). Identifying individuals who are at risk for poor mental health outcomes can facilitate interventions that reduce their likelihood before a chronic course of symptoms is established.

In many instances, FSR appears to be a primary impetus for subsequent health inequalities across the life course, which is evidence in support of macro-level policies and prevention efforts addressing early socioeconomic adversity (Center on Social Determinants of Health, 2008). Thus, at various levels (e.g., federal, state, and county levels) policies and programs aimed at reducing socioeconomic disadvantage and socioeconomic inequality are essential as they offer a way to potentially inoculate individuals from the consequences of early stressful contexts. More specific policies and programs that are comprehensive in targeting multiple mechanisms simultaneously are likely to develop from research testing aspects of the current heuristic organizing framework.

Relatedly, there is a need for local-level interventions aimed at reducing the impact of early adversity on the initial levels and shapes of physiological, behavioral, and resource trajectories. It is imperative that the efficacy of such interventions be evaluated so successful interventions can be adopted more broadly. For example, family-based interventions, such as the Family Check-Up (Fosco, Frank,

Stormshak, & Dishion, 2013) and Strong African American Families program (Brody, Miller, Yu, Beach, & Chen, 2016), have demonstrated efficacy in reducing exposure to life adversities and positively altering mental health trajectories. Implementing interventions to reduce experiences of early adversity may also be able to ward off early biological damages with long-term health impacts.

This review and heuristic framework can also inform the substance of local- or family-level interventions targeting early socioeconomic adversity and subsequent health disparity outcomes. First, interventions should target developmental mechanisms leading to offspring psychological problems earlier in the life course because childhood and adolescence have been identified as life stages that are more malleable to positive influences (e.g., parental attachment, cognitive stimulation). Targeting these mechanisms at earlier life stages can effectively reduce the incidence and severity of mental health risks in later years.

Also, the research informing the FSAMH model highlights intervention and prevention opportunities related to the psychosocial resources (e.g., self-control, mastery, and self-esteem) and elements of family processes (e.g., parenting affect and close relationships). These types of interventions may prove particularly efficacious because psychosocial resources and family processes appear to be primary mediators *and* moderators of multiple pathways responsible for the adversity-mental health association. Because these psychosocial resources and family resilience can bolster resilience to adversity, they represent protective factors that can be leveraged as buffers to protect offspring who do encounter socioeconomic adversity from experiencing its negative consequences. More applied research is necessary to identify promising procedures for impeding in the adversity-health association. In many instances, such procedures may already be active in prevention or intervention projects in various settings (churches, schools, community centers), although their efficacy has yet to be empirically demonstrated.

DISCUSSION QUESTIONS ●————————————————

1. What are examples of potential social, developmental, and biological pathways that connect family socioeconomic adversity to youth mental health outcomes?

2. Can you identify mechanisms that may connect family socioeconomic adversity to

youth mental health outcomes that are not included in the FSAMH model?

3. How does the FSAMH define *resilient factors*, and what are some examples of resilient factors specific to your own research interest?

REFERENCES

Attar, B. K., Guerra, N. G., & Tolan, P. H. (1994). Neighborhood disadvantage, stressful life events and adjustment in urban elementary-school children. *Journal of Clinical Child Psychology, 23,* 391–400.

Barker, D. J. P., Gluckman, P. D., Godfrey, K. M., Harding, J. E., Owens, J. A., & Robinson, J. S. (1993). Fetal nutrition and cardiovascular disease in adult life. *Lancet, 341,* 339–341.

Barker, M. P., Ornel, J., Verhulst, F. C., & Olde-hinkel, A. J. (2011). Adolescent family adversity and mental health problems: The role of adaptive self-regulation capacities: The TRAILS study. *Journal of Abnormal Child Psychology, 39,* 341–350.

Baumeister, R. F. (2002). Ego depletion and self-control failure: An energy model of the self's executive function. *Self and Identity, 1,* 129–137.

Belsky, J., & Beaver, K. M. (2011). Cumulative-genetic plasticity, parenting and adolescent self-regulation. *Journal of Child Psychology and Psychiatry, 52,* 619–626.

Berscheid, E., & Ammazzalorso, H. (2001). *Emotional experience in close relationships.* In G. J. Fletcher & M. S. Clark (Eds.), Interpersonal process. Blackwell handbook of social psychology (pp. 308–330). Malden, MA: Blackwell.

Bodnar, L. M., & Wisner, K. L. (2005). Nutrition and depression: Implications for improving mental health among childbearing-aged women. *Biological Psychiatry, 58,* 679–685.

Bowlby, J. (1988). *A secure base: Parent–child attachment and healthy human development.* New York, NY: Basic Books.

Broderick, C. B. (1993). *Understanding family process. Basics of family systems theory.* London, England: SAGE.

Brody, G. H., Chen, Y., & Kogan, S. (2010). A cascade model connecting life stress to risk behavior among rural African American emerging adults. *Development and Psychopathology, 22,* 667–678.

Brody, G. H., Miller, G. E., Yu, T., Beach, S. R. H., & Chen, E. (2016). Supportive family environments ameliorate the link between racial discrimination and epigenetic aging: A replication across two longitudinal cohorts. *Psychological Science, 27,* 530–541.

Brody, G. H., Yu, T., Chen, Y., Evans, G. W., Beach, S. R. H., Windle, M., . . . & Philibert, R. A. (2013). Cumulative socioeconomic status risk, allostatic load, and adjustment. *Developmental Psychology, 49,* 913–927.

Broh, B. A. (2002). Linking extracurricular programming to academic achievement: Who benefits and why? *Sociology of Education, 75,* 69–96.

Buck, A. A., & Neff, L. A. (2012). Stress spillover in early marriage: The role of self-regulatory depletion. *Journal of Family Psychology, 26,* 698–708.

Caspi, A., & Moffitt, T. E. (2006). Gene-environment interactions in psychiatry: Joining forces with neuroscience. *Nature Reviews Neuroscience, 7,* 583–590.

Carballo, J. J., Muñoz-Lorenzo, L., Blasco-Fontecilla, H., Lopez-Castroman, J., García-Nieto, R., Dervic, K., . . . & Baca-García, E. (2011). Continuity of depressive disorders from childhood and adolescence to adulthood: a naturalistic study in community mental health centers. *The Primary Care Companion to CNS Disorders, 13*(5).

Center on Social Determinants of Health. (2008). *Final report of the Commission on Social Determinants of Health.* Geneva, Switzerland: World Health Organization. http://www.who.int/social _determinants/thecommission/finalreport/en/

Chen, E., & Miller, G. E. (2012). "Shift-and-persist" strategies: Why low socioeconomic status isn't always bad for health. *Perspectives on Psychological Science, 7*, 135–158.

Choi, S., Hutchison, B., Lemberger, M. E., & Pope, M. (2012). A longitudinal study of the developmental trajectories of parental attachment and career maturity of South Korean adolescents. *The Career Development Quarterly, 60*, 163–177.

Clougherty, J. E., Souza, K., & Cullen, M. R. (2010). Work and its role in shaping the social gradient in health. *Annals of the New York Academy of Sciences 1186*, 102–124.

Conger, K. J., Williams, S. T., Little, W. M., Masyn, K. E., & Shebloski, B. (2009). Development of mastery during adolescence: The role of family problem-solving. *Journal of Health and Social Behavior, 50*, 99–114.

Conger, R. D., Conger, K. J., & Martin, M. J. (2010). Socioeconomic status, family processes, and individual development. *Journal of Marriage and Family, 72*, 685–704.

Conger, R. D., & Donnellan, M. B. (2007). An interactionist perspective on the socioeconomic context of human development. *Annual Review of Psychology, 58*, 175–199.

Conger, R. D., Rueter, M. A., & Elder, G. H., Jr. (1999). Couple resilience to economic pressure. *Journal of Personality and Social Psychology, 76*, 54–71.

Cox, M. J., & Paley, B. (1997). Families as systems. *Annual Review of Psychology, 48*, 243–267.

Cutrona, C. E., Russell, D. W., Abraham, W. T., Garder, K. A., Melby, J. N., Bryant, C., & Conger, R. D. (2003). Neighborhood context and financial strain as predictors of marital interaction and marital quality in African American couples. *Personal Relationships, 10*, 389–409.

Davila, J., Karney, B. R., Hall, T. W., & Bradbury, T. N. (2003). Depressive symptoms and marital satisfaction: Within-subject associations and the moderating effects of gender and neuroticism. *Journal of Family Psychology, 17*, 557–570.

Derogatis, L. R., & Melisaratos, N. (1983). The brief symptom inventory: An introductory report. *Psychological Medicine, 13*, 595–605.

Donnellan, M. B., Conger, K. J., McAdams, K. K., & Neppl, T. K. (2009). Personal characteristics and resilience to economic hardship and its consequences: Conceptual issues and empirical illustrations. *Journal of Personality, 77*, 1645–1676.

Edwards, M. E. (2002). Attachment, mastery, and interdependence: A model of parenting processes. *Family Process. 41*, 389–404.

Elder, G. H., & Giele, J. Z. (Eds.). (2009). *The craft of life course research.* New York, NY: Guildford Press.

Evans, G. W., & Kim, P. (2010). Multiple risk exposure as a potential explanatory mechanism for the socioeconomic status-health gradient. *Annals of the New York Academy of Sciences, 1186*, 174–189.

Evans, G. W., Wells, N. M., & Moch, A. (2003) Housing and mental health: A review of the evidence and a methodological and conceptual critique. *Journal of Social Issues, 59*, 475–500.

Fosco, G. M., Frank, J. L., Stormshak, E. A., & Dishion, T. J. (2013). Opening the "black box": Family check-up intervention effects on self-regulation that prevents growth in problem behavior and substance use. *Journal of School Psychology, 51*, 455–468.

Ge, X., Lorenz, F. O., Conger, R. D., Elder, G. H., Jr., & Simons, R. L. (1994). Trajectories of stressful life events and depressive symptoms during adolescence. *Developmental Psychology, 30*, 467–483.

Gould, E., McEwen, B. S., Tanapat, P., Galea, L. A. M., & Fuchs, E. (1997). Neurogenesis in the dentate gyrus of the adult tree shrew is regulated by psychosocial stress and NMDA receptor activation. *The Journal of Neuroscience, 17,* 2492–2498.

Guo, G., & Tillman, K. H. (2009). Trajectories of depressive symptoms, dopamine D2 and D4 receptors, family socioeconomic status, and social support in adolescence and young adulthood. *Psychiatric Genetics, 19,* 14–26.

Hatch, S. L. (2005). Conceptualizing and identifying cumulative adversity and protective resources: Implications for understanding health inequalities. *The Journals of Gerontology Series B Psychological Sciences and Social Sciences, 60,* 130–134.

Keenan, K., Feng, X., Hipwell, A., & Klostermann, S. (2009). Depression begets depression: Comparing the predictive utility of depression and anxiety symptoms to later depression. *Journal of Child Psychology and Psychiatry, and Allied Disciplines, 50,* 1167–1175.

Kenny, D. A., Kashy, D. A., & Cook, W. L. (2006). *Dyadic data analysis.* New York, NY: Guilford Press.

Kogan, S. M., Brody, G. H., Chen, Y. F., Grange, C. M., Slater, L. M., & DiClemente, R. J. (2010). Risk and protective factors for unprotected intercourse among rural African American young adults. *Public Health Reports, 125,* 709–717.

Kouros, C. D., & Cummings, E. M. (2010). Longitudinal associations between husbands' and wives' depressive symptoms. *Journal of Marriage and Family, 72,* 135–147.

Krishnakumar, A., & Buehler, C. (2000). Interparental conflict and parenting behaviors: A meta-analytic review. *Family Relations, 49,* 25–44.

Larson, R., Moneta, G. B., Richards, M. H., & Wilson, S. (2002). Continuity, stability, and change in daily emotional experience across adolescence, *Child Development, 73,* 1151–1165.

Lazarus, R. S. (1999). *Stress and emotion: A new synthesis.* London, England: Free Association Books.

Ledermann, T., & Kenny, D. A. (2012). The common fate model for dyadic data: Variations of a theoretically important but underutilized model. *Journal of Family Psychology, 26,* 140–148.

Lee, T. K., Wickrama, K. A. S., & O'Neal, C. W. (2019). Early socioeconomic adversity and cardiometabolic risk in young adults: Mediating roles of risky health lifestyle and depressive symptoms. *Journal of Behavioral Medicine, 42,* 150–161.

Lee, T. K., Wickrama, K. A. S., & O'Neal, C. W. (2020). Health continuity over mid-later years in enduring marriages: economic pressure as couple- and individual-level mediator. *Journal of Social and Personal Relationships, 37*(2), 377–392.

Lee, T. K., Wickrama, K. A. S, O'Neal, C. W., & Lorenz, F. O. (2017). Social stratification of general psychopathology trajectories and young adult social outcomes: A second-order growth mixture analysis over the early life course. *Journal of Affective Disorders, 208,* 375–383.

Lee, T. K., Wickrama, K. A. S., O'Neal, C. W., & Prado, G. (2018). Identifying diverse life transition patterns from adolescence to young adulthood: The influence of early socioeconomic context. *Social Science Research, 70,* 212–228.

Lewinsohn, P. M., Clarke, G. N., Rohde, P., Hops, H., & Seely, J. R. (1996). A course in coping: A cognitive-behavioral approach to the treatment of adolescent depression. In E. D. Hibbs & P. S. Jensen (Eds.), *Psychosocial treatments for child and adolescent disorders: Empirically based strategies for clinical practice* (pp. 109–135). Washington, DC: American Psychological Association.

Lewinsohn, P. M., Rhode, P., Seeley, J. R., Klein, D. N., & Gotlib, I. H. (2003). Psychosocial functioning of young adults who have experienced and recovered from major depressive disorder during adolescence. *Journal of Abnormal Psychology, 112,* 353–363.

Lorenz, F. O., Conger, R. D., Montague, R. B., & Wickrama, K. A. S. (1993). Economic conditions, spouse support, and psychological distress of rural husbands and wives. *Rural Sociology, 58,* 247–268.

Lorenz, F. O., Elder, G. H. Jr., Bao, W. N., Wickrama, K. A. S., & Conger, R. D. (2000). After farming: Emotional health trajectories of farm, nonfarm, and displaced farm couples. *Rural Sociology, 65,* 50–71.

Mossakowski, K. N. (2003). Coping with perceived discrimination: Does ethnic identity protect mental health? *Journal of Health and Social Behavior, 44,* 318–331.

Muller, D., Judd, C. M., & Yzerbyt, V. (2005). When moderation is mediated and mediation is moderated. *Journal of Personality and Social Psychology, 89,* 852–853.

Nam, Y., & Huang, J. (2009). Equal opportunity for all? Parental economic resources and children's educational attainment. *Children and Youth Services Review, 31,* 625–634.

Needham, B. L. (2009). Adolescent depressive symptomatology and young adult educational attainment: An examination of gender differences. *Journal of Adolescent Health, 45,* 179–186.

Nella, D., Panagopoulou, E., Galanis, N., Montgomery, A., & Benos, A. (2015). Consequences of job insecurity on the psychological and physical health of Greek civil servants. *BioMed Research International.* https://www.ncbi.nlm.nih.gov/pmc/articles/PMC4628735/

Orr, A. J. (2003). Black-White differences in achievement: the importance of wealth. *Sociology of Education, 76,* 281–304.

Palacios-Barrios, E. E., & Hanson, J. L. (2019). Poverty and self-regulation: Connecting psychosocial processes, neurobiology, and the risk for psychopathology. *Comprehensive Psychiatry, 90,* 52–64.

Pearlin, L. I., Schieman, S., Fazio, E. M., & Meersman, S. C. (2005). Stress, health, and the life course: Some conceptual perspectives. *Journal of Health and Social Behaviors, 46,* 205–219.

Prawitz, A., Kalkowski, J. C., & Cohart, J. (2013). Response to economic pressure by low income families: Financial distress and hopefulness. *Journal of Family and Economic Issues, 34,* 29–40.

Repetti, R., Taylor, S. E., & Seeman, T. E. (2002). Risky families: family social environments and the mental and physical health of offspring. *Psychological Bulletin, 128,* 330–366.

Risch, N., Herrell, R., Lehner, T., Liang, K. Y., Eaves, L., Hoh, J., . . . & Merikangas, K. R. (2009). Interaction between the serotonin transporter gene (5-HTTLPR), stressful life events, and risk of depression: A meta-analysis. *Journal of the American Medical Association, 301,* 2462–2471.

Ross, C. E., & Mirowsky, J. (2009). Neighborhood disorder, subjective alienation, and distress. *Journal of Health and Social Behavior, 50,* 49–64.

Rudolph, K. D., Flynn, M., Abaied, J. L., Groot, A., & Thompson, R. (2009). Why is past depression the best predictor of future depression? Stress generation as a mechanism of depression continuity in girls. *Journal of Clinical Child and Adolescent Psychology 38,* 473–485.

Rutter, M., Kim-Cohen, J., & Maughan, B. (2006). Continuities and discontinuities in psychopathology between childhood and adult life. *Journal of Child Psychology and Psychiatry, 47,* 276–295.

Sameroff, A. J. (2006). Identifying risk and protective factors for healthy youth development. In A. Clarke Stewart & J. Dunn (Eds.), *Families count: Effects on child and adolescent development* (pp. 53–76). Cambridge, England: Cambridge University Press.

Saphire-Bernstein, S., Way, B. M., Kim, H. S., Sherman, D. K., & Taylor, S. E. (2011). Oxytocin receptor gene (OXTR) is related to psychological resources. *Proceedings of the National Academy* of Sciences of the United States of America, 108, 15118–15122.

Shanahan, M. J., & Boardman, J. D. (2009). Genetics and behavior in the life course: A promising frontier. In G. H. Elder, Jr. & J. Z. Giele (Eds.), *The craft of life course research* (pp. 215–235). New York, NY: Guilford Press.

Seeman, T., Epel, E., Gruenewald, T., Karlamangla, A., & McEwen, B. S. (2010). Socio-economic differentials in peripheral biology: Cumulative allostatic load. *Annals of the New York Academy of Sciences*, 1186, 223–239.

Sun, Y., & Li, Y. (2001). Marital disruption, parental investment, and children's academic achievement: A prospective analysis. *Journal of Family Issues*, 22, 27–62.

Thoits, P. (1995). Stress, coping and social support processes: Where are we? What next? *Journal of Health and Social Behavior*, 35, 53–79.

Whitbeck, L. B., Simons, R. L., Conger, R. D., Lorenz, F. O., Huck, S., & Elder, G. H., Jr. (1991). Family economic hardship, parental support, and adolescent self-esteem. *Social Psychology Quarterly*, 54, 353–363.

Whitbeck, L. B., Simons, R. L., Conger, R. D., Wickrama, K.A.S., Ackley, K. A., & Elder, G. H. Jr. (1997). The effects of parents' working conditions and family economic hardship on parenting behaviors and children's self-efficacy. *Social Psychology Quarterly*, 60, 291–303.

Wickrama, K. A. S., & Bryant, C. M. (2003). Community context of social resources and adolescent mental health. *Journal of Marriage and Family*, 65, 850–866.

Wickrama, K. A. S., Bryant, C. M., & Wickrama, T. (2010). Perceived community disorder, hostile marital interactions, and self-reported health of African American couples: An interdyadic process. *Journal of Personal Relationships*, 17, 515–531.

Wickrama, K. A. S., Conger, R. D., Lorenz, F. O., & Elder, G. H., Jr. (1998). Parental education and adolescent self-reported physical health. *Journal of Marriage and the Family*, 60, 967–978.

Wickrama, K. A. S., Conger, R. D., Lorenz, F. O., & Jung, T. (2008). Antecedents and consequences of trajectories of depression symptoms from adolescence to young adulthood. *Journal of Health and Social Behavior*, 4, 468–483.

Wickrama, K. A. S., King, V., O'Neal, C. W., & Lorenz, F. O. (2019). Stressful work trajectories and depressive symptoms in middle-aged couples: Moderating effect of marital warmth. *Journal of Aging and Health*, 31, 484–508.

Wickrama, K. A. S., Kwag, K. H., Lorenz, F. O., Conger, R. D., & Surjadi, F. F. (2010). Dynamics of family economic hardship and the progression of health problems of husbands and wives during the middle years: a perspective from rural Mid-West. *Journal of Aging and Health*, 22, 1132–1157.

Wickrama, K. A. S., Lee, T. K., & O'Neal, C. W. (2018a). Genetic moderation of multiple pathways linking early cumulative socioeconomic adversity and young adults' cardiometabolic disease risk. *Development and Psychopathology*, 30, 165–177.

Wickrama, K. A. S., Lee, T. K., O'Neal. C. W., & Kwon, J. A. (2015). Stress and resource pathways connecting early socioeconomic adversity to young adults' physical risk. *Journal of Youth and Adolescence*, 44, 1109–1124.

Wickrama, K. A. S., Noh, S., & Bryant, C. M. (2005). Racial differences in adolescent distress: differential effects of the family and community for Blacks and Whites. *Journal of Community Psychology*, 33, 261–282.

Wickrama, K. A. S., Noh, S., & Elder, G. H. (2009). An investigation of family SES-based inequalities in depressive symptoms from early adolescence to emerging adulthood. *Advances in Life Course Research*, 14, 147–161.

Wickrama, K. A. S., O'Neal, C. W., & Lee, T. K. (2016a). Cumulative socioeconomic adversity, developmental pathways, and mental health risks during the early life course. *Emerging Adulthood, 4*, 378–390.

Wickrama, K. A. S., O'Neal. C. W., & Lee, T. K. (2016b). The health impact of upward mobility: Does socioeconomic attainment make youth more vulnerable to stressful circumstances? *Journal of Youth and Adolescence, 45*, 271–285.

Wickrama, K. A. S., O'Neal, C. W., & Lorenz, F. O. (2018b). The decade-long effect of work insecurity on husbands' and wives' midlife health mediated by anxiety: A dyadic analysis. *Journal of Occupational Health Psychology, 23*, 350–360.

Wu, C. I. (2007). The interlocking trajectories between negative parenting practices and adolescent depressive symptoms. *Current Sociology, 55*, 579–597.

Yuan, A. S. V. (2008). Exploring the changes in economic hardship and children's well-being over time: The "linked lives" of parents and children. *Advances in Life Course Research, 13*, 321–341.

CHAPTER 19

Families Coping With Alcohol and Substance Abuse

Kevin P. Lyness and Judith L. Fischer

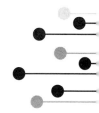

A biopsychosocial approach to the study of substance use disorders and families organizes the prediction of substance involvement through consideration of biological contributions, psychological factors, and social influences (Skewes & Gonzalez, 2013). Conjoining this model with the family stress and coping model (see McKenry & Price, 2005) acknowledges the contribution of these biopsychosocial factors at each juncture: stressor, resource, perception, coping, and managing.

The purpose of this chapter is to review research on children and adolescents and their parents coping with the challenges posed by substances and to discuss intervention strategies. Throughout the chapter, we put the emphasis on both the family stresses involved and the search for explanations of resilience in these situations of families coping with substance abuse. We pay particular attention to the mediating and moderating effects that intervene between two or more variables, such as those that occur when associations between parent drinking and offspring drinking work through (mediated) or are altered (moderated) by other variables. The chapter begins with an illustrative vignette that highlights many of the findings summarized.

Some definitions are in order. *Substance use,* as we use the term in this chapter, includes both experimental and regular use. *Substance misuse* refers to the excessive consumption of a substance. *Substance abuse* and *substance dependence* are clinical designations involving serious and persistent problems with substances. The recent revision to the *Diagnostic and Statistical Manual of Mental Disorders* (*DSM-5*; American Psychiatric Association, 2013) brings a significant departure from past editions in nomenclature. The only designation used is that of *substance use disorder* (with the substance name used, such as *alcohol use disorder*) along with a severity indicator (mild, moderate, and severe). For all substance use disorders (SUDs), there are four areas of behavior to assess: impaired control, social impairment, risky use, and pharmacological criteria (tolerance, and withdrawal where applicable). Designations used in this chapter reflect those chosen by the authors cited.

In organizing the following literature review, we take a family developmental approach. Timing is an important part of the stress and coping model. Stressors may be time limited, but they may also extend over long periods. Situations not considered stressors at one developmental period may be stressors at another. For example, Biederman, Faraone, Monuteaux, and Feighner (2000) found that *childhood* exposure to parental SUDs conferred a twofold risk on offspring, but *adolescent* exposure was associated with a threefold risk for the emergence of SUDs. Perceptions, resources, and problem solving may be greater or lesser depending on individual and family development. Coping that is effective in the short term may moderate the long-term impacts of a stressor or lead to a pileup of stressors over time. In any given family, the substance misuser(s) may be the parents, the offspring, or both. Treatments vary depending on whether the child in the family or the adult is the presenting patient. And when intervening with an alcoholic parent, the ages of the children in the family need to be taken into account (Kelley & Fals-Stewart, 2008).

Vignette

Karl is a 13-year-old boy who has been getting into trouble for drinking at school. This is not Karl's first time in trouble—he is often disruptive and aggressive and seems to lack impulse control. When he was younger, his parents (at the urging of the school) had him tested for ADHD, but the results were inconclusive, and the psychiatrist did not recommend medication. Karl's parents are typically punitive and often use physical punishment, and Karl has reported not feeling supported by his parents. Moreover, Karl's parents have been considering getting a divorce. His father is a heavy drinker, although he has never been diagnosed with a substance abuse problem. Karl sees his father come home from work each night and drink five to six beers as he complains about his day. Recently, his father reports that the stress of dealing with Karl has led to increased drinking in order to cope. Karl has learned from this that drinking is a good way to relieve stress and this reinforces his positive attitudes toward alcohol. Karl's parents do not know most of his friends, but the school reports that Karl hangs out with a slightly older group of kids who are known to drink and party. Karl has never felt that he fits in very well with his peers, but this current group of friends seems more accepting of his impulsive nature. Karl has an older sister who has not gotten into trouble with substances and who has always been more controlled and inhibited. The school has recommended that the family see a therapist.

The family therapist, knowing some of the literature on stress and coping as well as alcohol and substance abuse, engaged a multifaceted approach. The therapist first addressed parental behaviors and coping, including the quality of the marriage, parenting styles, and Karl's father's drinking, with a focus on increasing self-regulation capacities in both parents and in Karl—with Karl by specifically focusing on developing positive goal structures and increasing his focus on choices he makes in coping. Partly as a result of increased self-awareness, Karl's father decided to cut down on his drinking and made a commitment to work on the marriage. Both parents agreed to specific behavioral interventions designed to interrupt Karl's disinhibited behavior patterns. The therapist also helped Karl find less maladaptive ways of coping, along with implementing interventions with Karl at the school that helped him develop a different peer group (particularly focusing on Karl's propensity for aggression). Finally, the therapist intervened with Karl directly about his drinking behavior, knowing that Karl's early onset of drinking places him at risk for later serious substance abuse problems.

Children and Substance Abuse Problems

Most research on childhood (ages 6 to 12 years) substance abuse has focused on 8- to 11-year-olds. A number of scholars have documented the fact that children this young are using and even abusing substances (Acion, Ramirez, Jorge, & Arndt, 2013; Elkins, Fite, Moore, Lochman & Wells, 2014). According to research conducted by Elkins et al., between 5% and 7% of fourth through sixth graders consumed alcohol, used marijuana, or used tobacco in the previous 30 days. Past 30-day binge drinking among sixth graders ranged from approximately 2% to 7% (Acion et al., 2013).

Child Characteristics

Research on substance abuse prior to adolescence tends to focus on childhood predictors of *later* adolescent and adult use and abuse (cf., Zucker, 2008) rather than correlates of actual substance use *in* childhood. Early alcohol initiation is strongly predicted by the presence of conduct disorders as well as externalizing disorders, ADHD, parental alcohol dependence, and being male (Sartor, Lynskey, Heath, Jacob, & True, 2006). Age of drinking onset in adolescence is a strong predictor of later alcohol abuse and disorder (Aiken et al., 2018; Kim-Spoon et al., 2019). Associations between early drinking status and later problem behaviors remain even after controls are employed for a number of demographic and family variables (Ellickson, Tucker, & Klein, 2003). Findings such as these suggest that early drinking is an important risk in and of itself for later problems with alcohol.

A considerable body of literature suggests that behavioral undercontrol or behavioral disinhibition (failure to inhibit behavioral impulses) in childhood, especially among males, is an important precursor of later adolescent problems with substance use and abuse (Acheson, Vincent, Cohoon, & Lovallo, 2018; Chassin, Sher, Hussong, & Curran, 2013; Zucker, 2008). Recent work has focused on socialization (a willingness to follow rules and endorse conventional values) and on boldness (including thrill seeking) in childhood. Longitudinal research has demonstrated a link between low socialization at ages 11 and 14 and boldness at age 11 to substance abuse at age 17 (Hicks et al., 2014).

Cognitions (expectancies, beliefs, and values) about alcohol use appear in children as young as 3 to 6 years old (Zucker, Fitzgerald, Refior, Pallas, & Ellis, 2000), particularly among children in alcoholic families. Alcohol expectancies become more positive during the transition from childhood to early adolescence (Smit et al., 2018) and positive expectancies predict alcohol use initiation and drinking patterns over time. As an example, children's favorable attitudes toward alcohol and intentions to use alcohol at age 10 are associated with a higher probability of drug abuse and dependency at age 21 (Guo, Hawkins, Hill, & Abbott, 2001). Smit et al. (2018) found a range of factors influenced the development of alcohol expectancies, including psychopathology, genetics, environmental factors, parent and peer influences, and media. Furthermore, there are reciprocal effects (with expectancies influencing use and use influencing expectancies).

The child characteristics that scholars have found to be related to *childhood* substance use include a mix of behavioral and cognitive variables: less competence (Jackson, Henriksen, & Dickinson, 1997), more tolerance of deviance, more deviant self-image, more susceptibility to peer pressure, and greater reported peer use (Loveland-Cherry, Leech, Laetz, & Dielman, 1996). Eiden et al. (2016) found a developmental cascade model that links low child self-regulation in preschool years to continuing externalizing behaviors leading to early onset of drinking and higher engagement with substance-using peers.

Parent Factors

Jacob and Johnson (1997) conceptualize parenting influences on children as alcohol-specific effects and nonalcohol-specific effects. *Alcohol-specific effects* involve the behaviors of the parents with respect to alcohol and how these are related to the child's behavior and cognition. Frequently studied are the effects of being a child of an alcoholic (COA). The risks associated with parental alcohol use disorder (AUD) are likely additive (Mellentin et al., 2016)—children with two parents with AUDs were found to be at higher risk than those with a single parent (who were at higher risk than those with no parental AUD). Familial alcoholism has been linked to behavioral disinhibition and conduct problems in children, but this relationship is moderated by positive parenting practices (Su et al., 2018), and the overall effects of parental AUD on children is moderated by family cohesion (Finan, Schulz, Gordon, & McCauley Ohannessian, 2015), and socioeconomic status (SES) (Vermeulen-Smit et al., 2012). Higher levels of open adolescent–father communication in families with problem drinking predicted increased externalizing for girls, with the authors hypothesizing that in problem drinking families this open communication with fathers about the father's poor choices may actually increase risk for girls (Finan et al., 2015). For both boys and girls, family cohesion mediated the relationship between parental problem drinking and externalizing (Finan et al., 2015).

Similarly, family functioning mediates the effects of parental psychopathology on adolescent externalizing behaviors (particularly fathers' perceptions of family functioning; Burstein, Stanger, & Dumenci, 2012). In general, parents' substance-specific influences on preadolescents have predictive utility for later adolescent and adult use and abuse (Dishion, Capaldi, & Yoerger, 1999).

Nonalcohol-specific effects reflect the operation of such influences as parenting practices related to supervision, discipline, and nurturance of children; communication with children; parental divorce and remarriage; and clear family rules and monitoring (Guo et al., 2001). Nonsubstance-specific factors are studied as operating alone, together with alcohol-specific factors, and as part of feedback loops. For example, the combination of parental alcoholism (alcohol-specific) with parental antisocial behavior (nonalcohol-specific) predicts child externalizing behavior, itself a predictor of more harmful drinking as an adult (Fals-Stewart, Kelley, Cooke, & Golden, 2003). Parental comorbid mental illness and SUDs during childhood (especially in mothers) have also been linked to later substance abuse in adolescence (Ali, Dean, & Hedden, 2016), perhaps due to negative effects on parenting behavior (Seay & Kohl, 2015). A number of studies have provided evidence that negative parent reactions to children's difficult behaviors are followed by additional child maladaptation (Dishion et al., 1999).

Contextual Factors

In addition to personal and parental factors, there are a number of contextual factors that influence child substance abuse. For example, there are higher levels of substance use for children (age 10) who live in a neighborhood with more trouble-making youth, antisocial friends, frequent alcohol use by best friends, frequent contact with antisocial friends, and high levels of bonding with antisocial friends (Guo et al., 2001). Perceptions of higher disorganization, lower social cohesion, and more neighborhood problems are associated with higher odds for substance use (Shih et al., 2017). At the parental or familial level, low marital satisfaction can be a risk factor (Fals-Stewart et al., 2003) alone or in combination with other factors (Rothenberg, Hussong, & Chassin, 2016).

Much recent attention has focused on the role of childhood stress and childhood adverse life events or adverse experiences on the development of SUDs (Charles et al., 2015; Otten, Mun, Shawn, Wilson, & Dishion, 2018). Children from families with a history of SUDs experience more stress in childhood across multiple domains which contributes to risk of later substance abuse (Charles et al., 2015). Early childhood stress is also linked to poorer inhibitory control in childhood, which was subsequently linked to substance abuse in a developmental cascade (Otten et al., 2018).

In sum, children with conduct problems are at high risk for later substance use problems, exacerbated by parental substance abuse and other family and societal stressors. These stressors contribute to children's current and future substance use.

Adolescents and Youth and Substance Abuse Problems

In the United States, the period of adolescence, roughly ages 13 to 19, is characterized by dramatic increases in substance use. Although adolescent alcohol use has been declining dramatically since the 1980s, the period of youth or young adulthood, up to age 25, is generally the time during which substance use and abuse peak (National Institute on Alcohol Abuse and Alcoholism, 2000). Monitoring the

Future's annual surveys of 50,000 students in the eighth, tenth, and twelfth grades document the latest figures. "Despite recent declines, by the end of high school six out of every ten students (59% after a significant 3 percentage point drop in 2018) have consumed more than just a few sips of alcohol at some time in their lives; and about a quarter (24%) have done so by 8th grade" (Miech et al., 2019, p. 15).

Despite the overall decline in alcohol and illicit substance use, data from the Monitoring the Future surveys show large shifts in behavior from those in the eighth grade to those in the twelfth grade. Scholars' attempts to account for these age-related changes, and to explain the use of substances in adolescence, have generated a substantial body of literature in which certain themes stand out. Researchers have looked at (a) adolescent characteristics, such as expectancies, achievements, moods, behaviors, stressors, personality, roles, and clinical diagnoses, as well as demographics of gender, ethnicity, school, and neighborhood; (b) substance-specific family characteristics, such as parent and sibling substance use and alcohol-specific parenting practices; and (c) nonsubstance-specific influences such as parenting styles, family dysfunction, family stressors, family socioeconomic status, and parent-adolescent communication. It should be noted that most of the research documents factors that are involved in greater risk. However, research on moderating variables highlights areas where there may be factors involved in resilience (doing well despite adversity).

Fitting primarily within the resources component of the stress and coping model, four important models link family history of alcoholism to adolescent pathological alcohol involvement: positive affect regulation, deviance proneness, negative affect regulation, and pharmacological vulnerability (Sher, Grekin, & Williams, 2005). In research on moderators, scholars have sought to specify for whom and under what conditions associations hold between and among variables (Fischer & Wampler, 1994; Jacob & Johnson, 1997).

Adolescent Characteristics

Chassin et al. (2013) summarize research on the importance of the developmental periods of adolescence and emerging adulthood. There are several important considerations regarding adolescence that create increased risk for developing AUDs: heightened sensitivity to the neurotoxic effects of alcohol (Chassin et al., 2013) and gaps in neurobiology between a rapidly developing reward system and the more slowly developing cognitive control systems (see Kim-Spoon et al., 2019 and Martz, Zucker, Schulenberg, & Heitzeg, 2018 for recent studies on neurobiology and addiction risk and resilience).

Just as research has identified *childhood* behavioral disinhibition as an important factor in the onset of substance use, there is a similar influence of *adolescent* behavioral disinhibition (Zucker, 2008). The relationship between high sensation seeking or impulsivity and substance use has been found to be moderated by gender, with a stronger association for males than for females; societal pressures and expectations placed upon females may be protective for young women (Baker &

Yardley, 2002). There are also gender differences in exposure to and effects of risk in adolescence (Foster, Hicks, Iacono, & McGue, 2015). Males had higher exposure to risks but risk exposure was more predictive of alcohol problems in females (Foster et al., 2015).

Researchers have examined problems related to both delinquency and substance use (deviance proneness) in adolescents over time, with mixed results (Chassin et al., 2013). Generally speaking, conduct disorder or behavioral problems in adolescence are strong predictors of substance abuse (Mason, Patwardhan et al., 2017; Meier et al., 2015), and there is also a link from early adverse events to impulsivity, poor mood regulation, antisocial characteristics, and substance use risk, especially in families with a positive history of alcoholism (Sorocco, Carnes, Cohoon, Vincent, & Lovallo, 2015). Adolescents who lacked the self-control resource were more vulnerable to alcoholism (Barnow, Schuckit, & Lucht, 2002). There is a reduced likelihood that stressed parents or those who themselves engage in deviant behavior will encourage or teach their children self-control (Patock-Peckham, King, Morgan-Lopez, Ulloa, & Filson Moses, 2011).

Evidence for a negative emotion or internalizing pathway is mixed. For example, in the research of Englund, Egeland, Olivia, and Collins (2008), children with internalizing problems at age 7 reported less alcohol use in adulthood; however, at age 11, children with internalizing problems reported more alcohol use during young and middle adulthood for both genders and, for males, more alcohol use during adolescence. There is also a positive link between early adolescent alcohol use and reported internalizing symptoms, possibly gender-specific for females (Foster et al., 2015). Affect dysregulation mediates an association between childhood sexual abuse and substance abuse: Sexual abuse was associated with greater affect dysregulation, in turn, associated with more substance abuse (James, 2014).

Several recent studies have focused on specific coping mechanisms in adolescence and the link to substance misuse, generally finding that coping styles that involve avoidance, denial, or suppression are linked either directly to greater substance misuse or indirectly through increases in externalizing behaviors (Lyness & Koehler, 2016; Wong et al., 2013). Coping motives vary by SES, with higher SES adolescents drinking for increased confidence whereas lower SES adolescents drink to cope with low mood (Stapinski et al., 2016).

Risk factors also interact with other characteristics of the adolescent (e.g., race/ethnicity, sexual orientation, living arrangements). Rates of alcohol and other substance use have generally been lower for African American youth than for White or Hispanic youth (Miech et al., 2019). For rural African American youth, family risk factors include having family members who use alcohol or drugs and being raised by nonfamily members, whereas being raised by family members and having parents who talk with the adolescent about the dangers of drug and alcohol use were protective (Myers, 2013). Other risk factors found in studies of African American youth include low SES and social maladaptation in childhood (Fothergill, Ensminger, Doherty, Juon, & Green, 2016) and family stress (Voisin, Elsaesser, Kim, Patel, & Cantara, 2016).

Research demonstrates what has been called the "immigrant paradox" (Cristini, Scacchi, Perkins, Bless, & Vieno, 2015, p. 531)—that although immigrants to various countries often live in challenging conditions, they experience lower levels of substance abuse. A strong sense of ethnic identity may constitute a protective factor for ethnic minority youth (Banks, Winningham, Wu, & Zapolski, 2019). For Asian American youth, acculturation was a risk factor for alcohol use only in the absence of attachment bonds to parents (Wang, Kviz, & Miller, 2012). Parent–adolescent relationship factors have been shown to have a stronger influence on onset of substance abuse in Hispanic versus Caucasian families (Moreno, Janssen, Cox, Colby, & Jackson, 2017). Among Latinx youth, father involvement is a factor; there is a curvilinear association between a parent–child acculturation gap and increased risk for alcohol use (Cox, Roblyer, Merten, Shreffler, & Schwerdtfeger, 2013).

Sexual minority youth are at particular risk for alcohol and drug use, with this status conferring both direct risk and indirect risk through increased levels of depression (Day, Fish, Perez-Brumer, Hatzenbuehler, & Russell, 2017) and through higher levels of victimization (Coulter, Bersamin, Russell, & Mair, 2018; Day et al., 2017). Negative family interactions in the homes of sexual minority youth also increase risk for substance use and misuse (Rosario et al., 2014). Family rejection is a key risk factor for gender nonconforming individuals (Klein & Golub, 2016).

Substance-Specific Parenting and Family Factors

Associations between parental drinking and adolescent drinking are well documented (See Park & Schepp, 2014, for a review). Involved in these associations are all the elements of the stress and coping model. Not only is there greater risk for alcohol problems among COAs and earlier initiation of drinking, but the interval from first using alcohol to the development of alcohol disorders is shorter (Hussong, Bauer, & Chassin, 2008). As well, when children are involved in their parents' use (e.g., getting or pouring drinks for parents, getting cigarettes for parents), they are at higher risk for alcohol, cigarette, and marijuana use (Bailey, Epstein, Steeger, & Hill, 2018). A recent meta-analysis shows that parents' provision of alcohol, parental drinking, and parents' favorable attitudes toward drinking are factors (Yap, Cheong, Zaravinos-Tsakos, Lubman, & Jorm, 2017).

Considering the important transitions that accompany adolescence (graduating high school, employment, romantic involvements), experiencing an alcohol disorder could disrupt the timing and success of these events and relationships. There are pathways from alcohol misuse of parents both to young adults' difficulties with particular romantic relationships (e.g., Fischer et al., 2005) and to the initiation and maintenance of dating relationships in general (Fischer & Wiersma, 2012).

A family history of alcoholism is an important element in adolescent development of substance use problems; parental drinking has a causal effect on offspring drinking (Kendler, Edwards, & Gardner, 2015). Indeed, AUDs are approximately

50% heritable (Verhulst, Neale, & Kendler, 2015). Shared environments of children in the same family also contribute to AUDs but to a lesser extent.

There is some support for a deviance training hypothesis wherein older siblings influence younger siblings in deviant behavior such as drinking (Samek, Goodman, Riley, McGue, & Iacono, 2018; Samek, Rueter, Keyes, McGue, & Iacono, 2015; Whiteman, Jensen, Mustillo, & Maggs, 2016). Mediators that account for the association include co-drinking by the siblings and positive expectancies for alcohol use (Whiteman et al., 2016). However, there are exceptions in that some research indicated that younger adolescents influence older siblings when close in age (< 1.5 years), when they reported high sibling companionship (Samek et al., 2018), and when the siblings were in middle to late adolescence (Whiteman, Jensen, & McHale, 2017).

In addition to family, there are peer and friend influences as well (Scholte, Poelen, Willemsen, Boomsma, & Engels, 2008). The greater the number of parents, siblings, and friends who drink, the greater the regular drinking risk (i.e., consistently drinking a few times a month or more). The association between sibling modeling and similarity in alcohol use was stronger when the siblings shared friends (Whiteman, Jensen, & Maggs, 2013). In addition to not sharing friends, other protective influences for lower levels of drinking include closeness of sisters (but not brothers) (Samek et al., 2015). Social contagion appeared to play more of a role among brothers in increasing drinking (Samek et al., 2015). Buist, Deković, and Prinzie's (2013) meta-analysis indicated that sibling conflict was a stronger predictor than sibling warmth in predicting internalizing and externalizing (including drinking) behaviors.

Siblings from the same family may be concordant or discordant for alcohol use. The correlation between older and younger sibling for drinking was .33, sharing just 11% of variance (Whiteman et al., 2016). Fischer and Wiersma (2008) reported that 18% of siblings were different in alcohol use, primarily in adolescence, and that this difference appeared to reflect a niche-seeking strategy when there was more parental drinking. Understanding which sibling dyads pursue which pattern would enhance understanding of sibling dynamics and processes that are involved in alcohol use.

Mediators

Mediators of associations between parental substance abuse and adolescent behavior identify mechanisms and processes in the transmission of adolescent alcoholism. Monitoring and supervision constitute one dimension of parenting style (Shorey et al., 2013); warmth and support constitute another. When parents abuse substances, their ability to provide appropriate levels of monitoring and support may be compromised, thereby providing a mediating pathway to adolescent substance use and abuse (Su et al., 2018). Furthermore, because parents are regarded as sources of information for children, it is important to consider what parents tell their children about substance use and abuse (i.e., alcohol-specific parenting practices). The effectiveness of parental communication about substance use varies depending on whether or not the children have already begun to use. Ennett, Bauman, Foshee, Pemberton, and Hicks (2001) indicated that for adolescents who were already using substances, parent–child communication on the topic actually made the situation worse. Nonnemaker, Silber-Ashley, Farrelly, and Dench (2012) also found that parent–child communication about drug use may increase likelihood of marijuana initiation. Handley and Chassin (2013) concluded that "parental conversations about their own personal experiences with alcohol may not represent a form of parent–child communication about drinking that deters adolescent drinking" (p. 684). Parents should begin communicating with their children about substance use before the children initiate use and they should refrain from fondly discussing their own experiences.

Beliefs about risk for alcoholism may be modifiable and could be a target for intervention. Haller and Chassin (2010) indicated that adolescents with alcoholic parents who perceived that they were then at risk for alcoholism reported lower levels of drinking over time. For younger children, talking with the child about harmful consequences of alcohol use had an effect on later alcohol use initiation only in families where the parents drank more frequently (Ennett, Jackson, Bowling, & Dickenson, 2013).

Alcohol-specific parenting strategies could be a mechanism through which monitoring and other parenting practices work, that is, a mediation effect. Parental provision of alcohol and access to alcohol in the home increases the likelihood that adolescents will express greater intent to use as well as greater actual alcohol use (Yap et al., 2017). Parental approval of drinking or drug use is also consistently associated with greater adolescent drinking behavior, both directly and indirectly through effects on peers (Yap et al., 2017). Nonetheless, the findings have not been consistent from study to study, suggesting the presence of moderating effects.

Moderators

Gender of the drinking parent (as well as of offspring) is an important moderator (Homel & Warren, 2019). Consistently, associations of predictors with drinking outcomes are stronger and more stable for boys compared to girls (Zucker, 2008). Greater male vulnerability may be genetic (Zucker, 2008), but emotional distress and depressed mood in adolescence have also been found to be a stronger predictor of drinking for boys (McCauley Ohannessian, Flannery, Simpson, & Russell, 2016; Soloski & Berryhill, 2016) whereas negative family functioning (family conflict in particular) is a stronger predictor for girls and this relationship may be mediated by depressed mood (McCauley Ohannessian et al., 2016).

Maternal drinking is an often-overlooked factor in offspring drinking but it plays an important role (Mellentin et al., 2016; Vermeulen-Smit et al., 2012; Wolfe, 2016). For example, maternal closeness has been found to partially mediate the association between maternal problem drinking and adolescent alcohol use (Shorey et al., 2013), and maternal closeness was protective when there was maternal problem drinking. Maternal AUD had a significant negative effect on children's relationships with siblings and friends (Wolfe, 2016). Tyler, Stone, and Bersani (2006) attribute maternal influences to mothers' stronger role in child-rearing.

Other moderating factors that have been found to alter the association between parental drinking and offspring outcomes include expectations, peer orientations, ethnicity, family functioning, family structure, family cohesion, parental support, personality of the offspring, and family roles of the offspring (Fischer & Lyness, 2005). However parental support loses its effectiveness among adolescents with higher levels of undercontrol (King & Chassin, 2004). With respect to resilience, Fischer and Wampler (1994) investigated the buffering effects of personality and family roles (hero, mascot, scapegoat/lost child) on the associations between offspring alcohol misuse and both family history of addictions and family dysfunction. They found that personality was a moderator of the association of family addictions with offspring drinking for both males and females, but family roles such as hero buffered offspring drinking only with respect to family dysfunction. The kind of coping a child engages in, such as active coping, is important to adjustment (Lyness & Koehler, 2016; Stapinski et al., 2016); unfortunately, parental alcoholism is more likely to lead to children using avoidant coping, a tactic associated with poorer adjustment. Adolescent depression also interacts with parental substance abuse, such that depressed adolescents with substance abusing parents develop SUDs earlier (Gorka, Shankman, Seeley, & Lewinsohn, 2013). Andrews, Hops, and Duncan (1997) concluded that although a good parent–child relationship is important to positive child adjustment, it may not always be protective in situations in which parents use substances.

Nonsubstance-Specific Parenting Factors

Supervision and support are important parenting variables that operate regardless of parental substance use or abuse to influence adolescent outcomes (e.g., Shorey et al., 2013; Yap et al., 2017). Protective parenting factors include parental monitoring, parent–child relationship quality, parental support, and parental involvement (Yap et al., 2017). Among other benefits, these parenting practices may reduce stress, increase resources, and encourage active coping. Parental rules about alcohol are important in reducing adolescent alcohol use (Koning, van den Eijnden, & Vollenbergh, 2014; McKay, 2015). Koning, van den Eijnden, and Vollenbergh (2014) reported that stricter rules increased adolescent self-control and led to lower alcohol use only in families with high qualitative parent–child communication about alcohol. Parental rules were significant predictors distinguishing moderate drinkers from abstainers as well as moderate drinkers from problem drinkers (McKay, 2015). Abstaining youth have parents who convey warmth and do not use punishment to maintain control but instead clarify appropriate behavior and reinforce that behavior (Koning et al., 2014). Maternal warmth is especially protective (Eiden et al., 2016). At the other end of the spectrum, parental overprotection has been linked to regular alcohol use in adolescence (Visser, de Winter, Vollebergh, Verhulst, & Reijneveld, 2013). Increased family involvement, support, and bonding during adolescence are protective factors that predict less problem alcohol use in adulthood (Vakalahi, 2002). Parental consistency has been found to be protective for Latinx youth (West et al., 2013). Generally, family cohesion (Soloski, Monk, & Durtschi, 2016) and attachment to parents (McKay, 2015) are protective.

Adolescent demands for autonomy may create parent–child stressors and disrupted parenting. Monitoring is a delicate balance during adolescence as parents weigh the need for youth to be become independent while providing enough guidance and control (Dishion & McMahon, 1998). Parental monitoring can be a protective factor against alcohol and other drug use; however, for this protection to emerge, adolescents had to report high levels of parental monitoring (Branstetter & Furman, 2013). Monitoring seems to be more protective in middle childhood and early adolescence, although family relationship quality continues to be protective across the transition to high school (Van Ryzin, Fosco, & Dishion, 2012; Yap et al., 2017). High levels of monitoring work best in families that also exhibit a warm and supportive environment (Donaldson, Handren, & Crano, 2016).

Lindfors, Minkkinen, Katainen, and Rimpelä (2019) found significant protective effects for both maternal and paternal monitoring for boys and girls. However, others report gender-specific effects—monitoring by the opposite-gender parent mediated the link between parenting styles and impulsiveness (Patock-Peckham et al., 2011) such that monitoring decreased impulsiveness, which, in turn, was related to fewer alcohol-related problems. Poor relationships with parents were more predictive of substance use for girls but parental monitoring was more protective for girls (Rusby, Light, Crowley, & Westling, 2018).

Parental support is an important correlate of adolescent alcohol use, but the association is also mediated by other factors, such as religiosity, peer alcohol use, and school grades (Lindberg & Zeid, 2017). According to Bogenschneider, Wu, and Raffaelli (1998), mothers' responsiveness acted indirectly on adolescent alcohol use by helping to weaken adolescents' orientation to peers. Maternal depression, a condition that could reduce maternal support, contributed to adolescent and young adult problem drinking (Alati et al., 2005) and this effect is exacerbated in families where mothers have comorbid mental illness and substance abuse (Ali et al., 2016). There is also a complex interaction between genetic risk and family factors such as marital instability, alcoholism, and psychopathology in the home. Kendler et al. (2012), in a large-scale combination of data from adoption studies, found that the adverse environmental effects are stronger for those with high levels of genetic risk.

There are interactive effects of family and peer relationships on adolescent use as well. Family support moderates the effects of peers on adolescent substance use (Frauenglass, Routh, Pantin, & Mason, 1997). Parental knowledge about the children, such as their spending habits, their activities, and who the children's' friends were, had positive direct effects on adolescent use as well as indirect effects in reducing use through substance-using peers (Van Ryzin et al., 2012). The combination of supervision and acceptance, an *authoritative* parenting style, has been identified as a particularly important factor, both concurrently and longitudinally, in the reduced use of substances (Donaldson et al., 2016). Among older adolescents, having more indulgent and less controlling parents is more often associated with adolescent substance abuse compared to having authoritative parents. In general, the more the parent used alcohol, the more permissive were the alcohol rules for the adolescent, and the more permissive the alcohol rules, the more the adolescent drank (Tucker, Ellickson, & Klein, 2008). There were factors predicting less heavy drinking for these adolescents living in a permissive home: social influences, alcohol beliefs, and resistance self-efficacy (Tucker et al., 2008). Adolescents with parents who granted them more autonomy were found to engage in more substance use when they also were more highly engaged in disadvantaged communities (Russell & Gordon, 2017). However, cross-cultural research has found that in Europe, both authoritative and indulgent (or permissive) parenting styles are protective (Calafat, Garcia, Juan, Becoña, & Fernández-Hermida, 2014), primarily because of the high levels of support present within the indulgent-permissive parenting styles.

Contextual Factors

There is quite a body of evidence that drinking or substance using peers influence adolescent use in various ways (e.g., see Lindberg & Zeid, 2017 on interactive pathways to substance abuse and Shamblen, Ringwalt, Clark, & Hanley, 2014 on longitudinal growth trajectories). Furthermore, parenting and peer factors interact (Lindberg & Zeid, 2017). Kliewer and Zaharakis (2014) summarized the role of peers in family-based models of drug use progression, noting that multiple models support both the role of peers on drug use and interactions with family variables, including the quality of the parent–child relationship and identification with parents versus peers. Negative family factors can promote affiliation with deviant peers (Kliewer & Zaharakis, 2014). However, parental disapproval of drug use may moderate the negative role that drug using peers have on adolescent substance use (Chan, Kelly, Carroll, & Williams, 2017). Romantic relationships may also affect alcohol-related problems (see Fischer & Wiersma's 2012 review).

A number of factors operate directly and indirectly on adolescent substance use over time. Stressful life events were related to drinking to cope and to adolescent alcohol problems; and such events may interact with a family history of alcoholism (where there are higher levels of severe stressors; Charles et al., 2015). Specific stressful events linked to adolescent substance abuse include childhood sexual abuse (James, 2014; Mason, Russo, Chelan, Herrenkohl, & Herrenkohl, 2017) and exposure to violence in families and communities (James, Donnelly, Brooks-Gunn, & McLanahan, 2018; Schiff et al., 2014). Adverse childhood experiences have a cumulative effect, with individuals exposed to multiple adverse events demonstrating higher risks for substance abuse (Mersky, Topitzes, & Reynolds, 2013).

Trauma is another important pathway to adolescent problem behavior (Beal et al., 2019; Chassin et al., 2013). The dual risks of COA status and sexual abuse in adolescence have been related to higher levels of adolescent problems, including substance abuse, than that found in adolescents with only one risk factor (Fenton et al., 2013; Mason, Russo et al., 2017). Adolescents experiencing *current* abuse have been shown to have more problem behaviors, such as binge drinking, than adolescents with histories of *prior* abuse (Luster & Small, 1997). Employing a national data set, Kilpatrick et al. (2003) found connections between substance abuse and dependence during adolescence and (a) family alcohol problems, (b) having been a witness to violence, and (c) having been a victim of physical assault. Posttraumatic stress disorder (PTSD) occurred when sexual assault was added to the mix. Those who develop alcohol misuse subsequent to trauma are also more at risk for future assault (Mulsow, 2007). In a moderated-mediation model, distress mediated the relationship between childhood sexual abuse and alcohol consequences but only for those who reported coping motives for drinking, suggesting a tension-reduction model of alcohol use (Smith, Smith, & Grekin, 2014). It is also important to distinguish among unexpected tragedies, family instability, and family violence, which may have differing effects on adolescent substance use (Beal et al., 2019).

Some scholars have theorized that single-parent family structure creates distress in adolescents that may lead to greater affect and mood alteration through substance use. In addition, the lower levels of supervision and availability of parents in single-parent households may also lead to greater substance experimentation and abuse. Reflecting a stress approach, Jackson, Rogers, and Sartor (2016) and Russell and Gordon (2017) found clear evidence that parental divorce and separation are risk factors for adolescent substance use, magnified in situations involving high levels of parental drinking (Jackson et al., 2016). Arkes (2013) reported that youth were more likely to use alcohol 2 to 4 years *before* parental divorce, and that effects persisted after divorce as well. Other variables, including parent unavailability, family quality, peer acceptance or self-esteem, and deviant peer involvement, serve as mediators between parental divorce and adolescent alcohol use (Curry, Fischer, Reifman, & Harris, 2004). Divorce is not the only family structure risk factor; adolescents who transition from a single-parent family to a stepfamily increase their risk of initiating alcohol use (Kirby, 2006). There is some support, however, for the idea that parent and peer relationships are better at explaining adolescent alcohol consumption than family structure (Crawford & Novak, 2008).

Homelessness is another particular risk for adolescent substance abuse (James, 2014), particularly for those with poorer coping skills (Nyamathi et al., 2010), as is living in foster care (Brook, Rifenbark, Boulton, Little, & McDonald, 2014). Brook, Rifenbark, Boulton, Little, and McDonald (2014) found that risk factors played a greater role in predicting drug use than protective factors in foster youth, highlighting the vulnerability of these youth. Trauma can also make these contexts worse—Milburn et al. (2019, p. 37) found that "trauma, poor family functioning, and family conflict significantly predicted greater mental health problems, delinquent behaviors, high-risk sexual behaviors and substance use" in a population of homeless adolescents. Risks for foster care youth are amplified among girls (McDonald, Mariscal, Yan, & Brook, 2014). Although homelessness is a risk factor, among those in intact families, *higher* socioeconomic status (SES) is actually a consistent risk factor for increased use (Melotti et al., 2013). On the other hand, economic hardships affect families' ability to manage parenting. One longitudinal study found that economic pressure led to parental emotional distress and couple conflict, which led to harsh parenting, which then led to adolescent substance use (Diggs & Neppl, 2018). Another risk factor for minority youth is found in the effects of discrimination (Sanders-Phillips et al., 2014), although among Hispanic youth, a Hispanic orientation can be protective (Unger, 2014).

In sum, difficulties in making the transition from childhood to adolescence are compounded when alcohol and drugs enter the picture. Parents' use of substances increases adolescent risk by creating stressors, influencing perceptions, detracting from resources, and hindering coping. Parents' flexibility in coping with adolescents' emerging needs for autonomy and independence should be gender sensitive, given that socialization pressures continue to differ for boys and girls. More resilient adolescents in the face of parental alcoholism, poorer parenting, and trauma tend to be female, less disinhibited, and more parentally supported and monitored.

Bidirectional Processes

Throughout this chapter, the studies we cited have primarily focused on a particular direction of effects from parent to child: Alcohol abuse in parents *leads to* child and adolescent alcohol use and misuse; parenting practices help or hinder adolescent resistance to alcohol use. Other research suggests that bidirectional effects are at work. The title of one article put the issue as "Can Your Children Drive You to Drink?" (Pelham & Lang, 1999). A series of experimental studies documented an affirmative answer. Adoptive parents (Finley & Aguiar, 2002) of children whose biological parents had alcohol, antisocial, depressive, or other psychiatric disorders experienced double the risk of developing their own psychiatric or alcohol-related problems compared to adoptive parents of children without such a predisposition. Rather than parenting practices being a result of parental SUDs, parents' discipline was *elicited* by sons' neurobehavioral disinhibition (ND); this ND was in turn related to sons' SUDs (Mezzich et al., 2007). Commenting on studies such as these, Leonard and Eiden (2007) stated, "Alcoholic parents are at higher risk for having children with behavior problems, and children's behavior problems may increase parental stress and lead to more drinking" (p. 299). Elkins et al. (2014) looked at bidirectional effects of parenting and youth substance use during the transition to high school and stated, "findings indicated that higher effective discipline strategies decreased the likelihood of youth substance use in the subsequent grade, and engaging in substance use predicted lower perceived effectiveness of discipline in the subsequent year" (p. 481).

Issues in Prevention and Treatment

The family focus of the research cited in this chapter suggests that limiting prevention and treatment efforts to the individual in the family with the substance use problem is not sufficient to address the multiple levels of factors that are implicated in a person's substance use problem. There is no one place to start. In fact, alcohol misuse in families can extend back generations (Garrett & Landau, 2007). The substance-abusing parent certainly needs help but so do the children in the family. As this chapter illustrates, the stress and coping model highlights the importance of all the components—stressors, perceptions, resources, problem-solving skills, coping skills, and bidirectional effects—found in families dealing with substance abuse. Helping parents to effectively manage a behaviorally disinhibited child may interrupt the negative sequence of events from childhood to young adulthood. But helping children cope with a substance-abusing parent is also critical.

Prevention of both early onset of substance use and early conduct disorder problems is a key factor in positive youth development. Children from antisocial alcoholic families would benefit from interventions that begin in infancy (Fitzgerald, Puttler, Refior, & Zucker, 2007). Other pathways that children follow are sorted out in middle childhood, suggesting that interventions should begin before this critical time. Bolstering the case for early intervention, Aldwin's (2007) developmental approach identifies coping as embedded in the social ecology of the family throughout the lifespan beginning with infant and even prenatal coping behaviors. Feinberg, Sakuma, Hostetler, and McHale (2013) have introduced a school-based family prevention program that focuses on communication, especially communication of compliments to and from parents and siblings. Their program intends to interrupt the negative parenting, sibling conflict, and sibling deviance training contributions to adolescent alcohol use.

If children and adults are dually diagnosed (e.g., alcohol abuse or dependence with PTSD), it is important to treat both (Mulsow, 2007). For example, parental monitoring of their children may be particularly important in parenting youth with ADHD (Walther et al., 2012). It is also necessary to deal with such family background issues as stresses surrounding grief, loss, and trauma (Garrett & Landau, 2007) for which alcohol abuse is a symptom.

An important concomitant of recovery is the disruption of family dynamics, and programs need to address changes in family dynamics to prevent relapse and to prevent children in the family from experiencing additional difficulties (Lewis & Allen-Byrd, 2007). Fischer, Pidcock, and Fletcher-Stephens (2007) describe three evidence-based programs for alcohol-abusing adolescents that include the family as well as the adolescent. Hogue et al. (2019) describe common factors among three manualized family therapy programs for adolescents: focusing on interactional change, having a relational reframe, engaging the adolescent, and having a relational emphasis. Recent applications of attachment-based family therapies with adolescent substance use provide a promising approach (Downs, Seedall, Taylor, & Downs, 2015). Family recovery is a stressful endeavor, and attention needs to be given to children when other family members go through recovery (Lewis & Allen-Byrd, 2007). One positive effect of parents receiving treatment has been decreased child exposure to parental conflict (Rounsaville, O'Farrell, Andreas, Murphy, & Murphy, 2014).

Dealing with family dynamics is only one goal of comprehensive intervention, however. As we noted in an earlier version of this chapter (Fischer & Lyness, 2005), to prevent relapse, programs must also consider settings and situations beyond the family itself, such as (a) effective aftercare services; (b) safe havens for children of addicted parents; (c) school, college, and community policies (Cleveland, Harris, & Wiebe, 2010); (d) cultural and subcultural norms and behaviors; and (e) support for recovery.

Conclusion

An encouraging aspect of recent studies examining how families cope with substance abuse is the inclusion of multiple variables, multiple perspectives, multiple waves of data collection spanning infancy to middle age, and sophisticated data analysis techniques. This very richness presents challenges to the scholars who report such research because the findings are embedded in complex webs of interrelated results. Studies that examine the changing nature of predictors across different developmental ages provide valuable information for prevention and risk reduction (e.g., Guo et al., 2001). With this information, programs can begin to focus on the key developmental periods specific to identified predictors.

The literature we have reviewed in this chapter has largely reported on research with families of European heritage; however, the Monitoring the Future surveys repeatedly find lower rates of substance use among African American youth than among European American adolescents and higher rates among Hispanic youth (Miech et al., 2019). Even when similar rates are reported across ethnic groups, as with marijuana use, researchers should not assume that predictors and pathways to substance use are analogous. Furthermore, the consequences of use are greater for African American than European American youth (Jones, Hussong, Manning, & Sterrett, 2008). Future research must reflect the diversity of families coping with substance abuse, not just in terms of ethnicity and culture but also in terms of emerging understandings of the broad spectrum of close relationships covered by the term *families*. We have included in this review research on families with children and adolescents which we believe illuminates family scholars' understandings of families coping with substance abuse.

DISCUSSION QUESTIONS ●

1. What are important factors that contribute to child and adolescent alcohol use?

2. What are the mechanisms (mediators) and factors that alter associations (moderators) between family and alcohol use?

3. What are promising approaches to reducing and treating child and adolescent substance use?

REFERENCES

Acheson, A., Vincent, A. S., Cohoon, A. J., & Lovallo, W. R. (2018). Defining the phenotype of young adults with family histories of alcohol and other substance use disorders: Studies from the family health patterns project. *Addictive Behaviors, 77,* 247–254.

Acion, L., Ramirez, M. R., Jorge, R., & Arndt, S. (2013). Increased risk of alcohol and drug use among children from deployed military families. *Addiction, 108,* 1418–1425.

Aiken, A., Clare, P. J., Wadolowski, M., Hutchinson, D., Najman, J. M., Slade, T., . . . & Mattick, R. P. (2018). Age of alcohol initiation and progression to binge drinking in adolescence: A prospective cohort study. *Alcoholism: Clinical and Experimental Research, 42,* 100–100.

Alati, R., Kinner, S. A., Najman, J. M., Mamum, A. A., Williams, G. M., O'Callaghan, M., & Bor, W. (2005). Early predictors of adult drinking: A birth cohort study. *American Journal of Epidemiology, 162*(11), 1098–1107.

Aldwin, C. M. (2007). *Stress, coping, and development: An integrative perspective* (2nd ed.). New York, NY: Guilford Press.

Ali, M. M., Dean, D., & Hedden, S. L. (2016). The relationship between parental mental illness and/or substance use disorder on adolescent substance use disorder: Results from a nationally representative survey. *Addictive Behaviors, 59,* 35–41.

American Psychiatric Association. (2013). *Diagnostic and statistical manual of mental disorders* (5th ed.). Washington, DC: Author.

Andrews, J. A., Hops, H., & Duncan, S. C. (1997). Adolescent modeling of parent substance use: The moderating effect of the relationship with the parent. *Journal of Family Psychology, 11,* 259–270.

Arkes, J. (2013). The temporal effects of parental divorce on youth substance use. *Substance Use & Misuse, 48,* 290–297.

Bailey, J. A., Epstein, M., Steeger, C. M., & Hill, K. G. (2018). Concurrent and prospective associations between substance-specific parenting practices and child cigarette, alcohol, and marijuana use. *Journal of Adolescent Health, 62,* 681–687. doi:10.1016/j.jadohealth.2012.11.290

Baker, J. R., & Yardley, J. K. (2002). Moderating effect of gender on the relationship between sensation seeking-impulsivity and substance use in adolescents. *Journal of Child and Adolescent Substance Abuse, 12*(1), 27–43.

Banks, D. E., Winningham, R. D., Wu, W., & Zapolski, T. C. B. (2019). Examination of the indirect effect of alcohol expectancies on ethnic identity and adolescent drinking outcomes. *American Journal of Orthopsychiatry, 89*(5), 600–608 doi:10.1037/ort0000390

Barnow, S., Schuckit, M. A., & Lucht, M. (2002). The importance of a positive family history of alcoholism, parental rejection and emotional warmth, behavioral problems and peer substance use for alcohol problems in teenagers: A path analysis. *Journal of Studies on Alcohol, 63,* 305–312.

Beal, S. J., Wingrove, T., Mara, C. A., Lutz, N., Noll, J. G., & Greiner, M. V. (2019). Childhood adversity and associated psychosocial function in adolescents with complex trauma. *Child & Youth Care Forum, 48,* 305–322.

Biederman, J., Faraone, S. V., Monuteaux, M. C., & Feighner, J. A. (2000). Patterns of alcohol and drug use in adolescents can be predicted by parental substance use disorders. *Pediatrics, 106,* 792–797.

Bogenschneider, K., Wu, M., & Raffaelli, M. (1998). Parent influences on adolescent peer orientation and substance use: The interface of parenting practices and value. *Child Development, 69,* 1672–1688.

Branstetter, S. A., & Furman, S. A. (2013). Buffering effect of parental monitoring knowledge and parent–adolescent relationships on consequences of adolescent substance use. *Journal of Child and Family Studies, 22,* 192–198.

Brook, J., Rifenbark, G. G., Boulton, A., Little, T. D., & McDonald, T. P. (2015). Risk and protective factors for drug use among youth living in foster care. *Child & Adolescent Social Work Journal, 32*(2), 155–165.

Buist, K. L., Deković, M., & Prinzie, P. (2013). Sibling relationship quality and psychopathology of children and adolescents: A meta-analysis. *Clinical Psychology Review, 33,* 97–106.

Burstein, M., Stanger, C., & Dumenci, L. (2012). Relations between parent psychopathology, family functioning, and adolescent problems in substance-abusing families: Disaggregating the effects of parent gender. *Child Psychiatry and Human Development, 43,* 631–647.

Calafat, A., Garcia, F., Juan, M., Becoña, E., & Fernández-Hermida, J. R. (2014). Which parenting style is more protective against adolescent substance use? Evidence within the European context. *Drug and Alcohol Dependence, 138,* 185–192.

Chan, G. C. K., Kelly, A. B., Carroll, A., & Williams, J. W. (2017). Peer drug use and adolescent polysubstance use: Do parenting and school factors moderate this association? *Addictive Behaviors, 64,* 78–81.

Charles, N. E., Ryan, S. R., Acheson, A., Mathias, C. W., Liang, Y., & Dougherty, D. M. (2015). Childhood stress exposure among preadolescents with and without family histories of substance use disorders. *Psychology of Addictive Behaviors, 39,* 192–200.

Chassin, L., Sher, K. J., Hussong, A., & Currant, P. (2013). The developmental psychopathology of alcohol use and alcohol disorders: Research achievements and future directions. *Development and Psychopathology, 25,* 1567–1584.

Cleveland, H. H., Harris, K. S., & Wiebe, R. P. (Eds.) (2010). *Substance abuse recovery in college: Community supported abstinence.* New York, NY: Springer.

Coulter, R. W. S., Bersamin, M., Russell, S. T., & Mair, C. (2018). The effects of gender- and sexuality-based harassment on lesbian, gay, bisexual, and transgender substance use disparities. *Journal of Adolescent Health, 62,* 688–700.

Cox, R. B., Roblyer, M. Z., Merten, M. J., Shreffler, K. M., & Schwerdtfeger, K. L. (2013). Do parent–child acculturation gaps affect early adolescent Latino alcohol use? A study of the probability and extent of use. *Substance Abuse Treatment, Prevention, and Policy, 8,* 4. doi:10.1186/1747-597X-8-4

Crawford, L. A., & Novak, K. B. (2008). Parent–child relations and peer associations as mediators of the family structure–substance use relationship. *Journal of Family Issues, 29*(2), 155–184.

Cristini, F., Scacchi, L., Perkins, D. D., Bless, K. D., & Vieno, A. (2015). Drug use among immigrant and non-immigrant adolescents: Immigrant paradox, family and peer influences. *Journal of Community & Applied Social Psychology, 25,* 531–548.

Curry, L., Fischer, J., Reifman, A., & Harris, K. (2004, March). *Family factors, self-esteem, peer involvement, and adolescent alcohol misuse.* Poster presented at the biennial meeting of the Society for Research on Adolescence, Baltimore, MD.

Day, J. K., Fish, J. N., Perez-Brumer, A., Hatzenbuehler, M. L., & Russell, S. T. (2017). Transgender youth substance use disparities: Results from a population-based sample. *Journal of Adolescent Health, 61,* 729–735.

Diggs, O. N., & Neppl, T. K. (2018). The influence of economic pressure on emerging adult binge drinking: Testing the family stress model over time. *Journal of Youth and Adolescence, 47,* 2481–2495.

Dishion, T. J., Capaldi, D. M., & Yoerger, K. (1999). Middle childhood antecedents to progressions in male adolescent substance use: An ecological analysis of risk and protection. *Journal of Adolescent Research, 14,* 175–205.

Dishion, T. J., & McMahon, R. J. (1998). Parental monitoring and the prevention of child and adolescent problem behavior: A conceptual and empirical formulation. *Clinical Child and Family Psychology Review, 1,* 61–75.

Donaldson, C. D., Handren, L. M., & Crano, W. D. (2016). The enduring impact of parents' monitoring, warmth, expectancies, and alcohol use on their children's future binge drinking and arrests: A longitudinal analysis. *Prevention Science, 17,* 606–614.

Downs, A. B., Seedall, R. B., Taylor, N. C., & Downs, K. J. (2015). Attachment-based considerations for addressing adolescent substance use (ASU) in a family context. *The American Journal of Family Therapy, 43,* 28–43.

Eiden, R. D., Lessard, J., Colder, C. R., Livingston, J., Casey, M., & Leonard, K. E. (2016). Developmental cascade model for adolescent substance use from infancy to late adolescence. *Developmental Psychology, 52,* 1619–1633.

Elkins, S. R., Fite, P. J., Moore, T. M., Lochman, J. E., & Wells, K. C. (2014). Bidirectional effects of parenting and youth substance use during the transition to middle and high school. *Psychology of Addictive Behaviors, 28,* 475–486.

Ellickson, P. L., Tucker, J. S., & Klein, D. J. (2003). Ten-year prospective study of public health problems associated with early drinking. *Pediatrics, 111,* 949–955.

Englund, M. M., Egeland, B., Olivia, E. M., & Collins, W. A. (2008). Childhood and adolescent predictors of heavy drinking and alcohol use disorders in early adulthood: A longitudinal developmental analysis. *Addiction, 103*(Suppl. 1), 23–35.

Ennett, S. T., Bauman, K. E., Foshee, V. A., Pemberton, M., & Hicks, K. A. (2001). Parent–child communication about adolescent tobacco and alcohol use: What do parents say and does it affect youth behavior? *Journal of Marriage and Family, 63,* 48–63.

Ennett, S. T., Jackson, C., Bowling, J. M., & Dickinson, D. M. (2013). Parental socialization and children's susceptibility to alcohol use initiation. *Journal of Studies on Alcohol and Drugs, 74,* 694–702.

Fals-Stewart, W., Kelley, M. L., Cooke, C. G., & Golden, J. C. (2003). Predictors of the psychosocial adjustment of children living in households of parents in which fathers abuse drugs: The effects of postnatal parental exposure. *Addictive Behaviors, 28,* 1013–1031.

Feinberg, M. E., Sakuma, K.-L., Hostetler, M., & McHale, S. M. (2013). Enhancing sibling relationships to prevent adolescent problem behaviors: Theory, design and feasibility of Siblings Are

Special. *Evaluation and Program Planning, 36*(1), 97–106.

Fenton, M. C., Geier, T., Keyes, K., Skodol, A. E., Grant, B. F., & Hasin, D. S. (2013). Combined role of childhood maltreatment, family history, and gender in the risk for alcohol dependence. *Psychological Medicine, 43,* 1045–1057.

Finan, L. J., Schulz, J., Gordon, M. S., & McCauley Ohannessian, C. (2015). Parental problem drinking and adolescent externalizing behaviors: The mediating role of family functioning. *Journal of Adolescence, 43,* 100–100.

Finley, G. E., & Aguiar, L. J. (2002). The effects of children on parents: Adoptee genetic dispositions and adoptive parent psychopathology. *Journal of Genetic Psychology, 163*(4), 503–506.

Fischer, J. L., Fitzpatrick, J. A., Cleveland, B., Lee, J.-M., McKnight, A., & Miller, B. (2005). Binge drinking in the context of romantic relationships. *Addictive Behaviors, 30,* 1496–1516.

Fischer, J. L., & Lyness, K. P. (2005). Families coping with alcohol and substance abuse. In P. S. McKenry & S. J. Price (Eds.), *Families and change: Coping with stressful events and transitions* (3rd ed., pp. 155–178). Thousand Oaks, CA: SAGE.

Fischer, J. L., Pidcock, B. W., & Fletcher-Stephens, B. J. (2007). Family response to adolescence, youth and alcohol. In J. L. Fischer, M. Mulsow, & A. W. Korinek (Eds.), *Familial responses to alcohol problems* (pp. 27–41). Binghamton, NY: The Haworth Press.

Fischer, J. L., & Wampler, R. S. (1994). Abusive drinking in young adults: Personality type and family role as moderators of family-of-origin influences. *Journal of Marriage and Family, 56,* 469–479.

Fischer, J. L., & Wiersma, J. D. (2008, November). *Patterns of sibling drinking in adolescence and young adulthood.* Paper presented at the National Council on Family Relations Annual Meeting, Little Rock, AR.

Fischer, J. L., & Wiersma, J. D. (2012). Romantic relationships and alcohol use. *Current Drug Abuse Reviews, 5,* 98–116.

Fitzgerald, H. E., Puttler, L. I., Refior, S., & Zucker, R. A. (2007). Family response to children and alcohol. In J. L. Fischer, M. Mulsow, & A. W. Korinek (Eds.), *Familial responses to alcohol problems* (pp. 11–25). Binghamton, NY: Haworth Press.

Fothergill, K., Ensminger, M. E., Doherty, E. E., Juon, H., & Green, K. M. (2016). Pathways from early childhood adversity to later adult drug use and psychological distress: A prospective study of a cohort of African Americans. *Journal of Health and Social Behavior, 57,* 223–239.

Foster, K. T., Hicks, B. M., Iacono, W. G., & McGue, M. (2015). Gender differences in the structure of risk for alcohol use disorder in adolescence and young adulthood. *Psychological Medicine, 45,* 3047–3058.

Frauenglass, S., Routh, D. K., Pantin, H. M., & Mason, C. A. (1997). Family support decreases influence of deviant peers on Hispanic adolescents' substance use. *Journal of Clinical and Child Psychology, 26,* 15–23.

Garrett, J., & Landau, J. (2007). Family motivation to change: A major factor in engaging alcoholics in treatment. In J. L. Fischer, M. Mulsow, & A. W. Korinek (Eds.), *Familial responses to alcohol problems* (pp. 65–83). Binghamton, NY: Haworth Press.

Gorka, S. M., Shankman, S. A., Seeley, J. R., & Lewinsohn, P. M. (2013). The moderating effect of parental illicit substance use disorders on the relation between adolescent depression and subsequent illicit substance use disorders. *Drug and Alcohol Dependence, 128,* 1–7.

Guo, J., Hawkins, J. D., Hill, K. G., & Abbott, R. D. (2001). Childhood and adolescent predictors of alcohol abuse and dependence in young adulthood. *Journal of Studies on Alcohol and Drugs, 62,* 754–762.

Haller, M. M., & Chassin, L. (2010). The reciprocal influences of perceived risk for alcoholism and alcohol use over time: Evidence for aversive transmission of parental alcoholism. *Journal of Studies on Alcohol and Drugs, 71,* 588–596.

Handley, E. D., & Chassin, L. (2013). Alcohol-specific parenting as a mechanism of parental drinking and alcohol use disorder risk on adolescent alcohol use onset. *Journal of Studies on Alcohol and Drugs, 74,* 684–693.

Hicks, B. M., Johnson, W., Durbin, C. E., Blonigen, D. M., Iacono, W. G., & McGue, M. (2014). Delineating selection and mediation effects among childhood personality and environmental risk factors in the development of adolescent substance abuse. *Journal of Abnormal Child Psychology, 42,* 845–859.

Hogue, A., Bobek, M., Dauber, S., Henderson, C. E., McLeod, B. D., & Southam-Gerow, M. A. (2019). Core elements of family therapy for adolescent behavior problems: Empirical distillation of three manualized treatments. *Journal of Clinical Child & Adolescent Psychology, 48,* 29–41.

Homel, J., & Warren, D. (2019). The relationship between parent drinking and adolescent drinking: Differences for mothers and fathers and boys and girls. *Substance Use & Misuse, 54,* 661–669.

Hussong, A. M., Bauer, D., & Chassin, L. (2008). Telescoped trajectories from alcohol initiation to disorder in children of alcoholic parents. *Journal of Abnormal Psychology, 117,* 63–78.

Jackson, C., Henriksen, L., & Dickinson, D. (1997). The early use of alcohol and tobacco: Its relation to children's competence and parents' behavior. *American Journal of Public Health, 87,* 359–364.

Jackson, K. M., Rogers, M. L., & Sartor, C. E. (2016). Parental divorce and initiation of alcohol use in early adolescence. *Psychology of Addictive Behaviors, 30,* 450–461.

Jacob, T., & Johnson, S. (1997). Parenting influences on the development of alcohol abuse and dependence. *Alcohol Health and Research World, 21,* 204–210.

James, C. (2014). Childhood sexual abuse and adolescent substance abuse and sexual risk behaviours among homeless youth: The mediational roles of affect dysregulation and post-traumatic stress symptoms. *Dissertation Abstracts International: Section B: The Sciences and Engineering, 74(7-B)(E).*

James, S., Donnelly, L., Brooks-Gunn, J., & McLanahan, S. (2018). Links between childhood exposure to violent contexts and risky adolescent health behaviors. *Journal of Adolescent Health, 63,* 94–101.

Jones, D. J., Hussong, A. M., Manning, J., & Sterrett, E. (2008). Adolescent alcohol use in context: The role of parents and peers among African American and European American youth. *Cultural Diversity and Ethnic Minority Psychology, 14(3),* 266–273.

Kelley, M. L., & Fals-Stewart, W. (2008). Treating parental drug abuse using learning sobriety together: Effects on adolescents versus children. *Drug and Alcohol Dependence, 92(1–3),* 228–238.

Kendler, K. S., Edwards, A. C., & Gardner, C. O. (2015). Sex differences in the pathways to symptoms of alcohol use disorder: a study of opposite-sex twin pairs. *Alcoholism, Clinical And Experimental Research, 39(6),* 998–1007.

Kendler, K. S., Sundquist, K., Ohlsson, H., Palmer, K., Maes, H., Winkleby, M. A., & Sundquist, J. (2012). Genetic and familial environmental influences on the risk for drug abuse: A national Swedish adoption study. *JAMA Psychiatry, 69,* 690–697.

Kilpatrick, D. G., Ruggiero, K J., Acierno, R., Saunders, B. E., Resnick, H. S., & Best, C. L. (2003). Violence and risk of PTSD, major depression, substance abuse/dependence, and comorbidity: Results from the national survey of adolescents. *Journal of Consulting and Clinical Psychology, 71,* 692–700.

Kim-Spoon, J., Lauharatanahirun, N, Peviani, K., Brieant, A., Deater-Deckard, K., Bickel, W. K., & King-Casas, B. (2019). Longitudinal pathways linking family risk, neural risk processing, delay discounting, and adolescent substance use. *The Journal of Child Psychology and Psychiatry, 60,* 655–664.

King, K. M., & Chassin, L. (2004). Mediating and moderated effects of adolescent behavioral undercontrol and parenting in the prediction of drug use disorders in emerging adulthood. *Psychology of Addictive Behaviors, 18,* 239–249.

Kirby, J. B. (2006). From single-parent families to stepfamilies: Is the transition associated with adolescent alcohol initiation? *Journal of Family Issues, 27*(5), 685–711.

Klein, A., & Golub, S. A. (2016). Family rejection as a predictor of suicide attempts and substance misuse among transgender and gender nonconforming adults. *LGBT Health, 3,* 193–199.

Kliewer, W., & Zaharakis, N. (2014). Family-based models of drug etiology. In L. M. Scheier & W. B. Hansen (Eds.), *Parenting and teen drug use: The most recent findings from research, prevention, and treatment* (pp. 37–61). New York, NY: Oxford University Press.

Koning, I. M., van den Eijnden, R. J. J. M., & Vollenbergh, W. A. M. (2014). Alcohol-specific parenting, adolescents' self-control, and alcohol use: A moderated mediation model. *Journal of Studies on Alcohol and Drugs, 75,* 16–23.

Leonard, K. E., & Eiden, R. D. (2007). Marital and family processes in the context of alcohol use and alcohol disorders. *Annual Review of Clinical Psychology, 3,* 285–310.

Lewis, V., & Allen-Byrd, L. (2007). Coping strategies for the stages of family recovery. In J. L. Fischer, M. Mulsow, & A. W. Korinek (Eds.), *Familial responses to alcohol problems* (pp. 105–124). Binghamton, NY: Haworth Press.

Lindberg, M. A., & Zeid, D. (2017). Interactive pathways to substance abuse. *Addictive Behaviors, 66,* 76–82.

Lindfors, P., Minkkinen, J., Katainen, A., & Rimpelä, A. (2019). Do maternal knowledge and paternal knowledge of children's whereabouts buffer differently against alcohol use? A longitudinal study among Finnish boys and girls. *Drug and Alcohol Dependence, 194,* 351–357.

Loveland-Cherry, C. J., Leech, S., Laetz, V. B., & Dielman, T. E. (1996). Correlates of alcohol use and misuse in fourth-grade children: Psychosocial, peer, parental, and family factors. *Health Education Quarterly, 23,* 497–577.

Luster, T., & Small, S. A. (1997). Sexual abuse history and problems in adolescence: Explaining the effects of moderating variables. *Journal of Marriage and Family, 59,* 131–142.

Lyness, K. P., & Koehler, A. M. (2016). Effect of coping on substance use in adolescent girls: A dyadic analysis of parent and adolescent perceptions. *International Journal of Adolescence and Youth, 21,* 449–461.

Martz, M. E., Zucker, R. A., Schulenberg, J. E., & Heitzeg, M. M. (2018). Psychosocial and neural indicators of resilience among youth with a family history of substance use disorder. *Drug and Alcohol Dependence, 185,* 196–206.

Mason, W. A., Patwardhan, I., Smith, G. L., Chmelka, M. B., Savolainen, J., January, S. A., . . . & Järvelin, M. (2017). Cumulative contextual risk at birth and adolescent substance initiation: Peer mediation tests. *Drug and Alcohol Dependence, 177,* 291–298.

Mason, W. A., Russo, M. J., Chmelka, M. B., Herrenkohl, R. C., & Herrenkohl, T. I. (2017). Parent and peer pathways linking childhood experiences of abuse with marijuana use in adolescence and adulthood. *Addictive Behaviors, 66,* 70–75.

McCauley Ohannessian, C., Flannery, K. M., Simpson, E., & Russell, B. S. (2016). Family functioning and adolescent alcohol use: A moderated mediation analysis. *Journal of Adolescence, 49,* 19–27.

McDonald, T. P., Mariscal, E. S., Yan, Y., & Brook, J. (2014). Substance use and abuse for youths in foster care: Results from the communities that care normative database. *Journal of Child & Adolescent Substance Abuse, 23,* 262–268.

McKay, M. T. (2015). Parental rules, parent and peer attachment, and adolescent drinking behaviors. *Substance Use & Misuse, 50,* 184–188.

McKenry, P. C., & Price, S. J. (2005). Families coping with change. In P. S. McKenry & S. J. Price (Eds.), *Families and change: Coping with stressful events and transitions* (3rd ed., pp. 1–24). Thousand Oaks, CA: SAGE.

Meier, M. H., Hall, W., Caspi, A., Belsky, D. W., Cerda, M., Harrington, H. L., . . . & Moffitt, T. E. (2015). Which adolescents develop persistent substance dependence in adulthood? Using population-representative longitudinal data to inform universal risk assessment. *Psychological Medicine, 46,* 877–889.

Mellentin, A. I., Brink, M., Andersen, L., Erlangsen, A., Stenager, E., Bjerregaard, L. B., & Christiansen, E. (2016). The risk of offspring developing substance use disorders when exposed to one versus two parent(s) with alcohol use disorder: A nationwide, register-based cohort study. *Journal of Psychiatric Research, 80,* 52–58.

Melotti, R., Lewis, G., Hickman, M., Heron, J., Araya, R., & Macleod, J. (2013). Early life socio-economic position and later alcohol use: Birth cohort study. *Addiction, 108,* 516–525.

Mersky, J. P., Topitzes, J., & Reynolds, A. J. (2013). Impacts of adverse childhood experiences on health, mental health, and substance use in early adulthood: A cohort study of an urban, minority sample in the U.S. *Child Abuse & Neglect, 37,* 917–925.

Mezzich, A. C., Tarter, R. E., Kirisci, L., Feske, U., Day, B., & Gao, Z. (2007). Reciprocal influence of parent discipline and child's behavior on risk for substance disorder: A nine-year prospective study. *American Journal of Drug and Alcohol Abuse, 33*(6), 851–867.

Miech, R. A., Johnston, L. D., O'Malley, P. M., Bachman, J. G., Schulenberg, J. E., & Patrick, M. E. (2019). *Monitoring the Future national survey results on drug use, 1975–2018: Volume I, Secondary school students.* Ann Arbor: Institute for Social Research, University of Michigan.

Milburn, N. G., Stein, J. A., Lopez, S. A., Hilberg, A. M., Veprinsky, A., Mayfield Arnold, E. . . . & Comulada, W. S. (2019). Trauma, family factors and the mental health of homeless adolescents. *Journal of Child & Adolescent Trauma, 12,* 37–47.

Moreno, O., Janssen, T., Cox, M. J., Colby, S., & Jackson, K. M. (2017). Parent–adolescent relationships in Hispanic versus Caucasian families: Associations with alcohol and marijuana use onset. *Addictive Behaviors, 74,* 74–81.

Mulsow, M. (2007). Treatment of co-morbidity in families. In J. L. Fischer, M. Mulsow, & A. W. Korinek (Eds.), *Familial responses to alcohol problems* (pp. 125–140). Binghamton, NY: Haworth Press.

Myers, L. L. (2013). Substance use among rural African American adolescents: Identifying risk and protective factors. *Child and Adolescent Social Work Journal, 30,* 79–93.

National Institute on Alcohol Abuse and Alcoholism. (2000). Drinking over the life span: Issues of biology, behavior, and risk. In *National Institute on Alcohol Abuse and Alcoholism, tenth special report to the U.S. Congress on alcohol and health: Highlights from current research.* Retrieved from https://pubs.niaaa.nih.gov/publications/10report/chap01.pdf

Nonnemaker, J. M., Silber-Ashley, O., Farrelly, M. T., & Dench, D. (2012). Parent–child communication and marijuana initiation: Evidence using discrete-time survival analysis. *Addictive Behaviors, 37,* 1342–1348.

Nyamathi, A., Hudson, A., Greengold, B., Slagle, A., Marfisee, M., Khalilifard, F., & Leake, B. (2010). Correlates of substance use severity among homeless youth. *Journal of Child and Adolescent Psychiatric Nursing, 23,* 214–222.

Otten, R., Mun, C. J., Shaw, D. S., Wilson, M. N., & Dishion, T. J. (2018). A developmental cascade model for early adolescent-one substance use: The role of early childhood stress. *Addiction, 114,* 326–334.

Park, S., & Schepp, K. G. (2014). A systematic review of research on children of alcoholics: Their inherent resilience and vulnerability. *Journal of Child and Family Studies, 23*(2), 1–10.

Patock-Peckham, J. A., King, K. M., Morgan-Lopez, A. A., Ulloa, E. C., & Filson Moses, J. M. (2011). Gender-specific mediational links between parenting styles, parental monitoring, impulsiveness, drinking control, and alcohol-related problems. *Journal of Studies on Alcohol and Drugs, 72,* 247–258.

Pelham, W. E., & Lang, A. R. (1999). Can your children drive you to drink?: Stress and parenting in adults interacting with children with ADHD. *Alcohol Research and Health, 23,* 292–298.

Rosario, M., Reisner, S. L., Corliss, H. L., Wypji, D., Calzo, J., & Austin, S. B. (2014). Sexual-orientation disparities in substance use in emerging adults: A function of stress and attachment paradigms. *Psychology of Addictive Behaviors, 28*(3), 790–804. 10.1037/a0035499

Rothenberg, W. A., Hussong, A. M., & Chassin, L. (2016). Modeling trajectories of adolescent-perceived family conflict: Effects of marital dissatisfaction and parental alcoholism. *Journal of Research on Adolescence, 27,* 105–121.

Rounsaville, D., O'Farrell, T. J., Andreas, J. B., Murphy, C. M., & Murphy, M. M. (2014). Children's exposure to parental conflict after father's treatment for alcoholism. *Addictive Behaviors, 39,* 1168–1171.

Rusby, J. C., Light, J. M., Crowley, R., & Westling, E. (2018). Influence of parent–youth relationship, parental monitoring, and parent substance use on adolescent substance use onset. *Journal of Family Psychology, 32,* 310–320.

Russell, B. S., & Gordon, M. (2017). Parenting and adolescent substance use: Moderation effects of community engagement. *International Journal of Mental Health & Addiction, 15,* 1023–1036.

Samek, D. R., Goodman, R. J., Riley, L., McGue, M., & Iacono, W. G. (2018). The developmental unfolding of sibling influences on alcohol use over time. *Journal Of Youth And Adolescence, 47*(2), 349–368.

Samek, D. R., Rueter, M. A., Keyes, M. A., McGue, M., & Iacono, W. G. (2015). Parent involvement, sibling companionship, and adolescent substance use: A longitudinal, genetically informed design. *Journal of Family Psychology, 29*(4), 614–623.

Sanders-Phillips, K., Kliewer, W., Tirmazi, T., Nebbitt, V., Carter, T., & Key, H. (2014). Perceived racial discrimination, drug use, and psychological distress in African American youth: A pathway to child health disparities. *Journal of Social Issues, 70,* 279–297.

Sartor, C. E., Lynskey, M. T., Heath, A. C., Jacob, T., & True, W. (2006). The role of childhood risk factors in initiation of alcohol use and progression to alcohol dependence. *Addiction, 102,* 216–225.

Schiff, M., Plotnikova, M., Dingle, K., Williams, G. M., Najman, J., & Clavarino, A. (2014). Does adolescent's exposure to parental intimate partner conflict and violence predict psychological distress and substance use in young adulthood? A longitudinal study. *Child Abuse & Neglect, 38*(12), 1945–1954.

Scholte, R. J., Poelen, E. P., Willemsen, G., Boomsma, D. I., & Engels, R. E. (2008). Relative risks of adolescent and young adult alcohol use: The role of drinking fathers, mothers, siblings, and friends. *Addictive Behaviors, 33*(1), 1–14.

Seay, K. D., & Kohl, P. L. (2015). The comorbid and individual impacts of maternal depression and substance dependence on parenting and child behavior problems. *Journal of Family Violence, 30,* 899–910.

Shamblen, S. R., Ringwalt, C. L., Clark, H. K., & Hanley, S. M. (2014). Alcohol use growth trajectories in young adolescence: Pathways and predictors. *Journal of Child & Adolescent Substance Abuse, 23,* 9–18.

Sher, K. J., Grekin, E. R., & Williams, N. A. (2005). The development of alcohol use disorders. *Annual Review of Clinical Psychology, 1,* 493–523.

Shih, R. A., Parast, L., Pedersen, E. R., Troxel, W. M., Tucker, J. S., Miles, J. N. V., . . . & D'Amico, E. J. (2017). Individual, peer, and family factor modification of neighborhood-level effects on adolescent alcohol, cigarette, e-cigarette, and marijuana use. *Drug and Alcohol Dependence, 180,* 76–85.

Shorey, R. C., Fite, P. J., Elkins, S. R., Frissell, K. C., Tortolero, S. R., Stuart, G. L., & Temple, J. R. (2013). The association between problematic parental substance use and adolescent substance use in an ethnically diverse sample of 9th and 10th graders. *The Journal of Primary Prevention, 34,* 381–393.

Skewes, M. C., & Gonzalez, V. M. (2013). The biopsychosocial model of addiction. In P. M. Miller (Ed.), *Principles of addiction, Vol. I,* (pp. 61–70). San Diego, CA: Academic Press.

Smit, K., Voogt, C., Hiemstra, M., Kleinjan, M., Otten, R., & Kuntsche, E. (2018). Development of alcohol expectancies and early alcohol use in children and adolescents: A systematic review. *Clinical Psychology Review, 60,* 136–146.

Smith, K. Z., Smith, P. H., & Grekin, E. R. (2014). Childhood sexual abuse, distress, and alcohol-related problems: Moderation by drinking to cope. *Psychology of Addictive Behaviors, 28,* 532–537.

Soloski, K. L., & Berryhill, M. B. (2016). Gender differences: Emotional distress as an indirect effect between family cohesion and adolescent alcohol use. *Journal of Child and Family Studies, 25,* 1269–1283.

Soloski, K. L., Monk, J. K., & Durtschi, J. A. (2016). Trajectories of early binge drinking: A function of family cohesion and peer use. *Journal of Marital and Family Therapy, 42,* 76–90.

Sorocco, K. H., Carnes, N. C., Cohoon, A. J., Vincent, A. S., & Lovallo, W. R. (2015). Risk factors for alcoholism in the Oklahoma Family Health Patterns project: Impact of early life adversity and family history on affect regulation and personality. *Drug and Alcohol Dependence, 150,* 38–45.

Stapinski, L. A., Edwards, A. C., Hickman, M. Araya, R., Teesson, M., Newton, N. C., . . . & Heron, J. (2016). Drinking to cope: A latent class analysis of coping motives for alcohol use in a large cohort of adolescents. *Prevention Science, 17,* 584–594.

Su, J., I-Chun Kuo, S., Aliev, F., Guy, M. C., Derlan, C. L., Edenberg, H. J., . . . & Dick, D. M. (2018). Influence of parental alcohol dependence symptoms and parenting on adolescent risky drinking and conduct problems: A family systems perspective. *Alcoholism: Clinical and Experimental Research, 42,* 1783–1794.

Tucker, J. S., Ellickson, P. L., & Klein, D. J. (2008). Growing up in a permissive household: What deters at-risk adolescents from heavy drinking? *Journal of Studies on Alcohol and Drugs, 69,* 528–534.

Tyler, K. A., Stone, R. T., & Bersani, B. (2006). Examining the changing influence of predictors on adolescent alcohol misuse. *Journal of Child and Adolescent Substance Abuse, 16*(2), 95–114.

Unger, J. B. (2014). Cultural influences on substance use among Hispanic adolescents and young adults: Findings from project RED. *Child Development Perspectives, 8*(1), 48–53.

Vakalahi, H. F. (2002). Family-based predictors of adolescent substance use. *Journal of Child and Adolescent Substance Abuse, 11*(3), 1–15.

Van Ryzin, M. J., Fosco, G. M., & Dishion, T. J. (2012). Family and peer predictors of substance use from early adolescence to early adulthood: An 11-year prospective analysis. *Addictive Behaviors, 37*, 1314–1324.

Verhulst, B., Neale, M. C., & Kendler, K. S. (2015). The heritability of alcohol use disorders: a meta-analysis of twin and adoption studies. *Psychological Medicine, 45*(5), 1061–1072.

Vermeulen-Smit, E., Koning, I. M., Verdurmen, J. E. E., Van der Vorst, H., Engels, R. C. M. E., & Vollebergh, W. A. M. (2012). The influence of paternal and maternal drinking patterns within two-partner families on the initiation and development of adolescent drinking. *Addictive Behaviors, 37*, 1248–1256.

Visser, L., de Winter, A. F., Vollebergh, W. A. M., Verhulst, F. C., & Reijneveld, S. A. (2013). The impact of parenting styles on adolescent alcohol use: The TRAILS study. *European Addiction Research, 19*(4), 165–172.

Voisin, D. R., Elsaesser, C., Kim, D. H., Patel, S., & Contara, A. (2016). The relationship between family stress and behavioral health among African American adolescents. *Journal of Child and Family Studies, 25*, 2201–2210.

Walther, C. A. P., Cheong, J., Molina, B. S. G., Pelham, W. E., Wymbs, B. T., Belendiuk, K., & Pedersen, S. L. (2012). Substance use and delinquency among adolescents with childhood ADHD: The protective role of parenting. *Psychology of Addictive Behaviors, 26*, 585–598.

Wang, M., Kviz, F. J., & Miller, A. M. (2012). The mediating role of parent–child bonding to prevent adolescent alcohol abuse among Asian American families. *Journal of Immigrant Minority Health, 14*, 831–840.

West, J. H., Blumberg, E. J., Kelley, N. J., Hill, L., Sipan, C. L., Schmitz, K. E., Kolody, B., . . . & Hovell, M. F. (2013). The role of parenting in alcohol and tobacco use among Latino adolescents. *Journal of Child & Adolescent Substance Abuse, 22*, 120–132.

Whiteman, S. D., Jensen, A. C., & Maggs, J. L. (2013). Similarities in adolescent siblings' substance use: Testing competing pathways of influence. *Journal of Studies on Alcohol and Drugs, 74*, 104–113.

Whiteman, S. D., Jensen, A. C., & McHale, S. M. (2017). Sibling influences on risky behaviors from adolescence to young adulthood: Vertical socialization or bidirectional effects? In N. Campione-Barr (Ed.), *Power, control, and influence in sibling relationships across development. New Directions for Child and Adolescent Development* [Special issue], *156*, 67–85.

Whiteman, S. D., Jensen, A. C., Mustillo, S. A., & Maggs, J. L. (2016). Understanding sibling influence on adolescents' alcohol use: Social and cognitive pathways. *Addictive Behaviors, 53*, 1–6.

Wolfe, J. D. (2016). The effects of maternal alcohol use disorders on childhood relationship and mental health. *Social Psychiatry and Psychiatric Epidemiology, 51*, 1439–1448.

Wong, C. F., Silva, K., Kecojevic, A., Schrager, S. M., Bloom, J. J., Iverson, E., & Landenau, S. E. (2013). Coping and emotion regulation profiles as predictors of nonmedical prescription drug and illicit drug use among high-risk young adults. *Drug and Alcohol Dependence, 132*, 165–171.

Yap, M. B. H., Cheong, T. W. K., Zaravinos-Tsakos, F., Lubman, D. I., & Jorm, A. F. (2017). Modifiable parenting factors associated with adolescent alcohol misuse: A systematic review and meta-analysis of longitudinal studies. *Addiction, 112*, 1142–1162.

Zucker, R. A. (2008). Anticipating problem alcohol use developmentally from childhood into middle adulthood: What have we learned? *Addiction, 103*, 100–108.

Zucker, R. A., Fitzgerald, H. E., Refior, S. K., Pallas, D. M., & Ellis, D. A. (2000). The clinical and social ecology of childhood for children of alcoholics: Description of a study and implications for a differentiated social policy. In H. E. Fitzgerald, B. M. Lester, & B. S. Zuckerman (Eds.), *Children of addiction: Research, health, and policy issues* (pp. 109–141). New York, NY: Routledge/Falmer.

CHAPTER 20

Death, Dying, and Grief in Families

Colleen I. Murray and Jordan C. Reuter

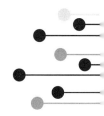

Vignette

Ella is worried about her two children. Her husband died suddenly in a car accident 1 year ago, and her school-age daughter and teenage son are struggling with the loss. Her daughter has developed anxiety and fear of other loved ones leaving her and is having difficulty focusing on her schoolwork. Her son has withdrawn from the family and his friends, spending much of his time alone in his room. While she expects disengagement from a teenager, she is concerned because he refuses to talk about his father, and recently she found drug paraphernalia in his backpack. The children don't want to hurt their mother any further so they don't argue with her, but, instead, they fight more with each other than in the past. Her own grief recovery has been affected by her geographical distance from family and a lack of community support; this has resulted in her feeling very isolated and alone. She has lost a great deal of weight and is unable to sleep more than a few hours at a time. In worrying about her children, she has neglected to address her many conflicting emotions including sadness, anger, and fear. She worries how she will keep their standard of living or send the children to college without her husband's income. Well-meaning coworkers tell her to read some popular psychology books and seek professional assistance in facilitating her children's grief as well as her own, but the resources she has found just don't seem right for her family.

The public images of death and grief that we see today are often those of terrorism, war, epidemics, natural disaster, or celebrity death. Many hold ambivalent views regarding displays of mourning for people one never knew in life or for publicizing one's grief, expressions Tony Walter (2008) calls the *new public mourning*. Although mourning may be a major source of social integration, most grieving is private and involves pain from personal relationships, even in cases where expression is vicariously triggered by a public tragedy. Most adults in industrialized countries today die from degenerative illnesses, and most young people die from sudden or violent causes. Overall, we live in an environment where death is invisible and denied, yet we have become desensitized to its vast media presence. These inconsistencies appear related to the extent we are personally affected by death—whether we define loss as happening to "one of us" or "one of them." This chapter addresses enduring processes and areas of change related to death in families.

Annually, there are more than 2.8 million deaths in the United States, affecting 8 to 11 million surviving immediate family members, including over 2 million children and adolescents (Kochanek, Murphy, Xu, & Arias, 2019). Death is a crisis that *all* families encounter and is recognized as *the* most stressful life event families face, although most do not need counseling to cope (Shear, Ghesquiere, & Glickman, 2013). However, the study of loss as a family system phenomenon has received modest visibility.

Etiology of "Invisible Death" and Its Consequences

From the Middle Ages through the 17th century, death was viewed as inevitable and natural (Aries, 1974). A movement to deny the realities of death began during the 18th century, and by the 20th century a lack of firsthand familiarity with death fostered an era in which death became sequestered, privatized, and invisible. Factors contributing to this lack of familiarity with death include increased life expectancy, changes in leading causes of death from communicable diseases to chronic and degenerative diseases (although there is renewed concern about increases in communicable diseases), redistribution of death from the young to old, decreased mortality rates, and increased duration of chronic illnesses. Geographic mobility and family social reorganization resulted in reduced intergenerational contact and fewer opportunities to participate in death-related experiences (Rando, 1993). As a result of the development of life-extending technologies, (a) most deaths occur in health-care settings rather than at home, (b) care has become dominated by efforts to delay death by all means available, (c) we question our assumptions of what constitutes life and death, and (d) families are confronted with decisions of prolonging dying or terminating life of loved ones (Doka, 2005).

Although families have limited direct contact with death, they are bombarded with its presentation via news media (Murray & Gilbert, 1997). These frequent, violent portrayals of death as unnatural contribute to desensitization, as well as personal traumatization of the bereaved. Media-orchestrated emotional invigilation in reporting of celebrity death and mass tragedies leaves viewers with illusions of intimacy and grieving or concern that their behavior differs from what everyone else is doing (Walter, 2008). Private grief coexists with the public expression of grief on social media in the online death space (Maddrell, 2016; Walter, Hourizi, Moncur & Pitsillides, 2012). Individuals who did not personally know the deceased can go through rituals of mourning, participate in Facebook memorials, and "virtually" attend celebrity funerals through television or the Internet, without feeling the depth of pain and depression of actual grief. Viewers may confuse their emotional response with the real grief experienced by loved ones of the deceased, and since their "recovery" is quick, they may be insensitive to the amount of time required to "return to normal" when they experience real grief.

These changes have increased the stress that families experience when coping with death. Those in industrialized countries do not view dying and bereavement as normal life-span experiences; rather, they compartmentalize death, frequently excluding children from family experiences. Adaption to loss has been hampered by lack of cultural supports that could assist families to integrate death into their ongoing life and the lack of instrumental social supports to help manage daily life disruptions in childcare, housework, and finances (Walsh & McGoldrick, 2004). Often a minimum of rituals exists surrounding death, roles of the chronically ill or bereaved are not clearly defined, and geographic distance hinders completion of "unfinished business" and dealing with the loss (Shapiro, 2001).

As illustrated in the opening vignette, although death and grieving are normal, the bereaved can experience physical, psychological, and social consequences as a part of the coping process or as related stressors. Even though few studies use physiological measures, research suggests that bereavement can result in negative consequences for physical health, including illness, aggravation of existing medical conditions, increased use of medical facilities, and presence of new symptoms and complaints (Maciejewski, Maercker, Boelen, & Prigerson, 2016; Stroebe, Schut, & Stroebe, 2007). During anticipatory bereavement and the months following a loss, physiological changes are indicative of acute heightened arousal (i.e., increased levels of cortisol and catecholamines, change in immune system competence, and sleep complaints) (Buckley et al., 2012). Sympatho-adrenal-medulla system changes during acute grief may even limit success of psychotherapy (O'Connor et al., 2013). There also are changes in neuroendocrine function, immune system competence, and sleep patterns that endure for years (Hall & Irwin, 2001). Intrusive thoughts and avoidance behaviors are correlated with sleep disturbances, which appear to intensify effects of grief, resulting in reduced immune functioning (Fried et al., 2015; Hawkley & Cacioppo, 2003). Although bereavement may be related to long-lasting changes, Rosenblatt (2000) found that the narratives of bereaved parents contained sparse reference to any personal health problems.

Epidemiologic studies cannot assess direct causal relationships between bereavement and illness, but researchers have suggested that bereavement is an antecedent of disease. Risk factors for increased morbidity and mortality include self-damaging or neglectful behaviors during bereavement, additional stress symptoms, elevated physiological arousal, and depression, as well as being male or Caucasian (Elwert & Christakis, 2006). Physiological resiliency appears to be related to coping strategies, social support networks, and healthy sleep.

Consequences of bereavement for mental health also are difficult to measure. Characteristics typically associated with grief are ones that would evoke concern in other circumstances. High rates of depression, insomnia, suicides, and anorexia may exist in conjunction with consumption of drugs, alcohol, and tobacco (Stroebe et al., 2007) as illustrated in the vignette of Ella's family. Lack of differentiation between grief and depression has been problematic as they represent distinct, although related reactions to bereavement (Scharer & Hibberd, 2019).

The challenge of differentiating grief and depression is reflected in two contentious changes related to bereavement introduced in the American Psychiatric Association's (APA; 2013) *Diagnostic and Statistical Manual of Mental Disorders* (DSM-5). One change is the elimination of the *DSM-IV's* bereavement exclusion (BE) that provided a 2-month window of bereavement before qualifying for a diagnosis of major depressive disorder (MDD), assuming that other criteria were not met. Scholars disagree as to whether the BE is valid (Zachar, First, & Kendler, 2017). In response to concerns, the *DSM-5* includes the diagnosis of MDD for bereavement after 2 weeks of symptoms commonly found in intense normal grief. To avoid misdiagnosis the *DSM-5* differentiates grief from MDD in three descriptive footnotes. The plan to remove BE met with sharp criticism and concerns that footnotes are inadequate, normal grief will be pathologized resulting in overdiagnosis, and there is a loss of recognition of cultural methods of adapting to loss (Bandini, 2015); as a result, "for reasons of economic profit and clinical efficiency, people will often be prematurely diagnosed with depression and put on medication" that interferes with the pathway to recovery (Balk, Noppe, Sandler, & Werth, 2011, p. 208). Ironically, there is also concern that elimination of the BE may lead a counselor to view all grief as normal, missing those whose grief warrants additional treatment.

The second *DSM-5* change added a single form of complicated grief, persistent complex bereavement disorder (PCBD), identified among trauma- and stressor-related disorders and included among conditions for further study. Validity and reliability of the criteria have been a focus of frequent criticism (Boelen & Prigerson, 2012; Bryant, 2014). PCBD criteria include those from existing inventories that examine complicated grief (Shear et al., 2011) and prolonged grief disorder (Prigerson et al., 2009), as well as other criteria with less empirical support. These inventories have primarily been developed with samples of older, White, conjugally bereaved women, and may not apply to other populations. Some of the criteria are so broadly defined that many bereaved persons, especially women and bereaved parents, may receive a false positive diagnosis for situations in which the normal grief response may be more intense and long-lasting than other losses (Thieleman & Cacciatore, 2014). Examples of these criteria include persistent yearning for the deceased, intense sorrow, frequent crying, difficulty accepting the death, feeling alone, or having anger related to the loss (APA, 2013). The list of symptoms results in 37,650 possible combinations by which a person could meet the diagnosis (Boelen & Prigerson, 2012). Although diagnostic criteria include symptoms that have persisted for at least 12 months for adults (6 months for children), there is no empirical evidence that this specific timing is warranted.

It also may be that yearning is more characteristic of grief than is depression (Klass, 2013), and bereaved who perceive a decline in their financial well-being are also at increased risk of psychological difficulties (Corden & Hirst, 2013). Research has suggested that individuals also identify bereavement as a social stressor, reporting lack of role clarity and support (Rando, 1993; Rosenblatt, 2000). Changes in social status, conflicts in identity, disputes over family inheritance, and loss of roles, income, or retirement funds that may result from the death of a family member can contribute to social isolation. Changes in family communication patterns and relationships with people outside the family are common. Several of these factors are illustrated in Ella's situation.

Paradoxically, growth may also be an outcome of loss. *Posttraumatic growth* is both a process and outcome in which, following trauma, growth occurs *beyond* an individual's previous level of functioning (Tedeschi & Calhoun, 2008). Growth outcomes occur in *perception of self* (e.g., as survivor rather than victim, and self-reliant yet with heightened vulnerability), *interpersonal relationships* (e.g., increased ability to be compassionate or intimate, to self-disclose important information, and to express emotions), and *philosophy of life* (e.g., reorganization of priorities, greater appreciation of life, grappling with meaning and purpose of life, spiritual change, and sense of wisdom). In contrast, terror management theory (Pyszcznski, Solomon, & Greenberg, 2003) suggests that what appears to be growth is actually cognitive coping, which protects or distances us from traumatic events and buffers fear of death.

Theories of Grieving

Theories are necessary for understanding complex response to loss and the sometimes counterintuitive phenomena that occur during bereavement (e.g., posttraumatic growth). They range from individualistic intrapersonal approaches to an interpersonal study of group influence. Scholars have proposed individual-based theories focusing on developmental stages or trajectories for the dying (e.g., Kübler-Ross, 1969) or survivors (e.g., Rando, 1993), derived from works of Freud (1957) or Bowlby (1980). Such theories differ in number of stages identified, but they all assume that grief follows three basic phases, including periods of shock, denial, and disorganization; extremes including intense separation pain, volatile emotions, and active grief work; and resolution, acceptance, and withdrawal of energy from the deceased and reinvestment. Critics of these theories question the definition of "normal" grief and assumptions about how people "should" respond, including beliefs that (a) intense emotional distress or depression is inevitable, (b) failure to experience distress is indicative of pathology, (c) working through loss is important—intense distress will end with recovery, and (d) by working through loss, individuals can achieve resolution and intellectual acceptance (Wortman & Silver, 2001).

Others purport that stage theories have not been supported in research and view these theories as problematic because they are population-specific and misrepresent progress toward adjustment as linear (Stroebe, Schut, & Boerner, 2017). Critics contend that progress is not always forward and that grief processes may have no definite ending (Rosenblatt, 2000). They argue that emphasis should not be on recovery or closure, but on continuing bonds, relearning relationships, and renegotiating meaning of loss over time (Neimeyer, Klass, & Dennis, 2014).

Concern regarding developmental theories also deals with viewing grief as passive, with few choices for grievers. Critics contend that grieving is active, presenting the bereaved with challenges, choices, and opportunities, and that the bereaved are active participants relearning the world in terms of physical surroundings, relationships, and who they are (Corr, 2019). They question the necessity of "grief work"—traditionally viewed as an essential cognitive process of confronting loss. Margaret Stroebe and her colleagues (2000) suggest that grief work is not a universal concept, its definitions and operationalizations are problematic, few studies have yielded substantial conclusions, and findings were intended for understanding of processes, rather than prescriptions for recovery. Archer (2008) suggests that it may be cognitive restructuring rather than grief work that is related to adjustment following loss.

Among individually centered process-based models is Rando's (1993) "Six R's" model, which assumes the need to accommodate loss. Processes include recognition of loss, reacting to separation, recollection, and reexperiencing the relationship with the deceased, relinquishing old attachments, readjusting to a new world without forgetting the old, and reinvesting (p. 45). In contrast, the dual process model of coping (Stroebe & Schut, 2010) suggests that active confrontation of loss is not necessary for a positive outcome, and there may be circumstances when denial, avoidance of reminders, and repressive strategies are essential. Minimizing expression of negative emotions and using laughter as dissociation from distress may improve functioning (Bonanno, 2004). The dual process assumes that most individuals experience ongoing oscillation between *loss orientation* (coping with loss through grief work, dealing with denial, and avoiding changes) and *restoration orientation* (adjusting to various life changes triggered by death, changing routines, transitioning to a new equilibrium, avoiding or taking time off from grief). There is movement between coping with loss and moving forward with differences for individuals, type of loss, culture, and gender.

Although scholars have focused on dying or bereaved individuals, death does not occur in isolation, and it includes a family context (Breen et al., 2019). Individual process models have not been broadened to aid in understanding families, except for some psychoanalytic attempts. Archer (2008) suggests that rather than using Bowlby's work to look at the breaking of attachment bonds, it can instead be used to address the relationship between styles of attachment and grieving, thus going beyond the individual. Mikulincer and Shaver (2008) argue that Bowlby's work on the attachment behavioral system and pair bonds as related to bereavement has been misunderstood, and there is recent evidence from experiments and clinical observations in support of these psychodynamic processes. The bereaved form new attachment bonds while maintaining a symbolic attachment to the deceased, and they integrate that relationship into their new reality (i.e., a focus on both the loss and restoration). Those with insecure attachments have difficulty in oscillating between this hyperactivation and deactivation of the attachment system, overemphasizing one or the other.

Social constructionist theory has become an increasingly popular explanation as it accommodates integration of three approaches to explaining grief: (1) continuing bonds and mental representations of the relationship, (2) meaning of the bereavement and maintenance of a meaningful world, and (3) loss of relationship supports from the deceased and the social network (Neimeyer et al., 2014). Work on grief from a family perspective has typically used elements of systems theories, particularly through integrative approaches to complex issues. Refined systemic models recognize that multiple types of grief exist simultaneously for individuals, families, and communities, and although some thoughts and feelings are shared, others are not (Bartel, 2019; Breen et al., 2019).

Family systems theory focuses on dynamics and provides concepts for describing relationships, offering a nonpathologizing conceptualization of grief as a natural process (Nadeau, 2008). The following premises of systems theory can be useful in examining families' adaptation to dying and death:

1. A family reacts to loss as a system. Although we grieve as individuals, the family system has qualities beyond those of individual members (Jackson, 1965), and all members participate in mutually reinforcing interactions (Walsh & McGoldrick, 2004).

2. Actions and reactions of a family member affect others and their functioning. Interdependence exists because causality is circular rather than linear (Shapiro, 2001).

3. Death disrupts a system's equilibrium, modifies the structure, and requires reorganization in feedback processes, role distribution, and functions (Bowen, 1976; Walsh & McGoldrick, 2013).

4. Death may produce an emotional shock wave of serious life events that can occur anywhere in the extended family in the years following loss (Bowen, 1976). Waves exist in an environment of denied emotional dependence and may seem unrelated to the death. They may trigger additional stressor events or increase rigid strategies to maintain stability (Shapiro, 2001).

5. There is no single outcome from death of a member that characterizes all family systems. Various family characteristics, such as feedback processes (Jackson, 1965), patterns of relationship (Shapiro, 2001), and family schema and family paradigm (Boss, 2006), influence the outcome.

Scholars have infrequently applied systems theory in examining death-related reorganization. Loss has traditionally been identified as a historical, individual, or content issue and inappropriate for traditional family systems work (which focused on process, homeostasis, differentiation of self from family, current interaction, and the present) (Nadeau, 2008; Walsh & McGoldrick, 2004). Recent versions of systems theory have focused on balance of change and continuity, as well as the negotiated inclusion of differences to balance self-assertion and cohesion. The family systems-based study of grief exists within a framework that includes intergenerational and family life cycle perspectives (Walsh & McGoldrick, 2013), focusing on change in structural factors such as boundaries, and family dynamics such as roles and rules, as well as meaning making and communication (Nadeau, 2008). An examination of the relationship between individual grief and family system characteristics found that grief symptomatology at 4 to 5 weeks postloss did not predict any family system characteristics or grief symptomatology 6 months later (Traylor, Hayslip, Kaminski, & York, 2003). However, perception of family cohesion, expression of affect, and communication were predictors of later grief.

Particularly useful models are those that simultaneously consider individual, family, and cultural dimensions. Rather than relying on traditional family systems, these models integrate family systems' concepts with other perspectives. Rolland's (1994) family systems–illness model examines the interface of individual, family, illness, and health-care team. Rather than identifying the ill individual as the central unit of care, it focuses on the family or caregiving system as a resource that is both affected by and influences the course of illness. This model can be useful for understanding experiences of the individual and family members during the terminal phase of chronic illness, in multiple contexts, and across time. Shapiro (2001) applied a systemic developmental approach to examine grief as a family process. This clinical model views grief as a developmental crisis influenced by family history, sociocultural context, and family and individual life-cycle stages. Grief is a crisis of identity and attachment that disrupts family equilibrium but provides an opportunity for developing growth and stability.

Popular interactionist approaches account for context by incorporating life course, social constructionism, and systems concepts. These models recognize the unique interpretation of internal and external worlds of individuals and families dealing with loss (Harvey, Carlson, Huff, & Green, 2001; Rosenblatt, 2000). They utilize narrative methods, focus on meaning making or account making, and recognize intimate losses as part of a changing identity. These models assume that the accuracy of meaning given to any particular event is of limited importance because it is *meaning itself* that influences family interactions. Interactionist counseling would not help families to just understand and manage grief symptomatology but would also help to reconstruct a meaningful narrative of self, family, and world.

Factors Related to Family Adaptation to Death

Characteristics of the Loss

Some characteristics of the death itself and societal interpretations of a loss can influence family adaptation. For example, when the duration of time before death is far longer or shorter than expected, or the sequence of death in a family differs from expected order, problems may occur. Elderly members are assumed to experience "timely" deaths. Early parental loss, death of a young spouse, and death of a child or grandchild of any age are considered tragic and evoke searches for explanations.

The initial grief reaction to sudden or unexpected death may be more intense than death that is related to illness (Bowlby, 1980), with survivors experiencing a shattered normal world, a series of concurrent stressors and secondary losses, with unfinished business more likely to remain (Lindemann, 1944). Factors existing along a continuum that can affect coping include (a) perceptions of whether the loss was natural or human made; (b) degree of intentionality or premeditation; (c) degree of preventability; (d) amount of suffering, anxiety, or physical pain experienced while dying; (e) number of people killed or affected; (f) degree of expectedness (Doka, 1996, pp. 12–13); (g) senselessness; and (h) whether the survivor witnessed the death or its aftermath or found out about the loss through the media. Differences related to suddenness of death appear short term once internal control beliefs and self-esteem are considered (Stroebe & Schut, 2001) and are lessened when families are present during emergency medical procedures, such as during efforts to resuscitate (Kamienski, 2004).

According to the National Center for Health Statistics (Kochanek, et al., 2019), nearly 80% of deaths of teens and young adults are sudden violent accidents, homicide, or suicide. A longitudinal study of parents surviving the sudden death of a child reported that marital satisfaction decreased during the first 5 years after the death; nearly 70% said it took 3 to 4 years to put their child's death in perspective; and at 5 years post death, 43% said they still had not found meaning in their child's death (Murphy, 2008).

Although popular works often discuss the suicide of an attachment figure as the most difficult loss, there is little empirical evidence to support this contention (Murphy, 2008). Homicide appears to be most directly related to posttraumatic stress disorder and grief marked by despair. In a mass trauma (a potentially life-threatening event experienced by a large number of people), adaptation appears to be influenced by whether it is a single event or recurring/ongoing; by emotional or geographic distance (with vicarious traumatization possible through media coverage, particularly for those who have experienced other unrelated losses); by attribution of causality; and by the interaction of personal, community, and symbolic losses (Webb, 2004).

Deaths following protracted illness can also be stressful. In such cases, family members have experienced a series of stressors before the death, including increased time commitments for caring, financial strain as a result of cost of care and lost employment, emotional exhaustion, interruption of career and family routines, sense of social isolation, and lack of time for self or other family members (Rabow, Hauser, & Adams, 2004). Although research findings on the existence, role, and multidimensionality of anticipatory grief are inconsistent, protracted illness appears to be associated with trauma and secondary morbidity—that is, difficulties in physical, emotional, cognitive, and social functioning of those closely involved with terminally ill persons (Rando, 1993). Deaths following chronic illness may still be perceived as sudden or unexpected by surviving adults who are not yet "ready," by children whose developmental stage inhibits their understanding that death is inevitable, and following multiple cycles of relapse and improvement. Deaths from trauma and illness have much in common. Similar to families who have witnessed or experienced death through violence, families experiencing prolonged or complicated grief, multiple deaths simultaneously, or a series of deaths in close proximity may display signs of posttraumatic stress disorder, with caregivers experiencing secondary traumatic stress (Anderson, Arnold, Angus, & Bryce, 2008).

Scholars have devoted increased attention to losses unacknowledged by society and *disenfranchised grief*—that is, grief that exists although society does not recognize one's right, need, or capacity to grieve (Doka, 2008). Examples include grief over the loss of unacknowledged personal relationships or those not recognized as significant, such as the death of a former spouse, lover, or extramarital lover; a foster child or foster parent; a stepparent or stepchild; a coworker; or a companion animal. In addition, deaths related to infertility (McBain & Reeves, 2019) or pregnancy (i.e., miscarriage, elective abortion, stillbirth, or neonatal death) may be disenfranchised. Professional caretakers and first responders, especially those labeled as "heroes" or competently focused on tasks of rescue and recovery, also may suffer unacknowledged grief when they lose those for whom they provide care. Bereaved grandparents, men in general (Gilbert, 1996), people of color whose family member died after police contact (Baker, Norris, & Cherneva, 2019), and families of deceased addicts or death row inmates may also be disenfranchised. Many people see others, such as young children, older adults, and people with mental disabilities, as incapable of grief or without a need to grieve (Doka, 2008). Disenfranchised grief also occurs when the transgender body of a loved one is treated with heteronormativity (detransitioning) after death (Weaver, 2018). Further, disenfranchisement occurs when bereaved persons are told they are experiencing or expressing grief in inappropriate ways. Societal expectations of who is entitled to grieve change over time; losses that are gaining in recognition involve cohabitors and partners in a gay or lesbian relationship. However, Robson and Walter (2012) argue that disenfranchised grief is not binary (yes/no) but is hierarchical and complex.

People who are grieving various types of death report that they believe their grief has been stigmatized. They feel the discomfort of others who distance themselves, and they experience direct or indirect social pressure to become "invisible mourners" (Rosaldo, 1989). Disenfranchised grief often results from stigmatized losses, particularly when there is the assumption that the death was caused by an individual's disturbed or immoral behavior, or a fear of contagion, such as with AIDS, Ebola, or cancer-related deaths. Survivors of those who died from contagious diseases may experience multiple losses among family and friends and isolation. Stigma also occurs in families that have lost a member to suicide or homicide, resulting in altered identities, provoking feelings of anger and guilt, and experiencing isolation, blame, and injustice—characteristics of revictimization (Bucholz, 2002). Resulting secrecy and blame can distort family communication, isolate members, and diminish social support (Walsh & McGoldrick, 2004).

Factors Affecting Family Vulnerability

Death-related loss involves many secondary losses including personal, interpersonal, material, and symbolic losses. Families have more difficulty adapting to death if other stressors are present, as dealing with a loss does not abrogate other family needs. When normative events associated with the family life cycle (e.g., new marriage, birth of child, or adolescent's move to increase independence) are concurrent with illness or death, they may pose incompatible tasks (Shapiro, 2001). The centrality of the deceased's role and the degree of the family's emotional dependence on that individual (i.e., function and position) influence adaptation. Shock waves rarely follow the deaths of well-liked people who played peripheral roles or of dysfunctional members unless dysfunction played a central role in maintaining family equilibrium (Bowen, 1976).

Complications in family adaptation can occur when there is intense and continuous ambivalence, estrangement, or conflict. Chronic mourning and depression have been reported by those with anxious-ambivalent attachments; somatization and cognitive suppression are more common among those with avoidant attachment styles (Mikulincer & Shaver, 2008). Grief after the death of an abuser can result in ambivalence, rage, secrecy, sadness, and shame (Monahan, 2003). During illness, there may be time to repair relationships, but family members may hesitate, fearing that confrontations increase risk of death.

Resources also influence the bereaved family's vulnerability and assist in meeting demands. They may be tangible (e.g., money or health) or intangible (e.g., friendship, self-esteem, role accumulation, or a sense of mastery). African American evacuees from the aftermath of Hurricane Katrina exhibited greater psychological distress (and a lower sense of recovery) if they were uninsured or experienced home destruction or a human loss (Lee, Shen, & Tran, 2009). The disruption that a bereaved family experiences is mediated by intensity and chronicity of family stress. Adaptation is facilitated by members' emotional regulation capacity, nonreactivity to emotional intensity in the system, cohesion and adaptability, and marital intimacy (Nadeau, 2008; Shapiro, 2001). Research findings on benefits of open communication about loss are mixed. Pennebaker, Zech, and Rime (2001) suggest that confiding in others is related to health after a loss. Others assert that the best predictor of emotional well-being is emotional regulation, not emotion-focused coping (Bonanno, 2004).

Social support networks appear to simultaneously complicate and facilitate grieving. Supporters may listen but hold unrealistic expectations. Availability of formal or informal networks does not guarantee support, especially in a society that does not sanction the expression of emotions surrounding loss. Some bereaved family members turn to face-to-face or online self-help groups composed of persons who have experienced a similar type of loss—a practice that may be predictive of finding meaning in death during the years that follow. However, rules of some family systems discourage members from sharing intimate information and feelings with persons outside the family. Religious belief also may simultaneously complicate and facilitate grieving. Belief in "God's plan" can help create meaning from loss, but it can create anger toward God for unfairly allowing the death and isolate the individual from familiar spiritual roots.

Family Belief System, Definition, and Appraisal

To understand how a family perceives a death or uses coping strategies, one must understand its assumptions about the world. A common paradigm is the "belief in a just world," which posits that the self is worthy and the world is benevolent, just, and meaningful (Janoff-Bulman, 1992; Lerner, 1980). This paradigm values control and mastery; it assumes fit between efforts and outcomes: One gets what one deserves. Such a view is functional only when something can be done to change a situation. Challenges to the just-world assumption make the world seem less predictable and can lead to cognitive efforts to manage fear of death. Such efforts can lead to blaming chronically ill persons for their conditions and lack of recovery, or to linking adolescent deaths to drug use or reckless behavior as a way of affirming, "It can't happen to my child." In contrast, for those dealing with loss, understanding the complexities, multiple levels of context, and short- or long-term effects of the event will facilitate grief.

Family members share some beliefs that are unintentionally but collectively constructed. Family history and experiences with death provide a *legacy* (a way of looking at loss that has been received from ancestors) that is related to how the family will adapt to subsequent loss (Walsh & McGoldrick, 2004). Particularly in relation to several traumatic untimely deaths, a family may have a legacy of empowerment (i.e., family members see themselves as survivors who can be hurt but not defeated) or a legacy of trauma (i.e., family members feel "cursed" and unable to rise above their losses)—either of which can inhibit openness of the system. Families may not recognize transgenerational anniversary patterns or concurrence of a death with other life events, and members may lack emotional memory or have discrepant memories regarding a death (Shapiro, 2001). Members may make unconscious efforts to block, promote, or shift beliefs to maintain consistency with the legacy.

Grief can also be viewed as a process of *meaning construction* that evolves throughout the life of the bereaved. Several factors appear to influence families' construction of the meaning of their losses, including family schema, contact, cutoffs, interdependence, rituals, secrets, coherence, paradigms, divergent beliefs, tolerance for differences, rules about sharing, and situational and stressor appraisals (Nadeau, 2008; Rosenblatt, 2000). Family members' language reflects the meaning of their loss, and it often involves the loss of the relationship system between or among people, not just the death of the individual (Rosenblatt, 2019). For example, one grieves the loss of a mother–daughter interaction system (e.g., the loss of being parented), not just the loss of the mother. Researchers are increasingly noting the importance of making sense of the event, finding benefits from the experience and shaping one's new identity to include the loss (Neimeyer et al., 2014). Irrational, violent death may result in meaning making expressed through activism or intense pursuit of numerous small actions.

Families may find additional challenges when experiencing a situation of family boundary ambiguity (i.e., confusion a family experiences when it is not clear who is in and who is out of the system) (Boss, 2006). Ambiguity rises when (a) the facts surrounding a death are unclear, (b) a person is missing but it is unclear if death has occurred, or (c) the family denies the loss. Degree of boundary ambiguity may be more important for explaining adaptation and coping than the presence of coping skills or resources. Both denial and boundary ambiguity initially may be functional because they give a shocked family time to deny the loss and then cognitively reorganize itself before it accepts the fact that the death is real. If a high degree of ambiguity exists over time, the family is at risk for maladaptation. However, evidence that bonds continue to exist after death and that conversations with the dead may be replacing rituals as the normative way bonds are maintained (Klass, 2013) may challenge the notion of boundary ambiguity, suggesting one can recognize loss while holding psychological, emotional, and spiritual connections to deceased loved ones.

Factors of Diversity

Despite Western cultural expectations, most couples experience incongruent grieving, often with one adult whose grief could be called *cognitive and solitary* and the other whose grief is more *social and emotional* (Gilbert, 1996). Perhaps this incongruence can be understood as a family system-level manifestation of Stroebe and Schut's dual process model (Murray, Toth, & Clinkinbeard, 2005; Stroebe & Schut, 2015). A functional system would require a *loss orientation* and *restoration orientation*. Earlier studies of incongruent grieving have suggested that women often display an intuitive grieving style, with more sorrow, guilt, and depression than men (Doka & Martin, 2010). Men are socialized to manage instrumental tasks, such as those related to the funeral, burial, finances, and property. Women are more likely to take on caregiving roles, which require them to engage in both dual processes. However, men are more able to immerse themselves in work and block other intuitive tasks. Reasons for gender-related differences are not well understood but seem influenced by expectations and socialization. Research in this area has been hampered by reliance on studies completed during acute stages of grief and lack of nonbereaved control groups. Doka and Martin (2010) cautioned that gender is only one factor that affects style of grief; rather than two categories, there is a continuum from intuitive (affective) to instrumental (cognitive and behavioral), as well as blended or dissonant styles. Longitudinal studies of bereaved persons who have suffered violent or traumatic losses found few gender differences (Boelen & van den Bout, 2002/2003).

With gender controls, despite differences in social support, widowers experience greater depression and health consequences than widows (Stroebe & Schut, 2001). It has been proposed that men have unrecognized problems because their socialization interferes with active grief processes (Doka & Martin, 2010). Men's responses to grief often include coping styles that mask fear and insecurity, including remaining silent; taking physical or legal action in order to express anger and exert control; immersion in work, domestic, recreational, or sexual activity; engaging in solitary or secret mourning; and exhibiting addictive behavior, such as alcoholism. Despite the assumption that gender roles are more relaxed than in the past, Worden (2018) confirmed that the double bind Judith Cook identified in 1988 as experienced by bereaved fathers still exists for grieving men: Societal expectations are that they will contain their emotions to protect and comfort their wives, but that they cannot heal their own grief without the sharing of feelings. This double bind is consistent with the pattern of grief involving dissonance between the way one experiences grief and the manner it is expressed (Doka & Martin, 2010). For example, some males may experience internal grief feelings but are constrained from expressing them. Much of the problem may not be in men's grieving but rather in our understanding of the mourning process (Cook, 1988; Proulx, Martinez, Carnevale, & Legault, 2016), which largely has been formulated through the study of women. As such, concepts of meaning making (Gilbert, 1996) and the dual process model (Stroebe & Schut, 2010) may be more relevant for men than concepts of grief work.

Grief is a socially constructed malleable phenomenon, and given current levels of immigration, transnational grief, and contact among diverse groups, mourning patterns in the United States can be expected to vary. In addition to commonalities, group differences in values and practices continue and present a wide range of normal responses to death. General areas in which differences exist include the following:

- Extent of ritual attached to death (e.g., importance of attending funerals, types of acceptable emotional displays, and degree to which these affairs should be costly)

- Need to see a dying relative

- Openness and type of display of emotion

- Emphasis on verbal expression of feelings and solitary or family expression of grief

- Appropriate length of mourning

- Importance of anniversary events

- Roles of men and women

- Role of extended family

- Beliefs about what happens after death, particularly related to suffering, fate, and destiny

- Value of autonomy/dependence in relation to bonds after death

- Coping strategies

- Social support for hospice patients

- Whether certain deaths are stigmatized

- Definition of when death actually occurs

- Barriers to trusting professionals

- Interweaving of religious and political narratives

- Appropriateness of the concept of recovery (Laurie & Neimeyer, 2008; McGoldrick et al., 2004; Rosenblatt, 2008)

Children's Grief

Children deal with many losses (e.g., death of pet, neighbor, peer, or grandparent; family move or divorce). From infancy onward, children recognize loss and do grieve, and their grief corresponds with the cognitive developmental stage that guides their other thinking processes (Murray, 2016). Like adults, they try to make sense of the situation and fit it into their understanding of the world. Also, like adults, they don't just "get over" a loss. Because of their cognitive development, children's understanding and remembrance of events and situations may seem fragmented and distorted to adults. They tend to be very concrete, focusing on physical and observable changes. Their understanding is further hindered by euphemisms that adults may use. For example, "going to see Grandma's body" may imply to the child that she has lost her head. "She is on vacation" or "went to sleep" can later manifest in a child who doesn't want to go to bed or worries when his parents plan a vacation. Similar to Ella's daughter in the vignette, children may fear losing other loved ones, and euphemisms may add to their confusion and fear of abandonment. Perhaps euphemisms serve a purpose in the denial of death that is existentially oriented (Becker, 1973), and that terror management theory scholars (Pyszcznski, et al., 2003) say most adults need most of the time.

A death that may not appear to "affect" a child may be revisited later in life and expressed in a new way. As they move into new stages of cognitive development, children gain skills and resources for making sense of the world, they revisit their losses, and their meaning of events incorporates their new level of understanding (e.g., their understanding of what *permanent* means). Their grief is renegotiated, not resolved. Thus, adults need to be prepared to repeat things several times over the days, weeks, and years after a death.

The experience of dealing with death in childhood can have positive and negative outcomes. Children, like adolescents and adults, may regress to an earlier stage of cognitive development and behaviors. Bereaved children must also cope with grieving adults in their family, and their fears can be heightened by adult reactions that seem unclear and unusual (adults who are not their "normal" selves). Developmentally appropriate coping strategies may seem odd or frightening to adults. Children seem sad one minute and playing happily the next; adults may misinterpret that as a sign that the child isn't really grieving. In reality it is just a reflection of how children deal with change, stress, or crisis in general. Children grow and mature from opportunities to grapple with understanding loss. Depression and emotional withdrawal are not inevitable outcomes of childhood bereavement, and most children do not require counseling. Bereavement does not necessarily affect school functioning; for some, school is a refuge from other issues in family life, but for others it is not.

Factors that appear to influence childhood grieving include positive relationships and ample emotional and psychological support with a parent or caregiver, as well as open, honest, and developmentally appropriate communication about the death. Instead of insulating and isolating children from loss, encouraging (but not requiring) them to participate in family rituals and death-related activities allows them to develop skills for coping with loss. Generally, children who do best following the death of a loved one are those who experience the fewest additional changes and disruptions in their lives (Shapiro, 2001). Some children, including those who choose not to discuss loss with their parent for fear of adding to the adult's pain, may benefit from interacting with other bereaved children in support groups, grief camps, or Internet grief chat networks (Bachman, 2013; Metel & Barnes, 2011).

Specific Losses

The death of one's child is viewed as the most difficult loss, for it is contrary to expected developmental progression and thrusts one into a marginal social role that has unclear role expectations. Deaths ranging from fetal loss to that of an adult child (who may also be a grandparent or a caregiver to older parents) can cause reactions similar to posttraumatic stress and produce differential outcomes for a marital relationship (Albuquerque, Pereira, & Narciso, 2016; Murphy, 2008). From an Eriksonian perspective, young-adult parents grapple with death-related issues of identity as a parent and spousal intimacy, middle-age parents deal with loss of generativity, and elderly parents deal with loss through a life review that includes wondering what it was worth and whether they have failed by outliving their children, resulting in either ego integrity or despair. Classic attachment and psychoanalytic models are inadequate to address experiences of bereaved parents.

Newer models focus on integrating the deceased child into the parents' psychic and social worlds (Klass, 2013).

Society expects spouses to provide support and comfort during times of stress; however, this may not be possible for bereaved parents who are both experiencing intense grief as individuals, with unique timetables, and may not be "in sync" with each other (Albuquerque, et al., 2016; Rando, 1993). Sexual expression between bereaved parents can serve as a reminder of the child and elicit additional distress (Rosenblatt, 2000). However, previously reported high divorce rates of bereaved parents appear to be erroneous; research on which they were based is neither longitudinal nor representative and confuses marital distress and divorce.

Most research on sibling death is recent, focused on children and adolescents. Prior work on sibling loss generally was confined to clinical studies; recent work differentiates normal and complicated sibling grief patterns. Even in the same family, sibling grief reactions are not uniform or the same as parents, but they can be understood best in relation to individual characteristics (e.g., sex, developmental stage, relationship to the sibling). Scholars have not reported consistent behavioral or at-risk differences in school-age children who experienced parental death or sibling death. Initial negative outcomes and grief reactions of siblings may include a drop in school performance, anger, a sense that parents are unreachable, survivor guilt, and guilt from sibling rivalry (even when siblings recognize the irrationality of their beliefs) (Rando, 1993; Schaefer & Moos, 2001). Adolescents who use religious coping ascribe more negative meaning to the death, especially when they try to reconcile belief in a loving God with a negative event such as sibling death (Hays & Hendrix, 2008). Although siblings report more family conflict than do parents, siblings rarely direct their anger toward parents, who they perceive to be vulnerable and hence in need of protection from additional pain. Long-term changes for bereaved siblings appear to be positive, especially in terms of maturity, which adolescents relate to appreciation for life, coping successfully, and negotiating role changes. Adults who lost siblings in childhood have reported that these losses fostered greater insights into life and death (Schaefer & Moos, 2001).

Siblings have unique bonds that continue following the death of a brother or sister (Marshall & Winokuer, 2018). Deceased siblings also play an identity function for survivors who may feel a need to fulfill roles the deceased children played for parents or to act in an opposite manner in an attempt to show that they are different. In later adulthood, sibling death is the most frequent death of close family members, yet researchers have largely overlooked this loss. Surviving siblings appear to experience functioning and cognitive states similar to those of surviving spouses (Moss, Moss, & Hansson, 2001). Unfortunately, research on sibling grief to date has consisted primarily of cross-sectional investigations that rely on retrospective data, data no more than 2 years beyond the loss, and longitudinal data treated as cross-sectional due to small sample sizes.

The death of a parent can occur during childhood or adulthood. Children's reactions to parental death vary and are influenced by emotional and cognitive development, closeness to the deceased parent, responses or interactions with the surviving parent, and perceptions of social support. Researchers have reported evidence of both complicated grief and posttraumatic growth in parentally bereaved children and adolescents (Melhem, Moritz, Walker, Shear, & Brent, 2007; Wolchik, Coxe, Tein, Sandler, & Ayers, 2008). Adolescents grieving the death of a parent appear to have heightened interpersonal sensitivity, characterized by uneasiness and negative expectations regarding personal exchanges (Servaty-Sieb & Hayslip, 2003). Teens tend to flee a grieving peer (Balk, 2014); thus family support may be especially important for bereaved adolescents. Although many adolescents live in single-parent, divorced, or blended families, researchers have largely ignored the topic of parental death in those contexts or have focused on surviving parents' grief and adjustment.

The death of a parent is the most common form of family loss in middle age. Adult response to this loss is influenced by the meaning of the relationship, roles the parent played at the time of death, anticipation, disenfranchisement, circumstances of the death, impact on the surviving adult child, and maintenance of the parent–child bond while letting go (Moss et al., 2001). Adults whose parents experienced protracted illness or lived in nursing homes prior to death exhibit multidimensional responses to their parents' deaths, including sadness, grief, relief, persistence of memories about the parent, and a sense that the protection against death provided by the parents has vanished. Adults who become "orphaned" may find their identities and remaining relationships impacted.

Adults with mental disabilities who experience parental death have some aspects of grief in common with others but also have unique concerns. When individuals with psychiatric disabilities are faced in midlife with the death of a parent, they often have no preparation for this event. They may suddenly find themselves faced with making funeral arrangements, and dealing with financial repercussions of the death, as well as possible residential relocation (Jones et al., 2003).

Among the family losses during adulthood, the death of a spouse has been the most intensively studied; however, less attention has been given to spousal death in early or middle adulthood, widowed parents with dependent children (McClatchey, 2018), or death of other life partners such as committed LGBTQ+ couples. Loneliness and emotional adjustment are major concerns of spouses who lose a companion and source of emotional support, particularly in a long interdependent relationship in which there was a shared identity based on systems of roles and traditions (Moss et al., 2001). Conjugal bereavement can be especially difficult for individuals whose relationships assumed a sharp division of traditional sex roles, leaving them unprepared to assume the range of tasks required to maintain a household. The death of one's spouse brings up issues of self-definition and prompts the need to develop a new identity. Despite these problems, many bereaved spouses adjust very well, and the death of a partner does not always result in grief for the other (Bonanno, 2004). Some derive pleasure and independence from the new lifestyle, feeling more competent than when they were married.

An additional loss involves death and the multidimensional families of those in the military. Sacrificing one's life in military operations has historically been extolled as honorable. Generally, family members of a fallen soldier are embraced by their surrounding community, as well as the military organization, with intense support shortly after the loss, and a sense of meaning is constructed to account for, and help justify, the loss. The military's standard operating procedures help create a supportive environment for the surviving family (Bowen, Mancini, Ware, & Nelson, 2003). However, the prevalence and social legitimacy of military deaths have led to a general desensitization of communities to the length of time needed for grieving and impatience in waiting for the family to move ahead. Survivors of military personnel who commit suicide may not receive the same support as other bereaved military families (Ramchand et al., 2015).

Among service members, the lasting impact of combat losses on grieving is often overlooked or assumed to be posttraumatic stress disorder (Papa, Neria, & Litz, 2008). Yet war veterans often experience complicated grief as a result of the deaths of close friends, unit members, or leaders; survivor guilt; witnessing the death of other security forces and civilians; or their own killing of enemy insurgents. The close relationships that form within military units reflect attachment, and their losses are subject to grief as with loss of other attachment and family figures. Adjustment difficulties and suicide rates, especially of those with lengthy deployments, are indications that early evidence-based interventions are needed (Figley, 2007).

Conclusion

Dealing with death involves a process, not an event. It is an experience that all families *will* encounter and is inherent in the nature of close relationships. Despite its importance in the experiences of individuals and families, death still appears to be a taboo subject, and no comprehensive theory exists to account for the complexity and contexts in which grief occurs. Families' adaptation to death varies; factors that influence the process include characteristics of the death, family vulnerability, history of past losses, incompatible life-cycle demands, resources, belief systems, and the sociocultural context in which a family lives.

Although loss is a normal experience, it has been treated by theorists and researchers as a problem. More work needs to focus on processes and strengths, such as the process of coping (rather than problems), and factors that facilitate growth from loss (rather than those that inhibit growth). Examination of posttraumatic growth is a first step, but it warrants application beyond the individual to assess its applicability to families. Promising areas of study involve the interface of grief with technology, including the role of social media, how the Internet is changing the way we die and mourn (from suicide bulletin boards and virtual funeral rites to virtual grief therapy), and the validation or humiliation that comes depending on whether one is "followed," shared, or ignored.

DISCUSSION QUESTIONS

1. What factors influence how a family member adapts to death?

2. In what ways can social media be used to support and facilitate grieving individuals? And in what ways can it result in hurting or discounting them?

3. What are some beliefs or activities related to death that exist in various religious or cultural groups? In what ways do they impact the experiences of bereaved people?

REFERENCES

Albuquerque, S., Pereira, M., & Narciso, I. (2016). Couple's relationship after the death of a child: A systematic review. *Journal of Child and Family Studies, 25*, 30–53.

American Psychiatric Association. (2013). *Diagnostic and statistical manual of mental disorders* (5th ed.). Arlington, VA: Author.

Anderson, W. G., Arnold, R. M., Angus, D. C., & Bryce, C. L. (2008). Posttraumatic stress and complicated grief in family members of patients in the intensive care unit. *Journal of General Internal Medicine, 23*, 1871–1876.

Archer, J. (2008). Theories of grief: Past, present, and future perspectives. In M. S. Stroebe, R. O. Hansson, H. Schut, & W. Stroebe (Eds.), *Handbook of bereavement research and practice* (pp. 45–65). Washington, DC: American Psychological Association.

Aries, P. (1974). *Western attitudes toward death: From the Middle Ages to the present.* Baltimore, MD: Johns Hopkins University Press.

Bachman, B. (2013). The development of a sustainable, community-supported children's bereavement camp. *Omega, 67*, 21–35.

Baker, D., Norris, D., & Cherneva, V. (2019). Disenfranchised grief and families' experiences of death after police contact in the United States. *Omega.* Advance online publication. doi:10.1177/0030222819846420

Balk, D. E. (2014). *Dealing with dying, death, and grief during adolescence.* New York, NY; Routledge.

Balk, D. E., Noppe, I., Sandler, I., & Werth, J. (2011). Bereavement and depression: Possible changes to the Diagnostic and Statistical Manual of Mental Disorders: A report from the Scientific Advisory Committee of the Association for Death Education and Counseling. *Omega: Journal of Death and Dying, 63*, 199–220.

Bandini, J. (2015). The medicalization of bereavement: (Ab)normal grief in the DSM-5. *Death Studies, 39*, 347–352.

Bartel, B. T. (2019). Families grieving together: Integrating the loss of a child through ongoing relational connections. *Death Studies.* Advance online publication. doi:10.1080/07481187.2019.1586794

Becker, E. (1973). *The denial of death.* New York, NY: Free Press.

Boelen, P. A., & Prigerson, H. G. (2012). Commentary on the inclusion of persistent complex bereavement-related disorder in DSM-5. *Death Studies, 36*, 771–794.

Boelen, P. A., & van den Bout, J. (2002/2003). Gender differences in traumatic grief symptom severity after the loss of a spouse. *Omega, 46,* 183–198.

Bonanno, G. A. (2004). Loss, trauma, and human resilience: Have we underestimated the human capacity to thrive after extremely aversive events? *American Psychologist, 59,* 20–28.

Boss, P. G. (2006). *Loss, trauma, and resilience: Therapeutic work with ambiguous loss.* New York, NY: Norton.

Bowen, G. L., Mancini, J. A., Ware, W. B., & Nelson, J. P. (2003). Promoting the adaptation of military families: An empirical test of a community practice model. *Family Relations, 52,* 33–44.

Bowen, M. (1976). Family reaction to death. In P. J. Guerin (Ed.), *Family therapy: Theory and practice* (pp. 335–348). New York, NY: Gardner.

Bowlby, J. (1980). *Attachment and loss* (vol. 3), *Loss: Sadness and depression.* New York, NY: Basic Books.

Breen, L. J., Szylit, R, Gilbert, K. R., Macpherson, C., Murphy, I., Nadeau, J. W., . . . & International Work Group on Death, Dying, and Bereavement. (2019). Invitation to grief in the family context. *Death Studies, 43,* 173–182.

Bryant, R. A. (2014). Prolonged grief: Where to after Diagnostic and Statistical Manual of Mental Disorders, 5th Edition? *Current Opinion in Psychiatry, 27,* 21–26.

Bucholz, J. A. (2002). *Homicide survivors: Misunderstood grievers.* Amityville, NY: Baywood.

Buckley, T., Morel-Kopp, M. C., Ward, C., Bartrop, R., McKinley, S., Mihailidou, A. S., . . . & Tofler, G. (2012). Inflammatory and thrombotic changes in early bereavement: A prospective evaluation. *European Journal of Preventive Cardiology, 19,* 1145–1152.

Cook, J. A. (1988). Dad's double binds: Rethinking fathers' bereavement from a men's studies perspective. *Journal of Contemporary Ethnography, 17,* 285–308.

Corden, A., & Hirst, M. (2013). Economic components of grief. *Death Studies, 37,* 725–749.

Corr, C. A. (2019). The "five stages" in coping with dying and bereavement: Strengths, weaknesses and some alternatives. *Mortality, 24,* 405–417.

Doka, K. J. (Ed.). (1996). Commentary. In K. J. Doka (Ed.), *Living with grief after sudden loss: Suicide, homicide, accident, heart attack, stroke* (pp. 11–15). Bristol, PA: Taylor & Francis.

Doka, K. J. (2005). Ethics, end-of-life decisions and grief. *Mortality, 10,* 83–90.

Doka, K. J. (2008). Disenfranchised grief in historical and cultural perspective. In M. S. Stroebe, R. O. Hansson, H. Schut, & W. Stroebe (Eds.), *Handbook of bereavement research and practice* (pp. 223–240). Washington, DC: American Psychological Association.

Doka, K. J., & Martin, T. L. (2010). *Grieving beyond gender: Understanding ways men and women mourn.* New York, NY: Routledge.

Elwert, F., & Christakis, N. (2006). Widowhood and race. *American Sociological Review, 71,* 16–41.

Figley, C. R. (2007). An introduction to the special issue on the MHAT-IV. *Traumatology, 13,* 4–5.

Freud, S. (1957). Mourning and melancholies. In J. Strachey (Ed. & Trans.), *The standard edition of the complete psychological works of Sigmund Freud* (Vol. 14, pp. 243–258). London, England: Hogarth Press. (Original work published 1917)

Fried, E. I., Bockting, C., Arjadi, R., Borsboom, D., Amshoff, M., Cramer, A. O. J., . . . & Stroebe, M. (2015). From loss to loneliness: The relationship between bereavement and depressive symptoms. *Journal of Abnormal Psychology, 124,* 256–265.

Gilbert, K. R. (1996). "We've had the same loss, why don't we have the same grief?" Loss and differential grief in families. *Death Studies, 20,* 269–283.

Hall, M., & Irwin, M. (2001). Physiological indices of functioning in bereavement. In M. S. Stroebe, R. O. Hansson, W. Stroebe, & H. Schut (Eds.), *Handbook of bereavement research: Consequences, coping, and care* (pp. 473–492). Washington, DC: American Psychological Association.

Harvey, J. H., Carlson, H. R., Huff, T. M., & Green, M. A. (2001). Embracing their memory: The construction of accounts of loss and hope. In R. A. Neimeyer (Ed.), *Meaning reconstruction and the experience of loss* (pp. 231–243). Washington, DC: American Psychological Association.

Hawkley, L. C., & Cacioppo, J. T. (2003). Loneliness and pathways to disease. *Brain, Behavior, and Immunity, 17,* supplement, 98–105.

Hays, J. C., & Hendrix, C. C. (2008). The role of religion in bereavement. In M. S. Stroebe, R. O. Hansson, H. Schut, & W. Stroebe (Eds.), *Handbook of bereavement research and practice* (pp. 327–348). Washington, DC: American Psychological Association.

Jackson, D. (1965). The study of the family. *Family Process, 4,* 1–20.

Janoff-Bulman, R. (1992). *Shattered assumptions: Towards a new psychology of trauma.* New York, NY: Free Press.

Jones, D., Harvey, J., Giza, D., Rodican, C., Barreira, P. J., & Macias, C. (2003). Parental death in the lives of people with serious mental illness. *Journal of Loss and Trauma, 8,* 307–322.

Kamienski, M. C. (2004). Family-centered care in ED. *American Journal of Nursing, 104,* 59–62.

Klass, D. (2013). Sorrow and solace: Neglected areas of bereavement research. *Death Studies, 37,* 597–616.

Kochanek, K. D., Murphy, S. L., Xu, J. Q., & Arias, E. (2019). Deaths: Final data for 2017.

National Vital Statistics Reports, 68(9). Hyattsville, MD: National Center for Health Statistics.

Kübler-Ross, E. (1969). *On death and dying.* New York, NY: Macmillan.

Laurie, A., & Neimeyer, R. A. (2008). African Americans in bereavement: Grief as a function of ethnicity. *Omega, 57,* 173–193.

Lee, E.-K. O., Shen, C., & Tran, T. V. (2009). Coping with Hurricane Katrina: Psychological distress and resilience among African American evacuees. *Journal of Black Psychology, 35,* 5–23.

Lerner, M. (1980). When, why, and where people die. In E. S. Schneidman (Ed.), *Death: Current perspectives* (pp. 87–106). Palo Alto, CA: Mayfield.

Lindemann, E. (1944). Symptomology and management of acute grief. *American Journal of Psychiatry, 101,* 141–148.

Maciejewski, P. K., Maercker, A., Boelen, P. A. & Prigerson, H. G. (2016). "Prolonged grief disorder" and "persistent complex bereavement disorder," but not "complicated grief," are one and the same diagnostic entity: An analysis of data from the Yale Bereavement Study. *World Psychiatry: Official Journal of the World Psychiatric Association (WPA), 15,* 266–275. doi: 10.1002/wps.20348

Maddrell, A. (2016). Mapping grief. A conceptual framework for understanding the spatial dimensions of bereavement, mourning and remembrance. *Social & Cultural Geography, 17,* 166–188.

Marshall, B., & Winokuer, H. (Eds.). (2018). *Sibling loss across the lifespan: Research, practice, and personal stories.* New York, NY: Routledge.

McBain, T. D., & Reeves, P. (2019). Women's experience of infertility and disenfranchised grief. *The Family Journal: Counseling and Therapy for Couples and Families, 27,* 156–166.

McClatchey, I. S. (2018). Fathers raising motherless children: Widowed men give voice to their lived experiences. *Omega, 76,* 307–327.

McGoldrick, M., Schlesinger, J. M., Lee, E., Hines, P. M., Chan, J. Almeida, R., . . . & Petry, S. (2004). Mourning in different cultures. In F. Walsh & M. McGoldrick (Eds.), *Living beyond loss* (2nd ed., pp. 119–160). New York, NY: Norton.

Melhem, N. M., Moritz, G., Walker, M., Shear, M. K., & Brent, D. (2007). Phenomenology and correlates of complicated grief in children and adolescents. *Journal of the American Academy of Child and Adolescent Psychiatry, 46,* 493–499.

Metel, M., & Barnes, J. (2011). Peer-group support for bereaved children: A qualitative interview study. *Child and Adolescent Mental Health, 16,* 201–207.

Mikulincer, M., & Shaver, P. R. (2008). An attachment perspective on bereavement. In M. S. Stroebe, R. O. Hansson, H. Schut, & W. Stroebe (Eds.), *Handbook of bereavement research and practice* (pp. 87–112). Washington, DC: American Psychological Association.

Monahan, K. (2003). Death of an abuser: Does the memory linger on? *Death Studies, 27,* 641–651.

Moss, M. S., Moss, S. Z., & Hansson, R. O. (2001). Bereavement and old age. In M. S. Stroebe, R. O. Hansson, W. Stroebe, & H. Schut (Eds.), *Handbook of bereavement research: Consequences, coping, and care* (pp. 241–260). Washington, DC: American Psychological Association.

Murphy, S. A. (2008). The loss of a child: Sudden death and extended illness perspectives. In M. S. Stroebe, R. O. Hansson, H. Schut, & W. Stroebe (Eds.), *Handbook of bereavement research and practice* (pp. 375–395). Washington, DC: American Psychological Association.

Murray, C. I. (2016). Young children's understanding of grief and loss. In D. Couchenour & K. Christman (Eds.), *The SAGE encyclopedia of contemporary early childhood education* (pp. 640–642). Thousand Oaks, CA: SAGE.

Murray, C. I., & Gilbert, K. R. (1997, June). *British and U.S. reporting of the Dunblane school massacre.* Paper presented at the meeting of the 5th International Conference on Grief and Bereavement in Contemporary Society/Association for Death Education and Counseling. Washington, DC.

Murray, C. I., Toth, K., & Clinkinbeard, S. S. (2005). Death, dying, and grief in families. In P. C. McKenry & S. J. Price (Eds.), *Families and change: Coping with stressful events and transitions* (3rd ed., pp. 75–102). Thousand Oaks, CA: SAGE.

Nadeau, J. W. (2008). Meaning-making in bereaved families: Assessment, intervention, and future research. In M. S. Stroebe, R. O. Hansson, H. Schut, & W. Stroebe (Eds.), *Handbook of bereavement research and practice* (pp. 511–530). Washington, DC: American Psychological Association.

Neimeyer, R. A., Klass, D., & Dennis, M. R. (2014). A social constructionist account of grief: Loss and the narration of meaning. *Death Studies, 38,* 485–498.

O'Connor, M.-F., Shear, M. K., Fox, R., Skirtskaya, N., Campbell, B., Ghesquiere, A., & Glickman, K. (2013). Catecholamine predictors of complicated grief treatment outcomes. *International Journal of Psychophysiology, 88,* 349–353.

Papa, A., Neria, Y., & Litz, B. (2008). Traumatic bereavement in war veterans. *Psychiatric Annals, 38,* 686–691.

Pennebaker, J. W., Zech, E., & Rime, B. (2001). Disclosing and sharing emotion: Psychological, social, and health consequences. In M. S. Stroebe, R. O. Hansson, W. Stroebe, & H. Schut (Eds.), *Handbook of bereavement research: Consequences, coping, and care* (pp. 517–543). Washington, DC: American Psychological Association.

Prigerson, H. G., Horowitz, M. J., Jacobs, S. C., Parkes, C. M., Aslan, M., Goodkin, K., . . . & Maciejewski, P. K. (2009). Prolonged grief disorder: Psychometric validation of criteria proposed for DSM-V and ICD-11. *PLoS Medicine 6(8)*: e1000121.

Proulx, M., Martinez, A., Carnevale, F., & Legault, A. (2016). Fathers' experience after the death of their child (aged 1–17 years). *Omega, 73*, 308–325.

Pyszcznski, T., Solomon, S., & Greenberg, J. (2003). *In the wake of September 11: The psychology of terror.* Washington, DC: American Psychological Association.

Rabow, M. W., Hauser, J. M., & Adams, J. (2004). Supporting family caregivers at the end of life: "They don't know what they don't know." *Journal of the American Medical Association, 291*(4), 483–491.

Ramchand, R., Ayer, L., Fisher, G., Osilla, K. C., Barnes-Proby, D., & Wertheimer, S. (2015). *Suicide postvention in the Department of Defense: Evidence, policies and procedures, and perspectives of loss survivors.* Santa Monica, CA: RAND.

Rando, T. A. (1993). *Treatment of complicated mourning.* Champaign, IL: Research Press.

Robson, P., & Walter, T. (2012). Hierarchies of loss: A critique of disenfranchised grief. *Omega, 66*, 97–119.

Rolland, J. S. (1994). *Families, illness, & disability: An integrative treatment model.* New York, NY: Basic Books.

Rosaldo, R. (1989). *Culture and truth: The remaking of social analysis.* Boston, MA: Beacon.

Rosenblatt, P. C. (2000). *Parent grief: Narratives of loss and relationship.* Philadelphia, PA: Brunner/Mazel.

Rosenblatt, P. C. (2008). Recovery following bereavement: Metaphor, phenomenology, and culture. *Death Studies, 32*, 6–16.

Rosenblatt, P. C. (2019). Responding to bereaved people's words about relationship system loss. *Mortality, 24*, 261–270.

Schaefer, J. A., & Moos, R. H. (2001). Bereavement experiences and personal growth. In M. S. Stroebe, R. O. Hansson, W. Stroebe, & H. Schut (Eds.), *Handbook of bereavement research: Consequences, coping, and care* (pp. 145–167). Washington, DC: American Psychological Association.

Scharer, J. L. & Hibberd, R. (2019, March 29). Meaning differentiates depression and grief among suicide survivors. *Death Studies.* Advance online publication. doi:10.1080/07481187.2019.1586791

Servaty-Sieb, H. L., & Hayslip, B. (2003). Post-loss adjustment and funeral perceptions of parentally bereaved adolescents and adults. *Omega, 46,* 251–261.

Shapiro, E. R. (2001). Grief in interpersonal perspective: Theories and their implications. In M. S. Stroebe, R. O. Hansson, W. Stroebe, & H. Schut (Eds.), *Handbook of bereavement research: Consequences, coping, and care* (pp. 301–327). Washington, DC: American Psychological Association.

Shear, M. K., Ghesquiere, A., & Glickman, K. (2013). Bereavement and complicated grief. *Current Psychiatry Reports, 15*, 406, 1–7.

Shear, M. K., Simon, N., Wall, M., Zisook, S., Neimeyer, R.A., Duan, N., . . . & Keshaviah, A. (2011). Complicated grief and related bereavement issues for DSM-5. *Depression and Anxiety, 28*, 103–117.

Stroebe, M., & Schut, H. (2010). The dual process model of coping with bereavement: A decade on. *Omega, 61*, 273–289.

Stroebe, M., & Schut, H. (2015). Family matters in bereavement: Toward an integrative intrapersonal coping model. *Psychological Sciences, 10*, 873–879.

Stroebe, M., Schut, H., & Boerner, K. (2017). Cautioning health-care professionals: Bereaved persons are misguided through the stages of grief. *Omega, 74*, 455–473.

Stroebe, M., Schut, H., & Stroebe, W. (2007, December). Health outcomes of bereavement. *Lancet, 370,* 1960–1973.

Stroebe, M., van Son, M., Stroebe, W., Kleber, R., Schut, H., & van den Bout, J. (2000). On the classification and diagnosis of pathological grief. *Clinical Psychology Review, 20,* 57–75.

Stroebe, W., & Schut, H. (2001). Risk factors in bereavement outcome: A methodological and empirical review. In M. S. Stroebe, R. O. Hansson, W. Stroebe, & H. Schut (Eds.), *Handbook of bereavement research: Consequences, coping, and care* (pp. 349–371). Washington, DC: American Psychological Association.

Tedeschi, R. G., & Calhoun, L. G. (2008). Beyond the concept of recovery: Growth and the experience of loss. *Death Studies, 32,* 27–39.

Thieleman, K., & Cacciatore, J. (2014). When a child dies: A critical analysis of grief-related controversies in DSM-5. *Research on Social Work Practice, 24,* 114–122.

Traylor, E. S., Hayslip, B., Kaminski, P. L., & York, C. (2003). Relationships between grief and family system characteristics: A cross lagged longitudinal analysis. *Death Studies, 27,* 575–601.

Walsh, F., & McGoldrick, M. (2004). Loss and the family: A systems perspective. In F. Walsh & M. McGoldrick (Eds.), *Living beyond loss* (2nd ed., pp.3–26). New York, NY: Norton.

Walsh, F., & McGoldrick, M. (2013). Bereavement: A family life cycle perspective. *Family Science, 4,* 20–27.

Walter, T. (2008). The new public mourning. In M. S. Stroebe, R. O. Hansson, H. Schut, & W. Stroebe (Eds.), *Handbook of bereavement research and practice* (pp. 241–262). Washington, DC: American Psychological Association.

Walter, T., Hourizi, R., Moncur, W., & Pitsillides, S. (2012). Does the internet change how we die and mourn? Overview and analysis. *Omega, 64,* 275–302.

Weaver, K. K. (2020). Paying your respects: Transgender women and detransitioning after death. *Death Studies 44,* 58–64. doi:10.1080/0748 1187.2018.1521886

Webb, N. B. (2004). The impact of traumatic stress and loss on children and families. In N. B. Webb (Ed.), *Mass trauma and violence: Helping families and children cope* (pp. 3–22). New York, NY: Guilford Press.

Wolchik, S. A., Coxe, S., Tein, J. Y., Sandler, I. N., & Ayers, T. S. (2008). Six-year longitudinal predictors of posttraumatic growth in parentally bereaved adolescents and young adults. *Omega, 58,* 107–128.

Worden, J. W. (2018). *Grief counseling and grief therapy* (5th ed.). New York, NY: Springer.

Wortman, C. B., & Silver, R. C. (2001). The myths of coping with loss revisited. In M. S. Stroebe, R. O. Hansson, W. Stroebe, & H. Schut (Eds.), *Handbook of bereavement research: Consequences, coping, and care* (pp. 405–429). Washington, DC: American Psychological Association.

Zachar, P., First, M. B., & Kendler, K. S. (2017). The bereavement exclusion debate in the DSM-5: A history. *Clinical Psychological Science, 5,* 890–906.

Index

social support and, 170–171
stress and, 159–161
stressor events in, 161–170
Aguirre, R. T. P., 315
Aid (social support), 170
Akosile, A. E., 411
Alcohol-specific effects, 456
Alcohol use and abuse. *See* Substance use and abuse
Alcohol use disorder (AUD), 456
Aldwin, C. M., 160, 161, 468
Alienation, 5, 132
Almeida, D. M., 36, 44
Alternative for Families: A Cognitive Behavioral Therapy (AF-CBT), 344
Ambiguous loss, 9–10, 108–109, 164
Ambivalence, 157, 242
American Association on Intellectual and Developmental Disabilities, 105
American dream, 259, 263–264
American Life Project, 44
Anderson, E. R., 216
Anderson, M. L., 359
Anderson, N. D., 58
Ando, A., 269
Andrews, J. A., 463
Anger, abusers, 363
Anne, S., 411
Anticipated everyday hassles, 28
Appraisals, 92–93
Archer, J., 486
Arias, I., 360
Arkes, J., 466
Armstrong, D. M., 241
Artelt, E., 223
Asian American parenting, 285
    expectations, 286–289
    family obligations and, 286–287
    involvement in education, 289–291
    perpetual foreigner stereotype and, 286–289
    technology and transnationalism, 287–289
Assimilation (acculturation type), 236
Attachment theory, 391, 436
AUD. *See* Alcohol use disorder (AUD)
Axsom, D., 391

Bacigalupe, G., 287
Bajaj, R., 239
Balanced coping, 412

Bandura, Alfred, 363
Baniban, J., 410
Bankruptcy, 265
Banks, A., 141
Banyard, V. L., 339, 341
Bao, W. N., 435
Baranowski, M. D., 112
Barner, J. R., 360
Batt, R., 45, 47
Battering, 358
Bauman, K. E., 462
Baumrind, D., 285
Baxter, C., 373
BE. *See* Bereavement exclusion (BE)
Beck, C. J. A., 200
"Belief in a just world" paradigm, 492
Belief systems, 12, 231, 491–493
Bell, C. C., 397
Benign appraisals, 92
Benzies, K., 392
Bereavement, 483
Bereavement exclusion (BE), 484
Berger, L. M., 264
Berger, R., 413
Berman, H., 372
Berry, J. W., 236, 237, 243
Bersani, B., 463
Best, C. L., 465
Bethell, C. D., 388
Bevens, W., 415
B factor. *See* Resources
Biederman, J., 453
Binuclear family, 218–219
Bioecological theory, 57
Birth control, 73
Bishop, S. R., 58
Black, K., 388
Blackwell, C. K., 410
Bobek, M., 468
Bodenmann, G., 41
Bogenschneider, K., 464
Bolger, N., 40, 41
Bonanno, G. A., 390
Bonomi, A. E., 359
Booth, A., 415, 416
Borderline personality disorder (BPD), 60
Borges, A. M., 366
Boss, P. G.

Couple subsystem, 212–214
Coutin, S. B., 233
Cowan, C. P., 41
Cowan, P. A., 41
Coyne, J. C., 29
CPP. *See* Child-Parent Psychotherapy (CPP)
Crane, R., 60
Creating a tenuous balance (CTB) theory, 410
Credit, 264–265, 270
Crisis, 13–14, 231
    color discrimination, 292–293
    IPV, 367–368
    law enforcement interactions and, 298–299
    MMM, 290–291
    single parent, 297
    transnationalism, 294
Crosby, D., 195
Cross, K. A., 110, 113
CTB theory. *See* Creating a tenuous balance
    (CTB) theory
Culture
    caregiving, 419
    community resilience factors, 393
    death/dying/grief and, 493–495
    divorce, 185
    family stress process and, 12
    IPV, 364
    parental stress and, 85
    skipped-generation families, 169
Cumming, J., 413
Cunradi, C. B., 363
Currant, P., 458
Custodial grandparents, 168
Czaja, S. J., 335, 342, 419

Daily hassles. *See* Everyday hassles
Daily Inventory of Stressful Events (DISE), 31
Daily stressors, 160–161
Daly, K. J., 33
Darity, W., 360
Dauber, S., 468
Davis, K. E., 360
DBT. *See* Dialectical behavior therapy (DBT)
Death, dying, and grief, 481–482
    belief system, family, 491–493
    child, 496–497
    diversity factors, 493–495
    family adaptation factors, 488–496

gender differences, 493–494
    invisible death, 482–485
    loss characteristics, 488–491
    parental, 497–498
    siblings, 497
    spouse, 498
    systems theory to, 487
    veterans, 317–318, 499
    vulnerability, family, 491–492
Deatrick, J. A., 411
Debt, 264–265
    management plan, 270
    repayment, 270–272
Deck, A., 141
Defenders in stepfamilies, 214
Definition of event/perceptions
    ABC-X model, 7, 11–13
    colorism, 292
    immigrant families and communication, 294
    IPV, 367
    law enforcement interactions and, 298
    MMM, 290
    parental stress, 91–93
    perception of self, 485
    perpetual foreigner stereotype and, 287–288
    physical illness, 412–413
    single mother, 296
De Genova, N. P., 234
Degree of exposure, 389
Deković, M., 461
De Livera, A. M., 415
DeLongis, A., 29, 40, 41
Delsol, C., 363
Dementia caregivers, 164
Demo, D. H., 189
Dench, D., 462
Denial of problem, 170
Deployment. *See* Veterans and veterans families
Depression, 434–435, 437–438
    grief versus, 484
Desai, S., 360
Developmental delay, 105
Developmental disabilities, 105
Developmental transitions, 82–83
Diagnostic and Statistical Manual of Mental Disorders
    (*DSM-5*), 453, 484
Dialectical behavior therapy (DBT), 59, 60–61
Diaz E., 383

Lau, M., 58
Lazarus, R. S., 29
Lee, C. C., 419
Legacy, 492
Leon, S. C., 339
Leonard, K. E., 456, 467
Leone, J. M., 365
Lesbian, gay, bisexual, and queer (LGBQ).
    See LGBQ-parent families
Lessard, J., 456
"Letting go" process, 83
Leung, P., 369
Levi, L. L., 393
Lewis, D. C., 242, 244
LGBQ-parent families, 127–128
    coming out and being out, 128–130
    experiences and challenges, 138–143
    health-care bias, 142–143
    legal issues, 133–134, 135, 137, 139, 144–145
    parent–child relationship, 138–139
    parents, becoming, 134–138
    planned/intentional, 134(n1)
    practitioners and, 143–145
    same-sex relationships. *See* Same-sex relationships
    school bias, 140–141
    sexual minorities and, 129–130, 133, 136, 137
    social support, 139–140
Life-course perspectives, 306–307
    children (individual transitions), 313–314
    family transitions, 306–307, 314–318
    FSAMH and, 430
    historical time, 306, 307–308
    prevention and intervention, 318
    spouses (individual transitions), 312–313
    veterans (individual transitions), 308–311
Life, philosophy of, 485
Liminal legality, 233
Lindfors, P., 464
Linehan, M. M., 65
Lingfors, H., 411
Linked lives, 307, 314–319, 430
Lipman-Blumen, J., 8
Little, T. D., 466
Little, W. M., 437
Littleton, H. L., 391
Liu, C., 388
Livingston, J., 456
LLATs (living apart together later in life), 156

Lloyd, A., 60
Lobo, M., 388
Lochman, J. E., 455, 467
Loewenstein, D., 419
Long-term immigrants, 241
Lopez, S. A., 466
Lorenz, F. O., 435, 437
Loss orientation, 486, 493
Lowenstein, A., 167
Loyalty binds, 213, 214, 215

Macrosystem level stressor, 159
Maes, H., 464
Maltreated children. *See* Child maltreatment
    resilience
Mamikonyan, E., 415
Mannarino, A. P., 317
Marginalization (acculturation type), 236
Margolin, G., 363
Marin, D., 413
Marital conflict, 85, 214, 265, 436
Marital quality
    deployment of service members and, 315
    physical illness and, 414, 415
    retirement and, 162
    stepfamilies, 212
Marital relationship
    deployment of service members and, 315
    economic stress, 267
    family economic hardship and, 435–436
    intellectual and developmental disabilities
        and, 110, 111
    parental stress and, 82, 88
    VSA model, 41–42
Marital satisfaction, 185, 315
Marital separation. *See* Divorce
Marquis, S., 111
Martin, T. L., 493
Marttunen, M., 391
Massey G., 298
Mass shootings, 383, 386
Mass violence, 382–387
    active shooter, 383–384, 385 (figure)
    attachment style and, 391
    communication and, 397
    defined, 381
    evidence-based practices, 399
    family resilience to, 387–389, 392–393

implications for professionals working, 393–399
mass shootings, 383, 386
media exposure of, 397–398
natural disasters versus, 383
parenting and, 396–397
resilience, 389–393, 394–396
resources, 391, 396
responding to, 394–396
social support, 390
terrorism, 386
theoretical framework, 387–389
therapy-based interventions of, 399
traumatic events and, 383, 386–387, 387 (table)
Mastery orientation, 12
Masyn, K. E., 437
Maternal and Child Health Bureau, 103
Maternal drinking, 462
Mavandadi, S., 415
Maxwell, K., 413
Mayfield Arnold, E, 466
Mazumdar, S., 242
MBIs. *See* Mindfulness-based interventions (MBIs)
MBSR. *See* Mindfulness-based stress reduction (MBSR)
McCubbin, H. I., 10, 12, 16, 56, 109, 284, 388, 408
McCubbin, L. D., 12
McDonagh, T., 390
McDonald, T. P., 466
McFarland, B. H., 311
McFarland, K., 360
McGonagle, K. A., 44
McGrail, K., 111
McGuire, A. P., 391
McHale, S. M., 468
McIntosh, D. N., 389
McLeod, B. D., 468
McNeil Smith, S., 12, 56, 284
McStay, R. L., 107
Mechanic, M. B., 200
Media exposure, 397–398
Mediation, divorce, 198–200
Mediators in stepfamilies, 215
Medicare, 418
Medina, L., 241
MEES. *See* Mundane extreme environmental stress theory (MEES)
Meghani, S. H., 411
Menjivar, C., 233
Mental health

children, 442–443
family, 429
FSAMH model. *See* FSAMH model
immigrant families, 243–246
interdependence, 432, 433 (figure)
parents, 434–436
youth, 437–438, 443
Mental Health First Aid, 393
Mental retardation, 105
Menzel, K. E., 199
Merged families. *See* Stepfamilies
Merighi, J. R., 130
Merritt-Gray, M., 371 (table), 372
Mersky, J. P., 338
Mesosystem level stressor, 159
Messinger, A. M., 368
Microsystem level stressor, 159
Middle-old years, 158
Mikton, C. R., 166
Mikulincer, M., 486
Milburn, N. G., 466
Miller, S. A., 339
Mindfulness, 55–56
ABC-X model, 56, 63, 64
acceptance and change, 65–66
chronic stress and, 62–63
as cognitive phenomenon, 61
DBT, 59, 60–61
as disposition, 61
family-based mindfulness programs, 59
home practice, 60
MBSR, 58, 59–60
mundane experience of stress and, 63–64
origin of, 58
overview, 57–58
perspectives change, 61
structural support for, 61–62
systemic oppressive practice, 64–65
Minkkinen, J., 464
Minority stress, 128
models, 56
MMM. *See* Model minority myth (MMM)
Model minority myth (MMM), 289–291
Modigliani, F., 269
Moen, P., 45, 47
Moffitt, T. E., 335, 338
Montoro-Rodriguez, J., 169
Monuteaux, M. C., 453

Mooney-Doyle, K., 411
Moore, K., 389
Moore, M. R., 130
Moore, T. M., 455, 467
Morris, A. H., 18
Morris, A. S., 388
Mortgage, 264
Moss, V., 371 (table)
Moxley, J. H., 419
MST for Child Abuse and Neglect (MST-CAN), 347
Mundane extreme environmental stress theory
    (MEES), 56, 298–299
Muruthi, J. R., 242, 244
Mychasiuk, R., 392

Naar-King, S., 114
Neate, S. L., 415
Negative resources, 86
Neglect (elder abuse), 166
Negrusa, B., 315
Negrusa, S., 315
Nelson Goff, B. S., 110, 113
Net worth, 262–263
Neuroendocrine, 438–439
Neurological mediating processes, 438–439
New public mourning, 481
NFP. *See* Nurse–Family Partnership (NFP)
Nielsen, R., 397
9/11 attacks, 389–390
Nonalcohol-specific effects, 456–457
Nonegocentric stress, 160
Nonnemaker, J. M., 462
Nonnormative economic stress, 258
Nonnormative stressor, 8, 83
   chronic stressors, 84–86
   initial awareness or diagnosis, 84
   off-time developments, 84
Normative economic stress, 258
Normative stressors, 8, 81
   daily hassles, 81–82
   developmental transitions, 82–83
Norris, F. H., 383
Nuclear family, 296
Nurse–Family Partnership (NFP), 345–346
Nussbeck, F., 41

Off-time stressor event, 84
Ohlsson, H., 464

Oksanen, A., 390
Oldest-old years, 158
O'Leary, S. G., 338
Olivia, E. M., 459
100,000 Jobs Mission, 319
Ongkasuwan, J., 411
Open adoptions, 136
Operation Enduring Freedom (OEF), 305
Operation Iraqi Freedom (OIF), 305
Operation New Dawn (OND), 305
Oshiri, A., 342
Otten, R., 455

Paik, S. J., 289
Pakanati, K., 411
Palmer, K., 464
Parent–adolescent conflict
   immigrant families, 240
   parental stress and, 83, 85
Parental adaptation, 90–91
Parental affect, 443
Parental competence, 87
Parental coping, 89–90
Parental efficacy, 87
Parental rejection, 443
Parental resources, 86–87
Parental stress
   adaptation/resilience, 90–91
   appraisals and, 92–93
   child effects perspective, 85–86
   co-parenting and, 82
   coping, 89–90
   culture and, 85
   defined, 78
   divorce and, 91
   family stress theory and, 77–80
   marital conflict and, 85
   marital relationship and, 82, 88
   of newborns, 82
   nonnormative stressor events, 83–86
   normative stressor events, 81–83
   parent–adolescent conflict and, 83, 85
   parent–child relationship and, 79–80
   parenthood and, 74–76
   poverty and, 85
   as reciprocal/multidirectional process, 78
   recovery factors, 86–91
   resources, 86–89

About the Editors

Kevin Ray Bush is a professor with a joint appointment in the Departments of Educational Psychology, and Family Science and Social Work; and codirector of the Doris Bergen Center for Human Development, Learning and Technology at Miami University in Oxford, Ohio. His research interests focus on child and adolescent development in the contexts of family, school, community, and culture. He has examined the relationships between parents, teachers, and child and adolescent development within diverse U.S. and international samples. Dr. Bush is also interested in program evaluation and has conducted evaluations of school, agency, and home-based child and family intervention programs. Dr. Bush has a master's degree in marriage and family therapy from Arizona State University and a PhD in human development and family relations from the Ohio State University.

Christine A. Price is a freelance editor and adjunct associate professor with the Department of Family Science and Human Development at Montclair State University, Montclair, New Jersey. She provides developmental editing and copyediting services and teaches online courses relating to family gerontology from her home in Charlotte, North Carolina. Prior to leaving academia, she was on the faculty at Montclair State University, The Ohio State University, and Missouri State University. She earned her master's and PhD in child and family development and graduate certificate in gerontology from The University of Georgia.

About the Contributors

Chapter 1: Families Coping With Change: A Conceptual Overview

Patrick C. McKenry was professor of Human Development and Family Science and African American and African Studies at The Ohio State University. His work focused on family stress and coping with particular interest in gender, cultural, and lifestyle variations. In addition to books, he published numerous articles in professional journals. He received his PhD from the University of Tennessee in Child and Family Studies and was a postdoctoral fellow at the University of Georgia in Child and Family Development. Pat and Sharon Price worked together for almost three decades and edited three previous editions of this book as well as the book, *Divorce* (1988, SAGE). He died in 2004.

    Sharon J. Price is professor emerita and former head of the Department of Child and Family Development at the University of Georgia. She has published extensively in professional journals and coauthored or coedited several books. She won several teaching awards including the Osborne Award, presented by the National Council on Family Relations, and the highest honor for teaching at the University of Georgia, the Josiah Meigs Award. She was active in several professional organizations, serving in many capacities, including president of the National Council on Family Relations, and is a fellow in NCFR. She earned her PhD from Iowa State University.

Chapter 2: Everyday Hassles and Family Relationships

Heather M. Helms is a professor in the Department of Human Development and Family Studies at the University of North Carolina at Greensboro where she has been recognized with research and teaching excellence awards. Her research focuses on marital quality in socio-cultural context. Funded by the National Center for Research on Hispanic Children and Families, an additional focus of her scholarship underscores policy implications of research findings for Mexican immigrant families. Her work has been published widely in scholarly journals (e.g., *Journal of Marriage and Family*, *Journal of Family Psychology*, *Journal of Family Theory and Review*, *Family Process*), edited volumes (e.g., *Handbook of Marriage and the Family*, 2013, Springer), and media outlets including the BBC and the *Wall Street Journal*. Recognized with a mentoring career award by the National Council on Family Relations in 2015, Dr. Helms has mentored students and faculty across these endeavors. She received her PhD from Pennsylvania State University.

Kaicee Beal Postler is a recent doctoral graduate from the Department of Human Development and Family Studies at the University of North Carolina at Greensboro. Her research centers around the connections between developmental or psychological outcomes and family processes. Specifically, she is interested in how atypical development, psychopathology, and adversity spillover to impact family processes, such as marriage. She is also interested in factors that promote and support the well-being of individuals, families, and relationships across various contexts and in relation to various systems. Her dissertation research examined linkages between marital quality and anxiety and marital instability and anxiety with meta-analytic techniques. She received her PhD in December 2019.

David H. Demo is associate dean and professor in the School of Health and Human Sciences at the University of North Carolina Greensboro. His research focuses on divorce and family transitions, changes in family relationships accompanying divorce, and the consequences of family transitions for family members' well-being. He has published widely in professional journals and he has authored or coauthored numerous chapters in edited volumes. He has also authored or edited several books, including *Beyond the Average Divorce* (2010, SAGE), *Handbook of Family Diversity* (2000, Oxford University Press); *Parents and Adolescents in Changing Families* (1995, National Council on Family Relations); and *Family Diversity and Well-Being* (1994, SAGE), which received the *Choice Magazine* Outstanding Book Award. He served as editor of *Journal of Marriage and Family*, and he is a fellow of the National Council on Family Relations. Dr. Demo received his PhD in human development and family studies from Cornell University.

Chapter 3: Family Stress and Intervention

Suzanne Klatt is director of the Miami University Mindfulness & Contemplative Inquiry Center; clinical associate professor, College of Education, Health & Society; Educational Leadership Affiliate. She has been practicing, training, creating, and facilitating mindfulness- and contemplative-based practices and programming both personally and professionally since 1997. Many of her current courses bridge mindfulness and contemplative inquiry themes with anti-oppressive practices. She is a licensed clinical social worker–supervisor who presents locally, nationally, and internationally about these partnerships, related faculty learning communities, engaged critical contemplative pedagogy, and creating the infrastructure for students to weave contemplative inquiry into their research process. She began utilizing mindfulness as a team member trained in and providing 12 month dialectical behavior therapy (DBT) with women in community mental health. She is a qualified mindfulness-based stress reduction (MBSR) teacher, certified in Mindful Schools, Mindfulness in Schools, Integrative Restoration Yoga Nidra (I-Rest), anti-oppressive practices, and cultural proficiency.

Chapter 4: Conceptualizing Parental Stress with Family Stress Theory

Gary W. Peterson is professor emeritus for the Department of Family Science and Social Work at the University of Miami in Oxford, Ohio. His areas of scholarly interest are parent–child/adolescent relations, cross-cultural influences on adolescent development, and family theory. His publications have appeared in numerous academic journals and edited book chapters. He is editor or coeditor of books on fatherhood, cross-cultural parent–adolescent relations, and adolescent development in families. The central focus of Dr. Peterson's research has been concerned with how aspects of parent–adolescent relationships influence dimensions of adolescent social competence using samples from several countries. He is a past coeditor of the *Handbook of Marriage and the Family* (2nd ed., 1999, Plenum), the editor (with Kevin R. Bush) of the *Handbook of Marriage and the Family* (3rd ed., 2013, Springer) and a previous editor of *Marriage and Family Review*. Dr. Peterson is a fellow of the National Council on Family Relations.

Chapter 5: Intellectual and Developmental Disabilities: Understanding Stress and Resilience in Family Systems

Kami L. Gallus is an associate professor in human development and family science at Oklahoma State University. She earned dual bachelor degrees in family science and psychology from Anderson University, a master's degree in marriage and family therapy from Kansas State University, and her doctorate in marriage and family therapy from Texas Tech University. Dr. Gallus's scholarship focuses on enhancing individual functioning and relationship outcomes among vulnerable, often marginalized, and traditionally underserved populations, including female trauma survivors, at-risk youth, and individuals with intellectual and developmental disabilities. Since 2013, Dr. Gallus and Dr. Jennifer Jones have collaborated to collect Oklahoma's In-Person Survey for National Core Indicators and to develop the IDD Network promoting research, education, and community engagement among individuals with intellectual and developmental disabilities (IDD), their families, and students, faculty, and staff at Oklahoma State University.

Briana S. Nelson Goff is a professor in the School of Family Studies and Human Services at Kansas State University. She earned dual bachelor degrees in life science and psychology and a master's degree in marriage and family therapy, both from Kansas State University and her doctorate from Texas Tech University. Dr. Nelson Goff's clinical experience and research specialization is with primary and secondary traumatic stress symptoms in trauma survivor couples, families, and children, with specific focus on military and disaster related traumatic events. Since 2010, Dr. Nelson Goff has conducted a national research study on the positive aspects of having a child with Down syndrome, which is both a personal and professional endeavor.

Chapter 6: LGBQ-Parent Families: Development and Functioning in Context

Abbie E. Goldberg is professor of psychology at Clark University. She received her PhD in clinical psychology from the University of Massachusetts Amherst. Her research focuses on parenting in diverse families, including lesbian/gay parent families, adoptive families, and families formed through reproductive technologies. She has received grant funding for her work from a range of private and federal agencies, including the American Psychological Association, the Alfred P. Sloan Foundation, the Spencer Foundation, and the National Institutes of Health. She has over 115 peer-reviewed publications in journals such as *Journal of Marriage and Family*, *Journal of Family Psychology*, and *Adoption Quarterly*. She is the editor of three books and the author of three books, the most recent being *Open Adoption in Diverse Families: Complex Relationships in the Digital Age* (2019, Oxford).

Nora McCormick is a second-year doctoral student in clinical psychology at Clark University. Her research interests include how minority stress affects health outcomes in the LGBTQ and other minority communities, especially where multiple minority statuses intersect with one another. Ultimately, she hopes to take this knowledge and determine how it can inform interventions that foster resiliency and reduce harmful effects in these communities. She has published on health outcomes among same-sex adoptive parents, adoptive parents' experiences with their child's pediatrician, adoptive parents' experiences with managing uncertainty surrounding their child's origins, transgender students' experiences in applying to graduate school, and on pediatric HIV-outcomes in sub-Saharan Africa. She has a MSc in epidemiology from the Harvard T. H. Chan School of Public Health and a BA in anthropology from Washington University in St. Louis.

Chapter 7: Stress and Coping in Later Life

Áine M. Humble is professor in the Department of Family Studies and Gerontology at Mount Saint Vincent University in Halifax, Nova Scotia, Canada. Her research interests focus on gender construction and family work, family rituals, women and healthy aging, same-sex couples and older LGBTQ (lesbian, gay, bisexual, transgender, queer) individuals, qualitative research methods, and computer-assisted qualitative data analysis. Her work has been published in scholarly journals such as *Family Relations*, *Journal of Family Theory & Review*, *Journal of Applied Gerontology*, *Journal of Women and Aging*, *Canadian Journal on Aging*, and *Sage Research Methods Foundations*. She and Dr. Elise Radina are the coeditors of

How Qualitative Data Analysis Happens: Moving Beyond "Themes Emerged," (2019, Taylor & Francis). She is a certified Family Life Educator through the National Council on Family Relations. Dr. Humble received her PhD in human development and family studies at Oregon State University in 2003.

Chapter 8: Divorce: Variation and Fluidity

David H. Demo is associate dean and professor in the School of Health and Human Sciences at the University of North Carolina Greensboro. His research focuses on divorce and family transitions, changes in family relationships accompanying divorce, and the consequences of family transitions for family members' well-being. He has published widely in professional journals and he has authored or coauthored numerous chapters in edited volumes. He has also authored or edited several books, including *Beyond the Average Divorce* (2010, Sage), *Handbook of Family Diversity* (2000, Oxford University Press); *Parents and Adolescents in Changing Families* (1995, National Council on Family Relations); and *Family Diversity and Well-Being* (1994, SAGE), which received the Choice Magazine Outstanding Book Award. He served as editor of *Journal of Marriage and Family*, and he is a fellow of the National Council on Family Relations. Dr. Demo received his PhD in human development and family studies from Cornell University.

Mark Fine is a professor in the Department of Human Development and Family Studies at the University of North Carolina at Greensboro. He earned his PhD in clinical psychology from The Ohio State University in 1983. He was editor of *Family Relations* from 1993–1996, editor of the *Journal of Social and Personal Relationships* from 1999–2004, and currently is the editor of the *Journal of Family Theory and Research*. His primary research interests lie in the area of adjustment to family transitions, such as divorce and remarriage, and family diversity. He has over 200 publications, including coediting or coauthoring 10 books, primarily on topics related to family diversity, divorce, and family theories. He has been a fellow of the National Council on Family Relations since 2000.

Chapter 9: Stress and Resilience in Stepfamilies Today

Chelsea Garneau-Rosner is an assistant professor in human development and family science at the University of Missouri. She received her PhD in family relations from Florida State University. Her work focuses on identifying factors that family processes (e.g., coparenting, parental monitoring, positive interaction, family cohesion) and individual, couple, and family well-being, particularly in complex family structures. Recent publications focus on the role of cognitions and in marital and family relationship quality and interactions in stepfamilies.

Dr. Garneau-Rosner has been invited to speak at national international meetings about relationships and family processes in stepfamilies. She is an active member of the National Council on Family Relations.

Braquel R. Egginton is a doctoral student in human development and family science at the University of Missouri. She earned her MS in family sciences from Brigham Young University in 2018. Her work focuses on understanding the complexity of divorce and stepfamily relationships and the impact of relationship education and responsible fatherhood programs on these relationships. Her research has been presented at the Research and Evaluation Conference of Self-Sufficiency, the National Council of Family Relations, and the European Network for Sociological and Demographic Study of Divorce Conference.

Chapter 10: Immigrant Families: Resilience Through Adversity

Bertranna A. Muruthi is an assistant professor in the Department of Counseling Psychology and Human Services at the University of Oregon. Her research and scholarly interests focus on community-based culturally responsive interventions and prevention programs for immigrant families in the United States. Central to her research activities is the examination of factors related to immigrant families in transition, and predictors for risk and resilient behavior. Her work has been published in several scholarly journals including the *Journal of Marital and Family Therapy, Journal of Family Theory & Review* and the *Journal of Family Issues*. She received her PhD from the University of Georgia.

Hyoun K. Kim is professor in the Department of Child and Family Studies at Yonsei University, Seoul. Korea. Her long-term research program centers around the development of psychopathology in at-risk youth and families. Her research has specifically focused on understanding the developmental trajectories and transmission of these behaviors within as well as across generations with a strong focus on the mediating effects of self-regulatory systems and social influence processes on the development of health risk behaviors. Her work has been published in several scholarly journals, including *Developmental Psychology, Development and Psychopathology, Journal of Family Psychology, Journal of School Psychology, Psychoneuroendocrinology, Prevention Science, Journal of Marriage and Family, Journal of Consulting and Clinical Psychology, Family Process, Emotion,* and *Criminology*. She received her PhD from The Ohio State University and worked as a research scientist for about 20 years at the Oregon Social Learning Center, Eugene, Oregon.

James R. Muruthi is an assistant professor in the Department of Counseling Psychology and Human Services at the University of Oregon. His main research interest focuses on family and neighborhood factors, social capital, and health disparities among marginalized older individuals and their families. He has conducted studies in Kenya, Ghana, South Africa, and the United States, and published in various peer-reviewed journals, such as the *Journal of Aging and Health,* and the *Journal of Applied Gerontology.* His current research interests involve health-care access, social capital and health among caregivers, and aging care recipients. In his current position, he teaches courses on diversity in human services, global health, health promotion, and equity. He received his PhD from the University of Georgia.

Jaehee Kim is an adjunct professor in the Department of Child and Family Studies at Yonsei University, Seoul, Korea and in the Department of Social Work at Gachon University, Gyeonggi-do, Korea. Her main research interest focuses on child social emotional development, family focused intervention programs, and social policy for young children, their families and childcare center. She has conducted studies in Korea and United States, and published in various peer-reviewed journals, such as the *Journal of Family Psychology* and the *Korean Journal of Child Studies.* Her current research interests include children's emotion regulation, educational programs for school readiness, and cyberbullying among youth. She received PhD from Ewha Womans University, Seoul, Korea.

Chapter 11: Economic Stress and Families

Suzanne Bartholomae is an assistant professor and extension state specialist in family finance in the Department of Human Development and Family Studies at Iowa State University. Her engaged scholarship focuses on financial education, financial wellness, and financial behavior based in local, regional, state, and national initiatives. Her work has been published in several scholarly journals including *Family Relations,* the *Journal of Family Issues,* the *Journal of Family and Economic Issues,* the *Journal of Adolescent Health,* and the *Journal of Consumer Affairs.* She earned her PhD from the Ohio State University.

Jonathan Fox is the Ruth Whipp Sherwin Endowed Professor in the Department of Human Development and Family Studies, director of the Financial Counseling Clinic, and program leader in financial counseling and planning at Iowa State University. His research focuses on financial education and financial socialization. He has served as PI for several financial education evaluations and his publications appear in journals such as *Financial Services Review, Financial Counseling and Planning,* the *Journal of Family Issues,* and the *Journal of Consumer Affairs.* He teaches consumer economics and personal and family finance and received his PhD in consumer economics from the University of Maryland.

Chapter 12: Race, Ethnicity, and Family Stress

Anthony G. James is director of the Family Science Program and associate professor in the Department of Family Science and Social Work at Miami University (Ohio). His scholarly work uses an interdisciplinary approach to understanding social interactions and human development, with an expertise in positive youth development, religion and spirituality, diverse family systems, family processes, and program evaluation. His works include publications in refereed journals and book chapters, on topics in the areas of youth development and family processes, including an edited book on Black family life using a systems perspective. He is the current deputy editor of the *Journal of Family Theory and Review* and a consulting editor for the *Journal of Research on Adolescence*. Dr. James is a certified relationship assessment facilitator through the PREPARE/ENRICH program, a certified family life educator through the National Council on Family Relations. He received his PhD from the University of Missouri.

Veronica R. Barrios is an assistant professor in the Department of Family Science and Social Work at Miami University (Ohio). Her primary scholarly work focuses on understanding and exposing the culture of nondisclosure of sexual violence. Dr. Barrios works with survivors of sexual violence and clinical practitioners to develop clinical tools that facilitate disclosure of sexual violence and elucidates family dynamics and socially mandated rules involved in silencing practices. Her secondary research area revolves around Latinx families and the educational experiences of Latinx students. She is a certified program evaluator who focuses on working with grassroots organizations. Dr. Barrios integrates theory, research, and practice to create scholarly work that can be used by communities. She received her PhD from Montclair State University.

Roudi Nazarinia Roy is an associate professor and area coordinator of the Child Development and Family Studies Program in the Department of Family and Consumer Sciences at California State University, Long Beach. Her research interests revolve around the transition to parenthood, cultural influences on family roles, and marital satisfaction. She recently coedited a book on biracial families. She currently serves as the book review coeditor of the *Journal of Family Theory and Review* and on the editorial board of the *Journal of Family and Economic Issues and Marriage and Family Review*. Dr. Roy is a certified family life educator through the National Council on Family Relations and consults for community agencies serving diverse populations of families. She received her PhD from Kansas State University.

Soyoung Lee is an associate professor in the Department of Family Science and Human Development at Montclair State University. She is a certified family life educator through the National Council on Family Relations. Her major research areas include ethnically and culturally diverse families' experiences within larger community and global settings and family life education in order to support the changing needs of families and communities in a diverse society. As part of her research program, she has conducted research on Korean immigrants' adjustments in the United States, multicultural families and family policies in South Korea, parenting experiences across various life courses of different ethnic and cultural groups, and effective teaching strategies in the fields of family science. She is currently serving as a member-at-large on the board of directors at the National Council on Family Relations. She received her PhD from Virginia Tech.

Chapter 13: The Newest Generation of U.S. Veterans and Their Families

Kyung-Hee Lee is a research associate and project manager to Dr. Ellen Kossek, Basil S. Turner Professor of Management and Director of Research for the Susan Bulkeley Butler Center for Leadership Excellence. She earned her PhD at Texas Tech and previously worked as a postdoctoral research associate at the Military Family Research Institute at Purdue University, at Virginia Tech as a postdoctoral research associate, and at Texas Tech as an adjunct professor. Her research interests include military families, work–family issues, dyadic and longitudinal processes of intimate relationships, and voluntary childlessness.

    Shelley M. MacDermid Wadsworth is a professor in the Department of Human Development and Family Studies at Purdue University, where she also directs the Military Family Research Institute and the Center for Families. Her research focuses on relationships between job conditions and family life, with special focus on military families and organizational policies, programs, and practices. She is an author of over 140 articles and chapters, and author or editor of five books. Dr. MacDermid Wadsworth is a fellow of the National Council on Family Relations. She has served on federal advisory committees for the National Academies of Science and the Department of Defense and has testified in Congress on multiple occasions. Dr. MacDermid Wadsworth is a recipient of the Morrill Award, Purdue University's highest faculty honor, and in 2019 was named a "Top Ten Extraordinary Contributor" among work–family researchers worldwide.

Chapter 14: Promoting Pathways to Resilient Outcomes for Maltreated Children

Margaret O'Dougherty Wright, PhD is a professor emeritus of psychology at Miami University (Ohio). She received her PhD in clinical psychology from the University of Minnesota in 1981 and completed a clinical internship at UCLA's Neuropsychiatric Institute. Her research focuses on understanding what promotes positive resolution of traumatic experiences as well as factors that lead to continued vulnerability. Her current research explores mothering as a survivor following childhood abuse or neglect; identification of mediating and moderating factors that account for the link between childhood maltreatment and intergenerational continuity or discontinuity of abuse; exploration of protective processes that foster resilience in child abuse survivors, such as attachment relationships and meaning making; and the wounded healer paradigm, exploring therapists' ability to use the knowledge acquired through their own suffering following trauma in the service of their clients' recovery.

    Lucy J. Allbaugh, PhD, is an assistant professor of psychology at the University of Dayton. She received her PhD in clinical psychology from Miami University (Ohio) and completed a doctoral internship and postdoctoral residency at the Emory University School of Medicine. Her research focuses on outcomes associated with trauma and on change in functioning across the lifespan, with a particular emphasis on resilient outcome and relational well-being. She is currently engaged in research to understand relational functioning, including change in quality of significant attachment relationships; factors that contribute to the efficacy of trauma-focused interventions; and psychosocial and biological predictors of risk versus resilience in families exposed to multiple forms of trauma.

Chapter 15: Stress and Coping With Intimate Partner Violence

Lyndal Khaw is an associate professor of family science and human development at Montclair State University, Montclair, New Jersey. Her academic research focuses on intimate partner violence, specifically on women's process of leaving abusive partners and strategies women use to resist violence. Dr. Khaw's work explores the impact of violence beyond the survivor, such as parenting, family dynamics, and intimate relationships. Her empirical and theoretical works have been published in peer-reviewed journals including *Journal of Interpersonal Violence, Family Relations, Journal of Family Theory and Review,* and *Family Process.* Dr. Khaw received her PhD in human development and family studies from the University of Illinois at Urbana-Champaign in 2010.

Chapter 16: Family Responses to School and Community Mass Violence

Amity L. Noltemeyer, PhD, NCSP, is professor and chair of the Department of Educational Psychology at Miami University (Ohio). Dr. Noltemeyer's research interests include positive behavioral interventions and supports (PBIS), school discipline disparities, and school-based mental health services. She comanages externally funded grants and is editor-in-chief of *School Psychology International* journal. Dr. Noltemeyer received her master's and EdS degrees in school psychology from Miami University and her PhD in school psychology from Kent State University.

    Courtney L. McLaughlin, PhD, NCSP, is a professor in the educational and school psychology department and directs the PhD program in school psychology at Indiana University of Pennsylvania. Her primary professional interests are in the areas of school-based mental health, cognitive-behavioral therapy, depression, geography and mental health, and social media. She serves as a senior associate editor for *School Psychology International* journal. Dr. McLaughlin received her master's degree and PhD in school psychology from Kent State University.

Mark R. McGowan, PhD, NCSP, is professor of educational and school psychology and director of the Child Study Center at Indiana University of Pennsylvania. His research interests focus on the provision of mental health services in educational settings, violence risk and threat assessment, school-based neuropsychological assessment, supervision, and graduate training in psychology. Dr. McGowan earned a master's degree in school psychology and a PhD in counseling psychology from Northern Arizona University.

Caitlin M. Johnson, MS, is a graduate student studying school psychology at Miami University (Ohio). Her professional interests include school-based holistic case management, school-based mental health services, equity in school systems, positive behavioral interventions and supports (PBIS), and crisis intervention. She serves as an editorial assistant of *School Psychology International* journal. Caitlin received her BS in psychology from The Ohio State University.

Chapter 17: Physical Illness and Family Stress

Jeremy Yorgason is a professor in the School of Family Life and director of the gerontology program at Brigham Young University. His research interests include later-life family relationships, with an emphasis on dyadic coping with illness. His recently published research explores how couples manage type 2 diabetes, sleep and exercise in couples relationships, and connections between cognition and marital interactions in later life. Dr. Yorgason received his PhD from Virginia Tech University in human development, and was a postdoctoral fellow at the Gerontology Center of Pennsylvania State University.

Stephanie Richardson is a master's student in the marriage, family, and human development program at Brigham Young University. She has taught a research methods course for undergraduates in the field of human development and family studies. Her research interests include how mental and physical health impact relationships, especially couple relationships. Topics that she has explored include type 1 diabetes and depression. She has presented research at various conferences, including the Gerontological Society of America, and the Society for the Study of Emerging Adulthood.

Kevin Stott is a doctoral candidate in the Department of Human Development and Family Science at the University of Missouri. He is currently a graduate instructor for various courses covering interpersonal relationships and family science. His research interests include the daily-life experiences of older adults and later-life family relationships. He is especially interested in the memorialization practices of families and promoting early discussions about end-of-life preferences and plans. He has presented original research at various professional conferences including the Gerontological Society of America and the International Association of Gerontology and Geriatrics.

Chapter 18: Family Socioeconomic Context and Mental Health in Parents and Children: A Heuristic Framework

Kandauda A. S. Wickrama is professor in the Department of Human Development and Family Science at the University of Georgia. His research focuses on life course social epidemiology, international health, and quantitative research methods. He has investigated how socioeconomic context and individual life experiences influence individual mental and physical health over the life course. He has published widely in professional journals and he has coauthored numerous chapters in edited volumes. He has also authored or edited several books, including *Higher-Order Growth Curves and Mixture Modeling with Mplus: A Practical Guide* (2016, Routledge). Dr. Wickrama has received Ruben Hill Award twice from the National Council on Family Relations and research award from the Rural Sociological Society. Dr. Wickrama received his PhD in sociology from Iowa State University.

Catherine Walker O'Neal is an assistant research scientist in the Department of Human Development and Family Science at the University of Georgia. Her research focuses on informing evidence-based outreach efforts through increased understanding of the interplay of risk and resilience among families facing acute or chronic stressors. Her research utilizes advances quantitative methods in evaluating contextual and ecological effects on individual and family outcomes, particularly their mental health, physical health, and relational well-being. She co-authored *Higher-Order Growth Curves and Mixture Modeling with Mplus: A Practical Guide* (2016, Routledge Press) and regularly publishes her research in well-respected family science journals, including *Journal of Family Psychology*, *Family Process*, *Journal of Marriage and Family*, and *American Journal of Community Psychology*. Dr. O'Neal received her PhD in child and family development from the University of Georgia.

Tae Kyoung Lee is a lead research analyst in the Department of Public Health Sciences at the University of Miami Miller School of Medicine. His research focuses on quantitative methods in family research. He has authored and coauthored over 50 publications in journals such as the *American Journal of Public Health*, *Child Development*, *Health Psychology*, *Development and Psychopathology*, and *Structural Equation Modeling*. He coauthored *Higher-Order Growth Curves and Mixture Modeling with Mplus: A Practical Guide* (2016, Routledge). Dr. Lee received his PhD in human development and family studies from the University of Georgia.

Chapter 19: Families Coping With Alcohol and Substance Abuse

Kevin P. Lyness is professor, chair of the Applied Psychology Department, and director of the Couple and Family Therapy PhD Program at Antioch University New England. Previously he was on the faculty in Colorado State University's

Marriage and Family Therapy Program. He is a former assistant editor of the *Journal of Marital and Family Therapy* and serves on the editorial boards of the *Journal of Marital and Family Therapy*, the *Journal of Feminist Family Therapy,* and the *Journal of Couple and Relationship Therapy.* He received his PhD from Purdue University, and his initial training was in substance abuse counseling.

Judith Fischer is professor emeritus of human development and family studies at Texas Tech University. She continues her research on family problems, addictions, and adult development. Her work has been published in addiction, family, and human development journals. She was coeditor of *Familial Responses to Alcohol Problems* (2017, Routledge) and serves on the editorial board of *Journal of Marriage and Family.* She is a past president of the Groves Conference on Marriage and Family and was the first holder of the C. R. & Virginia Hutcheson Professorship in Human Development and Family Studies at Texas Tech University. She is a Fellow of the National Council on Family Relations and a member of the Academy of the Groves Conference on Marriage and Family. She received her PhD from the University of Colorado.

Chapter 20: Death, Dying and Grief in Families

Colleen I. Murray is professor of sociology and the Interdisciplinary Social Psychology PhD Program, and adjunct professor in programs of human development and family studies, public health, justice management, and women's studies at the University of Nevada, Reno. She served as chair of the Grief Focus Group of the National Council on Family Relations. Her research focuses on the intersection of health and justice, with emphasis on parent and sibling grief following sudden loss or mass tragedy, mixed document status immigrant families, the interplay of posttraumatic growth and stress theories, civilian uses of drones and technologies, and media portrayal of adolescents. She has published numerous articles and chapters on family relationships, grief, adolescents, gender, and culture. She is a fellow in thanatology with the Association for Death Education and Counseling. She received her PhD from The Ohio State University.

Jordan C. Reuter is a doctoral student in the Interdisciplinary Social Psychology PhD Program at the University of Nevada, Reno. His current research broadly focuses on religion and nonreligion. He is particularly interested in nonreligious worldviews, and religion's and nonreligion's relationship to family, health, and identity.